ISAAC I. STEVENS

ISAAC I. STEVENS
Young Man in a Hurry

∾ **KENT D. RICHARDS** ∾

Washington State University Press
Pullman, Washington

Washington State University Press, Pullman, Washington 99164-5910

©1993 by the Board of Regents of Washington State University
All rights reserved
WSU Press Reprint Series, first printing 1993
Originally published by the Brigham Young University Press, 1979

Library of Congress Cataloging-in-Publication Data
Richards, Kent D., 1938-
    Isaac I. Stevens: young man in a hurry / Kent D. Richards.
        p.   cm.
    Originally published: Provo, Utah : Brigham Young University Press, c1979.
    Includes bibliographical references (p.   ) and index.
    ISBN 0-87422-094-7 (paperback : acid-free paper)
    1. Stevens, Isaac Ingalls, 1818-1862. 2. Governors—Washington (State)—Biography. 3. Generals—United States—Biography. 4. United States. Army—Biography. 5. Indians of North America—Washington (State)—History—19th century. 6. Indians of North America—Oregon—History—19th century. 7. Washington (State)—History—To 1889. 8. Oregon—History—To 1859. I. Title.
F880.S843R5   1993
979.7'03'092—dc20
[B]   92-41393
                                                                CIP

For
Vernon Carstensen

Contents

Illustrations

Foreword

In a perceptive talk at the 1991 Pacific Northwest History Conference held in Walla Walla, David H. Stratton of Washington State University lamented that the Pacific Northwest has generally been ignored by historians of the frontier and West.[1] His point is amply confirmed by the dearth of work that has appeared on early Washington history since the publication of *Isaac I. Stevens: Young Man in a Hurry* in 1979. Stevens remains as controversial as ever, but if anything he has become even more of a symbol to those with various agendas. This is particularly true for the Indian treaty era when Stevens often emerges as a villain incarnate rather than as an officer of the government carrying out its policy, the major thrust of which was the peopling of the American West.[2]

This new paperback edition corrects errors in the original edition and contains other minor editing. A major regret was the decision to use "Young Man in a Hurry" as the subtitle in the 1979 edition, a change from my original choice, "A Regular Go-Ahead Man." The former, insisted upon by the original publisher who rejected the latter as too arcane, abets the unfortunate impression that Stevens acted with excessive haste to force treaties upon the Northwest Indians. It is argued in the biography that this was not the case, with the possible exception of the Flathead council. However, even the most recent history of the American West states that Governor Stevens was "particularly eager to rush through the treaties" and that the treaties were the cause of the war that followed.[3]

Arcane though it may be, "a regular go-ahead man" was a common 19th century phrase that admirers applied to men like Stevens, who embodied those characteristics of energy, vision, initiative, and forcefulness necessary to move the fortunes of the nation forward. These men exemplified the spirit of "Young America" and would lead the way from the Mississippi Valley to the Pacific Ocean carrying with them the values of the age—republicanism, entrepreneurial spirit, energy, and opportunity. To Stevens' contemporaries the negative side of this advancing frontier was minimal. Recent practitioners of the "New Western History" would disagree, and argue that Stevens and his cohorts were imperialists who destroyed indigenous cultures and the environment—that they were exploiters rather than builders. Whatever the present generation's judgement of the consequences of the last century and a half of history in the Pacific Northwest, Stevens and his contemporaries, if they had had the benefit of foresight, would have been enormously pleased with the results.

xii

It took longer than they expected, but the five million people that Joe Lane in 1853 predicted would inhabit the region that now includes Washington, northern Idaho, and western Montana has come to pass, along with the farms, ranches, ports, cities, and industries that support them—Isaac Stevens would, I believe, offer no apologies for this legacy.

The dedication of this volume to a scholar and a gentleman, Vernon Carstensen, is perhaps even more apt with this new edition for he was teaching a "New Western History" that merged with but did not replace the "Old History" long before anyone knew that a new Western history existed.

In addition to reaffirming my acknowledgments to those mentioned in the original preface, I wish to thank Glen Lindeman and Keith Petersen of the Washington State University Press for suggesting reissuance of *Isaac I. Stevens* in a new format. Their efforts and those of their colleagues at the WSU Press have made it a better book.

Foreword Notes

1. The talk was later published; David H. Stratton, "Oh, Nova Albion, Ye Were Young So Long," *Columbia* (Winter 1991/92), pp. 2-3.

2. See for example, Clifford E. Trafzer, ed., *Indians, Superintendents, and Councils: Northwestern Indian Policy, 1850-1855* (Lanham, Maryland: University Press of America, 1986), chapters 1-3. Francis Paul Prucha in his magisterial magnum opus places Stevens and the Pacific Northwest treaties in the context of federal Indian policy; *The Great Father* (Lincoln: University of Nebraska Press, 1984).

3. Richard White, *"It's Your Misfortune and None of My Own": A History of the American West* (Norman: University of Oklahoma Press, 1991), p. 93. Among the few books published since 1979 pertaining to Washington Territory in the 1850s and 1860s or to the career of Isaac I. Stevens are: Murray Morgan, *Puget's Sound: A Narrative of Early Tacoma and the Southern Sound* (Seattle: University of Washington Press, 1979); covering some of the same period as Morgan, but methodologically deficient is J. A. Eckrom, *Remembered Drums: A History of the Puget Sound Indian War* (Walla Walla: Pioneer Press Books); a solid but brief history of Washington is Robert E. Ficken and Charles P. LeWarne, *Washington: A Centennial History* (Seattle: University of Washington Press, 1988). Other books on specific topics are Carl Schlicke, *General George Wright: Guardian of the Pacific Coast* (Norman: University of Oklahoma Press, 1988); Eugene Coan, *James Graham Cooper* (Moscow: University of Idaho Press, 1981); and Clifford E. Trafzer and Richard D. Scheuerman, *Renegade Tribe: The Palouse Indians and the Invasion of the Inland Pacific Northwest* (Pullman: Washington State University Press, 1986). William Lang's forthcoming biography of William W. Miller promises to be an excellent complement to *Isaac I. Stevens*.

PREFACE

There is an often-repeated apocryphal story of Governor Isaac
I. Stevens' initial appearance in Olympia in the fall of 1853. According to the story, a small, slight figure, bearded, begrimed,
and dressed in rough woolen clothing came to the entrance of
Olympia's unpretentious but crowded hotel to inquire about the
bustling crowd filling the rude structure. Brushing aside the ragged stranger a celebrant said they were waiting for the governor,
but suggested the traveler might find food in the kitchen. After
eating his fill, Stevens reappeared to dramatically announce his
true identity.

Drama and a penchant for the unexpected did typify the governor, but not the role of an unnoticed stranger. Despite his
small stature Isaac Stevens was most often in the center of activity, providing leadership, spewing out orders and ideas, shaping
events, or creating controversy. He was a man either loved or
hated, but seldom ignored. From his entrance into the United
States Military Academy in 1835 until his death at the battle of
Chantilly in 1862, Isaac Stevens pursued a career in public service as a cadet, an officer in the Army Corps of Engineers,
Coast Survey officer, territorial governor, superintendent of Indian affairs, head of a Pacific railroad survey, delegate to Congress, and Civil War general. In his varied capacities Stevens
participated in a broad spectrum of scientific, military, and political activities spanning the era from the age of Jackson to the
middle of the Civil War. He was directly involved in basic issues raised by America's westward expansion, the territorial system, sectionalism, and democracy. Among these were: new criteria for geographic reconnaissance and scientific observation;
Indian-white relations; the proper powers of a territorial gover-

nor; relations in the Northwest between the United States and Great Britain; civil-military confrontations; the sectional crisis; and policy toward the freedman during the Civil War.

Contemporaries bitterly divided as to how well Stevens met these challenges. Virtually all who knew him agreed that he possessed a brilliant mind, enormous energy, and a dominant personality. These characteristics were highly respected in the nineteenth century, particularly on the American frontier. A Minnesota newspaperman best captured the admiration for Stevens' character when he praised him as a true representative of the times, "a regular, go-ahead man;" but others castigated him as a Napoleonic dictator with delusions of grandeur and a narrow egotism that brooked no criticism or opposition. Stevens' career reflected these divergent opinions; he acquired many fast friends, but he also engaged in monumental feuds. Subsequent accounts have taken their cue from Stevens' contemporaries. The best known defense came from his son, Hazard Stevens, who published a biography in 1900 that virtually elevated his father to sainthood. Many late nineteenth- and early twentieth-century historians who have touched on Stevens' career are almost as laudatory as his son. The detractors were also numerous but have tended to focus upon certain aspects of his life such as martial law or the Indian treaties.

Isaac Stevens often said that history would be the most valid judge of his life, and he was convinced that nothing was more worthy of study than "the actions of the illustrious dead." History, in his view, allowed man to look at the actions of his ancestors and assess the causes of success or failure. Stevens believed that "biography may be regarded as a specie of history— as history on a small scale." In this last respect, at least, Isaac Stevens would approve of this biography although he would, no doubt, disagree with some of its conclusions. It has not been my intention to become a detractor or to be partisan, but to become acquainted with one man attempting to struggle with the often overwhelming problems of his time.

The author owes a debt to the many individuals and institutions who aided in this book's preparation. Particular thanks are due the North Andover Historical Society, the Huntington Library, the Bancroft Library, the Rutherford B. Hayes Memorial Library, the Library of Congress, the Smithsonian Institution, the Washington State Historical Society, the Washington State Archives, the Oregon Historical Society, and the manuscript division of the University of Oregon Library. Various sections of the National Archives assisted in every way possible during one extended and several brief visits to Washington D.C. I owe special thanks to John Porter Bloom, editor of the Territorial Papers of the United States and Senior Specialist for Western History, and to Jo Tice Bloom. Richard Berner, head of the manuscript division, and Robert Monroe, head of special collections, and their staffs at the University of Washington's Suzzallo Library extended invaluable assistance and many courtesies for which I am deeply appreciative. Hazel Mills, head of the Washington Room at the Washington State Library, and her former associate, now successor, Nancy Pryor, have made their facility a haven for researchers in Washington history and a model for others to emulate. Special thanks, also, to the staff of the Bieneke Library, Yale University.

Central Washington State College granted a summer research stipend, a faculty research grant, and a sabbatical leave which helped provide some of the time and money necessary. Millie Marchal, Gail McCartney, and Barbara Davis all served competently as typists for various drafts of the manuscript. Mr. and Mrs. Edmund Leland III graciously allowed me to examine the house where Isaac Stevens grew up and which is now their charming residence.

Special thanks must go to three individuals who share much of the credit for this book but none of the responsibility for errors of fact or interpretation. Gordon B. Dodds, now Professor of History at Portland State University, was my first mentor at Knox College. His encouragement was in large part responsible for my going on to graduate work in western history. Subsequently, he has remained a valued friend and advisor. Finally, he read the entire manuscript with his usual critical eye. Professor Vernon R. Carstensen, now at the University of Washington, guided me through all but the final stages of a graduate program at the University of Wisconsin before he moved on to the Pacific Northwest. The Carstensens generously extended the hospitality of their home on numerous occasions when I worked at the University of Washington Library, and Professor Carstensen read an earlier version of this manuscript with the candor his graduate students and colleagues expect and appreciate.

Carolyn E. Richards worked from the first day of our marriage to put me through graduate school and has since carried most of the burden of home and family. Although skeptical of history, and perhaps of historians, she has read the manuscript more than once with a keen eye for errors of omission and commission. Although it has at times seemed otherwise, I must assure her that she, not Isaac Stevens, is still the most important person in my life.

1 OF NEW ENGLAND PURITANS AND PIONEERS

Virtually every man who achieved even a modicum of political success during the nineteenth century claimed birth in a log cabin and an early life of unremitting toil. In so doing these men conformed to prevailing mores which insisted that most virtues were best nurtured by rural antecedents, poverty, and hard work. Isaac I. Stevens always reacted strongly to any suggestion that he did not spring from the log-cabin mold, and he often alluded to a youth spent scratching out an existence on his father's New England farm. Stevens boasted that he rose from humble, but honest, circumstances to win an education, forge a career, and emerge as a figure of national prominence.

The heritage of the sturdy yeoman cannot by itself explain the rich past of the Stevens clan and the influence it exerted on the personality and career of Isaac I. Stevens. The family occupied a secure and often distinguished place in colonial society with the lineage in the New World tracing to John Stevens, one of the first generation of New England pioneers. The Stevenses had their roots in Oxford where, for at least a century before John Stevens made his decision to emigrate, they owned and leased farm lands.[1] John Stevens grew to majority in the midst of political and religious intrigue. His family was among the uncompromising Protestants who rejected the feudal and aristocratic Anglican Church. By the time of his father's death in 1627, when John was twenty-two, Puritanism had become a way of life that insisted upon the sinful nature of man, but also stressed the importance of the individual. Many Englishmen viewed the Puritans as

generally aggressive and self-reliant, somewhat intolerant of human weaknesses, hostile to compromise, inclined to impose their views on others, and

1

actuated by a craving for self-expression and an eager desire to shape the course of human development toward spiritual ends.

John Stevens embodied these characteristics, and his descendent Isaac I. Stevens can be partially understood by reference to them.[2]

When John assumed responsibility for his father's family, Puritan opposition to Charles I and the Anglican Church had reached a fever pitch.[3] John Stevens resisted the temptations of the New World until his marriage in the mid-1630s gave him new responsibilities and apparently provided the catalyst that led him to take the fateful step. In the spring of 1638, with his younger brother, his wife Elizabeth, and her mother and brother, John Stevens traveled down the main highway from Caversham to the port at Southampton. They were crammed into the 200-ton *Confidence* along with 105 others, many of them friends and neighbors, and on April 11 the vessel hoisted sail for the unknown future. The cramped, dreary, and seemingly interminable voyage ended in safety at Newbury, where John Stevens disembarked in a mood similar to the vessel's bold name. He passed the screening tests applied by the magistrates to insure that new colonists were of good character and some material substance.[4]

Dissatisfaction grew among the 1630s emigrants to the Massachusetts Bay colony, who complained of overcrowding and discrimination in the division of land sites. John Stevens, who became a freeman of the colony in 1641, had not come all the way from Caversham to receive an allotment of three acres. New settlements began to spin off from the old, and Stevens, with his wife and the first two of an eventual eight children, joined the pioneers who ventured up the Merrimack River in the spring of 1642 to become the founders and first settlers of Andover.[5] Over the years he maintained his status as a leader of the community, serving in various capacities including militia officer and commissioner to settle the boundary with a neighboring town. The family prospered financially, and when John Stevens died in 1662, he left a substantial estate valued at 463 pounds sterling.[6]

The first Stevens in the New World established a pattern followed by the family for over 200 years. The line which led from John to Isaac I. Stevens remained rooted in Andover as farmers, military men, local political leaders, and officers in the church. John's fifth son, Joseph, was typical as he farmed, held town offices, and served as a deacon. His son, in turn, became one of the community's military leaders, acquiring the sobriquet "Captain James."[7] He lived up to his title by participating in the campaign against Louisburg during the French and Indian War although he was then in his seventies.[8] "Captain James" was characterized as one of the well-to-do men in North Andover, and at his death in 1769 he left several parcels of land in Massachusetts as well as a large tract in Maine, which he had received for his war service.[9] James' eldest son, named after his father, also served in the French and Indian War, but was less fortunate for he fell ill with typhoid fever and died near Fort Ticonderoga. The younger James left a wife and four children, among them his eldest son, Jonathan, who would become Isaac I. Stevens' grandfather.[10]

Traits found in the character of the Puritan immigrant John Stevens were also apparent in his descendents. A nineteenth-century member of the family catalogued the Stevenses' collective personality as comprising "a peculiar decision of character, a certain amount of pride, and a pronounced independence, coupled with a slight amount of reserve." It was a shockingly accurate appraisal. There were changes, however, as the generations rolled by. Perhaps the most noticeable was a diminishing of interest in spiritual affairs and a parallel increase in attention to the material and secular. This loss of religious zeal was typical for descendents of the first settlers, who found that fervor diminished under any circumstances but seemed particularly difficult to maintain on the frontier. John Stevens came to the New World at least in part to increase his worldly wealth, and he and his posterity discovered that rich opportunities existed for those willing to labor. The Stevenses also found it difficult to avoid military service as European conflicts began spilling over periodically into the New World, although the family proved more zealous than many others in their attention to martial affairs.[11]

Isaac I. Stevens' grandfather, Jonathan, continued family proclivities as he enthusiastically supported the American Revolution, rushing to defend Boston and firing when he saw the whites of the enemies' eyes at the battle of Bunker Hill. Unlike some "summer patriots" he did not lose faith. In 1777 he marched to meet the advance of General Burgoyne and in the course of the campaign trod much of the same Hudson Valley covered by his father in the French and Indian War. A successful farmer and tanner, Jonathan prospered financially—a fortu-

nate circumstance as he was equally successful in increasing the
clan by fathering fourteen children. He supported them all comfortably in a "substantial mansion" built to overlook Lake
Cochichewick, and he became a local philanthropist by donat-
ing land for Franklin Academy in 1799.[12]

Jonathan's seventh son, Isaac, arrived in 1783 just as the Revolution drew to a close. As a young man, Isaac sailed before the
mast to China; and soon after his return in 1800, he and two
older brothers headed for the Maine frontier, where their father
had added to the military grant by purchasing additional land
for six cents an acre. The brothers christened their new community Andover, in honor of their Massachusetts birthplace, and
began the laborious task of clearing the virgin timber. Within a
short time tragedy struck; a falling tree badly mangled Isaac's
left leg. A doctor urged amputation, but Stevens refused. After
weeks of agony his brothers carried him to North Andover. The
leg appeared to heal, but it also shortened and the kneejoint
stiffened. Throughout the rest of a long life, recurring pain, stiff-
ness, and abcesses in the limb plagued Stevens and confined
him to the house for weeks on end. His father had sufficient
wealth to support Isaac in a life of relative comfort, or at least
one free from work, but he never considered withdrawing from
the responsibilities of the world. As soon as he was physically
able, Isaac, no doubt financed by his father, leased twenty acres
at the south end of Lake Cochichewick, not far from the family
home. Soon thereafter he took a mortgage from the owner for
the land, home, and farm buildings, and after years of hard
work, paid off the mortgage and increased his holdings to 150
acres.[13]

Stevens took advantage of the farm's location on the main
road leading from Andover to Haverhill to establish a "store."
This "store" dispensed only liquid refreshment and provided a
stopping point for thirsty travelers and a gathering place for
neighboring farmers. He later expanded his activities with an
ingenious rent-a-horse service for travelers. The injury hindered
his economic progress very little, but it did restrict his social
mobility. It is likely that many young ladies objected to a
serious relationship with a partial cripple, and Stevens limited
courting opportunities by remaining close to his farm.

Hannah Cummings did not object; she married Isaac on September 29, 1814. The Cummings family had arrived in Massachusetts in 1638, the same year as John Stevens, and had become prosperous yeomen, much like the Stevenses.[14] The

Cummings family maintained close ties with the church: Hannah's father, Asa, carried the title "Deacon," and his brother a Doctor of Divinity, for many years published the *Christian Mirror* in Portland, Maine. Asa Cummings, a native of North Andover, moved to Maine in 1798 when Hannah was thirteen. It is likely that Isaac and Hannah were youthful acquaintances prior to this move, and that the friendship was reestablished not too long before the marriage.[15]

Hazard Stevens later described Hannah as a woman "who united to a warm and affectionate heart, noble and elevated sentiments, strong good sense, and untiring industry." Evidence to support or refute Hazard's judgment of his grandmother is primarily circumstantial. Hannah's children expressed nothing but sentiments of love and respect after her death, but the oldest child was only twelve when Hannah died in 1827. In addition, hostility arose between Hannah's seven children and their stepmother, which might account for a collective memory that selected only the favorable.[16] If "noble and elevated sentiments" meant piety, Hazard was probably correct for this came naturally from Hannah's Puritan heritage and upbringing. The same factors insured her "untiring industry." During thirteen years of marriage she bore Isaac five daughters and two sons, carried on the usual manifold household tasks and spun, wove, and sewed clothing for extra cash. Hannah exceeded even her husband's aspirations for economic success. Her sister Sarah observed that for all her excellent qualities, Hannah had "one great fault, an inordinate desire to lay up treasure on earth." Sarah accused her sister of planning to acquire property to such an extent that it became a "ruling passion." There is no reason to question Hannah's love for her children, and it is possible that her quest for wealth was partly motivated by a desire to provide for them. But in her zeal she at times ignored their emotional and physical needs.[17]

Prodded by his wife, Stevens expanded his economic ventures. He built a malt house and prepared malt for sale, harvested hay from a wet meadow at the end of Lake Chochichewick, and during the winter fattened cattle. The tavern closed, however, probably due to a growing repugnance to the selling of hard liquor on the parts of both Hannah and Isaac. (Isaac eventually became a temperance advocate.) Like many farmers, Stevens engaged in land speculation and moneylending. But unlike less imaginative neighbors, he relied primarily on cash crops (anticipating the trend to commercial agriculture) and kept in close touch with the latest scientific developments. He also experimented with fruit trees, and a widely praised apple orchard produced cider that Isaac's temperance sentiments seldom prevented him from enjoying.[18]

On March 25, 1818, in their substantial seventeenth-century home, Hannah gave birth to her third child and first son. The new child, Isaac Ingalls Stevens, was small and delicate at birth and his parents feared his ability to survive. Isaac's fragility was not typical of other children born into the Stevens family, and the exact cause of his early physical problems is not known. When mature, his large head and short, stumpy legs indicated a malfunction of the pituitary gland which allowed the cartilage to calcify and create a mild form of dwarfism. Perhaps other gland deficiencies also plagued the infant, but, whatever the cause of his frailty, Isaac's parents provided no special attention. They were busy with their many chores, particularly Hannah, who had two small children besides Isaac and another on the way.[19]

Isaac did not walk until he was three and may have learned then only because his grandmother, Susannah Stevens, took him into her home and gave the necessary attention and encouragement. According to family legend, Isaac, once on his feet, became extremely active as if to make up for a delayed start. Isaac, Sr., told how his son, while still very young, crossed a rickety footbridge made of two poles, one for footing and the other for a railing, and accomplished it carrying a string of fish between his teeth. The hired hand, who later appeared to help the boy across, assumed he had surely drowned. The family cited the story as evidence of youthful daring and adventurous spirit, although it also may have indicated impatience with delay and a desire to make his own decisions.[20]

Tragedy struck the family when Isaac was seven. His father loved fast horses and, perhaps compensating for his own locomotive inability, habitually drove the family carriage at a furious pace. One day, with his wife beside him, Stevens took the carriage around a corner at his usual speed and the conveyance overturned. Hannah hit the ground heavily, striking her head. She lived for two years but never fully recovered physically or mentally. Several months after the fall, Hannah gave premature birth to a stillborn infant and thereupon lapsed into a severe mental depression that her family described as a deep melancholy. During the last year of her life she became increasingly irrational, and on at least one occasion she attempted to throw herself from the second story of their home. Young Isaac verbally and physically restrained her until his father could come rushing from the fields. After this incident, Isaac, Sr., reluctantly decided that Hannah needed continual supervision, and he arranged for her to be taken into the home of a neighbor, where she died several months later.[21]

Hannah's death was a blow to the entire family. Young Isaac had become increasingly devoted to his mother during her illness, and after her death he and the other children remembered her as a saintly figure that cruel fate had snatched from them. They would tolerate no criticism of her, and in time their mixture of childhood remembrances and fantasies merged into a memory that they insisted was real. For Isaac, Sr., it was another cruel blow. His injury had not dimmed his optimism or weakened his will, but after Hannah's death he turned inward, dropped many of his business ventures, and seldom left the farm. Increasingly outspoken and orthodox in his religion, he also became a strong supporter of abolition and prohibition.

The relationship between Isaac I. Stevens and his father often was not harmonious. Isaac, Sr. prodded his eldest son, who frequently became the target of his sullen moods and ill temper. The circumstances of Hannah's death lay as an unmentioned, but formidable, barrier between them, and the marriage in 1829 of Isaac, Sr., and Elizabeth Ann Poor further increased the tension. The Poor family had cared for Hannah during her illness, and Ann had worked as the Stevens' housekeeper, a job she continued after Hannah's death. The marriage of widower and housekeeper was logical but the children harbored a deep-seated animosity toward Ann, an acrimony which did not diminish over the years. Her sullen nature did little to improve the morose atmosphere which often permeated the family.

Despite the tension in the family, the elder Stevens was proud of his oldest son, and ambitious for his future. Isaac, Sr., voiced suspicion of too much book learning but recognized his son's superior mental ability. Young Isaac started school when he was five and proved to be a prodigy in mathematics by mastering all the problems his teachers and available books provided. This confirmed the belief that Isaac was destined to be the intellectual in the family and thereafter the boy's education was promoted to such an extent that at times he rebelled.

Isaac attended rural schools a portion of each year until, at the age of ten, he entered Franklin Academy, the school built upon land donated by his grandfather. After a year there, he

tired of academic life and, without asking his father's permission, sought a job in his Uncle Nathaniel's woolen mill.
Isaac later explained his action as an attempt to escape the rigors of academic life. He even suggested that the strain of incessant mental activity was harming him physically. He may
have believed this, but it is likely that the unhappy family situation was at least equally responsible for his decision. During
the year he worked in the mill, Isaac boarded with his grandparents who lived near the mill across Lake Cochichewik from
his home. He started work at five o'clock and put in a ten- to
twelve-hour day. Hazard later said that when young Isaac returned home he presented his entire year's salary to his father,
who would not return even the penny requested to purchase a
hot gingerbread. This story may not be true, but Hazard correctly observed that the elder Stevens "did not appreciate the
sensitive nature of a child, and its needs of sympathy, recrea-
tion, and occasional indulgence." Young Isaac could be as difficult as his father. He once asked for a new cap but was put off
with the explanation that his old one had not yet begun to
show signs of wear. For the next several days Isaac beat the cap
against fenceposts and trees until it was in shreds, and his father
eventually relented and bought a new one. When matching
tempers, father and son were a standoff.[22]

Young Isaac complained of mental fatigue, but he had more
cause to protest the unremitting labor to which he subjected his
slight frame. He seemed determined to prove that size was no
deterrent to working as hard as or harder than anyone else. At
the end of one strenuous day in the fields he was prostrated by
a severe sunstroke that nearly took his life. When he was twelve,
pitching hay during the harvest, Isaac suddenly doubled over
with a stabbing pain in his groin. It was quickly diagnosed as a
rupture. A Boston physician fitted him with a truss which he
wore for several years. By the time he reached maturity it appeared that the injury had healed, and Isaac virtually forgot it,
but eighteen years later the injury recurred and continued to
plague him periodically for most of his life.

Despite the physical problems of his youth, his mother's
death, the acrimony with his father, the hard work, and mental
anguish, life was not entirely devoid of joy or comfort. Although
Isaac, Sr., watched his pennies carefully, the family was prosperous, if not as wealthy as Uncle Nathaniel the mill owner or
William Stevens the lawyer, banker, and state politician. The
family home, first built in 1680 but continually modified and

enlarged, was comfortable and filled with the boisterous activities of the seven children. The two main rooms downstairs were dominated by large fireplaces, twelve-inch-thick oak sills, and foot-square solid beams across the ceiling. Frequently, relatives stopped in to sip cider before the fire during the winter and to visit on the porch in warmer weather. Politics, religion, and social reform shared in the talk of crops and local personalities.[23]

Given the family heritage and position in the community, it is not surprising that the Stevenses were concerned with developments taking place outside the perimeters of North Andover. Isaac, Sr., differed in two basic ways from the majority of his New England peers—he was a Unitarian and, more surprising, a Democrat. During an era that began with New England opposition to the War of 1812 and continued with strong support for John Quincy Adams and hatred of Andrew Jackson, Isaac, Sr. and the other Democrats in the family were in a minority. Jackson's defeat of Adams in 1828 cast gloom over Massachusetts but resulted in great rejoicing in the Stevens home. Ten-year-old Isaac joined the celebration that may have marked the beginning of his political awareness. When he entered the Military Academy in 1835, the old soldier was still in the White House; Isaac grew to maturity in the midst of the ferment and exhilaration of the Age of Jackson.

Isaac, Sr. modified his social views during this era. He turned to moral reform and contemplated the role of the common man in a democratic society. On numerous occasions he cautioned his son that all forms of slavery were evil but that slavery to bad habits was the greatest evil. In the mid-1830s he boasted of working the entire summer and autumn "without using any intoxicating liquors except a few quarts of cider." He predicted that "the times for rum or ardent spirits are passing away no more likely to return than witch times." The elder Stevens was equally vigorous in his attacks upon special privilege, and equated the Federalists and the Whigs with a monopoly of wealth, power, and learning. He condemned the Whigs as "the most aristocratical and corrupt of any party in the country." Of particular concern to Isaac, Sr., was the Bank of the United States which appeared to be a distillation of all the ills of monopoly. But whereas Andrew Jackson at least in theory opposed all banks, Isaac Stevens, Sr. did not: members of his family were stockholders and officers in local financial institutions. Like others in a similar position, he objected only to the control exercised by the powerful Bank of the United States over the local

financial brokers. Isaac, Sr. fit the Jacksonian pattern in other
ways: he read the *Liberator,* the *North American Review,* and numerous other newspapers and journals in preference to literature; he often caught election fever but was cold to political
principles; and, like his contemporaries, he knew how to make
money but not how to spend it.[24]

Young Isaac was influenced by, but did not always conform
to, his father's social and political beliefs. As a teenager, Isaac
went a step or two beyond his father's liberal religious position
and declared himself a Universalist. His most vehement opinions were reserved for revivalists or other religious enthusiasts.
When his sister Susan became infatuated with the preaching of
a quasi-religious diet faddist who cautioned against eating meat,
Isaac questioned why so many farmers who consumed large
quantities remained healthy. He speculated that those who suffered indigestion should blame lack of exercise rather than car-
nivorous habits. Isaac was upset when Susan was converted by
Missouri Methodists who believed more in inner emotion and
enthusiasm than in an intellectualized theology. He lamented to
his sister that if "our feelings and sympathies get the better of
our judgment we shall certainly be objects of ridicule and perhaps deservedly." By the time he reached maturity, Isaac could
best be described as a freethinker who put his faith in human
reason, the rational, and the credible. The rational being, he argued, could decide for himself on all subjects. A necessary corol-
lary was a thorough education, he reasoned, for "what is education, if it does not elevate us?"[25]

Young Isaac adopted the Democratic party and particularly
the ardent nationalism of the Jacksonians. He was upset, however, by the federal government's inaction in the dispute with
England over the Maine boundary and condemned it as "fawning subserviency to expediency in a matter of principle." Isaac
added, with youthful bravado, "Better die in a just cause, than
live by an abandonment of it." But like his father, Isaac saved
most of his fire for the Whigs, whom he blamed for the nation's
ills. He also shared his father's belief in the need for social re-
forms, particularly the abolition of slavery. While at the Military Academy he read the *Liberator,* and participated in Saturday night debates in which he became "much excited" in the
avowal of his abolitionist principles. John Quincy Adams's fight
against the gag rule in the House of Representatives won his admiration, and Isaac declared that politically he supported the
"loco-foco abolitionists." During this same period he applauded

a campaign by northern Negroes who refused to obey "Jim Crow" laws assigning them to separate railroad coaches. Wendell Phillips's argument that the North could interfere with slavery because the institution interfered with the rights of Northern citizens won his endorsement, and he came away from a Boston rally praising Phillips as a "pretty orator." Isaac would eventually modify or reject these youthful beliefs—except his life-long allegiance to the Democratic party.[26]

From his eleventh year until he was fourteen, Isaac alternated attending school in North Andover and working on the farm. In the fall of 1832 he went down the road to Andover to enroll at Phillips Academy, the most prestigious school in the area. Nathan W. Hazen, a lawyer and state politician, provided room and board, and in return the young scholar tended the garden, cut wood, cared for several animals, and did household chores. Isaac, Sr., paid the tuition of fifty cents a week. Hazen was impressed by the energy and quick mind of his boarder and took time to provide encouragement and fatherly advice. He talked to the young pupil about his future career, and Isaac, with the example of Hazen and his Uncle William before him, spoke of the law as his first interest. But Hazen saw Isaac as too introverted, and perhaps as physically unimposing, and suggested that his talent might lie in another profession.

To Isaac's great advantage much of his work at Phillips came in algebra, geometry, engineering, and surveying. In theory the classwork was rigidly scheduled, but in practice the students could proceed at their own pace. This was also to Isaac's advantage, and his teachers, Samuel R. Hall and Fred A. Benton, reported that in their experience at the Academy no one of his age had ever made such rapid progress. They praised their pupil for not missing a single assignment during a two-year period and claimed that he had completed a mathematics course equal to that given in most New England colleges. A third instructor testified that in twenty years he had seldom met a student who was Isaac's equal. In all areas of study his mentors agreed that he showed "perseverance, application and faithful attention," and that he demonstrated "good natural and acquired talents" and possessed "an unblemished moral character."[27]

Not only Nathan Hazen and Isaac, Sr., but virtually all of the Stevens family believed that young Isaac was destined for a bright future. When he was twelve his Aunt Sarah Cummings cautioned, "You must consider that you will not be merely an idle spectator, but will have a personal interest in these events [of the world]." Even when in his early teens, Isaac was entrusted by his uncles to carry out chores that involved the collection of debts and other responsible business matters. William Stevens was the first to suggest an application to the Military Academy, but it is likely that Isaac came to the same conclusion independently. He rejected farming and the ministry, business held little interest, and Hazen discouraged him from choosing the law. The Military Academy had obvious appeal. Many of the Stevenses had been military men, but, more important to Isaac, the Academy offered the best mathematics and engineering program in the country. The decision made, Isaac immediately applied to Congressman Gayton Osgood, a good friend of the Stevens family. But in his enthusiasm he failed to realize that he lacked a year of meeting the minimum age of sixteen. He stayed at Phillips for a second year, reapplied, and in March 1835 received appointment as a cadet.[28]

2

FIRST IN
THE CLASS

In June 1835 a young man of seventeen, far from home for the first time, stepped from the small steamer onto the West Point dock. The beauty of the setting, its historical significance, the dignity of the cadets, and the regal bearing of the officers filled the youth with awe. He arrived in time to witness the impressive graduation ceremonies. As fireworks burst overhead, he melodramatically pledged to be worthy of the blood and tears shed by his Revolutionary forefathers. He prayed that he might cherish a love of freedom and "not disgrace my country, my state, and that character of proud disdain and patriotic valor which inspired the heroes of Andover...." Looking at the Military Academy's mementos of past battles and heroic deeds, a lump rose in Isaac Stevens' throat and he asked, "Can I remain unmoved?" His answer was a simple and emphatic "No."[1]

The Military Academy may have overwhelmed young Isaac, but it was less impressive to the Democratic party and the President. Andrew Jackson and his followers condemned West Point as one manifestation of the special privilege and aristocracy they saw rampant in the nation. The Jacksonians argued that liberty was best protected by a trained militia, that a professional army represented a threat to freedom, and that by fostering an elitist officer corps the Academy constituted a dangerous and suspect institution. Ironically, the Jacksonian attack came in the midst of the Academy's first great era under Colonel Sylvanus Thayer, who had brought the school from the brink of extinction to national prominence.

Thayer, dubbed the "Father of the Military Academy," arrived in 1818, the year of Stevens' birth, to take over an institution which had not fulfilled the destiny expected by George

Washington, Thomas Jefferson, and its other early patrons. Fresh from a survey of French educational methods, particularly military training, Thayer was picked by President James Monroe to revitalize the institution. Thayer saw revision of the curriculum, tightening of standards, and upgrading of the faculty as his most important tasks. At a time when most American colleges relied on the old standbys of Greek and Latin mixed with a heavy infusion of Christian ethics and morality, Thayer developed a course of study that was primarily scientific and mathematic. As most of the necessary texts were written in French, work in that language was also required. Other subjects, including philosophy, history, ethics, and government, were touched lightly, if at all, and military tactics and strategy appeared only as an afterthought.

Thayer built his curriculum on the assumption that the Academy's primary objective was to train engineers. This purpose had seemed implicit in the assignment of the Academy to the Corps of Engineers. Prior to Thayer's arrival any distinction credited to the school came from the achievements of its engineers. The complaint was heard that the Academy turned out good engineers but few professional soldiers, and General John E. Wool, for one, grumbled that the solution of a mathematical problem did not make an officer a competent commander. Thayer did not attempt to alter the purpose of the school, but he endeavored to make it more effective. During his superintendency the Military Academy achieved recognition as the preeminent scientific and engineering college in the nation.[2]

Thayer vigorously modified the Academy's lackadaisical entrance, course, and graduation requirements. In the early years men entered at any season, and often lingered for several years without advancing. The cadet ranks included all ages from young teenagers to middle-aged men. Under Thayer's system new cadets reported before the summer encampment, formal examinations were held twice a year, and graduation ceremonies came in June. The superintendent set up a merit roll which allowed him to rank each cadet in every subject and within his class. The cadets recited every day in all subjects, and this constant check on progress allowed the faster students to move ahead, and the slower to be kept behind in separate sections, while those who made no progress were dropped. The final class rankings guided Thayer in assigning those near the top to the Engineer Corps, the middle group to artillery or ordnance, and the bottom portion to the infantry.[3]

Thayer was less successful in upgrading the quality of students admitted to the Military Academy. The army was sensitive to the charge that the school favored New Englanders in its admission policy. This was true because the school system of that section was superior to those of other locales. Thayer began to select one nominee from each Congressional district, knowing that he was temporarily sacrificing quality for increased public support. Under this method many appointees arrived at West Point with only a common school education or less, and Thayer was forced to keep the entrance examination painfully simple. Wider distribution of appointments was only one way in which Thayer tried to win public support for the institution. He also took the cadets on tours to major cities where they entertained the populace with close-order drills and martial music. To a certain extent Thayer's strategy backfired, for by placing the Academy in the public eye and increasing its prestige, he made it a more attractive object of Jacksonian wrath.[4]

In addition to complaining that the Academy was undemocratic, enemies charged that it was unnecessary and overly expensive. They argued that only a small percentage of cadets continued in the army, and that no guarantee existed that those who did remain would be better leaders than volunteer officers. Thayer partially met the criticism by requiring cadets to sign on for five years. The army also pointed out that the school at West Point did the job more cheaply than comparable British institutions. Some critics made good use of periodic disturbances, most of them in the pre-Thayer years, to show that a poor moral climate prevailed. One hostile Congressional report noted that the government had paid $10,000 to buy out a tavern near West Point. This was proof, the Congressmen said, that the authorities could not control the activities of the cadets. Much of the attack was directed against Sylvanus Thayer, and a good portion of it came, ironically, because he refused to grant special favors to cadets with powerful Jacksonian friends. Thayer's greatest enemy was President Jackson, who flew into a rage when several men in whom he took a personal interest were all dismissed for misconduct or academic failures. In July 1833 Thayer resigned as superintendent and was replaced by Rene De Russey, who did not match his predecessor in ability or intellect, but who continued most of Thayer's policies. Despite the vigorous attack upon the Military Academy, its opponents could not deny the success of its graduate engineers, who by the 1830s were building public works throughout the coun-

try. With the nation in the midst of a canal-building craze and
with the railroad era following in its wake, Andrew Jackson
might curse the Academy, but even he dared not destroy it.[5]

In his first days at West Point, Isaac Stevens was a bundle of
mixed emotions. His patriotism reached inspired heights but he
sadly confirmed the Jacksonian charge that the moral climate
on the Hudson left much to be desired. Stevens admitted that
regulations were strict, but he protested, "The laws are not insisted upon with that rigor and firmness which ought to characterize a Military Academy." Smoking, swearing, and chewing
indulged in "to a really dangerous degree" shocked the new cadet, and he called his comrades "wild and immoral fellows."
Worse, he reported, several officers and most of the cadets were
"scoffers and deriders of the Christian religion." But with firm
resolve Stevens pledged to find strength to resist the many
temptations and to comply strictly with the regulations.[6]

A few days after arrival the prospective plebes faced the assembled professors, all stern and resplendent in full-dress uni-
forms, to take the entrance examination. The faculty asked Stevens to write a sentence on the blackboard in a "fair legible
hand," to read a page from a standard history, and to demonstrate a knowledge of common and decimal fractions. The six
men who managed to fail returned home, and the remaining
sixty-four entered summer encampment, which for the plebes
consisted of continual marching under the supervision of up-
perclassmen. Although hazing was minimal during this era, Stevens, like every other cadet, found the incessant marching tiring
and deadening. He often complained during the annual camps
that he was "heartily tired" of it all. But by the end of the first
summer Stevens could boast of vigorous health and proclaim he
was taller, straighter, and slimmer. Although he wrote bravely
to his sisters that he was not homesick for a moment and had
never passed the time more pleasantly, he later admitted that in
the first months he made few friends and that the life of a
"poor plebe" was not easy. His size made him the natural target
for bullies, and Stevens was not one to back away from any
confrontation. During the encampment he was in a number of
fights and quickly piled up a string of demerits that placed him
low on the conduct role. He soon forgot his resolve to obey all
the rules and admitted that he was always "wide awake for a
scrape or for any kind of fun." It is probable that the fights
were more fun for Stevens than his opponents as he made up
for his lack of size with quickness and bulldog determination.

While Isaac was still at home a large bully had tweaked his nose, whereupon Stevens lowered his head, rushed through the astonished opponent's legs, knocked him down from behind and stomped him with his boots. He did not provide details of his fights, but he was not challenged after the first few months.[7]

Stevens told his father that the life of a cadet was all work and no play but he was closer to the truth when he confided to his cousin Aaron that he and his roommates had resolved during free hours to "carry on like wild ones." One kind of carrying on involved nightly expeditions to steal corn and apples from the professors' gardens. No one was caught because the cadets who thought themselves so daring were only repeating the exploits of many predecessors, and the faculty had tacitly agreed to allow this small supplement to the cadets' dreary diet. In winter it was likewise traditional to raid the kitchens and steal bread, butter, sugar, and meat for midnight "hashes." Stevens, with pride and great exaggeration, insisted that they were "rather a wild set." Dances held periodically during the summer attracted belles who came north to escape the city heat, and the end of the encampment climaxed with a grand celebration including a band, wines, cakes, and fireworks. The first year Stevens complained that he was embarrassed to attend these functions because he did not dance. The next year he took lessons during the encampment, a practice encouraged by the faculty to cultivate the social graces, although he went protesting that he did not care "one cent for all the dancing in the world." Even after the lessons, Stevens admitted ruefully that he cut "rather a sorry figure" on the dance floor. The cotillions, Spanish dances, and waltzes did not suit the farm boy who could not quite overcome his shyness in fashionable feminine company. He took more readily to the comradery of the taverns near West Point which he once called "those repositories of good cheer and good morals,"—a decided change of opinion from his first days at West Point. During the 1830s, and for many years thereafter, the favorite spot for cadets to illegally bide their time was Benny Havens. So popular was the congenial Mr. Havens that one of Stevens' classmates wrote the verses of "Benny Havens, Oh!" which immortalized that watering spot for later cadet generations. Although he spent his share of time at Benny Havens, Stevens declared that he "heartily approved" when two cadets were suspended for drinking.[8]

At the end of the first summer encampment, Stevens took up residence in a barracks room of ten by thirteen feet along with two plebes from Maine, Stephen Carpenter and John Bacon. The room was obviously crowded, and they slept on mattresses which they rolled and stored during the day. Stevens characterized his roommates as hard workers and fine fellows, but each eventually dropped from the Academy in anticipation of academic deficiencies.[9] The superintendent attempted to allow the cadets little time for leisure activities. The first year's course work emphasized mathematics and French. Stevens, in contrast to his roommates, had no fear of the mathematics, but prior to arrival at the Academy he was entirely ignorant of French. At the suggestion of one of the officers, he sought tutoring in the language during the summer camp. With the start of classes, he had at least some of the basics in French, and in math he rose quickly to the top of the class and remained there.[10]

Most of the faculty during Stevens' cadet years had been collected by Thayer, and they formed a distinguished group. In selecting faculty, Thayer flouted tradition by picking men not for their piety, patriotism, or personal characteristics, but solely for knowledge of their field. Stevens' professor of mathematics, Albert E. Church, taught at the Academy from 1828 until his death in 1878. Some students found him "dry as dust," "cold of eye and manner," or an "old mathematical cinder," but Stevens praised Church as a fine man and an accomplished teacher. Church admired Stevens' abilities in return, particularly praising his talent for grasping the most general rule that applied to a problem and then using the rule to arrive at the solution. The French professor, Claudius Berard, first came to the Academy in 1815. A native of France, Berard, like Church, used his own texts in his courses. Stevens described his first-year French class for his sister Susan.

At every lesson we get about half a page of exercises, and are obliged to get them so that we can write any sentence our Prof. gives us upon the blackboard without referring to the books. We are now writing sentences upon the pronominal verbs.

In addition they translated from Voltaire's *Historie de Charles XII*, and although the cadets were only required to read and write the language, Berard also paid close attention to proper pronunciation.[11]

Hazard Stevens has emphasized the single-minded dedication, the hard work, and the obstacles that Isaac overcame to rank first in his class. There is no doubt of his dedication to achieve and retain the first spot, although when his Uncle William chided him for not standing higher in one of the early weekly rankings, Stevens responded that a final position of nineteenth would not only be respectable but "very high." He gave differing versions of the time spent studying on an average day, telling his sisters that both math and French lessons took half an hour, but later implying to Uncle William that twelve hours a day including two and one-half hours in class were devoted to study. The lessons, given his training and capacity to learn, were probably not difficult. He frequently wrote his brother and sisters recommending Carlyle, Plutarch, *The Spectator* and a variety of other works that he read in his spare time.

Hazard Stevens, in particular, has emphasized the superior educational background of several of his father's classmates and the edge this gave them. This was possibly true for Henry W. Halleck of New York and Henry Biddle of Philadelphia, both of whom had attended college and had training in French before they arrived at West Point. But, compared with the vast majority of his classmates, Stevens was far ahead by virtue of his previous education. As has been stated, Thayer succeeded in upgrading the instruction, the curriculum, the administration, and the prestige of the institution, but he failed, because of the Congressional appointment system, to significantly change the quality of entering cadets. It is possible that the average cadet was less well prepared in the 1830s than he had been earlier. When Henry Biddle left the Academy in his second year, it left Halleck and Stevens to contend for the top spot. Halleck was inclined to literary and philosophical pursuits and would later make his reputation as the author of a volume on the art of war. But these talents counted for little at the Academy. When ranking the cadets, a complicated weighted formula was used based on course performance and to a lesser extent on demerits which were subtracted from the academic record. Within the academic courses the most emphasis was placed upon mathematics, and for this reason Stevens had an advantage over Halleck or other pretenders to the number-one ranking. One cadet in the 1850s reported that no students to that date had stood at the head of a class except those who had an extraordinary talent for mathematics. This cadet further argued that all but the "down-east Yankees" lacked the necessary preparation in the subject. There is no doubt that Stevens applied himself in French and drawing, but his innate advantages should not be forgotten. He was not a poor farm boy of seventeen competing against cadets with superior educational attainments, but rather a young man from a prominent New England family with good political and economic connections, a sound educational background, a sharp mathematical mind, and a desire to excel. All of these factors brought him to the top of his academic class.[12]

The most important and trying time for the cadets came at the semiannual examinations. Stevens described the process as a grueling operation: "We were not lifted, we were ground." In contrast to the entrance questions, the course examinations were thorough, as the professors fired queries on theory as well as specific applications. Cadets might be asked, for example, to discuss the subject of friction, give its laws, and find a value for the coefficient of friction by means of the inclined plane. In natural philosophy they were required to draw a cross-section of a human eye and to explain its construction and the optical principles on which it was based. At one examination, Secretary of War Joel Poinsett, who served as a member of the board of visitors, expressed skepticism that the cadets could answer so precisely without knowing the questions beforehand. When Thayer learned of Poinsett's comment, he called the cadets and board of visitors to a special evening session and invited Poinsett and his associates to ask their own questions using the course outlines as a guide. They did, and the cadets performed equally well. The board of visitors that served during Stevens' last year as a cadet testified to the thoroughness of the examinations and the equity of faculty decisions on merit.[13]

Like the other cadets, Stevens approached his first examinations uneasy and excited. He was part of a group examined for four hours in mathematics and then for an equal time in French. A perfect score in mathematics placed him first and he ranked fourteenth in French. In December he stood first in the class despite demerits which placed him forty-third among about sixty students on the conduct roll. He was first in French as well as mathematics at the end of the second round of examinations in June. All agreed, even his rivals Halleck and Biddle, that he was best in mathematics, but Stevens confessed that he did not understand his top grade in French. He explained that he could translate from French to English very well, but could write the language only indifferently and speak it hardly at all. Apparently Stevens was not aware that only translating ability was considered in the grading process even though Berard also drilled the cadets in writing and pronunciation.[14]

In the second year, drawing appeared in the course of study, a subject that Stevens approached with trepidation. Fortunately, at least for Stevens, the Academy was interested in the practical application of art to engineering problems, and he observed, with much relief that "success in this branch depends as much (and perhaps even more) upon perservering application as on a natural talent." He set himself to the task and after much experimenting he developed a technique of drawing broad outlines and then adding considerable shading to produce an acceptable finished product. His professor, Thomas Weir, was not concerned with quantity, so Stevens put in long hours on a small number of drawings. At the end of the course he worked two or three hours a day for twelve weeks on a drawing of the infant Jesus. It took him a week to complete one eye, part of the other, and a curl of hair, but the finished product showed such attention to detail and subtlety in shading that he ranked fourth in drawing.[15]

In addition to the basic mathematics, French, and drawing curriculum, Stevens took courses in natural philosophy and engineering. His instructor in natural philosophy, William H. C. Bartlett, has been called the Academy's most brilliant nineteenth-century graduate. He was named a professor in 1834 and he published books on acoustics, optics, astronomy, mechanics, and physics. Many found both the course and the professor difficult, but Bartlett, like Church, praised Isaac for his ability to generalize and find governing principles. The course that had the most immediate application for Stevens upon graduation was engineering, which was taught by Dennis Hart Mahan, now the best known of the Academy's faculty of that era. Mahan, like Bartlett, graduated from the Academy during the 1820s, and Thayer brought him back as professor of engineering in 1832. His book *Course of Civil Engineering* first appeared in 1837, and it soon achieved general recognition as the best civil engineering text in the English language. Stevens learned the rudiments of building batteries and redoubts, field fortifications, gun placements, forts, and bridges. The Academy allotted little time for training in military tactics and strategy, but it was in these fields that Mahan made his greatest reputation, and the portion of his course spent on warfare proved popular with the cadets. Later in his career Mahan devoted more time to the art of war than he did in the 1830s (his classic work did not appear until 1843), but Stevens learned certain principles that he later attempted to apply in Indian wars and the Civil War. Mahan stressed the maintenance of strong positions to protect lines of supply, and urged vigorous pursuit of a defeated enemy. He drilled into his students the virtues of mobility, surprise, and boldness, and preached that "celerity is the secret of success," a maxim that Stevens adopted for his own.[16]

At the end of his second year Stevens, as was customary, received his only extended leave from West Point. He returned to North Andover for a month, and enjoyed parading before the home folks in his tight cadet jacket with black braid and gold fittings; the uniform was topped off with a high plumed hat that added several inches to his height. Many cadets complained that the heavy shakos gave them headaches, but this was a penalty Stevens was perfectly willing to pay. The homecoming was tarnished by the elder Stevens' chastisement of his son for extravagance in his personal expenditures. The unexpected attack hurt all the more because he had made an effort to economize, and only pleading by his sisters persuaded him not to cut the leave short and return to West Point. With the start of his third year Stevens was named as assistant professor of mathematics and assigned to instruct a group of the slower students in algebra. He found it tedious work, and the ineptness of his pupils taxed his limited patience. At the end of the first term only four of his twelve students passed their examination, and the rest returned home. He continued teaching until graduation, not because he enjoyed it, but because he received twenty-five cents an hour and was relieved from guard duty and other routine military chores.[17]

Stevens was active in the Dialectic Society, one of the few sanctioned extracurricular activities allowed the cadets. He realized that public speaking was not one of his strong suits for he spoke too rapidly and tended to be shy and withdrawn at large gatherings. After one of his early efforts he admitted to being "most woefully used up" by the critics. The Saturday evening meetings provided debate on a wide range of topics, such as the expediency of studying dead languages, the desirability of lynch law, and slavery. Stevens had strong opinions on most topics, and the weekly gatherings forced him to organize and present his arguments in a cogent, coherent manner.[18]

Stevens took the lead in obtaining subscriptions to start a collection of history, biography, and travel books which would supplement the Academy's limited holdings in nontechnical works. The project resulted from Stevens' recognition that the Military Academy did not provide a well-rounded liberal education. He complained that "some of the faculties are developed in a high degree, whilst others are almost entirely ignored; its effect is . . .

to cast the mind in a rough, strong mold, without embellishing or polishing it." Was it not, he once argued, of greater advantage to have a good idea of political economy or the principles of composition, than to be able to solve some abstruse problem in mathematics? He longed for more time to read history and poetry and to improve his writing style. The board of visitors, while generally favorable to the Academy, echoed his criticism when they complained that one professor and an assistant provided all the instruction in history, geography, ethics, constitutional and international law, rhetoric, and grammar. The school gave no examinations in history and totally ignored English composition. But the board's protest had little if any effect on the curriculum. Stevens was disillusioned by the lack of change, and in one bitter outburst he castigated the Academy as "the charnel house of mind [,] as the extinguisher of all those noble aspirations after self improvement and eminence which should characterize a man of liberal education." West Point, he averred, deadened fine qualities of heart and mind and turned men into machines.[19]

There was some truth in Stevens' complaint, but also an element of unfairness, for the Academy, as Thayer had recognized, could not possibly provide a complete liberal and technical education in four years. At least a portion of his ill temper can be dismissed as a typical display of undergraduate fault-finding, a tendency to which cadets were particularly susceptible after spending four years confined to West Point. But Stevens was entirely sincere in his desire to broaden his education. He conducted his own self-improvement program, reading ancient, European, and American history, and every work of biography, fiction, or poetry he could obtain. To provide experience in English composition for himself and others, he established an underground newspaper, *The Talisman*, of which he was editor and apparently the major contributor. In a prospectus issued for the newspaper, Stevens argued that composition best trained the mind "to deep thought and patient investigation," and he assailed his superiors for displaying "cold sovereign contempt" and not even a "smile of condescension" to his request to include writing instruction in the course of study. He called for essays on lofty subjects and warned that any paper not characterized by wit, dignity, and good sense would be rejected. Perhaps this warning scared off potential contributors, but Stevens wrote a series of papers including "Has Man a Conscience," "The Importance of a Good Style of Writing to an Officer of the Army,"

and "History—The Proper Study of Mankind is Man." The
journal also offered an outlet to satirize the faculty, administration, army, and fellow cadets. Stevens enjoyed it all immense-
ly, and once wrote a savage, anonymous rebuttal to one of his
own compositions, which produced a flood of sympathy for the
original article and its author. By the end of his four years he
had moved a long way toward providing himself the liberal
education necessary to complement the Academy's technical
training.[20]

During Stevens' years at West Point his sisters and brother
looked to him for guidance. They sought advice on family quarrels, educational decisions, courses of study, and career as well
as personal problems. He was more understanding, more knowl-
edgeable, and more approachable than their father on most of
these issues, and the family forced him to accept the role of ar-
biter and decision maker. In return the family sent much
unasked advice, most of which he ignored, at least after his first
weeks at West Point. Typically, Susan urged that he "not be induced by any to indulge in the dangerous practices of chewing,
smoking, or making use of any sort of spirit even wine." Any
one of these, she warned, would debase the man, weaken his
mind, and ruin the soul. Elizabeth warned against reading novels because they were addictive, and "they have a very per-
nicious effect on the mind."[21]

Stevens could ignore these pious warnings, but he could not
avoid being touched by the schism that his stepmother created
in the family. His father refused to interfere with Ann's rule
over household affairs or to intervene in her disputes with the
children. While at West Point, Stevens was particularly concerned by reports that Ann did not take proper care of his father when his leg forced him to take to his bed. She also refused
to hire an extra hand to help her hobbled husband because the
new man would need to sleep in her parlor. Stevens mused that
he wished his stepmother "could be fully conscious of how
much unhappiness she is the willful cause." But he urged his
sisters to do their duty and give no cause for complaint, and
suggested that "Mother is undeniably a woman of very strong
feelings and could we by any conciliatory course of conduct
turn them in our favor, the parental roof would be as it once
was, the abode of real happiness." Stevens took his own advice,
for he began inquiring about his stepmother's health, and he invited her to attend graduation ceremonies along with his father.
That occasion proved to be the high point of his relationship

with his stepmother. She and her husband were impressed by the high regard shown for their son at the Academy and they proudly basked in the reflected glory. But Ann began to suffer increasingly from ill health, and the old animosities returned, never again diminishing until she died of tuberculosis.[22]

Stevens also attempted to guide his sisters' educational development. They had attended local schools and had become country school teachers, but their knowledge was limited to the rudiments of reading, writing, and arithmetic. Their father had mixed feelings about education, but was convinced that one college graduate in the family was sufficient; he often urged his eldest son to study hard, but just as often he warned that he should avoid injury by too much study. Elizabeth confided to her brother that she wished to pursue Latin, but feared her father would protest. Isaac told her to go ahead, and promised that he would accept the blame if any was forthcoming. He sent continual advice on books to read and mailed home copies of the *Democratic Review* and the *Knickerbocker*.[23] Stevens urged his oldest sister, Hannah, to cultivate a taste for poetry. He confessed that he once had not liked it, but then discovered "it refines and polishes the mind," and that "truth always makes a deep impression when garbed in the fascinating garb of poetry." He even recommended novels, despite his sisters' pious objections that reading such literature was immoral.[24]

A particular concern was the welfare of his only brother, Oliver, the youngest member of the family, who was ten years old when Isaac left for West Point. Oliver displayed a personality almost the reverse of his older brother; he was extroverted, easygoing, not overly ambitious, and happy working on his father's farm. Stevens constantly urged his brother to read, often suggesting biography, and he sent books as presents, among them Washington Irving's *Astoria*. Isaac, Sr. was skeptical, muttering that too many men were ruined by college and that in any event they could not afford to send a second son to school. His eldest son pretended to agree but insisted that Oliver follow a program of self-education, which could be pursued during long winter nights otherwise wasted. Stevens reminded his father that one of his heroes, Benjamin Franklin, had followed just such a program of study, and asked, "How could Oliver . . . pass the time better than reading or studying till perhaps ten in the evening?" The year after he left West Point, Stevens submitted his brother's application to the Military Academy, and spent three weeks in Washington City lobbying on Oliver's behalf. He found that there was a reluctance to appoint brothers as it smacked of favoritism, although it had occurred on previous occasions. But Stevens did not have the necessary influence to make his brother one of the exceptions, although he did succeed in pressuring his father into sending Oliver to Bowdoin College in Maine.[25]

While at the Military Academy Stevens did not commit himself to the army as a permanent career. He believed only that his training was an important "first step" in his life. There is little doubt that he departed in 1839 with a better technical background and liberal education than the great majority of his generation. At the Academy he had been exposed to men like Church, Bartlett, and Mahan, who were preeminent in their fields and who provided excellent examples for scholars to emulate. The Academy's discipline confirmed his own predilections toward order, hard work, and fixed goals. Stevens gained enormously in self-confidence and in his opinion of his own worth. Countless class recitations, oral examinations, and debates left him unafraid of presenting his opinions before others. While still at the Academy he told a friend that he believed men like Milton and Napoleon achieved success as a result of hard work and study, not from inherited genius. He left West Point confident that the first step was prologue and that continued effort would propel him to greatness.[26]

3

THE YOUNG
LIEUTENANT

In the spring of 1839 the newly appointed Chief Engineer, Joseph G. Totten, requested four or five "eminently qualified" cadets for his corps. After summer graduation ceremonies the superintendent dispatched Isaac Stevens to Fort Adams at Newport, Rhode Island, most likely because it was "Totten's fort," and it was always good policy to provide the Chief Engineer with the best man available. Second Lieutenant Stevens was not consulted, but he could not have made a better choice if he had picked his own post. He had earlier told his father that he hoped for assignment to Boston, where he could work directly under Sylvanus Thayer, whom he praised as the "most scientific man in the Corps . . . in whose superior judgment and intelligence I can rely." But Newport also had great advantages. Colonel Totten had supervised construction of Fort Adams for twenty years, and although he would henceforth be stationed in Washington D.C., it was assumed that he would keep a close eye on the fort's progress, and that officers in Newport would have ample opportunity to secure his approbation. The other four men assigned to the Engineer Corps remained at the Academy as instructors. Stevens' good friend, Henry Smith, complained bitterly. "Blast West Point," Smith cursed, "I don't want to go back there." He protested that he would learn nothing new and lamented an existence subjected to the same old preaching. Stevens was properly sympathetic, but pleased that he had escaped his comrades' fate.[1]

Newport exceeded the young lieutenant's fondest expectations. It was the home of numerous families with wealth or position, and officers were in constant demand to participate in the city's active social life. Stevens' lot was far different from that of the typical Military Academy graduates of this era who in times of peace were usually assigned to isolated posts where amenities were few, the pay low, and promotion painfully slow. A friend reported to Stevens on the life of some of his comrades stationed on the Michigan frontier, who could do little except attempt to conduct drills and keep the post in order. The friend observed:

Nothing is so well calculated to stifle ambitions and palsy the energies of a young officer as to be thrown into a remote frontier fort, without society, without books ... and nothing so well fits him to plunge incontinently into vicious habits as to live a mere animal existence.

The army also suffered from negative public opinion during the two decades prior to the Mexican War. As the American Revolution and the War of 1812 became dim memories, the anti-militarism of the nation asserted itself. The Jacksonians trumpeted the virtues of the militia and viewed the new professionalism of the Regular Army as dangerous. Ulysses S. Grant told of proudly walking down a Cincinnati street soon after his graduation from the Military Academy, and suffering embarrassment when small boys hooted and jeered at his uniform.[2]

Antimilitarism was muted in Newport and the pleasures of the city's society were numerous, but Lieutenant Stevens seriously considered resigning. He would not have been alone, for by the eve of the Mexican War about one-third of his graduating class had left the army.[3] The prospects for young officers had worsened in 1838 when the Eighth Infantry was formed and, in response to political pressure, its officers selected from civilian life. Stevens had always viewed the Military Academy more as the source of an education than as preparation for an army career, and this fact, in addition to the seeming lack of opportunity for future advancement, led him to consider alternative professions. He came back to his earlier choice—law. He explained to his father that the reasons for this decision were "thick as blackberries," but most important, law suited him better than the army. He drew up a program whereby he would remain with the Engineer Corps for three years while studying history and ethics in his spare time and saving the money necessary to finance a three-year training period in a law office. Stevens told his unconvinced father that the decision to attend West Point was one "which circumstances and good luck ... forced upon me," and time would prove "the longest way round is the shortest way home." Knowing his father would think the four-year effort and expense wasted, Stevens argued that the Academy had developed the proper habits and faculties which would serve him well in any field of endeavor.[4]

A major reason for Stevens' return to the law was his acquaintance with Benjamin Hazard, whose daughter Margaret he had begun courting. Hazard was a prominent Rhode Island lawyer who had served in the state legislature for thirty-one consecutive years. He encouraged the young man's ambition, recommended a course of reading, and promised that he would secure him a place in the office of the well-known Jeremiah Mason of Boston when he was ready to devote full time to law studies. Stevens' family, his friends, and his old advisor Nathan Hazen were not enthusiastic about the plan as they believed it showed inconsistency of purpose to alter careers, particularly when he had barely embarked on the first. Hazen offered lukewarm encouragement, but advised that if he was determined to proceed he should acquire a solid backing in ethics, history, and general legal principles, areas in which he found most law students woefully weak. A former classmate, Henry Smith, said he would not try to persuade him to remain in the corps because "if you fear the struggle and think it too great for the prize then it would be so." But Smith then offered some persuasive arguments why he should stay. Smith believed that Totten would raise the status of the Engineer Corps, and he speculated that Stevens would someday have a good chance of replacing the Chief Engineer for he would be "in the prime of life when Col. Totten is no more." Smith suggested, only half-jokingly, that the pretty girl in Newport appeared to have upset his equilibrium; perhaps if he married her he could think more clearly. But Stevens was determined, and "as soon as I decided, I began to act." Fate stepped in and dealt the plan a severe blow when his patron Benjamin Hazard died early in 1841 from pulmonary tuberculosis.[5]

Hazard's death proved only the first of several circumstances that forestalled his intended resignation. Another was increasing responsibility within the corps, which not only made the army more palatable but made it difficult to find time for independent study. And Stevens became a husband and father who could not afford the luxury of changing professions. Soon after arriving in Newport, Lieutenant James Mason of the Engineer Corps, a native of the city, had introduced him to society. Stevens looked back at the West Point balls and dancing lessons with gratitude when he suddenly found himself the center of at-

traction at a series of social functions. One of Newport's young
ladies reported that some of her friends thought the new lieutenant homely. If she was correct, it was no doubt a consequence
of the large head on a slight body which made it appear that
each had become separated from a more logical counterpart.
But this factor aside, Isaac Stevens was a dashing young man of
twenty-one who possessed dark hazel eyes, thick black hair
which curled over his ears and collar, a small goatee carefully
trimmed, straight nose, and firmly set lips and chin. Whatever
their opinion of him, he was completely enamored of the young
ladies. After four years of relative isolation on the Hudson, the
splendors of Newport and the attentions of flirtatious young
belles were quite enough to set any young man's head spinning.
One former roommate, still pining away at West Point, en-
viously speculated that there must be "plenty of pretty ladies"
at Newport, and he warned his friend to "beware of Cupid's
shafts—they oft transfix the stoutest heart."[6]

The prophecy was accurate; Stevens appeared with increasing
frequency in the company of Margaret Lyman Hazard, a de-
scendant of two prominent Newport families. On the Lyman
side of the family, her grandfather had served as an officer in
the Revolution and later as chief justice of Rhode Island. Margaret's maternal grandmother, Mary "Polly" Wanton, descended
from colonial merchants and political leaders, including a governor. During the Revolution French officers stationed in the city,
bewitched by her beauty and vivaciousness, called her "Charming Polly Wanton." Margaret's mother was one of thirteen children but she inherited the Newport home when the rest of the
family moved to Providence.[7]

Margaret was a year older than Stevens, and she liked to be
called Meg, Margie, or Maggie—anything but Margaret. She
had a small, slight figure, and dark hair fell in ringlets over her
shoulders, framing an oval face set with expressive eyes, aquiline
nose, and a small mouth. Meg possessed an aristocratic bearing
and the charm of her grandmother Polly; she was well educated
and polished, but also bored with the confinement that prevailing social standards placed on her activities. Meg complained to her sister, "My life is composed of items and noth-
ings," and she made occasional half-hearted resolutions to spend
more time in reading and self-improvement. Stevens may have
met her for the first time at the reading society, an organization
she attended less for intellectual improvement than for company. Meg was not immediately impressed with the young lieu-

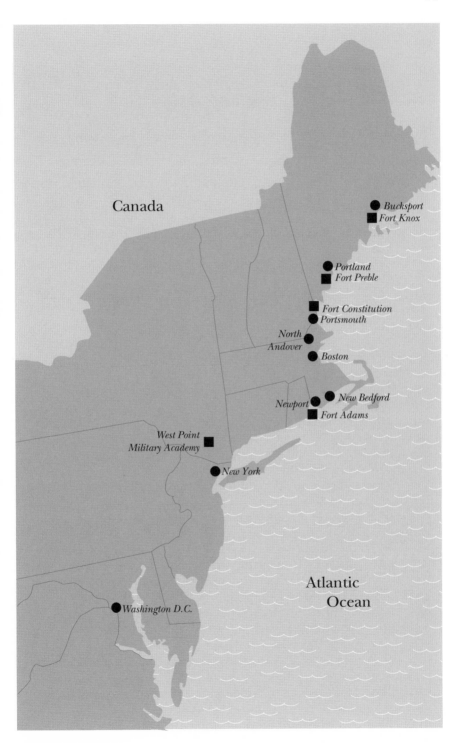

Canada

● Bucksport
■ Fort Knox

● Portland
■ Fort Preble

■ Fort Constitution
● Portsmouth

North
Andover ●

● Boston

Newport ● ● New Bedford
■ Fort Adams

West Point ■
Military Academy

● New York

Atlantic
Ocean

● Washington D.C.

Northeast Coast Forts

tenant, although he was smitten at once. Numerous suitors vied for her attention, which was not surprising for an attractive, charming young lady who had social position and a comfortably well-to-do family. She had been engaged briefly to a man deemed to be below the Hazards in social standing. Meg justified the match with the rationalization that "love is blind." Her father, "Black Ben," stormed that love was not reason enough, and the engagement was quashed.[8]

Meg's interest in Stevens blossomed after a particular reading-society meeting early in the winter of 1840. During the course of the meeting Stevens read with great feeling, and when the group started to break up at ten o'clock, Meg suggested to a few of the younger set that they stay to play Old Maid. It would be a shame, she said, to go home just when the evening was getting sociable. An early snow lay upon the ground and when they finally left, she jumped into a sleigh, and with Stevens pulling and others pushing, they "went like the wind down Touro St." The next day Stevens sent her some verses, and Meg took "a fancy" to the poems of Wordsworth. She also began to fancy the lieutenant, and she later confided to her sister Mary, "I like Stevens a great deal better. He improves so much on a nearer acquaintance." She saw "a strong undercurrent of soul refinement and honor in him." Meg confessed that she felt love, but, surprised that she would admit it even to her closest confidant, she then suggested a feeling closer to "devotion." Still, she was sure "the more I see him, the more I like him."

Meg saw a lot of Stevens for the next few months. There were sleigh rides, and in good weather there was horseback riding, a favorite pastime of Meg's, or they took long walks on the beach, where one evening, accompanied by another couple, they spent six hours looking at the moon on the water. They studied German under the tutelage of Charles Brooks, a Unitarian minister, who was also Meg's brother-in-law. Stevens began reading more poetry, although he was not so smitten that he could not rate Shakespeare and Milton superior to Byron. Inspired both by Meg and by a phrenologist who told him he had the makings of a poet, he set himself to writing verse. Henry Smith joshed Stevens with mock disbelief: "I heard . . . from good authorities that you are in love!!!!!" Writing from his West Point quarters, Smith sighed that "it must be delightful to ride out with a lady and talk German with her." Henry Stevens came to Newport to visit and complained that he could seldom find his cousin because he was always off somewhere with Meg. Stevens denied all these allegations, but he did not fool Smith, who concluded that his friend had fallen and was "not very much to be pitied since you are gone to such sweet ruin."[9]

The courtship continued throughout 1840. Even a trip to Washington D.C., where Stevens' old rival, Henry Halleck, showed him the town and introduced ladies that Halleck claimed to be the most attractive in the world, could not turn his thoughts from Meg. Benjamin Hazard approved the match, and even encouraged it, as Stevens appeared to be a good catch compared to his daughter's previous favorite. The engagement was announced early in 1841 with the wedding planned for the spring. Hazard's death in March forced a postponement, and it was not until September 8, 1841, that Charles Brooks presided over a quiet ceremony in the same parlor of the Hazard house where Meg's mother and grandmother had said their vows. From the Stevens family only Oliver and Cousin Henry attended the ceremony. The groom put on a brave front, explaining that only "something very unusual" would induce his father to leave the farm during the harvest season, but he was hurt and disappointed by his absence. Although Stevens had denounced the Military Academy throughout his cadetship, he took his bride to West Point for the honeymoon. They visited scenes of his cadet escapades, and climbed the hills to view "the grandeur of the Highlands." One walk turned into a four-hour hike to the highest point above the post, and Stevens boasted that it was "a pretty good feat for a lady." A week after the wedding they were back in Newport, where Stevens found orders sending him to New Bedford to supervise reconstruction of an old fort. He rode off the following day, leaving Meg at her mother's home.[10]

The works at Newport and New Bedford were part of a chain of coastal defenses that stretched from Maine to Texas. The real impetus for the fort system came from the War of 1812; there was no better example of the value of the forts than the embarrassing sack of unfortified Washington contrasted with the successful defense of Baltimore bulwarked by Fort McHenry. In 1816 Congress appropriated $838,000 and appointed a Board of Engineers that included the Chief Engineer, Joseph Swift, and Simon Bernard, once an engineer officer for Napoleon. John C. Calhoun, Secretary of War, presented their recommendations to Congress in 1818 along with his suggestion that construction be placed under the authority of the Corps of Engineers. In six years the corps spent over three million dollars in beginning works up and down the coast. After 1824 appropriations dwindled as the memory of the war faded and the Jacksonians tightened the budget. In the 1830s many of the works stood virtually completed but empty as the army lacked funds for either men or ordnance. The engineers took up some of the slack time by clearing harbors, improving river navigation, and constructing the wings and dome of the national capitol.[11]

When Stevens first reported to Newport in July 1839, he found Fort Adams under the immediate supervision of First Lieutenant James Mason, an 1836 graduate of the Military Academy and Totten's assistant for the previous three years, but Totten remained very much in command. Joseph G. Totten better than anyone except perhaps Sylvanus Thayer epitomized the Corps of Engineers in the first two-thirds of the nineteenth century. He graduated from the Military Academy in 1805, and was one of the bright officers often pointed to by early defenders of the school. Totten was a professional totally dedicated to the fortune of the corps, which he served through three wars and as Chief Engineer from 1838 until his death in 1864. In his personal relationships Totten was genial and urbane; professionally he directed the corps with firm authority, honesty, and integrity. Fair and impartial to subordinates, he did his utmost to remedy errors and grievances. Unlike many military leaders, Totten was not a primadonna and managed to avoid most of the bickering that took place within the upper ranks of the army. The Chief Engineer was a stickler for detail, as Stevens soon discovered. For example, Totten sent Mason and Stevens precise instructions on the type of latrines he desired at Fort Adams and explained fully the proper method of installation. He ordered that they use all iron, but later wrote, "I find on reflection, that it will be necessary to make the tops of wood, otherwise in cold weather, the skin might be taken off." As a consequence of this close direction, Mason's competent supervision, and the advanced state of construction, Stevens' duties were confined to routine supervision of bricklaying, plastering, and, no doubt, latrine installation. The routine was broken only by the Secretary of War's inspection tour in 1839, and visits to Washington and North Andover. This left time for study and for courting Meg, but it also left him dissatisfied with army life. He believed that he was overtrained for a position as overseer or straw boss.[12]

Prior to his marriage it appeared that Stevens' duties at Fort Adams would continue indefinitely because in August two companies of artillery were ordered to the post and substantial work was needed to complete the quarters. Thus he was completely surprised by the order issued during the honeymoon which assigned him to New Bedford; Meg was probably equally astonished at the alacrity with which her husband responded. Stevens described his method of operation.

We arrived at Newport about four o'clock on Thursday. I left the next day at two o'clock, made an inspection of the fort on Saturday forenoon, issued a hand-bill the same day for mechanics and laborers, and on Monday morning had a gang of about twenty men at work. I never was in New Bedford before, and knew not a single man in the place.... I went on Monday into a ledge of granite rock, and have already thrown out about two hundred tons of stone, and got about a hundred feet cut.... After I had been at work three days, I dismissed three men for idleness, which had a very good effect.

As for his bride of two weeks, whom he had not seen for seven days, Stevens was not perturbed, for "I have been so busy that I have had no time to miss her."[13]

New Bedford's resurrection as a part of the nation's coastal defenses resulted partially from the election of a Whig President in 1840 and partially from increased tension in relations with Great Britain and Mexico. Stevens took an active interest in the presidential canvass and sourly watched the successful progress of the log-cabin and hard-cider campaign. But the Whig victory proved a boon for both Stevens and the professional army as it resulted in a subtle shift in executive leadership and Congressional votes. Most significant for the Corps of Engineers was the first increase in appropriations for coastal works since the 1820s. However, the change in administration did not mean an end to attacks on the army or the Military Academy.[14]

But for the Corps of Engineers the threat in the early 1840s came not so much from outside as from within military circles. Other branches of the service, envious of the increased prestige of the corps, attempted to remove the Military Academy from its exclusive control and substitute a rotating leadership. A second battle developed with the Corps of Topographical Engineers, which claimed a monopoly over the construction of public works. A related issue was the plan of the engineers to train a company of sappers and miners who would replace civilian employees in construction of forts and other works; opposition arose from General Wool and other Regular Army leaders. Some military men even questioned the necessity of further coastal fortifications. Major General Edmund P. Gaines proposed a widely discussed plan under which forts would be maintained at only a few key points, with the bulk of the coastal defense to be taken over by naval squadrons and floating batteries. Totten rejoined that forts were more economical over the long haul because coastal works protected against land as well as sea attacks, and allowed the nation to maintain a smaller army and navy. The Chief Engineer argued that he would be glad to see a strong navy, but not at the expense of coastal works. Congress was inclined to accept Totten's view.[15]

All the threats to the Corps of Engineers were successfully met, and fortification proceeded with renewed vigor. New plans were made and old ones dusted off. For example, the Secretary of War, alarmed by the Maine boundary dispute, asked for defense plans for the Northeast coast. Totten discovered that the Board of Engineers had recommended defenses for the area in 1823, but had delayed specific plans until the War Department provided maps and surveys; Totten laconically resubmitted the map request which had never been filled. The Chief Engineer estimated that $10 million had been expended on coastal fortifications prior to 1840 and that an additional $23 million, plus $8 million for ordnance, was required to finish the job properly. He envisioned an eventual total garrison of 54,000 men manning 10,500 large guns.[16]

As at many points along the eastern coast, the defenses at New Bedford were pre-War of 1812 works that had fallen into disrepair. Totten requested $50,000 to restore New Bedford's fort, expecting and receiving only a small fraction of that amount, but enough to begin work. Lieutenant Stevens in his first examination found that the fort contained only a frontal embankment and even at its strongest was readily vulnerable to flank attacks. No powder magazine existed, and the structures within the walls trembled on the verge of collapse. The wooden gun platforms had decayed and bricks in the walls were so loose that many could be removed by hand. Stevens' initial orders required only that he repair the parapet and gun platforms to receive batteries, but with typical energy the young lieutenant began making plans to turn the work into one of the major forts on the Atlantic Coast. He even revived the old name, Fort Phoenix, which appropriately designated the new battlements rising from the old ashes. The War Department ignored his nomenclature and insisted upon the more prosaic "old fort at New Bedford." Stevens received $3,451 for the remaining months of 1841, a sum which limited his plans, but he began with twenty men blasting rock to use in the new parapet and scarp, and he put another eighteen to work building a road to the fort. Totten quickly drew in the reins and ordered his officer to confine work to preparing the fort to receive guns. In December they placed nine twenty-four pound guns with their carriages upon the new pintle plates.[17]

As the spring and a new working season approached, Lieutenant Stevens, unable to restrain his ambitions, renewed the plea to extend and expand the fort, arguing that as the third largest port in the country, New Bedford deserved a proper fortification. In addition to a general rebuilding, he urged construction of a magazine and a hot-shot furnace. But because New Bedford was close to the gigantic Fort Adams, it remained low on the priority list, and Totten only allowed completion of small tasks such as building a shingled roof over the guns and sodding the parapet. Suffering from enforced inactivity, Stevens proposed a topographical survey of the New Bedford area. His work at the fort would be no hindrance "to give proper attention to both duties," and he could gain valuable experience. As Totten had little patience with the Topographical Engineers, whose domain Stevens would be invading, he gave enthusiastic support, and praised the plan as indicative of the "zeal and spirit of inquiry by which the corps builds much of its reputation."[18]

Using the base lines of a state survey, Stevens proceeded with a general sketch that traced possible invasion routes and noted military obstacles, forests, swamps, rivers, and suitable defensive locations. Using triangulation, he plotted the primary points and then filled in the details with the assistance of existing maps augmented by personal reconnaissance. A second survey covered the harbor and outlying islands—a task that consumed countless hours in sounding to provide an accurate depth chart. It proved an exciting exercise in which Stevens could put much of his training to practical use for the first time. He failed only in his estimate of the time necessary for the project, initially telling Totten it would consume a few weeks. Stevens characteristically took the most optimistic view and often failed to allow for illness, bad weather, unexpected delays, or other contingencies. In the fall he reported the fort in good condition where he had been allowed to proceed, but pointed out that the scarp was in poor condition, the buildings leaky at best, and the magazine still nonexistent. A picket fence served as a temporary gorge wall to keep out invasions of sightseers. Stevens admitted that the topographical survey was still incomplete; he com-

plained that a seige of sickness in July and an old theodolite
which was constantly malfunctioning had slowed progress, but
promised completion by the next summer.[19]

The year and one-half that Stevens spent at New Bedford
passed pleasantly. His duties never became onerous, and, as the
sole officer at the post, he could test his judgment and professional abilities. He brought Meg, pregnant with their first child,
to Fairhaven in September 1841. They rented the front half of a
double house located near the fort and overlooking the harbor.
Often they sat before the fireplace on a large hair sofa drinking
London porter or watching from the window as whaling vessels
slipped in and out of the bay. Stevens mused that it, was just
the spot where he would like to build a cottage to enjoy the
"downhillside of life," when he had a head of gray hair and
could "hear little soft joyous musical voices call me grandpapa."
But he soon returned to the reality that he was "yet low on the
hillside and have scarce begun the laborious ascent." The Stevenses suffered the material inconveniences of newlyweds living
on a limited salary. Their home was small and sparsely furnished,
but they found more commodious houses rented for $400 a year,
or about one-fourth of Stevens' salary. Meg fussed that she had
never seen such an extravagant place to live, but her husband
praised her for "proportioning [our] style of living to our
means." Although Stevens did not consider his duties challenging, Meg complained that he often worked from six to six, and
then spent the evening drawing. She tried sitting up to the early
morning hours to keep him company but admitted "it was
rather tiresome," and "tis dull music for the bride." She asked
her sister Mary, in jest, "Would you not be divorced [?]" Meg
found that she would need to provide for her own entertainment. Novels filled many evenings, and she attended lectures in
New Bedford when her husband or someone else would accompany her. Meg was accustomed to living among a large circle of
friends and family, and New Bedford for her was "lonely . . .
sometimes," but she insisted "[I] cannot complain."[20]

In June 1842 Meg gave birth to their first child at the Hazard home in Newport. The proud father was present at this
"most interesting moment" only because a physician had prescribed calomel for a bilious condition and the cure prevented
his return to New Bedford. The new child, Hazard, unlike his
father, was a robust, healthy baby, but Meg remained weak and
ill throughout the summer and fall. Stevens assured his father
with uncharacteristic jocularity, "Now . . . you may fairly say

that you have a right to your grey hairs." Hazard, he claimed, was "superlatively beautiful, as he looks exactly like his father." With less humor, he fretted that the little fellow squalled unmercifully and "takes it for granted that no ones convenience is to be consulted but his own." While Meg remained in Newport, her husband rented a house in New Bedford for a reasonable $156 a year which provided more room and privacy, and, with the help of Meg's sister Emily, proudly furnished it before Meg returned.[21]

Stevens took Meg sailing on the bay, and they traveled to Providence to hear lectures by Ralph Waldo Emerson, Wendell Phillips, and William Ellery Channing. Stevens continued to support Phillips's stand on slavery, praised Emerson as giving solid satisfaction that few lecturers could match, and saluted Channing as "a great champion of human rights", whose work he read and collected at every opportunity. John Quincy Adams's conduct in the House of Representatives impressed Stevens for he overlooked Adams's former opposition to Andrew Jackson and exclaimed "how grandly" the old man conducted himself on the slavery issue. He agreed totally with Adams's argument that slavery jeopardized the North because laws protecting slavery threatened traditional liberties. It was a position that many, particularly those with a legalistic mind, found comfortable, but Stevens did not go as far as his father, who by the early forties was harboring slaves on the underground railroad.[22]

Stevens' reading program for the law dropped by the wayside when he assumed command at New Bedford, but he continued to read history and biography. He also shifted toward military works, indicating a conscious move away from the law. Friends in Boston sent him atlases, and he pondered Machiavelli, studied Jomini, read biographies of Frederick the Great, and pored over the Napoleonic campaigns. Enormously impressed by the Italian campaign, he believed the key to the Corsican's success lay less in his strategy than in his supremacy over the hearts and minds of soldiers, who followed "their leader to the death, never knowing fatigue." "Such," Stevens believed, "is the omnipotence of a great mind. Brute force triumphed not in Italy— but a master spirit, a sagacious intellect, a lofty and daring soul. . . ." This summed up his own philosophy of military command and indeed of political life as well.

While in Washington D.C., in an unsuccessful attempt to secure his brother's appointment to West Point, Stevens visited the Senate and listened to John C. Calhoun, Henry Clay, Dan-

iel Webster, and Thomas Hart Benton debate the issues. He left
unimpressed, dismissing Webster as a political opportunist and
Clay as a man more interested in sarcasm and invective than
solid argument. One can see Stevens contemplating his own future when he speculated that the efforts of both generals and
political leaders seemed attainable by industry if united with a
fair share of capacity; he well knew that he fit that formula for
success.[23]

In November 1842 the Chief Engineer ordered Lieutenant
Stevens north to assume command of repairs at Fort Constitution (near Portsmouth) and at Fort Preble (at Portland).
The order reflected increasing government concern over the
Maine boundary and a general deterioration of relations with
Great Britain. Stevens had once characterized the indecision
over the boundary location as "fawning subservience," an opinion most Northeast men shared; now it appeared in 1842 that a
resolution of the issue was at hand. Colonel Totten recommended a refurbishing of the coastal defenses from Bangor south to
Portsmouth. The absence of defensive works on Maine's northern frontier did not cause undue apprehension, for few people
and no military objectives encumbered the area, and overland
attack routes to the south were long and difficult. Totten wished
to cut off a possible attack by sea and prevent any drive down
the coast from the area of the Penobscot River or points farther
south. As a consequence, he recommended a new fort at the
mouth of the Penobscot and an arsenal at Bangor, as well as extension and repair of the Portland and Portsmouth works.[24]

Forts Constitution and Preble, like the installation at New
Bedford, had been constructed prior to the War of 1812, and by
the 1840s they were badly in need of repair. Stevens' orders required him to work in consultation with and under the general
supervision of Colonel Thayer. Stevens traveled to Boston in December, and Thayer agreed to his remaining in New Bedford
for the winter to complete his topographical survey. This would
allow the young officer to be with his family. In any event, no
work could be started until spring. No further construction was
attempted at New Bedford, and the fort was never manned, but
it remained under Stevens' nominal command with a caretaker
in charge until 1853. Returning north in March, Stevens first
concentrated on the repairs to Fort Preble (located on Cape
Elizabeth outside of Portland). He had instructions to rebuild
the powder magazine with walls and ceiling, to repair the gun
mountings, and to extend the parapet. Colonel Totten provided

Isaac Ingalls Stevens (1818-1862), first Governor of Washington Territory.
Manuscripts, Archives, and Special Collections, Washington State University Libraries,
Pullman, WA.

Isaac Stevens, probably when serving as Washington Territory's delegate to the U. S. Congress, 1857-1861. *Washington State Historical Society, Tacoma, WA.*

"Meg"; Mrs. Margaret Stevens in middle age. *Washington State Capital Museum, Olympia, WA.*

Portrait of Margaret Stevens; shortly after her marriage to Isaac in 1841. *Washington State Historical Society, Tacoma, WA.*

Charles H. Mason, Washington Territorial Secretary and close friend of the Stevens family. *Washington State Historical Society, Tacoma, WA.*

Olympia, July 3, 1857. Sketch by topographer James Madison Alden (1834-1922) of the U. S.-Canada boundary survey party. *Washington State Historical Society, Tacoma, WA.*

Governor Stevens welcomes the grand entrance of the Nez Perce to the Walla Walla council grounds, May 24, 1855. Eyewitness sketch by Gustavus Sohon (1825-1903). *Washington State Historical Society, Tacoma, WA.*

The fort and bustling community at Steilacoom on southern Puget Sound, circa 1860. *Washington State Historical Society, Tacoma, WA.*

Major General John E. Wool differed sharply with Stevens in regard to Indian and military affairs in Washington Territory. *Oregon Historical Society, Portland, OR.*

Edward Lander, Chief Justice of Washington Territory and Isaac Stevens' nemesis during the martial law episode. *Washington State Historical Society, Tacoma, WA.*

Stylized composite photograph/lithograph of Brigadier General Isaac Stevens.
Following the 1861-1862 Sea Islands Campaign on the South Carolina coast,
Stevens participated in the Second Battle of Bull Run, Virginia, dying
September 1, 1862, in a subsequent action not far from the nation's capital.
Inset: Hazard Stevens (Isaac's son); probably circa Civil War period. Hazard fell
wounded on the same battlefield where his father died. Hazard recovered to
serve with distinction, earning the rank of Brevet Brigadier General at age 23.
Washington State Historical Society, Tacoma, WA.

detailed instructions for each phase of the construction. For example, on the powder magazine he ordered Stevens to use boards one inch thick and cautioned him to construct the interior walls eight inches from the outer stone. Totten prescribed the construction of a cobble wall below ground level with clay and top sloped outward to provide drainage. Although Stevens chafed under Totten's tight rein and Thayer's scrutiny, he recognized his good fortune in having an independent command that many senior corps officers still sought. He did not complain and followed Totten's and Thayer's instructions closely. By summer two more works, Fort Scammel (on House Island in Portland harbor), and Fort McClary (at Portsmouth), were added to his command.[25]

Totten increased the young lieutenant's duties once again by sending him to Castine, on the east shore of Penobscot Bay, to inspect old fortifications. It had already been decided to build the new fort fifteen miles to the north at the narrows of the river, but Totten wished to salvage or sell any useable materials at Castine. Stevens found a sleepy village, one that still appeared to be part of the eighteenth century, protected by a large earthwork built during the Revolution but captured by the British in the War of 1812. He reserved 30,000 bricks for possible use at Bucksport and suggested that he could "see no reason why the battery should not stand for the antiquarian gratification of the people of Castine." Returning south, Stevens shifted his operations to Portsmouth and began repairs at Fort Constitution, which was located on the right bank at the entrance to the harbor. The fort needed bombproofing of the powder magazine, the lowering of the parade wall, the construction of new gun mountings, and the erection of a seawall to protect a corner of the fort threatening to fall into the bay. No sooner was the work under way than he found himself on the move again, back to the Penobscot River. Totten apologetically explained that no other officer was free to undertake the assignment and, "I have to call on you to take the steps preparatory to the purchase of the site." It was significant that he did not hesitate to call on Stevens to undertake delicate negotiations that would involve large sums of money. At a time when advancement and responsibility came to most officers slowly over a period of many years, Stevens had assumed unusually important duties only four years after graduation.[26]

Stevens eagerly responded to the new challenge. Although ordered only to select the site and negotiate for the land, he ob-

viously hoped that he would receive command of construction;
it was an exciting opportunity to begin a new fort and carry it
through to completion. Working from a map on which Totten
indicated the general site on the west bank of the river opposite
Bucksport, Stevens purchased several parcels of land that totaled
sixty-three acres for $4,323.43. The land did not come cheap.
Once word leaked out of the proposed fort, prices jumped in the
Bucksport area. Stevens expedited the sale by taking title in his
name and then transferring it to the government after completion of the lengthy approval process. The new work was
christened Fort Knox, and work was scheduled to begin in the
spring of 1844 with an appropriation of $15,000 for the first six
months. Stevens efficiently carried out each progressive step: the
purchase of the land, surveying, the clearing and leveling of the
site, and the beginning of actual construction. Totten, short of
good men as always, found it easiest to simply let him continue,
although it was extraordinary for any officer, and unheard of for
a junior officer, to have responsibility for five works all in the
process of construction. The Chief Engineer rationalized that although the duties were burdensome, the new fort was of simple
design and would not require much time once work was under
way. Totten certainly knew that he was being unduly optimistic.
Fort Knox was not in a class with Fort Adams, but the technical and practical problems involved in building a structure with
walls eighteen feet thick, two batteries, plus a wharf, roads, interior walls, and numerous support buildings, were substantial
and represented a full-time job. Totten had confidence that Stevens could handle all these duties and could be trusted to get
the most for the government's money while constructing sound
fortifications. The Chief Engineer often repeated the corps' two
major criteria.

Where so much has to be done in repairing these old forts and it is so difficult to get even a little to do it with, economy, economy, economy must be
the cry of this office. At the same time we must expect that everything be
done well, conditions not easy to reconcile and sometimes probably incompatible.

Stevens, as much as any officer in the corps, appeared able to
combine quality with economy.[27]
    After May 1844 Stevens spent most of his time in Bucksport,
leaving the other forts in the charge of supervisors. One of his
supervisors was his brother Oliver, who temporarily left Bowdoin College to work at Fort Scammel.[28] Stevens soon found

that he needed to be on the ground part of the time and decided to spend a week each month in the Portland-Portsmouth area, but Bucksport became his headquarters. At Fort Knox he immediately encountered major problems in constructing a wharf that would allow easy transportation of equipment and supplies. The steep bank required a retaining wall, and the strong tides necessitated the sinking of heavy piles which were then filled with stone. Stevens soon realized that a breakwater was essential to further protect the wharf. To complicate matters he could find no good stone quarries on government-owned land to provide cheap ballast for the wharf and material for the fort walls. While work on the wharf proceeded, Stevens drafted the preliminary plans for the fort. Totten approved most of his draft, although he reduced the batteries from three to two and warned Stevens that the road from the wharf offered an unobstructed path for an enemy as it could not be swept by the fort's guns. Although Totten made suggestions and dictated changes, the degree of freedom he allowed Stevens stands in striking contrast to his relationship with many of the corps' officers in the field. Totten believed he could trust few of his officers to carry out operations on their own initiative or even to follow detailed instructions from his office.[29]

As Totten's faith in Stevens grew, he pushed for increased appropriations and lent his support to the lieutenant's plans and projects. For the year beginning in July 1845, Congress, at Totten's urging, appropriated $35,000 for Fort Knox and $40,000 for the other works; the next year the figures were $20,000 and $12,000 respectively. Throughout this period, Stevens experienced few problems with the Chief Engineer or the department, and most of the difficulties were minor. For example, an expenditure of five dollars for a gold pen was disallowed as "an unusual and extravagant purchase," and Stevens, with usual persistence, appealed to the Secretary of War but finally had to pay for the pen out of his own pocket. The department also refused to pay for a twelve dollars subscription to the *New York Evening Post*, which he claimed was necessary to keep up on current prices.[30] The most serious dispute arose over construction of officers' quarters at Fort Preble. Totten had decided to rebuild the enlisted men's barracks at the fort, and Stevens suggested constructing the officers' quarters at the same time. Totten demurred that funds were not available, but Stevens persisted, arguing that the quarters formed part of the defensive perimeter, and that he could save $1,000 by beginning construction at

once. Totten cautiously agreed but warned that the cost could
not exceed the $6,000 estimated by Stevens. His figure proved
overly optimistic, and he later requested an additional $3,800 to
finish the work. The Chief Engineer made the appropriation
with great reluctance and admonished Stevens, "After your repeated assurances that it could be done for $6,000 we did not
anticipate further call for funds." The colonel added, "Indeed, if
I had anticipated that it would cost more than $6,000, it would
not have been undertaken at this time."[31]

Stevens found it difficult to oversee the work and keep it running smoothly at five separate forts. In addition to his duties as
architect, engineer, paymaster, and purchasing agent, he discovered that he needed to be involved in direct supervision of the
work. He also learned that he often represented the closest contact of many citizens with the federal government, and thus he
became the recipient of their complaints and problems. Monthly
trips to each fort and the appointment of trusted subordinates
helped alleviate the situation. In addition to Oliver, he placed
one of Meg's Newport cousins, and Isaac Osgood, a friend from
Andover, in key positions. Stevens tried to lure good men by
paying wages five to ten percent higher than the going rate for
comparable jobs. No one complained of nepotism, but an army
inspector questioned the high pay. Stevens replied that labor
was generally higher down east and that his bonus created a
better spirit and meant the men needed less close supervision.
Good morale, he contended, was as important in workmen as in
soldiers.[32]

A different type of pressure came from men seeking employ-
ment. One, William Dearborn, armed with letters of recommendation from Maine congressmen, demanded appointment as civilian supervisor of the two Portland forts. Stevens sent him
packing. Dearborn's friends appealed to the department, but the
young lieutenant held his ground and refused to break up his
organization or to replace a supervisor who had performed well
for three years. Dearborn, and perhaps other disgruntled applicants, then complained to Totten that morale was low at the
Portland forts and charged that Stevens required excessive hours
of work. Stevens admitted that the men at Fort Preble worked
twelve hours rather than the usual ten, but with his permission
they lived at the fort and thus saved a hard hour's row back
and forth. Spirit was good, he insisted, and complaints came
"from a few who fancy that appropriations are made for their
benefit, and that they have the right to be employed at their

terms." "It is not," he vowed, "in the power of any fomentor of discontent . . . to shake the confidence of the men in the justice and honesty which is dealt out to them." Stevens' version appears essentially correct. Totten instructed him to avoid paying wages higher than those prevailing locally, but in all other matters he supported his lieutenant. Significantly, the local newspapers, which vigilantly exposed excessive expense and mismanagement at the Portsmouth Navy Yard, made no complaints about Stevens' management.[33]

In the fall of 1846 Totten personally inspected all the works in Stevens' charge. At Bucksport he found the wharf completed, the road to the fort about two-thirds finished, the two batteries ready for guns, and the magazine intact, while some sodding, leveling, and work on the walls remained incomplete. Totten was impressed and reported, "On the whole . . . very good progress has been made, and . . . operations are pursued with judgment as well as energy." At Fort Preble the old hospital and gun house were gone, the battery was extended by four guns, the parapet was completed, and new hospital, barracks, and quartermaster buildings stood ready for occupants. Totten was concerned only with the officers' sanitary arrangements and suggested privies with deep vaults and two separate compartments, one for officers' families and the other for servants. At Fort Scammel a new battery was complete and the parade ground graded. Totten found all the works "advancing very well." The Chief Engineer's report was high praise as Totten was generally not lavish in his commendations and had an eye for the smallest error. Lieutenant Stevens could be rightly proud of his accomplishment on the northern frontier; he had placed four forts in readiness while completing a good portion of a fifth.

The only drawback to the scheme was the fleeting purpose, if any, served by the coastal forts. Despite the time, energy, and expense, Stevens' forts never repulsed any invaders, and by the Civil War, only fifteen years in the future, they were huge white elephants at the mercy of rifled shells, serving little purpose except (as Stevens had once said of the old fort at Castine) to provide for the "antiquarian gratification" of the neighboring inhabitants. Although Stevens could not peer into the future, he knew he had displayed judgment and energy, and had handled men and equipment with an efficiency that the Chief Engineer thought highly commendable. It seemed that Henry Smith had made an accurate prophecy; the young lieutenant appeared the right material to some day reach the top post in his profession.[34]

Stevens paid a price for his onerous duties. His health suffered from the debilitating Maine winters and the heavy travel schedule which took him on frequent 350-mile round trips, often in inclement weather, from Bucksport to Portsmouth. In addition there were journeys to Boston to buy supplies and collect vouchers, or to confer with Thayer, and annual winter conferences with Totten in Washington City. The constant travel also exacted its toll on Stevens' pocketbook as his bonus pay of $1.50 a day when away from Bucksport did not cover his extra expenses, and he reluctantly turned to his father for loans.

When compared with the placid existence of Newport and New Bedford, these years were also hectic for his family. When Stevens left New Bedford in the spring of 1843, Meg took young Hazard and their possessions back to Newport, and late in the summer they joined Stevens in a rented house in Portsmouth. For Meg life was not unpleasant as Hazard kept her busy, and although she was away from the Newport area for the first time, Portsmouth contained a good number of military officers and their families. In addition, Stevens' relatives from the Cummings family often visited, and they were close to the Stevenses in North Andover. Both Isaac and Meg were doting parents, and Sarah Ann could jokingly exclaim after a visit, "How nicely the Old Folks keep house."[35]

After only a year in Portsmouth, Meg moved to Bucksport where her husband had rented a drafty old house which was the best he could find in the small community. Stevens later purchased this house, which he also used as an office, although most days he was rowed across the river to the construction site. Meg was dismayed by Bucksport; its only similarity to any of her previous homes was its proximity to the sea. For entertainment they took long sleigh rides in the winter, and learned to make a festive occasion out of "fine old cider" for which they splurged twenty cents a bottle. Stevens attempted to enliven Bucksport society by establishing a lyceum and importing speakers who delivered lectures on subjects which included American literature and contemporary English poetry. Stevens delivered one of the papers, probably giving an address on Oliver Cromwell, which he had first prepared for the lyceum in Newport. He jokingly told his brother Oliver that they would be glad to have him give a talk and would pay expenses except for "drinkables" which they could not afford to underwrite. Stevens was soon recognized as the town leader and even found himself selected to lead the search for a new minister.[36]

The early years of Meg and Isaac's marriage passed smoothly and happily, but death hovered about like a dark cloud. Stevens' sisters suffered from tuberculosis. Hannah, who quarreled bitterly with her stepmother until the end, died in 1840, and Susan died in Missouri in 1841, one month after Meg's father had succumbed to the same disease. When Sarah Ann visited in 1843, Stevens could see that she was not well, and he arranged for her care in Portsmouth at the home of an aunt and uncle. The doctor assured Stevens that Sarah did not suffer from the consumption that had taken her two sisters, but his diagnosis was incorrect; her condition worsened and she too died. Meg returned to Newport early in the summer of 1844 to give birth to her second child, Virginia. The infant provided the family with the joy of new life to relieve the pall of Sarah Ann's death and their fears for the two remaining sisters. Stevens brought his family north to their new home in Bucksport in August, and on the way they stopped in North Andover. Mary and Oliver were there, and Elizabeth had just arrived from the West with her new husband, whom she had met and married in Tennessee. Stevens never saw either sister again. Elizabeth died in Tennessee at the end of 1846, outliving her stepmother by only a few weeks. Mary was with Elizabeth at the end and was herself too weak to leave Tennessee. In the spring, accompanied by Oliver, she tried to come home to die, but only reached Cincinnati before the disease which had killed all her sisters brought her also to the grave.[37]

In the midst of this unhappiness, Isaac and Meg's greatest tragedy occurred with the sudden death of their daughter in December 1845. Virginia had appeared healthy and normal, but suddenly she became violently sick and died three days later. Stevens, seeking a rational explanation, ordered an autopsy. He insisted on being present when the doctor opened Virginia's skull and was satisfied that the diagnosis of inflammation of the brain, or encephalitis, had been correct. Meg lamented that "few can judge what he suffered." She remained at home while her husband and a companion brought the small casket to the cemetery. Stevens returned with an "expressive silence which announced . . . that the last sad office had been done."[38]

IN THE
HALLS OF THE
MONTEZUMAS

Cadet George C. McClellan summarized Regular Army sentiment toward the outbreak of war with Mexico when he exclaimed, "War at last sure enough! Ain't it glorious! 15,000 regulars and 50,000 volunteers!" Isaac Stevens well knew that war could provide the opportunity to display courage and leadership on the battlefield, an increase in the army rolls, the chance for rapid promotion, and increased power and prestige for the entire military establishment. All these assumptions proved correct, but in the early months of the war it appeared that Stevens might languish in New England while the glory fell to others. General Zachary Taylor marched into Texas in August 1845 with 3,500 regulars who represented two-thirds of the army's total force. Inevitably incidents occurred between the hostile armies and in May 1846 the first battles took place at Palo Alto and Resaca de la Palma.[1]

During the summer and fall Stevens watched as several engineer officers departed for Mexico, and when Totten's September inspection tour passed with no hint of possible reassignment, his impatience increased. As early as May 1845 Totten had assumed that infantry and artillery regiments would be expanded, and he asked his officers if they wished transfer with promotion to the new regiments. Few did, as the Engineer Corps remained more attractive even without the promotion. Stevens' reply to the Chief Engineer swelled with self-righteous and patriotic hyperbole. He proclaimed his readiness to discharge any duty assigned, "promotion or no promotion, in my own corps or in any other corps or department of the public service, and whether the field of duty be in Oregon, California, or at the North Pole." But the next year, pining away in Bucksport, he dropped his disinterested stance and pleaded for assignment to the theater of war:

In the present condition of military operations against Mexico, three armies actively engaged in the field, two expeditions against the coasts of California, and rumors of a new expedition landing at Tampico and having San Luis Potosi for its objective point, I feel it due myself to state that any call made upon me having reference to any of the above or similar objects would be responded to, with the greatest promptness and alacrity.

Stevens argued that operations at the forts would soon close down for the winter, and continual office work in the severe northern climate would prove detrimental to his health; he prescribed an assignment that would provide moderate exercise in the open air. He realized that his request might be resented as too audacious and he told Totten, lamely, "I do not mean to make any application. I simply propose to communicate certain facts to the department."[2]

The only new orders Stevens received requested him to raise recruits for the Engineer Corps. He advertised extensively in the Maine and New Hampshire newspapers and interviewed candidates who responded.[3] A goal of the corps and a particular concern of Stevens was to upgrade the quality of army recruits. Stevens called for men of character, energy, and resource, promising advancement on merit and opportunity for professional distinction. He indicated they would receive training qualifying them for good jobs on civil works when their tour of duty ended. When the recruits found themselves in Mexico digging trenches in fourteen-hour shifts while exposed to enemy fire, some decided that they had been misled by the corps' recruiters. Seth Clark and Warren Lothrop, two of the first men enlisted by Stevens at Portland, were among those who asked for immediate discharge. They claimed Stevens overstated the rate of pay and implied they would be stationed at West Point with the opportunity to become cadets.

It is likely the recruits only listened to what they wanted to hear, for Stevens had promised training at West Point, but not as cadets, and he had warned that transfer was likely in time of war. Stevens defended himself and the corps by pointing to the instruction offered in reading, writing, and engineering theory to these men not only in the United States, but during the campaigns in Mexico. He claimed that every man in the Engineer Company could "if he chooses to study and do his duty, become a good clerk, overseer, or practical engineer." Lothrop was of-

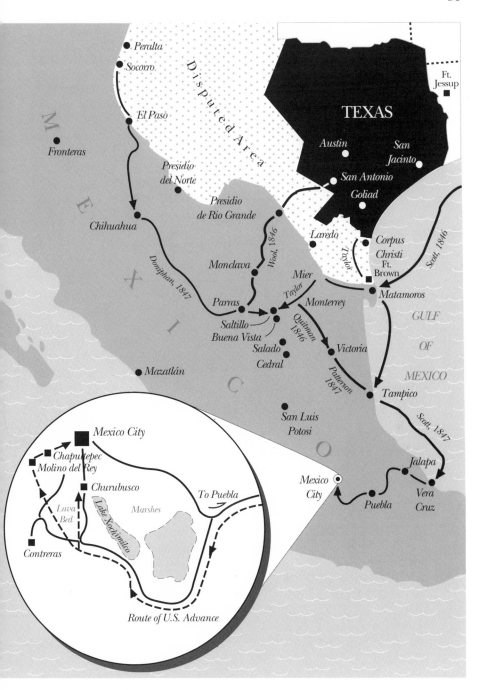

Peralta

Socorro

El Paso

Fronteras

Presidio
del Norte

Chihuahua

Presidio
de Rio Grande

Monclava

Wood, 1846

Donipha n, 1847

Parras

Saltillo
Buena Vista

Mazatlán

Salado

Cedral

Mier

Taylor

Quitman
1846

Laredo

Corpus
Christi
Ft.
Brown

Taylor

Monterrey

Victoria

Patterson
1847

Matamoros

Tampico

Scott, 1846

Scott, 1847

San Luis
Potosi

Disputed Area

TEXAS

Austin

San
Jacinto

San Antonio

Goliad

Ft.
Jessup

GULF

OF

MEXICO

Mexico City

Chapultepec
Molino del Rey

Churubusco

Lava
Bed

Lake Xochimilco

Marshes

To Puebla

Contreras

Route of U.S. Advance

Mexico
City

Puebla

Jalapa

Vera
Cruz

Scott, 1847

Scott's Central Mexico Campaign

fered as one example of an able man who had quickly been promoted to corporal, and who was a sergeant before the end of the war. The disgruntled men and their families appealed to Congress and the Secretary of War, but all remained in the army until 1849, when members of the company were allowed discharge before expiration of their enlistment. Ironically, Lothrop, who had vigorously condemned Stevens, was one who elected to remain in the company. In spite of disgruntlement expressed by some recruits, the effort to attract and train good men was largely successful. On numerous occasions during the war, observers testified to the intelligence and ability of the Engineer Company.[4]

In 1846 Lieutenant Stevens was paying the penalty for his responsible duties at the Northeast forts. The Webster-Ashburton Treaty in 1842 had settled the Maine boundary dispute, but failed to resolve other issues, most important of which was the Oregon question. The increasingly belligerent stance of the United States threatened the possibility of a two-front war. James K. Polk and the Democratic party heightened tensions, proclaiming "fifty-four forty or fight" and asserting that the only way to deal with John Bull was to "look him straight in the eye." Stevens supported the President and was all in favor of giving the one-year notice necessary to abrogate the 1827 treaty of joint occupation. Unlike some New England men, Stevens made no distinction between British claims in Maine and Oregon—he was a thorough-going Anglophobe unwilling to concede England an inch of ground anywhere. The outbreak of war with Mexico forced Polk to reverse his field. However, it took several months before the Oregon boundary settlement, the Walker tariff which lowered duties on British goods sent to the United States, and the new tone of American policy produced the desired result and tensions eased. In the hectic summer and fall of 1846 this new relationship was not yet apparent to the War Department. To the contrary, the announcement early in the year that a British fleet was preparing to sail for the St. Lawrence was sufficient to necessitate continued work on the Northeast defenses. It was only at the end of the year that Totten could consider removing the single engineer officer northeast of Boston.[5]

Less than a week before Christmas, Stevens unexpectedly received word that he would soon be on his way to Mexico. He placed all the forts under caretakers and closed down construction for the duration of the war. Within a week the eager Stevens was on his way to Boston to oversee the shipping of the engineers' equipment train he was assigned to accompany to Brazos Santiago. Before leaving, he and Meg agreed that she would remain in Bucksport with the children and her sister Mary until spring, when they would all move to Newport to await his return. Stevens arrived in Boston on December 29 eager to be under way at once, but delays prevented his sailing for three weeks. Embarrassed by his hasty flight from Bucksport, he wrote Meg to promise that he would use the time in a rational manner. He said good-by to friends and family, but as the sailing was postponed, the leave-taking seemed interminable. His father, Oliver, Uncle William, and cousins Charles and Henry came to see him off. While arguing with his father, who opposed the war as a slave holders' plot, and celebrating his departure with his free wheeling brother and cousins, Stevens outfitted himself with a new saddle, India-rubber leggings, and every conceivable piece of equipment he might need in the field. He even wanted to take a horse but could not raise the cash because he had already borrowed $500 to purchase his outfit.[6]

On January 11 the 200-ton barque *Prompt* was ready to sail when Captain David Vinton of the Quartermaster Corps announced a change in destination to the Chandeleur Islands (off New Orleans) before proceeding to Brazos Santiago. Stevens protested that his orders superseded Vinton's and ordered the vessel to proceed directly to its original destination. In that event, Vinton rejoined, the *Prompt* would not go anywhere. They might have sat out the war locked in verbal combat, but Totten intervened and ordered that they get under way, if possible directly to the Brazos, but if not, to the Chandeleur Islands. As the engineers proved they were open to compromise, the Quartermaster Corps indicated they could be equally magnanimous and ordered the captain to proceed directly to Brazos Santiago. The controversy had caused a week's delay. Once under way there was nothing Stevens could do but endure the long voyage. After suffering the usual seasickness, he relaxed, "enjoying mere existence," admitting that he "dreamed away many hours and built and pulled down air castles." After twenty-six days at sea, the *Prompt* put in at Brazos Santiago, a port located on the inland waterway just north of the Rio Grande River.[7]

Stevens stepped ashore into a scene of wild confusion. Thousands of troops appeared to be in constant motion, disembarking, drilling, or preparing to move out, while hundreds of laborers and teamsters sweated to unload and repack supplies for shipment to the front. The Quartermaster Corps, perhaps to Stevens' grim satisfaction, proved woefully inefficient, and the civilians in the army's employ were even worse. It was not a situation for which the Military Academy or the texts of Jomini had prepared anyone. In the midst of the turmoil, Stevens found Colonel Totten (who had arrived a few days earlier), his old friend James Mason, and Zealous Tower, who was once his West Point roommate.

At the center of the vortex was General Winfield Scott. "Old Fuss and Feathers" had been through it all before in the War of 1812 as well as in Indian wars in Florida and the Old Northwest; he was now calmly preparing the most daring exploit of his long career—an attack on Vera Cruz and a march inland to seize the Mexican capital. It would mean cutting his small army off from its base, dangerously extending lines of supply, and leading his men through hostile country without the aid of accurate maps. Critics of the plan called it suicide. The day after Stevens arrived, Scott and his staff left Brazos for the Island of Lobos, where forces were gathering for the attack on Vera Cruz. The Quartermaster Corps insisted that the engineers were responsible for their equipment and Totten left Mason, Tower, and Stevens in Brazos to organize the supply train. Stevens went to work with a will, worrying all the while that they would not reach the main force before it took Vera Cruz.[8]

Scott's force landed unopposed in a remarkable amphibious operation and was preparing to lay seige to the city when Stevens arrived. He was traveling much lighter (most superfluous equipment had been shipped home) and he had lost his servant to the lure of higher wages at Brazos. At Scott's headquarters, Stevens and his friends joined the other Engineer officers who soon formed a close-knit group that worked, messed, and enjoyed "a pleasant time" together. Scott and his staff had determined that the presence of a heavily fortified castle in the bay made a land attack on the city the most feasible. The Corps of Engineers, Stevens among them, set to work reconnoitering the terrain, laying out roads, and selecting sites for the mortar batteries. In mid-March the laborious work of digging zigzag trenches leading to the redoubts began, followed by construction of the batteries. The Engineer Company contained insufficient men for the task, so Scott assigned infantry companies to work under the engineers' direction in fourteen-hour shifts. The infantrymen took rifles and two or three cartridges and reported to the engineer depot where Stevens or another officer escorted them to the trenches. They worked under constant enemy fire, and one evening Stevens estimated that 200 shells fell near his party. He found that it was often impossible to get much work out of the volunteers. Some were drunk, all were tired, and they complained constantly of hunger and fatigue. More than once the regulars completed their assigned work, while the volunteers made little progress. On one occasion, when Stevens left momentarily to inspect a battery, the volunteers departed for camp. Work was further hindered by "northers" which filled the air with blinding sand and dirt, but eight days after work began, the batteries were ready to open fire on the city.[9]

Vera Cruz surrendered four days after the shelling began. When the army entered the city, Stevens saw that the guns had done their work efficiently by leveling most of the buildings nearest the batteries. He was depressed because "many inoffensive people [were] killed." The troops thought the city with its Moorish architecture romantic by moonlight, but wretched with filth and flies in the harsh light of day. As Stevens strolled the streets of Vera Cruz he speculated that the war was a contest between a people with a past and a nation with a future. For Mexico, "their future is in their past," and he was convinced they could not cope with the spirit of enterprise of the Americans, as they had fallen away from the stern virtues of Cortez. Mexico could not match the zeal of a nation "on a rapid march to greatness." Stevens believed the war started because Mexico had acted unreasonably in refusing to surrender Texas with good grace, and her insistence upon clinging to this territory made it necessary "to conquer a peace." Stevens was moved many times by the bravery and suffering of the Mexican people, but he had no doubt of the necessity or morality of the war.[10]

The army remained in Vera Cruz for two weeks. Stevens set himself up comfortably in the district's government palace in quarters he shared with Mason, Robert E. Lee, and John L. Smith, and the four feasted on hams, fresh fruit and vegetables purchased from the inhabitants. Stevens believed he had never worked so hard in his life as he had during the seige but congratulated himself that the Engineer Corps had done its duty. No one could deny that it had undergone its baptism of fire and emerged with flying colors, although George Meade of the competing Corps of Topographical Engineers groused that "the corps of engineers ... performed all the engineering that has been done." "This," he suggested, "is attributable to the presence of Colonel Totten, who wishes to make as much capital for his own corps, and give us as little, as possible."[11]

When the army left Vera Cruz, Scott sent Totten to Washington D.C. to carry news of the victory, present his plans, and make requests for additional men and supplies. Major John L. Smith assumed command of the Engineer Corps attached to Scott's army, and Lieutenant Stevens became his adjutant. Smith was less forceful in pushing the interest of the corps, but it had proved its worth and Scott would rely heavily on the engineers' reconnaissances and advice throughout the campaign. The responsibility for the corps' baggage and supply train rested primarily with Stevens, and during the days prior to their departure from the city, he worked himself to the verge of collapse. But by the appointed time all was in order. He joined the march toward Mexico City mounted on a newly purchased horse, a superb animal with a beautiful long-striding action which made him thankful he had lacked the funds for a mount when in Boston.[12]

A two-day march brought Scott's force to the Rio del Plan, beyond which the Mexican commander, Santa Anna, waited in a mountain pass with an estimated 12,000 men. Scott was proceeding without detailed maps and only crude information on topography, proper routes, and defensive positions. Thus the Corps of Engineers, which had the opportunity at Vera Cruz to demonstrate ability in selecting and constructing field works, were in constant service from Rio del Plan to Mexico City providing information on the terrain and reconnoitering enemy positions. The nine engineer officers worked together as a team and proved to be virtually indefatigable as well as being unusually dependable during the course of the campaign. The work of Robert E. Lee, P.G.T. Beauregard, and George McClellan is well known due to the fame each won in the Civil War, but the other six contributed in equal measure to the corps' success. Stevens boasted, "All our officers of engineers are superior men, and we stand by each other like a band of brothers."[13]

Because a frontal attack upon Santa Anna's fortified position would be foolhardy, the engineering officers searched for a route to allow a flanking movement. High ridges flanked by the river effectively protected the Mexican right, making it imperative to find a way over the hills and ridges to the left. Stevens, Lee, Beauregard, and Tower, accompanied by a troop of infantry, crept over the rough terrain to the vicinity of Cerro Gordo, the hill which became the key to flanking the Mexican force. The Mexicans believed they had nothing to fear from that direction and failed to post guards. The scouting party was able to look down into the Mexican camp and count the brass cannons glistening in the sun. For two hours the engineers sketched the position; then one of the infantrymen clumsily discharged his gun, and they had to beat a hasty retreat. Stevens reported that the route appeared promising but recommended a more extensive reconnaissance which would determine the direction of Santa Anna's retreat, if defeated, and the possibility of sealing off this line. He wished to observe the course of the national highway behind the Cerro Gordo and determine the location of a ford which he thought existed behind the Mexican position.

Scott approved, and the next morning Stevens set out with fifty dragoons and a wagonmaster who claimed to know a practical trail up the river. They proceeded over an almost impassable route, and it was soon clear the teamster was mistaken. Stevens ordered the force to double back, as he intended to cross the river and then proceed upstream. But when retracing their steps over the rough terrain, up and down steep ravines, the old rupture, which had not caused trouble for many years, suddenly broke through again, causing Stevens to collapse in excruciating pain. Suffering greatly, he rode four miles back to camp where cold water relieved the pain. An army surgeon fixed up a truss, and by evening the patient was resting comfortably. When General Scott heard of the incident, he rode to Stevens' tent and helped ease the pain by exclaiming, "You engineers are too daring—you require to be held back—my young friend I almost cried when I heard of your mishap." Buoyed as he was by the general's praise, the injury was a severe blow to Stevens' hopes for winning additional glory and distinction. Just as the real action was about to begin, he was ingloriously confined to his bed, and not even by a wound sustained in combat.[14]

Stevens could only watch the next day as Captain Lee led General David Twigg's division along the route they had scouted to flank the Mexican force. While these troops moved into position, General Gideon Pillow, guided by Lieutenant Tower, staged a frontal assault to provide a diversion. For the first of many times Pillow, President Polk's former law partner, displayed his incompetence when he ignored Tower's advice and attacked Santa Anna at one of his strongest points resulting in greater losses than necessary. However, the battle was won when

Twiggs took Cerro Gordo with Colonel William Harney leading the charge up the hill in a display of courage that won Stevens' admiration. Although part of the Mexican force was cut off and captured, the majority, including Santa Anna, escaped over the ford which Stevens had sought to find the previous day. In his report of the conflict Scott took particular care to mention the Engineer Corps and commended all of its officers by name. Captain Lee, however, was singled out for particular praise for his conduct in leading Twiggs to his successful attack. Although Stevens shared in the glory, he was despondent that fate had prevented his finding the ford and had kept him from an active role in the battle. He told Meg, "My hopes of distinction have in a measure vanished." But Stevens stoically accepted his condition and philosophized that in the future he would need to rely more on his brains and less on physical effort.[15]

The plan followed at Cerro Gordo was often used by Scott in the course of the campaign; after careful reconnaissance, troops were moved into a flanking position while other forces applied pressure to the center. The key to success was the skill of the engineers in finding practical routes, the placement and judicious use of artillery, and, of course, the courage of the troops making the assault. Scott's strategy made extensive use of artillery and engineers and both branches emerged from the war with increased prestige and widespread acceptance of their value in combat. When Scott's force continued its march toward Mexico City, Stevens rode in a wagon, and after a few days he was able to walk about if he moved slowly and cautiously. The danger remained that the intestine might become strangulated resulting in gangrene and certain death—a possibility that could have occurred at any time during the remainder of his life. As they followed in Santa Anna's wake, Stevens became well aware of the realities of war and the effects of gangrene; they periodically passed bodies disfigured and mangled with the wounds of battle.[16]

At Jalapa, Scott spent one night at Santa Anna's captured villa where he treated the engineer officers to a grand supper. Some elements of the army pushed over the divide of the Sierra Madre Mountains to Perote, but Scott remained in Jalapa to ponder the problem created by the twelve-month volunteers, who comprised forty percent of his force. As their enlistment period was nearly over, he decided to send them home before the malaria season began in the lowlands. It was a humanitarian act, but President Polk and Secretary of War William Marcy chastised the general for complaining of the inadequacy of his force and then returning men six weeks before their enlistments expired.

Scott ordered the remainder of his force to proceed to Puebla, where they would wait for reinforcements. The general's decision to move to Mexico City, and in the process cut his small army off from its supply base, dismayed military experts such as the Duke of Wellington who exclaimed, "Scott is lost." But the general's coolness and courage in the face of adversity won the admiration of Stevens and the other officers. They knew that Zachary Taylor's victories in the north and their own successes at Vera Cruz and Cerro Gordo had demoralized the enemy. Even a small army of ten thousand men could succeed if they struck with confidence while they possessed momentum and initiative. The danger remained that a blunder could produce disaster, but Stevens for one was supremely confident that Scott's army would make no mistakes.[17]

For two weeks Scott remained in Jalapa with his staff and a small guard while the rest of the army moved either toward Mexico City or back to the coast. Stevens made good use of this time to reorganize the engineers' supply teams, to replace worn-out mules, and to acquire new supplies. The latter proved the most difficult as the Quartermaster Corps refused to bring any Engineer Corps supplies from Vera Cruz and reminded Stevens that the engineers always insisted on providing their own supplies when in the states. But the engineers appealed to higher authority and the quartermasters reluctantly sent on the needed equipment. Despite these annoyances, Stevens had much free time to appreciate the beauty of Jalapa (which he called the Eden of Mexico) and to contemplate the past and future course of the campaign. He gathered information for a narrative on the battle of Cerro Gordo by interviewing numerous men and officers, and he wrote a memoir on the proper countermoves to any Mexican attempt to implement guerrilla warfare. Stevens concluded that the Mexicans liked to fight best from well-fortified breastworks and would not be very good at guerrilla tactics—an assessment as false as it was contemptuous. In other letters and memos he commented on the army's experience with volunteers. Although he admitted that frontiersmen were accustomed to the use of arms, in most respects he believed they would not equal regulars. Later he wrote:

Disciplined troops are far more effective, both for the multifarious duties of the campaign and the shock of battle than hastily collected levies, whether under an organization of volunteers or additional regulars. Such troops are more amenable to discipline, suffer less from disease, are more patient and enduring under hardship, and more firm and undaunted in a perilous crisis.

Stevens believed the war could have ended weeks earlier but for the small size of the army at the start of hostilities and the use of twelve-month volunteers.[18]

There was some discussion whether Stevens should continue with the army or return to the states to recover. Stevens convinced the doctors that he could ride or walk if he did not subject himself to extreme exertion. It was agreed, to Stevens' immense relief, that he could remain. As he prepared to leave Jalapa in early May with Scott, Stevens correctly assessed their situation:

I now hold myself in readiness to move forward at any moment. But in the present aspect of affairs, three regiments of Volunteers returning home, much sickness among the troops and no certainty as to the arrival of new levies, it is not certain that it will be possible to move beyond Puebla.

They went into camp in Puebla, as he had expected. The weeks of inactivity after Cerro Gordo aided the healing of Stevens' rupture, and by the end of May he reported ready to assume full duty. He participated, usually with Lee, Mason, or Tower, in scouting the roads from Puebla or helped set defensive positions to repel the attack which rumor predicted. The pause dragged on through June and continued into July as the new forces failed to arrive. Aside from the pressure of simply waiting, the greatest concern was the constant sickness which disabled up to one-fourth of the men at any given time. Stevens, who had once cautioned his sisters against diet fads, recommended the liberal use of chile peppers as the best guarantee of good health.[19]

Reinforcements arrived on July 8, but because the new volunteers had received no training, Stevens wondered if they would be of any help. Scott, too, had his doubts, and the army remained in camp to await the arrival of General Franklin Pierce with 2,000 veterans from Taylor's command. Peace rumors circulated through the army, but Stevens remained convinced that "Castilian obstinacy and pride" would overrule military considerations and force Scott to conquer Mexico city. He argued,

Another great blow must be struck. Learning wisdom from the past, it ought to be deferred till our resources be collected, organized, and in a state of complete preparation, not only to drive the enemy from the City, but also, taking his whole army prisoners, to push our forces in all directions, and by a most vigorous simultaneous movement, grasp the important places, disperse the whole organized force, and bind together the whole by well secured lines of communication.

But, Stevens lamented, Scott was hampered by the "imbecility" of the administration's insistence upon half way measures. He complained that the government, "impatient for immediate results," nevertheless doled out men and supplies grudgingly and forced the army to win with limited means. Stevens believed that a failure to push forward to a definite conclusion nourished "the hopes of the enemy that ere long some unexpected turn in the wheel of fortune will bring victory to his standard, and drive the invader from his soil."[20]

Scott finally ordered his army, over 10,000 strong, forward from Puebla on August 8. Four days later, as they were nearing the capital, Lee, Mason, and Stevens carried on a day-long reconnaissance of the eastern approaches to the city. They found the main road flanked by swamps and lakes on both sides and the city protected by El Penon, a heavily fortified hill. Stevens reported that the road passed through a narrow defile directly under the guns and the water prevented any detour. As Stevens, Mason, and an officer in the Kentucky Volunteers rode toward El Penon over the causeway, they approached eight or ten mounted Mexican officers. The two parties closed to within 300 yards, but when the Americans kept coming, the Mexicans abruptly wheeled and galloped back to the fortifications, a flight that carried a company of dragoons with them and produced great merriment among Stevens and his companions. Although exhausted from the long day's ride plus several hours of wading about through marshes, Stevens returned to the area the next day and spent seven hours riding completely around El Penon to determine possible approaches as well as the number of guns in the citadel. Scott praised his detailed report, although Stevens (with atypical modesty) protested, "I got more credit for it than I deserved." After considering the matter for three days, Scott decided to abandon the main road, turn south and west around Lake Chalco and Lake Zochimilco, and approach the city from the south or southwest. An arduous march over a rough, narrow road, which they had to repair as they marched, brought the army to San Augustin.[21]

Stevens, Mason, Tower, and Major Smith examined the route leading north from San Augustin while Lee and Beauregard explored the alternate route heading west. Major Smith reported

to General William Worth that the road north was passable and
recommended moving in that direction to turn the flank of the
enemy force at San Antonio. Stevens dissented vigorously and
received permission to extend the survey further. He found
Smith's route "was marshy, intersected with canals, and that operations . . . were not practicable." Late the same evening Scott
assembled the engineer officers, who advised a feint at San Antonio, a move to the west to Contreras, and a march north from
that point. Scott adopted their plan. The next day the engineers
found the Mexicans strongly entrenched at Contreras on the far
side of a ravine with a *pedregal* (lava field) further blocking the
American advance.[22]

August 19 was the first day of Scott's difficult, bloody drive to
enter Mexico City. Troops under General Pillow and Colonel
Riley attempted to cross the lava field and turn the enemy
flank, but the difficulty of the terrain caused dispersal of the
American force, and at nightfall the Mexicans still held their
position. For the battle Stevens was assigned to Twiggs's division, which applied pressure to the Mexican front. Along with
McClellan and Foster, he attempted to place batteries (commanded by Franklin Callender and John Magruder) in position
to rake the enemy. It was a frustrating day, and to Stevens' dismay Magruder was not able to come up in time to protect
Twiggs's advancing infantry. He fumed at the artillery commander that "everything seemed to go wrong with him." With
the artillery finally placed, Stevens guided the Ninth Infantry
forward over the open terrain to a protective ledge. As he returned to join General Twiggs on a small ridge overlooking the
enemy lines, a shower of grapeshot passed directly over their
heads. Twiggs did not move a muscle, and Stevens calmly suggested "the propriety of stepping down to a little depression
which afforded cover." Stevens volunteered to go forward again
to attempt to find the advanced positions of Colonel Riley, who
seemingly had become separated from the rest of the force in
the confusion of battle. Stevens struggled over the rough terrain,
but when he failed to locate Riley, he came back to the position
of the Ninth Infantry. Still later in the afternoon he returned to
field headquarters and found General Pillow, like everyone else,
confused and "somewhat perplexed with the posture of affairs."
It was clear that the attack had failed, and Pillow sent Stevens
to find the Ninth Infantry and bring them back from the front.
He tried to carry out the order but went only part way before
collapsing from fatigue. Lieutenant Foster happened by and

half-carried, half-dragged his friend back to the camp through a drenching rain that completed the misery of the day. To Stevens' great relief, the infantry made it back safely without his help, but he bemoaned his lack of stamina and the lingering debilitation of his hernia. Although Stevens lamented his inability to carry out orders, he had displayed remarkable energy, driving himself at a furious pace, under the most arduous conditions, from before dawn to late afternoon. His failure was an inability to realize that he was so near collapse when Pillow ordered him forward.[23]

Stevens stumbled into Scott's headquarters tent, wet and exhausted, and found most of the others in the same condition. The general sat them all down at a large table, laden with hot food, and one by one they gave their reports of the day's action. Stevens believed it was Scott at his finest; the general was "composed, complacent, weighing every word . . . finding fault with no one's blunders, and taking in all cases the best view of things, indulging in no apprehensions, and exhibiting entire confidence in the ultimate event." Stevens made his report and listened while General Persifer Smith convinced Scott to attack the Mexican rear. Major Smith and Lee dragged Stevens back to their camp and ordered him to get some rest. He reluctantly agreed and told a servant to wake him at three in the morning so he could reach the front before Smith's attack. To his dismay he was not roused until five o'clock, whereupon he rushed to headquarters. Scott sent him forward with reinforcements from General Worth's command, but nearing the front they learned that General Smith had already carried the field in a sharp, seventeen-minute engagement. Stevens sent the troops back and proceeded to the battlefield. There he met Tower, who already had found a route to the enemy rear, calmly eating his breakfast.[24]

That same morning Scott regrouped his forces in the village of Coyoacan and paused to plan the pursuit of Santa Anna's army. Stevens climbed the steeple of the village church from which he observed the Mexicans streaming down the road toward the capital. He told Scott the enemy rear was unprotected, and the commanding general quickly ordered General Twiggs to cut off the retreat while sending word to General Worth to advance from his position near San Antonio. Stevens was sent with Twiggs, who rushed after the rapidly retreating enemy. The American force was brought up short at Churubusco, where they encountered a fortified church and convent. Because Scott's army was swelled with optimism derived from their string of victories and the great success of the morning at Contreras, Twiggs and his staff confidently decided to "make a bold and quick matter" of the Mexican position. Stevens advised Twiggs to place a battery in front of the church to drive the enemy from the roof and then to carry the work by a charge from the front and the left. Twiggs followed his engineer's advice, but the troops on the left had difficulty moving into position and the battery of Frank Taylor, left exposed, took a dreadful pounding from the Mexicans, and was finally moved back to safety. Only after protracted artillery fire and a combined attack from front and rear by troops with bayonets fixed did the men in the convent surrender. Twiggs took more than a thousand prisoners from the church, although his men had suffered greatly in the sharpest and bloodiest fighting of the war to that point. But they also broke the resistance of the Mexican force, which retreated into the city. Scott could have continued the pursuit, but his own army was spent and exhausted, and he broke off the action.[25]

Stevens believed Churubusco "was the terrible and decisive conflict of the war." He had finally been in the midst of the action he had long sought, and it left him horrified at the terrors of war. He relived many times the day's events and shuddered at the ease with which life had been wasted. He thought of Taylor's battery and his part in the decision that had moved many of these men forward to death or injury. Stevens debated whether a pause by Generals Twiggs and Worth and a reconnoitering of the enemy position might not have produced the same result with fewer casualties. But such speculation, he finally concluded, came to no more than second guessing; they had seen the enemy in rapid flight and the best tactic was to pursue the advantage to a conclusion. Stevens could take solace in the final result as "most glorious to our arms," but he could not forget the terrible scenes of conflict. While the army sank into an exhausted sleep, Stevens lay awake haunted by "the mangled forms" of men he knew and respected; he found "I could not keep [them] from my mind." Before he finally slipped into a troubled sleep, Stevens recalled the observation of Benjamin Franklin, "I scarcely ever knew a good war or a bad peace."[26]

The day after Churubusco General Scott and Santa Anna agreed to an armistice for the purpose of negotiating peace terms. Although Stevens had predicted earlier that they would need to take the city by force, he now wanted to believe that the American negotiator, Nicholas Trist, would be successful. Stevens reminded his friends who wished to enter the city as conquering heroes that the objective was not to take the city but to effect a peace. He believed Trist was correct when he argued that a movement into the city would disperse the Mexican government and factionalize the country. Stevens speculated that if the United States confined its claims to California, New Mexico, and the line of the Rio Grande, and offered a cash payment in return, they could reach a settlement; these did become the major points in the final treaty. But his earlier prediction—that the army would need to move into the heart of Mexico City before there could be peace—was borne out. The peace commissioners failed to make progress, and numerous small violations of the armistice created a renewed climate of hostility. The lull did allow both sides to rest and regroup, and Stevens was among those who badly needed a respite to regain his strength.[27]

On September 7 Stevens wrote, "The ball is to be reopened," and he prayed, "God grant that a similar sacrifice may not be required of us as at Churubusco." The next day Scott sent Worth's division to capture a foundry at Molino del Rey on the supposition that it was used for casting cannon. It was a false premise and the taking of the foundry resulted in the American forces sustaining casualties totaling 25 percent of the attacking force. Stevens gloomily predicted "two or three additional victories of the same kind would annihilate our army." Stevens complained that Major Smith prevented the engineers from providing useful information prior to the attack. To his disgust, Smith was often content to make his observations from afar and in the case of Molina del Rey, the major observed the position from a distant housetop. Stevens believed, "All the facts of the ground and of the position and strength of the enemy could have easily been ascertained with officers so devoted and so efficient as ours, had they been directed by a vigorous chief." Mason and Foster accompanied Worth's forces and both fell seriously wounded. Late in the afternoon Stevens volunteered to take their place, and when the foundry was finally surrendered, he examined the works and reported to Scott the unhappy news that he could find no cannon or equipment for making guns. The heavy losses cast the army into gloom and even Scott became testy and snappish.[28]

At a "council of war" on September 11 Scott proposed the reduction of the fortified hill of Chapultepec, and further operations against the city as circumstances dictated. There was general agreement among the officers. Chapultepec, which stood about two hundred feet above the plain, was topped with guns and a large stone building used as the Mexican military college. After a heavy twenty-four-hour bombardment by the army's artillery, forces moved up the hill on September 13 and, after heavy fighting, stormed over the top. During the bombardment and attack Stevens, with Beauregard and Tower, reconnoitered approaches to the city through the Belen and San Antonio gates. When the citadel fell, Stevens took General Worth's command to the San Cosme gate while other forces attacked at Belen. Sharp fighting occurred in both places. Stevens reconnoitered the San Cosme suburb for enemy batteries, and early in the afternoon, while posting pickets and waiting for batteries to arrive to reduce two enemy gun positions, he was struck by a rifle ball which hit near the little toe and plowed diagonally across the foot to the instep. General Worth soon reduced the batteries and by late afternoon the suburb had fallen and troops were pouring into the capital. The next day Scott accepted the surrender of the city, and the fighting phase of the Mexican War ended.[29]

An army surgeon cut the ball from Stevens' foot, and he was placed in quarters in the government palace. The shattered bones and severed tendons caused intense pain. The doctor thought he would amputate, but after four days announced, "I can save the foot." He could do little to set the bones or repair the damage, but he tried to keep the wound clean and draining freely. Stevens remained flat on his back for over two weeks, and just as he seemed to be recovering the foot became infected, his temperature shot up, and new skin on the foot sloughed off. Blood poisoning almost claimed Stevens' life, as it did many of his comrades, but the crisis passed. Small bits of bone kept working out of the wound and in mid-November a piece of shoe leather the size of a large coin emerged. In early December Stevens was able to move about with crutches and he left his quarters for the first time in two and a half months. It was a lonely experience but he took solace from his comfortable room thickly carpeted and draped in damask. Stevens felt "as if I was in the Halls of the Montezumas." At one point, however, his old adversaries in the Quartermaster Corps attempted to eject him from the palace, but his friend Lee took the dispute directly to General Persifer Smith, who ordered that Stevens keep his quarters. On December 9 Stevens and Foster left for Vera Cruz in a small ambulance, and on December 26, one year after he left Bucksport, Stevens landed at New Orleans.[30]

General Scott again heaped praise on the engineer officers, stating that they had "won the admiration of all about them." Despite the cautious and unimaginative leadership of Major Smith, the competence and skill of the young engineers was recognized by General Scott and the other commanders. Stevens too had praise for each of his associates: Robert E. Lee, as not the most brilliant, but he was unsurpassed in constant labor, efficient service and good judgment; Beauregard was a forcible and independent personality and a fine soldier; Tower was remarkable for his ability to remain cool and decisive under extreme pressure; Gustavus Smith inspired the company of sappers and miners to great feats of labor; and Foster and McClellan were brave, intrepid, and resourceful. Stevens was most impressed by James Mason whom he found to be the most capable of making rapid, correct observations and decisions. There is no doubt that it was a distinguished group, and Stevens was certainly a well-qualified member. Some equalled, but none surpassed, his devotion to duty as he drove himself continually to the point of exhaustion. He won the confidence of Scott, Twiggs, and Worth, who knew that his observations were as accurate as they were meticulous.[31]

It was typical of Stevens' tour in Mexico that he would be wounded on the last day of fighting. As energetic, daring, and resourceful as his efforts were, Stevens was hampered to a degree by his physical limitations. His rupture removed him from the battle at Cerro Gordo, and he was struck down by exhaustion at Contreras. It often appeared that Stevens' reconnaissances, unlike those of Lee or Beauregard, produced negative results, such as his report on the fortifications at El Penon, and the infeasibility of the road north from San Augustin—even the discovery of no cannon at Molino del Rey. Although these reports were as thorough and as useful as a reconnaissance of the route eventually followed, there was a certain aura of negativism about them—it was not the same to point to a man who had successfully found the route to the enemy position at Contreras as it was to praise the man who found the route *not* taken to Mexico City. But although Stevens suffered some disappointments and lamented that "delicate health has much diminished my efficiency," he had nothing to apologize for. He demonstrated an excellent ability to analyze geography, enemy strength, and troop placement; he was cool and courageous in the heat of battle, and he had the will to act in the face of enemy fire. Stevens had sought glory in Mexico; he returned home as one of the heroes of the war.[32]

TO THE
COAST
SURVEY

Stevens traveled up the Mississippi and Ohio Rivers from New Orleans by steamboat and then proceeded overland to arrive in Washington D.C. in mid-January, 1848. Colonel Totten warmly welcomed the warrior home, and brimming with pride, the Chief Engineer boasted that the corps had accomplished all that was possible "to say nothing of several impossibilities." Contrasting the public image of the engineers before the war with his enthusiastic reception, Stevens exclaimed with surprise, "The services of the engineers have been so conspicuous that the corps has become popular." He was naturally eager to get home to Meg and his family, but Totten insisted that he remain two weeks to report fully on the corps' activities during the campaign. The Chief Engineer tried to secure three brevets for each of the engineers with Scott, but Congress and the Secretary of War balked and finally agreed to two brevets for each officer, except Robert E. Lee (who received three). Isaac Stevens was promoted to brevet captain dated from August 20, 1847, for gallant and meritorious conduct at Contereras and Churubusco, and brevet major from September 13, 1847, for Chapultepec. Congress theoretically assigned brevets for specific acts of bravery, but for the engineers they were in reality rewards for continuous meritorious conduct throughout the campaign.[1]

Meg waited anxiously in Newport while her husband visited with President Polk and accepted the "flatteries" the city's ladies showered on the "gallant Mr. Stevens."[2] The year had been the longest of Meg's life. She had had little to do but wait for mail that could easily contain tragic news. As early as February, only two months after Stevens left, she queried plaintively, "Haven't you had glory enough by this time?" During the

long and uneventful winter in Bucksport, the only conversation
seemed to be of sickness and ministers, and she predicted, "You
would have given up the ghost if you had been here." By summer she frequently complained that it was miserable to live
without her husband, particularly when he was "such an excep-
tional one as mine is." When Stevens finally returned to his
family in February, the old mansion in Newport overflowed
with joy and tears.

Two weeks later they traveled to North Andover, and whereas
young boys made snide remarks at the sight of a uniform prior
to the war, they now exclaimed, "I see him. There he goes. The
man that's been to Mexico." Stevens and his brother Oliver
"patronized" their father's hard cider, which they judged only
"middling," while battles were refought and the relative merits
of generals argued.[3] Isaac, Sr. had changed little; he was speculating in land, condemning the slaveholders, and hoping that
the nation had learned that "it is easier to begin than to leave a
strife." Stevens no longer agreed with his father on many issues,
particularly political questions, but he was generally more toler-
ant than he was in his younger years. Many of the old conflicts
were muted and as the oldest son he felt a responsibility toward
his father in his declining years.[4]

Stevens, like his father, continued to ponder the situation in
Mexico, as by spring neither side had as yet ratified the peace
treaty. The Mexicans, he confided to his brother, were "subtle
and treacherous," and the only safeguard to insure the peace
was the physical presence of troops on Mexican soil. He hoped
that he might be elected commander of a new volunteer regiment which he could take to Mexico while retaining his commission in the Regular Army. Virtually all the Regular Army
officers were upset by the rapid advancement of noncareer men
who had assumed command of most of the volunteer forces. Stevens had complained, "Our military organization is so wret-
chedly organized that it is difficult for a man of acknowledged
merit to rise," and as a reverse example he pointed to one man
designated a major of volunteers who earlier had been
drummed out of West Point for "extreme stupidity." But his
hopes of returning to Mexico were dashed when both sides ratified the treaty by midyear and all American troops returned
home before the end of the summer.[5]

The Chief Engineer allowed Stevens to remain in Newport
while his foot healed, and he continued desultory work on plans
for Fort Knox that had been left untouched during the war.

The sea breezes and the amiable society of the city made life pleasant, but his foot knitted slowly. By March he could walk about the house with a cane, but he still required crutches when venturing outdoors. The foot never regained normal strength, and for the next several years Stevens wore a shoe with a special thick sole. But he was not to savor Newport life very long; Totten ordered him to Savannah in March to estimate the funds needed to build bulwarks and a bridge at Fort Pulaski. Stevens enjoyed his two visits to the South and anticipated with some pleasure an assignment to works at Fort Pulaski and nearby Fort Jackson, but for the immediate future he wished only to remain in Newport. He complained to Totten that his foot troubled him during the trip, and suggested, "I am desirous in my crippled condition to remain quiet at Newport so long as the public service shall not be prejudiced."[6]

Totten appeared to agree and sent Stevens north to turn the forts at Bucksport, Portland, and Portsmouth over to Lieutenant Colonel Joseph F. K. Mansfield. The transfer took place at Bucksport late in April, but on the very day they completed the necessary paperwork, Totten changed his mind and sent orders for Mansfield to retransfer the works. Stevens could hardly conceal his displeasure—Bucksport was the last place he and Meg wanted as his station. In a private letter he hinted to the Chief Engineer that he would prefer another post and repeated his desire to spend at least the summer resting and recuperating. Totten replied that all orders needed to be flexible because many senior officers were still in Mexico and Congress had not yet made appropriations for the next fiscal year. He tried to mollify his officer by suggesting a one-year tour of duty on the Pacific, but the newly brevetted major coolly rejected this plan on the grounds that his physical condition would not allow it. Stevens seemingly forgot his earlier proclaimed readiness to return to Mexico with troops; his injury had seemed no hindrance then. The status quo prevailed until midsummer with Stevens officially responsible for Forts Knox, Preble, Scammel, Constitution, McClary, Pulaski, Jackson, and the old fort at New Bedford—eight works strung along the coast from Maine to Georgia. Though impressive on paper, the assignment was not only temporary, it was essentially an administrative technicality as no work was undertaken at any of the posts.[7]

Stevens' worst fears were realized when his good friend Zealous Tower took over the Portland-Portsmouth forts and Jeremy F. Gilmer went to Savannah, leaving him with Bucksport. For a man just returned from the sacrifices of war, the anticlimax of a return to Fort Knox was crushing. The appropriation for the fiscal year beginning in July 1848 amounted to only ten thousand dollars, and he was isolated at a minor post with duties far less than before the war. Oliver greatly understated his brother's mood when he observed that the assignment "must have been quite unexpected." But if it provided any solace, his situation was not unique: Robert E. Lee, a brevet colonel, found himself assigned to Fort Carroll, Maryland, where he remained for four years; James Mason needed a three-year leave to recover from his wounds and never did regain his health before he died in San Francisco in 1853; P. G. T. Beauregard built fortifications in Alabama and Louisiana; and George McClellan, to his utter disgust, went back to West Point with the Engineer Company. It appeared the war had changed the lot of the engineers only temporarily. After the conflict the same men filled the same old positions, but earlier they had built fortifications as lieutenants and captains; now they did so as brevet majors and colonels.[8]

Major Stevens eventually accepted his fate with relatively good grace. His acquiescence is partly explained by the effect of the hernia and foot wound on his health. Although many periods of his life were filled with frenetic activity, others were notable for ill health and relative leisure. With the spoofing good humor that Oliver alone often drew from him, Stevens reported to his brother from Bucksport:

We lead a quiet, rational, country life perhaps as much to be envied as the more attractive life of the great city. I want you to understand however that we do not shed our claws during the winter.... That is still further down East, I believe. We do not sleep more than twelve or at most fourteen hours a day. We manage to eat three meals per day.... We drink tea nights and eat apples morning.... By way of diversion we slide down hill on a moonlight evening. Then there are prayer and conference meetings.... What a consolation these ... would be to one of your serious turn of mind.

At thirty years of age Major Stevens was no longer an impetuous youth. He emerged from the Mexican War convinced that the army was a necessary and admirable profession, even "the first of professions," as he apparently rejected the traditional heir to that title. Stevens predicted more fighting in the future, perhaps with Mexico, but more likely with Great Britain in a struggle over Canada. He was willing to bide his time and wait for future opportunities.[9]

The year in Bucksport passed quietly as Stevens slowly recovered from his wound. Most labor at the fort involved the moving of stone and earth for the embankment in front of the work, a task that required little direct supervision. He could spend most days in his office at home, and he made certain that much of his time was devoted to Meg, to rapidly growing Hazard, and to young Susan, who was born in 1846.

Stevens also took great interest in political events. He closely followed the 1848 election, supporting Democrat Lewis Cass as a matter of course, but he took pleasure in Zachary Taylor's victory because it "indicated that we poor devils in the army are citizens of the country and eligible to civil offices of trust." General Taylor, Stevens predicted, would prove "a happy instance of the mingling of military and administrative ability." While in Washington City in February and March 1849 (consulting with General Totten), Stevens closely followed the debates that eventually resulted in the Compromise of 1850. Henry Clay and Daniel Webster, whom he ridiculed for lack of statesmanship in 1841, now received his praise, as did the rising star of the Democratic party, Stephen A. Douglas. Stevens remained opposed to slavery, but he now believed that other principles deserved higher priority. He sympathized with southern men who sincerely believed that the Constitution and the Union were being sacrificed to the abolitionists. If the issue became support of abolition or salvation of the Union, Stevens had no doubt of his choice. At the constant round of parties and receptions, he discussed the issues of the day with Stephen Douglas and many others and was convinced that the nation was in danger of splitting apart. If this happened, he believed that slavery would not be ameliorated, and he argued for continuation of the Union as the best way of ending that "terrible blight." He accepted the popular sovereignty position of Cass and Douglas and wondered why the South should be driven to the wall over an abstraction since the new territory acquired from Mexico would certainly remain free. Stevens anticipated Douglas's Freeport Doctrine eight years prior to its delivery when he argued that slavery could never exist where it did not receive protection from the state or territory. To break with the South, the major fiercely proclaimed, was not statesmanship—"It is popular clamor—and it may become fanaticism."[10]

The status of the Corps of Engineers and its officers was a political issue of more immediate concern. Most of the officers were happy with their brevet promotions, for an advance of two or three ranks usually came only after a full career in peacetime service. Joy disappeared when they became aware of the government's interpretation of the statutes of 1812 and 1818. The law required that officers of brevet rank hold commands considered normal for that rank before they could receive increased pay, and for a major or colonel an independent command was required. This did not appear to present a problem, for virtually all of the engineers who served in Mexico came back to independent commands, but the Treasury and War departments interpreted "command" narrowly, insisting that it meant only the command of a body of troops—thus eliminating the officers in the Engineer, Quartermaster, and Ordnance corps. Officers of these corps were also denied double pay when they were assigned to particularly burdensome duties. It appeared that they would still have to wait for the "Old Fogies" to die or retire before they could advance, and the older generation was notoriously reluctant to do either.[11]

Many of Stevens' colleagues turned to him for leadership in a campaign to redress their grievances. They respected his organizational ablity, knew that he would be outspoken, and recognized that he was close to General Totten, whose support was essential for success. During the war of 1848–49 Stevens considered various alternative plans, including a memorial of the engineer officers directed to Congress—or a cooperative effort with officers of the artillery and infantry. He visited Thayer and Mansfield in Boston, and once he had the support of these two officers (who were ranked only by Totten), he asked the other corps officers for their views and opinions. When he had heard from his colleagues, Stevens built his case and presented it first to the Secretary of War and then to Congress. He based his arguments on the general principle of equality with the other branches of the army, but he buttressed his case with previous examples of brevet pay granted to officers in the Engineer Corps. An 1835 decision of the Massachusetts District Court giving brevet pay to Thayer was of particular value. His efforts eventually proved at least partially successful; although a blanket ruling was not given, at least the War Department began to examine the merit of each individual's request for brevet pay.

Stevens was further shocked when the Engineer Company was reduced to its prewar limitation of 100 men. He thought the war had amply proved the need for a much larger body of able sappers and miners. A favorite dream was a four-fold increase in the company, with continued emphasis on recruitment of men with the potential to become officers. Then, if war broke out, the corps could undertake any engineering operation, and the enlisted men would be able to assume command if their officers fell in battle. Stevens hoped for a training program that would place the men in the field half the year and in the classroom for the other half. A change in station for the Engineer Company was essential, he argued, for it had always suffered second-rate status at West Point. In addition, explained Stevens, taking "human nature as we find it, the men of the company will be envious of the cadets."[12]

Major Stevens did not confine his thoughts or his activities to the Corps of Engineers. He proposed that camps or schools be established for all branches of the service, with officers spending every third year training and studying. Stevens believed the artillery branch needed drastic upgrading, and to this end he corresponded with artillerymen like James Duncan, whom he had known in Mexico. The Far West was also an area of increased concern for the army, and Stevens urged additional troops to protect emigrant trains and to keep a wary eye on Mexico and Canada. He warned, "There are numerous Indian tribes in the West and Northwest whose good behavior thus far has been occasioned by the presence of a strong military force." Stevens identified and attempted to correct many of the problems faced by a career officer in the nineteenth-century army. These included public apathy except in time of war, the poor quality of the average enlisted man, a tendency to downgrade the Artillery and Engineer corps, and the difficulty of securing relief from Congress without the application of vigorous effort or the use of powerful influence or public pressure. Although Stevens and his fellow officers failed to alleviate most of their grievances, he began to learn the art of politics. It was a lesson that would continue during his years in Washington D.C. with the Coast Survey.[13]

On August 7, 1849, Alexander Dalles Bache, the distinguished director of the United States Coast Survey, inquired of Major Stevens if he would be interested in accepting a position as his assistant. By law a portion of the Coast Survey's duties went to army and navy men, and the interrelationship of the engineers' work with that of the Survey made close ties with that branch particularly desirable. At any given time two or three engineers could be found in the field with the Survey. The number would have been higher because Professor Bache and General Totten maintained a close and cordial relationship, but the latter always complained of a shortage of competent officers. Captain Andrew A. Humphreys had served as Bache's chief assistant until ill health forced him to take an extended leave. Bache reluctantly let him go, comparing the sensation to taking a seat in the dentist's chair, and asked Totten if he could provide a replacement. It was a prestigious post with responsible duties that provided a likely stepping stone to even more important assignments. The greatest liability for most officers was the large amount of paperwork and constant office duty that the post demanded. Totten's first suggestion was George W. Cullum, then stationed at West Point, who after some thought opted to remain at the Academy. Bache asked for John Barnard, then at New Orleans, but the Chief Engineer claimed he could not be spared and denied the request. At this point Totten and Cullum both suggested Stevens as a man "in the highest degree qualified."[14]

The offer took Stevens by surprise, and his first reaction was to decline. He banked on the hope that several years of patient effort would result in an increase in the corps' scope and duties. Second thought suggested the potential opportunity, and a firm offer from the survey convinced him to give it a try. Stevens traveled to Boston to meet with Bache, and each came away favorably impressed. Neither realized it, but the meeting was the beginning of a close working relationship and a lifelong friendship. Stevens offered to accept the position on a provisional basis; if Totten and Bache were agreeable, he would retain command of Fort Knox until the next Congressional appropriation and then choose one of the two posts. In this way he could stay with construction if Congress made a generous appropriation, and if not, he would remain with the Coast Survey. Stevens also requested brevet pay if he joined the Survey, although the fate of the officers' petition to the Secretary of War had not yet been determined. Totten and the professor accepted this plan and the Chief Engineer even made the devious suggestion that Bache apply for *Major* Stevens in the hope that the Treasury Department would assume that to be his permanent rank and pay him accordingly. This deception did not pass unnoticed, but after months of haggling he received the higher compensation. In mid-September Stevens officially transferred to the Coast Survey and began work in Washington D.C. at the end of October.[15]

Reacting to commercial and navy pressure, Congress had created the Coast Survey in 1807 as an ad hoc agency under the directorship of Ferdinand Hassler with instructions to begin a general, comprehensive survey of the coast. One of the country's first pure scientists, Hassler was not given to compromise with the politicians. Consequently the Coast Survey was made part of the navy in 1818 and languished there until Congress returned Hassler to command in 1832 under the general supervision of the Treasury Department. Hassler struggled to make the Survey both a scientific and an independent enterprise and was successful enough that he provided a solid foundation for his successor, Alexander Dalles Bache, who proved a peculiarly happy choice. Under Bache's leadership the Coast Survey, in the estimate of the leading historian of the subject, became "the best example of the government in science" during the pre-Civil War period. The great-grandson of Benjamin Franklin, and grandson of Alexander Dalles, Bache was equally at home in scientific, educational, and political circles. He graduated from the Military Academy with highest honors and without receiving a single demerit, and he went on to teach at West Point and the University of Pennsylvania, to work on construction of Fort Adams, to study educational systems in Europe, and in 1836 to found Girard College. This impressive record of achievement placed Bache in an excellent position to make the public aware of the voice of the scientist through the medium of the Coast Survey. In 1850 Congress, in the name of economy, discussed returning the Survey to the navy, but Bache objected and pointedly testified that, in the future, unless survey work came "up to the demands of science and scientific men of the country, it could not long stand." Bache received strong support from the scientific community, and Congress allowed the Coast Survey to continue as an independent agency combining the talent of army, navy, and civilians, all under the direction of the professor.[16]

Hassler had started the surveys in New York and had worked north and south from that point, but he refused to publish any results until completion of the entire Atlantic coast. Bache divided the Atlantic and Gulf coasts into eight divisions and placed parties in each, a move that helped win the support of Congressmen in the affected states. The professor also began to publish results as they became available. Under Bache the Coast Survey broadened its scope to include scientific work related to the surveys. For example, Professor Bache had carried on research in terrestrial magnetism, and the Coast Survey collected data and conducted experiments at 103 stations across the country which resulted in publication of a table of magnetic variations. Hassler had worked to establish standards for weights and measures, and Bache continued these efforts and included time in the Survey's province. Under Bache the Survey developed a method for accurately determining longitude, a problem that had plagued explorers and surveyors. Working closely with Benjamin Pierce at Harvard College, the Survey tackled problems of astronomy and, despite protests from the navy, studied the Gulf Stream, measured tides in the Gulf of Mexico, and selected sites for lighthouses.[17]

Stevens began his new duties with characteristic optimism. He told Oliver, "The Coast Survey needs me to overhaul it. I feel that the army has a representative in me which it has not had in Washington for years." A "world of work" lay ahead, but the new assistant believed he could so arrange matters that subordinates could carry out most tasks and allow him to avoid becoming an "office drudge." But Stevens soon found that his desk was where most decisions stopped. The professor was often with parties in the field, so most of the Washington operation was left to the assistant; in addition Bache consulted him on general policies and relied on his help to lobby for the Survey. When Stevens came into the office the Survey was expanding rapidly because of Bache's policies and the Mexican War settlement, which had added Texas and California to the nation's coastline. The Washington office had not grown at the same pace as the field parties, and virtually nothing had been done to assure greater efficiency. Much of the fault lay with Stevens' predecessor, A. A. Humphreys, who had such a capacity for remembering detail that he and Bache carried most records and procedures in their heads. Expansion made this system no longer possible, and Stevens had to start from scratch to build an effective operation that would remain long after he had departed.[18]

Stevens set to work to bring order out of the chaos, and although he did not become precisely an "office drudge," the days of relative leisure he had enjoyed since the war were at an end. As its primary responsibility, the Washington office put into final form the rough maps, drawings, and computations that came from the hydrographic and topographic parties in the field. Stevens divided the office into engraving, drawing, and computing departments and named a supervisor for each. In addition all the clerks were placed under a fourth supervisor, and they began to centralize the records and establish a filing system. This arrangement put operations on a more systematic basis. But Stevens still was not satisfied; by the end of 1851 he had divided the office into eight divisions: computing, drawing, engraving, electrotyping, printing, sales and distribution, instrument making, and archives-library.

One basic task was to find and keep competent draftsmen and engravers. Henry Benner was a typical problem. Although a good engraver, he preferred to spend most of his time drinking and gambling. Stevens believed that Benner could be reformed through guidance and good influence plus hard work, all of which he vowed to provide. However, Benner did not improve, and frequent search parties would find him in the Bowling Saloon, "rolling balls, the most active of the set." After a year of warnings, lectures, and confidential talks, Stevens reluctantly gave up and released Benner from the office. It appeared to Stevens that the great majority of his employees had some personal defect which made them not completely desirable from his point of view.

In much the same way that he had attempted to upgrade the Engineer Company, Stevens tried to recruit apprentices who had education and ability. This program met with some success, but most young men were unwilling to submit to a long apprenticeship at low pay. One prospect, Samuel Manning, came from Philadelphia at Stevens' urging to interview for a position as apprentice electrotyper. The Survey offered an annual salary of $250 for the first two years and $500 for the next two years. Manning complained that the terms were illiberal and the work demeaning and suggested that the Survey wanted to hire a "white boy" to replace the "colored assistant." The offer, Manning sniffed, was not fit "for a man of 19 who has studied 18 months in chemistry at Harvard." Stevens would not accept that kind of talk from anyone, certainly not a young jape like Manning, and he summarily rejected the youth's counteroffer and declined to employ him on any terms. Stevens did realize, however, that apprentices could best be kept happy by setting them to responsible tasks, which he tried to do.[19]

At best, work in the Coast Survey Office was tedious and exacting. An accurate, industrious engraver could do less than one square inch of work a day, and Bache and Stevens insisted that the final results be near perfect. Stevens tried to make conditions as bearable as possible by permitting reliable men a certain flexibility in arranging their hours and by allowing liberal leaves of absence. One of his pet projects was a new building to replace the old, crowded, badly lighted, poorly ventilated firetrap. Stevens argued that a new fireproof building would increase morale and efficiency as well as provide safe storage for the charts and plates that could not be replaced without redoing the surveys. He drew up sketches and plans, but Bache, with an eye on Congressional concern for economy, would not make the new building a priority item, and the office remained in the old location. With the physical structure and the workers producing headaches, Stevens also found it was more difficult than he had expected to find competent supervisors for the office divisions. For example, he named Wilson Fairfax, an able, reliable engraver, as the head of that important section, but he was not cut out to be a supervisor, and there were constant complaints from Fairfax and the men under him. Stevens eventually recognized that his choice was "utterly incompetent" as a leader, but he could find no one any better to replace him. "If my health were good," Stevens muttered on one occasion, "I would take over supervision immediately," but he could only talk it over with Fairfax once again, knowing from past experience that it would do little good.[20]

The duties of the office increased enormously during Stevens' tenure, as expansion of the Survey came to full fruition. As the decade of the 1850s began, the Survey had twenty-seven parties in the field working between Delaware and the Rio Grande River, and a major effort on the Pacific coast was just beginning. Other government departments increasingly called on the Survey for aid, one being the newly created Department of the Interior, which asked for help in reproducing maps made from interior surveys. Stevens tried to reject this request, but Bache, desirous of establishing friendly relations with the new department, urged him to take on the additional work. The Corps of Engineers made numerous requests for charts to aid in river and harbor clearance, and Stevens must have thought back to his days at New Bedford when he made his own hydrographic survey. In addition there were demands generated by private sources for maps and charts. In 1851 Congress, at Bache's urging, assigned the task of locating shipping lights to the Coast Survey, and in that year the office prepared ten plates, each representing hundreds of man-hours of labor, devoted primarily to this purpose. Increased attention to tides and currents by the Survey led Stevens to demand as an absolute necessity one or two naval officers to handle these calculations.

In addition to his attempts to increase the staff and improve office organization, Stevens gave close attention to development of more efficient techniques. He brought Rufus Saxton, an 1849 graduate of the Military Academy, into the office to make and repair instruments, a procedure that proved cheaper and more efficient than jobbing the work out. Saxton had a talented and

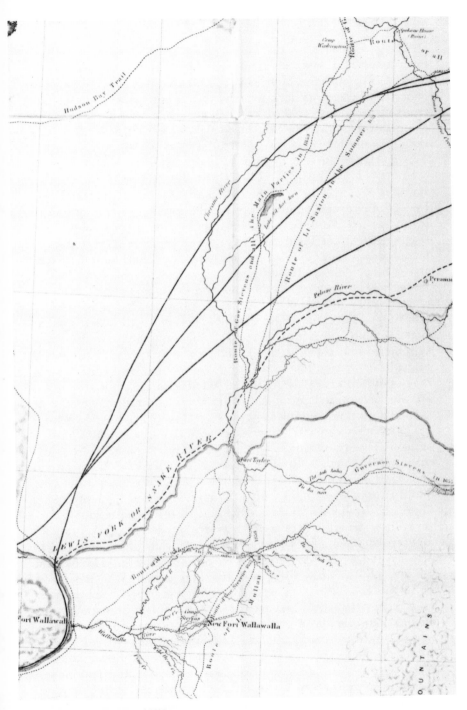

Columbia Basin, 1850s

Stevens' West Point training and his years with the Coast Survey provided him with the credentials to direct the northern Pacific transcontinental railroad survey in 1853. On this official map, solid lines indicate proposed railroad routes in eastern Washington.

inventive mind, and he made a number of improvements in Survey equipment as well as inventing the popular Saxton self-registering thermometer. Equally important was the work of electrotyper Francis Mathiot, a temperamental, moody genius whom Stevens hired in return for a promise that Mathiot would assign to the Survey his patent for a new electrotyping process. Through an improved heating method, Mathiot was able to reproduce engravings in a week for $100 when reproduction by an engraver would take months at a cost of several thousand dollars. Mathiot also made deep-sea thermometers and other instruments for the Survey. Bache remained suspicious of the melancholy inventor, but Stevens constantly pressed to obtain a higher salary and competent assistants for Mathiot as well as giving him "delicate handling."[21]

The work of the office, onerous and demanding as it was, did not constitute the whole of Stevens' duties. Bache relied on his assistant to push for appropriations, consult with other government bureaus, and explain Coast Survey policies to Congress and the public. At first glance the two men appeared to offer a study in contrasts: Bache was courtly, urbane, and unruffled as he worked his way through the intricacies of capital politics; Stevens was more direct, less willing to compromise, quicker to take offense, and more hostile toward opponents of the Survey. The two men differed more in style and temperament than in basic philosophy or goals however, as both were ambitious, dedicated professionals who were experts in military, administrative, and scientific problems. Neither was willing to compromise with quality or to excuse sloppiness and inefficiency. The professor, impressed by his assistant's dedication to the welfare of the Survey, knew he could rely on him to be honest and straightforward whether it be with Congressmen or an office boy. Bache in turn had a greater influence on Stevens than anyone outside his immediate family. The professor was a man who measured up to Stevens' ideals: his record at West Point had been as good as or better than Stevens', he was a successful military man and scientist, and he was a dedicated public servant. Most important were Bache's traits of patience, tact, understanding, and a willingness to delegate authority. He was a model Stevens could emulate—a father figure whom he could admire and look to for guidance more than to his real father. Although the relationship would be interrupted during Stevens' years in Washington Territory, in the last years of his life he again turned to Bache for support and advice.

The fall of 1850 was a typical period for Stevens. One project was to convince Congress to assign the task of lighthouse location to the Survey rather than the navy. A second issue was an increased appropriation to permit continuation and expansion of the Pacific coast surveys. Bache had rushed parties to the West when the ink had barely dried on the Treaty of Guadalupe Hidalgo, but surveys in that quarter proved expensive and Congress was skittish about making an additional appropriation. Bache and Stevens enlisted the support of Senator William Gwin of California. Stevens implied to Gwin that if the Coast Survey were given permission to locate lighthouses, the added funds might mean the difference in their parties remaining on the Pacific coast or coming home. Gwin quickly agreed to add a sentence in his lighthouse bill which would grant the responsibility of location to the Survey.

When this bill passed, Stevens turned his attention to the Senate Finance Committee. With the lighthouse funds secure he was able to reduce the Survey's supplemental request for the West Coast to $40,000. Stevens informed the Senators that wages were ruinously high in the West and that Bache had pared the budget to the bone. He pointed out that three officers of the Survey were making a total of only $150 more a year than the cook, and "he is a very poor cook at that." Stephen A. Douglas and John Charles Fremont came to his support, but Stevens deserved the most credit for convincing Senator Jefferson Davis that a vote for West Coast funds would not lead to a cut in Mississippi Delta appropriations. The appropriations passed the Senate, and in the process Stevens became closely allied with Douglas (an association which would last until the 1860 election campaign) and with Davis, who called Stevens "my friend." Stevens was out of town when the measure first came up in the House and was angered because Samuel Thurston of Oregon substituted a figure of $25,000 and introduced the measure when few members were in their seats. Stevens then set to work, and the House finally approved an appropriation of $40,000.[22]

By 1852 most of the responsibility for Coast Survey appropriations rested with Stevens; Bache congratulated him on passage of that year's deficiency bill and asked, "What was the opposition and from where?" Relative to the regular annual appropriation, the professor warned, "Be sure that some cranky amendment is not attached. I hardly think there is anyone ready to attack me just now, but one cannot be too watchful." This indicated the degree to which the old antagonisms of the Hassler era had disappeared, but it also illustrates Bache's confidence in Stevens' ability to handle matters vital to the existence of the Coast Survey. Stevens responded to this free rein by displaying a close personal loyalty to Bache that is unique in his career. He never wilfully disobeyed a direct order from a superior, but his allegiance to Bache went much beyond the usual relationship of a subordinate officer to his commander. After a year with the Survey he confided to Meg that he and Bache held "the same general view of things." In matters of appropriations they agreed perfectly on proper procedures and this, he reasoned, made him more efficient and judicious. Even in areas of disagreement Stevens kept an open mind. One major issue was the proposed new office building. With someone else, Stevens might have stuck to his position and perhaps would have pushed to the point of antagonizing his superior and straining the relationship. But he told Bache he understood his opposition and suggested deletion of any mention of the new building from the assistant's annual report so it would not conflict with the director's report.[23]

Despite the closeness of his personal and working relationship with the professor, Stevens attempted to leave the Coast Survey during each year of his tenure. According to the initial agreement, the first year was a trial period, and in the spring of 1850, after consulting with General Totten, Stevens decided to return to the Corps of Engineers and to Bucksport. One reason was his fear that constant office work was injurious to his health. This was probably a correct assumption, but the cause of his health problems may have been as much psychological as purely physical. As at Bucksport in the fall of 1846, Stevens could begin fretting about his health and confinement and perhaps cause the illness that he predicted. More important than health was his fear of professional stagnation. He commented, "I do not want to get involved in a routine that will exhaust all my energies and leave no time for professional studies and pursuits." It is also clear that after a year's separation he missed Meg and the family he had left behind in their Bucksport home. A rooming-house existence was not without its convivial pleasures of cigars, whiskey punches (for which Stevens achieved something of a reputation), and political conversation with Congressmen and bureaucrats, but it could not compare with the family life he had so much enjoyed after returning from Mexico. Stevens' loneliness was readily apparent when he wrote to

Meg, "It spoils a man on some accounts to be married—particularly if he gets a good lovable wife. He is not good for much away from her." Meg replied, "Oh dear me if this child doesn't want her old bed fellow back again. I hope you sleep cold nights and that you will make haste to relieve your better half from a state of frigidity." Stevens assured her, "I will never be separated from you again another winter unless it is an absolute impossibility for us to be together." Some of Stevens' letters became uncharacteristically sentimental and even maudlin during the year's separation:

> What a treasure I possess in your love. . . . I feel as if our recent trials had purified me and made me more worthy of you. They have shown to me your truth and trust. Your happiness I feel is in my keeping. . . . I feel that I can make you happy. . . . I know so well that your whole heart is filled with me, that the joy and triumph of my domestic life is complete.

In a rare moment of revealed passion, he looked forward to the time when "soft desire joins us in dear, sweet embraces. Our beating hearts, our responsive limbs, our bodies yearning and striving for each other, all these make us feel that we are really joined together." At the same time that Stevens informed Bache he was returning to Bucksport, Meg was about to give birth to her fourth child.[24]

Professor Bache applied all of his considerable charm to change his assistant's plan. He termed Stevens' decision a blow to the Coast Survey and a personal loss, as their relationship had "ripened into a warm friendship." The professor's pleas, although flattering, proved less decisive in Stevens' change of mind than the declining fortunes of the Corps of Engineers. The movement of the frontier westward and the lessening threat of European attacks led to drastic cuts in appropriations for eastern fortifications. Funds for the 1850 fiscal year were delayed by Congress until early 1851, and the appropriation eliminated funds for Fort Knox and numerous other installations. Totten and Stevens could see the handwriting on the wall in the spring of 1850, and he agreed to stay with the Survey at least one more year. He continued his control over Fort Knox with the understanding that his assistant, Abiel W. Tinkham, would supervise any construction under Stevens' general direction. Stevens had estimated that $420,000 would be necessary to complete the fort, but Congressional parsimony ended any further construction after early 1851. Stevens retained nominal command of Fort Knox and the old fort at New Bedford until his resignation from the army in 1853.[25]

His decision made, Stevens brought Meg and the three children to Washington D.C. in October 1850, and they joined him at Mrs. Kelley's rooming house opposite Lafayette Square. The other boarders were Congressmen and military men, including Commodore Matthew Perry, who took a fatherly interest in Sue and kept a stock of candy on hand for her benefit. The next summer Stevens leased a roomy brick house located on Third Street, a block north of Pennsylvania Avenue. They were joined by William Stevens' nineteen-year-old son, George, whom Stevens hired for the Coast Survey. With his family about him, one cause of discontent was removed, but unfortunately Stevens' gloomy predictions of poor health were substantiated. His rupture gave him renewed difficulty; excessive rubbing of the truss had produced an enlargement of his lymph glands. Consequently his doctor ordered him to bed for several weeks. Soon thereafter he was afflicted with a bad throat and miscellaneous colds and fevers. In the spring of 1851 he promised Bache one more year, but beyond that he claimed an obligation to let his health govern the decision. Explaining that he did not wish to sacrifice a useful life by remaining too long in one position, Stevens lamented, "Health, health is the trouble." He hinted to Bache that he was also vexed by the lack of opportunity to advance in the Survey. Stevens was glad to gain the valuable experience the Survey offered, but he had no intention of ending his career as an office bureaucrat.[26]

Stevens continued to believe, as he had since the Mexican War, that the army might be his lifelong career, but politics occupied a considerable portion of his time. He maintained his close relationship with the Corps of Engineers by acting as an unofficial lobbyist for corps measures, and by engaging in an extensive correspondence with army men in all branches of the service. As for politics, he viewed it as an extension of life—there were "trials to encounter [and] victories to achieve." He believed, "We must contend with evil. We must accomplish good." Meg observed, "Politics are important now and Mr. Stevens enters right into the spirit of things." She thought their location in the capital fortunate because her husband could "look out for his own advancement." Meg proudly boasted, "I think him rather ambitious."[27]

Major Stevens worked hard during his years in Washington D.C. to advance the interests of his country, the army, the

Corps of Engineers, and his career, although not necessarily in that order. Stevens directed his efforts to three interrelated political goals: reorganization of the army, increased appropriations for engineers, and passage of the Fourteen Year Bill designed to speed promotions for young officers. The latter measure paralleled his earlier efforts to secure full pay for brevet rank, as the bill required automatic promotion to captain after fourteen years for lieutenants in the Engineer, Artillery, Ordnance, and Topographical Engineer Corps. These corps were assigned the most talented West Point graduates, who quickly received responsible duties. They usually acted as their own paymaster and quartermaster and were often accountable for large sums of money and valuable property, yet promotion came more slowly than in the line. Stevens told Congress that in his corps first lieutenants had served an average of thirteen years at that rank, and had held duties usually assigned to a captain for at least eight of those years. He warned that if the bill failed, many officers would either leave the service or lose their ambition. Congress looked to military men for information on army measures, and Stevens was in a good position to use his influence and friendship with numerous Congressmen to advantage. General James Shields, the Senator from Illinois who became a close friend, and Armistead Burt of North Carolina, chairman of the House Military Committee, who lived at Mrs. Kelley's rooming house, proved particularly helpful. Despite opposition from officers of the line, the bill moved through the Senate and was passed unanimously out of the House Military Committee, but failed to reach the floor before Congress adjourned. Stevens pressed his fellow officers to keep writing their Congressmen and predicted the bill would pass easily the next session. He was right. Stevens proved himself an able manager in guiding the bill through Congress as he had learned since his earlier effort for brevet pay that constant attention was necessary even if the merits of a measure were just. One officer observed that the opposition was unanimous but unorganized—Stevens had the proponents' forces marshalled with drillmaster precision. He benefited little personally, however; by the time Congress acted, Stevens had left the Army.[28]

From his vantage point in Washington, Stevens was also in the forefront of an attempt to restore at least a portion of the Engineer Corps' budget, which had been so drastically reduced in 1851. He kept his fellow engineers, who were scattered across the country, informed of current Congressional opinion, and he coordinated propaganda efforts. Stevens rejected the suggestion of one officer to send literature to the public schools, but he did conduct an extensive newspaper campaign. General Shields and Commander Samuel F. DuPont each wrote articles that he circulated widely, and in particular he tried to bring public attention to DuPont's argument that a series of small forts would prevent an enemy from overwhelming the coast in a sudden attack. Stevens collected funds from army officers to pay for publication of various materials, and he convinced Totten that it would not be a conflict of interest for him to chip in twenty dollars. A series of articles published in a number of New England newspapers, including those in Boston, Bangor, and Providence, came from Stevens' pen. He admitted that Fort Adams and Fortress Monroe were overly large and expensive but placed the blame on an initial tendency to follow the European system too closely and suggested that smaller works could best protect key coastal points. But the engineers faced powerful sectional opposition, as Westerners saw no need for coast defenses and Southerners wished to keep the public expenditures low to prevent an increase in tariff duties. Even some of the engineer officers began to see that the time for coastal defenses had passed. J. M. Scarritt warned from his vantage point in the South that agitation was useless, and, "We should not be led away by a false 'esprit de corps.'" George Cullum believed fortifications obsolete, and G. A. Gilmore contended that permanent works had fallen under the bane of ill-guided popular opinion, with a portion of the public relying on steam power for protection and others believing the "millennium is at hand when the saints shall reign."[29]

The shifting priorities of national defense led Stevens to return to questions of military organization. His West Point professors had once noted that he usually attempted to place a problem in its broadest context. He continued to do so as he saw the brevet pay controversy, the Fourteen Year Bill, and declining Engineer Corps appropriations as parts of larger issues— the military's role in American society and the most efficient army organization. He considered methods to improve army operations, means to attract and keep competent officers, protection for the frontier, and effective use of artillery, ordnance, and engineers. Stevens renumerated some of his earlier plans for training schools for all branches of the service. For the Engineer Corps he suggested six companies with one at West Point, two in training at Old Point Comfort, one assigned to various forts, and two engaged in construction of forts on the West Coast. He urged that the practice of appointing officers from civilian life be discontinued and that career officers be granted increased responsibility for their commands. Minor posts and forts could be placed in the hands of caretakers and infantry regiments replaced by cavalry that could be rushed to needed areas. Many of his thoughts reflected the increasing role of the West and the problems that distance and a scattered white population imposed on the military. He sought the ideas of William Hardee, E. O. C. Ord, and other officers stationed in the West, and for perhaps the first time, he began to think not only of the military problems of the frontier, but also of the opportunities that might exist there for men of energy and vision. In pushing for all these measures, Stevens assumed the role of a political manipulator. He asked Gustavus Smith, "Why cannot you go into the broad question of General Camps of Discipline," and he urged George McClellan to prepare a memoir on the best use of the Engineer Corps in times of peace. He once spelled out his method of operation for securing army reform: correspondence with officers of sense and intelligence, an alliance of engineer and artillery officers, an intensive propaganda campaign through the newspapers, and the support of men with "weight and established reputations."[30]

One of the primary vehicles that Stevens used to advance his views on the army and society was his book *Campaigns of the Rio Grande and Mexico*. The work began as a short critique of Major Roswell S. Ripley's *History of the Mexican War,* which appeared late in 1849. Ripley's account was a good military history that has survived as a standard reference on the war, but Stevens rightly believed that Ripley gave undue credit to General Gideon Pillow, on whose staff he had served, and too little to General Scott. Stevens in private characterized Pillow as "a contemptible egotist and a consummate ass" and set about to rectify the slight to his hero, Winfield Scott. Encouraged by Joseph Mansfield, Robert E. Lee, and others, he expanded the review into an article and submitted it to the *North American Review,* which rejected it as too personal and controversial. The editor thought it read like an argument presented to a court martial and concluded, "'I wish to keep clear entirely of these controversies among military men." Stevens put the work aside for some months, but then revised it and added introductory comments which placed the war in historical context and summarized his plan for army reorganization. Although the work

still critiqued Ripley, Stevens believed it more important as a
case history of the weaknesses in an army which did not have
proper training or adequate numbers of competent officers. He
subsidized publication of 1,000 copies of the 108-page book,
which emerged from the presses of D. Appleton and Company
in July, 1851. Stevens pleaded with his army friends to "give it
a sufficient circulation to prevent it being much of a bill of expense to me." He later told Meg that most copies had been
sold, but he may have been trying to ease her fears that they
had lost heavily on the project. If the book cost Stevens money,
and if it did not have much effect on public policy, it did further enhance his reputation within the military—except, ironically, with General Scott, who was miffed because the book, despite its fulsome praise, was not completely laudatory.[31]

Although the campaign to reorganize the army and elevate its
public status brought some gains, it was on the whole a failure.
Stevens and his fellow officers were most successful when they
worked on specific and limited measures such as the Fourteen
Year Bill. The time was not right for a substantial change in
the nation's military system. Old suspicions of the Regular
Army still lingered, and those suspicions in addition to sectional
interests worked to preserve the status quo. Stevens was never
very hopeful that sectionalism would be put aside, and he had
to admit that even his Southern friends Jefferson Davis and Armistead Burt were lukewarm on army reform.[32]

In his work for the army as well as in his duties with the
Coast Survey, Stevens gained invaluable experience. Washington
D.C. was challenging Boston as the intellectual as well as the
political center of the nation in the mid-nineteenth century. Stevens had an opportunity, unusual for a young army officer, to
rub shoulders, converse, debate, and socialize with the great and
near-great during a period of three and one-half years. He became intimate with scores of Congressmen and military leaders;
in addition he had a foot in the intellectual world, where he
was acquainted with Joseph Henry, director of the Smithsonian
Institution, and numerous other scientific leaders. The single
most important person from this period of his life was Professor
Bache, who reinforced Stevens' zeal, enthusiasm, zest for excel-
lence, and impatience with shoddiness or deception. Stevens
learned from Bache, although he would at times forget the lesson, the necessity of tact in dealing with others, the art of gentle
persuasion, and the wisdom of respecting both sides in a controversy. The Coast Survey years marked a pivotal point in Ste-

vens' life as his military career merged into politics and resulted in a decision to opt for the latter profession. He came to see that much of the power in a democratic society rested with the political leaders, and as always, Stevens wished to be in the center of action. If Stevens received much from his Washington years, he also gave a great deal in return by putting the Coast Survey office on an efficient basis and offering able support to Bache's attempt to make the Survey the most important scientific organization in the country. Stevens also proved a capable spokesman for his profession, and during most of his time in the capital, he ably carried on both duties, either of which was ample to tax the stamina of an ordinary man.

IN THE
FOOTSTEPS
OF LEWIS
AND CLARK

During the 1852 presidential campaign Isaac Stevens plunged into the mainstream of national politics. His longtime interest in political issues, his lobbying on behalf of the Coast Survey and army, and his more than three years' residency in the nation's capital led him to take the step. As in 1848, the Whig party turned to a war hero, none other than General of the Army Winfield Scott, while the Democrats chose Franklin Pierce, whose military record came under scornful attack from the opposition. The necessity to choose between the two placed Stevens in a predicament which led to perhaps the first purely political decision of his career. He not only supported Pierce but became the leading champion of "Young Hickory's" military record, in the process somewhat revising his earlier opinion of the candidate. When assessing various generals late in 1847, Stevens had observed that Pierce as a military leader was "not particularly distinguished," but in a series of letters to the *Boston Post* in 1852, the budding politician argued that Pierce's leadership had won him "golden opinions," that he was a counselor and friend to the troops, and that he was a confidant and close advisor of General Scott. He defended Pierce's leadership at Contreras as a deliberate holding action to keep the enemy occupied, and praised his charge at Churubusco over marshy ground and watery ditches in the teeth of fierce opposition. Stevens' defense suggested that Pierce had served valiantly, or at least as well as opportunity allowed, and implied that his innate military ability equalled Scott's. A pamphlet titled *Vindication of the Military Character and Services of General Franklin Pierce* combined Stevens' letters with testimonials from others on Pierce's service in Mexico.[1]

Oliver Stevens, then an aspiring young lawyer and politician in Boston, told his brother that Pierce's military record was not "worthy of being particularly dwelt upon" and that the articles "perhaps do injustice to others by overpraising Pierce." The vain and temperamental Winfield Scott certainly would have agreed, even if Isaac Stevens did not, for the general-in-chief had earlier been miffed by *Campaigns of the Rio Grande and Mexico,* which Stevens had intended in part to be a defense of Scott. The general had bristled because Stevens did not consult him during the writing and because some criticisms crept in amongst the ample praise. Stevens was not in the general's favor even before the 1852 campaign began, but it is unlikely that he would have publicly opposed Scott if he had not been seriously contemplating leaving the army. Pierce's political supporters were ecstatic that a military man of Stevens' credentials would step forth to shield their standard-bearer from the fierce pounding he was absorbing on the military question. Word came that Pierce was "gratified," and other Democrats told Stevens the *Post* letters were "just the thing to stop the slander in the Whig papers." It was natural for the Democrats to turn to Stevens as their military expert and to put him on the stump during the climactic weeks of the campaign.

In this endeavor he received little support from his family; his father muttered darkly that Pierce seemed "friendly to the intoxicating cup," and Oliver warned that taking the stump meant becoming a complete partisan. A boardinghouse friend from the days at Mrs. Kelley's issued a similar warning when he pleaded, "I beseech you to eschew politics. You have enough to do in your profession. In that you can preserve your honor. But where is the successful politician who has not compromised his." Stevens nevertheless took to the campaign trail, speaking mostly in Massachusetts and New Hampshire during the weeks from August until the election. He also consulted directly with Pierce on campaign strategy. His tour won praise from friends and strangers with one of the former exclaiming, "You ought to have been a politician. In that element you were born." Most pleasing was the encouragement from political leaders, who averred that his speeches had "done much good," and who urged, "You should be in politics and free from the restraints of the army." "Perhaps," one suggested, "you may find it to your advantage to change your profession." These words were music to Stevens' ears.[2]

The Whig view of Major Stevens' efforts was expectedly less complimentary. They complained that although he was technically on leave from the army during his political appearances, his remarks were nevertheless offensive to the general-in-chief. The Whigs asked, "Is it decorous, is it right, is it customary for officers of the army to leave their posts and . . . make political speeches," and they concluded that it "may be allowable, but certainly not proper or respectful." Stevens' efforts caused sufficient furor that the Secretary of War investigated and hinted at disciplinary action. William Rosecrans assured his fellow officer that "it was all for Buncombe," and that once the election passed the matter would be dropped. Rosecrans was correct, but Stevens had overstepped the line of propriety and probably would have been called to account if Scott had won. Certainly he realized this and was prepared to resign from the army if necessary.[3]

But Pierce prevailed and more than one friend asked Stevens, perhaps only half facetiously, if he would be named the new Secretary of War. Despite Pierce's warm professions of friendship, Stevens knew he was not in line for a cabinet post, but that he could claim any reasonable political reward. One fact was certain—the long years of training and apprenticeship were over; he was ready and eager to become a leader in the expanding America of the 1850s. Stevens decided to break cleanly with the East and to cast his fortune with the emerging territories of the Far West. The lure of the frontier had begun tugging at him after the Mexican War. It began as a faint glimmer and grew to a belief that the West was the land of opportunity for a young man with ambition. Stevens' slow and tedious efforts to promote the interests of young officers added to the conviction that advancement to positions of power in the East would come, if ever, only with the advance of old age. Like countless others, he was not content to wait but wished to move boldly to the West. Like John Stevens, who migrated from England in 1638, he did not join the westward-flowing tide without careful consideration and preparation. Hasty "Don Quixote" expeditions to the California gold fields were not suited to Stevens' style or temperament. But Stevens was very much a part of the "Young America" element within the Democratic party, which pressed for the rapid expansion of the nation's boundaries and insisted upon the Manifest Destiny of American institutions to cover the Western Hemisphere.[4]

After the Mexican War, Stevens' work for the Coast Survey and the army brought him into contact with western issues, problems, and opportunities. One major issue in the capital during the 1850s was construction of a transcontinental railroad. As early as 1849 Stevens had predicted that a railroad would not be possible until there was "a careful examination of the route" and an estimate of the costs. He speculated that railroads would follow, not precede, population, and he foresaw the first transcontinental as twenty-five years in the future. During the last weeks of Millard Fillmore's administration, Congressmen hotly debated the transcontinental issue, and on March 3 a measure passed calling for the survey of several routes under the general supervision of the Secretary of War. One day earlier President Fillmore had signed the measure which created Washington Territory, a huge political division stretching from the Rocky Mountains to the Pacific Ocean and from the Columbia River to the 49th parallel. On March 4, Franklin Pierce, standing slim and handsome, delivered his inaugural address from memory; he reiterated his campaign pledge to support the Compromise of 1850 and promised vigorous expansion of the nation. Stevens wove the events of these three March days into a plan which would implement the expansionist tendencies of "Young America" and place him in a position to guide the destiny of the Far West. The key to his design was the northern railroad survey, which he hoped would lead to early completion of a transcontinental line, rapid settlement, and the emergence of Puget Sound as the entry port to Asia. Americans had looked longingly at the potential trade of the Orient for many decades, and Matthew Perry was at that moment on his way to Japan. If Stevens could gain command of the railroad survey as well as the governorship of the new territory, development of the Northwest and the expansion of his own power and influence would be virtually limitless. He might become the spokesman for the Pacific Northwest as William Henry Harrison and Thomas Hart Benton had been representative of earlier frontiers.[5]

Stevens did not reveal all his plans at once; he first applied only for the governorship of Washington Territory, a move that puzzled his friends. Historically the territorial governorships did not fall to the first rank of politicians, although there were exceptions, particularly in the early years of the century, when Meriwether Lewis, William Henry Harrison, Lewis Cass, and other notables held the office. Although the territories acquired increased political importance as the sectional crisis developed, appointments to territorial posts still went, as a general rule, to mediocrities. Able men like James Shields rejected appointments and even Abraham Lincoln, when still an unimportant Illinois politician, refused the governorship of Oregon Territory. On the face of it, Washington appeared one of the less attractive territories as it was isolated from the center of power and contained within its vast expanse only a scattering of settlers around Puget Sound. There was little doubt that Stevens could secure the governorship if he wanted it. No other prominent person applied, and it is possible that Stevens scared off potential applicants; the men who did seek the job were the type who applied for any known vacancy with the hope that someday lightning might strike.

In addition to Stevens' work on Pierce's behalf, he appeared to have all the necessary qualifications: military experience which could prove valuable in dealing with the Indians or in meeting any threat from England, the ability to handle men successfully, and honesty and integrity demonstrated during many years of public service. A number of powerful men supported his application including Stephen A. Douglas, Robert J. Walker (a former Secretary of the Treasury and a leader in the Democratic party), and Congressmen James Shields, Solon Borland of Arkansas, Jeremiah Clemens of Alabama, and Hannibal Hamlin of Maine. Some of the descriptive terms these men applied to Stevens were: "high administrative powers," "zeal," "energy," "fixedness of purpose," "probity," "uprightness," "political, civil, military, and scientific knowledge," "firmness," "high intelligence," "high tenor gentleman," "cool," "industrious," and "gentlemanly deportment." According to Douglas, his "education, tastes, and habits . . . fit him peculiarly" for the post. In one of his first acts as president, Pierce sent Stevens' name to the Senate, which quickly endorsed the appointment, and on March 17 the new governor accepted his commission and resigned from the army.[6]

With the governorship in his pocket, Stevens turned next to the northern railroad survey. The transcontinental railroad project was only one of a number of economic issues with sectional overtones, and Congress had authorized the surveys in an attempt to find a way out of a political deadlock. It was hoped that nature and science would determine the final route, thereby removing the railroad issue from the political arena. Initially four surveys were contemplated, including the northern route between the 47th and 49th parallels. This route was suggested

by Asa Whitney in 1844 when the transcontinental scramble
first began, and it was favored by economic and political interests in Minnesota, Wisconsin, and Michigan. The second survey
ran between the 37th and 39th parallels from the headwaters of
the Arkansas River through Chochetopa Pass to Salt Lake. A
third followed the 35th parallel from Fort Smith to Albuquerque and then to California, and the fourth ran through the
Tulare and San Joaquin Valleys with the objective of finding
passes to connect with the 35th and 32nd parallel routes. The
latter survey was not included initially, but Jefferson Davis favored it, and he ordered two parties to look into this route
across Texas, along the Gila River, and through the Gadsden
Purchase. One alternative not surveyed was an examination of
passes in the Sierra Nevada north of the 35th parallel which
might permit a direct route from Salt Lake to San Francisco—
the route eventually followed by the first transcontinental line.

Stevens submitted his application for leadership of the northern survey to the new Secretary of War, Jefferson Davis, and
based his claim on three factors: first, his training as an engineer, including practical experience in Mexico and work with
the Coast Survey in all phases of topographic and hydrographic
surveys; second, his position as governor, which included the superintendency of Indian affairs, which would complement his
work on the survey; and finally, he banked on his good personal
relationship with the Secretary of War as well as with other
powerful Southern politicians. Stevens told Davis that he could
have a report to Congress by December and estimated that the
survey would cost $48,120. He assured Secretary of State Wil-
liam L. Marcy, who had the primary responsibility for territorial officials, that a delay in his arrival would not hurt the territory because in any event it would be necessary first to conduct
a census and elect a territorial legislature. Secretary of the Interior Robert McClelland, whose department contained the Bureau of Indian Affairs, received promises that Stevens would
gather valuable information on Indian tribes during the course
of the railroad survey.[7]

Jefferson Davis confronted a delicate political problem in his
assignment of personnel to the surveys. When serving as a Senator from Mississippi, he had been an outspoken advocate of a
southern route, but as Secretary of War, he sought to avoid
charges of partisanship. A second but less urgent problem was
the bitter rivalry between the Corps of Engineers and the Topographical Engineers. Congress had indicated that the topographic

branch would have the prime responsibility for the railroad surveys, but Davis had the power to select qualified personnel from
any source. General Totten was not bashful in pressing the
claim of his corps to at least one of the routes. From Davis's
point of view Stevens was an admirable choice because of his
association with the Engineer Corps and because he was a
Northern Democrat acceptable to Southerners. Although Stevens
had resigned from the army upon his appointment as governor,
the engineers could still claim him as one of their own and bask
in any success he might achieve. One point led Davis to hesitate: Would the army personnel necessary for the expedition
balk at serving under the command of a civilian? Military men
were notoriously touchy on this point, but Stevens assured the
secretary that he was "now quite certain that a sufficient number
of Army Officers will volunteer to go with me. . . . Several accomplished officers would be glad to be detailed." Thus assuaged, Davis handed the job as commander of the northern
survey to Stevens, who on his thirty-fifth birthday found himself
in possession of a three-pronged assignment to open the Pacific
Northwest to American civilization.[8]

General Totten was not as easily convinced that Stevens' appointment was a judicious move. He had every confidence in
the major's ability, but, preferring an officer still in the corps,
he had suggested George McClellan. When Stevens, in one of
his first acts, requested McClellan as his subordinate in charge
of the western party, Totten refused unless his officer received a
separate command. He hinted that this might be accomplished
by making the eastern and western parties into separate surveys.
Stevens quickly countered that it was "exceedingly important
that the whole exploration . . . be placed under the charge of
the same person." Totten tried to placate his former officer
when he told Stevens that his appointment had provided the
survey with "all the military and engineering talent and all the
energy and enterprise necessary," and he then added, "With
your zeal for command, which is laudable and natural, you
should understand how McClellan would feel." But Stevens insisted that many officers and particularly McClellan would be
happy with the duty, and Totten reluctantly relented, releasing
McClellan but warning, "I hope he will receive the credit due
to him."[9]

Stevens threw himself into the multifarious preparations for
the survey. Haste was essential, as Congress had set January
1854 as the deadline and he had personally promised Davis to

be finished by the end of 1853. His presence in the capital gave
Stevens an advantage in the scramble for the available scientific
talent which was in short supply because Perry had taken some
to Japan and because Arctic expeditions would lure others. Stevens' contacts with the Smithsonian, the Coast Survey, and the
Engineer Corps allowed him to gather an able scientific and
military cadre. In addition to McClellan, he pried Andrew Jackson Donelson away from the reluctant Totten and placed him
in charge of the advance party, which was dispatched to Fort
Union by riverboat. With McClellan assuming command of the
western party, the three main divisions were in the hands of Engineer Corps men. Stevens also hired two civilian engineers,
Abiel W. Tinkham, who had been chief assistant at Fort Knox,
and Frederick West Lander. A self-trained Yankee, Tinkham
had won Stevens' confidence through hard work, shrewd intelligence, and loyalty. Faith in Tinkham had allowed Stevens
in good conscience to retain command of Fort Knox while he
was with the Coast Survey. Lander had built a reputation for
his work as a civil engineer on eastern railroad construction. For
the remaining military personnel, Stevens turned to the Artillery
Corps, whose officers he had held in high esteem since the Mexican War. Lieutenant Johnson Duncan, who had commanded a
battery in Scott's army and whose coolness under fire had impressed Stevens, was sent immediately to Fort Vancouver to
gather supplies for the western party and to serve as second in
command to McClellan. Lieutenant Rufus Saxton, who was employed in the Coast Survey office, and Lieutenants Cuvier Grover, Beekman DuBarry, and John Mullan, all of the Artillery
Corps, were assigned to the eastern party. The only line officer
was Captain John Gardiner of the First Dragoons, who established a base camp near St. Paul and began collecting supplies
prior to the arrival of the main party. In addition Stevens received sixteen privates, one sergeant, two corporals, and a musi-
cian from the First Dragoons then stationed at Fort Snelling.[10]

For chief geologist, Stevens assiduously wooed Dr. John
Evans, who had recently traveled over a portion of the survey
route while on duty with the Department of the Interior. Evans
agreed to provide detailed instructions, to travel at least part
way with the party, and to write the final geological report, but
he wished also to continue his work for the Interior Department
and intended to travel west by a more southerly route across the
Badlands and to join Stevens somewhere up the upper Missouri.
Spencer Baird of the Smithsonian, whom Stevens knew, agreed

to prepare instructions for the collection of natural history specimens and to supervise the final report, although he would not
accompany the survey. Lorin Blodgett, also of the Smithsonian,
was given the task of writing the meteorological report. The responsibility for making the field collections of natural history
material went to Dr. James G. Cooper, who joined the western
party, and to Dr. George Suckley, who was with the eastern
group. Both men were army doctors who had served at Fort
Vancouver and Fort Steilacoom and thus had the advantage of
western experience. "As naturalist," Stevens informed each man,
"it will be your duty to make as full collections as possible of
specimens . . . relating to the various departments of Natural
History including Zoology, Botany, Mineralology, Ecology, Eth-
nology, etc." The survey's chief artist was John Mix Stanley, a
thirty-nine-year-old painter who had spent much of his life
drawing and painting on the western frontier. Stanley had been
in Oregon in 1847, narrowly escaping involvement in the Whitman massacre. In 1852 Joseph Henry accepted the artist's offer
to display his work permanently in the Smithsonian Institution.
Stanley was still in the East when the surveys were authorized
and Stevens snatched him up. Stevens named a number of
young men as special aides, including his cousin George Stevens,
Isaac Osgood from North Andover (who had worked for Stevens
on the New England forts), and James Doty, the son of a former Wisconsin governor.[11]

    While he gathered personnel, Stevens attempted to master all
existing information on the territory between the 47th and 49th
parallels. For the eastern portion he relied on the reports of Joseph N. Nicollet's three reconnaissances in the 1830s and 1840s
and Lieutenant John Pope's 1849 report on Minnesota. He consulted with John Evans, who provided extensive information on
distance, terrain, Indians, and possible guides. Stevens pored
over Washington Irving's *Astoria,* the writings of Father De
Smet, George Simpson's account of his journey around the
world, and, of course, the journals of Lewis and Clark. Lieutenant Donelson was dispatched to Montreal to query Sir George
Simpson of the Hudson's Bay Company on the location of posts
and Indian tribes, the availability of guides, and the possibility
of buying supplies from the Company. (Simpson must have
wondered at the temerity of the Americans, who had forced the
Company north of the 49th parallel, and then turned to it for
help.) The prospect of selling supplies no doubt cooled Simpson's temper, but Stevens later resolved to divorce the expedi-

tion from any reliance upon the Company except in an emergency; he instructed his lieutenants, "While we exchange courtesies and hospitalities with the Hudson's Bay Company, the people and Indians of the Territory should see that we have all the elements of success in our hands."[12]

Congress had appropriated $150,000 for all the surveys, and the northern route had received $40,000, almost the amount Stevens had predicted as necessary, but costs quickly began to mount. The problem was partially offset by drawing upon the Quartermaster Corps for transportation, clothing, and rations for all members of the expedition except the scientific employees. Lieutenant Grover went to St. Louis to draw on the quartermaster there for the necessary supplies. Unfortunately, the quartermaster turned out to be David Vinton, with whom Stevens had quarreled while preparing to sail for Brazos Santiago. Stevens admitted that the army was "exceedingly liberal" in supplying the expedition, but despite this help and constant efforts to keep expenditures to a minimum, expenses continued to exceed the budget. The major problem lay in the scope of the expedition. Congress conceived of the surveys primarily as general reconnaissances of the topography, and secondarily as sources of scientific information. Because the task called for such a variety of information and because the scientific community saw a tremendous opportunity to collect data, all the railroad surveys broadened in scope. But Stevens more than any other survey leader assumed the task of providing complete geographic, geologic, botanic, zoologic, and meteorologic information for an area of several hundred thousand square miles. The heads of the other parties were all officers in the Topographical Engineers who approached the duty as one of significance, but Stevens was much more committed personally to the success of his assigned survey. It was his nature to be exceedingly thorough as well as optimistic about what could be accomplished in a given period of time. For example, when Baird and Henry urged him to gather copious data for the Smithsonian, he wholeheartedly agreed—because their interests corresponded with his. Stevens was determined that the northern railroad survey would be the greatest scientific, topographic expedition since Lewis and Clark and would provide a fitting opening chapter to the new era about to dawn in the northwest quarter of the nation.[13]

Stevens attempted to devote his personal attention to the most minute details of the preparations. For example, he checked on various types of equipment including rifles and insisted that only the new, more accurate Sharps model would meet their needs; he succeeded in bluffing the army into parting with a number of these precious new weapons. Construction of the transits, barometers, and other crucial equipment proceeded under his watchful eye while he dispatched letters to subordinates filled with detailed instructions. Stevens cautioned T. S. Everett, who was assisting Grover at St. Louis, to make individual selection of the mules and to choose only strong, active, well-trained, medium-sized animals. He went on to specify methods of mule packing, the proper material for tent flooring, and the type of tent poles he wished to purchase. Still, he told Everett, "Details must be left to your judgment and discretion." These typical instructions illustrate both Stevens' strength and weakness as an administrator. He displayed tremendous energy and a great capacity for detail, but he found it difficult to delegate authority. When forced by circumstances to rely on subordinates, he would issue very precise instructions, but he would also stress the importance of reacting to circumstances and relying upon individual judgment. This often left his men undecided as to the proper course to follow, and if the final result did not meet Stevens' approval, he could and often did castigate his employees either for not following directions to the letter or for not exercising independent judgment.[14]

After six weeks of frenetic activity, Stevens left Washington D.C. for St. Louis. On May 8, the day before Stevens' departure, McClellan finally arrived from his post in Texas and, after hasty consultation with Stevens, left for New York to catch a steamer to Panama. In mid-April, because the time factor gave Stevens increasing concern, he put a fourth party in the field under Rufus Saxton, who was ordered to take a supply train from Fort Vancouver to St. Mary's in the Bitterroot Valley and to act as a connecting link between the western and eastern parties. A. J. Donelson had preceded Stevens to St. Louis and had departed upstream on an American Fur Company steamboat loaded with supplies. Ten sappers assigned to the survey by the Engineer Corps were also aboard. Donelson made a navigational survey of the Missouri River and after arriving at Fort Union undertook a reconnaissance of the divide between the Souris and Missouri rivers. Accompanied by Stanley, Stevens arrived in St. Louis on May 15 and found preparations well under way but everything in great confusion. The young, unbroken mules provided by Quartermaster Vinton caused particular concern, and strenuous searching failed to produce seasoned animals to

Stevens' 1853
railroad survey
expedition,
John Mix Stanley

replace them. After a week some order began to emerge from
the chaos, and Stevens traveled up the Mississippi toward St.
Paul, pausing at Galena to purchase additional equipment, including a few precious well-broken mules.[15]

The situation was somewhat less chaotic in St. Paul and at
Camp Pierce, the base camp established by Captain Gardiner
nine miles from town. One St. Paul resident assessing the prepa-

rations a day or two before the survey leader arrived was impressed by Stevens' efforts to that point. He reported that

Governor Stevens is said to be a regular go-ahead man and so far the work shows for itself. His men, baggage, and about 150 mules have already arrived, and the work has been going on for over a week. How he has managed so to expedite affairs is a problem. The shipments of merchandise and emigration to St. Paul this spring have been enormous; so that many of our merchants,

who purchased even in the winter, have not yet received their supplies. The
Governor has crowded them off and hurried his effects along. It is not easy to
define how much the people of the West admire such a character.

Arriving at St. Paul in the early morning hours, Stevens immediately rode out to the camp, and as he told it, "I . . . had the
pleasure of arousing the gentlemen of the expedition from their
sleep" at 4:30. The gentlemen were quickly apprised, as the citizens of St. Paul already knew, that this survey would be no
Sunday stroll.[16]

The next day Governor Stevens sat in his tent with rain
dripping outside and assessed the immediate future, which he
had to admit was gloomy. Four straight days of rain had turned
everything into a sea of mud; the barometers arrived broken
and James Doty (with another young assistant, Benjamin F.
Kendall) had to travel to New York for replacements; and the
mules were presenting a serious problem. The governor estimated that of two hundred animals, about a hundred were
completely unbroken and most of the rest were "quite wild."
After pondering the situation, Stevens made a key decision. Although he was accustomed to a society in which there were
sharp divisions between gentlemen and laborers, officers and enlisted men, and those who worked with their hands and those
who did not, he decreed that the manual labor of the expedition would be shared by all and that they would start by breaking the mules with each person responsible for his own animal.
They herded several animals into a corral and lassoed each in
an attempt to wear the mules down by allowing them to drag
half a dozen men around the arena. The mules were then picketed on a short rope on which the animals turned "summersets
both before and behind." The real action started when the men
put on the saddles and mounted. George Stevens described the
fun:

Behold some fifteen or twenty of us mounted; off we start, and in a moment
all sorts of scenes are being enacted. Here one is thrown headforemost; here is
one borne through the air with lightning speed. . . . Some of the mules lie
down, and some persist in running among a number of picketed animals, tan-
gling themselves in the lariats; the riders—however good—are sent "bounding
through the air."

George Suckley called his animal "demonically wild" and lamented that it had a habit of purposely running into trees and
bushes; he claimed that he cured the beast by aiming it at obstacles, which the mule would then take pains to avoid. Stevens

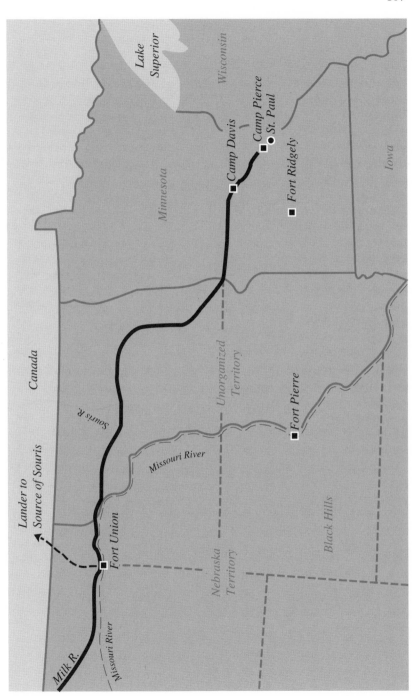

Eastern Half of Railroad Survey Route.

made light of the mule breaking and suggested that in the gloom and rain it provided a "source of mirthful enjoyment." But some incidents were not so mirthful, for Suckley was kept busy treating bruises and kicks and Frederick Lander suffered a dislocated shoulder that required the combined strength of three men to snap back in place. Most of the mules needed several weeks on the trail before they became resigned to their fate, and, during the breaking period, each morning provided its share of wild rides and dislodged riders. Quartermaster Vinton, safe in St. Louis, probably enjoyed a satisfying laugh at the expense of his old Engineer Corps adversaries as he imagined the scene. Suckley suggested that the experience had its good side, for it prepared all members to be ready to undertake any task, and the efforts of the gentlemen set a good example for the habitually grumbling teamsters and wagonmasters.[17]

Frederick Lander had explored the Mississippi River before Stevens' arrival at Camp Pierce and reported that the best railroad crossing was at Sauk Rapids. The governor sent Lander and Tinkham on ahead with advance parties at the end of May and the main party left Camp Pierce on June 6. Four days later Stevens reported that the mules were fairly well broken and all was proceeding smoothly, but that "All I can do is see what a day will bring forth, bringing to the duties of each day all that previous experience has suggested."

At Camp Davis, on the Sauk River two miles from its juncture with the Mississippi, Stevens paused to make final plans and to reorganize the party for the long march to Fort Union. He assigned Lieutenant Cuvier Grover to take a small party from Pike Lake west to the James River and to then turn north and rejoin the main party near the Souris River.[18]

During the first leg of the journey Stevens weeded out the men he believed to be too lazy, too ineffective, too insubordinate, or of insufficient physical strength. One of the latter was Captain Gardiner, who returned to Fort Snelling suffering from gout. Max Strobel, hired in St. Paul as an artist, was sent back as "inefficient," and Lieutenant Beekman DuBarry was released for the same reason. Captain Remenyi and Mr. Jekelfaluzy, whom Stevens had hired in Washington to make meteorological observations and to care for the instruments, proved to be totally incompetent; they joined a number of other rejects making the trek back to St. Paul. As replacements, the governor hired French-Canadian voyageurs, who as a group had made a favorable impression. Stevens enthusiastically praised them as

"thorough woodsmen, and just the men for prairie life also, going into the water as pleasantly as a spaniel, and remaining
there as long as needed; stout, able-bodied, and willing to put
their shoulders to the wheel." Stevens hired as chief guide and
informal leader of the voyageurs Pierre Boutineau, a man he believed had the talent and broad view of an engineer. Stevens
quickly grasped that the Canadians wished to be treated with
"kindness and a certain degree of familiarity," which would result in their becoming the "most obedient and hard-working fellows in the world."[19]

Once the deadwood was eliminated, Stevens issued his general
instructions and method of operation for the exploration. With
the party drawn up in military formation, the governor read the
orders:

Cook fires to be made at two o'clock a.m.; the cooks and teamsters called at
three, and the animals to be put in good grass; reveille to be sounded at four,
and all the officers to be called by name; the whole camp to breakfast about
four, and the teamsters immediately to commence harnessing up; tents struck
at half-past four, and camp in motion by five; the sentinels instructed to fire
upon any prowling Indians.

As the mule breaking had already indicated, no one would be
excused from camp duties. Each man would also take his turn
at guard duty, and no one was allowed more than twenty-five
pounds of personal baggage. Stevens denounced the notion of a
military escort and declared that each man would serve as escort for every other. All, including civilians, received a military
rank so that when rapid decisions were necessary, it would be
clear who was in command. Stevens gave a speech which by his
own admission exaggerated the difficulties that lay ahead; he
spoke of bogs, rivers, mountains, snows, and hostile Indians and
tried to impress upon the party the necessity of loyalty and cooperation if they were to reach their objective and accomplish
the mission. A few grumbled, but the majority accepted the
strict orders without complaint as a matter of necessity. Dr.
Suckley endorsed Stevens' instructions and assessed him as "a
smart, active, ubiquitous little man, very come-at-able."[20]

Expedition Moves West

With Stevens leading the way dressed in a red flannel shirt
and slouch hat, the 120 men of the northern railroad survey
moved across the prairies of western Minnesota accompanied by
the peculiar music of the creaking, oversized wheels on the Pem-

bina wagons. The first portion of the survey covered relatively well-known ground, and the main negative feature was the boggy nature of much of the terrain. Stevens did not believe this would cause a problem, and he enthused that the country west of St. Paul for 120 miles "presents facilities for railroad construction seldom, if ever, exceeded." He tried to set a good example by rushing to lend a hand with the ropes when a wagon needed help in fording a stream or crossing a bog. He praised the young lieutenant who informed him one morning that he had four minutes to finish his breakfast, and at the end of the time struck the tent over his head so they could be under way on schedule.

The first major personnel problem occurred at Pike Lake when Grover was preparing to leave the main party for the James River. Because of the delays incurred by the unbroken mules and encounters with Minnesota mud, only twenty days' rations remained for a journey to Fort Union that would take about twice that long. Stevens argued that an abundance of game and eight oxen made starvation impossible, and a threatened strike ended without "any open demonstration." The governor ordered regular rations cut when they had game or fish available, and his prediction proved correct as they encountered a plentiful supply of birds and buffalo as they moved west. But he had to cut the bread ration drastically and "this state of affairs caused considerable grumbling"—except among the voyageurs, who preferred the all-meat diet.[21]

The terrain continued to exceed Stevens' fondest expectations as he found the divide between the Mississippi and Red Rivers "a gently undulating and exceedingly rich prairie country," and further west the prairie in the valley of the Red River presented a horizon as "unbroken as that of a calm sea." On July 1 they met a train of half-breed Red River traders headed to St. Paul with goods acquired from the Meteis, and the survey party traded with them for pemmican, moccasins, beaded clothing, and, most important, carts and oxen. The traders also helped the survey by leaving a bridge they had constructed over the rapidly rising Sheyenne River. Although they were traveling over ground mapped by Nicollet, Stevens found it was necessary to correct some mistakes such as the proper course of the Sheyenne River. Most of the party's difficulties continued to come from mud and rain-swollen rivers, but there were numerous annoyances such as the loss of their best compass and the malfunctioning of the chronometers, which prevented computations of longitude. West of the Sheyenne River they encountered vast herds of buffalo; on one occasion various individuals estimated a herd to contain between 200,000 and 500,000 animals. Stevens sent hunters ahead to clear a safe passage, but despite precautions they lost several animals who became irretrievably mixed with the buffalo. The wet, warm weather brought out mosquitoes that hit the sides of the tent "with a noise like the pattering of rain, while the inside is perfectly black with them."

As the expedition proceeded, Lander and Tinkham explored north and south of the line of march to plot rivers and determine the general lay of the land. Tinkham and a small party alarmed the camp when they became lost in fog for two days. While awaiting their return, Boutineau stumbled on an Indian encampment of over a thousand lodges and threw many of the men into near panic when he announced that they were hostile Sioux. They prepared for the worst, only to discover that Boutineau, who had Stevens convinced he was the finest woodsman in North America, was mistaken—they were Meteis on a hunting expedition. For Stevens the greatest calamity happened on July 12 when, exerting himself to keep a herd of buffalo turned away from the wagons, he was prostrated by his old rupture. Once again in the midst of an exciting expedition he was forced to take to the wagons, and although he claimed substantial recovery after a few days, it was apparent that the injury troubled him for the remainder of the journey.[22]

The party first encountered Indians on the Souris River (in present North Dakota), where they came upon an encampment of 1,200 Assiniboines. This was Stevens' first contact with a tribe relatively untouched by white civilization, and the meeting provided a number of surprises. He was impressed by the friendly reception and the chiefs' invitation to visit the camp. Using American standards as criteria, the governor observed that numerous horses and well-stocked cooking pots gave the appearance of plenty, but he judged the camp on the whole as "very filthy and miserable." Stevens smoked the pipe, ate buffalo soup and turnips, and listened to a speech given by an elderly chief. The Assiniboine asked what would happen when the railroad was completed and the buffalo disappeared. He complained that his tribe had abided by the Treaty of Fort Laramie (1851) but in return for good faith had been raided by Sioux and had found half-breeds hunting in their territory. It was a theme on which Stevens would hear many variations in the next three

years. He was ready with a reply: Whites who settled along the railroad would bring goods to replace the game, and the President would provide agricultural implements so they could till the soil and "obtain food with less labor than now." The Assiniboines must have been skeptical, but they said nothing, and the governor believed that his remarks made "a very favorable impression." He departed with a rich present of thirty-two dressed

Herd of bison
near Lake Jennie,
John Mix Stanley

skins and two buffalo robes and mused, "I was very much
pleased with these Indians . . . their hospitality I shall long remember."[23]

On August 1, as the expedition neared Fort Union, the men
marched toward the post carrying a home made American flag
and smaller banners indicating the occupation of the bearers;
the engineers' banner was decorated with a locomotive running

down a buffalo and the motto "Westward Ho." Stevens mounted his horse for the first time since his injury three weeks earlier so he could lead his men into the American Fur Company post in proper fashion. When they reached the Missouri, "the whole party gave three cheers as its beautiful bluff banks, dotted with timber, came in view." The men fired off a rifle volley, and the fort answered with a thirteen-gun salute. At the fort Stevens found Lieutenants Donelson and Grover encamped with their men awaiting his arrival. That evening the combined parties assembled before the governor's tent. Stevens offered congratulations to his men on their zealous performance to that point, noted the difficulties that lay ahead, and offered each man the opportunity to return east with the fur company. All opted to go on, and the only member left behind was Private White, an engineer-company sapper fatally wounded by the accidental discharge of his gun. Stevens happily reported to Jefferson Davis that the route to Fort Union was made to order for a railroad with the greatest obstacle being the Sheyenne River crossing.[24]

The survey party remained at Fort Union for ten days to repair equipment, mend clothing, rest the animals, and make additional Pembina carts. Stevens had found that these carts pulled by ox teams provided the best transportation, and he purchased two additional teams from the fur company. The party could have avoided much difficulty and delay by an earlier awareness of the superiority of oxen for western travel, but they naturally relied on the old army standbys, the mule and horse. As preparation for the next leg of the journey ended, some of the men who had been so zealous to continue began to have second thoughts. Stevens blamed fur company employees who spread "bugbear stories" of snow knee deep at Fort Benton and twenty feet deep in the Rocky Mountains in September. The men were acquiring "cold feet." The threatened "stampede" was averted when Stevens quoted contrary evidence from De Smet's writings, and the officers of the fort labeled the stories as unfounded. Some of Stevens' officers were also disillusioned with the governor's leadership, although none threatened to leave.

While at Fort Union Stevens sent Frederick Lander on a jaunt into Canada to find the source of the Souris River. Stevens admitted that "this reconnaissance was a very extended one," but he believed the effort justified because it added to their knowledge of the upper reaches of the Souris. However, he did not mention the obvious fact that they were straying without permission into a foreign country, that the territory lay out-side the boundaries assigned to the survey, and that at best it was an arduous and dangerous venture that could provide mar-ginal return to the expedition. The danger was amply illustrated by Lander's encounter with several hostile bands of Indians and avoidance of an incident in one case resulted only from the exercise of considerable tact by Lander and his men. In addi-tion, Stevens would soon report to Davis that the appropriated funds were exhausted, yet he made no effort to save on expense by curtailing nonessential operations.[25]

As the survey left Fort Union and headed for the next check-point at Fort Benton, it was joined by sixty Blood and Piegan Indians. Stevens desired to make contact with as many tribes as possible, but a particular objective was the various divisions of the Blackfoot nation (Blood, Piegan, Gros Ventre, and Black-foot). The warlike nature of these people was legend; their hos-tility to whites dated from Lewis and Clark and had continued through the fur-trade era. Stevens hired Alexander Culbertson, an employee of the American Fur Company, to act as an advi-sor on Indian relations. He could not have made a better choice: Culbertson was married to a Blood and had for many years acted as a mediator between the two races. The fur trader was not optimistic for the future; the Blackfoot Indians believed that the United States gave the most goods to those who took to the warpath, and he stated that peace had been difficult to maintain during the previous year. It soon appeared that Cul-bertson's gloomy prediction was accurate when a minor misun-derstanding at their camp on the Little Muddy River nearly re-sulted in violence; Culbertson and his wife needed all their wiles to restore calm.

Stevens promised this band, and all the Blackfoot Indians he met, that a council would convene at Fort Benton the next year for the purpose of establishing peaceful relations with the Amer-icans, the Flatheads, and other tribes further west. The Black-foot tribe was not included in Stevens' jurisdiction as superin-tendent of Indian affairs for Washington Territory, but he believed it of first priority to initiate a treaty to remove any possible objection to the northern railroad route, and also to re-move this powerful tribe as a threat to Indians who lived within the boundaries of Washington Territory. Despite the near in-cident on the Little Muddy, Stevens remained optimistic as he was met cordially by the chiefs and received the impression that they approved of his plans.[26]

Stevens continued to suffer from his rupture and turned command of the daily routine over to Donelson while he tried to recover his strength for the mountain passes. As they proceeded west along the Milk River, Tinkham, Lander, and Grover continued on expeditions that took them away from the main route. They determined that the courses of the Missouri and its tributaries were incorrect on existing maps; for example, the

Fort Union and
distribution of
goods to the
Assiniboines,
John Mix Stanley

Milk continued almost directly west rather than heading off in
a northerly direction. The route continued to be promising although the governor noted a number of ravines and coulees that
would require bridges.

Tempers were not as even as the terrain, and a number of
quarrels and disputes arose. One issue was the relationship between civilian and military members of the survey and the au-

118

thority the former had to give orders to the latter. The governor reaffirmed the command system, but the necessity of taking orders from civilians left a bad taste in the mouths of the army men. Suckley, who had earlier agreed with Stevens' policy of putting all on an equal basis, objected to an order requiring all members to walk part of each day to conserve the animals. The doctor argued that his letter of appointment was a contract that promised transportation which he did not interpret to mean his own two feet. After a heated debate, Suckley agreed to "cheerfully obey" but grumbled that Stevens should have made his wishes known by "politic suggestion," rather than by peremptory order. Suckley had put his finger on a weak point in Stevens' ability as a leader—his tendency to be curt when tact and courtesy could better have accomplished the desired result. To Stevens such courtesy was unnecessary nonsense, and that attitude resulted in his offending many and acquiring enemies needlessly. Another incident occurred when it came to light that instrument observations were not taken on longitude. Stevens insisted that he had given Donelson verbal instructions specifically on this point, but the lieutenant denied it, and argued that he could not be expected to supervise personally every detail of the march. Neither would compromise, and the misunderstanding eventually resulted in an open split between the two men.[27]

The party circled north of the Bears Paw Mountains and dropped down the west side to the Missouri River, arriving at Fort Benton on September 1. The men at the fort fired a fifteen-gun salute, outdoing their counterparts at Fort Union by two guns. According to George Stevens the trip to that point had been "made with ease and comfort as if at home." The difficult portion lay ahead in the passes of the Rocky and Bitterroot mountains, and as they paused to rest the animals for the assault, Stevens attempted to gather information on the snows and possible routes from the employees and Indians at the fort. As usual, the information was contradictory, with some asserting that the passes would prove impenetrable by November and others predicting snow only on the peaks by then. Stevens typically decided they would have to determine the facts by their own observations. The northern Rockies and the Bitterroots had been traversed by explorers from the time of Lewis and Clark, and had been combed throughly in the search for beaver since the 1830s. But no one had made a systematic survey of the various routes and passes, nor had there been any attempt to gather information on snow depth, temperature, grades, rainfall, soil

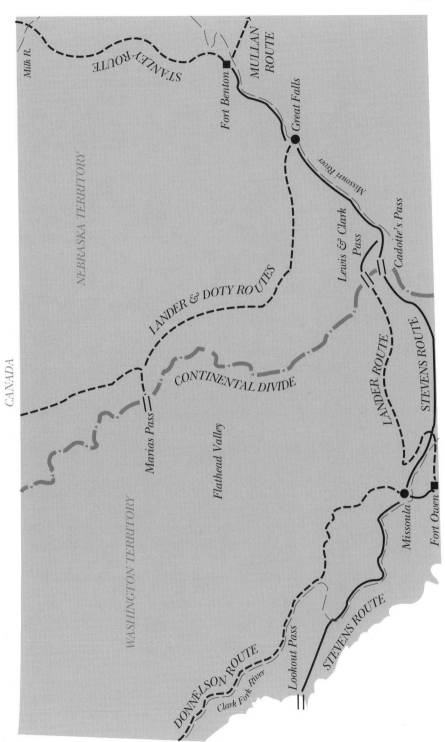

Railroad Survey Route through Western Montana

Crossing the
Hellgate River,
May 5, 1854,
Gustavus Sohon

quality, or other geologic and topographic information. It was
Stevens' task to supplant myths, opinions, and guesses with
facts. He rightly argued that this could be accomplished in most
cases only by examination over an extended period as long as
several years. This, of course, required time and money which
were both becoming precious to Stevens in the fall of 1853.[28]

Stevens informed Jefferson Davis from Fort Benton that the $40,000 appropriation would be exhausted by the end of October, with many vital tasks still remaining. The governor announced that he was not justified in suspending operations and would continue with the hope that Congress would make a deficit appropriation. He projected the work to continue until June

1855, and suggested an additional $80,000 would allow completion of the necessary tasks. This would not include the cost of making the Blackfoot treaty, which would assure that "a single man will be able to go unmolested through these vast plains." To Stevens the proposal was entirely practicable, for he continued to think in terms of his grand design for the Pacific Northwest. But to Jefferson Davis the request was absurd. The Secretary of War had no choice but to adhere closely to the timetable mandated by Congress. Davis coldly informed Stevens, "The department very much regrets . . . you have made your arrangements as to absorb all your funds so long before the completion of the work;" the survey was to be completed and a report submitted no later than the first week in February, 1854. Still the secretary was sympathetic to the necessarily high costs of the expedition, and he asked Congress for an additional $25,000 to cover the deficit.[29]

At Fort Benton the survey divided into several sections for the attack on the Rocky Mountain passes. Stevens sent Grover ahead to the Bitterroot Valley to make contact with Rufus Saxton, who he hoped was waiting with supplies brought from Fort Vancouver; Donelson took a party to reconnoiter the approaches to Cadotte's Pass; the governor remained temporarily at Fort Benton to have a conference with a group of Piegans; and a fourth party under Frederick Lander started north to explore Marias Pass, which Stevens believed might offer the best rail route. While still in Washinton D.C. he had guessed that this pass, along with a crossing of the Cascade Mountains just south of Mt. Baker, appeared practical, and his opinion was confirmed by Little Dog, a Piegan chief, who said that Marias Pass was once the main route over the mountains but had been abandoned for superstitious reasons. A fifth party under the command of John Mullan departed on an extensive reconnaissance to the southeast of Fort Benton. Mullan had come up the Missouri with Donelson, and this was the young West Point graduate's first independent assignment with the survey. With it he began a career of extensive exploration of the Rockies and Bitterroots that would culminate with construction of the Mullan road from Walla Walla to Fort Benton.[30]

Lieutenant Mullan traveled east from the fort to the Judith River and then turned south in an attempt to make contact with the Flathead Indians hunting in this area. After some effort he found them south of the Musselshell River (written by Stevens as Muscle Shell) and used his West Point French to communicate through a member of the tribe who claimed to know the language. They appeared to understand his message, which urged them to attend the grand peace council the next year, and Mullan was grateful for the first time that he had undergone the "many and frequent annoyances" of learning French. Mullan's Piegan guide deserted him, but he persuaded four Flathead scouts to accompany him westward. They followed a river that the lieutenant correctly guessed to be Lewis and Clark's Smith River, and crossed the Missouri at Gate of the Mountains (near present Helena). He headed up Prickly Pear Creek (now Sevenmile Creek) which took him through Mullan Pass, one of a group that Stevens called the Hell's Gate passes. The pass was six thousand feet high, and Mullan pronounced it practical for wagons or railroads. Across the pass, he took the Little Blackfoot River to Clark Fork (called by the survey Hell Gate River) and found a mile-wide valley, covered with a "beautiful and luxurious growth of fine grass," which he followed to the Bitterroot Valley. He concluded quite correctly that Clark Fork provided a potential major route through the mountains.[31]

On September 11 a messenger galloped up to Stevens, then two days out of Fort Benton, with the happy news that Grover and Saxton had met near the divide on Cadotte's Pass. Less happy was the report that the route could not be traversed by wagons. Stevens decided to return to Fort Benton and await the arrival of his two lieutenants. Saxton received a joyful welcome when he arrived tired but happy, and even the governor seemed a little surprised that "a party from the Atlantic and one from the Pacific . . . had met by appointment . . . at the foot of the dividing ridge between the oceans." The spirit of the whole party was buoyed up, and Stevens believed "daylight now breaks through the struggles of three months." The same day Tinkham, who had gone up to the Milk River as far as the 49th parallel, returned. Stevens immediately sent John Stanley, who had accompanied Tinkham, back north with instructions to find the main Piegan band and escort them to Fort Benton for a talk. Stanley had to travel north of the 50th parallel before he found the Piegans and their chief, Low Horn, on the Bow River. They agreed to come south with him, and when Stanley returned, the governor observed that "in eleven days he had gone 160 miles and back, effected the business he was sent for, made a number of sketches of the country and the Indians, and collected a partial vocabulary." While Stanley made his forced march north,

Stevens conferred with Grover and Saxton and it was agreed that with time growing short it would be best to abandon the wagons and push ahead with the mules. Saxton and Culbertson returned down the Missouri to report in person on the state of the railroad survey and on Indian affairs. They were accompanied by most of the dragoons and several other men Stevens believed were no longer needed. A messenger was sent to bring Lander in, as the governor had reluctantly decided to abandon, at least temporarily, the survey of Marias Pass. They would all move immediately through Cadotte's Pass or nearby Lewis and Clark Pass to the Bitterroot Valley.[32]

While Lander, Donelson, Tinkham, and Stevens moved west into the Rockies, Cuvier Grover and James Doty remained at Fort Benton. Stevens ordered Grover to make a detailed examination of the Missouri River between Fort Union and Fort Benton, and then to make his way to the Puget Sound in midwinter using dog teams to cross the mountains, measuring snow depths as he traveled. Doty remained at Fort Benton to establish a meteorological post and to act as a contact with the Blackfoot Indians until the great council. He proved to be one of the pleasant surprises of the expedition. The governor had not expected much from the young man when he agreed to take him on the expedition as a concession to Doty's father, but young Doty showed himself to be cool, intelligent, and hardworking. His assignment to an important duty indicated Stevens' faith in his assistant, and Doty amply rewarded the governor's confidence. In May and June 1854 he made a forty-one day reconnaissance up the Sun River, north along the eastern slope of the Rockies, across the 49th parallel and back to Fort Benton. He was unable to cross Marias Pass but deemed it worthy of future examination, although he did not endorse the eastern approaches as either a good railroad or packtrain route. Doty visited the various Blackfoot tribes, made a census, took note of customs and characteristics, and worked to preserve friendship. When it became apparent that the great council would not take place in 1854, Doty gathered up his meteorological observations and traveled to Olympia to rejoin the governor.[33]

While the main party moved ahead, Stevens waited at Fort Benton for Stanley to return from the north with Chief Low Horn and his Piegan band. At a hasty council with thirty chiefs representing the Blackfoot and Blood as well as the Piegan, the governor praised the Indians' generosity to the survey and stressed the importance of the upcoming council. Presents valued at $600 were distributed, and everyone departed, Stevens hurrying to catch his main party. On September 24 the survey party moved up to the east slope of the divide following a creek filled with the lodges and dams of numerous beavers. As they ascended, the men could see small tributaries of the Missouri flowing far below with their banks lined by deciduous foliage beginning to show fall colors. To Stevens it was a scene "full of interest to the eye of one who could appreciate the beauties of nature." The party reached the summit of Cadotte's Pass at four o'clock in the afternoon, just as a pelting rain accompanied by hail, severe wind, thunder, and lightning broke suddenly upon them. In the midst of nature's wild orchestration, Stevens turned to his companions to "cordially and heartily" welcome them to Washington Territory. The survey party came down into the valley of the Clark Fork, where they struck the trail followed by Meriwether Lewis, who on his eastward journey had crossed the divide a few miles to the north of Cadotte's Pass. Rumors circulated that gold existed between Clark Fork and the Bitterroot River, but Stevens avoided a delay by promising that the men stationed at St. Mary's could investigate later. On September 28 they arrived in the Bitterroot Valley and moved on to Fort Owen, a trading post converted from an old Catholic mission by mountain man John Owen.[34]

Frederick Lander and his exhausted party had preceded their arrival by one day. Stevens had sent Lander to explore the pass used by Lewis (Lewis and Clark Pass), but after crossing the divide Lander mistook Clark Fork for the Bitterroot and began traveling east on a course that would have eventually collided with Stevens moving west. Lander finally recognized his error, but rather than turning around and following the river to Hell Gate (near present Missoula), he decided to head overland on a shortcut to the Bitterroot Valley. It was a feat that few have been tempted to duplicate, for it has been observed that "to this day, reaching Fort Owen ... by Lander's shortcut presents a mountaineering problem." Stevens was disgusted and complained that Lander left Fort Benton with the best animals but they had "been much pushed" and "came in exceedingly jaded." The large, vain Lander was not one to let mere mountains stand in his path, and it was not the first or last time he would live up to his reputation as a good engineer but a hard driver of men and animals.[35]

The combined parties regrouped once again at Cantonment Stevens, established twenty miles south of Fort Owen, and the governor plotted the division of labor for the final push over the Bitterroots. He was increasingly optimistic: first, Flathead Indians indicated that they crossed the mountains during all seasons, and snow and cold appeared less of a problem than he had feared; second, they now had the 2,000 rations Saxton had brought to Fort Owen; and third, the mules, although needing a rest, were in good condition to continue. After hearing Mullan's report of his successful expedition to Flathead country, and the crossing of Mullan Pass, he named the young lieutenant to remain behind in the Bitterroot Valley. Like Doty, Mullan collected weather data and acted as an unofficial agent to the Flathead Indians with whom he had developed a relationship of mutual respect. Also like Doty, the lieutenant conducted extensive explorations during his year in the mountains. Mullan believed that a day not spent in the field was a day wasted. After a preliminary journey up the Bitterroot Valley, Mullan crossed the divide at Gibbons Pass in early December and traveled east through the Big Hole Valley to the Jefferson River and thence to Medicine Lodge Pass near the present Montana-Idaho border. He crossed the pass in below-freezing temperature in a strong wind through three-foot drifts, and in typical understatement declared the day's travel "uncomfortable." Mullan hit tributaries of the Snake River, went as far south as Cantonment Loring, five miles above Fort Hall, and then returned to Cantonment Stevens by a somewhat different route. Tinkham also remained behind to explore north along the west side of the Rockies for Marias Pass, on which Stevens' mind "had been so long fixed." He managed to miss Marias Pass and crossed to the east side through Cut Bank Pass (now Pitamakan Pass). (Doty was able to point out the mistake in his expedition of the next spring.) Tinkham returned to the Bitterroot Valley over Mullan Pass and was even more pleased about the possibilities of this route than Mullan had been. Through their dedicated and thorough explorations, Doty, Mullan, and Tinkham were able to provide Stevens with a good understanding of the Rocky Mountain passes and the intermountain region.[36]

With operations in the mountains secured, Stevens turned to preparations to survey the Bitterroots and make the connection with McClellan, who he assumed was nearing completion of his labors in the Cascades. George Suckley wished to collect specimens in the mountains, but the governor argued he could not spare any animals, whereupon the doctor suggested he take a couple of men and a canoe and travel by Clark Fork and the Columbia River to Fort Vancouver. An Iroquois Indian who had once worked for the Hudson's Bay Company built the canoe of three bullock hides, and Suckley with two boatmen pushed off, confidently expecting to beat the others to the Columbia. It proved a cold, wet voyage but they emerged safely, although two weeks after the main party. Still Suckley could report that he had gained thirty pounds during the otherwise arduous venture.

The governor sent Lander to Hell Gate with instructions to wait for Donelson, but, impatient as usual, Lander moved north to an area between Clark Fork and the Jocko River. Stevens wearily sent a messenger to bring him back and determined to send one party over the Bitterroots under Donelson and to personally accompany a second group. Donelson followed the Jocko River and the Clark Fork across the mountains while Stevens left the latter river at present St. Regis and struck to the west to Coeur D'Alene or Stevens Pass (now Lookout Pass). He spent the night of October 10 on the divide and woke on a clear morning to a spectacular view of the Rockies and Flathead Lake, a scene that he asserted could not be matched anywhere else in the country. Two days later Stevens' party visited with Father Anthony Ravalli at his mission, where the governor observed Indians hard at work farming, and left convinced that they could adapt readily to agrarian pursuits. The survey traveled along the Spokane River until October 18, when Stevens learned that McClellan was near Fort Colville. He immediately decided to ride the sixty-five miles to the Hudson's Bay Company post. After a few miles his hernia became so painful that he had to lie flat on the ground to rest, but he finally struggled back on his horse and completed the journey. McClellan was camped only a few miles from the fort and by evening the two main parties of the survey were united for the first time.[37]

The Cascade Mountains Problem

When Stevens discussed his plans for the survey with Jefferson Davis in March 1853, he correctly assumed that the Cascade Mountains would be the most difficult and time-consuming section. His decision to start a party east from Fort Vancouver was sensible; Portland and the fort could provide the necessary supplies and men and an immediate start would allow completion during the summer months. Despite the area's long contact with the fur trade, and increased numbers of permanent settlers after 1835, little was known of the Cascade Mountains because the Columbia River had provided a convenient highway to the interior. Stevens requested that an old acquaintance from Mexico, Captain Benjamin Alvord, write from his station at Fort Dalles to McClellan. But Alvord had to confess that he knew nothing of the passes except the generally known fact that Naches Pass north of Mt. Rainier was often used by Indians and occasionally by white travelers. Thus, as with the Rockies and Bitterroots, the survey had to start virtually from scratch in an attempt to find the best route.[38]

George McClellan seemed an obvious choice to command the western portion of the survey. Young, carefree, and always ready for new adventures, he was also a competent engineer who had impressed Stevens in Mexico. The two men were personality opposites, but they shared characteristics of pride, ambition, and a desire for command. Stevens knew McClellan's preference for work in the field as he had written often to grumble of his station at West Point, and, when sent to Texas, had asked that Stevens persuade Totten to let him remain there rather than returning him to work on a fort. Stevens had no doubt that his friend would be glad to join the survey, and he wrote to explain that the duty would be "arduous" but "will bring reputation." He anticipated correctly: even while the offer was in the mail, McClellan was requesting a transfer to duty in Oregon. When he heard of the survey, he told a friend, "I look forward to the trip with great pleasure—I would not miss it for a great deal." He asked his friend if he should bring back as a present "a live grizzly or a tame Indian chief."

McClellen arrived at Fort Vancouver at the end of June and assisted Saxton in supplying his train for the Bitterroot Valley. McClellan was left with reduced stocks as well as a barely adequate allotment of horses and mules. His forthcoming mission was impaired further by a worthless transit, two "indifferent" sextants, and one unreliable chronometer of only two available. Perhaps questioning the wisdom of outfitting two parties on the Columbia, McClellan grumbled that the annoyance of preparation was beyond imagination, and he declared, "I shall be as pleased as a child with a new toy when I get started." He finally left Fort Vancouver on July 18 with more than sixty men and 160 animals of various descriptions and serviceability. Other members of the party, in addition to his chief assistant, Lieutenant Johnson Duncan, were meteorologist Lieutenant Sylvester

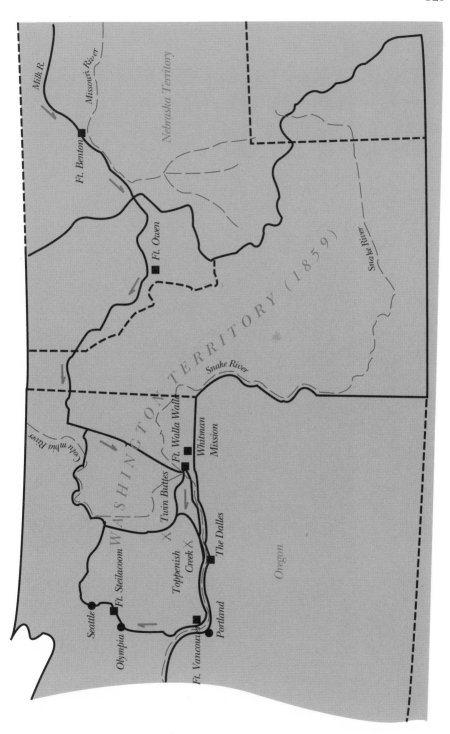

Western Half of Railroad Survey Route. Territorial boundaries as of 1859.

Mowry, ethnologist George Gibbs, assistant engineer J. F. Minter, and surgeon/naturalist Dr. James G. Cooper—a remarkably able group of scientists and engineers.[39]

The party headed north to the Cathlapootle River (now Lewis River) and turned east to follow its valley over Klickitat Pass south of Mt. Saint Helens and Mt. Adams. It proved an arduous start to the expedition. In twelve days they covered

Fort Vancouver,
Washington
Territory,
Gustavus Sohon

only seventy-eight miles over an often nonexistent trail through rugged, heavily forested terrain. The animals were further weakened by the lack of good grass. Like Stevens, McClellan had to weed out misfits during the first days; he sent one packer back as a constant grumbler and later released a young civilian assistant who had forged McClellan's name to drafts in Olympia. Before leaving camp the young man stole a revolver which necessi-

tated McClellan's sending a party back on the trail to retrieve
it. Smoke from forest fires cast a pall over the landscape, making it difficult to get a clear view of mountains that could be
used as landmarks. However, the smoke was not thick enough to
discourage large horseflies, which drove the animals to dis-
traction—or to bother the clouds of mosquitoes which attacked
the men. The pack saddles began breaking under light loads,
causing McClellan to stop the party while Duncan went back to
Vancouver to retrieve some old Ringgold army saddles that
someone remembered were piled in a storeroom at the fort.[40]

Upon reaching the Klickitat River, McClellan decided they
had not gone over a pass but rather through a pocket between
the mountains which contained poor timber and nothing to
"tempt settlement and civilization." Turning north over a ridge,
they came into the Yakima Valley and stopped at the Ahtanum
mission of the Oblate fathers Charles Pandosy and Louis
D'Herbomez. The eastern side of the mountains appeared unim-
pressive to McClellan, who mused, "To what useful purpose this
country can be put it is difficult to imagine." While in the valley he met on a number of occasions with the Yakima Indians
including Kamiakin and his brother Skloom. McClellan and
Saxton, who had passed that way earlier, found the atmosphere
hostile because the rumor had gone ahead (allegedly spread by
a French-Canadian employee of the Hudson's Bay Company)
that the exploring party would take the land and punish the Indians if they resisted.

McClellan explained to the Indians that they were looking for
the best road location emigrants would use on their way to the
Sound. There is little doubt he believed this to be true: McClellan could not conceive that any white would want to settle in
the region east of the Cascades. Talk of a road was in itself
alarming to the Yakimas, but they said nothing; however, when
Stevens later began to speak of treaties and opening parts of
eastern Washington to settlement, it appeared that McClellan
had deliberately deceived them. Kamiakin and Skloom suspected as much, for during their talks with McClellan they reminded him that their neighbors south of the Columbia had
been told many things in the past and were often paid only
with promises. They were assured that when Governor Stevens
came he "would only tell them the truth." Kamiakin professed
that he wished friendship and as proof sold McClellan cattle
(although at a high price) and provided a guide to Naches
Pass.[41]

While setting up camp on the Wenas River, McClellan pondered the future of the expedition and became convinced that the rugged terrain and poor condition of the animals required sending to Steilacoom for fresh mules. He explained, "I must do so at all risks in order to carry out my orders this fall—at least as far as the Cascade Range is concerned." On August 21 a party departed for the Sound via Naches Pass with orders to bring as many mules as could be found and 3,690 rations. The following day McClellan set out to make his examination of the pass and found the grade steep, with a need for many cuts through solid rock, plus the prospect of numerous bridges and four or five tunnels near the crest. A railroad could be built through the pass, McClellan decided, as modern engineering made virtually nothing impossible, but he concluded, "It seems doubtful to me whether I shall ever ride down the valley of the Nachess in a railroad car." On August 31 bad news arrived from Steilacoom that his men could find no animals and few provisions. McClellan decided to reduce the party by half, sending back thirty men and all the horses. The remainder would push on using the mules.

With the reduced party he crossed the dividing ridges into the Kittitas Valley and followed the Yakima River to Snoqualmie Pass, the pass described by the Indians as less desirable than Naches, but declared by Father Pandosy as the far superior route. The wide, open expanses of the lower valley encouraged McClellan. Although time was running short, he decided that he "must at all events go as far as the divide and examine that." On September 7 he crossed the divide at a point thought to be Snoqualmie Pass that was actually Yakima Pass five miles to the north. The party continued for three miles down the east side, then returned to the summit, where visual and instrument observations were made from a peak 2,000 feet above the pass. Thick smoke limited visibility, but McClellan and George Gibbs surveyed the western approaches and examined Lakes Keechelus, Kachess, and Cle Elum before rejoining the rest of the survey of the Kittitas Valley.

McClellan thought Snoqualmie (actually Yakima) Pass was a possibility, but he believed an examination of the west side was necessary before determining the superiority of any route. He was criticized later for not surveying the west side himself, particularly as the party remained idle in the valley for three days. McClellan had not been instructed to examine the western approaches to the passes. He expected his party to join him at any moment with supplies from Steilacoom, and he wanted his men to be ready on short notice. While McClellan waited, gold fever struck the camp and Duncan took some of the men "on a wild goose chase" which turned up traces of precious metal but not enough to make panning profitable.[42]

Accompanied by the Yakima chief Owhi and supplied with twenty-nine fresh horses and some additional provisions, the survey party marched north over the Wenatchee Mountains via Colockum Pass to the confluence of the Wenatchee and Columbia Rivers. Probably because the Indians did not use the present Stevens Pass (at the origin of the Wenatchee River), and failed to point it out, the party heedlessly struck north along the Columbia River. McClellan, worried by the approach of winter, tried to hurry his men on. He complained that cold weather could be very nice "in a tight house with a whisky punch, but in tents and on cold water it is a different affair." The Indians expressed doubt that any pass existed in the vicinity of Mt. Baker, as Stevens hoped, and told McClellan that the next pass to the north was in British territory. McClellan established a camp at Fort Okanogan and then set off up the Methow Valley on a route that seemed promising, but the Indian guides' reports were corroborated when the valley narrowed and the trail became rugged. The party returned to the fort, followed the Okanogan River as far north as Lake Okanogan, then doubled back down the river until they reached the same parallel as Fort Colville, where they turned east, marched over the mountains, and arrived at the fort one day before Governor Stevens. Stevens was greatly relieved at the successful juncture of both main parties although he was near collapse from fatigue and from the pain caused by his rupture.[43]

Angus McDonald, in charge at Fort Colville, anticipated the arrival of the survey party by laying in an extra ration of fifty gallons of wine and brandy; he would not have conceived of departing from the Company's tradition of playing gracious host to all visitors. After a dinner of beefsteak washed down with a plentiful supply of liquor, and a long evening of talk and more drink, Stevens mumbled, "Mac this is powerful wine" and fell fast asleep. A short time later McClellan slipped off the sofa onto the floor. McDonald, well satisfied that he had been an adequate host, left them snoring. For the next several days they partook freely of the Company's food and drink while waiting for Donelson to arrive from his venture on the Clark Fork–Lake Pend Oreille route. They exchanged stories of their recent adventures and listened to McDonald weave tales of his many years in the wilderness. Stevens relaxed and contemplated their success to that point: no major problems or catastrophies had occurred; there was little sickness or disability in either party; relations with the Indians appeared excellent and the way had been paved for future treaties; they had completed the most difficult work before winter; and the route appeared practical and even highly desirable for a transcontinental railroad. He was pleased at the work accomplished by McClellan and praised his party as well organized and efficient. An unexpected dividend was the copious material George Gibbs had gathered on the Indians along that route. To Stevens it appeared that the only major task remaining was to run a line or lines through the most promising Cascade passes down the west side to the Sound.[44]

Stevens decided to meet Donelson south of the Hudson's Bay Company's old post at Spokane House. There the party would split again, with McClellan and Lander striking due west via the Snoqualmie Pass and the remainder proceeding to Fort Vancouver by way of the Walla Walla Valley and the Columbia River. His major concern was the condition of the animals, all of which were beginning to show the effect of their long journeys. When they left Fort Colville on October 21, McDonald presented a keg of cognac "to cheer the hearts of the members of all parties" and threw in a generous supply of port for good measure. Stevens went into camp on the Spokane River, and three days later Donelson arrived after coming around the north end of Lake Pend Oreille, down the west side to the Little Spokane, and on to the camp. He was welcomed with a grand feast; the governor had a table set up under a canopy and had it loaded with roast beef, bread, coffee, a plentiful supply of McDonald's good cheer, and a beef head that had been wrapped in leaves and cooked in a hole "Texas style." McClellan called it a political-type barbecue with "the devil played generally." But Donelson could not help solve the animal problem, as he had lost twenty on the trail (five while crossing Clark Fork), and the rest were in poor condition. Both McClellen and Donelson argued that the condition of the pack trains vitiated any attempt to cross the Cascade Mountains that winter. In addition they noted that most of the barometers and other necessary equipment had been broken or had malfunctioned. After a long discussion everyone agreed that the animals were thin and leg-weary, and Stevens acquiesced to his subordinates' wishes.

He explained, "I was unwilling, after so much labor and fatigue ... to assign the gentlemen to duty, when they did not have confidence in their means, unless it was a case of imperative necessity." He believed, however, that the decision may have been unduly influenced by the several inches of snow that fell when they had moved from Fort Colville to the Spokane. He reluctantly ordered that the entire party would remain intact and would proceed to Fort Vancouver via the Walla Walla Valley and the Columbia.[45]

Although he suffered constant pain, Stevens rode on ahead, accompanied by one or two men. On a typical day it took three hours "to get my courage to the sticking point so that I could bear the pain growing out of travelling faster than a walk." The lack of snow on the Blue Mountains and the luxurious, well-watered soil of the Walla Walla country began to persuade him that he had been misled about the region's climate. William McBean of the Hudson's Bay Company fort at Wallula showed him potatoes weighing two pounds each as well as carrots and beets of extraordinary size. McBean said that emigrants were casting longing glances at the Walla Walla Valley but were afraid to settle because there was no "arrangement with the Indians." Because the weather in the valley was mild, Stevens decided that snow would not provide a problem in the Cascades, and reconsidered his decision not to attempt at least one of the passes. In the hope that he could persuade one of his lieutenants to volunteer for the assignment, he wrote to McClellan, who was still two days from Fort Walla Walla, "If you are disposed to try Nachess Pass I can get you 20 fast horses." But McClellan had made his decision and argued strenuously that it would serve no "earthly advantage" in running a line over the pass at that time of year. McClellan once again was convinced that the project had been abandoned, but the next day the governor speculated that Lander might agree to go and hinted that McClellan should give him instructions.

The issue became not so much a question of practicality but a contest of wills, and McClellan was not going to budge. He insisted that it would mean "heavy expense and some danger without any compensating object to be obtained," for they already knew all they needed to know about Naches Pass, and it had been agreed it would not be the railroad pass; if they did succeed, it would be "a matter of stupid luck not judgement." He told Lander to go if he wished, but warned that the odometer would not work in the rough terrain, that he had lost ani-

mals on the Naches, and that snow would only increase the difficulty. McClellan extended "best wishes in whatever you choose
to do." It was no surprise that Lander declined the assignment.
On November 8 Stevens, again ahead of the party, left for The
Dalles, where he renewed his acquaintance with Major Gabriel
Rains and other old comrades from his military years. He arrived at Fort Vancouver on November 20 and five days later he
was in Olympia. The last two days were spent in a drenching
rain that soon turned his buckskins wet and soggy; he wryly advised that the others coming to the west side of the mountains
should first remove their buckskin clothing or suffer the uncomfortable consequences.[46]

As Donelson, Lander, and McClellan followed down the Columbia in Stevens' wake, they became increasingly disillusioned
with their leader. McClellan had convinced himself that Stevens
viewed the survey primarily as a political tool. With the others
he concluded they had been asked to take unusual risks but that
most of the credit and glory would go to Stevens. McClellan
proved Totten a prophet when he vowed that he had learned
his lesson and would never again serve under civilians, particularly politicians. He was also annoyed, as Lander and Donelson
had been for some time, at Stevens' habit of appearing to give
his lieutenants broad responsibilities but then restricting their
freedom with numerous specific instructions. After receiving orders for disposing of animals at The Dalles, which local circumstances made impossible to carry out, McClellan stormed, "I
will not consent to serve any longer under Governor S unless he
promises in no way to interfere—merely to give me general orders and never say one word as to the means, manner, or time
of executing them." The criticism had a certain validity, but
another factor was the irritability resulting from an arduous expedition. Relatively minor matters assumed major importance,
and there was a tendency to lose sight of the accomplishments
of the survey.[47]

The main party arrived at Vancouver on November 18,
where most of the men were paid and released. George Gibbs
traveled up the coast to examine Shoalwater Bay and the sur-
rounding area before returning to Olympia, while Dr. Cooper
continued collecting specimens in the area of the lower Columbia. McClellan, assigned the survey of the west side of Snoqualmie Pass, complained of the prospect of a winter in
Olympia, "a flourishing city of ten or twelve houses." With his
ardor for the survey cooled, he protested, "As I never saw a

snowshoe in my life (except in a museum or a picture book), I
don't anticipate much pleasure during the jaunt, and am desirous of finishing it as soon as possible." He declared that he
would try his best to reach the summit but appeared dubious
that his best would be good enough. McClellan first appeared
in Olympia in mid-December protesting that his arrival was delayed because a horse had fallen on his foot. After looking at Snoqualmie Falls and peeking at the western approaches to the pass,
he returned to Olympia, and in March he made his escape from
the Pacific Coast.[48]

Governor Stevens finally had his crossing of the Cascade
Mountains when Abiel Tinkham arrived in Olympia at the end
of January. After the journey that took him east through what
he thought was Marias Pass, Tinkham had gone to Fort Benton
and then had completed the full circle by returning to Cantonment Stevens. There he exchanged his mules for fresh animals
and headed west on November 20. He rode to the head of the
Bitterroot Valley, crossed over the mountains to the south fork
of the Clearwater River (which he followed to the Snake), and
then continued overland to the Walla Walla Valley. Crossing
the Bitterroots, he had encountered heavy snow that accumulated to a depth of six feet, but Tinkham was undeterred and
simply sent his mules back to Cantonment Stevens while he and
his men made snowshoes and pushed ahead on foot. Stevens
had sent a message to Fort Walla Walla for Tinkham to cross
over to the Sound through Snoqualmie Pass, which seemed like
child's play after his experiences in the Bitterroots. Although
Stevens stressed the importance of Tinkham's crossing, it essentially confirmed McClellan's observations, for Tinkham did not
have instruments, and his report made extensive use of McClellan's measurements. He was able to measure snow depth of two
to four inches in the lower valley which increased to six feet at
the summit and decreased to eight inches fourteen miles west of
the pass.[49]

The final survey party to reach the Sound was Cuvier Grover's. After examining the upper Missouri, he left Fort Benton
on January 2, 1854, with dog sleds. Crossing the Rockies to Hell
Gate, he found snow only a foot deep but temperatures as low
as thirty-eight degrees below zero. Stevens, writing before his
warm fire, calmly observed, "This intensely cold weather was
not, however, disagreeable for traveling on foot, [if one took] the
precaution to rub the nose and ears frequently." Grover followed Donelson's route to Fort Walla Walla, finding less than a

foot of snow in the mountains and in many places an insufficient pack for the dog sleds. Grover's arrival closed the survey for the winter, although Doty and Mullan continued operations in the Bitterroot Mountains and at Fort Benton. For Stevens the survey did not end until he published his final report in 1859, and in it he drew on his extensive travels through eastern Washington during his treaty making and in the Indian war. But for Jefferson Davis and the War Department the survey was officially closed as of the spring of 1854.[50]

Consequences

A leading historian of western explorations has contended that Jefferson Davis made only two mistakes in his selection of personnel for the railroad surveys and one of them was Isaac Stevens, who "as the new governor of the Washington Territory, was almost certain to overstate the case for a Northern route." McClellan voiced the same suspicions when he muttered during the march that the survey had become more political than topographical. Although the reports of 1853 and 1859 do in part overstate the advantage of the northern route, they contain little, if any, more special pleading than the reports of the other surveys. Each leader presented the case for his survey and the natural tendency was to put the best light possible on one's work. If Stevens demonstrated an excess of zeal, it was not in inflating his route's desirability, but rather in his exceeding somewhat the scope of his instructions by attempting to produce a report on an entire region.[51]

In his report to Jefferson Davis, Stevens emphasized that the northern survey offered several alternatives and he urged further examinations to find the best. However, he sketched the line he thought superior based on the reconnaissance to that point.

The railroad route from St. Paul keeps up the left bank of the Mississippi, crosses at Little Falls, continues along the dividing ridge between the Mississippi, Red River, and the Minnesota, until entering upon the prairie at Bois des Sioux, pursues its same general direction through this prairie, passes thence on the summit grounds between the James and Shayenne rivers, and finally, without losing its elevation, enters and passes the great plateau of the Missouri by a coulee connecting the two valleys of the Mouse [Souris] and Missouri rivers, and for a time piercing the barrier which separates them.

This route avoided the Black Hills and Badlands and did not require a crossing of the Missouri; the rise in elevation was gradual, and the only problem was a lack of wood in some areas. For the Rockies, Stevens recommended any of the passes leading into the valley of Clark Fork but chose the Hell's Gate Passes of the Northern and Southern Little Blackfoot as most desirable because they would not require any tunnels. For the Bitterroots he suggested either the Coeur d'Alene route through Stevens (Lookout) Pass, which would require a six-to-eight-mile tunnel, or a line following Clark Fork, which would be seventy miles longer but would require no tunnel. He estimated the cost as equal for either alternative. The Cascade Mountains could be penetrated via the Columbia River or Snoqualmie Pass. He argued that debris from ledges could be used to build up the embankment along the Columbia and that only one tunnel was required where the mountains came down to the river. On Snoqualmie Pass the grade was eighty feet per mile for a short distance and could be overcome either by a tunnel or, at least temporarily, by using additional engines. He estimated the tunnel's cost at $5 million. Even with this expense, he believed Snoqualmie preferable as it resulted in the saving of between sixty-four and eighty-seven miles. By adding 25 percent to eastern costs for areas west of the Red River and forty percent west of the Rockies he arrived at an estimate of $105,076,000 to build the railroad line.[52]

Stevens made it a point to counter fears that winter weather would be a severe handicap to the northern route. He used observations taken at The Dalles, Fort Vancouver, Fort Benton, and on Puget Sound in the winters of 1851–52 and 1853–54 to indicate that temperatures were milder at any of these places than at Fort Snelling, Fort Laramie, Milwaukee, Buffalo, or Boston. He argued that Puget Sound's climate was comparable to San Francisco's and that temperatures on Snoqualmie Pass were equivalent to those on the railroad line running between Montreal and Portland, Maine. He dismissed Indian legends describing heavy snows and, with a pun that was probably unintentional, characterized the Indians as "lying" in their lodges all winter. He used the information gathered by Doty, Mullan, Tinkham, and Grover to show that snow depth could be much less than opponents of the line estimated. He argued further that much of the precipitation fell along the coast as rain before it reached the mountains and turned to snow. All but the last rather immaterial point were valid arguments.[53]

Stevens was not content only to counter objections to the route; he took the offensive in presenting advantages that were peculiar to the northern latitudes. He picked up a prominent

theme of nineteenth-century expansionists when he spoke of the
Pacific Northwest as the gateway to trade with Asia. Stevens
pointed to Puget Sound, standing "midway between the great
centres of Asiatic and European population," and he enthused,
"Facing our Pacific possessions and separated from them by the
smooth Pacific, is a vast region covering an area of over twelve
millions of square miles, and having a population of over six
hundred millions." Echoing Thomas Jefferson, Thomas Hart
Benton, and many others, the governor averred that the Asia
trade "has been the greatest commercial prize in ancient and
modern times" with Persia, Carthage, Rome, Venice, Amster-
dam, and London all dominating the world at one time by con-
trolling that trade. He pointed out that Shanghai, the gateway
to one-third of China, was only five thousand miles, via the
great circle route, from Puget Sound, and that Japan was on
the same line of latitude. To Stevens the only logical connection
from Europe and North America to East Asia lay on the northern route across the Atlantic, the Great Lakes, and Puget
Sound. In addition, coal deposits and numerous deep, safe harbors made the Sound ideal as an all-season port.[54]

Stevens' arguments had little impact on Jefferson Davis, who
seized upon the snow factor and cost estimate as two decisive
weaknesses in the northern route. He thought the estimates were
too low and suggested that an increase of 100 percent over eastern prices for the area west of the Rockies would be more accurate—bringing the total cost to $140 million. But either man's
estimate could be only a wild guess. Davis indicated as much
when he freely juggled figures for all the routes. For example,
he decided that Captain Amiel Whipple overestimated the cost
of the 35th parallel route by $75 million, a sum greater than
the total expenditures of the federal government in any given
year during the 1850s. The surveys could give indications of topography or of particular problems, but the final cost could be
determined only by actual construction. Davis ignored Stevens'
weather data when he spoke of the "severely cold climate
throughout the whole route, except the portion west of the Cascade Mountains." He also disregarded Tinkham's snow measurements on Snoqualmie Pass and relied entirely on McClellan's
guess that there would be twenty feet at the summit. Like costs,
the snow question was moot. Time proved that Snoqualmie Pass
did have a snow pack greater than six feet (but less than twenty
feet) during most winters, but time also proved that the snows
were not a serious deterrent, just as they did not prevent trans-

continental lines through the Rockies or Bitterroots. Davis and
McClellan assumed that snow depth was a key determining factor in deciding if a pass was feasible, but Stevens argued that
evidence from European and United States railroads indicated
that snow and cold were not major considerations. Stevens was
not alone in this belief. Lieutenant E. G. Beckwith, who did
much of the work on the 38th parallel route, argued that snows
would present no particular problem and warned of the danger
in "overestimating the obstructions arising from snow in mountain passes, where its fall over the general surface of the country
is not sufficiently great to offer a general obstruction to the operation of railroads."[55]

Davis also found fault with descriptions of the soil (which he
labeled generally sterile) and noted that "the proximity to the
dominions of a powerful foreign sovereignty" was a negative factor. Additionally, he spoke of the lack of timber on certain portions of the route—the only point of agreement with Stevens.
The Secretary of War gave most of his praise to McClellan and
conceded only that Stevens' efforts might be of some future use
as he had covered a wide area and had collected "a great
amount of topographical and general information." It was clear
that the Secretary of War was prejudiced against any northern
route and that he used only the negative portions of Stevens' report.

When all the information was in, Congress was more divided
on the railroad question than it had been in 1853. The Kansas-
Nebraska Act had widened the sectional split, preventing the
separation of the transcontinental route from the several serious
economic and political issues that afflicted the nation. When
transcontinental railroads finally came to the Northwest, long
after Stevens' death, new surveys were made, and although at
times the lines followed the route recommended by Stevens, at
other points they deviated from it considerably. Even Stevens
Pass in the Cascade Mountains, through which the Great Northern built its main track, does not commemorate the leader of
the great railroad survey; rather it acknowledges John F. Stevens, the chief engineer for the railroad company.[56]

It remains to ask if the railroad survey made any contribution
to scientific knowledge of the northern Rockies and the Pacific
Northwest. The work of the survey quite naturally took place
within the context of the American scientific community, which
in 1853 stood at the end of one era symbolized by men like
Hassler and Bache and on the threshold of another marked by

the appearance of Darwin's *Origin of Species* in 1859. Before the 1860s, American scientists concerned themselves mostly with collecting and cataloguing the remarkable numbers of new species in the New World. The railroad surveys continued the work begun by early explorers, and it was as collectors of such information that they contributed their greatest service.[57]

The drawings of John Mix Stanley and Gustavus Sohon, which were reproduced in Stevens' final report, made a significant contribution to art as well as providing an accurate pictorial record of the West. Although they were reporters first and artists second, they ably fulfilled both objectives. Stanley proved to be a master at capturing perspective and distance, and at depicting geological phenomena. His drawings illustrate terrain, mountain passes, and important geographic or geologic features such as the Marias River, the Falls of the Spokane and Flathead Lake. Dramatic incidents experienced by the party along the route, as well as numerous illustrations of Indians, were recorded by his pen. One of his most striking drawings, "Herd of Bison, Near Lake Jessie," captured the vast spaciousness of the plains filled with enormous herds spreading to the horizon. Using a spyglass, he could see the horizon fifteen miles in the distance but still not see the entire herd. According to one art historian it is the best existing illustration of a large pre-railroad buffalo herd. Stevens, recalling his efforts as a struggling artist at West Point, admired Stanley's talent, which he declared "above any commendation we can bestow." He was equally grateful to the artist for his services as explorer and emissary to the Indians. Stanley returned to Washington D.C. carrying the preliminary reports of the survey and later worked to prepare his sketches and those of other artists for publication in the final reports. He also prepared a panorama of forty-two paintings, based on his drawings, which went on display in September 1854 in the capital. The exhibit subsequently drew large crowds in Baltimore, Boston, and other eastern cities. The panorama, as well as most of Stanley's other paintings, either burned in the 1865 Smithsonian fire or have disappeared.[58]

Except for two or three drawings credited to Dr. Cooper, the other sketches for the survey were executed by an army private, Gustavus Sohon. He was a lucky find, for Stevens had fired the man originally picked as Stanley's assistant. Sohon was assigned by the army to accompany Rufus Saxton on his journey to the Bitterroot Valley, and when his artistic ability was discovered, Stevens arranged for him to remain in the valley with Mullan

144

Cantonment Stevens,
looking westward,
Gustavus Sohon

during the winter. He later accompanied the governor to the
Blackfoot Council, where he was listed as an interpreter. (Subsequently he served in the Northwest until 1862, often under
Mullan's command.) Stevens characterized Sohon as intelligent
and faithful with "great taste as an artist, as well as a good student of Indian languages." A number of his drawings of present
eastern Washington, Idaho, and the Rockies appeared in the

J. Bien N. Y lith.

railroad report, and Mullan later included Sohon's work in his report on the Mullan Road. His drawings, like Stanley's, provided an accurate portrait of the land and its people, and included sketches of Cantonment Stevens, the Big Blackfoot Valley, and numerous other scenes.[59]

Spencer Baird of the Smithsonian supervised the natural history data of all the railroad surveys, with his office acting as a central clearing house for the collections. Before the survey started, Baird issued specific instructions for handling various specimens, suggesting that small quadrupeds could be preserved whole in alcohol, while animals the size of a prairie dog required skinning with the skull and skin preserved. For a large beast the skin needed only to be rolled in arsenic and salted. He advised the skinning of large snakes, and asked that all the lizards, and small frogs "that can be caught should be secured and preserved," and required that birds should be captured with their nest and eggs if possible. Baird provided drying papers for plant specimens and sent the survey off burdened with copper kettles, India rubber bags, specimen kits, alcohol, and arsenic. Suckley, Gibbs, and Cooper were all dedicated collectors, and in both parties the men eagerly brought in specimens of all kinds for the collections.[60]

Under Baird's direction the Smithsonian staff prepared a report based on the findings of all the expeditions, which consisted primarily of a listing of specimens with a description of the specie. For the northern survey a more extensive account was included as book two of Stevens' final report. Some expedition members resisted Stevens' efforts to include their work in the final volumes for fear that the Smithsonian would subsume materials without giving proper credit to the field men. Others were upset or peeved at the governor, and George Gibbs turned over his specimens reluctantly, vowing to provide additional information only if Stevens behaved properly. The crux of the dispute, however, was mutual suspicion between the survey scientists and those at the Smithsonian. In the field report Stevens heaped ample praise on Suckley, Cooper, and Gibbs for unstinting efforts and thanked the Smithsonian for their magnanimous assistance. A greater problem arose from the geology report that John Evans was to prepare based on his observations supplemented with information gathered by other members of the survey. Evans had taken a southerly route through the Badlands and Black Hills and had met Stevens at Fort Benton. Stevens thought it was agreed that Evans was jointly employed by the survey and the Interior Department, but Davis insisted Evans would have to rely on the Interior for compensation and refused to publish his report. Both Stevens and Evans expended a great deal of effort in an attempt to reverse the decision but failed, and the completed survey lacked a geology report. Stevens ably compensated by interspersing extensive comments on geology through his narrative.[61]

Before 1853 John Torrey of Princeton College and his younger protégé, Asa Gray, had engaged in the classification of botanical specimens gathered by western expeditions. Through their labor many western species had been classified earlier, and the railroad surveys only completed the work. Torrey and Gray did all the classifying for the several surveys, although for the northern route Dr. James G. Cooper contributed the section west of the Rocky Mountains. Gray, who would later become one of Darwin's leading defenders, did not stray from his catalogue lists, only occasionally adding a comment, usually to suggest that a specimen was related to a plant already classified. Cooper proved more adventurous, attempting in a preliminary way to differentiate between types of plant life found in various zones and regions. He made separate listings for specimens found east and west of the Cascade Mountains and estimated that his 400 identifiable species represented about one-third of the total for Washington Territory. Cooper's work also served as a practical guide for settlers, for he commented on the edibility of fruits and plants, the types of soil and climate favored by various species, the best time to plant and harvest, and suitability for grafting.[62]

The zoology report also represented a cooperative effort between the men of the survey and the scientists of the Smithsonian. Professor Baird prepared most of the report on birds, and his colleague John T. Leconte wrote the chapter on insects. Dr. Cooper contributed sections on mammals, land birds, reptiles, and crustacea; his nephew William Cooper wrote the chapter on mollusca; Suckley and Gibbs collaborated on mammals, and Suckley wrote chapters covering water birds, fishes, and additional mammals. The work of James Cooper, Gibbs, and Suckley provided not only a catalogue of animal life; they also compiled information on Indian and white customs, with anecdotes and personal observations to document their conclusions. In a section on the coyote, Gibbs and Suckley were diverted to a tangential account of the great smallpox epidemic of 1853, which so devastated the Indians north of the Columbia River that they fled in panic, leaving their dead unburied. The two scientists surmised that the coyotes ate the corpses, contracted the disease and suffered from infections caused by blowing dirt and sand, which worked into open sores. A consequence, they concluded, of the smallpox epidemic was decimation of the coyote population. Gibbs and Suckley also speculated on the origins of Indian dogs, tentatively endorsing the notion that they were a mixture of coyote and canine blood, although they puzzled whether such a hybrid would be able to perpetuate itself. Such lines of inquiry did not interest the eastern scientists.[63]

The western-oriented scientists also included bits of practical advice for interested readers. For example, in the section on the red lynx, Suckley noted that the Indians frequently ate the meat and had persuaded him to try it, but after tasting a broiled steak he had "no hesitation in pronouncing the creature not good." Suckley was also intrigued by the great number of skunks in western Washington and was surprised to learn that many settlers, accustomed to the animals living under their cabins, liked the distinctive odor. He concluded that it was comparable to a chemist who came to appreciate the odor of hydrogen sulphide. Suckley was told that picking up a skunk by the tail prevented it from emitting its scent. "This is an experiment," he confessed, "which I have not had the hardihood to make." One of the most notable contributions was Suckley's report on the Pacific Northwest salmon, in which he classified, discussed Indian methods of catching and preparation, and detailed the spawning habits of the various species.[64]

All of the zoological work was marked by zealous effort and extensive collections. Although the scientists could fall into error, they displayed a scientific spirit of testing and inquiry. Legends such as the supposed existence of a mountain creature that resembled a cougar, but which was said to be much larger and more ferocious, were checked and quickly discarded. Perhaps most important, they attempted to apply their research to ends that would be of practical value to the settlers. This goal went beyond the guidelines of the Smithsonian, but reflected the western experiences of the scientific members of the northern survey.[65]

Perhaps the most important contribution was the review by Stevens of the geography of the route and the possibilities for adequate transportation and settlement in various regions covered by the survey. Although Lewis and Clark had written of good soil in some areas, they had also remarked on general aridity, and public opinion reflected the latter assumption. To most Americans the northern plains and the Pacific Northwest, except for the area west of the Cascade Mountains, were part of the Great American Desert. Stevens divided the survey route into five sections with subregions within each: from the Mississippi River to the great bend of the Missouri; from the great bend to Fort Benton; the mountain and intermountain region;

the great Columbia Plain; and the land west of the Cascades. The first and last regions were already well known, and the fact of existing settlement required little additional comment on the geography. Stevens did attempt to rescue the remaining three regions from their contemporary disfavor. He admitted that Davis, McClellan, Humphreys, and many others disputed his estimates of the extent of arable land, and he conceded that "nothing but the detailed surveys of the land office can furnish minute detail [and thus determine the exact available acreage]," but, he argued, "the eye of the experienced observer . . . can discern whether it is adapted to agriculture or to grazing, or to a union of the two."[66]

Looking first at the land west of the great bend of the Missouri, Stevens dismissed the notion that the Badlands and Black Hills formed an impassable obstacle; he reported they were inconsequential and easily avoided. Numerous areas in the region once thought sterile were now, he claimed, "pronounced arable by geologists who pass over them." Stevens recognized that many people still considered grasslands to be infertile, and he wrote, "To guard against misconception . . . it must not be inferred, when I speak of a country being covered with excellent grass, that it is not an arable country, for I suppose it will be admitted that all arable countries ought to furnish grass of some kind." Turning to the Rockies and Bitterroots he took pains to comment on the luxurious grasses in the valleys between the two major ranges, and concluded that all the valleys would provide excellent grazing and that some could be cultivated. In addition he found this country "not being as broken as one would have anticipated," with gently sloping hills in many places. The governor emphasized the "unbelievable" number of buffalo and horses that grazed in these valleys and on the plains of present eastern Montana. The mountain region and the land from Fort Union to the Rockies was in his opinion "extraordinarily fine grazing country." When purging the land along the northern route of its bad reputation, Stevens did not allow his enthusiasm to carry him to the opposite extreme. He did not label all the land as fertile and salubrious. Although lack of information and the rapidity of the survey led him into some errors, he tried to make the most objective assessment possible. The narrative is dotted with negative comments, as in Stevens' summary of Mullan's account of the route from the Bitterroot Valley to Fort Hall. He wrote, "The soil generally is fertile and productive and well adapted to grazing, except for that portion from the Snake

River divide to Fort Hall, whose whole characteristic might be described in one word—sterility."[67]

Stevens directed much of his attention to the Great Columbia Plain stretching from the Bitterroots to the Cascades. He divided this area into five subregions and noted the characteristics of each. The most favorable area was the Walla Walla Valley, whose many streams and fine soil he carefully detailed "in order to show that this region is not the barren desert it has been represented to be" but "a remarkably fine grazing and wheat country." He found the western portion of the plain near the Columbia less promising for agriculture, but good grazing land for sheep, and he stated that the plain in areas west of the Bitterroots was suitable for wheat growing without the use of irrigation. Because he took a view that contrasted so greatly with prevailing opinion, Stevens drew upon Lewis and Clark's assessment of the Columbia Plain and said, "I will refer the reader to the narrative of Lewis and Clark. . . . I have sometimes thought . . . that it was a work of supererogation to do anything more than simply quote their narrative." Stevens also pointed out that many early travelers who came away from the Great Columbia Plain unimpressed had seen it in the heat of summer from the vantage point of the Columbia River and the coulees that led through the least promising areas. Stevens did not change the opinions of Jefferson Davis or George McClellan, but he did convince numerous prospective settlers, some of whom were already aware of the potential richness of at least the Walla Walla area. Ironically Stevens' efforts to promote settlement and bring a railroad helped build the pressure that resulted in an Indian war and delayed both of the goals he so greatly desired.[68]

The Pacific railroad surveys closed the old era and anticipated the dawning of a new age in American science. The surveys amassed an immense amount of data, as the scientists were still more concerned with collection than analysis. The northern survey departed from this pattern in that the three major scientists looked for explanations and practical applications for the phenomena they observed and collected. Isaac Stevens, as much as anyone connected with the surveys, looked at his assignment as an endeavor bringing together all possible facts about a region into one grand treatise. He believed that his survey would allow federal and territorial authorities to plan the orderly growth of the territory by drawing upon the information provided to locate proper routes for roads, railroads, and water transportation, to formulate Indian treaties and land policy, to ascertain settlement patterns, and to plan proper use of the soil. In some of these endeavors Stevens failed, and in other areas his actions complicated events, but the report of the northern railroad survey remains as the record of an extraordinary exploration, scientific effort, and regional evaluation.

Stevens was satisfied that the survey was a success, although he admitted that the expedition met "with the usual embarrassments and difficulties." Given the limitations of time and money, the final report was more extensive, detailed, and accurate than any previous report on the Northwest. The personal differences Stevens experienced with Lander, Donelson, Suckley, and McClellan, which loomed so large at the time, now appear relatively inconsequential, and the survey proceeded smoothly for an operation of such scope. The survey proved the expanse of Stevens' vision, and rather than being a liability, his dual appointment as governor and head of the survey was an asset for both duties.

Stevens also demonstrated his energy and tenacity in pushing projects to conclusion when confronted by enormous problems and personal hardships. But he also indicated a certain perversity, an inability to abandon an idea or to postpone a project to a more favorable moment. He did not have the gift of patience, and this characteristic proved both a strength and weakness during the survey and in his later career. In his relationships with other individuals, Stevens at times failed to communicate his zeal and enthusiasm, and he appeared at such times as harsh and unreasonable. He commanded best when surrounded by subordinates who shared his vision and his goals—men like Tinkham and Mullan who possessed energy and courage and who were willing to place these attributes at Stevens' disposal. But individuals like Lander and McClellan, whose egos matched Stevens' and who easily became restive under the command of another, were destined to find life with Stevens filled with misunderstandings and clashes of will. The governor may have dimly perceived it, but he never fully understood why he could not maintain a good relationship with some individuals. He explained it as a weakness in the other person's personality or moral fiber. Stevens was proving to be better suited to an army position, where his talents could be utilized within a clearly defined chain of command. In embarking upon a political career, he was treading on slippery ground.

Railroad Reports Excerpts

EXPLORATIONS AND SURVEYS FOR A RAILROAD ROUTE
FROM THE MISSISSIPPI RIVER TO THE PACIFIC OCEAN.
WAR DEPARTMENT.

REPORT

of

EXPLORATIONS FOR A ROUTE
FOR THE PACIFIC RAILROAD,

NEAR THE

FORTY-SEVENTH AND FORTY-NINTH PARALLELS
OF NORTH LATITUDE,

FROM

ST. PAUL TO PUGET SOUND.

BY

I. I. STEVENS,
GOVERNOR OF WASHINGTON TERRITORY.

NORTHERN PACIFIC RAILROAD EXPEDITION

The special object of the exploration is the determination of a railroad route from the headwaters of the Mississippi river to Puget Sound. In consequence of the meagreness of the information in reference to the country to be gone over, particularly in the Rocky and Cascade mountains, a general topographical survey must be had of these mountains between the 46th and 49th parallels, and most of the intervening country, in order to determine the general course of the railroad and furnish data to guide civil engineers in determining the route . . . [*Introductory paragraph of Stevens printed instructions to all expedition members*]

GENERAL ORGANIZATION OF THE EXPEDITION.

1. The expedition is in charge of Isaac I. Stevens, governor of the Territory of Washington.
2. There will be two main parties in prosecuting the work. One party, under the immediate direction of Governor Stevens, will proceed from the Mississippi river, and surveying rapidly the intermediate country, will reach as early as practicable the Rocky mountains, and examine all the passes to ascertain the most practicable one. The second party, under the command of Brevet Captain George B. McClellan, will organize at Puget Sound, or on the Columbia, and operate for a similar purpose in the Cascade range of mountains. The parties will operate in the mountains until they are thoroughly explored, or till driven away by the snow, when they will be applied, with probably a somewhat reduced organization, to the survey of the intermediate region . . .
3. All officers detailed on the survey are on topographical duty, and will in the field receive one dollar per day.
4. Lieutenant Rufus Saxton, jr., is the acting assistant quartermaster and commissary of the expedition. His most important duty as such is, as early as practicable to cross the [Panama] isthmus [to Ft. Vancouver], and establish a depot of provisions at the Flathead village of St. Mary's, just west of the Rocky mountains, and then crossing the mountains by the Blackfoot trail, meet the eastern party at Fort Benton, at the sources of the Missouri river . . .
7. Each officer and scientific man of the expedition will keep a daily journal, noting everything worthy of observation of a general character. These journals will be deemed a part of the results of the expedition, will be turned over as a part of its archives, and will be made use of in preparing the report. This is not intended to preclude copies being taken and published by the writer, after the publication of the report and proceedings of the expedition . . .

CAMP REGULATIONS

1. There is no such thing as an escort to this expedition. Each man is escorted by every other man. The chiefs of the scientific corps will equally with the officers of the army act as officers of the guard . . . The quartermaster employees will stand guard equally with the privates, and sappers and miners, and dragoons. It is confidently believed, that every member of the expedition will cheerfully do his duty in promoting all the objects of the expedition, sharing its toils of every description.
2. Each man of the expedition will habitually go armed. The chief of each party and detachment will rigidly inspect arms each morning and evening. Except in extraordinary cases, there shall be no march on Sunday. On that day there will be a thorough inspection of persons and things. Clothes should be washed and mended, and, if water can be found, each man will be required to bathe his whole person. This course is taken to secure health.

3. [In] The Indian country . . . There is no danger to be apprehended, except from the want of vigilance of guards, and the carelessness of single men. The chief of a party or detachment will inspect the guard from time to time in the night, and report every case of inattention to duty.

4. It will be the habitual rule of each member of the scientific corps to take charge of his own horse, and to take from and place in the wagon his own personal baggage. As private servants are not allowed, the necessity of this rule will be apparent . . .

5. There will be no firing of any description, either in camp or on the march, except by the hunters and guides, and certain members of the scientific corps, without permission of the chief of the expedition, or, in case of detachments, of the officer in charge of the detachment.

[Order No. 8.]

CAMP NEAR LIGHTNING LAKE,
July 19, 1853.

The most rigid economy in the consumption of provisions being necessary, the caterer of each mess will carefully note, in a book kept for the purpose, the daily amount consumed of the various articles constituting the ration, which book shall be daily inspected by the chief of each party . . .

[Order No. 9.]

NORTHERN PACIFIC RAILROAD EXPLORATION AND SURVEY,
9 degrees N. W. Fort Union Camp, August 16, 1853.

The most careful attention to animals is enjoined upon all persons engaged in the expedition, and will be rigidly enforced. The animals must not go beyond a walk, except in case of necessity; and each mounted man must walk some four or five miles each day to rest his animal, unless it be impracticable, in consequence of his duties. At halts, men must dismount. This direction will be enforced, as well in regard to private as to public animals.

I. I. STEVENS,
Governor of Washington Territory,
in Command of Expedition.

[Order No. 12.]

NORTHERN PACIFIC RAILROAD SURVEY,
Camp Atchison, Mouth of Milk River, August 20, 1853.

On the march the train will keep as much together as possible; the speed of the wagons will be regulated by Governor Stevens's ambulance or wagon, or by the instrument wagon. The acting quartermaster will regulate the pace of the leading team in such a manner that all other teams can keep up without forcing the mules. No person except guides, or those having permission, will precede the train by more than one-fourth of a mile, or go farther from it than that distance, unless in case of necessity, or for the performance of some duty.

ISAAC I. STEVENS,
Governor of Washington Territory,
in Charge of Expedition.

TAMIAS TOWNSENDII.
Townsend's Striped Squirrel.

The ground squirrel, or "chipmunk," inhabiting the neighborhood of the coast in Washington Territory, resembles closely in its habits that common on the Atlantic border. It differs, however, considerably in colors, and has not the shrill cry of the eastern species. About the first of April it emerges from its winter nest and soon after great numbers are seen where none appeared before. In summer they will often sit on some prominent stump or rock, and make a shrill barking noise for hours together, answering each other from distant parts of the woods. They become very mischievous in the garden, being especially fond of peas either green or ripe, for which they will come from their burrows several rods distant, as I have observed from the scattered pea-vines growing along the path where they have dropped the seed from their overloaded cheek-pouches. In November they retire to their burrows to sleep through the long rainy season . . . Their principal food on the eastern slopes of the Cascade mountains was the pine nut, and during September I observed them very busy extracting these from the still hanging cones, ascending the trees to a considerable height . . . [Dr. James G. Cooper]

HALIAETUS LEUCOCEPHALUS, Savigny.
The Bald Eagle; the White-headed Eagle.

The white-headed eagle is one of the most abundant of the falcon tribe in Washington Territory, particularly along the Columbia river, and other smaller streams, as well as the salt water. I was astonished at their numbers on the day of my arrival in the Territory in June, 1853. As the steamer ascended the Columbia river, a light rain falling constantly, I could see three or four at any time, sitting on the gigantic spruces that lined the banks, occasionally sailing off, circling around over- head, uttering their shrill scream, as if to dispute our right to navigate the great river . . . [Dr. James G. Cooper]

Sub-Family GARRULINAE.—The Jays.
PICA HUDSONICA, Bonap.
Magpie.

This magpie is abundant throughout the central region of Oregon and Washington Territories . . .

This bird is mischievous and gluttonous, but not so tame or so fond of the society of man as the European species. They are so much disliked by the frontier traders and mountain men of interior Oregon on account of their vile propensity to alight on the sore backs of broken-down and chafed horses and mules, most unceremoniously picking and feeding upon the raw, sore flesh, notwithstanding the moans, kicks, and rolling of the poor tortured animals. In this manner many disabled beasts have been most irretrievably injured, and probably a vast number even killed. It is said that the mountain men and trappers of former times so hated this bird, on account of its evil propensity for horse flesh, that when one of them possessed but two bullets he was sure to fire *one* at a magpie if he had an opportunity . . .

As with other birds of the genus, carrion affords its principal food. The dead cattle, so numerous along the great Oregon emigrant trail some years ago, afforded them an abundant supply of food during half the year . . .

One of the chattering cries of our magpie resembles much a peculiar call uttered by a Steller's jay . . .

When in the Rocky mountains I frequently noticed these birds assembling on the trees around us, just before we were to leave our camp. Instinct, or, perhaps, experience, had taught them that on our departure they would have "full swing" at the rinds of bacon and other culinary refuse of the deserted camp . . . [*Dr. George Suckley*]

CYANURA STELLERI, Swainson.
Steller's Jay.

Steller's jay is very common in all the forests of the Territory on both sides of the Cascade mountains . . . It seems to depend upon the forests chiefly for its food, but in winter visits the vicinity of houses, stealing potatoes and almost anything eatable. During these forages on the garden, made during the early morning, they are very silent and watchful, evidently conscious of the criminality of their actions, and when discovered fly off to the concealment of the forest. They will visit Indian lodges while the owners are absent, and enter them if possible, one all the time keeping watch. In the forests they are not shy, but often rather boldly follow intruders, screaming and calling their fellows around [*Dr. James G. Cooper*] . . .

The nickname given to this bird by the Nisqually Indians is "Sky-ky," or *the chief* . . . This jay is remarkable for its varied cries and notes, having one for nearly every emotion or pursuit in which it may be engaged. I think it also has a fondness for mimicing the cries of other birds. I have frequently been most pleasantly excited in hopes of obtaining a rare bird, the cry of which I had never heard before, and which was then issuing from some clump of bushes or thicket; but was almost invariably disappointed by finding that the strange notes had issued from this jay. It mimics the principal cry of the *Mimus felivox* perfectly. The males and females of this species are alike in appearance . . . [*Dr. George Suckley*]

BASCANION VETUSTUS, Baird & Girard.
The Green Racer.

Three specimens of this handsome snake were caught in or near the Yakima valley, in August, 1853. Like its relative, the black snake of the Atlantic States, it is perfectly harmless, and does not even bite usually when handled. It runs with great rapidity [*Dr. James G. Cooper*]. . .

It has the same habit of climbing in bushes common to the black snake of the eastern States. Found sparingly at Puget Sound. [*Dr. George Suckley*]

ASTOR CANADENSIS, Kuhl.
Beaver

The beaver and the land otter, particularly the former, have multiplied rapidly since the fur trade has become of such little value. I am told that they are now in greater numbers than they have been at any time since the first flush of the trade. The natives no longer seek them, as they get clothing from the whites, and also because the skins bring such small returns, a dollar being the present price of a large beaver skin in the stores. The Hudson['s] Bay Company give much less for them in trade . . . [*George Gibbs*]

CANIS OCCIDENTALIS, var. GRISEO-ALBUS.
Gray Wolf.

These wolves are very abundant in the neighborhood of the sources of the streams flowing into the Columbia from the Cascade, and Blue mountains. In the winter, until March, they come down into the valleys, where they are very destructive to horses, hunting them singly or in packs. They destroy the largest horses by hamstringing them while running. This is their favorite way of hunting. They are about 3 feet high . . . [*Dr. George Suckley*]

[Extract from "Topography" of the Clark Fork River Valley— Thompson Prairie, MT, to Pend Oreille Lake, ID]

. . . The traveler through the valley frequently passes through tracts of timber where the tall trunks stand denuded of their limbs and foliage, scarred and blackened by destructive fires which are sometimes started by lightning, but as probably by negligence or the nefarious purposes of hostile Indians. It is one of the grandest sights by night to watch the progress of the fearful element through the close-grown trees; the hissing of the flames enveloping the green limbs; the crashing of falling logs, and the clouds of belching smoke that darken the star-lit sky; the lurid glare and fitful light, in which the outlines of the hills and woods are seen starting from obscurity into view, to sink again into thicker darkness: these, with all the minor concomitants of such a scene, make an impression on the mind which can never be effaced. Though these fires be so terrible in appearance, they are rarely of any great extent, as the mountain-spurs and jutting rocks, with the winding of the river, form impassable checks to the most furious fire; they are soon succeeded by a growth of young trees, and are of but slight importance, compared to the devastating effects of a fire on the prairies.

Among the few disagreeables of such a mountain trip is one, it should hoped of rare occurrence, which perhaps may not improperly be mentioned here. While the studious observer of nature is feasting his imagination with the varied scenery of the mountains, he suddenly stumbles on the scalped remains of some poor Indian warrior, left hastily on his last battle-ground by his vanquished tribe, his horse having shared his fate, lying near by; horribly mutilated by obscene birds and beasts, the loathsome objects are found, it may be, festering in the sun or stiffened in the frost—the most deplorable evidence of the unceasing hostilities which seem to be the most important purpose of the red man's life . . . [*John Lambert*]

[Lt. Rufus Saxon en route up the Columbia with supplies for the main Stevens party in the Bitterroot Valley]

Monday, July 25 [*1853*] . . . In consequence of the great heat we advanced but fifteen miles, and encamped in a pleasant spot on the banks of the Umatilla river.

Near our camp we were met by a delegation of Cayuse braves, sent by the chief of the Nez Perces, to ascertain our object in passing through their country. They had been told that we were coming to make war upon them, and take away their horses. We assured them that such was not our object . . . In the evening the old chief came and smoked the pipe of peace with us, promised to always be friendly, and said that he was glad our "hearts were good." The Nez Perces are a rich and powerful tribe, and own a great many horses. They cross the mountains yearly to hunt buffalo on the plains of the Missouri . . .

Tuesday, July 26 . . . encamped on the Columbia, within ten miles of Wallah-Wallah [River]. It has been the hottest day of the season; men and animals suffered severely. Twelve miles of our route was over burning sands, destitute of vegetation; the animals sunk deeply into it at every step . . .

There is a beautiful island in the river near our camp covered with luxuriant grass, on which a large number of horses belonging to the Nez Perces are now feeding. They are driven here to pasture and fatten for the annual trip across the mountains . . .

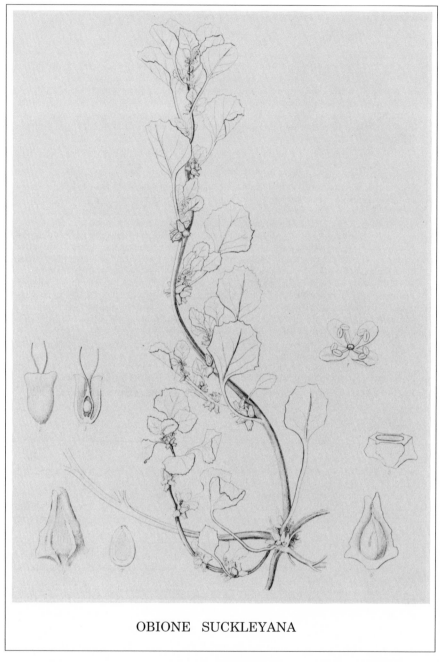

OBIONE   SUCKLEYANA

[Collected by Dr. George Suckley in Montana's Milk River Valley,
August 19, 1853]

7

THE GOVERNOR

Washington school children know that their state emerged from the Monticello Convention of November 25, 1852. At this hamlet at the mouth of the Cowlitz River, forty-four hardy settlers drafted a petition asking Congress for a new territory north of the Columbia River. Bowing to Montesquieu, whose philosophy was assumed still to prevail in the nation's capital, the petitioners argued that the people's needs could best be satisfied in a territory of moderate size. The settlers north of the Columbia protested that their peers in the Willamette Valley ignored their wishes and that "Northern Oregon has never received any benefit from the appropriations made by Congress for said Territory." The settlers objected to inadequate transportation and mail facilities, called for a university and public buildings, and complained, "Our whole territory is alive with Indians, who keep up a most provoking and unceasing broil about the lands which they say the 'Bostons' are holding without a proper and legitimate right and title to the same."[1]

To one unfamiliar with the patterns of American territorial expansion, the demands of fewer than four thousand citizens in a remote corner of the nation might appear audacious. There was insufficient settlement to support even one town deserving of the name. One settler lamented that Olympia boasted only one saloon and that it consisted of only a keg and three glasses. An army officer at Fort Steilacoom, even though accustomed to frontier life, observed that everything on the Sound existed in the crudest possible state. But the citizens north of the Columbia were merely following patterns started in the colonial period and firmly established with the initiation of the territorial system. When they complained of distance from seats of govern-

153

ment and control by a distant clique, the Puget Sound settlers were repeating formulas and—at times—the exact words of earlier petitioners in Tennessee, Maine, Illinois, Minnesota, and other areas previously carved from existing states or territories. John R. Jackson, Quincy Brooks, Charles Hathaway, and their fellow visionaries of Puget Sound saw territorial status as the first step toward statehood and looked for immediate benefits which would include a capitol, improved postal service, roads, navigational aids, increased protection from the Indians, land surveys, and new wealth brought by the men who provided these services. Separate political status seemed the easiest way to insure quick growth of new frontier areas.[2]

Although the demands of the Puget Sound settlers may seem logical in the context of American expansion, it is less logical that Oregon politicians would give their blessing because territories, like nations, often protested any diminution of their land mass. But Joseph Lane, Oregon's delegate in Congress, enthusiastically supported the division, and the territorial House voted 20–3 for the split. William Strong, reminiscing many years later, explained that Oregon's magnanimity was due to a bargain struck by Francis Chenoweth and Isaac N. Eby, the two representatives to the Oregon legislature from north of the Columbia, who cast the key votes in a dispute over the location of a penitentiary and asylum in return for support for the new territory. There may be some truth in Strong's recollection, but it does not fully explain the overwhelming support of the Oregon legislators, for surely Eby and Chenoweth angered many members with their votes. More important as an explanation was the Northwest's position in national and international political strategy. Oregon's citizens chafed under the restrictions of territorial government. Like most territories they desired statehood, but in Oregon the pressure was greater because they had enjoyed self-government for five years under the Oregon Provisional Government. It appeared unlikely that Congress would create a new state larger than any existing state, and a reduction of Oregon's boundaries would thus enhance immediate prospects for statehood. The Oregon politicians could also see that the creation of new territories would lead eventually to a bloc of Pacific coast states which could wield considerable influence in the councils of the national government. In addition, British claims created an unsettled political climate in northern Oregon. In sum, it was not charity but rather a desire to promote statehood ambitions that led Oregon to support the petitioners on the north side of the Columbia.[3]

On December 6, 1852, even before he received the petition of the Monticello Convention, Joe Lane requested the Committee of Public Lands to consider separation of the territory. On February 8 the measure came before the House, and Lane (now armed with the citizens' petition) argued the case. He rattled off the advantages of the proposed new territory, which included a "salubrious and healthy" climate and an agricultural capacity that he claimed could support a population of five million within a generation. In the Oregon delegate's opinion the harbors of Puget Sound assured the development of a great commercial center, and even in the near term "the revenues that will be collected at Puget Sound alone will in a very short period of time more than equal all the expense of the new territory." Lane neatly sidestepped a question on the size of the existing population and agreed to change the name from "Columbia" to "Washington," which Congressmen erroneously thought would eliminate confusion of the nation's capital with the new territory. The bill passed the House, and, with the support of Stephen A. Douglas, chairman of the Committee on Territories, the Senate added its assent. President Fillmore signed the Organic Act before his term expired.[4]

The measure had moved through the necessary steps with surprising smoothness. Aside from Lane's influence, which was considerably greater than that of the average territorial delegate, there were other important reasons for the relatively painless birth. Political leaders in Michigan, Wisconsin, and Minnesota could readily see the connection between new territories along the 49th parallel and the northern railroad route. Also, Lane and the Puget Sound settlers fortuitously picked a time when the Compromise of 1850 had muted sectional strife. Washington Territory's isolation was a primary reason for its failure to reopen the old wounds, and the Washington experience may have lulled Douglas into believing that the Kansas-Nebraska Act of 1854 would pass with as little difficulty.[5]

Amid numerous patronage questions, President Pierce and his advisers considered federal appointments for Washington Territory. As with other territorial positions, the key requirements were past service to the party in power, and support from one or more influential members of the administration. The first appointees to territorial office in Washington met these requirements and most also met a third criterion, service in the Mexican War. None were residents of the Northwest, although several indicated that they were bound for the new territory whether or not they received a federal appointment. Washington's first attorney general, John S. Clendenin, a native of Mississippi, had served under Jefferson Davis during the Mexican War and in 1852 had applied for the post of charge d'affaires to Peru. He later altered his application, and his close friend Davis, as well as Joe Lane, who knew him from Buena Vista, gave warm support to the Mississippi lawyer. Another member of the Mississippi bar, James Patton Anderson, became territorial marshal although he sought one of the judgeships.[6]

The three federal judges were Edward Lander, Victor Monroe, and Obediah B. McFadden. Lander, brother of the northern survey's Frederick Lander, received his law degree from Harvard, practiced law in Massachusetts, and became prosecuting attorney for several Indiana counties. He served with Lane in Mexico and returned to Indiana as a judge until a new state constitution reorganized him out of his job. Quieter, more reserved, and less volatile than his brother, Edward Lander deservedly possessed a reputation as a dignified and scholarly gentleman. Victor Monroe of Virginia was championed by his brother-in-law, E. Louis Lowe, Congressman from Maryland. The need to placate the upper South and particularly the Old Dominion state explained Monroe's appointment, an appointment soon to be regretted. McFadden initially received a post in Oregon, but a mixup led to cancellation of his commission, and he was sent instead to Washington.[7]

The only appointment Isaac Stevens influenced was that of territorial secretary. He recognized that patronage was dispensed by individuals more powerful than himself, but because the governor and secretary worked together closely, Stevens asked Charles H. Mason, the younger brother of his close friend James Mason, if he would like to fill that position. Mason, a lawyer in Providence, readily agreed, but the next news he received announced the appointment of Major Robert Farquharson of Texas as secretary. The Texan declined and Stevens wrote from St. Louis to James Mason to have the papers prepared for his brother as "I cannot doubt that place would be given to him." This time the Mason brothers relied on more than Stevens' word and sought the endorsement of Rhode Island's governor and that state's Congressional delegation. The governor recommended Charles Mason as fully qualified and said he "would be acceptable to our friends." This time the appointment was made.[8]

Although the list of appointments did not include anyone from Washington Territory or from the West, the territory's citizens were seemingly too surprised or awed by their new status to protest. The officials possessed considerable talent; each man administered his office with energy and ability, and some of the clashes that took place during Stevens' administration resulted from differences of opinion between intelligent, honest public servants who took their duties seriously. One possible exception to these generalizations was Victor Monroe, a man who possessed fine legal talent but who also possessed an excessive devotion to alcohol. Pressure from the other federal office holders, as well as Stevens, resulted in his removal in 1854. Later in the territorial period a sufficient number of incompetents more than balanced the talent of the first appointees, but whether through chance or good judgment by the Pierce administration, the new territory was launched by administrators of comparatively high quality.

Governor Stevens arrived in Olympia for the first time on the evening of November 25, 1853. The apocryphal story of his unnoticed arrival contained an element of truth, for although a formal reception was planned, the governor arrived unexpectedly in a drenching rain. Thoroughly surprised and somewhat taken aback by the rough garb and the bedraggled, diminutive appearance of the new governor, the citizens nevertheless quickly ran up the American flag, gathered at the Washington Hotel, and received Stevens "into the arms of a warm-hearted, patriotic people." The governor addressed his constituents in a masterful performance. He expressed pleasure that despite his belated arrival all citizens appeared to agree that the greater good of the territory was served by the railroad survey, and he promised, "I have come here not as an official for mere station, but as a citizen as well as your chief magistrate to do my part toward the development of the resources of this territory." Stevens urged his fellow citizens to labor with the conviction that "from your hands an imperial domain will descend to our children, and power ascede [sic] to the country, and all too in the cause of humanity and freedom." There could be no more succinct statement of Isaac Stevens' vision of his misson in the Pacific Northwest. Judge Victor Monroe welcomed the governor in a long, flowery speech, Marshal J. Patton Anderson and Judge Edward Lander added appropriate remarks, and Secretary

Charles Mason brought the festivities to a close with light-hearted comments. Most citizens left the meeting convinced they had the best set of officials on the coast and a "model" governor. The territory was launched, and it was confidently asserted, "The future is pregnant with noble achievement." Some saw "a new, gallant, dashing, sparkling . . . momentum to the march and swagger of 'progress' hereabouts."[9]

At least one aspect of their future "progress" began to bother some of Washington's citizens—the very nature of the territorial system itself. They suspected that the problems of Puget Sound under Oregon rule might not have resulted from the tyranny of the Willamette Valley cabal, but from the deficiencies of the territorial process. Some suggested that their system, although perhaps sufficient in the past, needed necessary and indispensable change. The editor of the *Columbian* wrote complaining of a serious absence of sovereignty in the western territories. This editor, like others in Washington Territory, believed it right and necessary for the federal government to pay the territory's expenses but he also believed that the citizens possessed the same rights of sovereignty as those in the states.[10]

The editor had valid reason for complaint. The Organic Act that created Washington Territory followed a pattern that had solidified many years earlier. Federal authorities reserved the right to treat with the Indians, retained the public domain, prohibited territorial debt, reviewed all territorial legislation, and appointed, paid, and removed territorial officials. Congress made appropriations for a territorial library and for public buildings and paid for contingent expenses, but for additional sums the territory had to petition a parsimonious Congress. The citizens could elect a delegate to Congress, but he did not have a vote. The governor was usually the main link between the territory and the federal government, and in many territories his power was substantially increased by his appointment as superintendent of Indian affairs. The problem of sovereignty that bothered the editor was never resolved in Washington Territory or elsewhere, but it remained a nagging issue particularly during the Indian war and martial law controversy that soon beset the territory. For the moment, however, most citizens were content in the assumption that they would achieve statehood in five or ten years.[11]

Immediately after his appointment as governor, Stevens began to build a working relationship with the leading citizens of the territory. Relying primarily upon Lane's advice, he compiled a

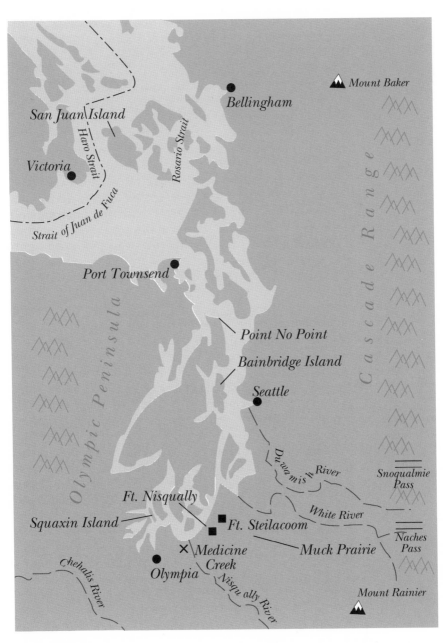

Puget Sound

list of some thirty men who might provide information or services or who exercised power and influence among their peers. The list included William Fraser Tolmie, a British citizen and chief factor of the Puget Sound Agricultural Company; settlers Michael Simmons, Arthur A. Denny, and David S. Maynard; collector of customs Isaac N. Eby; William Strong, a former Oregon judge; prominent Whigs E. D. Warbass and William Miller, and brothers A. Jackson and Benton Moses. The governor wrote to each of these men asking them to confer with Marshal Anderson, George McClellan, or any other official to convey their previous experiences and to suggest future needs and requirements for the territory. He ordered the federal appointees who would precede him to consult freely with the citizens, and he particularly urged Anderson, in the course of taking a census, to become personally acquainted with the people of each community, to ascertain the number of stores, mills, mines, and factories, and to obtain any other information that might prove useful to the government.[12]

While Anderson, aided by Benton Moses, took the census, and the territory waited for the governor to complete the railroad survey, the citizens began to struggle with one problem—the proposed wagon road from Steilacoom to Walla Walla via Naches Pass. Governor Stevens, local citizens, and federal officials agreed that immediate improvement of this Indian trail over the mountains was necessary to prepare for the large number of emigrants expected to detour north from planned destinations in California or Oregon to the newest territory on the Pacific slope. Congress appropriated twenty thousand dollars for this "military road," and the Secretary of War placed it under the direct control of Governor Stevens, who in turn asked McClellan to take charge and to spend up to fifteen thousand dollars on improvements during the summer months. He explained to McClellan that he would need to explore Naches Pass for the railroad survey and that the road work would complement this task; further, he could charge part of the survey costs to the road fund because that appropriation totaled half of the amount for the entire railroad survey. Before he left Washington D.C., Stevens issued instructions for the entire road to be put in sufficient shape to allow passage of wagons and for the remainder of the funds to be reserved for improvement the next year. Jefferson Davis suggested that perhaps McClellan could do the "hard part" and leave the rest for the emigrants to complete as they traveled along the road.[13]

The Puget Sound settlers learned of the road appropriation at
the end of April 1853, but were not confident that the funds
could have any effect that season. Believing that "thousands will
come to Puget Sound if they can get here," subscription papers
began to circulate for pledges of labor or supplies to construct
the road. But before they were completed, news arrived from
the governor that McClellan, "the best military roadbuilder in
the country," would begin work during the summer. The captain arrived at Fort Vancouver, but the settlers waited in vain
to hear his plans, and they finally began without him in the
hope that the government would reimburse them for their expenses. Under the general supervision of Edward Allen, parties
commenced work to open the trail on the west side of the
mountains.[14]

McClellan's party encountered the workers, but it was only
when the superintendent of the western party came to visit
McClellan at his camp in the Kittitas Valley that the captain
agreed to help. His attitude indicated that he knew neither of
the road nor that he was to play any part in its construction,
despite the fact that he had received detailed written and oral
instructions from Stevens regarding the road. McClellan crypti-
cally noted in his journal entry for September 12, "[I] determined to afford a little assistance to the road cutters for what
yet remains to be done on the western portion of the road—subject to the approval of the governor." He agreed to pay twenty
men $2.50 a day for up to three weeks' work and to provide all
provisions during the same period. This proved to be the extent
of McClellan's involvement in the road.[15]

After the McClellan agreement, it was reported the workers
"are going it like fire," and in early October thirty-five wagons
struggled over the road, bringing among others Judges Lander
and Monroe, Secretary Mason, and District Attorney Clendenin
to the Sound. It proved to be the first and last wagon train of
the season, and the optimistic predictions of thousands of new
settlers disappeared into the mists. But a rough trail had been
hacked out at a cost of five thousand dollars, leaving most of
the funds for future improvements. Some were not satisfied with
the season's work. Indians claimed the "Bostons'" road was
worse than their former trail, and at least one white agreed that
the path was a tangle of brush and downed trees at many
points. When McClellan left Olympia, Lieutenant Richard Arnold took charge of construction. He resumed work in May
1854 and continued the project through the summer but ex-

pressed doubt of the route's practicality because the west side had many steep and dangerous sections and the east side required forty-four crossings of the Naches River. The remaining fifteen thousand dollars melted away, and at the end of the year some portions still remained unimproved.[16]

Stevens suggested that the counties assume responsibility for completion of the road. Also, because he was concerned that long stretches of the route did not provide good grass, he asked the legislature to plant grass at intermediate points, including the appropriately named Bare Prairie, and La Tete Mountain. Neither the counties nor the legislature acted, and many ridiculed the governor's grass proposal (although in retrospect it does not appear humorous). Pioneers were unaccustomed to improving upon nature, but the suggestion was typical of the imaginative, practical proposals of which Stevens was capable. By the end of 1854 there was less enthusiasm for the Naches route. The railroad survey concluded that Snoqualmie Pass was superior and future efforts to improve east-west transportation shifted to the more northerly route. The first venture to improve transportation in the territory was not a great success, but the project had indicated the beneficial impact of federal funds on a struggling frontier area. It is not surprising that subsequent Congresses were bombarded with military road requests from the territorial delegate, the legislature, and private citizens.[17]

After the governor's warm welcome by the citizens of Olympia in November 1853 he plunged immediately into the various tasks of his new position. To Stevens the most important were completion of the railroad survey and rapid construction of a transcontinental line, disposition of the Indian question through the treaty-making process, and settlement of disputes relating to or resulting from the 1846 boundary agreement with Britain. Governor Stevens first turned his attention to the British "intruders." The treaty of 1846 had appeared to settle the long-standing dispute which had placed the two nations close to open conflict. In actuality it also led to subsequent disputes over the exact boundary in the vicinity of the San Juan Islands, and the rights of the Hudson's Bay Company, and its subsidiary the Puget Sound Agricultural Company, south of the 49th parallel. Throughout his career Stevens had predicted future hostilities with Great Britain and had often appeared to welcome the prospect. However, as governor, although careful to protect the rights of Americans, he adopted a conciliatory posture toward the Crown and the Hudson's Bay Company. Stevens never backed down from a fight, but a realistic assessment indicated that the Americans could not match British military strength in the Pacific. The governor could be pugnacious, but he was not a fool. The issue of the correct boundary arose soon after the signing of the 1846 treaty. The terminology in the treaty spoke of "the channel which separates the continent from Vancouver's Island," but two channels existed. Between 1846 and 1853 both parties recognized the discrepancy but dragged their feet in initiating new negotiations. In 1850 the Hudson's Bay Company established a fishing station on San Juan Island and added a sheep ranch in 1853, both clearly intended to strengthen the British claim to the islands north of Rosario Strait. When Secretary of State William L. Marcy issued instructions to Stevens in June 1853, he devoted virtually the whole document to questions likely to arise over the 1846 treaty. Marcy did not wish to press the boundary issue but observed that it was "important that there should be no mistake in determining with accuracy this line." As with the railroad question, the Secretary of State hoped a complicated political problem could be settled by the surveyors, and he ordered the Coast Survey to chart the proper channel. Thus, at least for the moment, Stevens' hands were tied on the boundary question.[18]

Of immediate concern to the Pierce administration were the claims of the Hudson's Bay Company in Washington Territory. The treaty left room for various interpretations of the rights retained by the Company. Marcy's position was that the Company had forfeited the right to trade with the Indians but had retained all lands acquired before 1846 with any improvements; these lands, however, could be appropriated by the United States if proper compensation were given. Marcy instructed Governor Stevens to ascertain the location and fair value of all property held by the Company or any other British subjects in the territory. In December 1853 Stevens relayed his government's position to Peter Skene Ogden and Dugald MacTavish at Fort Vancouver and William F. Tolmie at the Puget Sound Agricultural Company farm at Nisqually, and set July 1, 1854, as the date they must cease trading with the Indians. Ogden and MacTavish forwarded Stevens' letter to Montreal, but Tolmie "solemnly" protested, averring that the treaty protected the Company in "all the rights" possessed in 1846. Tolmie used the occasion to launch an attack upon American settlers who squatted on Puget Sound Agricultural Company lands, took fence poles, plowed up pasture lands, and shot horses and cattle—all of which caused "great and increasing loss." In March 1854 Company officials sustained Tolmie, noting the language of the treaty confirming "possessory rights," which they insisted included not only land and improvements, but also trade rights and free entrance to and egress from their various posts.[19]

The dispute was primarily a consequence of the treaty language and, more important, of the fact that different articles appeared to grant different rights. Article IV pertained only to the Puget Sound Agricultural Company and granted its rights to "farms, lands, and other property," but with the provision that the United States could obtain possession at any time "at a proper valuation, to be agreed upon by the parties." Article III, pertaining to the Hudson's Bay Company, directed that "the possessory rights . . . shall be respected." Stevens and Marcy unfairly included the Hudson's Bay Company under Article IV, and Company officials unjustly brought the Puget Sound Agricultural Company under the protection of Article III. A further complication arose from the language of Article II, which gave all British citizens, including the Company, the right to use the Columbia River and its portages "on the same footing as citizens of the United States."[20]

In June 1854 Stevens submitted a description and valuation of British property in the territory, but also took the opportunity to give Marcy his view on the impasse. He admitted that Article III appeared to grant a broad spectrum of rights to the Company but he was not willing to concede that the treaty provided the final word on the subject. Stevens developed a sophisticated argument which relied on the definition of sovereignty. He began by looking at earlier treaties in which he found that private companies surrendered their rights and sovereignty to the new nation, and he listed the Louisiana Purchase and the Adams-Onís Treaty of 1819 as specific examples. He argued that if the Company possessed the same rights as prior to the treaty, it then could make laws, exercise a trade monopoly, and enjoy other privileges that obviously could not be tolerated. The real issue, Stevens said, was whether the treaty conveyed sovereignty to the Hudson's Bay Company or to the United States. The claim of the Americans to the territory was superior to that of the Company, he believed, because "it has been the policy of the company to discourage agricultural emigrants, and to keep the greater portion of the territory a mere wilderness or a vast preserve for game." Cultivation was a prime requirement for possession of the soil, and, using that criterion, it was difficult to distinguish the rights of the Company from those of the Indians who were "fast disappearing before the steps of civilization on this continent." Stevens equated the Company with savagery and the American with the advancing forces of civilization. This was not an entirely new position; the Willamette Valley settlers had used the same argument in their boundary dispute, and Oregon's first delegate, Samuel Thurston, had made the comparison in the halls of Congress. But Stevens had a valid point when he noted that sovereignty could not be divided, that either the Company or the United States would have to yield.[21]

Stevens based his estimates of the value of Hudson's Bay Company (and its wholly owned affiliate, the Puget Sound Agricultural Company) property upon his personal observations or reports of territorial officials or members of the railroad survey. He valued the property on its 1853–54 condition, whereas the Company based its calculations on the value in 1846—before the treaty had necessitated withdrawal from most posts, virtually had ended the fur trade, and had diminished trade with the Indians. The governor found that the buildings at Fort Vancouver had been allowed to decay and that only one thousand acres, as compared with twice that amount earlier, remained under cultivation. He also found that the former hub of the fur trade had been reduced to a country store that imported only two shiploads of goods in 1853. Isaac N. Ebey fixed the value of Fort Vancouver and the adjacent lands at $32,000, but the governor raised the figure to $50,000. At the other posts, the governor found similar decay and diminished operations. He characterized a farm near Fort Walla Walla as a hovel and found the fort in indifferent repair. The Puget Sound Agricultural Company claim of 800 square miles of grazing land was valued by Stevens at $150,000, which, added to the total for the Hudson's Bay Company posts, came to $300,000, a figure that Stevens claimed resulted from "giving liberal estimates in all instances." He urged rapid settlement of the claims and hinted that he should be named as the chief negotiator because as governor he had "public position, local knowledge, and experience."[22]

Although Stevens arrived at a sum lower than Company estimates, it was an amount higher than many in the Northwest believed the foreign properties were worth. Throughout his tenure as governor and delegate, Stevens was less anglophobic than in his earlier career and less militant than prevailing public antipathy toward the British seemed to dictate as good political policy. Unlike Samuel Thurston and others, Stevens did not make a political reputation by twisting the lion's tail. In a typical speech on the subject to the Thurston County Democratic Convention, he promised only that the rights of the Company would be strictly construed. The governor found much to admire in the attitude of Company officials who had cooperated with the railroad survey, and he appreciated the friendly treatment the party received at Company posts, particularly the rousing reception of Angus McDonald. Invariably the Company's servants, from Sir George Simpson down through the factors and traders, were the type of men Stevens admired—straightforward, competent, honest individuals who took business seriously but knew how to relax when the occasion arose. The governor was also impressed by the Company's previous efforts on behalf of all white settlers in the Northwest, efforts that many of his contemporaries, particularly the politicians, chose to forget. Significantly, in his report to Marcy, the governor emphasized that the Company "has always sustained whites in every matter between a white man and Indians." Referring to the Whitman massacre, he noted that the Company never requested or received payment for its efforts and expenditures on behalf of the survivors. Stevens' praise of Hudson's Bay Company actions at the time of the Whitman affair contrasted sharply with the charge still heard in the 1850s that the Company had actually instigated the massacre.[23]

Governor Stevens remained firm in his determination to remove the British presence from south of the 49th parallel as quickly as possible, but he proceeded with a minimum of nationalistic rhetoric and took no precipitate actions. Although he insisted that the Company stop the Indian trade, he did not enforce this demand before the Indian war effectively settled the issue in 1855. In January 1854 Stevens journeyed north down the Sound to pay a courtesy call on Governor James Douglas at Victoria. The two men, who possessed similar temperaments, held amiable discussions and agreed to avoid any hasty or intemperate actions. When he arrived back in Washington D.C. in the spring of 1854, Stevens urged the administration to settle the "possessory rights" by paying the $300,000 he had recommended. Sir George Simpson, who earlier had set a value of $500,000 on the Company's properties, recognized the weakness of his position. Trade with the Indians was declining and would eventually cease when they came under treaties, and import duties made it difficult to compete with American merchants for the white trade. Simpson probably would have settled quickly at a figure near that proposed by Stevens had Congress acted. But despite the governor's effort and the administration's support, the appropriation failed, primarily because many Senators saw opposition to the measure as a way to establish their anti-British position on an issue that did not appear potentially explosive. Politicians in Washington Territory were equally happy to make political capital, and the legislature asked Stevens to explain his position on the British claims. He defended his figure as a maximum amount designed to be used in opening negotiations. The governor further argued that all Company rights would cease in 1863 with the expiration of its charter. In this Stevens confused the License of Exclusive Trade, which did expire, with the Company Charter, which did not—a mistake which might have been unintended, but was more likely an effort to placate the legislators with a piece of good news. Stevens did not entirely convince the citizens of his territory that he had acted rightly on the Company claims, and found himself for some time defending his attempts to deal fairly with both sides.[24]

As they argued the question of Hudson's Bay Company rights, the San Juan boundary issue began simmering. Marcy had wished to avoid a confrontation, and when Stevens had pressed for more detailed instructions on this point in May 1853, the Secretary of State testily dismissed the governor's emissary with the comment that the governor had all the instructions he needed. But local events forced the Pierce administration to take a position as each side took steps to bolster its claims to the islands. The Hudson's Bay Company dispatched Charles Griffin to San Juan Island and in January 1854 named him justice of the peace and magistrate. The latter action was an answer to Collector of the Customs Isaac N. Ebey, who claimed that Company sheep were subject to seizure when they entered the island without payment of the duty. Ebey named his own special agent in May, and for several days both the British and American representatives loudly claimed sovereignty, each threatening to arrest the other. But both men stopped short of physical action, and Ebey declared the authority of the United States had been established and successfully maintained. Ebey had always been strongly anti-Hudson's Bay Company, and he acted without consulting Stevens or other territorial officials. Stevens, who was in the nation's capital when he learned of the dispute over the islands, immediately went into consultation with Marcy. By this time the Secretary was armed with Coast Survey charts of Haro and Rosario straits, but he cautioned the governor to preserve the status quo until an international commission could be formed to run an official line. President Pierce urged the formation of such a commission in his State of the Union address, but Congress again failed to act.[25]

Upon his return to the territory, Stevens again conferred with James Douglas and suggested that they leave the boundary issue to their respective governments, a sentiment with which Douglas heartily agreed. But Stevens and Douglas could not mute local tensions, which reached a breaking point in March 1855 when Sheriff Ellis Barnes of Whatcom County landed at San Juan Island with a party of ten armed men and demanded that Griffin pay eighty dollars in taxes. When the Hudson's Bay Company agent refused, Barnes confiscated more than thirty Company sheep. An alarmed James Douglas protested to Stevens and asked if he sanctioned Barnes's actions. Douglas warned that the sheriff's activities "must ultimately lead to bloodshed." Stevens had not approved of Barnes's move but felt compelled to uphold a territorial official. He insisted that the United States government, the Oregon legislature, and the Washington legislature all understood the boundary to be Haro Strait. Douglas replied by demanding 2,990 pounds sterling for damages and added, sarcastically, that it appeared Governor Stevens "takes for granted that the acts of the legislative assembly of the Territory of Washington confers on the United States a substantial right to that part of the British dominions." Marcy warned Stevens that he should restrain territorial officers and "should abstain from all acts on the disputed grounds calculated to provoke conflict." The Secretary assured the governor that he would inform British officials that forebearance did not indicate any concession by the United States pending mutual agreement to a boundary. The British ambassador concurred with Marcy and promised equal forebearance by his subjects. This brought the incident to a close, and the islands remained in limbo until the Pig War in 1859 brought the San Juans to the foreground of international diplomacy once again.[26]

Although Governor Stevens began his efforts to settle Hudson's Bay Company claims in the days after his arrival at Olympia in November 1853, he also set the machinery of government in motion and began to establish a political organization. He fixed January 30, 1854, as the day for election of a delegate and territorial legislators. During the interim Stevens worked to insure the success of the Democratic party in this and subsequent polls. The most important step was to bring the territory's only newspaper into the party fold. And Stevens succeeded: on December 3, in the first issue to appear after the governor's arrival, publisher J. W. Wiley sported a new banner, the *Washington Pioneer*, a new partner, A. M. Berry, and a new philosophy as an "all out Democratic paper." Henceforth, the newspaper (which two months later became the *Pioneer and Democrat*) championed the candidates and policies of its party with single-minded intensity. But despite the efforts of the governor and Editor Wiley, the voters paid little attention to party affiliation in the first legislative election, preferring to vote for the men of standing in their localities without regard to national parties and politics. The Democrats won a two-to-one majority in the House but captured only five of nine Council seats.[27]

In the election of a delegate to represent the territory in Congress, national issues and national parties assumed greater importance. The Democrats nominated Columbia Lancaster, a veteran of the Oregon legislature, who emerged victorious when the delegates from the Puget Sound split their votes and the Columbia River delegates solidly supported Lancaster. One of the unsuccessful candidates for the Democratic nomination was Marshal J. Patton Anderson, who had the backing of Stevens and the other federal office holders. The Whigs nominated William H. Wallace, a lawyer and politician who had settled in Steilacoom. He attempted to make issues out of the location of polling places (which had been selected by Anderson and Stevens) and the apportionment of representatives to the House (in which Wallace charged that Clark County was slighted). If mistakes were made in locating polling places, they were probably more a result of ignorance than chicanery, and the Democrats rightly claimed that Clark was not discriminated against in relation to the other populous counties. The Whig charges fell flat, and Lancaster won with 690 votes to 500 for Wallace. Most surprising was the dismal showing of Michael Simmons, one of the first Americans to move north of the Columbia, who ran as an independent and received only eighteen votes. The territory was started on the road to adoption of the two-party system.[28]

Stevens delivered his first message to the legislature on February 28. The document accurately reflected the interests and personality of the new governor while indicating his sure grasp of the major issues that would face the territory during his tenure. He opened the address with a fine burst of mid-century rhetoric characterizing the Northwest as a land destined for great development in commerce, manufactures, agriculture, and the arts. Stevens claimed, "The emigrant looks forward to it as his home; princely merchants as the highway of the trade of nations; statesmen and patriots as a grand element of national strength and national security." Extending his own outlook on life to the territory, he asserted, "In this great era of the World's history, an era which hereafter will be the theme of epics and the torch of eloquence, we can play no secondary part if we would. We must of necessity play a great part if we act at all."[29]

Stevens touched only briefly on the mechanics of organizing the territorial government—referring the legislators to the Organic Act and leaving new counties, a legal code, the organization of judicial districts, and passage of an election law to their discretion. He moved quickly to the broad problems he saw confronting the territory, beginning with a plea to the legislature to petition Congress for continuation of the railroad survey "until the whole geography of the country and its resources be entirely developed." A related issue of more immediate concern was wagon roads; he called for roads from Fort Benton to Walla Walla, Vancouver to Walla Walla, and Vancouver to Bellingham Bay, with feeder roads as necessary. The lack of roads made mail service irregular and often impossible, leading Stevens to complain that ships brought by word of mouth news that arrived by mail six weeks later. He asked for regular mail service by steamer from San Francisco to various points on the Sound.

Transportation and communication were of vital concern. Alienation of the land was also important. The governor discussed the problem of the northern boundary, Hudson's Bay Company claims, and Indian title. He pointed out, as the legislators were well aware, that Indian claims had not been extinguished in any part of the territory even though the government had induced emigration by the provisions of the 1850 Oregon Donation Land Act. The solution was immediate settlement of Indian titles through treaty negotiation except "such portions as are indispensable to their comfort and subsistence." Stevens estimated that ten thousand Indians lived in the territory, Indians who were "for the most part a docile, harmless race, disposed to obey the laws and be good members of the State." He urged, once foreign and Indian claims were settled, that surveys be carried out quickly and that a separate surveyor general for Washington be appointed. He predicted that "by a vigorous effort, the land surveys may be kept in advance of settlement." The governor anticipated the Homestead Act by urging a law that would allow a settler to take a claim in one of several ways: by paying the minimum valuation, by continuous residence for one year, or by making improvements equal to the land's value. He wanted single women eligible to participate and he advocated curbing speculation by allowing settlers to take advantage of the law only once; that is, if they sold their claim they would be forced to buy new land. Stevens hoped that liberal land legislation would attract the large migration that he confidently predicted would settle the territory within a few years.[30]

Governor Stevens concluded his message with two subjects closely related to his own career, education and military defenses. He reported on his efforts to establish the territorial library and asked for the creation of an educational system that would "allow each individual to develop to his fullest potential." Stevens declared, "Let every youth, however limited his opportunities, find his place in the school, the college, the university, if God has given him the necessary gifts." The legislature was called upon to form a committee to report on a public school system and asked to memorialize Congress for land to support a university. With equal fervor Stevens called for a militia system, which he deemed particularly important in an isolated territory. He reminded the citizens, "The nation depends on the patriotism and valor of its citizens for defence in time of war," and urged military training in the schools, the enrollment of able-bodied men as artillerists or riflemen, and the building of batteries at exposed points on the coast.[31]

This was Stevens' program: settle the Indian and foreign claims, conduct rapid surveys, and provide adequate transportation, educational opportunities, and military protection. With the accomplishment of those tasks the territory would grow and prosper. Few could disagree. However, the limited resources of the territory and the great expense of most of the proposals as well as the national or international ramifications of some meant that the key to success or failure lay not with the territory's citizens or legislature, but with the federal government. Stevens could look down his list of suggestions—continuation of the survey, roads, railroads, land surveys, Indian treaties, improved mail service, schools, armaments—and it became obvious at a glance that all required federal authorization or support.

The legislature and governor could do little beyond establishing the machinery of government and a workable judicial system, and sending petitions to Congress.

Stevens knew from previous experience that petitions accomplished little without the right person to lobby in their behalf in the nation's capital. It did not take him long to decide to return to Washington D.C. to present personally his program to the men who could make it work. There is no doubt that Stevens hoped eventually to become territorial delegate, but there were good reasons for him not to seek the office in 1854. For one thing it was not certain that he could be nominated in the still-unsettled political climate, particularly as he had not yet had the opportunity to make himself well known throughout the territory. Secondly, he wished to accomplish certain tasks, particularly the completion of Indian treaties, before he took up permanent residence in the capital. Stevens recognized that Columbia Lancaster, an amiable frontiersman, would prove a babe in the woods among the political professionals, and he desired to reach Washington D.C. as soon as possible. The governor delayed only long enough to see that the legislature was properly launched on its duties before he departed by steamer for the East. Stevens had spent only four months on the Sound, but it was long enough to assess the problems and the opportunities; he saw no reason to change his earlier opinion that the Sound was "just such a place as I have for many years proposed to myself one of these days to carve out a home. I am satisfied my family will be pleased with their new home and that we will be willing to settle down there for life."[32]

During the weeks before he left Olympia, Stevens paved the way for his arrival in Washington D.C. by firing off letters to the Postmaster General, Surveyor General, other high government officials, and Congressmen, alerting them to the needs of the territory. He also completed one of the few tasks capable of solution while he was still in Olympia, the establishment of the territorial library. By 1853 it was customary for an organic act to include a provision providing for a library, and Stevens received $5,000 to purchase books. While in the midst of preparations for the railroad survey, he began the collection, and it is probable that few governors gave as much thought or care to the job. Stevens had two guidelines for his selections: first, works which would prove of use to legislators and other government officials, and second, books that would provide the core for a

good general library. Various state officials were asked to con-
tribute copies of their statutes, legislative journals, law codes,
and other records to the library, and a number responded favorably. Through publishers and book dealers he purchased the remainder of the collecton. The number of volumes eventually totaled twenty-eight hundred, of which about twelve hundred
were either government documents, law books, or travel works.
Included were the writings of numerous maritime and overland
explorers of the American West and the Pacific Coast, among
them Fremont's reports on his explorations, Farnham's *Travels in
the Great Western Prairie,* and Parkman's *California and Oregon
Trail.* Noticeably absent were the works of Daniel Lee, Gustavus
Hines, Alexander Ross, and Nathaniel Wyeth. Stevens purchased a complete set of *Niles' Weekly Register* and subscribed to
the *North American Review, DeBow's Review, Harper's Magazine,* and
other contemporary journals, as well as one New York and two
Washington D.C. newspapers.[33]

Many purchases for the library reflected Stevens' interests although he attempted to include a broad spectrum of works. The
library contained books in most scientific fields, including
twenty-two on engineering. There were about two hundred volumes of literature, including some in French and Spanish.
Among the authors were many of Stevens' favorites such as Carlyle, Swift, and Addison. It is not surprising that he included
about three hundred titles (555 volumes) of history or biography, including works on most of the founding fathers and several biographies of Napoleon. The history ranged from ancient,
through modern European, to contemporary American represented by the works of George Bancroft. On the whole the governor did a remarkable job in stretching the available funds to
provide a collection which included the classics, books in most
fields of knowledge, and works particularly suited to the needs
of the new territory. That he accomplished the task while in the
midst of numerous other duties makes it all the more remarkable. In subsequent years, after Stevens departed the territory,
few additional purchases were made, and at the time of statehood in 1889 the library remained essentially as he had left it.
In his first message to the legislature, Stevens wrote, with understandable pride, "I have purchased the library of the Territory
... and the books, which reached the territory in excellent order, have been placed in a suitable room, in the charge of a
gentleman, until the legislature might make some suitable provision."[34]

Stevens' diligent efforts in assembling the library reflected his concern that each individual should have the opportunity to acquire knowledge. Despite his staunch allegiance to the Democratic party, his social philosophy closely followed the thought of John Adams. Each believed that in a republic an elite should govern, but that all should have the opportunity to join that elite without regard to the station of their parents. The best way for an individual of modest origins to rise in society was through education. There is no doubt that Stevens would have agreed with Chancellor John Lathrop of the University of Wisconsin, who argued, "Knowledge is the great leveller. It is true democracy. It levels up—it does not level down." Although most citizens of Washington Territory shared this concern for educational opportunity, few were attuned to recent trends. When in the capital, Stevens was eager to take advantage of the growing sentiment in Congress to support university education, just as it had supported the common schools since 1785.[35]

The governor left the Columbia River on March 26, and in San Francisco, while awaiting the vessel for Panama, he took advantage of his time to deliver an address on the northern railroad route. Stevens reached New York in May and once again rejoined his family after a year's absence. The family had increased by one with the birth of Kate in November 1852, and Meg had stayed most of the year with the three girls at her mother's home in Newport. Hazard, now twelve, began to follow in his father's footsteps by attending Phillips Academy in Andover. Meg and all the children had spent several weeks visiting Isaac's father in North Andover, and the old man reported proudly that the three girls were "sprightly, sensible" children and that Hazard made "good progress" at school. Stevens took his family immediately to the capital and set up headquarters in the National Hotel on Pennsylvania Avenue.[36]

Stevens did not have much time to enjoy his family during the summer months as his days were filled from early morning until late in the evening consulting with Joe Lane and Columbia Lancaster, lobbying with Congress, and working on a compilation of the railroad survey reports. Rested from the enforced leisure of his sea voyage and less troubled by his hernia, he plowed into the necessary work. The first order of business was the survey, for which he needed to procure a supplementary appropriation for the deficit as well as to prepare the report. Stevens argued that he had faithfully attempted to carry out the true intentions of Congress. He asked,

What did Congress request by the exploration of a route? Did it intend to restrict the examination to a mountain pass and a trail, or by a route did it expect the general feeling of a belt of country, its rivers, its passes, its plains, the soil adapted to settlement, the Indian tribes, the materials of cultivation, the population which would grow up, and their means of subsistence?

Jefferson Davis came to a similar conclusion, and although he did not officially sanction Stevens' cost overruns, he testified that they were prompted by zeal and asked Congress to pay for "arrearages necessarily incurred." Congress approved payment with certain exceptions such as disallowing salary or per diem for any member receiving payment from another agency while on the survey. Stevens, whose salary as governor and superintendent of Indian affairs started from the date of his commission, was not allowed a claim for eight dollars per diem, and John Evans was not given any compensation beyond payment he received from the Interior Department. Neither was Stevens successful in his quest for new funds to continue the work of the survey. In part he was defeated by the thorough work of his party: the voluminous sets of notes, documents, and collections seemed to indicate that little remained for a new party to accomplish. Davis hinted that the War Department might grant new funds if Stevens would indicate the specific purpose of the request. The governor made several suggestions, such as the need to compile Indian vocabularies and grammars, but Davis rejected these as falling outside the scope of the surveys or the War Department. The failure to receive additional funds did not stop Stevens from continuing the survey work on an informal basis, and his final report of 1859 included materials and observations made after 1854.[37]

Although he tried to provide for the future of the survey, the immediate problem that faced Stevens was to put in shape the information already gathered for the report being prepared under the supervision of Captain Humphreys. Most of the leaders of the northern survey were reunited in the capital in the spring of 1854. Saxton and Stanley, who had arrived earlier with some of the reports, were joined by Stevens, Donelson, McClellan, Tinkham, and Isaac Osgood. Numerous problems arose, including the sheer bulk of the various reports (which Humphrey's assistant estimated to total fifteen hundred pages). Some reports were lost, the most important being the meteorological and astronomical observations the governor had sent east with Lieutenant Donelson. As all his baggage was in the care of an express company, Donelson knew only that the valise containing the documents had disappeared somewhere between San Francisco and New York. Stevens had the lieutenant retrace his route, but after an exhaustive search on the Isthmus of Panama and in San Francisco, Donelson returned empty-handed.[38]

Although the assemblage of survey personnel in the capital produced some good results, it also led to renewed bickering. George McClellan once again provided problems for the governor. Stevens had shown considerable restraint in his relations with his subordinate while in Washington Territory. He had ignored McClellan's grumbling and considered their differences an honest divergence of opinion. Certainly he had never failed to give McClellan ample credit for his accomplishments in the Cascade Mountains.[39] When the governor arrived in the capital, he politely asked McClellan if he would join him on a visit to Professor Blodgett, the meteorology expert at the Smithsonian, and suggested, "[You] may modify your views of snows, and your suggestions may modify mine." And McClellan, who was staying just down Pennsylvania Avenue at the Willard Hotel, received invitations to dine with the Stevens family at the National Hotel. The relationship cooled when McClellan refused to allow the governor to read the journal he had kept during the exploration. Stevens insisted, for he had ordered McClellan and other leaders to keep journals as an aid in preparing the final reports. Finally, with some bitterness on each side, they compromised, and McClellan gave Stevens a summary of his notes. The relationship was further strained by rumors that McClellan would be named to head any new survey work in the Northwest. It is probably no coincidence that the first letter from Stevens to McClellan that was less than cordial was written one day after the governor testily protested to Humphreys that any further surveys "will obviously best be done under my supervision, I know the whole field." Jefferson Davis did send McClellan to Philadelphia and Boston to consult with various engineers on their views of the railroad routes, but Congress did not appropriate further funds for survey work, and McClellan was sent to Europe to observe the Crimean War.[40]

Stevens' dispute with Donelson over his responsibility for longitudinal observations while on the upper Missouri continued to simmer, and Donelson pleaded with Humphreys to give him a new assignment. Abiel Tinkham was also unhappy because he believed Stevens wrong in taking excerpts from his and other engineers' field reports and incorporating them in one narrative rather than publishing their work in separate segments. Tink-

ham left in a huff for Illinois and had no future contact with
the governor. A related issue was Stevens' fear that some members of the party might publish certain materials independent of
the survey report. George Gibbs was one who indicated he
might do this, but Stevens insisted that it would be illegal at
least until after the work appeared in the final survey report.[41]

These disputes, the voluminous details connected with the
survey report, and a seige of illness during a hot, sultry summer
provided sufficient cares for one man. But Stevens also acted,
unofficially, as delegate from Washington Territory. Columbia
Lancaster did his best to represent the territory, but he admitted that he had not been able to get his bills on the Congressional agenda and had found himself anxiously awaiting the arrival of each steamer in the hope that it contained the governor.
When he arrived, Stevens tackled the list of objectives outlined
in his address to the territorial legislature. He visited the Postmaster General with a proposal for mail service by steamer to
the Sound direct from San Francisco. He complained that the
outgoing mail left Rainier on the Columbia River once a
week with the local carrier often missing the connection because of high water and a lack of roads. The governor enlisted
Davis's support by suggesting that a mail steamer providing local service on the Sound could also provide protection from the
Indians. The Postmaster was not enthusiastic, but Davis responded and Stevens got his steamer from the War Department.
The Secretary of War reluctantly denied a request for arms and
ammunition, because under the law the territory first had to legally establish a militia. Another matter relating to the improvement of navigation was establishment of lighthouses on the
Sound, and Stevens visited his old acquaintances on the Lighthouse Board to successfully outline his proposals.[42]

A measure of vital concern was the appointment of a surveyor
general for the territory. The Oregon surveyors had not ventured many miles north of the Columbia River and in 1854
were carrying their surveys into the southern end of the Willamette Valley. Stevens argued that the large emigration coming
the next season made immediate work in Washington an absolute necessity and that even existing settlement required surveys
near Puget Sound and in the corridor between Vancouver and
Olympia. In another burst of originality the governor suggested
that the surveyor for Washington Territory depart from the rec-
tangular method (in use since 1785). Although this system had
served admirably for the generally flat lands of the East, Stevens

believed the mountainous, wooded terrain of the territory lent itself more readily to the geodetic method. This involved the use of triangulation, as practiced by the Coast Survey, in which large areas could be mapped by reference to a mountain peak or other prominent point. Stevens argued that large valleys and grazing areas could be surveyed rapidly with more difficult terrain left until later. The plan received a hearing from the Commissioner of the General Land Office and the Secretary of the Interior, who suggested that the method might be used in some instances, but they were not enthusiastic and the idea was dropped. But working closely with Lane, the governor was able to push through Congress a bill creating a separate surveyor general for the territory. James Tilton, a native of Indiana, veteran of the Mexican War, and a former surveyor in Minnesota, received the appointment. Able and industrious, Tilton would serve until removed in 1861 by the Lincoln administration. Although he began work immediately, progress was slow for the reasons that Stevens had suggested. Tilton found that he could not let all of his contracts to deputies because they were "often ruined by their losses" occasioned by the difficulty of the work and the low rate of pay. Stevens and Tilton asked Congress to allow increased compensation per mile, which was eventually granted.[43]

Stevens was less successful in his attempt to secure new appropriations for military wagon roads. But he laid the groundwork, and in the next session of Congress, Washington received $25,000 for the road from The Dalles to Fort Vancouver and $30,000 for the Fort Steilacoom-Fort Vancouver road. Congress gave supervision of construction to the newly created Pacific Coast Office of Military Roads (headquartered in San Francisco), which made preliminary examinations of the routes but was then forced by the Indian war to delay construction until 1856. The governor's disappointment at not receiving any road funds in 1854 was partially allayed by approval of funding for treaty councils with the Indians.[44]

After an arduous but profitable summer, Stevens prepared to return to Olympia with his family. He had accomplished many of his goals, including funding for the survey deficit and for the Indian treaty councils, and he had laid the groundwork for future progress on other programs. His only real disappointment was the failure of Congress to extend the life of the railroad surveys. Stevens' experience in the ways of Washington D.C. politics and his friendship with men like Lane, Gwin, Douglas, and

Henry Rice of Minnesota, as well as with Jefferson Davis and President Pierce, had placed him in a strong position to lobby for the interests of Washington Territory. Rice suggested Stevens' value as an effective lobbyist when he lamented that little could be done to push the interests of the northern railroad line once the governor left the city. Stevens sailed from New York on September 20 in fine spirits. He had made a positive impression in the capital and could return to the Northwest, settle the Indian question, open the territory to settlement, and await the glorious future.

THE GREAT
WHITE
FATHER

Stevens left New York with Meg, their four children, and an Irish nurse named Ellen in an overcrowded steamer packed with thirteen hundred passengers, most of whom were bound for California. Meg and Isaac received the best stateroom and ate at the Captain's table, but the children sat at the second table and received food of poor quality. The vessel put in at Aspinwall (on the Isthmus of Panama) in hot, humid weather, and the Stevenses found it a squalid village with numerous "pools of dirty, green, stagnant water." The next day a train took them to the summit of the isthmus where the tracks ended and mule transportation began. Only a few mules at exorbitant rates were available, and the family stayed the night in the hope of negotiating better and cheaper transportation the next day. After a sleepless night, during which they were first entertained by the California-bound Christy's Minstrels, and then disturbed by the musicians' drunken arguments, the mules arrived to take them to the coast—at a rate little reduced from the previous day. Meg later complained bitterly, and perhaps unfairly, that the yellow fever which later struck her and the three girls was a result of that overnight stay at the summit. The already farcical situation became calamitous when on the journey to the coast, young Kate and Maude, being carried on the backs of bearers, became separated from the rest of the party during a tropical rainstorm. When the mule train arrived in Panama City, the two girls could not be found, and Stevens returned to the jungle, where he spent a rainy evening in a fruitless search. It was not until the next morning that the girls were reunited with their frantic parents. The bearers explained that they had decided to wait out the storm in a village near the trail.[1]

181

Yellow fever broke out on board ship, and Meg and the three girls were in serious condition when they landed in San Francisco two weeks later. They moved into a hotel and Stevens located two army doctors he had known in Mexico to attend the family. Meg, Sue, and Kate soon passed the crisis, but the doctors gave up for four-year-old Maude. As a last resort, Stevens gave his daughter hot baths and forced her to take liquids from an eyedropper. Slowly she began to recover. In November they sailed to Vancouver, where the family rested at the army barracks for two weeks before making the difficult trip to Olympia.

That trip (of only slightly more than one hundred miles) matched even the rigors of the Isthmus of Panama. The rugged, virtually roadless, tree-choked and uninhabited territory was not what Meg had anticipated. A pleasant trip down the Columbia brought the family to Rainier, where they transferred to canoes to cross to Monticello on the north bank at the mouth of the Cowlitz River. Here they spent a wet night, and the next morning, huddled in one canoe with their belongings in another, they glided upstream.

At first Meg found the dexterity of the Indian paddlers exciting, but at the end of a long, wet day in the cramped canoe, she could hardly stand. They put ashore at Cowlitz Landing and walked through ankle-deep mud to the inn run by U. B. Warbass. There Meg saw a number of men with "so much hair upon their heads and faces they all looked alike." The white men seemed to her to be a rough, dirty lot that could only be cleaned "by boiling and scraping." At the inn one bed was provided for Meg and the children while the governor was shown the dank sleeping loft crowded with men rolled in wet, steaming blankets. Stevens opted instead for a stool next to the bed, where (to Meg's amazement) he slept soundly through the night.[2]

The next morning everyone piled into wagons, and soon the horses were sinking deep into the mud with every step. Rivers were forded with water coming up over the wagon bed, and the driver's jumping the team across wide holes brought the springless wagon down with a tremendous impact. "Surely," Meg shuddered, "there were no worse roads to be found in the world." Finally, when the team could not negotiate one of the larger holes, the wagon sank deep into the morass. The men pulled the wagon out with brute strength, and the weary travelers stopped, exhausted, at the home of John R. Jackson, whose genial hospitality and well-stocked larder provided a welcome respite. The difficulties of the journey were commonplace to the governor, but to his wife the initial introduction to the primitiveness of the territory that she had heard described in such glowing terms came as a rude shock. For two more days they continued toward Olympia over roads that improved somewhat as they neared the capital. But then came the final disappointment. Cresting a small rise on a dreary December evening, they looked down the muddy road at a clearing of tangled timber and tree stumps which contained a scattering of twenty or thirty rough-hewn cabins and an Indian village: Olympia. Meg's heart "sank with bitter disappointment" as she surveyed the dismal site of their new home.[3]

Wet and tired, they were escorted to the Washington Hotel for a repeat performance of the welcome extended to the governor one year earlier. This occasion was not as felicitous because Meg and the girls were still weak and Maude was ill and querulous. When one woman exclaimed, "What a cross brat that is!" it proved the last straw for Meg's nerves; she rushed into another room and collapsed in a flood of tears. For the next two months she kept to the house, even refusing to attend the ball given for her and the governor. Her illness, the incessant worry over the children, the rigors of the journey, and the initial disappointment at the crude state of the territory were nearly too much for the Newport belle.

As she and the children regained stength, prospects in Washington Territory appeared brighter, and Meg emerged from her uncharacteristic melancholy and depression. For an exorbitant $900 a year, Stevens had rented office and living space from Father Ricord. Although the two long, low buildings, situated on the beach near the Indian camp, were often enveloped by an overpowering "stench of dried clams and salmon," the family could look out over the bay, which was often covered with waterfowl, and the children could amuse themselves on the beach. Meg's household chores were light because Ellen cared for the children and the governor hired two men—one as a cook, and another, W. F. Seely (who had come west with the survey) as a gardener and general handyman. Meg found the officers' wives at nearby Fort Steilacoom to be pleasant company and discovered that many of the settlers came from similar backgrounds despite their crude outward appearances. Her position as the governor's wife made her the center of attraction, with even the Indians pointing to her as "the big woman." She often visited Father Ricord, who was delighted to converse in "pure" school

184

Puget Sound and
Mt. Rainier, from
Whidbey Island,
James G. Cooper

French, and she spent many hours on horseback riding through
the woods. She also planned their new house, which was to be
constructed a mile south of town on eight lots purchased by the
governor. Highlighting her routine were occasional trips north
down the Sound to shop at the Hudson's Bay Company store in
Victoria.[4]

Meg also enjoyed the company of the men who came to visit
or confer with her husband in the office adjoining the house.
Frequent visitors were Benjamin Kendall, Elwood Evans, Michael Simmons, Charles Mason, George Gibbs (whom she called
"accomplished and educated"), and George Stevens, who was
serving as the governor's private secretary. In the evening these
men would often come to dinner and stay to play cards; it
seemed "quite like old times." Meg was amused when relatives

said, "Only think of poor Margaret in that Indian country—
poor thing I pity her." Although she had pitied herself at first,
Meg could eventually reply, "I never was so well or happy in
my life as now." This serene existence was broken only when
George Stevens drowned crossing a river on his return from a
visit to Portland, and by the Indian war, which forced a brief
move to Fort Steilacoom. For a time Stevens, too, shared this
home life, but he was increasingly absent, and after the spring
of 1855 he was usually in the field or deeply involved with official duties.[5]

When the governor was absent, Charles Mason remained in
Olympia as acting governor, and he and Meg became close
friends. They shared a Rhode Island heritage, and the young,
soft-spoken, courteous bachelor was a hard man for anyone to

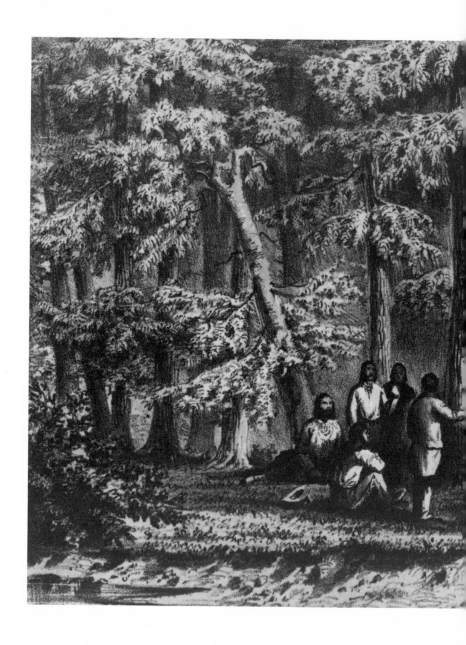

dislike, even among the administration's enemies. Meg admitted, "I never knew a young man that I liked so well." She believed he liked her equally well, and once confessed that she was "running on at a furious rate for a married woman concerning a young man." It is unlikely that the relationship was anything but platonic, but there is no doubt that the secretary filled a need for a young woman who, despite her protestations

Nez Perces,
John Mix Stanley

of happiness, was removed from the close family ties and relationships that had meant so much in her life.[6]

When Stevens returned to the East in the spring of 1854, he
left Mason, the other territorial officials, and the legislature to
shift for themselves. The legislators were typical for a new territory in that the average age was a young twenty-eight, and
among the twenty-seven members there were more farmers than

lawyers. During the session individuals and factions jockeyed for position and laid the groundwork for future political alignments. The assembly consistently followed the policies spelled out by the governor in his message, but the council displayed an independence that marked the beginning of an opposition party. Council President Donald N. McConaha became the leader of this incipient faction; he was one of three council members who refused to sanction the governor's return to Washington D.C., and he took the lead in winning legislative approval for Frederick Lander's reconnaissance of the South Pass route as an alternative line for the northern railroad. One of Stevens' friends complained that McConaha was "a perfect nuisance." Both houses passed the memorials the governor had requested, and they made two additonal requests of Congress: reimbursement for the party that rescued the Queen Charlotte Island victims, and annexation of the Sandwich (Hawaiian) Islands. Congress ignored the latter request, but approved the first. A major issue of the session was the status of French Canadians formerly employed by the Hudson's Bay Company who continued to reside in the territory. Some legislators argued that most of the Canadians were pioneers who helped open up the country and who paid taxes. Some citizens, however, petitioned for the denial of voting privileges to anyone who could not read and write English, and, after hot debate, the legislature granted the vote to half-breeds who the election judges determined had adopted the habits of civilization, a compromise that allowed Canadian farmers to vote but excluded those living among the Indians.[7]

The major work of the session was accomplished outside legislative halls as Edward Lander, Victor Monroe, and lawyer William Strong put together a code of criminal and civil law. The three, with Lander and Strong doing most of the work, relied heavily on the New York code, although adjustments were influenced by experience with the law in Indiana and Ohio. The legislature postponed hot issues such as the location of the capital, penitentiary, and university and adjourned well before the allotted one hundred days with the solons returning home to await the second session beginning in December. One who would not return was McConaha, who, along with other legislators, participated in a session-ending party presided over by Acting Governor Mason; immediately after the celebration he left for Seattle and drowned in a canoe accident during the trip.[8]

When the legislature adjourned, life on the Sound returned to its normal, placid existence, although one observer noted, "All

sorts of factions rage here against the absentee [governor]." Most
of the burden, in Stevens' absence, fell to Charles Mason, who
"groaned under the trials of office." One of Mason's greatest
problems was persuading the federal government to approve territorial expenditures and forward the necessary funds. Most important was the legislative printing expense which totaled $5,000
for the journals and $6,488 for laws, bills, resolutions, and mis-
cellaneous items. Mason had decided to print the laws in the
Pioneer and Democrat rather than in pamphlet form as his instructions required. He explained that any pamphlet work had to be
sent out of the territory and he chose the quickest and cheapest
way to distribute the laws to the general public. The auditor
paid half of the printing expenses and told the secretary that
the rest would be adjusted, leaving him to fret about the eventual consequences. When the Treasury Department did send
money, it came in large drafts that could not be cashed by anyone in the territory. Mason engaged the express company of
Parker and Cotter to take the drafts to Portland, but on one trip
temptation proved too great and Henry Cotter took a steamer
to San Francisco with $3,875 of the territory's money. With Ste-
vens' help, Mason, after great difficulty, persuaded the government to absolve him of any blame for the loss. The secretary
also was chagrined to find that the Treasury and Auditor disallowed payments he made under their authorization. In addition he protested that his salary once went to Chicago, once to
New Mexico, and finally stopped altogether. He complained
that all these factors were hindering his ability to carry on the
business of the territory and were shaking the confidence of the
citizens in the financial stability of the government. Mason was
overjoyed to see the governor return; he could finally take the
advice of a friend who had earlier told him to forget his troubles and go fishing.[9]

The second session of the Washington territorial legislature
gathered in Olympia on December 4, 1854, with the membership swelled by members from several new counties. The governor returned from his whirlwind trip to the nation's capital in
time to deliver his second message but added little that was
new. He repeated his concern over Hudson's Bay Company
claims, the need for improved transportation, and the necessity
of a militia, although he referred to the latter more in the context of European difficulties than in anticipation of Indian problems. Stevens made it clear that his major duty in the coming
months would be the Indian treaties.

I believe the time has now come for their final settlement. In view of the important duties which have been assigned to me, I throw myself unreservedly upon the people of the territory, not doubting that they will extend to me a hearty and generous support in my efforts to arrange, on a permanent basis, the future of the Indians of this territory.[10]

As superintendent of Indian affairs, Stevens soon became a key figure in the new reservation policy that federal officials had proposed as the latest in a long series of attempted solutions to the perplexing problem of dealing with the native inhabitants. Stevens' views on Indians had been shaped by the prevailing assumptions of his fellow Americans during the Jacksonian era. Their attitudes fell into two broad categories: one group believed that the natives were savages who, for their own protection as well as that of white society, needed to be isolated beyond a permanent Indian frontier. The other group argued that the Indians should be assimilated into white culture—taking the best from Indian and white civilizations. Common to both points of view was the assumption that all Indians were essentially the same—an assumption which lumped vastly diverse cultures under one label.

Historically, conflicting viewpoints, abetted by the realities of an advancing frontier, resulted in a vacillating Indian policy which had begun with the British government's Proclamation of 1763. This pragmatic decision to create a barrier to "Indian country" beyond the Appalachians was based on the experience of more than a century of bitter and bloody conflict—warfare in which Isaac Stevens' ancestors had often been participants. The new nation continued this policy, but it broke down under the pressures of white settlement, and, during the latter years of the eighteenth century, the government began moving in new directions. Under the Northwest Ordinance of 1787, the federal government reserved the right to extinguish Indian land title, and, with the Treaty of Greenville in 1795, there began a systematic process of treaty negotiations. Once the lands were purchased, the Indians became the responsibility of the government, and, at least in theory, they were to be instructed in farming and given the benefits of a common school education. In this way there would be assimilation. Some confidently predicted the process would take only a generation or less.

The assimilation policy often met with Indian resistance, the failure of agents to provide promised services, and the reluctance of Congress to appropriate funds. Even when the policy bore fruit, as with the Cherokees of Georgia, white greed placed enormous pressure upon the government to force the tribes from the rich land they occupied. President Andrew Jackson, who called for removal of all Indians west of the Mississippi River, argued that, even in the case of the Cherokees, "All previous experiments for the improvement of the Indians have failed. It seems now to be an established fact that they cannot live in contact with a civilized community and prosper." The removal of the "Five Civilized Tribes" led to the establishment of a new permanent Indian boundary running from northern Wisconsin across Iowa and following the present western borders of Missouri and Arkansas. Opinion differed in the 1830s as to the eventual fate of tribes sent to the West. Washington Irving predicted that a new, mongrel race would develop as "the amalgamation of the debris and abrasions of former races, civilized and savage; the remains of broken and almost extinguished tribes; the descendants of wandering hunters and trappers." It was visitor Alexis de Tocqueville who most accurately foresaw the future. He described how the Americans would take the Indians "by the hand and transport them to a grave far from the lands of their fathers," and he noted that it would be accomplished "with a singular felicity; tranquilly, legally, philanthropically." Tocqueville predicted they would remain undisturbed in their new homes only until the whites needed the land. He erred only in placing that need at a point in the distant future. In the early 1840s settlement pushed west from Missouri, following the river valleys—and trails cut across the continent to California and Oregon. By 1850 it was impossible to draw a straight line that would separate Indian and white settlements even if the government had wished to.

Before 1853, Isaac Stevens' direct contact with Indians was limited to viewing the survivors of tribes in Maine, but he was well aware of frontier conflicts such as the Seminole War. To the extent that Stevens had a philosophy of Indian-white relations, he assumed the superiority of European civilization and the necessity of removing the Indian from its path. He hoped the removal could be accomplished peacefully and that, during a period of benevolent care, the Indians could be educated to cultivate the soil and become productive, valued members of white society.

One anomaly of American Indian policy was the treaty system, which assumed an equality between the contracting parties that did not exist. It was suggested to President James Madison in 1811, as it was often suggested to other political leaders, that the treaty process was a farce and that it would be more equitable for the United States to dictate benevolent terms without negotiation. Madison, and other presidents, hesitated—partially because they did not wish to leave the nation open to charges of aggression or nondemocratic procedures. The fiction of negotiations between equal, consenting parties continued and Superintendent Stevens was obliged to work within this well-established treaty framework. The movement of settlers to the Pacific Coast had ended any real possibility of a permanent Indian frontier, and, beginning with the Treaty of Fort Laramie in 1851, the federal government moved toward the reservation system as an alternative to the frontier line. In 1854 Stevens was charged with the responsibility of extinguishing Indian title in Washington Territory under the basic policy then in operation: placement of the Indians on reservations under the treaty process.[11]

The Pacific Northwest differed from the typical American frontier in that extensive Indian-white contacts existed for many years prior to widespread agrarian settlement. Under the aegis of the Hudson's Bay Company, a pattern of Indian-white relationship began in the 1820s. Sir George Simpson and John McLoughlin, who disagreed on many matters, at least agreed that the Indians should receive fair treatment from the Company. This meant consistent policies, fixed prices for furs, and an end to the liquor traffic. The relationship benefited both sides: the Company provided goods, which raised the Indians' standard of living, and the Indians provided the Company with furs. Employees of the Company, including leaders like McLoughlin, tended to take Indian wives, and this brought the two races closer as time passed. During his long tenure in the Northwest, John McLoughlin became a larger-than-life figure respected by whites and Indians alike; he ruled with a firm hand, but he did not interfere much with the Indian way of life. For most tribes the arrival of the Hudson's Bay Company was a positive factor as it brought stability and economic progress. The major negative factor was the appearance of influenza, smallpox, measles, and syphilis, which took a heavy toll.

The first American missionaries who came to Oregon in 1834 did not disrupt the pattern. Jason Lee, for example, was steered to the Willamette Valley by McLoughlin, and Indians who wished contact with the Americans had to visit the mission posts. The American community grew for a few years without having a serious negative impact on the Indians, and efforts to bring cattle up from California proved to be beneficial. Significantly, the first American settlement of consequence in Indian country—that of Marcus Whitman—led to the first major conflict in the Northwest. Many American settlers believed that the Hudson's Bay Company encouraged the Indians to oppose the "Bostons." The charge was false. McLoughlin had warned Whitman that he was in danger; and, in any open conflict, the Company always sided with the Americans. But the contrast between the Company's impact on the region and the effect of American settlement was readily apparent. The Whitman mission was a permanent agricultural settlement, and the many settlers who stopped there indicated to the Indians that it was only the first of many settlements. In addition, the missionaries frankly admitted that they wished to destroy the Indians' traditional way of life and replace it with white culture. The outbreak of disease was only the last straw leading to the massacre and, subsequently, the Cayuse War.

By the 1850s the future of Indian-white relations in the Northwest was clear to experienced observers and incidents began to occur with increasing frequency. According to one government estimate, sixteen whites in Oregon were killed by Indians during the 1847–48 Cayuse War. In the next two years no deaths were reported, but in 1851 and 1852 there were six fatalities each year, and in 1853 the number ballooned to forty-seven. Most of the deaths resulted from squabbles and misunderstandings between individuals, and, more often than not, one or both parties were under the influence of alcohol—another exacerbating influence contributed by the Americans. Indians reacted to physical abuse from whites, and the settlers often objected to Indian thievery. The Indians quickly discovered that, unlike McLoughlin, the Americans would seldom if ever punish a white for harming an Indian. In addition, many "Bostons" made it clear that they were determined to remove the Indians from their neighborhood, if not from the face of the earth. One outspoken but not atypical Oregon settler called for an end to the "sickly sentimentality" of "pseudo—philanthrophists who seek to disguise the real Oregon Indian by representing him as possessing such ennobling traits of character as are seldom found within the realms of civilization." This Oregonian suggested that it was time for vigorous action: " 'Lo! the poor Indian' is the exclamation of . . . love-sick novel writers. 'Lo! the defenseless men, women, and children, who have fallen victims and suffered more than death itself at their hands' is the immediate response of the surviving witnesses of the inhuman butcheries perpetrated by this God-accursed race."[12]

The problem of Indian-white relations was further complicated in 1850 with passage of the Oregon Donation Land Act which allowed new families to claim as much as 320 acres of land. The act did not state specifically that these claims could be taken before extinguishment of Indian title or completion of land surveys, but it implied immediate settlement. The new settlement brought greater pressures, and in 1851 the Rogue Indians of southern Oregon lashed out against miners and settlers. At the same time the Snake Indians (along the Oregon Trail) were becoming increasingly hostile to emigrants. After 1851 military officers and Catholic priests in the Northwest frequently warned their superiors, government officials, and settlers that Indian outbreaks were not only possible but probably. A typical alarm was sounded by Major Gabriel Rains, who wrote from Fort Dalles to the headquarters of the Department of the Pacific, "The time has arrived when it becomes necessary to determine the question of peace or war between the citizens of the United States and Indian tribes on this frontier." Rains reviewed Indian complaints, noted the presence of an extensive liquor traffic, protested that Indians had no rights in the courts, and concluded that it would be best if the area east of the Cascade Mountains remained Indian country. But even as the major warned, "prompt action is required . . . to prevent an Indian war," Wasco County, south of Fort Dalles and east of the Cascade Mountains, was in the process of organization.[13]

Governor Stevens was aware of all the above factors, but he tended to play down the danger signals for a variety of reasons. Above all, he had great confidence in his own ability to handle the Indians. This cocksureness had developed as he came west with the railroad survey; he had expected the worst, particularly from the Blackfeet, but the survey party had come through with no serious incidents. Stevens did not recognize that their good fortune resulted in large measure fom the excellent liaison work of Alexander Culbertson. Stevens exaggerated his own role and assumed that other whites either had not known how to handle the Indians successfully, or had overestimated the danger. He became even more sanguine upon arrival west of the Cascade Mountains. Before coming west he had read George Simpson's *Narrative of a Journey Around the World,* in which the Puget Sound Indians were described as "quiet, inoffensive, and industrious people" who did well as agricultural helpers. When Stevens

reached Olympia it appeared that Simpson's assessment was correct for he found the various tribes trading with the whites, acting as guides, and working as servants. The Nisqually Indians,
who camped in and near Olympia, seemed anything but a
threat to the settlers. Meg echoed her husband's view that the
Indians could be easily controlled when she declared that they
"think so much of the whites that a child can govern them."
She boasted, "Mr. Stevens has them right under his thumb—
they are afraid to death of him and do just as he tells them."
On one occasion, as Meg told it, when their night-long singing
and chanting, which she likened to the howling of a band of
wolves, kept the governor's family awake, he took a club, walked
into the center of the group, and threatened to knock down the
first one who opened his mouth. The singing ended, Meg said,
at least for that night.[14]

Soon after arriving in the territory, Stevens outlined his plans
for the Commissioner of Indian Affairs, George Manypenny. He
noted the conflict that apparently existed between the Donation
Act and laws governing Indian affairs and urged speed in defining Indian lands before settlers spread over the whole territory
and further complicated the situation. Stevens knew that most
tribes would not wish to move very far from their existing locations, but he also knew that the federal government still tended
to think in terms of an Indian-white frontier as clearly defined
as possible. (Treaties made by Anson Dart in Oregon in
1851–52 were disallowed because they provided for numerous
reservations located near settlements in the western part of the
territory.) Stevens cautiously suggested that it would be imprac-
tical to move the Puget Sound tribes east of the Cascade Mountains and argued that it would be more humane and less expensive to locate them on the Sound where they could catch fish,
dig roots, and pick berries. Although confident of his ability to
resolve the Indian question, Stevens constantly urged the government to act quickly because delay would only complicate a
solution equitable to both whites and Indians.[15]

Events in 1854 confirmed the truth of Stevens' position. Conditions on the Oregon Trail worsened as Shoshone Indians attacked the "Ward party" on the Boise River and killed seventeen in a particularly shocking massacre. The rescue party
reported that many victims showed signs of the "most brutal
violence." Violence occurred periodically near Seattle and at
Bellingham Bay, where several whites lost their lives in 1853–54.
In most instances the white settlers retaliated against the In-

dians they assumed to be guilty of the crimes. For example, in July 1853 three white men hanged an Indian near Seattle. The hangmen were brought to trial: one man was acquitted and charges against the other two were dismissed.

Stevens became involved in one incident when a party of men from Seattle arrived in Olympia in March 1854 with the news that a man named Young had been murdered and a second, Dr. Cherry, had died during a subsequent skirmish at Holmes Harbor. The governor, with George Gibbs, Michael Simmons, and a squad of soldiers under the command of Lieutenant William Slaughter, sailed north down the Sound. Stevens met with Chiefs Seattle and Patkanim of the Duwamish and Snoqualmie bands. The chiefs told him that Young, a new settler headed for Whidbey Island, and two hired Indians had become drunk and had quarrelled. Young killed one Indian with his sword and wounded the other. The son of the dead man later killed Young for revenge. The young Indian was seized, and the fight at Holmes Harbor resulted when friends came to his rescue. In the ensuing battle Cherry and an Indian with the white party were killed. Testimony from whites made it clear that they feared a general uprising, and they pleaded with the governor to take strong measures to prevent further deaths. Stevens judiciously declared both sides at fault and promised justice would be meted out to all. Chiefs Seattle and Patkanim named the Indians involved in the Holmes Harbor affair but claimed they had disappeared into the woods. The governor then took his party to Holmes Harbor, where a number of Snohomish Indians were encamped, and demanded they give up the guilty parties. When they refused Stevens ordered their canoes burned and returned to Olympia empty-handed. Stevens reported that his action had a salutary effect, which may have been true, but the Indians must have wondered why only they received punishment as a result of the incident.[16]

Federal officials reacted positively when confronted with the urgent demands of Governor Stevens, Oregon officials, army officers, and a number of private citizens. Commissioner Manypenny, with masterly bureaucratic prose, informed Congress,

An enlightened forecast indicates that the present is a favorable time to institute and establish definite relations of amity with the wild tribes of Indians. . . . With many of the tribes in Oregon and Washington territories, it appears to be absolutely necessary to speedily conclude treaties for the extinguishment of their claims to the lands now or recently occupied by them.

Manypenny reminded Congress that it had promoted settlement in the Northwest, "Yet the Indian tribes still claim title to the lands on which the whites have located, and which they are now cultivating." This, the commissioner reported, led to hostilities and resulted in "the murder of white settlers, and in hindering the general growth and prosperity of the civil communities of these territories." Manypenny supported Stevens' plan to conduct negotiations with the Blackfeet and other tribes east of the Rockies not covered by the Treaty of Fort Laramie. He suggested that, as a railroad might go through these latitudes, it was "proper that all hostile Indian tribes or bands along such routes be permanently pacified." When Stevens arrived in the capital in the spring of 1854 prepared to argue vigorously for funds for treaty negotiations, he found the bills about to receive favorable action from Congress. To his great surprise the amounts requested were raised to $45,000 from $30,000 for negotiations west of the Bitterroots and to $100,000 from $60,000 for treaties east of those mountains.[17]

The Medicine Creek Council

After returning to Olympia in December 1854, Stevens set to work on his program to conduct treaty negotiations. He planned to treat with the tribes on the Sound during the winter and then to move east of the Cascade Mountains in the spring and work his way to the Blackfoot council. The governor and his associates had attempted to prepare the tribes for the treaties during 1853–54 when they advised all to keep the peace, promising that treaties would soon be made that would provide justice for all. Most Indians in the territory had forewarning of the treaty councils, although in some instances this increased rather than lessened fears. The first council took place at the mouth of Medicine Creek (on the Nisqually Flats between Olympia and Fort Steilacoom). While men rode out to escort the Indians to the councils, set up the council grounds, and procure the necessary supplies, the governor gathered his negotiating team in Olympia. In addition to Michael Simmons (who had been named as Indian agent for Puget Sound), the group included James Doty as secretary, Benjamin F. Shaw as interpreter, George Gibbs as surveyor, and Hugh A. Goldsborough as commissary. Simmons and Shaw were veteran frontiersmen and early settlers on the Sound. (Shaw was alleged to be the only man in the territory who could translate from English into the Chinook tongue while a man talked at normal speed.) Gibbs was rapidly becoming the most apt student of Indian language and customs in the Northwest, and Doty had just arrived on the Sound after his year's residence among the Blackfoot Indians. Goldsborough, an eastern lawyer who had been in the territory for several years, was the only member of the commission who lacked previous experience in Indian relations.

Several of these men later concluded that the policy of treaty councils was a mistake. Benjamin Shaw argued that the United States in fact had the land and erred in letting the Indians think they were equal parties in decisions relating to land disposal. Stevens' thoughts on this question in December 1854 are not known, but his earlier statements would indicate that given a choice he would have dictated a policy that would speed settlement yet offer protection for the Indian. This hypothetical policy could not have brought worse results than the treaties; whether it would have produced a more favorable climate for Indian-white relationships is open to conjecture. A consistent policy largely under the supervison of one man (McLoughlin) had earlier produced an environment acceptable to whites and Indians, but although there were similarities between Stevens and McLoughlin, the territorial system was not the Hudson's Bay Company's style, the American settlers were not Company employees, and 1855 was not 1825. In any event, there was no alternative to the treaty process. It was fixed government policy, and Stevens realized that he would have to work within its framework. There was no question as to if or when the Indians would be brought under treaties; the only issue open to discussion was how.[18]

Drawing on their knowledge of the Puget Sound region, its tribes, and previous treaties, the commissioners adopted nine principles as guidelines: to concentrate the tribes as much as practicable; to encourage soil cultivation and other civilized habits; to pay for the land with annuities consisting of useful goods rather than cash; to furnish teachers, doctors, farmers, blacksmiths, and carpenters; to prohibit war between the tribes; to end slavery; to halt the liquor trade; to allow the Indians to hunt, fish, and gather berries until the civilizing process was complete; and, in time, to allow division of the reservation lands in severalty. It was an enlightened policy in that it allowed for a transition period and a process of gradual assimilation. The policy was, however, based on several assumptions that the commissioners erroneously accepted as truisms: that it was best for the Indians to be converted to the European way of life; that this transition could be accomplished by an economic shift from hunting and fishing to farming; that the federal government and its agents would faithfully provide the goods and services stipulated in the treaties; and that the Indian could be persuaded that all of the above were in his best interests.[19]

On Christmas Eve, Stevens arrived at the council ground, where the Nisqually and Puyallup bands had already assembled. Sidney S. Ford and Orrington Cushman, two settlers employed as assistant commissaries, had stocked the camp with beef, mutton, deer, elk, wild geese, ducks, and salmon—all of which gave evidence that the talks would be interrupted by abundant feasting. The next day Stevens, Doty, Shaw, Gibbs, Mason, and Lieutenant Slaughter assembled at a table in front of the governor's tent, and the Indians gathered in a semicircle before them. The other whites sat off to one side on campstools "as a small cloud of witnesses." The governor was dressed in a red flannel shirt with his pants tucked into the boots "California style," but as a concession to the Indians, who preferred that important people dress the part, he wore a dark frock coat and black felt hat with a clay pipe stuck in the band. After the treaty draft was read, the council adjourned until the next day, when the governor opened the proceedings with an address which became the prototype for many speeches during the next year. He informed the Indians that it was

a day of peace and friendship between you and the whites for all time to come. You are about to be paid for your lands, and the Great Father has sent me today to treat with you concerning the payment. The Great Father lives far off. He has many children—some of those children came here when he knew but little of them, or of the Indians, and he sent me to inquire into these things. We went through this country this last year, learned your numbers and saw your wants. We felt much for you, and went to the Great Father to tell him what we had seen. That Great Father felt for his children. He pitied them and he has sent me here today to express those feelings and to make a treaty for your benefit. The Great Father has many white children who come here, some to build mills, some to make farms, and some to fish. And the Great Father wishes you to have homes, pasture for your horses and fishing places. He wishes you to learn to farm and your children to go to a good school. And he now wants me to make a bargain with you, in which you will sell your lands and in return be provided with all these things. You will have certain lands set apart for your homes and receive yearly payments of blankets, axes, etc., all this is written down in this paper which will be read to you. If it is good you will sign it, and I will then send it to the Great Father. I think he will be pleased with it and say it is good. But if not, if he wishes it different, he will say so and send it back, and then if you agree to it, it is a fixed bargain and payment will be made.

This speech was translated into Chinook by Shaw and then re-translated into the Indian dialects by natives. Stevens asked, "Is it good? If it is good we will sign it; but if you dislike it, in any point, say so now." He promised a distribution of goods after the signing, and more the next summer, with any further distributions coming after approval of the treaty in Washington D.C. After a period of deliberation, the Indian representatives gave their assent. All the goods were passed out, but towards evening James Swan appeared with twenty-nine Indians and said twenty more were on the way. Satisfied that they had been delayed by rainy weather, the governor sent to Olympia for more presents for the latecomers. The council had taken only two days.[20]

Under the terms of the Treaty of Medicine Creek the whites gained the land bounded by the Cascade Mountains, Puget Sound, the present southern suburbs of Seattle and the Skookumchuck River. The Indians received three small reservations (each containing two sections or 1,280 acres) located at Squaxin Island at the south end of Puget Sound; an area south of Commencement Bay on the present site of Tacoma; and the Nisqually Flats. They were to move to the reservations within a year after ratification of the treaty or "sooner if the means are furnished them." The tribes retained the "right of taking fish, at all usual and accustomed grounds and stations . . . in common with all citizens of the Territory . . . together with the privilege of hunting, gathering roots and berries, and pasturing their horses on open and unclaimed lands." Payments for the land were spread over twenty years, decreasing gradually from $3,250 the first year to $1,000 each of the last five years—the money to be spent at the discretion of the President for items that would most benefit the tribes. In addition, a sum of $3,250 was allotted for the initial expenses of settlement and breaking the land. The President retained the authority "when the interests of the Territory may require, and the welfare of said Indians be promoted," to move them to another reserve if they were compensated for improvements and moving expenses. In addition to giving up the land the Indians agreed to eight other provisions: (1) their dependence upon the United States; (2) friendship with whites and other Indians; (3) delivery of lawbreakers to white authorities; (4) prohibition of the sale or use of liquor on the reservations; (5) deductions from annuities to pay for stolen property; (6) abolition of slavery; (7) prohibition of trade outside the United States; and (8) exclusion of foreign Indians from the reservations. The United States promised to maintain an agricultural and mechanical school in the Puget Sound region for twenty years. In common with other tribes on the Sound, there would be access to a farmer, a blacksmith, and a carpenter who would offer occupational instruction, as well as a physician who would provide free care and medicine. Leschi, Stahi, Quiemuth, and fifty-nine other chiefs and subchiefs joined nineteen whites in signing the treaty.[21]

Governor Stevens was pleased with the results of the Medicine Creek council. He had gained title to 2,500,000 acres in exchange for widely separated and concentrated reservation lands totalling 3,840 acres. Some of the chiefs had asked for more land during initial council sessions, but Stevens held firm and objections ceased. Stevens believed the reservations adequate because they were so situated that the Indians could hunt, fish, and participate in the "labor of the Sound." When the treaty was submitted to the federal government, Stevens emphasized the severalty provision which allowed an eventual break up of the reservations in favor of individual allotments. He believed this provision, along with the authority granted to the President to combine the reservations if necessary, would remove any objection to three separate reserves. The governor, in anticipation of objections to the allowance of payments for improvements, noted that such costs would be minimal as only the chief Quiemuth could have qualified at the time. Stevens also defended the Indians' right to continue fishing, hunting, and berry picking off the reservation. These activities could, he argued, allow the Indians to remain largely self-supporting and would not create any problem for the settlers. The governor noted, for example, that the Indians usually fished with spears in the deep water rather than using seines or weirs like white fishermen. He emphasized the importance of the training school and claimed that some Indians had asked him to include a compulsory apprentice system in the treaty. Stevens did not want to make the school compulsory, but he informed his superiors that the Sound Indians would become excellent artisans. To provide a doctor and medicine was, the governor said, "an act of simple justice since the disease resulted from their contact with the whites." Governor Stevens was later criticized for giving the Indians too little, but his primary fear as he concluded his first treaty was that the government would reject it because he had been overly generous.[22]

After the Medicine Creek council the commissioners met to discuss future policy before moving on to other council sites on

Puget Sound. The point which produced the most debate involved the number of reservations west of the Cascades. Simmons and Gibbs argued vigorously that different customs, languages, and the need for sufficient fishing stations dictated that they continue creation of numerous small reservations scattered about Puget Sound. Stevens recognized the validity of this position, but fresh in his mind was the explicit instruction from the Commissioner of Indian Affairs that the tribes be placed "on a limited number of districts in country apart from the settlement of whites." The Commissioner had suggested a maximum of six treaties for all the tribes in the Washington Superintendency. These orders and the specter of recent failures to ratify Oregon treaties overrode all other considerations in the governor's mind. He suggested that they make one more treaty with the remaining tribes on the Sound, but this was voted down with only Doty supporting the governor. "Considerable argument" followed as the governor received more opposition from his own commission than he had from the Nisqually or Puyallup Indians. In an attempt to reach a compromise between the Indian Bureau and his advisors, Stevens proposed one additional treaty with the Indians on the east side of the Sound and one with those on the west side. All agreed, and they also decided to locate one school, one hospital, and a training center for all the Puget Sound tribes. The Indians also were to be allowed fishing rights at accustomed places (in common with whites) as well as the use of unclaimed land for pasture.[23]

Stevens speculated that if the whole treaty program proceeded as smoothly as Medicine Creek, and if Congress acted promptly, the next year would find the Indians from the Missouri River to the Pacific at peace. He sent Doty to the east side of the Cascade Mountains to prepare the way for treaties in the spring, and he named Gibbs as the new secretary of the commission. As the new year began, the members of the team scattered through the Puget Sound region to bring the tribes on the east side of the Sound to the council scheduled for late January at Point Elliott.

The Point Elliott Council

The only sour note came from the Duwamish Indians, who insisted upon meeting on their land east of Seattle. Simmons and Gibbs concluded that "cultus [evil] whites" were exerting a bad influence on this tribe. The influence of half-breeds and disaffected whites upon Indian relations was nothing new in American history, but in the Northwest the long period of the fur trade and many years of miscegenation made this group one of unusual size and potential power. When the governor and his agents spoke of "cultus whites" they clearly had two groups in mind. One group consisted of French Canadians (who might have Indian blood or Indian wives) most of whom had been employed by the Hudson's Bay Company. To many Americans these men were doubly suspect because of their relationship with the British. Their power may have been exaggerated or their motives misread, but there is little doubt that many did have influence, even if it might have been only to the extent of spreading rumors among the tribes. Some half-breeds wished to prevent the Indians in Washington Territory from making the same mistake as other Indians who had signed treaties only to regret it later; others sought to increase their power and wealth. The second group consisted of liquor dealers who might or might not also belong to the first group. Their motivation was clearer: absence of a reservation system made it easier to ply their trade with a minimum of risk, and they worked to diminish the authority and credibility of territorial officials in order to keep a disorganized political and social system.

In mid-January many of the Indians began to gather at Point Elliott. The Snohomish and Snoqualmie Indians welcomed newcomers with impressive ceremony as they lined up on the beach in single file and greeted each man with the sign of the cross. After dark there was continuous singing and preaching, and George Gibbs commented, "They did very well as regards tune and in the open air their hymns or rather canticles have quite a good effect. The Indians are all at present in an exceedingly pious frame of mind and are evidently brushing up their religion for a grand display on the Governor's arrival." On January 17 the Duwamish Indians made their appearance, and four days later Stevens arrived. Gibbs drew up a draft incorporating the same general provisions as the Medicine Creek treaty with the reservations based on investigations Gibbs had made the previous week. Of 3,000 Indians covered by this treaty about 2,300 were on the treaty grounds; those missing were mainly children and old people—and the Nooksack Indians, who were not contacted because of cold weather and frozen rivers. On January 22 the council began with the four chiefs whom the whites considered most important seated in the front rank: Seattle (Duwamish League), Patkanim (Snoqualmie), Goliah (Skagit), and Chow-its-hoot (Lummi). The subchiefs were seated next and the rest were grouped behind without specific order. Stevens, as usual, opened the council with an address. He began, "My Children! You are not my children because you are the fruit of my loins, but because you are children for whom I have the same feeling as if you were the fruit of my loins. You are my children for whom I will strenuously labor all the days of my life until I shall be taken hence." The father-child analogy became a favorite with Stevens, and he stressed it in subsequent councils on the Sound. Whatever reactions the Indians may have had, it is the key to understanding Stevens' view of the Indians. He believed that they, like children, had not yet reached the status of adulthood with its rights and responsibilities, and that they needed care and guidance until they achieved full growth and maturity. He did not assume that they were inherently inferior, but that they had not yet reached the full potential of human development. Also, like children, they should obey their father— which meant that good behavior should be rewarded and bad conduct punished. As at Medicine Creek, Stevens carefully explained the desires of the "Great Father," the provisions of the treaty, and the necessity to send the treaty to the nation's capital for final approval before it could take effect.[24]

After the governor finished, each of the four chiefs spoke, and all indicated their approbation. The commissioners went through the treaty item by item, and before evening the document had been signed. The next morning the governor's men distributed presents while Chief Seattle in return presented a white flag to Stevens and declared, "Now by this we make friends and put away all bad feelings if we ever had any. We are the friends of the Americans. All the Indians are of the same mind. They look upon you as our father. We will never change our minds."

The Point No Point Council

Word arrived that the Indians across the Sound had gathered at Port Gamble. A heavy wind delayed Stevens' departure until the next morning, when the commissioners made the short sail across the Sound.[25] When the schooner dropped anchor at Point No Point, the governor sent for the Clallam, Skokomish, and Chimakum Indians at Port Gamble and announced that the council would begin the next day. January 25 dawned windy and threatening, but as all the expected Indians were present, Stevens decided to begin. He gave virtually the same address that he had delivered at Point Elliott, but in deference to the weather he cut the speech short and went on to the reading and explanation of the treaty. The governor then asked if any of the chiefs wished to speak, and to his surprise an old Skokomish chief, Che-lan-teh-tat, rose to deliver a brief, frank address.

I wish to speak my mind as to selling the land Great Chief! What shall we eat if we do so? Our only food is berries, deer, and salmon. Where then shall we find these. I don't want to sign away all my land. Take half of it and let us keep the rest. I am afraid that I shall become destitute and perish for want of food. I don't like the place you have chosen for us to live on. I am not ready to sign the paper.

A Toanhooch chief expressed fear that he would die if his band left the site of their traditional burying ground. This was the first opposition to the treaties.[26]

Another Skokomish chief raised the issue of land value when he claimed, "I do not want to sell my land because it is valuable. . . . Formerly the Indians slept but the whites came among them and woke them up and we now know that the lands are worth much." The commissioners replied that only labor and improvements made the land valuable and that the lands under consideration were poor at best. The Skokomish continued to list objections as they complained they did not want to live with the Clallams, who they disliked and who outnumbered them. Finally Jim, a Skokomish chief, bitterly exclaimed that most of the Indians were afraid to speak openly, but that he would tell the governor that he did not wish to sell his home or lands: "It makes me sick to leave it." At this point the Clallam chief, The Duke of York, came to the commissioners' rescue. Because he suffered from a pronounced stutter, the chief had his message spoken by one of his tribe. The Duke of York pointed to the increase in their material wealth since the arrival of the whites and indicated that he would approve the treaty if the governor would stop bad men from beating the Indians and driving them off the land. On this favorable note, Stevens adjourned until the next day with instructions to the Skokomish to discuss the treaty provisions in their councils.[27]

The next morning Stevens used the bright, clear day as an omen that the council would come to a favorable conclusion. He again stressed the father-child analogy insisting that he would care for the Indians as he did his own children. The Duke of York presented a white flag, followed by a Skokomish chief who announced that he had put aside the bad feelings of the previous day and was satisfied. All came forward to sign the document and the schooner fired a salute to commemorate the occasion. There is no complete explanation why the Indians who vigorously objected to the Point No Point treaty one day came forward the next day and signed with professions of complete satisfaction. Much the same thing would happen in future negotiations. Part of the answer derives from the ambivalence of many Indian leaders. They could agree with The Duke of York that the whites had brought certain goods and economic advances which they considered not only desirable but necessary. In addition, the power of the settlers and their government was evident to the Indians of the Puget Sound region, and white strength had been amply demonstrated on earlier occasions when there were difficulties between the races. Although the Indian chiefs did not like many of the treaty provisions, they probably knew that there was no alternative but to sign. Seattle and Patkanim believed it not only fruitless but bad policy to object, and they signed the documents with professions of amity. Others like the Skokomish wished to have their voices heard before they succumbed to the inevitable. If they signed, the good things that the governor predicted might come to pass; if the promises were false, at least good relations were assured for the immediate future, and any long range problems resulting from the treaties could be dealt with as they arose.[28]

To Governor Stevens the signed treaties became legal agreements binding both parties. In conducting the treaty sessions, he did not think it necessary to pay much heed to Indian complaints that traditional customs, habits, superstitions, or religious mores would be violated by the treaties. After all, the long-term consequence of the treaties, in Stevens' view, was to replace the traditional pattern of Indian life with the superior white civilization. There was no doubt in his mind that the Indians would have to sign and that it was in their best interest to sign. The treaties offered certain guarantees and protections—without the treaties they would be swallowed up by white settlement and would receive nothing in return. Stevens ran the treaty sessions as if he were a judge in a court of law. Though all had the opportunity to speak, to ask questions, and to demand explanations, and though there was room for minor modifications of the treaty drafts, the end result of the councils was inevitable.

In certain respects Stevens was a good choice as superintendent of Indian affairs: he was an efficient, hard-working, honest administrator. In his own words, he was a stern but just "father" to the Indians. However, despite Stevens' constant assertions to the contrary, the Indians were not his children, and he did not always understand (or try to appreciate) their desires—or their best interests. He was a father who interpreted his "children's" welfare as corresponding to his own. In many parental relationships this can be a serious flaw; for Stevens and the Indians of Washington Territory it was fatal.

Governor Stevens reluctantly modified his original intention to make only one treaty with the tribes west of Puget Sound because the Makahs and other bands living in the northwest corner of the Olympic peninsula would not make the long journey to Point No Point. The small schooner carrying the commissioners beat up the Strait of Juan de Fuca through foul weather and reached Neah Bay on the evening of January 28. Two days later the Makahs, their relatives from Tatoosh Island, and the Ozettes gathered on the schooner, and Stevens informally explained the purpose of his visit. The Indians expressed concern that they would be forced to abandon their fishing grounds and become farmers. Stevens assured them that he would provide fishing equipment and asked only that they share the whale fishery with whites. The next day they met formally in council to sign the treaty. A hitch occurred when Stevens insisted that one man be named head chief. The Indians refused, but when the governor named an Ozette as the official head of all the bands in the treaty area, apparently the chiefs concurred, albeit reluctantly. The commissioners then returned to Olympia where the governor paused briefly to attend to business that had accumulated from the legislative session.[29]

Most white citizens on the Sound approved of the whirlwind treaty negotiations of the governor. They remarked on the energy with which the treaties were pushed and observed that extinguishment of Indian title was "a consummation devoutly to be wished." The *Pioneer and Democrat* published a list of reservations that had been surveyed or were "defined by natural boundaries," and declared, "Information is given to the public, that settlers may take action accordingly in locating claims." Subsequent settlement caused de facto ratification of treaty boundaries even though Congressional approval of all but the Medicine Creek treaty was delayed until 1859.[30]

While the commissioners were active on the Sound, William Tappen, Indian agent for southwest Washington, attempted to prepare the Indians in that area for the next round of negotiations. Stevens stated his preference for one reservation in the vicinity of the Quinault River and a second somewhere on the

Columbia. Tappen was anything but encouraging; in his first report he declared, "Such a mass of drunken Indians, I never before saw." As time went on, he became more pessimistic. The Indians in that area had maintained close relationships with the whites for a number of years. Liquor flowed freely and numerous half-breeds worked to spread distrust and suspicion. Their work was made easier because the Columbia River Indians had been included in an earlier Oregon treaty rejected by Congress. (One rumor in general circulation held that the Indians who signed treaties would be put on a great ship which would deposit them on a barren island far out at sea.) As the time for the council drew near, the Chinooks refused to travel to the treaty grounds (near Gray's Harbor) protesting that it was too far, that they could not leave their families for so long a time, and that they did not wish to undergo the dangers of a canoe trip on the open sea.[31]

The governor moved ahead with his plan to bring all of the tribes in Southwest Washington under treaty. Tappen, who was blamed for the reluctance of the Chinooks, was eventually dismissed as incompetent. During the third week of February, Indians living along the coast began gathering on the Chehalis River a few miles from Gray's Harbor. James Swan escorted the Indians from Shoalwater Bay, and the indefatigable Benjamin Shaw persuaded some of the reluctant Chinook and Cowlitz Indians to attend. When the governor arrived on February 24, he found that most groups or tribes were represented.[32]

The council began as usual with the governor's speech and the explanation of the treaty, but, when given a chance to speak, the chiefs echoed the objections raised at Point No Point with greater persistence and determination. The most objectionable point was the combination of several tribes on one reservation. As the land picked belonged to the Quinaults, that tribe expressed their satisfaction and willingness to sign, but all others insisted they would not move and offered instead to sell the whites some land while they continued to live in their traditional localities. The council dragged on for three days and Stevens' patience began to wear thin as the successful conclusion he anticipated did not materialize. Particularly infuriating to the governor was Tleyuk, son of the Chehalis chief Carcowan, who was offended because he was not named a head chief. The Chehalis Indians disliked and mistrusted the Quinaults, and Tleyuk increased his standing by vigorously attacking the treaty, particularly the contemplated removal of his people to Quinault country. On the fourth day of the council, Carcowan made his appearance in a drunken condition. Stevens, having banned liquor from the council grounds, in a fit of anger seized the paper that declared Tleyuk a chief, ripped it to shreds, and adjourned the council. For the first time the governer went home with his mission unaccomplished.

Although the setback at Chehalis was regretted, Stevens regarded the Indians of Southwest Washington as relatively unimportant people, who could be brought under treaty at a later time. Michael Simmons did return to conclude treaties with the Quinault and Quillayute tribes in July, which Stevens signed in January 1856, but the Chehalis, Cowlitz, and Chinook Indians never signed a formal treaty.[33]

Stevens then turned his attention to the tribes east of the Cascade Mountains. Although circumstances east and west of the Cascades were not identical, sensitivity to the objections raised at the various councils in the west could have better prepared him for future negotiations. Naming chiefs to represent people over whom they could claim no authority, grouping incompatible tribes on one reservation, removal from traditional lands, and pressure to become farmers were features which rankled the Indians whether or not they accepted the treaties. The experience of the treaty commissioners on the Sound also should have indicated the complexity of the treaty process. The situation varied from tribe to tribe, but the commissioners attempted to apply essentially the same terms to all. Some of the Sound Indians were perfectly willing to sign the treaties. The Makahs, once assured that they could continue hunting whales, were happy to dispose of interior lands; anything that they received from the white governor would be an asset, and they gave up nothing useful in return. Most of the other tribes also were willing to agree to treaties if the terms appeared favorable. They resisted, however, when they were asked to give up much in return for promises which they believed might never be fulfilled. To Stevens the most important lesson of the Sound negotiations appeared to be that his methods and terms had been largely successful. He was convinced that the one failure had resulted from the personal treachery of Tleyuk and his father.

There is little doubt that some type of treaty system contained the only realistic alternative for the Indians in western Washington in the 1850s. It is even possible that Stevens' treaties, although containing features objectionable to the tribes, might have been reasonably successful if they had been faith-

fully and conscientiously administered. If Stevens had made administration of these treaties one of his primary objectives, and
if he had closed to settlement the area east of the Cascade
Mountains, war might have been prevented and needless tragedy averted. But Stevens was bent on constructing a vast new
American empire, and, without pausing to ruminate on the
Sound treaties, he rushed east of the mountains to add to the
kingdom.

AMID
FLUTTERING
PLUMES

Stevens was joined in the negotiations east of the Cascade Mountains by Joel Palmer, superintendent of Indian affairs for Oregon Territory. Both faced the special problem of assigning to a single jurisdiction tribes straddling the Washington-Oregon territorial boundary. A second problem involved the gathering of numerous widely separated tribes at one location at the same time. More important were the contrasts between the history and culture of the coast tribes and that of the interior Indians. The tribes of the Columbia Plain were more mobile and far-ranging, and the treaties would bring a sudden and dramatic change in their way of life. It was Stevens' task to convince them that this change was in their best interests.

Stevens had instructed George McClellan to establish friendly relations with tribes encountered during the course of the railroad survey. Accordingly McClellan consulted with the Yakima chiefs residing near the Oblate mission in the Yakima Valley. Although McClellan tried hard not to be overly impressed by anything he saw, he was forced to admit that the Yakimas were "very fine looking," particularly the tall, regal Kamiakin who appeared to be the most powerful leader. McClellan tended to exaggerate the chief's power for, like most whites, he thought in terms of European rulers who exercised absolute control over their people. This assumption led McClellan to instruct Kamiakin that it would be his responsibility to punish any Yakima Indian who harmed a white, just as he assured the chief that Stevens would bring bad whites to justice. Kamiakin's power was substantial, but McClellan did not know that it was based on allegiances that could shift or diminish as the circumstances of the moment might dictate. Other Yakimas such as Teias, Owhi,

and even Kamiakin's brother Skloom were ready at any opportunity to increase their power and prestige at the expense of
other leaders. Because Kamiakin's father was a Palouse Indian,
some Yakimas harbored a suppressed feeling of uneasiness as his
prestige grew. Jealousy and maneuvering among leaders was apparent in other tribes also, and these struggles had a significant
effect on the treaty negotiations.[1]

As Kamiakin listened, quiet and dignified, perhaps wearing
his long green coat covered with patches of varying hues,
McClellan explained his mission, the necessity for amity, and
the desire of the governor to discuss a treaty. He concluded by
offering some gifts as tokens of friendship. After pondering
McClellan's remarks, Kamiakin replied that the English had
told him that the Americans would one day come with a few
presents and then say that they had bought the land. Although
McClellan tried to reassure him, Kamiakin refused the presents
but sent the captain on his way with assurances of his friendship. McClellan told Stevens that he could rely on the chief
"far more than the generality of Indians." But if the captain
was satisfied by the meeting, the Yakimas were not, for McClellan's words offered proof that American settlers were on the
way. Although courteous and friendly, the Yakima chiefs had
let McClellan do the talking, and he had assumed that their silence (or nods and grunts) indicated approval. In fact the Yakimas wished information as they attempted to glean the truth
from the rumors they had heard. To that point the Yakimas,
like most other tribes in the Columbia Basin Plateau, had benefited from the white presence. Horses and cattle had made
leaders such as Kamiakin rich, and the general economic status
of the tribes had risen. At the same time their traditional lands,
fishing stations, and root and berry grounds had not been disturbed. The Indians did not wish to turn the clock back to the
pre-white period, but they did fear a sudden change in the status quo.[2]

In March 1854 Stevens appointed Andrew Bolon, who had
been a member of McClellan's party, to be the agent for the
tribes between the Cascade and Bitterroot mountains. Bolon was
to confer with the various tribes and prepare them for the treaty
councils. The governor instructed him to "throw the weight of
your influence in the scale of those chiefs who are best affected
towards the American government and people." Bolon was to
determine when fragments of tribes could be coalesced with
large bands; he also was to decide which chiefs were important

enough to receive commissions which would allow them to speak at the treaty councils. Stevens told his agent that any tribe resisting the laws of the territory would be broken up and payment for their lands disregarded. Stevens emphasized in his instructions that the United States was sovereign—and had been sovereign even before the treaty process began.[3]

Stevens picked Bolon because he was a frontiersman who had some familiarity with the territory east of the Cascade Mountains. Bolon, a powerfully built, athletic man with a full red beard, had a reputation for physical strength, honesty, and an appetite for hard work. His notoriety had been enhanced as the result of his having run a footrace against a horse a few months before. Still, Bolon was not a tactful man, and one of his acquaintances claimed he had "great contempt" for Indians. Bolon met with all of the Yakima chiefs except Kamiakin (who probably avoided the agent purposefully), and was able to gain the confidence of some chiefs whom he favored, though he antagonized others. Bolon's relationship with the Oblate fathers (Pandosy and D'Herbomez) was rancorous and, at the end of 1854, the priests' superior, Father A. M. Blanchet, demanded the agent's removal on the grounds that he had insulted the priests and the Indians while generally conducting himself in a manner not fit for a federal official. Stevens, harboring the suspicion that the priests were jealous of this secular intrusion into their domain, defended his agent, but promised to appoint a man experienced in Indian affairs to conduct an impartial investigation.[4]

The "impartial" observer was James Doty, whom the governor had sent east of the mountains upon conclusion of the Medicine Creek council. Doty, accompanied by Bolon, met with Teias and Kamiakin on April 1 at the Ahtanum Mission. Teias was friendly and agreeable, but Kamiakin was "silent or sulky." Doty decided not to mention the charges against Bolon, leaving it to the chiefs to complain of Bolon's presence or previous actions if they chose. They did not, and Doty dropped the investigation. Silence on the part of the two chiefs regarding Bolon prompted Stevens to assure the Commissioner of Indian Affairs that the priests' complaints were unfounded.[5]

Doty invited the leading chiefs to meet in his camp, but Kamiakin declined. Teias, Shumaway, and Skloom agreed to attend, and a messenger was sent for Owhi. The next day Kamiakin sat alone in a clump of willows near the camp while Doty waited with the other chiefs for Owhi. When Owhi arrived the next day, Kamiakin also came into camp to hear Doty explain the reservation system. Doty emphasized that whites could not enter a reservation without permission and that tribes could continue their traditional customs but that their children could learn reading, writing, and trade skills. Kamiakin repeated the concerns he had conveyed to McClellan regarding land payment, but he expressed relief when Doty assured him that all payments would be fair. Recalling that in the days of Lewis and Clark the Walla Walla Valley had been the traditional council ground, Kamiakin suggested that they meet there with the Nez Perce, Cayuse, Walla Walla, Palouse, and Okanogan Indians at a time set by the governor. The others endorsed this plan, and Doty offered presents—which Kamiakin rejected just as he had refused the gifts brought by McClellan. The next day Teias reappeared to tell Doty that he was not subservient to any man and would accept presents for himself and Owhi. Skloom and Shumaway, who had spent the night in Doty's camp, also accepted their share of the gifts.[6]

Doty immediately left for William Craig's farm (near Lapwai) to meet with the Nez Perce Indians. On April 18 about two hundred of the tribe, including most of the chiefs, gathered and raised an American flag (given to them during the Cayuse War) to the top of a large pine tree. Doty explained the purpose of the Walla Walla council, and they readily agreed to attend. As a result of these conferences, Doty suggested to the governor that he hold a grand council in the Walla Walla Valley (rather than two or three separate meetings in the Columbia Basin), followed by separate meetings with the Spokane and Blackfoot Indians to the north and east. He continued his pre-treaty negotiations with a visit to the Walla Walla chief, Peopeomoxmox, who was reluctant to commit himself but admitted that it would be better to sell for a good price than to wait until settlers came and receive nothing. Doty observed, "This is a shrewd old chief." After his talks, Doty was convinced that there would be no difficulty in arranging treaties if the Indians received fair payment for the land, adequate pasture for their stock, and the right to fish in accustomed places. He was correct, but he ignored other issues such as combining tribes on one reserve or moving Indians from traditional lands. For Doty, as for most whites, Indians were either friendly or hostile. But leaders like Kamiakin and Peopeomoxmox stood in the middle; they did not want hostilities, but they were skeptical of what the treaties would bring. They had decided only to attend.[7]

Stevens, satisfied with Doty's arrangements, announced as he left Olympia, "I confidently expect to accomplish the whole business, extinguishing the Indian title to every acre of land in the territory." The governor met Joel Palmer at Vancouver, and they traveled to The Dalles—where Stevens encountered his first opposition. It came from the United States Army, which did not assume that it was subject to Stevens' orders. Doty had earlier complained that army officers would not sell him supplies unless they received permission from the commanding general; more important, Major Rains was reluctant to send troops to the Walla Walla council ground. Stevens believed that troops were necessary as Doty had reported that the Cayuse and Walla Walla Indians might try to disrupt the proceedings. It was generally believed that their chiefs still sought revenge for the Cayuse War and that they were angered by encroachment on their lands in eastern Oregon. By the time Stevens arrived at The Dalles, tension had mounted as the result of incidents perpetrated by individuals on both sides. He ordered Bolon to bring in a number of white renegades who had been stealing Indian-owned horses and cattle, but he also insisted that the Cayuse were in a violent mood and that a show of force was necessary. He promised Major Rains, "The American flag will be raised on the treaty ground, and will never be pulled down except at the sacrifice of our lives, and those of our men."[8]

Rains relented and, as the force marched toward the council grounds, Stevens instructed Doty to prepare Chief Peopeomoxmox for the arrival of troops. The governor suggested that Doty employ a carrot-and-stick tactic by offering to make the chief head of both the Cayuse and Walla Walla and by threatening to treat all hostiles as "conquered people." Doty did not heed these suggestions, but he tried to persuade Peopeomoxmox that the troops were not a show of force, although it was clear to all that they were meant to be just that. Though Stevens boasted in a letter to the Commissioner of Indian Affairs, "There is scarcely a doubt that the negotiations will be successful," he knew that he faced a wide variety of moods ranging from the Nez Perce Indians who appeared to welcome the council to the Cayuse Indians who were openly hostile.[9]

The Walla Walla Council

Stevens and Palmer reached the treaty grounds (on Mill Creek not far from the old Whitman mission) on May 21 in a drenching rain. The camp included a special dining structure set up next to Stevens' tent for the chiefs. Nearby a rough pine table was placed under an arbor to shield the negotiators from the elements. Though tired and wet, Stevens held a meeting the first evening with Doty, Dr. Richard Lansdale (who was assisting Doty), Palmer, and Nathaniel Olney (Indian agent for eastern Oregon). The main subject for discussion, as it had been on the Sound, was consolidation of the tribes. Stevens asked how many reservations there should be, with what boundaries, and who would be assigned to each. For several days they debated these issues, often pausing to consult with the chiefs (and other whites).[10]

On May 24 the Nez Perce Indians made a grand entrance to the treaty grounds. The commissioners went out onto the prairie where a flagstaff carried the same banner used during Doty's earlier meeting with that tribe. Five or six hundred warriors filled the plain with a splash of color as they rode forward gaudily painted and decorated. "Their plumes fluttered about them, while below, skins and trinkets of all kinds of fantastic embellishments flaunted in the sunshine." They approached two abreast until Lawyer rode forward with two other chiefs to shake hands with the commissioners, followed by twenty-five lesser chiefs. The warriors wheeled by with drums beating, galloped to the white camp and then returned to the flagpole The younger warriors dismounted, danced around the commissioners, and then rode off while the headmen accompanied Stevens to his tent for a smoke.[11]

Two days later as many as four hundred Cayuse warriors made an equally impressive entrance, whooping and singing as they rode around the Nez Perce camp. One of the white onlookers ominously suggested it looked and sounded like a war party. The Cayuse chiefs came to Stevens' tent where they shook hands but refused to smoke or accept provisions, and Dr. Lansdale described their manner as "decidedly offish." Word arrived that the Palouse Indians would not attend, and Peopeomoxmox informed the commissioners that the Walla Walla and Yakima tribes would not accept any gifts or provisions during the council. The only encouraging news amid the continuing rain was a report that the Yakima Indians had reached the mouth of the Snake River and would arrive soon.[12]

The next day (Sunday), Stevens attended church services in the Nez Perce camp where Timothy, one of the chiefs, presided according to the Presbyterian forms once taught by Henry Spalding and the Lapwai missionaries. The failure of Peopeomoxmox to come into camp, as he had promised, as well as the thinly veiled hostility of the Cayuse Indians, disturbed Stevens to the extent that he held another meeting with the commissioners on Sunday evening. The next day prospects brightened. Peopeomoxmox (called Yellow Serpent by the whites) finally appeared and talked cordially with Stevens and Palmer. The chief expressed concern about the council interpreters, but he was assured that anyone he wished could be used. Peopeomoxmox complained that he had been unfairly associated with Cayuse hostility; he averred that he had always been friendly to the whites, denouncing as false any rumors to the contrary. The Yakimas also arrived, and, unexpectedly, so did some of the Palouse Indians. Kamiakin and Skloom appeared to be "moderately friendly" but reserved. Still, Dr. Lansdale believed that prospects for a treaty with any but the Nez Perce were "dull."

On May 29 the council formally convened with about 1,800 Indians present. Stevens named the interpreters, who included William Craig and Nathan Olney, and asked if there were any objections. Hearing none, Stevens, with great ceremony that was mainly for Peopeomoxmox's benefit, swore the interpreters to do their job well and faithfully. Rain precluded further negotiations that day; the governor adjourned the council, predicting that the next day would bring clear skies and dry ground.[13]

The council continued on May 30 under the clear skies forecast by Stevens. Stevens and Palmer sat on a bench under the arbor with the official reporters stationed at a table behind them. The Indians sat in the familiar semicircles facing the governor. After smoking for a half hour, Palmer introduced the governor, who spoke for more than two hours, much of that time spent in translation. Unlike his negotiations with the Sound tribes, Stevens did not come to the point quickly; rather he spoke in generalities in an attempt to ease tensions. He spoke of his earlier travels through their country and again expressed his gratitude for the many favors extended to the survey party the year before. Continuing with a review of Indian-white relations in the New World, Stevens concluded that whenever large numbers of Indians and whites occupied the same ground, friction developed. He also reviewed the removal policy and the beginning of the reservation system.[14]

The second day Stevens concluded his opening remarks, noting that whites had made a positive impact on the Indians by bringing horses, cattle, wheat, and potatoes. Palmer, following Stevens, gave his version of the history of Indian-white relations, admitting that the United States had made many mistakes, but blaming the lack of prosperity of some tribes on the Indians' failure to take advantage of opportunities. Palmer reserved his strongest criticism for half-breeds, accusing them of marrying Indian women and then running off with horses and cattle when it was advantageous. The Oregon superintendent's frank talk provided something to mull over as the council adjourned. A Cayuse chief complained that his young men were becoming restless from too much talk and asked that the next day be set aside for general feasting and games. The governor, though he believed that the Cayuse chiefs wanted the delay so that they could plan further strategy, reluctantly assented. On the feast day all the principal chiefs ate with the commissioners, a gesture they interpreted as favorable. But the final outcome remained in doubt. Dr. Lansdale's assessment of the prospects for the treaties shifted from "more favorable" on one day to "not so good" on the next.[15]

On June 2 Joel Palmer continued his aggressive tactics. The land was not made only for Indians, Palmer declared. The Indians could not stop the whites from coming, and the only hope for peace was the success of the council.

Peopeomoxmox was the first chief to reply to the commissioners. The chief was clearly impatient, complaining that he could not see the point of the speeches. It was as if there were a barrier between himself and the speakers. He hinted that he would like to get down to specifics and learn what the Indians would have to give up in return for the things promised. The Walla Walla chief ominously warned, "Goods and earth are not equal; goods are for using on the earth; I do not know where they have given land for goods."[16]

After another rest day on the Sabbath the bargaining process began in earnest on June 4. Chief Lawyer, in a long rambling speech, indicated that the Nez Perce Indians endorsed the words of the commissioners. The Yakimas, as throughout the negotiations, were reluctant to speak at the formal sessions, but Kamiakin briefly declared that he harbored suspicions of white intentions and was not very optimistic that right would be done. Peopeomoxmox, clearly disgusted with generalities, again turned to specifics. Where, he asked bluntly, were the lines? The commissioners had "not spoken of any particular ones." Stevens had purposely avoided making any specific proposals until he was able to gauge the mood of the chiefs. He realized by June 4 that many, perhaps most, were willing to negotiate, but the

words of Peopeomoxmox indicated that he would be faced by
some hard bargaining. Stevens explained that he had two land
reservations in mind. One was in the Nez Perce country running roughly from the Blue Mountains to the crest of the Bitterroots, and from the Palouse to the Grande Ronde rivers. On
this reserve the Spokane, Nez Perce, Walla Walla, Umatilla,
and Cayuse Indians would each have separate territories but
share the right to pastureland and the privilege of fishing at the
accustomed places. The second reservation was a triangular
piece of land bounded by the Ahtanum Creek on the south, the
crest of the Cascades on the west, and the Yakima River from
Snoqualmie Pass to the mouth of the Ahtanum. This reserve
would hold the Yakima, Palouse, and Klickitat Indians, and the
tribes on the Columbia as far as White Salmon. Stevens knew
that the proposal would please the Nez Perce and Yakima Indians whose support was essential for success, but he also realized that it was extremely unlikely that he could force the
Cayuse, Walla Walla, and Umatilla Indians to move to Nez
Perce country. But the proposal provided a bargaining position
from which he could begin, and the two reservation proposals
would protect him from potential criticism in Washington D.C.
if or when he was eventually forced to grant additional reserves.
Many of the chiefs were obviously displeased, and Stevens adjourned the council before they could reply.[17]

The next day the governor defended his proposal. A few large
reservations would allow the agents to afford better protection
from white encroachments than would be possible if there were
many scattered areas. Stevens dwelt on the benefits the treaties
would give to the chiefs personally, including houses, annual salaries, and the power to select the goods to fill tribal allotments.
One Cayuse chief replied that he would never leave the land of
his mother, but at this point the chiefs asked for adjournment
with a day's recess to further discuss the governor's proposals. It
was evident that all except the Nez Perce were unhappy. That
evening, when Lieutenant Kip and another officer tried to ride
into the Cayuse encampment, they were stopped by warriors
who roughly grabbed the horses' bridles. The officers continued
to press forward, "riding around Indians, where it was possible,
and at other times forcing our way through." Kip wondered, "If
. . . this hostile feeling at the Council increases, how long will it
be before we have an actual outbreak?"[18]

While the chiefs conferred on June 6, a messenger arrived in
camp with the disturbing news of extensive gold discoveries in

the Colville area. A successful conclusion of the council now seemed even more imperative to the commissioners. The session opened the next day in a tension-filled atmosphere. Stevens told the chiefs, "Let us have your hearts straight out." Chief Lawyer made another long speech in which he agreed with Chief Eagle from the Light (who had spoken earlier) that they had had problems with the whites and still retained some suspicions, but he concluded that the Nez Perce Indians were satisfied and would accept the treaty. The governor's proposal meant that they retained their traditional lands and possibly could benefit from other provisions in the document. (This assessment was correct until the discovery of gold in Nez Perce country in 1860—only one year after ratification of the treaty—negated their assumptions.)

Other chiefs were not so conciliatory. According to Doty the council became "somewhat stormy." Young Chief lamented that the earth and grass would protest if he sold, and Peopeomox-mox suggested that they adjourn again until a more favorable time. As the discussions continued it became apparent to Stevens that there were two major objections. The Cayuse, Walla Walla, and Umatilla Indians adamantly opposed the move to Nez Perce country, and many of the chiefs protested that the commissioners did not offer enough for the land. Chief Skloom told Stevens that Yakima garden lands, such as those near the Ahtanum mission, were worth eight hundred dollars a mile (a section of 640 acres) and uncultivated lands were worth forty dollars a mile. He concluded, "I have understood what you have said; when you give me what is just for my land you shall have it. That is all I have to say." In private conversations Kamiakin indicated that he agreed with his brother. Even Young Chief seemed to suggest that monetary terms were his major concern when he declared, "If I had the money in my hand then I would see [the treaty]." Another Cayuse chief complained that "poor lands" were offered in return for "fine lands." The chiefs' words indicated the extent to which Indian society had changed by 1855. Stevens was dealing, not with naïve primitives, but with Indian leaders who owned horses, cattle, and cultivated lands. The Walla Walla Council was a negotiating session between parties whose capacity to draw upon a common set of assumptions about the past and future was closer than often assumed. The eventful day ended with the dramatic appearance of the Nez Perce leader, Looking Glass, who had been absent three years hunting buffalo. Riding into the council ground, he exclaimed, "My people what have you done? While I was gone you sold my country."[19]

That evening produced furious negotiations. Stevens realized that compromise was necessary, and he made his best offer. He agreed to set aside a separate reservation in Oregon Territory for the Cayuse, Walla Walla, and Umatilla Indians with the funds initially allotted to the Nez Perce reservation divided into payments of $200,000 to the tribes on the Nez Perce reserve and $150,000 to those on the new reservation. The Yakima reservation would be restricted only to those who accepted the authority of that tribe, and they would receive $200,000. Stevens met the chiefs' major objections and sweetened the pot, but he also reminded them that the whites would be coming with or without the treaties. As Lansdale laconically noted, "All possible influences [were] made to operate . . . and a bargain was made."[20]

Internal power struggles became apparent the next day. Peopeomoxmox returned to the governor's tent and confirmed that he would sign no matter what effect the return of Looking Glass might have on the Nez Perce tribe. Stevens then chided Kamiakin that, even though he was said to be the most powerful chief, he refused to speak and represent the interests of his people. Kamiakin protested that Owhi, Skloom, and others were also leaders, but he finally asserted that he was indeed the head chief of the Yakima, Palouse, and related bands. Once he had openly laid claim to power, Kamiakin appeared to steel himself to make the decision he and the other Yakimas had avoided. He told Stevens, "Well let it be so. It is well. I will make the treaty as you wish." Kamiakin listed the tribes who would accept his authority and promised that once the reservation was established he would bring in his people who were scattered across the Northwest from the Willamette Valley to the upper Columbia. He added that when the President signed the paper, and they moved to the reservation, he would accept goods from the government. When the chief left, Doty predicted that none of the Yakima leaders would dare oppose Kamiakin's decisions.[21]

After his satisfactory talks with Peopeomoxmox and Kamiakin, Stevens reopened the council in a confident tone, announcing, "My friends, today we are all I trust of one mind." He explained the decisions made during the night and morning, described the new reservations and the payments, and concluded with the promise that they would not be called upon to move to the reserves for two or three years. At this point Stevens would have called for signatures except that Looking Glass had been promised a chance to speak, and, as Lansdale put it, he "kicked the fat into the fire." Looking Glass protested that he did not come to scatter the whites from their settlements and asked the same respect for his people. He proposed that the Nez Perce reserve be expanded west into the Walla Walla Valley. As Stevens debated with the chief he realized that one man might destroy all that had been accomplished by days of hard effort. Finally Looking Glass said the line satisfied him, and Stevens announced with a sigh of relief, "Looking Glass is satisfied." But the chief quickly dashed this hope by indicating the line referred to was his, not Stevens'. The Cayuse Indians, who had reluctantly accepted the acquiescence of Peopeomoxmox, then began to rally about Looking Glass. Young Chief declared that the head chief of the Nez Perce, Looking Glass, could draw the boundary line where he wished, and the Cayuse and some Nez Perce chiefs began talking of sending the treaty to the President for his signature before the Indians signed. In the midst of a speech by Looking Glass, Lawyer, who had remained silent, rose and left the council as a sign of contempt for his rival. Lawyer's followers sprang to his defense, insisting that he was the head chief and had been appointed the Nez Perce spokesman for the council. Stevens adjourned the session with the hope that during the evening Lawyer could subdue his rival in the struggle for power.[22]

While the Nez Perce Indians retired to their camp to continue their dispute, Peopeomoxmox, Kamiakin, Owhi, Skloom, and lesser chiefs remained to sign the treaties. The next day all observed the Sabbath, and when they convened on Monday it was clear that Lawyer had prevailed in the Nez Perce council. Apparently the interpretation that the Lawyer-Looking Glass quarrel was a prearranged ploy to improve the bargaining position of the tribe is incorrect. Looking Glass (the most powerful chief before his three-year buffalo hunt), hurt by his loss of status, used the treaty council as a forum to regain his preeminence. It is quite likely that if Lawyer had taken a position against the treaties, Looking Glass would still have opposed him. When the council reconvened Stevens quickly called upon Lawyer, "who all say is head chief," to sign the treaty before any further complications could arise. The chief signed, followed by Looking Glass and Joseph, and it was confirmed that Looking Glass had lost the struggle and had accepted his new station in the second rank. This left only the Cayuse Indians to sign, and they affixed their signatures reluctantly in the belief that they had no other alternative. Chief Eagle from the Light delivered a fitting benediction for the council: "The Lord will reward us both when our hearts are good [so] that we will look and care for each other."[23]

The three treaties signed at Walla Walla were nearly identical, and most of the main provisions corresponded to those in the Treaty of Medicine Creek. The Cayuse, Walla Walla, and Umatilla treaty provided houses and gardens for the head chiefs, with the same privileges extended to the son of Chief Peopeomoxmox. In the Yakima treaty the reservation remained the same size as originally proposed, but its boundaries extended south rather than north from Ahtanum Creek, and at Chief Kamiakin's request the Wenatshpam fishery was reserved for the tribe. Kamiakin was named as head chief of all parties to the Yakima treaty and received a salary of five hundred dollars a year, as did the head chiefs of the tribes named in the other two treaties. The only unusual provision in the Nez Perce treaty was the exclusion, at the tribe's request, of William Craig's claim from the reservation lands.[24]

Governor Stevens believed that he had achieved a great victory for the settlers, for the Indians, and for the cause of peace by successfully concluding the council. He wrote the Commissioner of Indian Affairs that the "effect on the peace of the country hardly admits of exaggeration," and Doty was equally convinced that the treaties were "absolutely necessary to prevent blood." Stevens seemingly had good reason to congratulate himself. Although technically he and Joel Palmer possessed equal power as co-commissioners, in fact Stevens was the moving force in the negotiations. Faced with hostility by the Cayuse Indians, and uncertainty among the other tribes, he had convinced all that the treaties were necessary. Assailed by hostile speeches, unexpected calamaties such as the arrival of Looking Glass, and indecisiveness on the part of many Indian leaders, he had remained calm and in control during the thirteen days of the council. Although the Cayuse Indians were still unhappy, Stevens expected that without Nez Perce or Yakima support they would do little to disrupt the peace.[25]

Both Stevens and Palmer had argued during the course of the council that a major reason for the treaties was the expected influx of settlers and miners east of the Cascade Mountains during the summer months. Stevens had recognized as early as the spring of 1854 that this could be a sticky point. He had instructed Andrew Bolon to make sure that the Indians under-

stood that the treaties would not go into effect until ratified in
Washington D.C. and suggested that he tell the chiefs that dur-
ing the interim they should "let whites settle if they wish."
Whether Bolon raised this point is not known, but it appears
that the issue was avoided during the official sessions at Walla
Walla.

Whites west of the Cascade Mountains had little doubt that
the treaties would open the land to immediate settlement. In
April 1855, as Stevens was making preparations to leave for the
council, the *Pioneer and Democrat* announced that, if the governor
were successful, the treaties would

open immediately a large scope of country to our stock raisers, wool growers,
and farmers, for settlement and cultivation. Many people, we understand, design removing there, the present season, from the west side of the Cascade
Mountains, and an important line will then be furnished in the chain connecting the settlements on the two sides of the mountains.

The final drafts of the treaties included a provision that the Indians would not move to the reservations until one year after
ratification, "guaranteeing, however, the right to all citizens of
the United States to enter upon and occupy as settlers any lands
not actually occupied and cultivated by said Indians at this
time, and not included in the reservation."[26]

By August some Willamette Valley farmers had already
moved east; it was predicted that 8,000 gold seekers would go
over the mountains before October; and at The Dalles there was
a call for a convention to establish political machinery for a
new county. At the same time a notice signed by Palmer and
Stevens appeared in Northwest newspapers announcing that the
ceded lands east of the Cascade Mountains were open to settlement. The official record of the council and subsequent events
indicate that these consequences were not made clear to the Indians, who came away from the council believing that the status
quo had been confirmed until the treaties were ratified and returned. Stevens either neglected to explain this point fully in
the negotiations during the final days of the council or, more
likely, he decided to slip quickly over this provision, fearing that
a full explanation might block Indian approval of the treaties.[27]

The optimism that pervaded the treaty commissioners at the
end of the council was understandable as it appeared that only
the Cayuse Indians were still dissatisfied. Peopeomoxmox had
proved to the whites that he was a hard bargainer, but also a
statesman and a powerful force for peace between the races.

The good will of the Nez Perce had been amply demonstrated. The position of the Yakimas had changed very little since the time they had conferred with George McClellan in 1853. They were suspicious, but they were willing to accept the treaties if the whites followed their good words with equally good actions. Stevens' mistake was to assume that the council was the last, rather than the first, step toward peaceful relations. Most important was the need to keep settlers and miners west of the mountains. It would not have been possible to keep all whites out of eastern Washington, but strong warnings by the governor and emphasis on negative news from the mining areas could have discouraged many. Another important provision would have been to prescribe one route, guarded by army troops, for miners who did come east.

Within three days after the treaties were signed the Indians had scattered, and Joel Palmer, with the Oregon commissioners, had returned to the Willamette Valley. The Oregon superintendent had been invited by the commissioner of Indian affairs to join Stevens and Alfred Cumming at the Blackfoot council, but Palmer was not enthusiastic about a long trip to treat with Indians far from his jurisdiction, and, pleading that affairs at home needed attention, he took his leave. Stevens did not reflect on the completed council but immediately plunged into the details of organizing men and supplies for the journey across the mountains to the Blackfoot country. Concerned that he would not arrive at Fort Benton by the appointed time in midsummer, Stevens postponed the Spokane and Colville treaties until the return journey in the fall. He assigned Bolon to stay behind to gather supplies for the Spokane council and to make a reconnaissance of the Yakima reservation to ascertain its capability for sustaining additional tribes in the future.

As the governor made preparations at his usual frenetic pace, Dr. Lansdale, who was not accustomed to Stevens' methods, complained that he was not only arbitrary, "which is necessary at times, but also tyrannical which is not." On June 16 the governor moved out of the Walla Walla Valley accompanied by Hazard, Doty, Lansdale, Gustavus Sohon, C. P. Higgins (the head packmaster), fifteen teamsters, and two Indian guides. To save the mules, many of which had been with the railroad survey parties, they traveled only from midmorning to midafternoon, which allowed more time for the animals to graze. The party followed the Palouse River east to Camas Prairie and then headed north to the Coeur d'Alene mission. Stevens and

Doty, as usual, made careful observations of the geography along the route.[28]

On June 25 they reached Father Ravalli's mission, where Stevens talked briefly with Coeur d'Alene chiefs explaining his intention to hold a council with the Coeur d'Alene, Spokane, Colville, and Okanogan Indians in September. They agreed and accepted presents but demurred when the governor asked them to accompany him to the Blackfoot Council. Their long-standing fear of the eastern tribes could not be overcome by Stevens' promise to provide protection.

The Flathead Council

On July 7 Stevens reached the camp of the Flathead, Upper Pend d'Oreille, and Kutenai Indians (located near Hell Gate). Three hundred warriors rode out to greet the party, firing salutes and shaking hands all around. Stevens went into camp nearby.

Thomas Adams, who came west with the railroad survey, had been appointed by the governor as temporary Indian agent for the tribes east of the Bitterroots with his headquarters at Fort Owen. The Flathead tribe was located in the Bitterroot Valley near Fort Owen whereas the other three tribes lived to the north (the Kutenai on Flathead River and the shores of Flathead Lake and the two bands of Pend d'Oreille south of the lake on the Jocko and Clark Fork rivers). He had managed to bring three of the tribes together, but the fourth, the Lower Pend d'Oreille, was on a hunt with their head chief, Victor, who had refused to come in. Although Doty and Adams were familiar with these Indians, Stevens was not. When the governor met the Flathead chief (also named Victor) in 1853, he had dismissed him as "rather wanting in energy." Stevens thought the Flathead Indians were "very poor", and predicted that, as they relied primarily upon hunting, their main source of sustenance would likely be severely diminished in the near future. Stevens believed that they could be saved in the short run by negotiating with the Blackfoot Indians to allow them safe hunting in the buffalo country east of the Rockies; and in the long run he hoped they could be taught to be farmers or herders. Stevens met informally with the Flathead Chief Victor and stressed the necessity of peace with the Blackfoot Indians, which could be guaranteed only through the proposed treaties. Stevens believed that the prospect of intertribal peace would be a primary treaty negotiating point for the tribes at Hell Gate.[29]

After the usual day of rest on Sunday, the council opened officially on July 9 with Victor (Flathead), Alexander (Upper Pend d'Oreille), and Michelle (Kutenai) the primary spokesmen for their tribes. Stevens reviewed the Walla Walla treaties, which were already known to representatives of the Flathead tribe who had attended as observers. It was later suggested that the governor should not have mentioned Walla Walla, but to him there seemed no reason not to; it was only later that the Indians became critical of that council. Stevens then reviewed the proposed treaty, taking care to point out that missionaries would be allowed on the reservation only with Indian permission—this in deference to alleged Flathead antipathy toward priests.

Immediate controversy erupted over the provision for a common reservation for the four tribes. Chief Alexander said that they were well satisfied with the priests, that they had their own laws and way of life, and that they were not anxious to move from their lands. Flathead Chief Red Wolf was even more direct, asserting that he would have no part of the talk about a common reservation. The governor was somewhat surprised by the heat of the opposition, and he adjourned the council with his usual admonition to the Indians to discuss the proposals during the evening.[30]

By the third day Stevens was rapidly losing patience. He was anxious to consolidate these tribes, whom he considered relatively unimportant, on a single reservation and to move on to the Blackfoot council. When Chief Alexander insisted on land near the Jesuit mission in the Flathead Valley, the governor lectured the chief on the virtues of the Bitterroot Valley. Stevens fumed, "The agent [Adams] had examined both places; do you know about farms? The agent does. The [Bitterroot] valley is much the best land." Though he was determined to come to an agreement that day, he adjourned the council for two hours to let the chiefs reach a decision. But when they reconvened, Chiefs Alexander and Victor stated that they would not object to other tribes moving onto their land, but that they would not leave their traditional homes. The governor was forced to adjourn without an agreement. Stevens seethed at this impasse. The tribes gathered at Hell Gate appeared weak and unimportant compared to the Yakima, Nez Perce, or Blackfoot Indians, and he expected them to fall into line.[31]

As Stevens tried to ascertain why the chiefs were proving so recalcitrant, it occurred to him that the Jesuits might be the

logical villains. He had always been suspicious of the relationship of the Catholic priests with the Indians, although he at
times gave the fathers (such as Ravalli) credit for civilizing the
Indians with whom they labored. At the Walla Walla council
he had tolerated the presence of two priests because they put
their stamp of approval on the treaties. Father Adrian Hoecken,
a Jesuit stationed at St. Ignatius, had traveled to Hell Gate, but
left when Stevens did not arrive by the expected date. He was
needed at his mission as it had been moved only recently from
Clark Fork (on the west side of Lake Pend d'Oreille) to a new
location on the Flathead River. In addition, the priests were
fighting cholera that still persisted after the great outbreak of
1853. When Stevens arrived at Hell Gate, he asked Hoecken to
return, but the harried father was slow to respond. Stevens concluded that the Jesuit had influenced the Indians against the
treaty and was continuing to indicate disapproval by remaining
absent from the council. The governor curtly wrote to Hoecken
that he had earlier requested his presence, but now, "[I] require
you to come." He then declared a day of feasting and rest to allow time for the Jesuit to return.[32]

Stevens had misinterpreted the intentions of Hoecken, although it was true that the missionaries often harbored mixed
emotions toward the treaties. They believed that it was not their
business to involve themselves in secular matters by endorsing or
condemning the actions of the government. But some involvement was inevitable; the religious and the secular could
not be separated easily. However, there is no evidence that
Hoecken influenced the tribes against the treaty, and, once the
conference concluded, Stevens admitted that the father in fact
had been a positive influence.

When Hoecken arrived, Stevens again described the treaty in
detail and offered to place the reservation in the Flathead Valley with the land extending from the Flathead River to the
Rocky Mountains, but he continued to insist on one reservation
because "These are the terms of the government." Chief Alexander protested that the area was too small, and he blistered Stevens for talking "like a Blackfoot." Stevens shot back that Alexander had gone back on his word by first agreeing to the
Flathead reservation and then changing his mind. The chief patiently explained that he had agreed to the general area but
had not known the specific boundaries. Chief Victor then broke
in to point out that regardless of what Alexander had said, the
Flatheads had not agreed to that reservation. The governor be-

came angry and attempted to humiliate Victor by calling him an old woman who was "dumb as a dog." Flathead Chief Ambrose tried to calm Stevens by suggesting that if they continued to talk peacefully, they might work something out. Ambrose made a long speech in which he defended the treaty and concluded, "I say to the white chief, don't get angry, maybe it will come all right." Somewhat mollified, Stevens agreed that Ambrose was right; they would continue to talk.[33]

After a recess of two days they met again on Monday, July 16. Victor indicated that he had not changed his mind, and he reasserted his right to all the land. He suggested that the Great Chief of the whites might come and look at the reservations. The governor quickly seized on Victor's comment and asked the other chiefs if they would agree to let the Great Father look at the Bitterroot and Flathead valleys and decide on a reservation. Alexander demurred that the Lower Pend d'Oreille might not agree, but Stevens said he would talk with them later. The chief then insisted that he would not leave the Flathead Valley near the St. Ignatius mission. Stevens made a counter offer—let the Upper Pend d'Oreille and Kutenai tribes settle permanently in the Flathead Valley, and let Victor go there temporarily; then, after the President looked at the land, the Flathead tribe could either stay or move back to the Bitterroot Valley as the Great Father thought best. The governor had this provision written into the treaty, and the chiefs agreed to sign. The Flathead council had finally ended, and a relieved governor could hasten to the main business at Fort Benton.[34]

Charges that Governor Stevens was impatient, arbitrary, and untruthful have more validity for the Flathead council than they do for previous negotiations. For example, at the Walla Walla council Lieutenant Kip marveled that the governor's patience had not been utterly exhausted. Stevens could be firm, cajoling, stern, or angry, depending on circumstances, but he was always in control of his emotions until the Flathead council. The delays at Walla Walla, and then the recalcitrance of the Flathead and Upper Pend d'Oreille chiefs, led him to believe that the capstone to his treaty efforts, the Blackfoot council, would be sabotaged by his late arrival. Stevens convinced himself that two small tribes endangered the whole treaty structure. This belief led him to lash out in personal attacks, and finally to resort to deception to win the approval of the chiefs. He rationalized that the treaties were in the best interest of the tribes, and that the Pend d'Oreille and Flathead Indians eventually

would be grateful for his efforts. As Stevens left the Flathead
council grounds, he boasted that 11,300 of 15,000 Indians in his
jurisdiction were under treaties.[35]

The Blackfoot Council

The governor traveled rapidly over the mountains via Lewis
and Clark Pass to arrive at Fort Benton on July 26. He was astonished to find no evidence of Commissioner Cumming or the
supplies that were being shipped up the Missouri from St.
Louis. His furious drive to arrive on time was unnecessary and
made his impatience appear absurd. An angry Stevens started
down the Missouri River and on August 15 met Alfred Cumming at the mouth of the Milk River. His fellow commissioner
explained that the American Fur Company boat had discharged
the goods at Fort Union, and men were laboriously towing the
supplies upriver on flatboats. Stevens chastised Cumming for
not dispatching the goods earlier or for not forcing the fur company to send their boat on to Fort Benton. He pointedly reminded Cumming of his earlier warning to hire a special boat
rather than relying on the fur company. But the American Fur
Company had been employed, not because of a conspiracy, as
Hazard Stevens later charged, but because it was the cheapest
alternative. The governor urged that a work party be sent back
to hurry one of the boats along, but Cumming, who claimed the
goods were his sole responsibility, refused to sanction the plan.
This left the whites and Indians who had gathered near Fort
Benton seriously short of food. All that remained in the fort was
some jerked meat, left by the survey party two years earlier,
which was so hard that it was chopped out of the parfleches
with axes. The governor sent a party, which included Hazard,
to the Judith River to hunt buffalo, and he instructed the tribes
to scatter in search of food until the supplies arrived. He then
set up a complex messenger system to keep the Indians informed of events. William Tappen, camped with the Nez Perce,
Flathead, and Pend d'Oreille representatives who had agreed to
observe the council, found it difficult to keep them from returning home to lay in supplies for the winter. Thomas Adams was
sent to find the Crow Indians, whom the commissioners had be-
latedly decided to include in the council, but he returned without making contact.[36]

The relationship between Stevens and his co-commissioner
went from bad to worse. Alfred Cumming was the son of a politically and socially prominent Georgia family and had served

as mayor of Augusta. At the time of the Blackfoot council he was fifty-two years old, portly, white-headed, cultured, "refined," and "pompous in manner and jealous of his personal authority." When the supply boat finally arrived at Fort Benton, Stevens distributed the liquor to the men in his party, and for the next few days the fort was a scene of "fighting, cursing, and general uproar." Cumming was furious and accused the governor of acting irresponsibly, but Stevens responded that his party had been engaged in continuous, arduous duty since April and deserved an opportunity to let off steam.[37]

The delay of the goods gave Stevens an opportunity to reflect on the upcoming treaty, a luxury that had not been possible prior to the Flathead negotiations. He took issue with certain of the instructions from the Commissioner of Indian Affairs, such as a maximum allocation of $500,000 to the Blackfoot, Piegan, Blood, and Gros Ventre tribes. Stevens pointed out that this would average less than fifty dollars per person for the more than ten thousand natives whereas the Walla Walla treaties allowed two hundred to two hundred fifty dollars for each individual, and Joel Palmer had made at least one treaty in the Willamette Valley that provided over three hundred dollars. The governor also wanted a revision of expenditures so that in the first years most of the annuity would go for food and farm implements. Later, as herds and farms were developed, there could be a shift of funds to schools and similar cultural objectives. Stevens developed a detailed plan with a total expenditure of $750,000 which, he insisted, would best "fit them for civilized life." Stevens was convinced that all the tribes were capable of eventual assimilation, but he was certain that the Blackfoot Indians in particular had the necessary qualities to become citizens. He admired them for their character in keeping the promises made in 1853, and he was determined that their good faith should not go unrewarded. Cumming did not share this view; he believed the Blackfoot Indians were barbarians who required isolation from whites and other Indians. When Cumming argued that they were incurably bloodthirsty, Stevens rejoined that in the previous ten years they had killed no whites within their territory.[38]

The commission formed to conduct the Blackfoot council met almost daily from August 24 through the first week in October. Most meetings consisted of wrangles over proper Indian policy, council procedures, reservation boundaries, use of interpreters, and the respective power of the two commissioners. They discovered they could not agree on virtually any point. Finally, in early October, Cumming acquiesced to Stevens' plan to speed the council by moving to the mouth of the Judith River. The goods eventually arrived at that point, the Indians were brought in, and the proceedings began on October 16. About thirty-five hundred Indians were present including representatives of the Blackfoot, Cree, Nez Perce, Flathead, Kutenai, and Pend d'Oreille tribes.

Stevens emphasized that the theme of the council was peace between all the tribes, but he then dispensed with the usual oratory and got quickly to the treaty provisions. All went smoothly until the governor reached the point defining the buffalo areas open to the western tribes. At the insistence of the Blackfoot Indians, the region around Three Buttes had been reserved for their tribe, but other areas were unrestricted. Alexander (Pend d'Oreille) was immediately on his feet protesting bitterly that Stevens had promised at the Flathead Council that all the buffalo grounds would be open. Lame Bull, the Piegan chief, blandly replied that his people were not imposing conditions upon anyone, but merely agreeing to the whites' proposal. It appeared that another bitter, protracted council was at hand.[39]

But the next day an amicable agreement was quickly reached. Stevens persuaded the Blackfoot chiefs to grant the western tribes the right to come down the Musselshell as far as the Yellowstone in their search for buffalo as well as retaining the right to hunt on the east slopes of the Rocky Mountains except in the Three Buttes area. The western tribes agreed to this compromise. Stevens explained the rest of the treaty, and when he finished, Three Feathers (Nez Perce) asked the Blackfoot Indians to "show their hearts" as the western tribes had done at earlier councils and pledge that they were for peace. This the Blackfoot chiefs did, and the only remaining concern was the future conduct of the absent Crow Indians. Ironically, the treaty that Stevens had fretted over since 1853 had been the least difficult to conclude; his most serious disputes had been with Cumming. The treaty provided for peace and amity between the signing tribes and allowed all to hunt on a common ground extending south from a line drawn ten miles north of the Musselshell River. Below this line the Blackfoot chiefs agreed not to establish any permanent villages. The Blackfoot tribe received a guarantee of $350,000 over a ten-year period, with the provision that an additional $150,000 would be expended if necessary. Stevens had argued for salaries for the chiefs as well as higher annuities, but Cumming vetoed both.[40]

Although Stevens was furious that Cumming had blocked certain of his efforts on behalf of the Blackfoot Indians, he was enormously pleased that his long-sought-for objective of bringing peace to the northern Rockies had been consummated. The provisions of the treaty were adhered to during the ensuing months despite the pressures that war in Yakima country placed on the peace. For several years it appeared that the goals Stevens sought were being realized. The agent from 1857 to 1861, Major Alfred Vaughan, worked hard for the benefit of the Indians in his charge. He distributed the yearly allotments honestly and fairly, although he complained that some of the goods were shoddy and others were of no use to the Indians. Vaughan attempted to establish farming in the Sun River Valley, where he found a convert in Little Dog, a Piegan chief who had met Stevens in 1853. Although both the Blackfoot Indians and their western neighbors tried to keep the peace, incidents did occur. Some chiefs had pointed out during the treaty council that it often was easier for the old chiefs to agree to peace than it was to keep the young warriors in check. But until the Civil War the spirit of the treaty was maintained. After this time various factors—including the war, gold discoveries, and agents less capable or honest than Vaughan—began to destroy the treaty.[41]

As Stevens left the Judith River for Spokane country (and the final projected treaty), he was satisfied that his negotiations had succeeded even beyond his own optimistic predictions. In a period of ten months he had brought the majority of Indians living between Sioux territory and the Pacific coast under treaties, and in the process he had opened thousands of square miles to settlement. Stevens believed that he had stayed sufficiently within the guidelines set by the Bureau of Indian Affairs and that ratification would not be a problem. The Indian reaction to his proposals had run the gamut from wholehearted approval to outright rejection. But, for the most part, he thought that the chiefs considered the treaties necessary and beneficial for their people. Stevens could rationalize that the Indians who had been most hostile were those of whom he had never held a very high opinion. On the other hand, the Blackfoot and Nez Perce chiefs had proved as staunch as he had predicted. The Chehalis, Cayuse, and Pend d'Oreille Indians, in Stevens' opinion, ultimately would be forced to conform.

Though Stevens' treaties of 1854–55 gave every indication of general success, unfortunately they became negative symbols for both whites and Indians. Stevens and other whites believed that the Indians could not be relied upon to keep their word, and the Indians believed the eventual breakdown of the treaties proved white treachery. Perhaps the greatest tragedy was that Stevens might have stabilized Indian-white relations in the Northwest. Certainly he abundantly possessed the energy and the persistence to do so. But he allowed his dogged determination to obscure reality. As a result, the treaties did not bring peace to the territory, but instead provided a stimulus for further hostilities.

BROKEN
FAITH OR
BROKEN
PROMISES?

The murder of Andrew Bolon on September 23, while Stevens was still in Blackfoot country, was the catalyst that shattered the fragile relationship between the Indians and whites in the Northwest. Many whites believed that an Indian conspiracy had existed to drive them out of the territory. Some thought a plot was set in motion after the Walla Walla council, while others placed it earlier at any one of several dates in the 1850s. Like many historical interpretations which rely on a conspiracy theory, this view of the Indian war of 1855–56 is misleading. Like rumors of gold, reports of Indian uprisings and the fear of war were rife on the frontier. It was exceedingly difficult for citizen, soldier, or politician to know when to give credence to the reports and when to dismiss them as idle gossip. Just prior to the Walla Walla council, Indian Agent Michael Simmons complained that he was being called constantly to investigate alleged incidents which proved to have little or no foundation. He observed that rumors "spread rapidly among whites relative to Indian matters." Rumors aside, although some Indian leaders were apprehensive during the summer of 1855, there is no evidence that their uneasiness was substantially greater than in previous years. A council of representatives from various tribes met in the Grande Ronde Valley after the Walla Walla council, but the Indians could come to no agreement on a course of action because opinions varied so greatly. If anything, the Walla Walla treaties had further divided the tribes east of the Cascade Mountains rather than bringing them together in a grand anti-white alliance.[1]

The whites placed the major share of blame for the supposed conspiracy upon the Yakima Indians—specifically Kamiakin.

But, just as the chief was pressured by circumstances to decide
for or against the 1855 treaty (when he preferred to forego a decision), so was he forced into a war that he wished to avoid.
During the summer of 1855 the prominent Yakima chiefs did
not advocate war, and Skloom claimed that he spoke for peace
at the Grande Ronde council. But the steady stream of miners
going to the Colville gold fields placed pressure on the chiefs
and sorely tempted many of the young warriors. Most prominent and active of the younger generation was Qualchan, son of
Owhi, who led attacks upon at least two groups of miners. Henry Matisse and two companions were killed after crossing Snoqualmie Pass, and a short time later five men were murdered
near the juncture of Wenas Creek and the Yakima River. The
chiefs neither condoned nor condemned these murders, but
whites who had traveled through the Yakima country warned
prospective miners that they took a serious risk if they attempted to reach Colville.

The reaction of whites on the Sound to these incidents was
subdued even when the eight deaths were confirmed. Murders
were not unusual in the wilderness, and most recognized that
small parties traveling through Indian country faced potential
danger. Virtually no one at this time gave credence to the notion that a vast Indian outbreak was imminent. After all, hundreds of men had traveled between the Sound and Colville, and
only two incidents had occurred. There were rumors reporting
that Governor Stevens' party, or the detachment under the command of Major Granville Haller sent to protect the Oregon
Trail, had been massacred. The *Pioneer and Democrat* reported the
current gossip but gave scant notice to the tales. As fall approached, the stream of miners slowed—not because of fear of
Indians but because of discouraging news from the mines. Reports of a new Eldorado had been greatly exaggerated. Despite
the absence of the governor, the gold discoveries, the movement
of a few settlers into the Walla Walla Valley, and the death of
Matisse and the other miners, it appeared by mid-September
that there would be no serious Indian difficulties. The citizens
of the territory prepared for another winter by complaining
about dull economic prospects and wondering why most of the
emigrants again had gone to California. George Gibbs, a shrewd
observer of the Indians, predicted that an outbreak of hostilities
would not occur except through "great mismanagement."[2]

Bolon's death dramatically altered this situation. Adhering to
Stevens' orders, Bolon had spent the summer in Yakima country

until September when he rode to The Dalles to gather supplies for his rendezvous with the governor's party on the Spokane River. When he heard of the miners' deaths, he altered his plans and returned to the Yakima country in an attempt to prevent further bloodshed. Bolon left The Dalles on September 20. At Toppenish Creek he met Shumaway (Kamiakin's younger brother), a man with whom Bolon had a good relationship. Shumaway urged Bolon to turn back because at that moment Qualchan's band was out for blood and no white was safe. Though relieved by the report that only one Yakima band was on the warpath, Bolon took Shumaway's advice and turned back, after a brief stop at the Ahtanum mission. While on the trail he encountered Moshell, the son of Shumaway, with two companions, who were also headed toward The Dalles, reportedly to trade. Bolon knew and trusted them and rode along with them toward their common destination. Unbeknown to Bolon, Moshell was jealous of the reputation that his peer and potential rival Qualchan was acquiring by his exploits. To kill an important white would give him as much prestige as Qualchan. Moshell gained the support of his friends, and, when Bolon stopped to rest, he was seized from behind by one man while another cut his throat. They then killed Bolon's horse and took his gun and saddle bags back to the Toppenish Valley.[3]

Shumaway cried in shame when he heard that his son had killed a friend. At a tribal council Shumaway argued that his son and his friends should be turned over to white authorities, but the other chiefs, although also expressing shame at the murder, refused to consign the young men to certain death. That decided, the chiefs correctly predicted a vengeful reaction on the part of the whites. The *Pioneer and Democrat* spoke for most when it condemned Indians who violated treaties and killed agents assigned to them; the editor concluded that there was only one recourse—"the extreme measure." The citizens on Puget Sound now suddenly assumed that the rumors of an Indian conspiracy were correct, and that the ringleaders were the Yakima chiefs under Kamiakin's leadership. Thus Kamiakin, who had sensed trouble long before the Walla Walla council, unfairly was made the symbol of the so-called "Yakima War."[4]

In 1855 the United States Army's Department of the Pacific stretched from Mexico to Canada and from Utah to the Pacific Ocean. Organized after the Mexican War, it was, as General Wool often said, a "veritable empire." But the empire contained only a scattering of white settlers concentrated in California, the

Willamette Valley, and in the vicinity of Great Salt Lake. No
more than a thousand soldiers (mostly infantry) were assigned
for their protection against an Indian population far superior in
numbers, more or less evenly distributed throughout. Brevet
Major General John E. Wool, the second-ranking officer in the
army, took command of the department in 1854. Wool, a self-
educated native of New York State, began his army career at
the outbreak of the War of 1812. He raised a company in Troy,
received a captain's commission, served gallantly, and was severely wounded. Wool decided on an army career and quickly
climbed in rank and esteem. He received the brevet rank of
brigadier general in 1826. In 1836 Wool was named to supervise
the removal of the Cherokee to their new home across the Mississippi. Wool attempted to protect the Cherokee, but he also
wanted to convince them to obey the government's order to
move. His position as a mediator resulted in his condemnation
by a number of militia leaders, and politicians from several
states. The political pressure eventually resulted in a court martial which cleared him of all charges. There is little doubt that
these events, though they had occurred nearly two decades earlier, were still fresh in Wool's mind when he was faced with the
Yakima War.[5]

Although he was seventy years old in 1854, Wool remained a
vigorous, capable officer—apparently the logical choice for the
large, politically sensitive Department of the Pacific. He proved
to be capable of running the huge department with as much efficiency as circumstances allowed, but he was less suited to
handle political problems. Thoroughly professional, completely
honest, and imbued with a sense of public service, Wool believed that the army was in the best position to deal with various
problems caused by American expansion. The general would
brook no interference from outside sources—which included
state, territorial, and local officials within his broadly conceived
sphere of influence. In addition he held a high opinion of his
moral infallability, which at times led him to ignore or question
the motives of others. His critics (there were many) called him
pompous and arrogant. But criticism did not deter Wool. He
was not concerned with public relations; he would do his duty
as he saw it, whatever the objections or ultimate consequences.

When General Wool arrived at Benicia (on the Sacramento
River) to assume command, he was already convinced that Indian hostilities usually resulted from actions by the whites that
provoked retaliation. His observations during his first months on

the West Coast confirmed that opinion. Wool complained of white "cupidity" and suggested that the Indians were goaded by men who considered them "no better than wolves and take as much pleasure in killing them." He suspected that militia companies often were raised not to meet alleged Indian violence but rather to provide local entrepreneurs an opportunity for quick profits by selling supplies and equipment at exorbitant prices; such suspicions were supported by reports from army officers stationed in Oregon.[6]

Early in 1855 General Wool boasted that, with the exception of the Ward party massacre, the record in the department during the previous year had been good, with fewer total murders than major cities in the East. But he feared that increased emigration could bring trouble, particularly along the trails, and he knew that a force which allowed an average of one soldier for every 700 square miles of territory was insufficient to provide adequate protection. Wool asked for at least six more regiments which would allow the manning of posts at Boise, Grande Ronde Valley, Walla Walla Valley, Colville, and Port Townsend.

The officers in command on the Columbia River (Major Gabriel Rains at Fort Dalles and Lieutenant Colonel Benjamin L. E. Bonneville at Fort Vancouver) conveyed to Wool nearly opposite assessments of the Indian situation in the Northwest. Rains was convinced, as he had been for some time, that hostilities were inevitable, and he advised, "There must be an extensive war at no long period on this frontier, but I shall try to put off the evil as long as possible." Bonneville, whose fur-trade ventures had acquainted him with the Indians, sided with James Doty, who criticized Rains for giving credence to vague rumors. Bonneville admitted that increased immigration excited the natives, but he believed that mild, parental control similar to that long exercised by the Hudson's Bay Company would forestall any outbreak. He suggested that placing the Indians on reservations as soon as possible, in the care of good agents, would result in pacification. Obviously Governor Stevens shared Bonneville's opinion; Wool was inclined to think that Rains was right.[7]

The Yakima War

Major Rains first heard of Bolon's death from an old Indian woman whom Shumaway had sent to The Dalles. It appeared that Rains' worst fears finally had been realized. He immedi-

ately ordered Brevet Major Granville Haller, with 102 men, to
march into Yakima country. Haller was a thirty-six-year-old career officer who had been in the service for sixteen years. He arrived at Fort Dalles in the summer of 1853, and he led the 1854
expedition into Snake Indian country to chastise the murderers
of the Ward party. He led another punitive expedition in the
summer of 1855, 150 miles beyond Fort Boise, where his men
killed or executed Indians equalling the number of whites massacred in 1853. Haller and his men arrived back at Fort Dalles
in late September, footsore and weary after a march of 1,700
miles, only to be sent back into the field immediately.

Haller's force left Fort Dalles on October 3 and met a large
party of Yakima warriors three days later near Toppenish
Creek. Kamiakin and other older chiefs had hoped to talk with
Haller in an effort to persuade him to turn back. It is likely
that the chiefs would have offered to do their best to restrain
their young men in the future if the troops did not enter their
country. They also wished to explain that Bolon's death did not
occur as a consequence of tribal policy, but as the act of a few
misguided young men. But as soon as Haller's force appeared,
firing began and the chance for a parley was lost. The skirmish
lasted from three o'clock until sunset, when Haller broke contact
and moved his force back to a hill where they spent a sleepless
night with little water or forage. The major sent an urgent express back to The Dalles requesting additional troops and a
howitzer at once. The next evening Haller, who estimated that
the Yakimas had increased from six hundred to fifteen hundred
men, determined that the odds were too great to wait for reinforcements and ordered a retreat. Some of the chiefs believed
they should let Haller go, as their objective had been to drive
him out of the country, but about two hundred fifty warriors
took up the chase and fought sporadically with Haller's rear
guard until they reached the safety of the mountain ridge just
north of and across the Columbia River from The Dalles.[8]

Haller's command suffered casualties of five killed and seventeen wounded, while the Indians admitted losses of two killed,
four wounded, and one captured. Wool criticized Major Haller
for proceeding "without the precautions necessary against savage
warfare," and expressed doubt that he had actually faced fifteen
hundred warriors. The general's skepticism about the actual
number of Indians was justified, but the march into Yakima
country with 102 men was not a particularly reckless or unusual
movement for the frontier army. Haller had just spent two sum-

mers campaigning in the heart of hostile Indian country with a force of less than 150 men, and during much of that time his units had been several hundred miles from any possible relief force. Rains and Haller assumed that 100 men could handle virtually any eventuality. They knew that the Indians were not conditioned to fight sustained battles and that the army could make better use of its firepower. Though Haller met a larger force than anticipated, he obviously overestimated its size. If all men of fighting age had been present at the battle, the Yakima tribe could barely have mustered 1,500 men. Haller was not in immediate danger, and his decision to retreat rather than wait for reinforcements was, on purely military grounds, questionable.[9]

Haller's retreat freed the now enraged Yakima warriors to turn their attention to Lieutenant William Slaughter, who had left Fort Steilacoom with fifty men intent on crossing Naches Pass and making contact with Haller. One of Slaughter's scouts, a trader named Edgar, was married to Chief Teias's niece. Teias encountered Edgar on the east side of the pass and warned him that Haller had been defeated and that 250 men were on the way to meet Slaughter. Edgar turned back in time to warn Slaughter, who returned with his force to Fort Steilacoom. If Haller had not retreated, it is possible that the combined force could have dispersed the Yakimas at Toppenish. A defeat at first might have deflated young warriors such as Qualchan and might have strengthened the hand of those who advocated peace as well. As it happened, Haller's retreat further emboldened the Yakimas and encouraged other tribes to join in the war.[10]

News of Haller's defeat spread, seemingly on the wind, to the white and Indian populations throughout the Northwest. When the word reached Benicia, Wool sent seventy men immediately to Fort Vancouver, and requested a regiment from the East Coast (a request that was promptly honored). On the Sound there was a call for massive retaliation against the Yakimas. The *Pioneer and Democrat* cried, "We trust they will be rubbed out—blotted from existence as a tribe." Governor George Curry of Oregon and Charles Mason (acting for Stevens who was still in Blackfoot country) issued calls for volunteers who enlisted eagerly. One loud dissenting voice appeared in Steilacoom where the *Puget Sound Courier,* a Whig paper launched the previous May, attacked the treaties as the cause of the war and placed responsibility squarely on "King Stevens I.I." The *Courier* complained that the Indians had been treated as brutes and robbed of their land by a governor who paid them nominal amounts because he wished to be known as the man who had bought the most land at the lowest price. The editor of the Olympia paper countered that the charges constituted "a libellous, scurrilous, and ill-timed attack upon Governor Stevens," as well as affording evidence to the Indians that the settlers were not united in the war effort. Such a position, the editor charged, was treason. Most citizens agreed with the *Pioneer and Democrat* as they prepared to face what they feared would be a protracted war.[11]

During its second session, the Washington legislature had authorized the formation of militia companies, and Stevens had urged the local communities to form units. None had done so. When Major Rains learned of Haller's retreat, he asked Charles Mason to call for two volunteer companies "to act in concert" with the regulars. Mason complied, but the territory had no arms or ammunition. The acting governor frantically appealed to James Douglas of the Hudson's Bay Company and to Captain William Pease of the United States revenue cutter *Jefferson Davis* for munitions. While the *Jefferson Davis* and the *Decatur,* along with Hudson's Bay Company vessels, patrolled the Sound as visible deterrents to the local Indians, Mason sent one of the volunteer companies to Fort Vancouver.[12]

In Oregon, Governor Curry did not wait for the army to request militia. He sent out a call for five companies totaling 800 men to proceed east of the Cascades under the command of James W. Nesmith, colonel of militia. During the previous year General Wool and Oregon officials had quarreled about the need for militia forces in the territory, and Curry determined to preempt further argument by simply ignoring the existence of the Regular Army. Rains was clearly alarmed when he told Wool that Curry's action "disappointed" him, and, he added, it appeared that many of the Oregon militia were interested only in plundering Indian horses and cattle. "How far this feeling is rife I am unable to say," the major admitted, "but fear it has much to do with the state of things here." He concluded that in any campaign against the Indians, he would not be able to rely upon the Oregon troops for any assistance. General Wool agreed and severely chastised Governor Curry for presuming to send volunteers to another territory; Wool pointed out that the life or property of Oregon citizens was not threatened. There was truth in Rains's and Wool's charges although there were some among the Oregon volunteers who believed that immediate punishment of the erring tribes was necessary to prevent a general uprising throughout the Northwest. And Haller's defeat had indicated that the Regular Army did not have the necessary force to do the job.[13]

Mason conferred with Rains at The Dalles and placed him in command as brigadier general of Washington Territory volunteers. Rains spoke for both when he averred, "We must not be defeated again or the country is ruined, every defeat doubles the force of the enemy." The Washington volunteers, who believed their families and property were threatened by Indian hostility, did not pause to consider the reasons for the outbreak. They knew they were faced with a war and they were determined to return the territory to peace. William Fraser Tolmie aptly described the first recruits: "I saw the volunteers set out . . . yesterday evening . . . a goodly company of stalwart fellows, who at close quarters would rout ever so many Yakimaws."[14]

The temporary use of volunteer soldiers was a well-established practice in the United States. It reflected the Founding Fathers' apprehensions about a standing army with a professional officer corps, an apprehension that still prevailed in the 1850s. Stevens had in fact expended considerable effort to encourage expansion of the professional army—with little success. As governor he discovered that, though it was difficult to raise volunteers when peace prevailed, able-bodied men were quick to spring to arms when hostilities threatened. Stevens (during his years in active service) and Wool both had observed volunteers in combat conditions and were well aware of the problems created. That they strongly preferred regulars is not surprising. Lieutenant George Crook, who served in Oregon in the early 1850s, expressed the usual professional contempt for militia laxity and informality when he described his experience with one company of volunteers. According to Crook, when the militia captain bawled, "attenshun the company," his command answered with "go to Hell," and similar epithets. Only after the captain made a fumbling attempt to mount and accidentally hit his chin on the saddle horn did the company finally move forward. It is unlikely that Crook endeared himself to those within earshot when he remarked that he did not care to ride in the rear of the column because in the event of an Indian attack, he would likely be trampled to death. It was true enough that the volunteers were usually plagued by chaotic organization that created supply and command problems. Part of the difficulty arose from the haste with which the volunteers were usually organized; a second liability was an excess of democracy which permitted the men to elect their officers and to remove them at will.[15]

Twin Buttes

As the Oregon volunteers were moving east from Portland, Major Rains readied an expeditionary force near The Dalles. Unlike Haller, he planned to follow the north bank of the Columbia to a point near the mouth of the Yakima River and then move up the river into the Yakima Valley. Rains was a West Point graduate who, during a long military career, had proved himself an able, imaginative officer. He had been wounded in the Seminole War, had fought in Mexico, and later was to become an expert on land mines while serving the Confederacy in the Civil War. Rains's force of nineteen officers and 351 men was organized from regular detachments in Oregon and California. (As did Rains, a number of these men played key roles in the Civil War.)[16]

The major hurried his hastily organized command forward because he wished to chastise the Yakima before winter set in or other tribes came to their aid. The campaign was not helped when the Oregon volunteers arrived and began following in Rains' footsteps with the result that the horses and supplies of each command were mixed together. As they moved along the Columbia, officers unfamiliar with the country led their troops astray down blind canyons and civilian packers refused to guard their animals at night, which resulted in a loss of twenty-five horses and five mules.[17]

On November 7 the regulars, still accompanied by the unwelcome Oregon volunteers, arrived at the mouth of Toppenish Creek. Several miles to the north, where the Yakima River flowed through a break in the Ahtanum Ridge at Twin Buttes (Union Gap), Kamiakin was camped with 300 veterans of the Haller fight. On November 8 Rains made contact with 50 braves led by Kamiakin who retreated across the Yakima River. The army pursued, lost two men in the shallow but swift current, and moved north along the river over swampy ground and through heavy underbrush. At twilight the sound of scattered firing in the distance prompted Rains to push his men ahead in the dark, but the command became so weary and widely scattered he was forced to order a halt. (Rains later learned that the firing came from mounted volunteers pursuing a small band of Indians.) The next day Rains arrived at Twin Buttes where he was met by the beating of Yakima drums and small-arms fire from warriors concealed near the top of a high ridge. Rains's mountain howitzers bombarded the hill at long range until the late afternoon when Haller and Captain Ferdinand Augur led two companies in a charge up the ridge, accompanied by volunteers who "joined it as a free fight," to drive the Yakima off the crest of the hill. This ended the "battle."[18]

That night Kamiakin decided the only alternative in the face of superior numbers and firepower was to take advantage of their fresh horses and outrun the attackers. Leaving a rear guard to delay the troops, the Yakimas moved quickly with families and livestock to White Bluffs where they swam the Columbia, losing a large number of animals in the swift, icy waters. Some members of the tribe went into winter camp near Moses Lake while others continued north to the country of their relatives, the Isle des Pierres. Rains, considering that further pursuit might be futile in the increasingly wintry weather, ordered his command to begin the march back to The Dalles. A temporary halt was ordered near the Ahtanum mission, and a detachment under Colonel Nesmith and Lieutenant Sheridan was sent toward Naches Pass in an attempt to make contact with Captain Maurice Maloney, who was marching from Fort Steilacoom with a force of regulars and Washington volunteers. Unknown to them, Maloney had turned back to the Sound several days before without attempting to cross the pass. The troops remaining at the mission took out their frustration over the escape of the Yakimas by plundering and burning the mission station. Strict orders had been given to respect the property, but the volunteers ignored their officers and, during a short absence from the camp by Rains, even some of the regulars joined in the looting.[19]

The action at Twin Buttes, despite its apparent indecisiveness, should have been conclusive. Rains had amply demonstrated white military power and the Yakima chiefs had been convinced that further resistance on a large scale would be futile. Unfortunately, the fear of a general Indian uprising led to further actions by volunteers from both Washington and Oregon, actions which provoked Indians of several tribes to defend themselves or to retaliate. The fears were exaggerated. Significantly, up to and beyond the November 9 confrontation at Twin Buttes, the Yakimas fought alone. Tribes such as the Cayuse and Walla Walla, which had shown their hostile proclivities in seasons past, remained quiet and uninvolved until provoked by militia action in December and on into 1856.

On November 8, the day Rains first made contact with the
Yakimas, General Wool left San Francisco bound for the Northwest. After a brush with disaster when his vessel nearly swamped
in stormy weather upon crossing the bar of the Columbia River,
Wool set up headquarters at Fort Vancouver and began to assess the military situation. He discovered that east of the mountains only the Yakimas had killed a white man, although deserted property in the Walla Walla Valley had been plundered by
other tribes. Wool reasoned that the Indians could do no further
harm in the interior if the whites stayed out of the area. A winter campaign would only scatter the Yakimas into the territory
of friendly tribes. The general also found that the condition of
the army's animals made a winter campaign virtually impossible. Most had come across the plains in 1849 and had been
hard used in the marches to the Snake country as well as the
two expeditions to Yakima country. Complaining that he could
not purchase fresh horses or other supplies in the Northwest as
the volunteers had depleted all the stock, Wool decided to dispatch supply requisitions to California and to establish a fort in
the Walla Walla Valley and another in the Yakima Valley.
These forts would allow the army to keep an eye on the Indians
and still have easy contact with The Dalles. Wool was confident
that the Indians would choose peace in the face of the army's
increased presence.[20]

While at Fort Vancouver the general made no effort to contact territorial officials in Oregon or Washington, and they likewise avoided him. Fuming, Mason vowed, "I'll see him d—d . . .
before I write first." Wool chastised the Oregon volunteers for
creating a potentially dangerous situation and termed the fall
expedition up the Columbia River "one of the most unwise, unnecessary, and extravagant . . . ever fitted out in the United
States." Wool sailed for California in mid-January, and while
off the Oregon coast he met the vessel carrying the Ninth Infantry sent from the East. He conferred with the regiment's officers on board ship and ordered Colonel Silas Casey to Fort Steilacoom with two companies and Colonel George Wright to Fort
Dalles with the rest of the troops. Wright was further ordered to
prepare for a spring expedition into the Yakima and Walla
Walla Valleys. Wool had decided on a cautious course, a course
that opened a chasm between himself and the political leaders
of Oregon and Washington. The bitterness was to continue long
after the hostilities had ended.[21]

Death of Peopeomoxmox

Wool's fear that the Oregon volunteers would create serious problems for his Indian policy was confirmed in December. Volunteer forces commanded by Thomas Cornelius (who had replaced Nesmith as colonel), William Kelly, and M. A. Chinn converged in the Walla Walla Valley. The apparent reason for their presence was to keep the hostiles out of the valley, but the Yakimas had already scattered to the north, and reports had been received indicating that the Cayuse and Walla Walla tribes were remaining at peace. The intentions of the latter tribe were confirmed when Chief Peopeomoxmox, with forty warriors, appeared at Kelly's camp on December 5 with a white flag and asked for a parley. Kelly responded by demanding that the Walla Walla tribe surrender all its livestock and arms as a condition of peace. Peopeomoxmox protested that they had signed a treaty with Governor Stevens and that as far as his tribe was concerned, there was no war. The reply of the volunteers was to seize the chief and five of his men.

The next day the volunteers attacked the main force of the Walla Walla tribe and a running fight ensued with the Indians retreating until they made a stand near the Whitman mission. One volunteer was killed when a howitzer exploded in an attempt to fire at a farmhouse in which a few Indians had taken refuge. The fighting ceased that evening; the Indians withdrew and the volunteers camped at the farm. That night Peopeomoxmox and the other prisoners were killed under disputed circumstances. One witness reported that the prisoners objected to being tied for the night and were shot in a struggle which ensued when guards tried to bind their hands. Peopeomoxmox was scalped, his body skinned, his ears cut off and preserved in alcohol, and the corpse buried. Apparently not yet satisfied, some volunteers exhumed the body for further mutilation. The grisly trophies later appeared in Portland, where it was reported that the volunteers drank toasts with the same alcohol in which they had preserved the ears. Not all the volunteers condoned this mutilation, but critics of the volunteers' campaign would often refer to Peopeomoxmox's death as a prime example of volunteer brutality.[22]

More than anything else, the death of the prisoners alarmed all Indians in the Northwest and brought many tribes to the brink of war. Before, during, and after the Walla Walla council, Peopeomoxmox had proved an intelligent, perceptive leader; he had bargained for the best treaty for himself and his people, and after the council he had resisted the blandishments of those who spoke for war. Peopeomoxmox had not been able to prevent looting in the Walla Walla Valley, but he had sent word to The Dalles that restitution would be made. The chief had come to the volunteers' camp to confirm his good faith and his intention to keep the peace. But the volunteers had signed up to kill Indians and were not particular as to who, where, or how. Whatever the details of Peopeomoxmox's death, there is no doubt that his capture, execution, and mutilation were acts of treachery which said clearly to the Indians of the Northwest that it mattered little if they were friendly or hostile, for in either event they would be subjected to attack by the whites. It was not the Walla Walla treaties which brought the Cayuse and Walla Walla into the war, or clouded the friendship of many other tribes; the volunteers deserve the dubious credit.

After the death of the prisoners, fighting continued for three more days, but when additional volunteers arrived from Fort Henrietta with ammunition, the Indians once again withdrew. The volunteers tried to pursue, but their steeds were no match for the Indian horses. Estimates varied widely as to the number of Indians killed, with some reports ranging as high as 100 or more. Whatever the number, it was true that there were sufficient corpses about to cause pestilence. On December 20 Governor Stevens arrived from the Spokane country and the volunteers proudly accepted his praise as men who were not "summer soldiers," but hardy fighters who braved winter cold and snow. Their hardiness was to receive a maximum test. By the end of December, temperatures plunged to almost thirty below zero, and, as the cold continued, the men quarreled among themselves and criticized or ignored their officers. The volunteers strayed from camp only to look for food or round up horses and cattle, ignoring orders not to touch the stock of friendly Indians. By March the country had been stripped clean, and the volunteers had consumed most of the cattle and one hundred horses. They drove the rest of the stock before them when they returned home in the spring, looking, according to one officer, like "Ragged Dismounted Volunteers." It had been a long, hard winter for the volunteers, who came to believe that Indian fighting was not as glamorous or as profitable as they had assumed when they left home in the fall. Most vowed they would not do it again.[23]

Meanwhile, Governor Stevens left Fort Benton and headed west with twenty-five men on October 28, 1855, three weeks after the Haller fight at Toppenish Creek. The delay in the Blackfoot council had placed him more than two months behind schedule. If the goods for the council had arrived as planned, Stevens would have been in the Spokane country when hostilities commenced. The night after Stevens left Fort Benton, his expressman, William Pearson, rode into camp and breathlessly announced that the Yakima had murdered Bolon and had "declared a war of extermination upon the whites." Stevens sent Doty back to Fort Benton for additional animals, arms, and ammunition while he and the rest of the party hurried on to the Bitterroot Valley, covering the 230 miles in four and one-half days. He overtook the Nez Perce observers returning from the Fort Benton council. Stevens requested the delegation, which included Chiefs Looking Glass, Spotted Eagle, and Three Feathers, to acompany him to the Spokane council. Doty, also traveling as fast as his animals would go, caught up and all headed for Lookout Pass. Stevens possessed little factual information except that the Yakimas were at war, but he surmised that other tribes may have joined them. However, he believed that his party of forty men was strong enough to deal with any hostile force they might encounter before they reached the Spokane River. There he could take stock of the situation; if the worst were true they could seek protection among the Nez Perce Indians who he was certain would not join in any alliance against the whites.[24]

The pass through the Bitterroot Mountains was choked with three feet of new snow, and they were saved from severe hardship only by the fortuitous passage of a Coeur d'Alene party which had preceded them and had beaten a path. The governor found the Indians at the Coeur d'Alene mission greatly excited by events in the Yakima country and stunned by his arrival. Rumors were flowing rapidly through Indian country with each new report seemingly contradicting earlier information. There was one piece of accurate news. The four men whom Bolon had sent with supplies for the Spokane council were patiently waiting at Antoine Plante's farm near the Spokane River, and they had been joined by fifteen miners. Stevens decided to push ahead, retrieve the supplies, join forces with the miners, and hold a council to calm the Spokane and Colville Indians. He asked three of the Nez Perce delegation (including Looking Glass) to accompany him while the others returned home to report on events. Stevens reached Plante's farm on November 28. The Spokane Indians, who had just heard that the governor had returned to the East Coast, said that it could not possibly be Stevens, rather it was probably his ghost. He organized the miners into a militia company called the Spokane Invincibles, and then put his own party on a military footing (the Stevens Guards) with himself as commander-in-chief of territorial forces.[25]

The governor sent word to Angus McDonald to escort the Indians near Fort Colville to Plante's farm for a conference. While waiting he talked with Chiefs Spokane Garry and Vincent of the Spokane tribe, as well as some of the Coeur d'Alene Indians who were present. He referred to the many rumors and lies circulating concerning his actions. Stevens denied that he had ever threatened to take the land: "I have said to every Indian—I say to you—nothing will be done without your full consent." He remarked that he had just returned from east of the mountains where he had concluded a treaty giving them safe access to buffalo country. Stevens pleaded, "I trust you will ever remain my children, that you will look to me as a father." By December 4 a number of Colville, Spokane, and Isle des Pierres Indians had gathered. The latter group became a problem for the governor because he failed to recognize that they were essentially a separate tribe; he tended to link them with either Yakimas or Colvilles, an impression that Kamiakin had tended to confirm. (They had not been included in the Walla Walla Council; when they were ignored again at the second Walla Walla Council in 1856, they led an attack on the governor's party.) At the Spokane council, Isle des Pierres Chiefs Big Star and Moses were among those most hostile to Stevens, but he ignored them because he did not think they had any influence.[26]

The Indians brought news of the fight at Twin Buttes and the subsequent retreat of Kamiakin across the Columbia. Stevens welcomed the news, but the Spokane and Colville chiefs took alarm because it might mean that the Yakimas were headed for their country to winter. In late afternoon, with snow falling heavily, the governor began the conference by suggesting that it was not a good time to talk of lands as they had originally intended, but that he wished to discuss the war. Spokane Garry replied for his people. Because of his command of English, his long acquaintance with whites, and his education and travel outside the Northwest, Garry more than any other chief was able to explain the Indians' hopes and fears in terms that whites could understand. He told the governor that he believed both the whites and Yakimas were responsible for the war, and that he would be willing to ignore the whole business except that he knew that in time the fighting would spread "like the waters of the sea." Garry explained that the Yakimas might be forced into Spokane territory, an event his people did not relish because their supplies would be stretched dangerously thin. He concluded, "You want peace here—good—but also make peace in the Yakima country."[27]

Garry seems to have known Stevens' true mind on the matter. Even before he arrived at Plante's farm, Stevens had determined that a vigorous military campaign would be necessary to bring the Indians to terms. He had sent an express to Fort Dalles which urged the army to take to the field. He believed, as he had earlier in Mexico, that once one party to an agreement broke faith and began hostilities, the only alternative was to "conquer a peace."[28]

Garry, once he had addressed the war, turned to his real interest—land. He complained that French Canadians in that region were registering claims in a book. Garry pointed his finger accusingly at the settlers who were present and asked why they were so eager to write down their claims even before a treaty was signed? He suggested that the Indians, rather than the governor, define the reservations, and he posed a final question: Who would assure that they would be well treated after the treaties; who would guarantee that they would not be murdered as Elijah, the son of Peopeomoxmox, had been in California? (Two days after Garry's speech Peopeomoxmox was brutally killed by the Oregon volunteers.) Garry had summarized the position of most of the tribes. He had no reason to wish war; he was for treaties in principle; he was concerned over the division of lands; and he wanted guarantees of Indian rights after the treaties were signed. The speech contained the implication that Stevens would not (or could not) treat the Indians like his own children as he so often promised. The governor was on the defensive and he answered with some difficulty. He replied that he had only suggested reservation boundaries at Walla Walla and that he had modified his position until the chiefs were satisfied. Why, he asked Garry, did Kamiakin tell the commissioners he was happy, if in fact he was not? Stevens was less able to give satisfactory answers to the remaining points, and he adjourned the council until the next day when other chiefs were scheduled to speak.[29]

The next day's session indicated that the tribes held a variety
of opinions both on the treaties and the war. Chief Big Star of
the Isle des Pierres, whose country was in the Okanogan Valley,
criticized Stevens for not making a treaty with his people the
previous summer. Another chief objected because the whites had
banned the sale of ammunition to all Indians, an action that
Chief Peter John (Colville) defended as a necessary step by the
whites who did not yet know the disposition of various tribes.
But all of the chiefs agreed on two points: the war with the
Yakimas should end, and troops north of the Snake River would
not be tolerated. After everyone had spoken, Garry returned to
the land questions and persisted in arguing that the chiefs
should be allowed to draw the reservation lines. The chief and
the governor both knew that the Indians held the upper hand,
and Stevens tried to avoid the issue by pleading that he needed
to return to the Yakima country as quickly as possible to deal
with the war. He agreed to talk about the land, but he argued
that it would be better to put it off until another time. Garry
consented to meet in the future to discuss a treaty at leisure.
Stevens quickly said, "I agree with Garry," and adjourned the
council. The next day the governor crossed the Spokane River
and marched toward Lapwai.[30]

Stevens believed that some gains were made at the Spokane
council. In particular, he was confident that he had headed off
a coalition between the Yakimas and the Spokane-area tribes.
But, as with the treaties that hitherto had been consummated,
much depended on future actions, and Stevens again paid too
little heed to the points emphasized by the Indians.

The Spokane Invincibles and Stevens Guards marched
through snow eight inches deep to reach Lapwai in five days.
Two thousand Nez Perce had gathered at William Craig's
claim, where Stevens discussed the existing state of affairs with
Lawyer, Looking Glass, and the other chiefs. They met in an atmosphere that sharply contrasted with the Spokane conference.
Stevens accepted the Nez Perce as allies, and the purpose of the
talks was to convey information and to decide on a joint course
of action. Lawyer said that the Cayuse and Walla Walla chiefs
did not want to fight and explained that a few young men had
been responsible for plundering the Walla Walla Valley. Stevens
suggested that they march immediately to the valley, but Lawyer cautioned, "Hush my friend—do not say you are going at
just such a time." When they met the next day to feast on roast
ox and talk in the grand council lodge, the situation was altered

by the news of the Oregon volunteers' fight in the valley. Determined to go, Stevens offered any warriors who accompanied him the same pay as white volunteers. He left Lapwai on December 15 with about fifty-five whites and ninety-nine Nez Perce. The Nez Perce chiefs were ready to come to Stevens' aid because they did not yet have all the facts of the Peopeomoxmox affair, and because they blamed the Yakimas for the outbreak of the war. The chiefs, as much as the governor, accused the Yakimas of bad faith, particularly Kamiakin (because he "did not speak from the heart").[31]

Stevens was outraged that the Yakimas had "broken their solemn obligation." In his view the Indians either abided by the treaties or they did not, and, in the latter case, they could only be treated as enemies of the state. When he conferred with the Nez Perce chiefs, the governor made it clear that, in the case of doubtful tribes or individuals, the burden rested on the Indians to prove good faith. For those who waged war, "Utter submission to the will of the conquerer should be required." Hostiles would forfeit rights or annuities provided by treaty, and their word would not be trusted in the future. Stevens promised that the "most vigorous course" would be followed "as long as one of the enemy have not submitted to our will." He did not believe, or would not admit, that the treaties or any other official action had caused the outbreak. If there was a rational explanation, he found it "in the native intelligence of restless Indians, who, foreseeing destiny against them, that the white man was moving upon them, determined that it must be met and resisted by arms." More important to Stevens than the cause of the war was the fact of its existence.[32]

Stevens rode into the Oregon volunteers' camp on December 20. The somewhat disheveled troops compensated for lack of military precision with enormous enthusiasm as they fired off howitzers and small arms while giving three lusty cheers. The governor told them that 600 to 800 warriors were gathering (he did not say precisely who or where) and predicted that a winter campaign was in the offing. When the governor concluded his remarks, he retired to his tent and opened a verbal war with General Wool and the army by drawing up resolutions which censured the regulars for leaving "the citizen soldiery alone to fight the battles and gain the victories." Stevens further charged that the army (Wool in particular) had refused to send troops to his aid and had left him stranded in the midst of hostile Indian country.[33]

When hostilities commenced in the fall, no one knew exactly where Governor Stevens was, let alone what action he would take if the express bearing news of Bolon's death caught up to him. Some suggested that he would travel east to New York (or New Orleans) and take a steamer to the Sound, but those who knew him well had little doubt that he would return to the territory by the most direct route. With this in mind, Mason suggested to Rains that troops be sent to the Spokane country, where he expected the governor by the end of September or early October. Haller's defeat made this impossible, and Mason raised a special company of volunteers (under the command of Benjamin F. Shaw), which he assigned to meet Stevens. Shaw took his small force to the Walla Walla Valley instead and joined forces with the Oregon volunteers. In November General Wool sent Major Edward Townsend (his aide) on an inspection tour that took him as far as The Dalles. In his report, Townsend suggested that there should be troops in the Walla Walla Valley to meet the governor if he returned from that direction, but he believed that such an eventuality was "a bare possibility and not likely to occur." By the time Wool received this recommendation, the Oregon volunteers had moved into the valley, and the general assumed that they could give Stevens any aid he required. If anyone deserved blame for not meeting the governor, it was Shaw and the volunteers. But all believed the governor was not in any danger, and Stevens shared this view. He had assessed carefully the situation at each step of his journey from Fort Benton; he was not so rash that he would rush unprotected into the midst of hostile forces. The governor was never in danger; his assertion to the contrary was merely propaganda in his battle with General Wool.[34]

Stevens interrogated a number of the men in the volunteer camp in an attempt to piece together events of the previous five months and to plan what to do next. When Stevens and Major Chinn met on Christmas Day to plan future operations, they were forced to conclude that the bitterly cold weather, coupled with the miserable condition of the animals, precluded any campaign in the immediate future. Still, Stevens decided to remain in Walla Walla country, hoping that the weather would moderate enough to allow a march to the Palouse River. But during the last week of the year there was no change, and several horses froze to death each night. On January 1 the governor reluctantly gave up and headed for The Dalles.

The same day he ordered his Nez Perce allies to return to their country and to prevent any hostiles from entering their domain during the winter. Despite the warning at the Spokane council, he informed them that troops would probably cross the Snake River in the near future. His inflexible position was further illustrated when he refused permission to allow 100 friendly Walla Walla and Cayuse Indians (disciples of the Oblate Father Eugene Chirouse) to accompany the Nez Perce to Lapwai. Looking Glass and the other Nez Perce chiefs had agreed to take them in for the winter, knowing that their fear of being attacked by the volunteers had some justification. The Nez Perce did not dispute the governor's decision (which may have been motivated by an apprehension that the Walla Walla-Cayuse band might draw hostiles to Nez Perce country), but it must have appeared that Stevens did not trust them to stay completely out of the war. The governor further insisted that all individuals of hitherto hostile tribes would need to prove that they had not participated in any fighting before they would be pardoned. (He failed to explain how that might be done.)[35]

After Haller's retreat in early October, an uneasy quiet had fallen over Puget Sound. Charles Mason, left to his own wits, dispatched requests to the captains of the naval ships *Jefferson Davis* and *Decatur*, commissioned militia, and tried to quiet fears and persuade settlers to carry on business as usual. The status of the Indians in western Washington was unclear. None of the treaties (except Medicine Creek) had been ratified by Congress, and even the Indians covered by that treaty had not yet moved to their reservations. Except for special Indian agents Michael Simmons and A. H. Robie, no bureaucracy existed to provide for the tribes or to mediate between the races. As Mason raised troops and gathered supplies, the tribes became alarmed by the war preparations. (Their alarm reached near-panic proportions amid rumors that they would soon be exterminated by the whites.) Harried territorial officials did not visit the tribes to squelch the rumors, and in the chaotic final months of 1855 a few warriors took advantage of the confusion to raid farms and create mayhem. By the end of the year several whites had been killed in separate incidents, including three families on White River and two members of a party carrying dispatches from Captain Maurice Maloney to Mason.[36]

In October Major Rains ordered Maloney (at Fort Steilacoom) to cross over Naches Pass and join the troops from Fort

Dalles in the Yakima Valley. Maloney was even less eager than Slaughter had been to face the uncertainties of a campaign across the mountains. After marching up White River toward the pass, he stopped and sent word to Rains on October 29 that his force would return to the Sound because he had learned that Rains would not leave The Dalles for two more weeks. (Rains left The Dalles on October 30.) Maloney had not seen any Indians, but he pleaded, "There are from two to three thousand Indians well armed and determined to fight, in my front, and, after considering the matter over, have concluded that it is my duty to return to Steilacoom." He rationalized that snow could close the pass at any time. As Maloney fell back to the Sound, he learned of the deaths of the White River settlers (and his messengers), which led him to speculate that his return had saved the Sound from destruction. Lieutenant John Nugen, who assumed command of Fort Steilacoom in the absence of Maloney, joined the panic by reporting that 250 Indians were advancing on his post. Nugen sent out an urgent plea for additional troops.[37]

War West of the Cascades

Maloney deployed his troops on the Sound and on November 3, Lieutenant Slaughter, with fifty regulars and an equal number of volunteers commanded by Captain Gilmore Hays, fought a skirmish on the White River. Indians and whites fired across the river, which was too deep to cross, but even though the fighting took place at long range, Slaughter optimistically estimated that they had killed at least thirty warriors while losing one soldier. Maloney complained that in the high water and heavy woods the Indians "have the advantage of us, but still I think we can clean a good many of them out yet before we close the winter's campaign." They continued to patrol the area between the Green and White rivers and gratefully accepted a reinforcement of twenty-five men from the Fourth Artillery. The hostile Indians (made up of Puyallup, Nisqually, and Klickitat bands) remained out of the army's path until December 4 when a party under Klickitat Chief Kanasket came upon Slaughter's force camped for the evening between the Green and White Rivers forty-five miles east of Fort Steilacoom. The troops had built campfires to dry their sodden clothing. Slaughter, while sitting in his tent behind a fire just outside the entrance, was killed instantly by a shot through the heart. The attackers kept up the fire for three hours, killing three others and wounding several. Captain Erasmus Keyes, who had assumed command, ordered a withdrawal to Fort Steilacoom.[38]

Slaughter's death broke the courage of many of the settlers in the Sound area. At one time Lieutenant Slaughter's wife had been the only woman at Fort Steilacoom; the charming, intelligent, young couple was often in demand for social events and had developed a large circle of friends. Charles Mason spoke for all when he told George Gibbs that Slaughter's death left him "sick at heart." In late November Keyes found the Sound in a "condition of wild alarm," and James Tilton looked on with disgust as the streets of Olympia "filled with a timid ignorant fault-finding mob of Pikes, who terrify each other by horrid exaggerations about Indians, and whose claims are going to hell." Despair became pervasive and panic spread throughout western Washington. Settlers moved into the large communities or gathered behind hastily constructed fortifications and blockhouses. Many shared the apprehension of Margaret Chambers of Yelm, who was "about as badly frightened as I ever was in my life," and who spent many sleepless nights waiting for Indian attacks that never came. Some families moved to Portland or left for California. Even Mason succumbed to the prevailing mood when he dispatched Captain Sterrett north to seize all the Snoqualmie Indians in or near Seattle. Arthur Denny, with other citizens, persuaded Sterrett to abandon his mission by assuring him that the Snoqualmies had not participated in any fighting. When Sterrett withdrew, Denny remarked with relief that they had enemies enough without attacking friends. One of the few men able to assess the situation dispassionately was James Tilton, who continued to predict that there would be no general uprising on the Sound, but rather "sulking [sic] ambuscades and an occasional murder." He believed there were fewer than two hundred hostile warriors west of the mountains and suggested the best defense would be to maintain forces at key points so as to give confidence to the settlers and maintain a show of force.[39]

The year 1855 came to a close with Washington Territory shrouded in gloom. The great hopes that had arisen from the acquisition of territorial status were consigned to a seemingly distant past. But new hope came with the new year in the person of an express rider who brought news that the governor had returned to the territory and would soon appear on the Sound. "Glorious news," the *Pioneer and Democrat* proclaimed, "Little bandy-legged 'Rough and Ready' is in the field." Editor Wiley predicted that Stevens would "take off his coat and roll up his

sleeves, and if the Indians do not think the water is deep, just
let them pitch in." A citizen, who adopted the pen name Giles
Scroggins, knew that the governor would turn the situation
around, "Fer they say he is sum at sterin up tigers with a long
pole." Scroggins prophesied, "I reckin it will be I. I. Stevens instead of I. I. anybody else." When Stevens reached Olympia on
January 19, he was greeted with a thirty-eight gun salute, seventeen more than the number usually given to a head of state.
Most of the townspeople gathered at the legislative hall, where
they competed in offering praise and welcome to their hero. The
vast majority seemed to have boundless faith in the ability,
sagacity, and bravery of their leader. To Wiley it seemed that
the citizens looked upon the governor "as their deliverer—their
hope—in speedily freeing them from the evils of Indian hostilities, which for months past has cast such a thick gloom over
this portion of our devoted territory." That evening Stevens addressed a large throng, who interrupted with "deafening cheers"
when he vowed, "The war shall be prosecuted until the last hostile Indian is exterminated." Even the governor's political opponents agreed that "they must conquer peace."[40]

Stevens called for a campaign in February or March, as the
snow began to disappear in the valleys, with a mind to striking
the ·Indians before they could escape through the mountain
passes. Army arguments against the governor's plan for an eastern campaign before late spring were overwhelming. There was
no guarantee that the cold would abate or that the snow would
melt by the end of March. Even if it did, there would not be
enough grass for the animals. The Indians had a large area in
which they could maneuver without the need of crossing mountain passes, and any pressure could drive the hostiles into the
camps of friendly Indians. Although Stevens began preparations
to send an expedition east under the command of B. F. Shaw, it
is unlikely that he intended this force to take to the field before
late spring. He was too well acquainted with military campaigns
and wilderness travel to believe that even a well-disciplined
force could succeed in a winter campaign without proper forage.
But Stevens' bold talk gave proof to the white settlers of his determination, kept the Indians on the defensive, and pressured
Wool and the army to adopt a more vigorous policy. During the
winter months Shaw and Stevens raised supplies for the eastern
expedition, but in March the governor officially transferred the
men to Olympia and announced postponement of the campaign. By this time regulars were preparing to move into Yak-

ima country and the Walla Walla Valley, and Stevens was willing to allow the regulars a chance to end the war in that sector.
However, he kept a quartermaster busy at The Dalles preparing
supplies for the volunteers.[41]

The governor also moved to preempt further hostilities in the
Puget Sound region. He agreed with Tilton that those on the
warpath represented only a small fraction of the region's Indians, and suggested that the few warring Indians be isolated.
Stevens called for six-month volunteers to be organized into
Northern, Central, and Southern Battalions, each responsible for
a section of western Washington. He also called for the formation of home guards in all communities, and, in isolated areas,
he urged that wherever three or four families lived within a reasonable distance, they should move to the most easily fortified
farm. Stevens asserted that he was ready to cooperate with the
army and expressed hope that "the most cordial spirit of cooperation may exist between the regulars and the volunteers." But
he warned that the volunteers would act under his orders and
not those of Regular Army officers. He admitted that previously, volunteers had always been mustered into the service of
the United States Army "whenever it is practical or expedient,"
but he argued that the normal practice no longer applied because the volunteers sent to Rains had been mistreated and
were then mustered out—an act which constituted "a breach of
faith." The governor informed the legislature that he would take
the responsibility for raising troops independent of the army—
and he promised that the federal government would sustain
him. Stevens' actions amounted to a denial of Wool's authority
to determine military policy within the Department of the Pacific.[42]

Before Stevens could raise any troops, the dire predictions of
the preceding weeks appeared to come to fruition when Indians
from east and west of the Cascade Mountains joined forces to
mount an attack on Seattle. Those from the Sound who participated were primarily Nisqually Indians led by Leschi and Kitsap. They had been in continuous contact with the Yakimas,
who had applied pressure upon them to enter the war. The defection of these chiefs to the side of the warring tribes was a
shock to settlers who considered the Nisqually people as mild
and tractable. Leschi, in particular, had been known for his
friendship and kindness to many early settlers. His apparent
treachery was to be punished ruthlessly.

Leschi, like most chiefs west of the Cascade Mountains, found himself in a hopeless position after the beginning of hostilities. He had been subjected to many pressures as the white population increased and the early good relationships between his people and the whites had deteriorated. Leschi had hoped the treaties would solve many problems, but in the months after the Medicine Creek council the situation worsened. Reluctantly he joined in the hostilities, yielding to pressure from Yakima and Klickitat chiefs as well as his own warriors. The whites quickly labeled Leschi, his brother Stahi, Kitsap, and Nelson as the primary leaders of the disaffected Indians on the Sound, although there was not the clearly definable division between friendly and hostile Indians the governor and other whites believed.[43]

Leschi attempted to launch a strike when the *Decatur* (under a new captain, Guert Gansevoort) struck a reef and was beached in Seattle for repairs. The primary object of the attack was to seize the powder and ammunition on the vessel. Leschi was joined by Yakimas who had come over the mountains with Owhi. But the attack was delayed, and, by the time they finally acted on January 26, Gansevoort had been forewarned by an Indian spy. Seattle was a difficult target for the Indians; the vessel could protect the town with its guns, and the 150 sailors and marines, plus the local citizens, composed a formidable force. After firing into the town for most of the day, the Indians had made no headway and had lost at least ten men. The disgruntled warriors retreated to the Duwamish Valley and burned a few deserted farms. The attack had no hope of success, but the sheer audacity of the Indians further disheartened settlers. The battle at Seattle was the psychological low point of the war for the whites on Puget Sound.[44]

Stevens' most pressing problem was to revitalize the spirit of the settlers. He traveled to settlements around the Sound, promising vigorous pursuit of the hostile Indians, and pleaded, "Do not now talk of leaving us in our hour of adversity, but stay till the shade of gloom is lifted." He asked the settlers to "gather heart" to "rescue the territory from its present difficulties," promising the faithful that the end of the war would bring great prosperity. When Stevens returned to Olympia, he set up headquarters in his combination home-office and began to organize the volunteer forces.[45]

Stevens soon discovered that the territory did not contain enough able men to fill the numerous important and sensitive positions needed in the volunteers and the Indian service. He drew his staff mostly from the group of officials holding territorial office.

By the end of January Mason was on his way to Washington D.C. to report on the war, to vilify Wool's policies, and to seek Congressional support for the governor's measures. Surveyor James Tilton became a key advisor to Stevens and William W. Miller, an astute Olympia businessman, was the happy choice to serve as quartermaster and commissary general of volunteers. James Doty provided his usual competent services until March, when he was dismissed for drunkenness.[46] Stevens often worked eighteen to twenty hours a day in an attempt to keep control over the smallest details of volunteer and Indian agent operations. Virtually every decision came from the office of the governor. Although Stevens lived in the same building with Meg and the children, they saw little more of him than when he had been in Indian country.[47]

When he issued the call for volunteers, the governor stipulated that the enlistment contract would be for sixty days, subject to service anywhere in the territory. This was unacceptable to many who were willing only to serve and draw their pay if they could remain in their home community. Isaac Ebey, who recruited several volunteers by promising local assignments, was removed promptly as an enrolling officer by Stevens. The commander of the Nisqually blockhouse (William Packwood) reported that all his men walked off when he informed them of the governor's policy. Packwood also mentioned that family men refused to enlist because they did not want to be marching when the time came to put in the spring crop.[48]

Bickering and dissension broke out among those who did sign on as volunteers. Andrew Chambers, an elected lieutenant, rebuked his men for appropriating settlers' horses that had been rounded up as a precaution against theft. The volunteers reluctantly returned the horses—and they replaced Chambers with a new lieutenant. A more serious quarrel developed between Captain Joseph White, commander of the Pioneer Company, and Captain Calvin Swindal of the Central Battalion. The Pioneer Company—mostly manned by former soldiers, sailors, and whalers—had been established by the governor as an engineer force charged with building roads, bridges, and blockhouses. Urban Hicks, the second in command, characterized them as a tough bunch who were kept in constant motion to avoid insubordination. At a time when the Pioneer Company was working with the Central Battalion, nine of Captain White's men demanded his removal from command. The dissidents were supported by Captain Swindal, who urged Stevens to grant the petition. The governor refused, admonishing Swindal that the "first duty of a commander is to exact obedience to orders from his command, and any departure from this principle . . . especially to the extent of recommending the yielding to a mutinous spirit will lead to suspension from command of the officer offending." In a more conciliatory tone, Stevens urged Swindal to work with White because, "Every patriot and citizen must see that little differences ought now to be laid aside."[49]

Stevens found that even his direct commands were often ignored. On one occasion a volunteer company defied his order to move from Camp Montgomery to Yelm Prairie on foot. Instead, they rode their horses. The governor dispatched ten men to bring the horses back and warned that further disobedience would lead to dishonorable discharge. Still, Stevens exercised considerably more restraint than he would have had he been commanding regular troops.[50]

Recruiting the volunteer force was only the beginning of the problem. As in the other territories, the volunteers had to be financed primarily by the issue of scrip because territories lacked hard money as well as authority to issue currency or to incur debt. Because Congress was not legally obligated to redeem the scrip, it typically circulated at a discount which in turn boosted prices. Prices were also driven up because the territory usually needed the goods immediately and was in no position to bargain. Still another factor was the scarcity of certain essential items such as grain, beef, ammunition, arms, and horses. Quartermaster Miller found that most citizens in Washington and Oregon would accept the territorial scrip, although firms in San Francisco as well as the Hudson's Bay Company were at times reluctant to take the risk.[51]

As troops were raised and supplies gathered, Stevens ordered the construction of blockhouses and other fortifications at key points from Bellingham Bay to the Columbia River, with volunteer headquarters established at Camp Montgomery (a post constructed several miles southwest of Fort Steilacoom). All ablebodied citizens were required to work on the fortifications until completed. The first force into the field under the governor's reorganization plan was the Central Battalion (commanded by Major Gilmore Hays), which set up headquarters at Camp Montgomery in late January and established a ferry at the crossing of the Puyallup River. The Northern Battalion under

Major J. J. Van Bokkelin operated out of Port Townsend, and the Southern Battalion (commanded by H. J. G. Maxon) was based in Vancouver.

These forces were hampered by the usual problems of organization, the difficulty of the terrain, and the elusiveness of the enemy. Captain Keyes (Regular Army) advised territorial officials that it was fruitless to march around through the wet forest in winter unless they had a particular objective. He reported that many of the troops who had campaigned with Slaughter the previous fall were suffering from rheumatism. Keyes also suggested that "further forward movement . . . might antagonize the Indians to further depredations." In addition to giving unwelcome advice, army (and navy) officers hampered volunteer operations by refusing to furnish arms and supplies. Keyes explained that he had offered all possible assistance when a state of emergency existed but could no longer do so without specific orders from his superiors. Navy Captain Pease of the *Jefferson Davis* also refused further aid; he even requested the return of the two cannon he had loaned the territory. More important, the military storekeeper at Fort Vancouver, who earlier had issued rifles, muskets, and ammunition to the volunteers, was severely chastised for his action by the chief of ordnance stationed at Benicia. That source of critical supply ceased also.[52]

Captain Keyes was an accurate prophet. Although the volunteers did considerable marching, the results were negligible. The only hostile action occurred in late February and early March. On February 24 William Northcraft, a teamster, was killed near Olympia. Six days later William White, a farmer, was murdered in the same vicinity; his family escaped only because their team bolted and carried them to the safety of a neighboring farm. Stevens called upon the Southern Battalion to make a forced march to Olympia while the Central and Pioneer commands were to move to the White River to build a blockhouse. On March 8 they were surprised at Connell's Prairie by Indians whose number was estimated to be as high as 150, and, after a two-hour fight at long range, the volunteers charged and forced the attackers to withdraw. From twenty-five to thirty Indians were reported killed in the battle; the volunteer casualties numbered four wounded.[53]

Although Stevens touted the volunteers as saviors of the territory, he privately believed that their efficiency had been impaired by lack of cooperation from the army. By the time Stevens arrived in Olympia in January, he held out little hope that

Wool could be relied upon. His fears were substantiated when the general replied to Stevens' prompting for a vigorous winter campaign with the comment that he could not comply because "you should have recollected that I have neither the resources of a territory nor the treasury of the United States at my command." Wool promised the governor that the army would conduct the war with promptness and vigor *"without wasting unnecessarily the means and resources at my disposal by untimely and unproductive expeditions."* The general continued to assail Stevens and the Oregon civil authorities by predicting that he could end the war in a few months if the volunteers withdrew from the field and if settlers and volunteers refrained from a policy of Indian extermination. He agreed with one of his officers who reported, "Unless the friendly Indians can be protected against the very frequent attempts made to deprive him of his life and property this war may be protracted to an indefinite period of time, for he will be driven to hostility, if not from a sentiment of revenge, from sheer desperation."[54] Not content to limit his criticisms to private correspondence, Wool took to the newspapers to condemn the settlers for beginning the war and to charge that the volunteers were raised primarily to fill the pocketbooks of war profiteers.

Stevens publicly condemned Wool and called upon the Secretary of War to remove him from command. The *Pioneer and Democrat* echoed the governor's view when it suggested that the charitable explanation of Wool's conduct was insanity, or, less charitably, "criminal" neglect of duty. Stevens completely rejected the general's interpretation of the causes of the war and his recommendations for further action; the governor concluded, "I am . . . too old a soldier . . . to do otherwise than to press forward with all my energies."[55]

Stevens believed that Wool's policies could be circumvented to a considerable extent by securing the cooperation of the army commanders in the Northwest: Colonel George Wright and Colonel Edward Steptoe on the east side of the mountains and Colonel Silas Casey and Captain Erasmus Keyes on the Sound. All were West Point graduates with whom Stevens had previously developed friendly relationships. Colonel Casey had arrived at Fort Steilacoom in mid-January with two companies of the Ninth Infantry. Casey, an 1826 graduate of the Military Academy, had served with distinction in Mexico. (During the Civil War he was to write a two-volume work on infantry tactics which was officially adopted by the Union Army.) Casey had been briefed by Wool when their ships met off the Oregon coast, and he knew that he would need to be circumspect in his relationship with the governor to avoid the general's wrath. Wool had emphasized that volunteers should be called only in an emergency—an emergency the general predicted would not occur once reinforcements from the Ninth Infantry reached the Northwest.[56]

When Casey arrived at Fort Steilacoom, Stevens made every effort to convince the colonel that Wool's interpretation of the war was incorrect. He pleaded that the volunteers and regulars needed to cooperate, and he provided Casey with detailed memorandums on the current movements of volunteers. He also began to requisition supplies and men from the army post. Although cooperative and friendly, Casey had his own views on the proper way to conduct the Indian war. He and Keyes attempted to develop the tactics best adapted to the climate, terrain, and methods of the hostile Indians. Casey emulated Indian strategy by sending out patrols which moved swiftly in an attempt to surprise the enemy, and if unsuccessful, they were to return immediately to the fort. Keyes, who led many of the patrols, also established small ambushes (usually three men) at points at a distance from the main body during the night. The tactic trapped Chief Kanasket (leader of the raid on Slaughter's camp), who was mortally wounded by fire from one such ambush. His death subsequently demoralized the Klickitat tribe. On March 1 the regulars drove Indians from a fortified blockhouse they had occupied on the White River. It appeared to Casey and Keyes that their policy had had an effect, and by mid-March they announced that the Indian threat was virtually ended on the Sound.[57]

In February Casey attempted to cooperate with the governor by granting some of his requests and suggestions while politely turning away others. By March, however, he had become convinced that the volunteers were draining the area of transportation and supplies which could be utilized better by the Regular Army. On March 12 he refused Stevens' request for twenty-five tons of oats, and on the same day he told Tilton that the volunteers could not borrow arms stockpiled on the *Decatur*. Three days later Casey asked Stevens to turn two companies of volunteers over to the army and to remove the remainder from the field. With this force, he assured the governor, the army could "protect this frontier without the aid of those now in the service of the territory." Stevens was shocked by Casey's temerity; the governor asserted that a disaster would occur if the volunteers abandoned their positions, and he claimed that his troops were poised to strike the "decisive blow." Stevens swore that if additional volunteers were raised they would remain under his control and not that of the army because, he claimed, the governor was the ultimate authority in any emergency.[58]

Stevens further made his dispute with Casey a personal vendetta. He chastised the colonel for not treating a superior with proper respect and claimed to have waived personal etiquette in his desire to cooperate; he vowed that he would humble himself no longer by journeying to Fort Steilacoom to offer advice. Stevens' arguments touched a key issue in the dispute: both the governor and General Wool claimed to have the higher authority in times of emergency. Unfortunately, the Organic Act did not define the limits of the governor's or commanding general's power. It was obvious, however, when an emergency existed, that cooperation between civilian and military authorities was essential. Both the governor and the army were at fault by assuming that one could operate without the other. But Wool and Casey had precedent on their side when they assumed that volunteers would be under the command of the Regular Army. Stevens swept aside traditional legal procedures when he unilaterally divorced the volunteers from army operations.

The governor predicated his Indian policy in western Washington in 1855–56 on a separation of hostile and friendly bands. This proved to be an arduous task. In the fall of 1855 Michael Simmons was agent for all the Indians north of the Skookumchuck River. When the war started, Mason and Simmons established temporary agencies under the supervision of local settlers in an attempt to keep the Indians together at specified locations. They hoped that this arrangement would keep contact between the friendly and hostile Indians to a minimum. Most of the responsibility rested with Simmons who dashed about in a futile effort to quash rumors and to keep a lid on the volatile situation. Simmons's counterpart south of the Skookumchuck (Andrew Cain) did nothing.[59]

When Stevens arrived in Olympia, he immediately began appointing Indian agents and tried to secure emergency funds from the Bureau of Indian Affairs. His pleas to Washington D.C. were acted upon with unusual dispatch, and in March 1856 he was authorized to spend ten thousand dollars each month on behalf of the friendly Indians, although he was cautioned that the money could be used only for preserving the peace. The Chehalis and other tribes south of the Skookum-chuck who had refused to sign a treaty in 1855 were placed in the charge of Travers Daniel, Sidney Ford, Sr., and Simon Plo-mondon. Ford had lived among the Chehalis people for a number of years, had their confidence, and was sympathetic to their plight. If a man of Ford's stature had been available for each of the tribes, Stevens' job would have been considerably easier and many misunderstandings could have been avoided. But even Ford had to muster all his courage and powers of persuasion to prevent the Chehalis Indians from joining the hostile forces. After the defeat of Haller, the Yakimas maintained close contact with the Chehalis chiefs, using persuasion and threats to attempt to bring them into the war. The Chehalis Indians did not want war, but every new incident made it more difficult for them to maintain neutrality. They feared either destruction by the whites or enslavement by the Yakimas. Ford persuaded the Chehalis chiefs to move the tribe to his farm, and, once Stevens returned to the Sound, Ford was able to keep them supplied with meat purchased with Indian department funds. Either Ford or his son remained with the Chehalis tribe from the start of the war until the end of 1856. When some of the young braves became restless, Ford told them they could join the hostiles if they wished, but he would no longer protect them and they would become hunted men. He reported that none left.[60]

Unfortunately, for a variety of reasons, most of the other agents were less successful than Ford. Unlike Ford, Travers Daniel did not have the confidence of the Indians and could not speak their language. He spent most of his time attempting to stop the liquor traffic on Shoalwater Bay. Though he was able to make some headway when he offered a bounty to informers, the traffic resumed soon after he left. Stevens applauded these efforts, recognizing that liquor was the evil at the bottom of many incidents between whites and Indians, but he was distressed by rumors that Daniel often ignored the Indians or threatened them with his gun. Daniel did not deny that his efforts were minimal, but he suggested that the Indians were too drunk to pose any threat to the whites. He labeled the accusation that he had drawn his gun "a damned lie—for when I do draw my pistol on anybody, I use it." This did not ease the governor's fears, and after Ford conducted an investigation, Daniel was removed from office. Plomondon, who had responsibility for the Cowlitz Indians, like Daniel, also had liabilities that seemed to outweigh his assets. A French Canadian, he had become closely associated with the half-breed liquor sellers as well as having gained the trust of the Indians. Stevens complained to Ford that Plomondon was a lackadaisical record keeper who mixed private and public business to such an extent that an outside auditor would surely charge fraud. But no one was available to replace Plomondon, and Stevens, bemoaning the "great difficulties" the agent caused, was forced to retain him until the crisis had passed. Ultimately he was dismissed.[61]

The situation was much different at the northern end of the Sound, where conditions varied from the assessment of "nothing to rouse our drowsy settlers" to periods of panic when reportedly hostile Indians from Vancouver Island appeared or were rumored to be in the vicinity. The tribes north of the Snohomish River were neither under the influence of the Indians east of the mountains, nor dissatisfied with the assistance they were receiving from the Indian agents at Bellingham Bay and Port Townsend. According to Edmund Fitzhugh (the agent at Bellingham Bay), the local Indians were happy and "completely under my control." But the Fort Simpson, Haida, Stikene, and Queen Charlotte bands, which appeared periodically from across the 49th parallel, threw both local Indians and whites into consternation. Fitzhugh complained that these incursions caused panic among the local Indians, who ran to him for help. The agent was completely nonplused when Indians from British territory appeared in March 1856 to offer their services as mercenaries against the hostile tribes. Fitzhugh cheerfully suggested that the governor employ them as scouts to "give them a lively chance for being killed." Stevens was skeptical, but he finally accepted the services of a few. These mercenaries proved extremely effective; Fitzhugh grudgingly admitted that they were admirable soldiers—when serving the right side.[62]

Of greatest concern was that area, from Olympia to just north of Seattle, where most of the hostile Indians west of the Cascade Mountains resided. A representative agency within this sensitive area was Holmes Harbor (Whidbey Island), run by Nathan Hill, who had responsibility for as many as 1,800 Snohomish and Snoqualmie Indians. Hill had settled on the island in 1853 but had had minimal contact with the Indians until Stevens named him agent. He admitted, "I was but little acquainted with the Indians' character and did not understand their language and but little of the jargon." In an effort to separate these tribes from the hostile Indians, Stevens had ordered them moved to the island. In the first days after the transfer a plot developed to kill Hill, but he feigned indifference to the threat and the Indians eventually agreed to place themselves under his care. Hill made a determined effort to help the Indians, but he found it difficult to secure the necessary food and supplies. At one point he could dole out only a quarter pound of flour per person per day. He ruefully admitted, "Though I pretended to feed them, yet it was merely pretension." In May the conscientious agent submitted his resignation to Stevens and suggested that a better-qualified man be appointed. The governor knew that the patient, hard-working Hill was by far the best man available and persuaded him to stay on. By the end of the year Hill could report with some satisfaction, "By preserverence, attention to duty, and rectitude, I won their trust."[63]

The most sensitive agency was near Seattle. The situation there was complicated by feuds among the white settlers as well as divisions within the Indian tribes. The first agent in Seattle, Dr. David Maynard, was trusted by Chief Seattle, but he was irresponsible, inebriate, and disliked by most, Indians and whites alike. Maynard sent Chief Seattle and his men on scouts through the neighboring woods and casually told Stevens that he had offered to pay $100 for every Indian scalp they brought in. There is no evidence that the bounty was ever collected, though apparently the offer stood while Maynard remained in office. At the end of March Maynard resigned under pressure but continued to offer advice to Chief Seattle and to make his presence felt. Maynard complained to Stevens that he had not received payment from the new agent for services as a physician to the Indians. When the governor supported the agent, who said that Maynard had treated only one Indian, the doctor drafted a petition in which the Indians purported to request that only Maynard be allowed to treat them.[64]

Maynard's successor (H. Haley) attempted to improve the economic base of the local tribes. He developed a plan allowing them to cut timber for wages with the excess profit going to the tribe; in addition the logged-over land could be planted with potatoes. The project was scuttled when a settler claimed that he owned the land in question. To Stevens the most important duty of the agents near Seattle was to keep off the temporary reservations the Indians suspected of participating in hostilities. He advised his agents to learn the names of all the Indians in their charge and to call role every day, a difficult procedure to put into practice. One agent complained that, although he would be glad to comply, he would first have to assign names

that both he and the Indians could remember. Haley was removed when the captain of the *Decatur* accused him of harboring two deserters. The charge was denied, but Stevens felt obliged to make yet another change.[65]

George Paige became the third agent in Seattle in less than
six months. As he was reported not to be a party "to local feuds
and divisions," Stevens hoped he could bring some order to the
agency. Paige proved to be intelligent and efficient, but he too
encountered problems. As part of Stevens' policy to isolate the
friendly Indians, the Duwamish tribe had reluctantly moved to
Bainbridge Island (across the Sound from Seattle). The move
failed when the Indians could not find adequate fishing sites
and Paige was unable to provide enough food from agency resources. He was forced to allow the tribe to move back to the
mainland, where they resettled along the shores of Elliot Bay
(present-day Seattle). Later (fall 1856) many of the Duwamish
tribe left Seattle and moved to fishing spots on various rivers in
the general vicinity. Army officers approved of the move, but
Paige protested to Stevens, who in turn criticized Casey for in-
terfering with the Indian Department. Casey retorted that he
was only protecting the friendly Indians from harassment by the
volunteers. On another occasion he told Stevens that a company
of regular troops was protecting Indians fishing on the Black
River. He pointedly added, "Permit me to remark that I would
consider it extremely inexpedient and entirely unnecessary for
you to order volunteers to take these Indians' lives, or to commit any violence on them." The governor heatedly reminded
Casey that, in his capacity as superintendent, he had ordered all
Indians out of the area between the east shore of Puget Sound
and the Cascade Mountains, and any Indian who remained did
so at his own risk. Casey sarcastically remarked that if the governor was so jealous of his responsibilities as Indian superintendent, he would be glad if Stevens would take charge of 100 Indians who were eating army rations at Fort Steilacoom. But the
Indians in Paige's charge had the last word when they insisted
that they "would see Governor Stevens and all the agents in
hell before they will move [from the fishing locations]."[66]

Governor Stevens' Indian policy on the Sound in 1856 was
simple: first, isolate the friendly Indians and care for them when
they could not feed themselves by their usual methods; and second, harass the hostiles into defeat. In addition Stevens wished
to seal off the tribes on the Sound from any contact with the
hostiles east of the Cascade Mountains by using the volunteer

battalions to block off routes through the passes. He made it clear on numerous occasions that the only terms offered to the hostile Indians were the "mercy and justice" of the government, which meant that suspected Indians would be tried, with the guilty punished and the innocent returned to the reservations. Typically, he told a delegation of Indians from Seattle that his terms were those of "a father who punishes his children to make them good." Stevens did not appreciate suggestions that tensions could best be eased by promising a conciliatory policy toward all Indians in exchange for a halt to hostilities. Wool had recommended such a course, as did the Commissioner of Indian Affairs, who asked Stevens to exercise "restraint," and to "avoid vindictive and unnecessary bloodshed." The Commissioner urged that Indians "who are criminal may be treated with magnanimity after laying down arms." Stevens denied accusations that he meant to exterminate all Indians, but he modified his position only to the extent that he promised, once the war ended, to punish only "those who can be clearly proved to have been chief instigators of the war and most determined opponents of peace."[67]

Though simple, Stevens' policy was arbitrary in that he failed to take into account the cruelly conflicting pressures and loyalties the various tribes had to deal with. Stevens did not perceive that the Indians found it virtually impossible to take a neutral stance. Bands of Indians supported either one side or the other, in some cases as if they didn't care which. Whatever Stevens' perceptions were, he took advantage of the ambivalence of the Indians by hiring some of them as auxiliaries. This met with some success. Although most of these auxiliaries did little fighting, at least they were prevented from joining the hostiles.[68]

The other part of Stevens' policy, the sealing off of the Puget Sound country and the isolation of the friendly Indians, was impossible from the outset. A massive army could not have closed the mountain passes any more than they could have guarded the vast forests that crowded the Sound's shores.

Stevens' policy toward the friendly tribes was not, however, a total failure. He started with virtually no organization and no funds in January 1856 and managed to build a network of reserves and agencies throughout western Washington. Although there were occasional shortages in some areas, sufficient food was supplied to prevent starvation or suffering. Men such as Nathan Hill, Sidney Ford, and Robert Fay (at Penn's Cove) were honest, faithful agents who attempted to serve the Indians well. Working under enormous handicaps, Stevens deserves credit for a monumental effort to keep the Sound Indians supplied during the winter.[69]

By the summer of 1856 an uneasy peace existed on Puget Sound and Stevens claimed his strategy had been proven effective. Many Indians, however, although discouraged by their lack of military success, were still unvanquished. In addition the governor had expended vast sums of money to support the militia as well as the Indian service in an effort that regular army authorities claimed was largely unnecessary. General Wool argued that the presence of the Ninth Infantry—not the militia—had sufficiently discouraged further hostilities. The volunteers, he exclaimed, had had an opposite effect. Although Stevens would not publicly admit it, he recognized that much of his policy had failed. The volunteers had not won the successes he predicted, the army was in control on the east side of the mountains, and he had been charged with extravagant expenditures to conduct an unnecessary Indian war. Stevens needed a dramatic victory or a scapegoat if he wished to emerge with an unblemished image.

MARTIAL LAW

Throughout the nation the 1850s marked the quickening of opposition to races or religions deemed out of step with Americanism. Settlers in the western territories shared these prejudices. The Know-Nothing party, which became the political spokesman in the East for those who feared the rise of anti-American groups, did not develop a strong organization in Washington Territory, but many citizens were sympathetic to its platform. Slavery and the free Negro were one concern (the first legislature debated the issue), and, more important, antagonism toward half-breeds and Catholics was another. The power of Catholic priests, as well as the presence of numerous half-breeds (many of whom were Catholic and had once worked for the Hudson's Bay Company) gave credence in the Northwest to the beliefs of the Know-Nothings. The start of the Indian war increased concerns as many citizens suspected that the Indians were influenced by the Catholic, half-breed population.

To a degree, Stevens shared the prejudices of his era. But he preferred to judge men as individuals in the context of particular actions or circumstances. He was willing to work with Catholic priests or half-breeds in settling the Northwest if they supported his goals and programs. The governor had availed himself of the good services of priests at his treaty councils, and he had at times praised their work with the Indians. His dispute with Father Hoecken (prior to the Blackfoot council) indicated that minorities, as well as others, would suffer his wrath if he suspected any wavering in their support.

In the spring of 1856 Stevens realized that the volunteers were not bringing the war to a rapid conclusion. He began to fear that critics such as General Wool would be able to discredit his policy and destroy his credibility as a political leader in the territory and the nation's capital. Stevens was reluctant to admit, even to himself, that the policy was in error. He settled on two reasons for the continuance of the war: first, the obstinance of General Wool, who had frustrated his military efforts; and second, the half-breeds living on the Sound, who he believed had given aid to the Indians and who had thrown insurmountable obstacles in the path of the volunteers. The half-breeds earlier had attempted to thwart the governor at the treaty councils, and he concluded that a concerted, well-organized plot existed to oppose his policies.

When the Indian war began, the men in question, either by words or actions, declared their neutrality in the contest. To the governor this was unacceptable; just as he classified Indians as hostile or friendly, so citizens of the territory either supported the war or they did not. He considered the latter to be traitors. But the half-breeds pleaded that they did not have a quarrel with anyone and that they intended only to live peacefully on their claims. Although half-breeds either lived with the Indians or on isolated claims throughout western Washington, Stevens focused on those living at Muck Prairie, east of the Nisqually River. Some of these men were former Hudson's Bay Company employees living on lands included in the Puget Sound Agricultural Company claim, and at least two (Lyon A. [Sandy] Smith and Charles Wren) had Indian wives. During the winter months Indians passed through or stopped at the Muck Prairie claims on numerous occasions.

Two incidents in particular aroused the governor's suspicion. On Christmas night 1855 nine Indians stopped to visit at the home of John McLeod (a half-breed), where four settlers were celebrating the holiday with a game of cards. Several weeks later, hostile Indians (including Leschi) spent several days in the same vicinity. When they had departed, McLeod forwarded a message from Leschi indicating that he desired hostilities to cease. Sensing perfidy, Stevens charged that the half-breeds had given the Indians supplies and had concealed their presence from the volunteers. The settlers rejoined that they provided only such hospitality as was necessary to keep the Indians from turning on them. They also made the point that the Indians were quite capable of taking supplies, with or without permission. Later, after the killings of William Northcraft and William White on February 24, the Indian perpetrators traveled through Muck Prairie and stopped briefly at the claim of

Charles Wren. This was the last straw for Stevens; the half-breeds at Muck Prairie were ordered to move to Fort Nisqually.[1]

The governor's action was the first of a series of arrests and trials—and the declaration of martial law in Pierce and Thurston counties. The consequent political and legal battles soon overshadowed the Indian war.

It is doubtful that Stevens knew much about the legal intricacies of martial law. He merely assumed that the Organic Act gave him emergency authority to employ extreme measures in time of war.

Although Stevens would have disputed any charge that he was not a thoroughgoing democrat (as well as a Democratic party faithful), his temperament, training, and professional career best prepared him to operate as a monarch. He had always viewed his responsibilities broadly, and his overlapping duties and titles after 1853 led him to assume that he had absolute power. He defended his actions as a military necessity; he even portrayed himself as the territory's only hope for salvation.[2]

The martial-law declaration created a wave of reaction which Stevens had not expected. Yet his considerable knowledge of American history and politics should have alerted him to the danger of tampering with long-held principles and precedents, particularly those based on fear of too much power in the hands of the executive. This fear had led the framers of both national and state constitutions to delegate a major share of political power to legislatures on the theory that they were more responsive to the wishes of the people. Only the legislature could abrogate traditional civil rights and suspend the right of habeas corpus to declare martial law. Even the President did not possess this power. Stevens' assumption that he had these powers elicited vigorous reactions from his own constituency and from the federal government.[3]

When Stevens ordered the Muck Prairie half-breeds off their claims, he asked William F. Tolmie to keep them at Fort Nisqually because they would be most amenable to staying at the Puget Sound Agricultural Company post. Stevens explained, "I have determined to have placed under guard for a limited period all the persons suspected of intercourse with Indians between this place [Olympia] and Puyallup." The governor sent Doty to bring in the men, but he went only as far as Steilacoom, where he launched into a four-day drinking spree which led to his dismissal.[4]

The half-breeds agreed at first to follow Stevens' orders, and, after taking a few days to collect their belongings, they began to leave their homes the first week in March. Most went to Steilacoom rather than Fort Nisqually, but they were in the settlements at least, and the governor could turn his attention to other duties. On March 10 the volunteers fought the battle of Connell's Prairie; many settlers took heart from this victory and began to move back to their claims. The panic that had existed during the fall and winter began to subside, although most believed that danger still existed, particularly at the more isolated locations. A number of the half-breeds removed from Muck Prairie, refusing exile at Fort Nisqually, left the territory for Vancouver Island and Oregon, but men like Wren, McLeod, and Sandy Smith owned prosperous claims; they saw no reason why they should remain in the settlements and allow their farms to fall into ruin while other settlers were returning to the land. By the end of the month these men, and others who had not left the territory, returned to their homes.[5]

On the last two days of March, Major H. J. G. Maxon, patrolling with the Southern Battalion, arrested seven men on their Muck Prairie claims for violation of the governor's orders. Maxon, and Indian agent Wesley Gosnell (who accompanied the troops), admitted that they had no proof of wrongdoing by those arrested; they could only repeat the earlier rumors of alleged cooperation with the hostiles. Stevens ordered the prisoners—Sandy Smith, Charles Wren, John McLeod, Henry Smith, John McField, Henry Murray, and Peter Wilson—to be placed in the custody of the army at Fort Steilacoom (the territory did not yet have a jail). Stevens, convinced that disobedience to his orders gave proof that they were guilty of collusion, decided to try the men as soon as evidence could be collected. He explained to Colonel Casey that the men were all half-breeds and discharged servants of the Hudson's Bay Company who were connected by marriage to the Indians, and "We have reason to believe, from their immunity from danger, [that they] have been giving aid and comfort to the enemy." But the courts needed evidence, not supposition, and Casey agreed to hold the men only for a short time.[6]

When Stevens realized that he did not have proof that would be acceptable in a civil court, he shifted the cases to a military tribunal which might be more amenable to a guilty verdict, a verdict that would amply demonstrate that men could not aid the Indians with impunity—or disobey the governor's orders. A conviction also would provide an explanation to government officials as to why the volunteers had not been more successful in their campaigns. When the governor's intentions became known, a number of citizens, led by a group of lawyers in Steilacoom, came to the defense of the prisoners by insisting they had the right to trial in the civil courts. Frank Clark and William Wallace, two of the lawyers, headed for the home of Territorial Judge Francis Chenoweth (on Whidbey Island) to secure a writ of habeas corpus. The governor countered with a declaration of martial law for Pierce County which was posted in Steilacoom on April 3. It read:

Whereas, in the prosecution of the Indian war, circumstances have existed affording such grave cause of suspicion, such that certain evil disposed persons of Pierce county have given aid and comfort to the enemy, as that they had been placed under arrest and ordered to be tried by a military commission; and whereas, efforts are now being made to withdraw, by civil process, these persons from the purview of the said commission. Therefore, as the war is now being actively prosecuted throughout nearly the whole of the said county, and great injury to the public, and the plans of the campaign be frustrated, if the alleged designs of these persons be not arrested, I, Isaac I. Stevens, Governor of the Territory of Washington, do hereby proclaim Martial Law over the said county of Pierce, and do by these presents suspend for the time being and until further notice, the functions of all civil officers in said county.[7]

Judge Chenoweth issued the writ of habeas corpus before he learned of the governor's declaration. Meanwhile, Stevens asked Casey to continue to hold the prisoners and to disregard any writ that might come from the civil authorities. He indicated further that if the judge took no action on a writ, he would not put martial law in effect, thereby making it clear that his declaration had less to do with the military state of the county than with an attempt to keep the prisoners under military jurisdiction. Casey quickly recognized that he might find himself in an uncomfortable position between the governor and the territorial judiciary. He told Stevens, "I doubt whether your proclamation can relieve me from the obligation to obey the requisition of the civil authority." The governor responded by sending Indian agent Samuel McCaw with volunteer troops to remove the prisoners to Camp Montgomery, and soon thereafter six of the men were taken to Olympia and placed in the charge of Warren Gove of the volunteers' commissary department. Stevens delayed the trial because he had no evidence. Even a military commission would require more proof than supposition or rumor. But the governor had publicly stated that they were "evil disposed persons;" he had gone too far to drop the charges. However, when the prisoners continued to press for permission to return to their homes, Stevens relented to the extent of letting them ride out with a military escort to pick up personal items.[8]

As time for the regularly scheduled session of the Third District Court in Steilacoom drew near, Stevens realized that he had placed himself in a difficult position. He cautioned Benjamin F. Shaw, who had become his representative in Steilacoom, to see that martial law was enforced, but he also indicated that he was "desirous at the earliest practical period to allow the ordinary functions of the civil authorities." By May 5, the day court was scheduled to open, the governor was even more concerned; he stayed up through most of the night debating whether he should revoke his proclamation. He decided to wait, but implored of Shaw, "Have you new evidence against the accused?"[9]

Having become seriously ill, Third District Court Judge Chenoweth asked Lander to substitute for him at Steilacoom. Lander had been serving as a lieutenant colonel in the volunteers under a commission issued by Mason and had participated in the defense of Seattle in January. When he learned that he would be holding the court session, Lander resigned his commission, but Stevens refused to accept it, telling Lander that he was bound to obey the orders of the commander-in-chief. The judge ignored the governor, and when Lander arrived in Steilacoom on May 5, Shaw (acting on orders from Stevens) warned that he would use force if necessary to prevent the court from frustrating the governor's plans for the prisoners. He urged Lander to adjourn the session for two or three weeks. The judge agreed to delay for two days, but only to allow Shaw to persuade Stevens to end martial law voluntarily.[10]

Others also applied pressure on Shaw, particularly George Gibbs, who was then a sutler at Fort Steilacoom and a friend of both Shaw and the governor. A direct, earthy frontiersman, Shaw had not thought to question the governor's actions. But Gibbs was persuasive, and Shaw began a letter which advised the governor to rescind his edict. The governor might have followed the advice of one of his closest associates, but he never received the letter. As Shaw wrote, he had second thoughts and went outside to confer with some of the volunteers, men who had no doubt that the half-breeds were guilty and should be brought to trial. Shaw declared himself

satisfied that if martial law was not enforced, and the prisoners tried before a
military commission, that great injury would result to the public service, and
the confidence of my troops destroyed, in consequence of men being at large,
who men believe to be the worst enemies of American citizens and the progress of the war.[11]

Lander attempted to head off the impending clash by personally appealing to the governor. In an attempt to be conciliatory,
he agreed that martial law was necessary at the time of its declaration, but "The present condition of the country does not
seem to require it as strongly as before." Lander warned of the
"imminent danger of collision between the civil and military
authorities. Nothing could be more disasterous." Stevens
countered that cases had been transferred previously to Chenoweth's district because of charges that Lander was prejudiced,
and it would hardly be proper for him to decide as to the legal-
ity of the martial-law edict. As Lander prepared to open court
on May 7, the governor told Shaw to use good judgment and
discretion, "But martial law must be enforced."[12]

Tension ran high. Colonel Casey, deciding to keep the army
as far as possible from the disputing parties, confined his men to
the post. The sheriff of Pierce County gathered a posse com-
itatus (consisting primarily of local lawyers) to protect the court.
When Lander arrived he cautioned against any precipitate actions and confidently predicted that the weight of law and tradition would prevent any physical disruption of the court. However, soon after the judge took his seat on the bench, a company
of volunteers, many of whom were residents of Oregon, charged
into the room while a second company stationed itself outside.
Lander coolly proceeded to impanel a grand jury, but after a
few minutes, Shaw suddenly announced that by order of the
governor he was closing the court and arresting Lander as well
as the clerk of the court, John M. Chapman. Lander could see
that the volunteers were determined, and he pleaded with the
local posse not to offer resistance. Shaw immediately took the
judge, clerk, and court records to Olympia. The Pierce County
lawyers in the courthouse were stunned by the governor's action.
All had previously witnessed courtroom tactics that were une-
thical, or that bent the law, but they, like Lander, were totally
unprepared for the use of naked force by the volunteers. When
the shock wore off, they vented their anger by drawing up resolutions which were immediately dispatched to Congress and the
President. Later the same day they called a second meeting
which was more widely attended by citizens of Pierce County.

The arrest of Judge Lander was characterized as "an outrage ... subversive of our liberties," a course of action "without precedent in law or justice," and a "violation of every principle of constitutional privilege." The governor's suspension of habeas corpus was labeled a "usurpation unheard of in the history of our country," and the citizens accused Stevens of "a most despotic assumption of authority."[13]

Among the men who framed the resolutions were George Gibbs, Hugh Goldsborough, Benjamin F. Kendall, and Frank Clark, all members of the Democratic party or former associates of Stevens. Their participation indicated that the uproar was not merely a partisan political move against the governor, and many citizens began to have second thoughts or to think for the first time about the implications of Lander's arrest and martial law. Stevens was painting himself into a tight political corner. He reacted by taking the offensive. He was not going to let a coterie of lawyers disrupt his policies any more than he would tolerate opposition from Indians or half-breeds. One concession was made when he released Lander and the court records as soon as they arrived in Olympia—on the grounds that martial law was only in effect in Pierce County. Chapman, however, remained under arrest for several days.

The governor replied to the strictures of the Pierce County meetings with a statement entitled, "Vindication of Governor Stevens for Proclaiming and Enforcing Martial Law in Pierce County, Washington Territory." Stevens defended his action as necessary and right. It was necessary, he argued, because an Indian war was raging in which "whole families had been inhumanly massacred; alarm and consternation pervaded the whole territory" with "families living in blockhouses . . . and a majority of the citizens in arms, actively pursuing the enemy in order to end the war." The governor went on to state that a few men were found visiting with the hostiles, acting as spies, giving supplies, and "in every way furnishing them aid and comfort." Stevens, who had previously declared these men guilty of treason, now added a new charge: "There is grave cause of belief, not only that these persons fraternized with the hostiles, but that they were the main original cause of the war." Further, it was necessary to declare martial law because to allow the writ of habeas corpus to take effect "would have been to paralyze the military in their exertions to end the war, and to send into their midst a band of Indian spies."

It is likely that Stevens consciously exaggerated the role of the accused men in the war, but there is no doubt that he believed that he had the right to enact martial law. He assumed that the executive power and military authority of the territory were not only vested in him but that the two responsibilities were in fact inseparable and that those who thought otherwise were "public committees of citizens without law," who would bring a reign of vigilante terror upon the territory. Stevens professed confidence that the people would sustain his actions "as an imperious necessity growing out of an almost unexampled condition of things." He assured Shaw that if they presented their case in the strongest terms, all would go well.[14]

Judge Lander refused to become involved in public debate with the governor in the hope that tempers would cool sufficiently to allow a settlement that would satisfy all parties. Others, however, were not so conciliatory. The Steilacoom lawyers began to do their homework, and Benjamin F. Kendall discovered, to his surprise, that the existence of a state of hostility in Pierce County was irrelevant because neither the military commander nor the chief executive could suspend habeas corpus; such was the prerogative of the legislature. Other lawyers discovered that Stevens' power to declare martial law was suspect because the volunteers and their commander-in-chief did not have a legal existence; the troops were not regularly enrolled militia operating either under the laws of the territory or the federal government.[15]

Armed with this powerful ammunition, George Gibbs and Hugh Goldsborough, who became the most vocal spokesmen for those opposed to martial law, fired off a letter to Secretary of State William Marcy. They dismissed Stevens' rationale for martial law and asserted that the attempt to blame the war on the half-breeds was a fiction that "found birth in Governor Stevens' own brain." The governor's former associates then leveled a blistering personal attack. They charged that he was "actuated by an arrogant and unbridled love of power that unfits him for any trust in which life or liberty is concerned," and that "The sole object of the Proclamation was to get half a dozen obscure individuals into his absolute control and to demonstrate that he, Isaac I. Stevens could on the field offered by a small territory enact at second hand the part of a diminutive Napoleon." Gibbs and Goldsborough believed that Stevens missed the main issue in his "Vindication," which was "simply whether a public servant shall be allowed to over-ride all law, even the highest; to

usurp, at his sole and egotistical discretion, absolute power over
life and liberty, or whether the LAW OF THE LAND is to
control him." They demanded that the governor be immediately
removed from office.[16]

Stevens' friends charged that the two men, in attempting to
raise themselves from a well-deserved obscurity by attacking a
great man, were turning on Stevens after displaying "sickening"
and "fawning" behavior when in his employ. The governor reacted by stiffening his resolve. On May 12 Judge Lander
opened the regular session of the Second District Court in
Olympia, and the next day (upon request of the arrested men's
lawyers) issued a writ of habeas corpus on behalf of Wren,
McLeod, Sandy Smith, McField, and Henry Smith. The governor countered by extending martial law to Thurston County. On
May 14 Lander issued an order for Stevens to appear and explain why he had defied the writ of habeas corpus. Stevens ignored this communication until George Corliss, the territorial
marshal, attempted to serve the judge's order. When he approached the governor's office, Corliss was met by a dozen volunteers led by Captain Bluford Miller, who suggested in strong
terms that it would not be healthy to carry out the mission.
Corliss returned to the courthouse, followed by the volunteers,
who were acting under Stevens' orders to use good judgment
but to "attain the ends necessary." Miller called upon Lander
to surrender, but those in the courtroom replied by bolting the
door. After a pause the volunteers smashed in the door and
Lander, for the second time in eight days, was marched out of
court under armed guard. The judge was escorted to the governor's office, and while Lander was held outside, Miller went in
to confer with Stevens. Miller emerged to offer Lander parole if
he promised not to hold court while martial law was in effect.
The judge refused. He was then taken to Camp Montgomery
and imprisoned.[17]

On May 12 Stevens' supporters had held a public meeting in
Olympia to endorse his policies to that point. The second arrest
of Lander, however, marked a turning point in public opinion.
Pressure was building against martial law. Although most of the
citizens were not certain of the legal rights of the executive or
judicial branches, they knew that something was wrong when a
judge could be summarily removed from his courtroom and imprisoned. Stevens, acting quickly to resolve the affair, set May
20 as the court-martial date for the arrested men, although he
had no more evidence than when they had been seized at the

end of March. On the appointed day the military commission convened at Camp Montgomery with Lieutenant Colonel J. S. Hurd, Major H. J. G. Maxon, Captain Calvin Swindal, Captain W. W. DeLacy, and Lieutenant A. Shepard, all volunteers, serving on the board. The governor's opponents contemptuously claimed that none of the men were "acquainted with law, martial or civil."[18]

Victor Monroe, who had been relieved of his judicial position in 1854, was employed by the governor as judge advocate. Monroe accused Sandy Smith, John McLeod, and Charles Wren with having given food and shelter to the Indians, having failed to report their movements, and having given information injurious to the volunteers. Monroe also charged that the men had pretended to be neutral in a time of war and had failed to obey the governor's orders. Sandy Smith was tried first. His lawyers, William Wallace, Benjamin F. Kendall, and Frank Clark, protested that military commissions lacked the power to try crimes of treason. Also, they contended, the governor had acted illegally in constituting the body. The board agreed with the first objection and threw out the treason charges, but they judged that they were a legal body to try crimes which normally came under the jurisdiction of military tribunals. These preliminary motions occupied the first several days of the commission hearing.[19]

Meanwhile, the Steilacoom lawyers appealed to Judge Chenoweth, who had recovered his health but who remained on Whidbey Island. Chenoweth had been a strong supporter of the war effort, and, although he termed the martial-law declaration a "monstrous assumption of arbitrary power," he delayed in the hope that the governor could satisfactorily explain his motives. When Chenoweth received the governor's "Vindication," it appeared to him "more like a confession of his error than a justification of his course." Chenoweth then announced that the civil courts had been, and still were, willing to hear any charges the governor might bring against the accused. On Saturday, May 24, he arrived in Steilacoom to reopen court. Stevens did not see Chenoweth's letter announcing this decision, but the news spread quickly to Olympia. The governor again told Shaw, "Martial law must be maintained." He ordered him to prevent the court from meeting and to "arrest the judge on his attempting it." It appeared that the situation was farther from solution than ever, and Gibbs darkly predicted that blood would be shed. Elwood Evans, another former friend who opposed the governor's actions, was equally pessimistic when he cried, "Where this may lead God only knows." Stevens' opponents, like the governor, were convinced that they were in the right. Evans summed up the position of Stevens' opposition with the statement, "Military despotism is as hard to bear now as it was in 1776."[20]

Stevens seemed determined to make the predictions of Gibbs and Evans come true. He asserted that the "commission for the trial of the prisoners is the crisis of the war on this side. It must go on at all hazards." Lander was accused of a "high misdemeanor in endeavoring to subvert the civil authority of the territory in time of war." Stevens even claimed that Lander had usurped the power of the President. The governor boldly affirmed, "I have a right in law to pursue the course I have pursued, and the exigency demanded it." But Stevens did modify his position slightly when he ordered Shaw to allow Chenoweth to preside, subject to arrest if he issued any writ in favor of the prisoners.[21]

Chenoweth opened the court on May 24, while outside the building an angry group of local citizens faced a body of volunteers commanded by Lieutenant Samuel Curtis. Some of the troops had threatened to tear down the town if court convened, and Chenoweth had issued writs of habeas corpus for the three men held by the military commission even before the day's session began. Colonel Casey refused to bring regulars from the fort (as requested by the townspeople), but he came alone to act as a mediator. It was probably only the efforts of Casey, as a disinterested third party, that prevented the showdown (and the bloodshed) Gibbs had predicted. He convinced Curtis that force would be foolish and persuaded him to withdraw until his superiors settled the dispute. With this crisis averted, the writs were served on Shaw, who refused to hand over the prisoners. Expecting Shaw's refusal, Chenoweth had prepared a long opinion which reviewed the controversy and concluded that the writ superseded any order of the governor. The judge told Shaw and the other volunteers that they were right in obeying the orders of their superior officers, but that when such orders were illegal, they did not have to obey; indeed they had to disobey or be "guilty of a violation of the criminal law."[22]

Chenoweth's well-reasoned opinion, the failure of the volunteers to act, and the determination of the citizens of Steilacoom forced the governor to retreat. Stevens began to realize that he was in error legally and that his actions could have disastrous effects on his own career as well as vitiating the policies he had worked so hard to implement. On Sunday, May 25, while an uneasy calm prevailed in Steilacoom, Stevens made perhaps the hardest decision of his life. He ordered Lander and the other prisoners released, revoked martial law, and allowed the civil courts jurisdiction over any criminal proceedings. Although Stevens no longer argued that he had been legally correct, he continued to assert that absolute necessity demanded the actions. Still, he had had to back down, and it was a bitter pill to swallow. Ultimately, Stevens took his case to the people and, in 1857, won their verdict at the polls. Though he had been redeemed through the democratic process, Stevens did not forget those who supported or opposed him during the martial-law controversy.

The governor's letter announcing the repeal of martial law reached Steilacoom just as Benjamin Shaw was being arrested for violating Chenoweth's court order. Stevens cleverly, but weakly, explained that martial law was no longer necessary as the removal of the troublemakers had resulted in peace. The most surprised man in Steilacoom was Shaw, who had expected the governor to muster all the troops necessary to effect his release. Instead, a polite letter from Stevens asked Chenoweth to release Shaw on bail because he was needed to command an expedition to the Yakima country. The judge complied, asking only that Shaw promise to appear at the next court term to answer contempt charges. Stevens suggested to Judge Advocate Monroe that his best course might be to dissolve the military commission and turn the prisoners over to the civil courts because, he lamely explained, the trial was taking "too many officers from the command of the troops." Elwood Evans summed up the sudden turn of events.

What a fizzle! Well did the governor's great exemplar Napoleon predict "'Tis but one step from the sublime to the ridiculous," and sure he must have expected such an advent as I.I.I.I.S. and just such a denouncement to a farce so contemptable.[23]

Sandy Smith, John McLeod, and Charles Wren were brought before a hearing conducted under Judge Chenoweth's jurisdiction by United States Commissioner J. M. Batcheler. After hearing testimony for a week, Batcheler ruled that there was insufficient evidence to warrant a trial and the men were released. There was one final round in the territorial courts. In July Judge Lander cited the governor for contempt, but fined him a

nominal fifty dollars. With typical bravado, Stevens pardoned
himself, but this well-publiciz̧d action was primarily for the
benefit of the newspapers. By this time he knew that, legally,
Lander was right. He allowed associates to pay the fifty dollars,
observing that the honor of the court had been cheaply assuaged.[24]

While the final scenes were played out in Washington Territory, political figures in the nation's capital reacted to reports of
the controversy and the charges of the Steilacoom lawyers. Senator Lewis Cass of Michigan, a friend of Stevens and a power in
the Democratic party, expressed dismay and called upon the
President to provide the Senate with the facts on martial law in
Washington Territory. From the information available to Cass,
it appeared that there had been a usurpation of civil authority
by the military. Cass admitted that Andrew Jackson had declared martial law in New Orleans prior to the British invasion
in 1815, but excused this as an extreme circumstance in which
Jackson relied on public opinion to sustain his actions. The Senator warned that anyone who followed Jackson's course took the
same risk of forfeiting all future public office or positions of
trust. Cass thundered, "I do not want an officer on the border
of this Republic, under ordinary circumstances, to follow the example of General Jackson, to proclaim martial law on every Indian incursion. It is not to be tolerated." Cass admitted that "in
the presence of the enemy extraordinary transactions may take
place," but he was disturbed that Stevens "assumes to have the
power" to declare martial law.[25]

Andrew Johnson, perhaps the leading spokesman in the Senate for democracy and the common man, noted with alarm a
trend toward increased military control over civil authorities.
Never, Johnson asserted, since the attempt to crown George
Washington, had the military "shown so strong a disposition to
assume to itself the control of government," and, he explained,
"Though the army has not declared martial law in this case, the
authority which did declare it is connected with the authority of
the commander-in-chief in that Territory. I hope it will be
called to account." In a later debate several Senators (including
Samuel Adams of Mississippi, who had recommended Stevens
for the governorship) insisted that the Superintendency of Indian Affairs for Washington Territory be assigned to another
person before they would approve the yearly appropriation for
that department.[26]

President Pierce and Secretary of State Marcy were embarrassed by the martial law uproar, but they said and did little at first in the hope that it would not become a public issue. The debate in Congress, and the publication of letters by Gibbs, Goldsborough, Lander, and Evans in the *New York Times* brought the governor's actions into the political arena. Pierce was bombarded by demands from the anti-Stevens group in the territory to remove him as governor. Some of the attacks charged t'..t Stevens was a man

of a naturally arrogant and domineering character, of overwhelming ambition, and even unscrupulous as to the means requisite to effect his objects, [and] he has been further inflamed by the immoderate use of ardent spirits, and in fits of intoxication knows no bounds to his language or to his actions.

But Pierce was reluctant to remove a friend who had served him well in the past. He delayed a decision until word arrived that martial law had been revoked and the civil courts had been reinstated without injury or riots. He allowed Stevens to remain as governor, although the administration acquiesced in the move to combine the Washington superintendency of Indian affairs with that of Oregon. However, Marcy and Pierce did not condone the governor's action, and on September 12 the Secretary of State sent a stinging rebuke. He noted that after examination of Stevens' arguments, the President "has not been able to find in the case you have presented a justification for that extreme measure." Marcy avoided a commitment on whether or not a territorial governor could declare martial law, but he emphasized that if it were possible it would only be in dire circumstances "involving the probable overthrow of the civil government," and, "While the President does not bring into question the motives by which you were actuated, he is induced, by an imperative sense of duty to express his distinct disapproval of your conduct so far as respects the proclamation of martial law." Marcy concluded that Stevens' action appeared to diminish the civil government rather than to save or restore it. "Your conduct in this respect, does not, therefore, meet with the favorable regard of the President."[27]

Martial law had implications not only for Stevens' career, but also for the American political system. Prior to 1856 American politicians had dealt gingerly with martial law or the suspension of civil liberties. Stevens, however, during his military career, had been accustomed to military tribunals and courts-martial. His dual position as commander-in-chief of the volunteers and as governor muddled the issues in Washington Territory and allowed Stevens to act interchangeably as governor and military commander. Observers were unable to decide if martial law was an attack by the military upon civil authorities or a conflict between the judicial and executive branches. The realization that he did not have the power, either as governor or military commander, to inflict military justice on civilians came as a shock to Stevens, but he recouped his political fortunes by appealing to the people and winning their support. Perhaps most important is the fact that Stevens did not succeed in imposing martial law or subverting the jurisdiction of the courts. Faced with a threat to traditional rights and liberties, several citizens along with Judges Lander and Chenoweth struggled to preserve the separation of powers and the supremacy of civil authorities over the military. They amply demonstrated that unilateral assumptions of power would not be tolerated. The martial law fight in Washington Territory marked the beginning, not the end, of a struggle in the United States to retain the supremacy of civilian authority, separation of powers, and civil liberties. With the start of the Civil War, all these traditions came under attack—both from Abraham Lincoln and from the Confederate government of Jefferson Davis. Governor Stevens' conduct in 1856 in many respects adumbrated the broad use of executive power during the decade which followed.

RETURN TO
WALLA WALLA

During the first six months of 1856 Isaac Stevens labored under a crushing load of responsibilities. His burden was increased
by the absence of men in whom he could confide or seek valuable counsel. Mason was in Washington D.C., Doty was disgraced, and Gibbs, Goldsborough, Evans, and others had deserted the cause because of disagreement either on war policy or
martial law. Some charged that the governor turned to drink to
ease the pressure. Although he professed prohibition sentiments
in his youth, Stevens had learned the pleasures of social drinking at West Point, and in subsequent years he was ready to
drink his share on convivial occasions. No one, however, accused
him of drunkenness until 1856, when Gibbs and Goldsborough
claimed that he had delivered intoxicated harrangues at Camp
Montgomery and in Portland. Charges of drunkenness were
hurled frequently by political foes in the nineteenth century;
such charges often proved completely unjust or greatly exaggerated. Stevens denied that he drank heavily, but he did not dispute overindulgence on the two occasions cited by Gibbs and
Goldsborough. It is likely that he drank excessively at times, but
these lapses were relatively rare, seldom disrupting his daily
routine of constant labor.[1]

Meg and the children were a rock of stability in the governor's life. Meg's resolve had stiffened considerably during her
year and a half in the territory. She professed, for instance, that
the war disturbed her only because it drove up the price of butter and eggs. The Stevenses discussed the new house they
planned to build on the edge of Olympia once the crisis passed,
and Meg attempted to keep the mood festive by giving parties
and dances. On one occasion, a party for the men of the *Mas-*

sachusetts, she decorated the house, and the path leading to it, with lights and evergreens. Stevens did not consult his wife on specific decisions relating to official duties, but he relied on her support, which she always gave, no matter what his decision might be. She exclaimed to her sister, "I am interested in seeing the Governor plan and order the men about. Almost every man far and near have put themselves under his control." Stevens did confide his hopes and fears to Meg. He acknowledged his possible recall as governor and confessed, as he would have to no one else, deep distress that his policies had alienated many old friends and allies. His dedication to work must have placed strains on their marriage, but Meg did not question the priorities even when he declared that, if removed from office, he would not sit idle for a single day. Meg's love for her husband had matured from a youthful, tender devotion to a love based more on respect and admiration. Stevens' love for Meg, on the other hand, allowed him to take sustenance from her support and stability—perhaps more than he realized.[2]

Though hostilities on the Sound and the martial-law controversy consumed much of his energy, Stevens could not ignore the still dangerous situation east of the mountains. His concern mounted when the frustrated Oregon volunteers returned home in the spring from the Walla Walla Valley. By that time he had given up hope that the regulars would accomplish anything positive, and, in any event, Stevens had never entirely abandoned the notion of an eastern campaign. Although he postponed the expedition during the winter months, he maintained a correspondence which left little doubt that the Washington volunteers would march when the governor thought the movement opportune. In late May, at about the same time that he rescinded martial law, Stevens determined to mount an expedition of 200 men commanded by Benjamin Shaw. It is likely that the martial law controversy was partly responsible for the timing as the governor could regain his prestige with a victory east of the mountains. Stevens asked Oregon officials for their cooperation and dispatched recruiters into the Willamette Valley to find men, wagons, "first rate horses," and weapons. In February he had told governor Curry, "The volunteers have been left to do all the fighting; ... let us now finish the war before those who have been so backward shall be able to take the field." Stevens expressed complete confidence in Shaw. Surely Shaw, unlike Captain Haller, would not be so timid as to overestimate the opposition and retreat before he had won a victory.[3]

Martial law may have affected the timing, but the activities of the Regular Army were a more important element in Stevens' decision to send Shaw east. General Wool had returned to the Northwest (in March) in fine fettle because he believed the army could take credit for abatement of the war. Also, he had been informed that General Winfield Scott supported him in the quarrel with territorial officials. Wool stopped briefly at Fort Steilacoom where he rebuked Casey for allowing the volunteers to continue in the field and for being overly cooperative with the governor. He made no attempt to contact the governor. (Stevens considered, but then rejected, sending an invitation through Tilton asking the general to visit Olympia.) Satisfied that Casey could handle affairs on the Sound, Wool moved on to Vancouver to consult with Colonel George Wright. They confirmed the earlier decision that Wright should march into Indian country to establish peace—through talks if possible or by fighting if necessary. Wright was also directed to select sites and construct posts in the Yakima and Walla Walla valleys. Wright was a veteran career officer who had graduated from the Military Academy in 1822 and had served for the next thirty years on the frontier, in the Seminole War, and in Mexico. Wright was the type of officer Wool admired: he balanced an excellent combat record, and a reputation as a rigid disciplinarian, with intelligence and tact. One of his fellow officers praised him as "every inch a soldier and a gentleman," and there is no evidence that anyone disputed this assessment.[4]

On March 25 Wright left his camp at the Cascades of the Columbia for The Dalles and the march into the interior. He was aware that the Indians were displeased by army occupation of the Cascades fishing grounds, but he believed that a garrison of nine men (plus the local settlers) was sufficient to keep the peace. The day after Wright's departure, a large number of Klickitat Indians struck the small, separated settlements known as the Upper, Middle, and Lower Cascades. They attacked at the Lower Cascades just after most of the men had left to work on two railroad bridges then under construction. Most killed or wounded fell in this initial assault. One of the men ran down the railroad track to the blockhouse at the Middle Cascades and later jested, "I bet I made the best time that was ever made on a railroad." One or two others also made it to the protection of the blockhouse, but most fled to a store at the Lower Cascades. Some were not as fortunate as the man on the railroad tracks; in the mass confusion James Sinclair, a frontier veteran employed by the Hudson's Bay Company, was killed while peering out the door of the store. Fortunately for those who made it to the store, nine army rifles and several boxes of ammunition that had been deposited for shipment down the river were found and used.

Forty settlers were trapped for two days while the Indians burned the other buildings and attempted to fire the store with torches thrown from a nearby hill. One man, weakened by an arm wound, was pinned behind a rock on the bank of the Columbia midway between the store and the Indians. As neither side wished to traverse the open ground to reach him, the settlers (including his wife and children) watched a gruesome drama; he frequently fainted and fell into the river which revived him enough that he could again crawl behind the rock. He was still alive when rescuers arrived, but died two days later. During the initial attack, several men managed to fire up steam in the *Mary*, and the vessel headed upstream, overtaking Wright's Column five miles beyond The Dalles. Wright reached the Cascades forty-eight hours after the attack had begun. Driven off, the Indians retreated into the hills. At the same time, troops led by Lieutenant Philip Sheridan arrived from downstream and rescued the Lower Cascades settlers.[5]

Wright charged the Indians with treason. Nine, including Chief Chenoweth, were hanged as examples. When the noose was placed around Chenoweth's neck, he gave a war whoop and muttered, "I am not afraid to die." The hangmen failed and the gruesome affair came to an end when the chief was dispatched with a bullet. The treason charge was questionable, but no one protested Wright's action, an action considered to be just reprisal for the killing of sixteen and the wounding of twelve more.

The Cascades encounter was the costliest of the war for the whites, and, while Stevens deplored the loss of life, he and Governor Curry attempted to make political capital of the tragedy by citing it as proof of army incompetence.[6] The *Pioneer and Democrat* chided the army for wasting five months preparing Wright's expedition and then allowing disaster to strike twenty-four hours after its departure; the newspaper smugly suggested that the Indians were better generals than those in the army. The press jibed that maybe Wool, who was in California when the Indians struck, would finally admit that there were hostile Indians in the Northwest. Referring to a comment allegedly made by Wool that his headquarters was in the saddle, one newspaper editor facetiously remarked, "We have not learned whether or not he brought his saddle along." Curry charged flatly that Wool was responsible for the heavy casualties. The general retorted that the governor might as well blame him for the killing of Peopeomoxmox or other atrocities perpetrated by the volunteers. It was a telling rebuttal. After the Cascades affair, Oregon volunteers killed a number of friendly Indians, including one family of six who were strangled. Wright demanded to know how he could bring peace if these acts continued. He pointedly told Curry to withdraw all the Oregon volunteers to the south side of the Columbia—if they would still obey orders. Newspaper attacks notwithstanding, Wool was convinced that the attack on the Cascades was an aberration and directed Wright to restart his campaign when satisfied that the Cascades and other Columbia River points were secure.[7]

As the regulars prepared to move, the governor (who hoped that he might be more successful with Wright than he had been with Casey) suggested a "strong understanding between the regulars and volunteers" on operations east of the Cascade Mountains. He predicted that only "energetic and united" action would prevail as "we have the worst country in the world for operations." Wright had been acquainted with Stevens in the Mexican War. In fact, he had helped to carry him from the battlefield when he was wounded at Molino del Rey. The colonel responded cordially. He reported that his strategy was to concentrate on the Yakima Indian threat. In particular, a permanent post would be established in the Yakima country near the fisheries. He went on to state that he was confident that the Indian victory at the Cascades settlements would not be a stimulus sufficient to precipitate future large-scale warfare; rather, his strategy would soon produce an agreement for permanent peace. Stevens pressed for information on army plans for the Walla Walla Valley. He was told that, as those tribes were peaceful, Wright would concentrate on the Yakimas.[8]

Stevens, however, was convinced that the tribes in the Walla Walla Valley were hostile, despite their consistent attempts to avoid involvement in the war. Wright's attitude persuaded the governor that Shaw, his ever-willing lieutenant, would need to march a volunteer force to the Walla Walla country. Wright crossed the Columbia at The Dalles on April 28, and this news led the governor to press ahead with preparations. Six weeks later Shaw left Camp Montgomery with 175 mounted men, thirty-six packers, eighty-two pack animals, twenty beef cattle, and thirty days' rations. Stevens sent a dispatch to Wright, offering the volunteers' aid if he were in trouble. Wright responded that the regulars could handle the operation without help, adding, in a tone as condescending as the governor's offer, that he had no doubt the "volunteers would do good service if necessary to call for them."[9]

Granville Haller, with many veterans of the fall 1855 campaign, led Wright into the Yakima Valley by the same route taken before the October battle. On May 9 Wright reached the south bank of the Naches River opposite a large encampment of Yakimas. There he was reinforced by a detachment under Edward Steptoe which brought his total force to 500. Wright sent messages to the Yakima chiefs indicating that he came not to fight but to talk of peace. The chiefs were hesitant and cautious. Twice they promised to parley but failed to appear. Finally, on May 18 Owhi sent his son to Wright, and later the same day Owhi and Teias made an appearance. Wright, like the governor, spoke of unconditional surrender, but it soon became clear to the Yakimas that the army's terms differed from those of the civilian authorities. The colonel's essential terms were merely a promise to keep the peace.[10]

Wright puzzled over the hesitancy of the chiefs, but he soon understood that there were deep divisions within the tribe, and that the situation was further complicated by the presence of Klickitat, Walla Walla, Umatilla, Palouse, and John Day Indians in the Yakima camp. All had their own assessment of the reasons for the war and the proper policy for the future. The Indians in the Yakima camp were confused because the governor and Army followed different courses. As Wright patiently carried on negotiations, he came to the conclusion that those who favored war had tried mightily during the winter to muster support from the tribes in the Northwest, but only a few representatives of the Yakima, Walla Walla, Cayuse, and Umatilla tribes favored war, although some young men in all tribes wanted to fight. Most leaders, like Garry of the Spokane, promised resistance only if troops invaded their country. A serious split between war and peace advocates among the Yakima chiefs was obvious.

It became apparent also that the white factions were working at cross purposes. Wright learned that Stevens had been carrying on parallel negotiations with Chiefs Teias and Owhi since May. These chiefs had indicated a desire for peace and claimed that they spoke also for Chiefs Skloom and Shumaway. The governor had also received information that Kamiakin was attempting to secure support from the Spokane Indians, which was correct. Kamiakin's liaison with the Spokanes convinced Stevens that the peace overtures made by Teias and Owhi were a plot to gain time while the Yakimas collected reinforcements. Apparently, Stevens did not consider (and would not have believed) that the chiefs were acting independently; he still thought in terms of one tribe, one chief, one policy. Stevens directed Simmons to tell Teias and Owhi that negotiations would take place on the west side of the mountains (near Snoqualmie Falls), but not until the Yakimas had surrendered unconditionally and had given up the murderers to the authorities. Alarmed, the chiefs refused. Wright, angered by the effect of the double negotiations, complained that "it was indispensably necessary that the war be in the hands of one individual." Further angered by the arrival of Shaw's volunteers, Wright gritted his teeth and tried to ignore the governor and his troops. He informed Wool, "My efforts have been retarded, but not defeated by the volunteers."[11]

Although Owhi (and others who at one time supported the war) argued for conciliation during the summer, Kamiakin was reluctant because Stevens blamed him for the war and would demand that he be hanged. In addition, the hostile faction looked to him for leadership, a role that would have been difficult to abandon regardless of the threat to his life. By midsummer Wright correctly guessed that Kamiakin and the war group had insufficient strength to dare an attack against his force. He therefore decided to march north as far as the Wenatchee River to show the flag and to extend peace offerings.[12]

After building a bridge over the Naches River, Wright left three companies at the Naches camp and marched north with the remainder of his troops. In the Kittitas Valley he met with Chiefs Nelson, Leschi, and Kitsap who had fled from the Sound. Wright did not officially pardon these leaders but he allowed them to move freely in and out of his camp. Wright further weakened the power of the hostile faction by sending the Klickitats, who disliked living in Yakima country, to a reservation in Oregon. Father Pandosy, who had remained with the Yakimas during the war, trusted Wright and urged the Indians to cooperate. By mid-July Wright had a large percentage of the Yakima tribe pledged for peace. Many turned from the warpath to begin laying in supplies for the winter. By August 1 the regulars were back in the lower Yakima Valley where Wright reported that he had talked with the Indians, the situation was quiet, and "the war in this country is closed."[13]

Wright agreed with the recommendation of Major Townsend to locate a permanent post on Simcoe Creek (twenty-one miles southwest of present-day Yakima) as it was a crossroads with good wood, water, and climate. He predicted that the post would insure peace in the valley. It was Wright's contention that the area between the Cascade Mountains and the Columbia River should remain Indian country where the natives could maintain themselves without aid once peace was established. However, he asked Stevens to supply 10,000 pounds of flour for the coming winter because the usual food-gathering activities had been disrupted by the uncertainties of that spring and summer. Stevens approved the requisition, but did not agree with Wright's plan for the Yakima country because such a plan would maintain the status quo. It would keep the Indians in their savage state, he protested, and violate "the spirit of the treaty providing for vigorous measures to civilize the Indians." More than one hundred years later, cultural assimilation versus cultural autonomy still provided material for hot debates, and no one can say whether Wright or Stevens proposed the better policy. In the short run, however, Wright's plan was no doubt the wiser as only separation of the races and a cooling-off period could prevent further fighting.[14]

Benjamin Shaw crossed Naches Pass with his command on June 16. Seeing that peace prevailed in Yakima country, contrary to Stevens' predictions, Shaw pushed on immediately to the Walla Walla Valley. The command was plagued by the usual incidents of inefficiency and insubordination that afflicted volunteer units. Most serious was the dispute between Shaw and H. J. G. Maxon, one of three company commanders. Contrary to orders, some of Maxon's men fired off their rifles (as a precaution to prevent misfires from dampness). Shaw blamed Maxon and ordered his arrest, but the company commander countered by attempting to lead a mutiny which would oust Shaw from command. Maxon could not rally support outside his own company, but his men refused to obey anyone but their leader. After this incident Maxon kept his force about one hour's march behind the main party and maintained separate bivouacs. Both Shaw and Maxon wrote to the governor for support. Stevens suggested compromise and cooperation, although he advised Shaw that he had the power to arrest anyone for insubordination.[15]

On July 9, with Maxon still lagging behind, Shaw camped one day's march beyond the Whitman mission. Here they rendezvoused with 750 Nez Perce who had been informed by William Craig of the volunteers' impending arrival. The volunteer leader conveyed Stevens' professions of friendship and appreciation for their steadfast devotion to peace, but Shaw also announced his determination to fight the hostiles. The Nez Perce chiefs wondered aloud who he referred to, and warned that if he meant the Cayuse, the Nez Perce would be sorry to see an attack on their relatives. Shaw ignored these remarks and promised his men that they would not go home "without striking the enemy"—although he felt obliged to add, "if they can be found." It was clear to anyone who cared to listen that the Nez Perce were increasingly unhappy with white treatment of the Walla Walla and Cayuse since the 1855 council. They believed that these tribes had been goaded into war, that their chiefs and warriors had been murdered, and that even those who remained at peace had been harassed. The young men were becoming restive, and some of the older chiefs speculated that the Nez Perce might soon suffer the same fate as their brothers.[16]

The day after the conference with the Nez Perce, some of Maxon's men pleaded with Shaw to replenish their diminished supplies. He refused unless they promised to obey orders. They reluctantly agreed to allow Maxon to be placed under arrest—to be replaced by Lieutenant Curtis. With his force reunited, Shaw's first thought was to pursue Kamiakin who was rumored to be near the Palouse River. But sober reflection convinced him that the elusive chief could not be caught. Instead he decided to move southeast into the Grande Ronde Valley of Oregon where a number of the Walla Walla, Cayuse, and Umatilla bands were camped. The volunteers gladly marched out of the intense heat of the Walla Walla Valley and into the Blue Mountains. After crossing into the Grande Ronde Valley, they spotted a cloud of dust indicating an encampment. A Cayuse messenger approached to report that the camp contained mostly women, old men, children, and a few young men, but that the chiefs were absent and no one present was qualified to hold a conference. When the Cayuse brave returned to the Indian camp, he reported that the force was not Colonel Wright (as they had thought), but volunteers. Remembering the previous actions of the Oregon volunteers, the Indians took alarm and began packing their goods. Meanwhile, Shaw interpreted the remarks of the Cayuse messenger as evasive and hostile, and, when he saw the Indians preparing to flee, he ordered an immediate attack. The volunteers swept through the Indian village, scattering the inhabitants and killing at least sixty, many of whom were women and children. The Indians sought the refuge of nearby gorges, while the volunteers took possession of 300 horses and burned 120 lodges. To one volunteer it was "a good jolly time." Some expressed concern for the absence of Maxon, who had been reactivated, and sixteen other men. When the force returned to the Walla Walla Valley, they found the missing volunteers had preceded them. Maxon claimed that they had been cut off by a large body of hostiles during the attack, but Shaw suspected that they had run in fear. Shaw had had enough. Maxon, and his company, were ordered back to the Sound.[17]

Stevens was overjoyed at the news that Shaw had defeated a large hostile force. It was the great victory he had been hoping for since the beginning of the war. He exulted that now the fighting would come to an end because the Indians knew that the whites would prevail. The volunteers' victory would also vindicate the governor's war strategy. But despite Stevens' joy, the so-called Battle of the Grande Ronde was one of the sorriest affairs of the war. Unlike the December 1855 campaign of the Oregon volunteers, who at least encountered warriors on a field of battle, the Grande Ronde was a massacre of women, children, and old men that foreshadowed similar events at Sand Creek (Colorado) and Washita (Indian Territory) in 1864 and 1866. Grande Ronde did not become as well known as the later massacres, but it is deserving of an equal share of infamy.[18]

During the summer, before he learned of Shaw's victory, Stevens had seriously considered holding a second Walla Walla conference in late summer or early fall. The victory at Grande Ronde convinced him that such a council would be highly advantageous. Though he had obligated himself to return for a treaty with the Spokane, Colville, and Coeur d'Alene Indians, he was now motivated by the possibility that a second Walla Walla council held soon—while the whites enjoyed a perceived increased prestige garnered at Grande Ronde—could result in solidifying relations assured by the first council, as well as persuading the Indians to turn over to the whites all those guilty of precipitating the war. After his return from the Blackfoot council the governor had had to rely upon his Indian agents. He wished now to reestablish personal contact with the chiefs. One agent was Dr. Lansdale who remained in the Bitterroot Valley after the signing of the Flathead treaty. Lansdale also was appointed as the President's agent to make the final determination as to where the reservation was to be located. After a reconnaissance, Lansdale recommended that the tribes remain in the Flathead Valley. Though Stevens had argued for a Bitterroot Valley location, at least Lansdale had been able to honor Stevens' desire to consolidate these tribes on one reservation. The treaty had little effect on the tribes during the winter of 1855–56; Lansdale only received enough supplies for himself and his men while the Indians provided for their own needs (as they always had done previously). The government's inability to provide supplies notwithstanding, the Indians honored their pledge of intertribal peace. Lansdale reported that the Indians traveled freely in search of buffalo and did not tie their horses at night. The treaty was also advantageous in that it clearly defined Indian territory before a large influx of settlers.

Lansdale was not able to bring the Lower Pend d'Oreille Indians under the Flathead treaty, although he held a conference with Victor and other chiefs in March 1856. In addition the failure of the Congress to ratify the treaty delayed the goods that Stevens had promised. By 1857, John Owen, who replaced Lansdale as agent, reported the Indians were discouraged because they had given up the land but had received nothing in return. Victor, the Flathead chief, complained to Owen that "friend Stevens" had said that they would hear about the treaty before many months had passed. While the war delayed ratification of the treaties, and indirectly affected the tribes east of the Bitterroots, neither Lansdale nor Owen was concerned that the Indians in their charge would join the conflict to the west. Rather, Owen's fear was that a lack of food might drive the hostile tribes east into his area of responsibility.[19]

The relative lack of concern of the Flathead agents indicated that the Bitterroot Mountains formed an effective barrier separating events east and west of that line. Thus the governor could concentrate on the Indians closest to the conflict. Of particular concern was keeping the Spokane and Colville tribes from joining forces with the Yakimas. Father Ravalli said that Stevens' council in December 1855 had had a good effect on the tribes in his area. The priest reported, "his words, his manner toward them enraptured the Indians, they believe and comfort themselves repeating his words." Ravalli warned, however, "You well know how quick are the Indians to change their wills," and he suggested that the governor write to Garry and the other chiefs. The tribes in the Colville area feared a renewal of the gold rush that would bring in the volunteers. Knowledge of volunteer activity in the Walla Walla and Grande Ronde surely justified that fear. Above all, Ravalli cautioned, the whites should not send troops into the Spokane country. Angus McDonald attempted to second Ravalli's valuable counsel. He suggested that the Indians should be allowed some ammunition as they no longer had the ability or desire to hunt with bow and arrow. Stevens, ignoring the advice, responded by asking him to raise a militia company in Colville. McDonald was appalled; he warned bluntly that nothing would alarm the Indians more than to be denied ammunition while an armed force was created in their midst. McDonald lamented the recent atrocities committed by the volunteers which had greatly alarmed the tribes, particularly the treatment of Peopeomoxmox, which McDonald sarcastically suggested was "an historical feat 'tis worth salting to show our progress.' "[20]

Stevens took McDonald's advice to refrain from raising volunteers in Colville, but the governor paid little heed to other useful information he had received. He believed that the peaceful Indians could, and should, accept his decisions without question, and he continued to ignore the warning to keep all troops south of the Snake River. That neither the Oregon volunteers nor Shaw's forces crossed this line was accident not design. In addition, the governor's goal of keeping the hostile and friendly Indians apart was unrealistic as free movement between the tribes could not be prevented. Stevens had created bad feeling among the Nez Perce by refusing to allow the friendly Cayuse and Walla Walla Indians to leave the Walla Walla Valley, but they had nevertheless made efforts during the winter to keep known hostiles from living in their territory. However, when the Nez Perce welcomed friendly Cayuse Indians sent to them by Oregon Indian agent Nathan Olney, Stevens was furious and ordered Craig to send the Cayuse away and see that the Nez Perce did not listen to the Oregon agent in the future. The Indians obeyed, but reluctantly. Stevens was straining the friendship and forbearance of the Nez Perce chiefs to the breaking point.[21] Difficulties in moving supplies to the tribes east of the Cascade Mountains created further problems. William Craig distributed 3,000 pounds of beef to the Nez Perce in February, but received no additional supplies until the summer.

Despite these factors, most of the tribes on the Great Columbia Plain continued to reject hostility in favor of continued cooperation with the whites. Preoccupation with troubles on the Sound, and the inability of the Oregon volunteers to move from the Walla Walla Valley, were partly responsible for the relatively favorable situation. Even Wright's nonhostile campaign served to have contributed to the lessening of tensions. Garry assured Stevens that reports that the Spokane Indians would go to war were false. The chief affirmed, "We have always been and still are friendly."[22]

A second Walla Walla council could have been an excellent vehicle to solidify relations—if Stevens had departed from Olympia in June and if Shaw's volunteer force had remained on the Sound. A pledge of amnesty by the governor at a council convened as early as possible may well have brought peace. But despite the truce proposal from the Yakima chiefs, the reception accorded Wright, and other favorable developments, Stevens did not deviate from his original conviction that peace would have to be conquered. Only after the Battle of Grande Ronde did he announce that the war had ended on both sides of the mountains—and begin to muster out the volunteers. He then planned his triumphant return to Walla Walla to reaffirm the treaties which symbolized the validity of his policies. But Stevens, blind to the realities of the Grande Ronde massacre, banked on the wrong battle. Grande Ronde had been the last straw for many former Indian friends. They did not break out into open hostility—that would occur in 1858—but they seethed in anger at the treachery of the volunteers, volunteers whom they knew had received orders from the governor. When Shaw left the Grande Ronde Valley, he heard reports that the Nez Perce wished to fight. He let it be known that the volunteers were eager for battle. The Nez Perce murmured that they were a peaceful nation, but it was clear that they were angered and that only the size of Shaw's force deterred some of the chiefs from accepting the challenge.[23]

The governor called upon all the tribes between the Cascade and Bitterroot Mountains to attend a second Walla Walla council. As proof of his good intentions, he ordered that 40,000 pounds of flour be sent to White Salmon for the use of Indians on the Columbia as well as for those in the Yakima nation who had surrendered to Wright. He proclaimed, "It is not proposed to exterminate the Indians now at war, nor punish any but those who can be clearly proved to have been the chief instigators of the war and most determined opponents of peace." The Indians who fell into each category would be determined by the government. Stevens still insisted that the only terms were "unconditional submission and surrender of murderers" to "justice and mercy as decided by the authorities." While the governor expected that the Indians would submit to his will, Captain Pinkney Lugenbeel, commanding at Fort Dalles, was not as optimistic. He warned Wright, "The volunteers are accumulating troubles for you in the Walla Walla country." Indian agent A. H. Robie would have agreed with Lugenbeel; he had arrived at the main Nez Perce camp four days after the battle at Grande Ronde where he found the mood "impudent and hostile." The chiefs held a council, and, while Lawyer maintained a discreet silence, Looking Glass, Three Feathers, Eagle from the Light, and others condemned the volunteers' actions. One chief declared that the treaties were invalidated because their relatives, the Cayuse, had been murdered, and others averred that they would take no goods and allow no whites to enter their country. Even William Craig was threatened—an indication of how much the Nez Perce mood had shifted. Lawyer confided to Robie that only about a fourth of the Nez Perce remained friendly. Looking Glass apologized for his harshness at the council, but it was clear that the tribe was deeply disturbed. Robie returned quickly to the safety of the volunteer camp.[24]

Governor Stevens and Colonel Wright met at Vancouver and traveled together to The Dalles in mid-August. They were able to lay aside their differences, at least for the moment. After a series of cordial conversations, Stevens agreed to call no more volunteers—and to remove his men from the Walla Walla Valley when regulars arrived.

Stevens reached Shaw's camp on August 23. By that time he was aware that the mood of the Indians was not conducive to a council. As usual, he decided to go ahead nevertheless, reasoning that at least he could strengthen the bonds of friendship with the Spokane and Nez Perce. Messages sent to all the tribes had some positive response. It was even rumored that Kamiakin might attend. Stevens began to believe that stories of the tribes' hostility were no more than the usual exaggerated tales. Then a message arrived from Garry stating that the Spokane would not attend because they had to put up salmon for the winter. Garry remarked that the whites had appeared unfriendly lately toward all Indians. He also indicated that he had heard of threats against himself.[25]

When Wright returned to his headquarters at Fort Vancouver, Major Haller and Major Robert Garnett remained in the Yakima country to supervise construction of Fort Simcoe. Colonel Edward J. Steptoe was ordered to take five companies to establish a new Fort Walla Walla near the Whitman station. Stevens had known Steptoe in Mexico and had admired his coolness and efficiency as an artillery officer. Steptoe had a reputation as a conscientious, dedicated officer destined for increased responsibilities. He was also a close friend of President Pierce and had stayed in the White House as a guest in 1855. While there, Pierce offered Steptoe the governorship of Utah which he declined—upon learning that he was on the army promotion list. Steptoe left Fort Dalles with troops of the Fourth Infantry on August 22. Movement was slow as they were burdened with all the equipment necessary for the new post. The colonel remarked that all the cattle and chickens made him feel like an emigrant. Stevens began to fear that the warnings of Indian hostility were accurate. He ordered Shaw's men to remain until the army arrived, but suspected that they would depart when their enlistments expired on September 8. Stevens urged Steptoe to move as fast as possible to a camp near the council ground. Stevens' fears of hostility was confirmed when a pack train carrying supplies for the volunteers was attacked only a few miles from camp. The unescorted packers had fled for their lives, leaving the goods for the Indians. Though Stevens had not expected such audacity, others were not surprised. Lugenbeel, for instance, had predicted that Grande Ronde would either cow the Indians or drive them to new attacks. Still in the dark, Stevens lamented that the successful foray on the pack train meant a loss of prestige that would "negate much of the effect of Grande Ronde." He again prodded Steptoe to come quickly. Not only was he needed for security; loss of the supply train now necessitated borrowing food from Steptoe's stocks. Steptoe agreed to make the loan if the governor would promise to keep it secret. The colonel confided that Wool would interpret it as disobedience of "stringent orders . . . to give no aid or encouragement to your military operations."[26]

On September 5 Steptoe began to prepare his winter quarters on Mill Creek, six miles west of the council grounds. Per agreement, the volunteers, less one company of sixty-nine men, returned to the Sound. Although tension was mounting, Stevens announced that the conference would begin on September 11. The Nez Perce had the greatest number of representaives on the grounds, but there were also Yakima, Cayuse, Walla Walla, Umatilla, John Day, and Des Chutes Indians present. On the

304   ISAAC I. STEVENS

eve of the council, Stevens received a report that hostile Cayuse
warriors would appear the next day. He pressed Steptoe to
come immediately with two companies. The note arrived at
Steptoe's camp at nine in the evening, and the colonel refused
to move troops in the dark as it would alarm the Indians. He
also told Stevens that there would be no trouble, that he had to
prepare his camp for the winter, and that Wool had ordered
him not to participate in the council. Steptoe suggested that it
would be wise to adjourn the talks until a more favorable time.
Still, he promised the governor aid in an emergency. Stevens
huffily announced he would hold the council "whatever be the
consequences as regards my own personal safety. Such I regard
to be my duty to the public, to the Indians, and to my own
character."[27]

A Cayuse attack did not materialize, but tensions did not ease
during the first two days of talk. The governor sternly lectured
the Indians. He blamed Kamiakin for the war and insisted once
again that the hostiles would have to give up murderers and
surrender unconditionally. Though he admitted that whites and
Indians had died in open, legitimate battle, he argued that certain deaths (such as Bolon's) fell into a different category. The
Indians seethed in silence the first day, believing that they and
the governor were so far apart that there was little common
ground for meaningful discussions. The next day, after some
vague expressions of discontent and a desire for peace, Eagle
from the Light asked about a Nez Perce hanged by the Oregon
volunteers: would these men be treated the same as the killers
of Bolon? Stevens had not heard of the incident and asked for
time to investigate. The second day ended with nothing accomplished.[28]

Early the next morning, Stevens again implored Steptoe to
send troops. The colonel, perturbed by the continual requests,
replied, "Allow me to say that your request for troops embar-
rasses me fully as much as you can be by their absence from
your council ground." The governor went ahead with the day's
session, opening with a rather lame explanation that the Nez
Perce hanged by the volunteers was a spy who deserved his fate.
The Nez Perce then began questioning provisions of the First
Walla Walla Treaty, forcing the governor to turn in desperation
to his old friend Lawyer. The chief produced a copy of the
treaty, reviewed its provisions, and concluded that all would either obey the articles or suffer the consequences. Looking Glass
had refused to attend, but his adherents attacked Lawyer's po-

sition, charging that he had acted unwisely when he made the treaty. The next day, clearly alarmed by the lack of progress and the mounting hostility, Stevens moved the council to a location a few yards from Steptoe's camp. During the move they met 100 Yakima warriors who had just arrived. The party included Kamiakin and Owhi, though apparently Qualchan was in command. The meeting was cool, but not hostile, and the Yakimas, along with the other Indians, camped across Mill Creek from the governor's new location.[29]

Two days later Stevens reopened the council. It is not clear what he hoped to gain by further talks. Perhaps he believed nothing positive would come from them but wished to convince the Indians that they could not force him to abandon the council. He would speak his mind even if, as rumored, the Indians appeared with guns under their robes. The council dragged on for two more days without success. The governor did meet privately with a number of chiefs, including Owhi who again proclaimed that he and the Yakima were for peace. Another who came to the governor's tent was Quil-ten-e-nock of the Isle des Pierres, who had supported Qualchan's attacks on miners in the fall of 1855. He was one who believed the governor had ignored his people at the time of the first Walla Walla council. Quil-ten-e-nock had visited Wright on the Wenatchee River, and had received a letter from the colonel stating that he had made peace. The chief tried to tell these things to Stevens, but once again the governor snubbed the Isle des Pierres still considering them to be an unimportant band under Yakima hegemony. It is apparent that Stevens never realized that Isle de Pierre warriors, not Yakimas under Kamiakin, had wreaked havoc on the miners in the weeks before Bolon's death. The governor dismissed Quil-ten-e-nock by firmly repeating that Kamiakin was the head chief.[30]

On September 18 Stevens, convinced that the council had failed, began preparations to march to The Dalles. He decided that even the Nez Perce were so hostile that William Craig, who was to continue as that tribe's agent, would have to remain at Steptoe's post during the winter. On the same day, Steptoe held his own council with the Indians to assure them that he came in peace and friendship and would not fight unless provoked. The next morning Stevens left for The Dalles with the company of sixty-nine volunteers, about fifty packers, and fifty Nez Perce (led by Lawyer). At 1:00 p.m. they were attacked about three miles from Steptoe's camp. The hostiles included

Nez Perce, Yakima, Palouse, Walla Walla, and Umatilla, led by Qualchan and Quil-ten-e-nock, who had instigated the attack in retaliation for the governor's continued shabby treatment. Stevens estimated the Indians to number 450, which was approximately correct, but most, including Owhi and Kamiakin, were only observers. The actual fighting force was a much smaller number, mostly the younger braves. The governor charged that Steptoe's conciliatory attitude had led the Indians to believe the army would not aid the volunteers. The Indians, however, took the precaution of firing the grass around the army camp in an attempt to keep Steptoe occupied. Steptoe believed that the attack on Stevens was an act of bravado by some of the young warriors for, despite the hostility at the council, none of the major chiefs had participated in the battle.[31]

Stevens swiftly drew the wagons into a defensive corral at the edge of a stream when the attack came. The hostile Indians asked the Nez Perce band accompanying Stevens to withdraw, and the governor agreed for fear that they would be shot by his men in the confusion. Thus the battle began in peculiar fashion with the Nez Perce allies leaving the camp to become observers. The fighting dragged on through the afternoon with the volunteers mounting two charges, one led by Benjamin Shaw. Stevens sent a message to Steptoe asking for aid. With apparent cruel irony, the colonel replied that the volunteers should come to him as his men were busy locating a new camp near fresh grass. After nightfall Stevens reluctantly acquiesced and moved back to join forces with the Regular Army. The Stevens party suffered one killed and two wounded. Indians killed were estimated at thirteen.

The next day the same Indians continued to make threats from a distance but they withdrew when the regulars mounted an assault. Seeing that Stevens' party would need protection during their withdrawal west, Steptoe ordered a blockhouse built for the defense of one company to be left behind while he and the main force escorted Stevens to The Dalles. Stung by the bitter failure of the council, and humiliated by the attacks against his party, Stevens had reason to lament such a sour and undramatic conclusion to that strange war.[32]

The second Walla Walla council did not smooth relations between the governor and the Indians—or the governor and the army. A perturbed Steptoe told Wright that he had tried to dissuade Stevens from holding the council but that his advice had led to "almost angry discussions." Steptoe labeled the council "premature and inopportune," and pleaded, "I did my utmost to keep out of that trouble between the Indians and Stevens and only took part in it when it was evident that the latter must be destroyed unless rescued." But Wool was unhappy, and Steptoe admitted ruefully that the general found little to commend in his actions. That Stevens could find even less to commend was no surprise to anyone. Still, Steptoe and Wright were confident that, with the governor back in Olympia, they could restore order quickly and bring peace. They were correct. Wright returned to the valley with Steptoe, and while work continued on Fort Walla Walla, Wright held a council with the Nez Perce to smooth over the ruffled feelings that the Grande Ronde massacre—and the governor's council—had created. The Indians expressed confidence that they could expect justice from the army. A little more than a month after the Stevens skirmish, Steptoe reported that all was peaceful, and he was spending his days shooting grouse and fishing for trout. For the first time the army enjoyed a free hand east of the Cascade mountains. Unfortunately, Wool's successor, General Newman S. Clarke, determined on a policy similar to that of Stevens, which led inevitably to renewed hostilities in 1858. By that time Stevens was in Washington D.C., embroiled in the political battles which had resulted from the earlier Indian conflict.[33]

After the second Walla Walla council, Stevens was forced to focus his attention on Indian problems west of the Cascades. General Wool closed the territory beyond The Dalles to settlement and ordered Steptoe to keep former settlers from returning to their homes in the Walla Walla Valley. Stevens exploded that this was a "clearly illegal order" which settlers did not have to obey, but with five companies of soldiers stationed in the middle of the valley, it was army policy that prevailed. The governor condemned Wright's council with the Nez Perce, fuming that the colonel had surrendered to the demands of the Indians. He called army policy not only "unprecedented in history, and most discreditable to our government," but also a "usurpation of my duties, for which [it] will be held to account." The sole object of the army, Stevens charged, was to destroy his influence among the Indians and to establish military authority regardless of "propriety and honor." The governor even claimed that the military's conciliatory stance had frustrated the second Walla Walla council because the Indians saw the whites as disunited. He predicted that the Indians would plunder and kill at will because they believed that the whites were "a nation of old women." The governor consciously exaggerated. He was clearly building a case against the army's efforts and in behalf of his own. It was a fight that would continue for the next four years.[34]

Although Stevens abandoned eastern Washington to the army in all but a rhetorical sense, he continued to insist that the military capture Indians such as Kamiakin, Qualchan, and others whom he deemed murderers. He was particularly interested in Leschi, Quiemuth, Stahi, Nelson, and Kitsap, all Puget Sound Indians who had fled to eastern Washington. The arrest of these leaders would, Stevens insisted, insure continued peace on the Sound. They were, according to the governor, "outlaws or banditti" who could not be treated as ordinary participants in military warfare. In August 1856 Stevens had asked Wright to capture these chiefs when they came into his camp, but the colonel refused because he had at least implied that they had safe conduct. In October Wright advised that "in the present unsettled state of Indian relations it would be unwise to seize them and send them to trial." Stevens retorted that they were notorious murderers whose "acts of atrocity under circumstances almost beyond example" could not go unpunished. To the proposition that punishing those he termed offenders might precipitate more war, Stevens responded, "the sooner the better."[35]

Receiving little encouragement from Wright, the governor asked Casey for his aid to save the Sound from "death and devastation." He hinted that his scouts had information that Leschi was planning to rekindle the war. But most people on the Sound were not so easily motivated to panic at this kind of talk as they were in 1855, and Casey coolly replied, "Permit me to say, that I am firmly of the opinion that if the Indians of the Sound are treated with kindness and justice, and lawless men restrained from violence toward them, there will be no danger of any outbreak on their part." Casey added that the chiefs in question had made their peace with Wright and it would be "bad policy, if not bad faith" to overturn his colleague's decision. He advised Stevens, "With due deference to you sir, I would suggest that the better way would be to consider that we have been at war with the Indians, and, now, we are at peace."[36]

Stevens was not to be deterred; the chiefs he had branded as murderers were to die. He told his Indian agents that Wright had not promised amnesty to the Indian leaders, which was technically true, and he offered a $500 reward for the capture of

Leschi. The governor asked Sidney Ford, Jr., to set appropriate bounties on the heads of Nelson, Kitsap, Stahi, and Quiemuth, and added, "Should force have to be resorted to in the attempt to secure any of the above and death ensue, the reward will still be paid." In November, Quiemuth, who was Leschi's brother, voluntarily surrendered to four whites who brought him immediately to Stevens' home. They thought they had crept into town undetected (they arrived at two o'clock in the morning), and the governor told them to sleep in his office until daybreak when they could take the chief to Fort Steilacoom. But the news leaked out through a settler who had observed them riding through town. Several men, including the son-in-law of a man killed by Leschi at the start of hostilities, broke into the office at dawn and fired one shot that wounded the chief. In the confusion that followed, Quiemuth was fatally stabbed. Although Stevens was outraged that citizens would take the law into their own hands, the shabby episode offered further proof for Wool's claim of white atrocities, and it was another blow to Stevens' prestige. Associates claimed that they had never seen the governor so angry. There is little doubt that he desired that the perpetrators be brought to justice. The son-in-law of the murdered settler was arrested, but, although it was generally acknowledged that he had been in the office, no one was able (or willing) to make positive identification. Still, despite his "mortification" at failing to win a conviction, Stevens continued efforts to bring the other chiefs to trial.[37]

At the time of Quiemuth's murder, his brother, Leschi, was already in custody, having been betrayed by two of his braves (they received a reward of some blankets rather than $500). Leschi was charged with killing A. Benton Moses. At the governor's request, Judge Chenoweth held a special session of the district court to try the case. The result was a hung jury. The *Pioneer and Democrat* could not understand the lack of unanimity, but speculated that some jurors might be squeamish about meting out the death penalty. A second trial in March 1857 resulted in conviction, and the governor, who had criticized the courts after the first trial, now had nothing but praise for the system. Stevens declared that Leschi's conviction, which in his opinion resulted from a fair trial in every respect, would prevent future Indian outbreaks. The attitude of the Sound Indians was predictably different. An agent reported that the Indians felt that the murder of Quiemuth paid for any crimes the two men had committed.

Some of the same citizens who jousted with the governor on martial law also took him on over the Leschi case. Included were Frank Clark, William Wallace, and Elwood Evans, but not Hugh Goldsborough or George Gibbs. The Steilacoom lawyers appealed Leschi's conviction to the Supreme Court. As Lander was in California, the case was heard by Judges Chenoweth and Obediah McFadden, who upheld the conviction because the verdict was consistent with the evidence presented. This was valid as far as it went, but the court did not consider whether Leschi was improperly tried because his deeds occurred in time of war. Colonel Wright urged that the chief be pardoned, arguing that, when it came to massacres, "It is hard to say which side has the advantage." "In Indian warfare," Wright reasoned, "barbarous acts must be expected, at least on one side—it is the nature of the red man—but unfortunately our hands are stained with innocent blood, and the perpetrators are free." Wright suggested, "Let impartial justice be meted out to both parties, or cast oblivion over all." Stevens, solidly supported by public opinion, held firm.[38]

Other aspects of Stevens' Indian policy after he returned from the second Walla Walla council were less dramatic than his attempt to bring certain chiefs to trial. He expended much time and patient effort in an attempt to put the Indian service on a working basis. Severely limited in both funds and personnel, Stevens designed an austere program that concentrated on staving off starvation among the many dispersed tribes and bands of Indians in his charge—and preventing further hostile incidents. He ordered all his agents to spread the word that whites who harmed Indians without being attacked "are guilty of murder and nothing else."[39]

As his four-year term as superintendent drew to a close in the spring of 1857, Stevens reminded the Commissioner of Indian Affairs that he had tried to do his duty, and had often stayed up until three in the morning working on department accounts even in the midst of the war. He promised his successor, James W. Nesmith, the Oregon superintendent, that the affairs of the office would be in perfect order. (When Nesmith officially took over on June 2, he confirmed that the governor had kept his word.) As a parting shot, Stevens informed his superiors in Washington D.C. that they were asking Nesmith to assume an impossible task. Rather than combining the two superintendencies, he proposed that three superintendencies be formed: one for western Washington, another for western Oregon, and a

third for eastern Washington and Oregon. This sensible proposal
was ignored.[40]

Stevens left the superintendency with mixed feelings. It was
clear that the merging of the Washington and Oregon offices
was a personal affront, yet he was happy to be free of the heavy
responsibilities. He realized too that he had worn out his welcome with most Indian leaders; he had no desire to subject himself to further embarrassments such as the second Walla Walla
conference and its aftermath. Stevens could also see that, having
accomplished the major task—the treaties—he might serve better
himself, the superintendency, and the territory by going to
Washington D.C. as the territorial delegate. Whatever his motives, it is to that end that he next turned his attention.

Stevens left one significant loose end of his Indian policy to
others—the hanging of Leschi. Governor Fayette McMullin, Stevens' successor, refused to pardon Leschi, and his execution was
fixed for January 22, 1858. The large crowd that had gathered
that day to watch the hanging went home disappointed. The
previous night a group of citizens, led by William Wallace and
Frank Clark and supported by army officers at the fort, arrested
the sheriff and his deputy on a trumped-up charge of selling liquor to the Indians. The two law officers were held at the fort
until the time set by court order for the execution had expired.
It may have been fortunate that Stevens was in Washington,
D.C., for it is difficult to predict how he might have reacted to
these machinations. Perhaps he would have enjoyed the dis-
comfort of his martial law opponents as they now found themselves in a situation where they, rather than he, were accused of
taking the law into their own hands. Although the defenders of
Leschi believed they acted rightly, public opinion was against
them. McMullin denounced the arrest of the sheriff as "trod-
ding underfoot" the highest court in the territory, and public
meetings in Olympia and Steilacoom seconded the position of
the governor. The *Pioneer and Democrat* tore into the rescuers of
Leschi with obvious gusto as it condemned the "notoriety seeking army" and "knavish, pettyfogging" attorneys. The Olympia
paper piously concluded, "Whatever may be said of martial law,
late occurrences show that it is the only law of any effect in
Pierce county—the civil is inoperative."[41]

The territorial legislature immediately requested that the
court hold a special session to resentence Leschi, which it did
with February 19 set as the new date for the execution. Elwood
Evans, who had earlier published a pamphlet in newspaper

form called the *Truth Teller* to summarize the Leschi affair, brought out a second issue in February to defend the arrest of the sheriff and to protest the hanging. Public opinion, however, continued to oppose Evans and his friends as most citizens believed that justice would be served if the sentence were carried out. On the appointed day the chief marched to the gallows, ill and weary from his long confinement, resigned to his fate; this time the sheriff carried out his duty without interference.[42]

THE
DELEGATE

Stevens' primary objective during the winter of 1856–57 was to win election as delegate to Congress from the territory. He had had this goal in mind since 1853. Thoughts of running in 1854 were dismissed as premature and a decision to run in 1855 was preempted by the Indian treaty negotiations. There is little doubt that he would have run in 1857 in any event, but circumstances left him no other alternative. By August 1856 Stevens was convinced that he would be replaced as governor as a consequence of the martial law debacle. He confided to his closest political advisor, William W. Miller, that removal would be a "relief." Stevens was probably rationalizing, but he did believe that removal would have little negative effect on his race for delegate; sympathy among the voters generated by a dismissal could even have a positive effect. The martial law dispute had also revealed the "men of will and judgment who came up to the mark," and Stevens was certain that these citizens would rally around his political banner. A friend assured him, "The game is not lost by no means. I think if you play your hand well you will win."[1]

Stevens began his campaign for delegate in earnest after his return from the second Walla Walla council. He possessed an enormous advantage over his critics; the *Pioneer and Democrat* gave weekly support to his program, and until April 1857 there was no opposition paper to counter its arguments. The *Puget Sound Herald* had suffered financial problems from its initiation in May 1855, and the demise of the Whig party, plus the dislocations of the Indian war, had forced its closure early in 1856. In addition, the governor's supporters organized mass meetings and circulated petitions that defended him. "Giles Scroggins"

314314ISAAC I. STEVENS
314 ISAAC I. STEVENS

spoke for many when he condemned "all those lawyer fellers" for criticizing the governor when he was trying to fight a war. Scroggins predicted that when Stevens "gits dun fighting the war we want him to help folks get their pay for it." Other correspondents of the newspaper sprang to the governor's defense. "Charley" wrote:

I am proud to say he still pursues his course with that untiring industry and unwavering firmness which he possesses in so eminent a degree, and which he adheres to with the unflinching confidence of one who believed his course is just and honorable, and will ultimately receive that due mede of praise which is certain, soon or later, to be lavished upon the deserving.

"A Bystander" was convinced that Stevens had proved himself "to be a genuine limb of old Hickory—not only good for ram rods, but first rate for cabinet furniture." Stevens' campaign strategy tied martial law, Indian policy, the war, and the volunteers into a single interrelated package; it became a question of sustaining all of these actions or none. Martial law, even if technically wrong, was defended as a necessity demanded by the exigencies of the time. It was a situation, Stevens' friends said, that could not be assessed correctly from Washington D.C. Those politicians, as well as opponents in the territory, were elitists who possessed "sheep-skins," but no "brains."[2]

The Republican party officially appeared in Washington Territory in January 1857. Former Whigs and opponents of Stevens' "Olympia clique" joined the new organization, which announced its intention of naming a candidate for the delegate race. It was clear that the new party had less to do with national politics than with Isaac I. Stevens. Faced with this challenge, Stevens' supporters urged all Democrats to "pour oil on troubled waters," and join in a common front. In April the new party began to publish the *Washington Republican* in Steilacoom. The editor was Frank Balch, a close associate of the local lawyers. A battle of words was soon engaged by the two newspapers—the hottest issue being martial law. All the old arguments were rehashed, and the *Republican* added new fuel to the attack by publishing Marcy's rebuke to Stevens, and by alleging that delegate J. Patton Anderson had said that no man identified with martial law should be sent to Washington D.C. because he would be an outcast there. The *Pioneer and Democrat* asserted that the opponents of martial law were "a few selfish and interested lawyers, whose sordid hearts and souls are beneath the contempt of patriotic men." The editor charged that these lawyers were gamblers and drunkards who hatched their schemes while "steeped in the fumes of their midnight revels."[3]

Stevens easily controlled the territorial Democratic convention. The delegates passed resolutions that praised the governor's conduct in the Indian war, protested the continued presence of the Hudson's Bay Company in the territory, called for construction of a northern transcontinental railroad, and condemned slavery agitation as unnecessary and "tending to nothing but mischief." Stevens was nominated on the first ballot with fifty of the sixty votes. The major opposition came from King County (Seattle). Stevens' friends charged that the King County delegates were really under the control of Arthur Denny, a Republican leader. When a motion was made to declare the nomination unanimous, one of the delegates objected, but he was ignored and chairman Edmund Fitzhugh declared the motion adopted.[4]

The *Pioneer and Democrat* hailed the nomination of a zealous, trustworthy, intelligent, high-minded public officer. The newspaper predicted that with Lane and Stevens in Congress, "our territories will not be assailed with impunity, while our positions will be rendered invulnerable." The Republicans sourly complained that the Democratic convention was packed with public officeholders and Indian agents who owed their jobs to Stevens. There was some truth in the charge, but in a sparsely populated territory it was difficult to avoid overlapping the responsibilities of the few capable men in public service. Stevens argued, also with justification, that he had not hesitated to dismiss incompetents. This actuality, coupled with dismissals necessitated by postwar cutbacks, created as many political enemies as friends.[5]

The Republicans had difficulty finding a candidate willing to take on Stevens. Finally they turned to Alexander Abernethy, whose brother had headed the Oregon provisional government for several years. Abernethy was an intelligent, modest farmer who did not delude himself into thinking that he had much chance of winning. He was an able, witty writer, but a poor public speaker, and he accepted the nomination with the understanding that others, like William Wallace, would take the stump in his behalf. Stevens took no chances. He spoke every day in a different community and spent virtually all the time between appearances traveling. The governor admitted that he had made mistakes, but he called them errors of the head rather than the heart. His zeal and candor reaped benefits from the outset. For example, his trip to the Columbia River proved to be a triumphant procession. One supporter predicted a three-to-one margin in Clark County where, he boasted, they were verbally attacking the "woolly heads with a sharp stick."

The *Washington Republican* mounted a counterattack which included a political obituary of the governor that satirized his earlier career.

At early age suffered a disordered imagination—imagined himself a great man with the military genius of Alexander and Napoleon. Education at public expense where he learned all about martial law. Remained in U.S. Army until he found better paying office. Wrote a book about Scott and earned 2 brevets. In 1852 wrote about Pierce as greatest military Chief of Age. Made Pierce President and Stevens governor and chief of railroad survey.

Aside from martial law, the *Republican* hammered most on intemperance. They called a speech at Olympia apologetic, begging, and self-congratulatory, and noted, "It seemed to lack the infusion of *Spirit,* which on ordinary occasions, has made so large an ingredient of all the speeches the gentleman has made in the territory." They made capital of a letter signed by the Reverend George Whitworth (a neighbor of Stevens) stating that he did not believe the governor was in the habit of becoming intoxicated. The Republicans charged that Stevens had solicited the letter, and that it amounted to a pledge to remain sober until after the election. Stevens' supporters did not deny that he drank; but, like Whitworth, they vigorously refuted the charge that he was habitually drunk.[6]

In June and July Stevens campaigned down the Sound, accompanied by William Wallace, a Republican who had responded to a challenge by Stevens to debate the issues. On June 22 they arrived in Steilacoom, where the governor was met by a group of men beating on tin pans, blowing horns, and shouting insults. Stevens appeared unperturbed, but some of his friends engaged in a shoving match with the hecklers. One of the officers at Fort Steilacoom called the incident shameful, but credited the affair to some of the town ruffians. The *Pioneer and Democrat* sniffed that it was the typical blackguardism they had come to expect in Steilacoom. The newspaper declared primly that nothing of that nature had ever occurred in Olympia; everyone there was allowed to state his views in a climate of unfailing courtesy. The campaign drew to a close in July with the charges becoming more heated and the language more colorful, but with neither side interjecting any new issues. In its parting shots, the *Republican* claimed that intemperance made Stevens unfit for office. The *Pioneer and Democrat* countered that the pages of the opposition paper were written by "dirty dogs who disgrace the columns with foul-mouthed slander and low billingsgate language."[7]

Stevens won easily, having gained 65 percent of the vote (1,024 to 548). Abernethy carried Pierce County by a two-to-one margin and narrowly prevailed in King County, but Stevens won the rest, including Thurston (Olympia), where he gained 63 percent of the vote (222 to 133), and Clark (Vancouver), where he gained an overwhelming 88 percent majority (241 to 33). The margin in Clark County is explained by the large number of volunteers living there who supported Stevens as the best man to persuade Congress to pay the war debt. Abernethy confessed that he had not expected "such a horse foot and dragoons defeat," but he took it in good humor, telling Wallace, "A delegate is no great shakes anyhow, especially when I can't be elected." He believed, quite correctly, that it was a contest in which the real candidates were Stevens and General Wool (a vote for Abernethy was a vote for Wool's more conciliatory position regarding the Indians). Most frontiersmen were not particularly concerned if the governor did or did not drink heavily—most drank heavily themselves. For the same reason they did not condemn him for strong language or heavy-handedness. Apparently two-thirds of the white populace felt that such measures were necessary under the circumstances.[8]

J. W. Wiley, in a perceptive editorial in the *Pioneer and Democrat,* attacked eastern politicians for not understanding the westerner. The East, Wiley declared, was "old fogy" country which had been left behind by the "spirit of enterprising, go-ahead 'Young America'." Stevens represented this spirit, and he was supported by the citizens of Washington. Senator Cass, when he spoke of martial law, had said that it was only justified when a man was willing to submit his judgment to the mercy of the people. Stevens had done just that and could return to Washington, D.C., armed with the mandate of his constituents.[9]

First Term: Territorial Problems

Once the vote was counted transforming Governor Stevens into Delegate Stevens, he did not tarry long in Olympia. Stevens made a brief trip to the Willamette Valley to consult with James Nesmith, his new colleague Joe Lane, and other Oregon politicians, and returned to the Sound long enough to greet his successor, Fayette McMullin of Virginia. In mid-September the

Stevens family boarded a steamer on the Columbia River. Except for a delay of two weeks in San Francisco caused by the breakdown of their vessel, the journey to Washington D.C. was without incident. They arrived at the capital in time for the opening of the congressional term in December 1857. Meg had confidently predicted that her husband would be elected, but she had protested that she preferred to remain in her new home on the edge of Olympia with its garden, dogs, hens, and turkeys. Later she agreed to return to the East, and once she had settled into a comfortable brick house located between the Capitol and the White House, Meg declared, "I like the city and society and comforts one gets here after all."[10]

The Stevenses were caught up in the whirl of society when they renewed acquaintances with old friends like the Baches, Stephen Douglas, Jesse Bright, John Mullan, and Montgomery Meigs. Their relationship with professor Bache and his wife became particularly close as they frequently attended Trinity Church, visited, or dined together. The Baches enjoyed children and acted like grandparents to Hazard and the girls. A typical evening found Meg and Isaac at dinner with the Baches or other friends, and, after the ladies retired, the men discussed the Kansas question, slavery, filibustering expeditions to Central America, and other issues of the day. On one such evening Stevens had a long discussion with Robert Walker, the well-known adventurer then involved in Central American escapades—and one of the few men in public life who was as small in stature as Stevens. On another night John Mullan accompanied the Stevenses home from a reception at Senator Douglas's residence and remained until after three in the morning discussing possible wagon and railroad routes for the Northwest. They frequently attended balls, receptions, and soirees, and during one week Meg commented that they were scheduled to attend four parties plus dinner at the White House. She explained, "We did not mean to visit much this winter, but the governor stands out prominent and is thought so much of in truth, it is necessary for us to appear in public. We cannot slight the numerous invitations." For Meg it was more than a duty; she enjoyed it thoroughly, and soon she announced, "I want the governor to buy me a home in Washington [D.C.]"

At first Meg was shocked by the lavish feasts and elaborate entertainment which had escalated markedly during her absence. She was astounded that ladies spent so much time calling that they carried their cards in cigar boxes and even wore dresses that cost between $500 and $2,000, an amount greater than the annual salary of most territorial officials. To Meg the Cass and Douglas homes were like "palaces" to which the White House could not be compared. Meg envied the "beautiful" Mrs. Douglas, but she competed on even terms when, before a reception at the Douglas home, she engaged a French hairdresser then showed up in an elegant new dress with a head dress of white feathers tipped with gold.[11]

Stevens was equally happy to be back in the capital; it offered a more congenial arena for talents that he believed were not fully appreciated by some among his varied constituency in the territory. He enjoyed matching wits with the leading politicians in the country, and he thrived on long discussions of politics and public policy. And the dinners and parties offered additional opportunities to lobby for the territory. His predecessor had served well and had prepared the way, although Stevens criticized him for not having done more. Anderson had left most of the debate on the Indian war and other topics of concern to Joe Lane of Oregon because, he said, it was not good for new members to take the floor. Anderson conversed frequently with his old friend Jefferson Davis and may have prevented the Secretary of War from actively taking Wool's part in his controversy with the governor. The delegate was embarrassed by martial law, which raised such "a breeze" that President Pierce called on Anderson one evening to solicit his views. Anderson did not defend Stevens' actions, but he argued that the governor should be retained. He built a reputation as an honest, reliable man, but he was only beginning to learn the techniques of effective lobbying when his term ended.[12]

Like every other territorial delegate, Anderson also discovered that the position had inherent liabilities and ambiguities. The Northwest Ordinance of 1787 had provided that each new territory would elect one delegate to the House of Representatives but had greatly limited his power by denying the right to vote. By the 1850s it was still not clear what powers the delegates possessed beyond the right to speak on the House floor. Could they serve on committees, propose legislation, and become involved in issues that did not pertain to their territories? Custom ruled in the negative on all these points, although there were some exceptions. The territories depended upon the generosity of Congress for financial aid, but the inability of delegates to trade votes on measures that affected their territories made the job extremely difficult.

From his years of lobbying on behalf of the Engineers, army officers, and the Coast Survey, as well as his work for the territory in 1854, Stevens was much better prepared for the position than most new delegates. In addition to an understanding of proper techniques and procedures, Stevens was acquainted with many, if not most, of the influential politicians in the capital. The new delegate arrived in the city on the evening of November 18, and the next morning he was discussing outstanding expenses of the Washington territorial superintendency with the Commissioner of Indian Affairs. Within the next few days he had held conferences at the Interior, Navy, War, and State departments, and had scheduled two meetings with President Buchanan. Stevens told Nesmith, "Years since I learned brevity and directness in the transactions of business here, and I find no difficulty whatever in effecting a good deal in very brief interviews." He hired James Swan, then living in the capital, as his secretary and set up an office in the Irving Hotel. At the end of December he rented a house and brought his family down from Newport. During his first term Stevens concentrated on three problem areas: Indian policy, including ratification of the treaties, payment of the territorial war expenses, and punishment of his political enemies; final settlement of the Hudson's Bay Company claims and boundary problems; and continued lobbying for a railroad and other improvements that could make the territory more attractive to settlement.[13]

Because the "Salem Clique" developed a powerful political machine in Oregon during the 1850s, it is usually assumed that the "Olympia Clique" arose as the Washington counterpart with Isaac Stevens the mastermind and boss. In fact, Stevens never had a political machine in the sense of a tightly-knit organization with specific interests and goals. When he was thrust on the political scene of Washington Territory, Stevens was alone. The only individual in the territory who became and remained a close political confidant was William W. Miller; their alliance could hardly be called a machine. Stevens was too individualistic, too volatile, too much oriented to sweeping political designs, and too little interested in the detailed work required to build a political organization. He made decisions based on his perception of the issues rather than on the political benefits that he might gain. Though he had many strong supporters, he was not backed by a political machine. Even after he became a delegate he made no effort to use patronage to build an organization. Rather, he used his power to punish enemies and reward those who had served him well during the Indian war—even if their adherence to Democratic party principles might be questioned. Major targets of his wrath were those who opposed him during the martial law controversy. Judge Lander's term expired in 1857 and Chenoweth's expired in 1858. Both men knew that Stevens' election made reappointment doubtful. Chenoweth took the initiative in a letter to Attorney General J. S. Black in which he predicted that the delegate would oppose him because of his martial law decisions. The judge claimed that control of the newspaper, the volunteers, the Indian service, and territorial appointments meant that "there has never been an instance in our country in which a man has so much of the force of circumstance to confer unlimited power and influence as have clustered around Governor Stevens." Chenoweth claimed that he had done his duty, but that Stevens in return had threatened to "nail me to the counter and teach me whose path I had crossed." To Chenoweth's dismay, Black passed the letter on to the delegate, who flatly denied the allegations and claimed that he had lost faith in Chenoweth's competence as early as 1855 because he was a false and unscrupulous man.[14]

Stevens had hoped that Lander would seek forgiveness because he admired the judge despite his role in martial law; but he was angered when Lander joined Chenoweth in circulating petitions calling for their joint reappointment. William Miller quickly initiated counter-petitions which charged that the two judges had not only hindered the war effort, but that they had since joined the Black Republican cause. Both judges arrived in the capital in the spring of 1858, but it was already too late; Stevens had pulled the rug from under them. In June they were replaced by Edmund Fitzhugh, the former Bellingham Bay Indian agent, and William Strong, a respected lawyer from Clark County who had played a large role in drafting the territorial code. A hitch developed when it was discovered that Fitzhugh had killed a man in 1857, although he had been acquitted on grounds of self-defense. The opposition was quickly quashed by Senator William Gwin, a friend of Stevens who had known Fitzhugh in California. The two ousted judges left Washington D.C. sadly acknowledging that in a democracy the will of the majority could count for more than constitutional principles.[15]

The purge of the two offending judges was most satisfying to Stevens but he also accounted for other political enemies. Marshall George Corliss was replaced in 1858 by Charles Weed. When the Attorney General asked for more evidence of support

than Stevens' recommendation, the delegate said it was not necessary because the territorial legislature and the people wished
"to leave me entirely free to act according to my best judgement of their interests." Weed was approved without further
dissent.

Some appointees were able to create difficulties for Stevens,
however. One was Morris Frost, collector of customs at Port
Townsend. Because Frost was almost blind from an eye inflammation, his assistant, J. J. Van Bokkelin, who had commanded the northern battalion of the volunteers, did most of
the work. One aspirant for Frost's job was Travers Daniel,
whom Stevens had fired as Indian agent. Daniel had once been
Fayette McMullin's private secretary in Virginia. He also had
an uncle, Peter Daniel, on the United States Supreme Court.
Frost, according to Daniel, was incompetent and illiterate, but
Stevens, who "almost has the appointing power," blocked his removal. The delegate vigorously defended Frost (who was literate
but indeed not very competent) because he knew that his friend
Van Bokkelin's job depended on maintaining Frost in office.[16]

The biggest fight arose over the reappointment of Charles
Mason as secretary. Governor McMullin unexpectedly held up
approval by charging drunkenness. The relationship between the
new governor and the supporters of the old had been cool from
the start. McMullin, a courtly Virginian, was condescending in
his personal relationships. Worse, he possessed a strong Purita-
nical streak which led him to make a major issue of the use of
the legislative hall for dances, a custom that had developed because it was the only place available. McMullin had served a
term in Congress and was well known to Buchanan, but Andrew Cain, who was in Washington D.C. in 1857, was not impressed by the "wide-mouthed Virginian" who was "hanging on
the administration for some appointment." He found the new
governor "affable but not deep," and predicted that McMullin
would be disappointed in his belief that he could spend two
years in the territory and then become delegate. Cain's father
met McMullin when he first arrived in Washington Territory
and his opinion was similar to his son's. "He will not sute the
people and the people will not sute him." "If you have any use
for him," he told Miller, "you may be able to use him for a
time but I do not think he amounts to mutch in this climit."[17]

McMullin soon realized that it would not be easy to take
over the Democratic party in the territory. He quietly supported
the reappointment of Lander and Chenoweth, but in March

1858 he decided to assert his independence openly by asking the Secretary of State to hold up Mason's reappointment because he indulged "too freely in the social glass." Mason was in the East when he learned of the governor's action; he calmly observed that it was a charge "very easily made, and very difficult completely to refute." Citizens in the territory knew that Mason was not a heavy drinker, and they rallied behind the popular secretary. McMullin could not have picked a worse target. Stevens vowed to fight the removal tooth and nail, while in the territory petitions on Mason's behalf were signed, not only by political partisans and all but three members of the legislature, but by Army officers like Haller, Kautz, and Malony as well. Mason made a good impression when he appeared in the capital, and McMullin admitted defeat by withdrawing his complaint. Although the secretary was reappointed, his original objective in coming east had been to secure appointment as governor if McMullin resigned (as he anticipated). Although the governor did leave the territory in the summer of 1858, he did not submit his resignation until early 1859; Buchanan passed over Mason and paid off one of his political debts by appointing Richard Gholson of Kentucky.[18]

Territorial appointments were a continuous, time-consuming problem, but they constituted only a small portion of Stevens' total responsibilities. The transcontinental railroad continued to loom large in Stevens' plans, but he realized that the sectional dispute made a charter for any railroad unlikely until the political crisis moderated. Instead he worked to continue the road-building program, the improvement of navigation, and more efficient postal service—projects he had helped to initiate in 1854. He secured buoys for the Columbia River and pushed through a new semi-weekly postal service to Olympia. During his first weeks in Washington, Stevens and John Mullan thoroughly analyzed the territory's wagon-road needs and were particularly intrigued by a proposal that the governor had first made in 1853 to build a road connecting Walla Walla with the head of navigation on the Missouri at Fort Benton. The clouded future of the railroad made this wagon route appear even more imperative. The delegate, with Mullan's valuable help, immediately began to lobby for the road, although he expected that it might take two or three years to win congressional approval. To his great surprise the measure sailed through the necessary channels, and Mullan was soon on his way with an initial appropriation of $30,000 to begin work on the road that would bear his name.

Stevens exulted that it proved the wisdom of acting boldly In a letter to the *New York Journal of Commerce*, published unsigned, Stevens explained the importance of the new road for commerce and immigrants. He gave himself credit for the bill's passage, and claimed that Secretary of War John B. Floyd "acceded to the views of Governor Stevens, and promptly issued the requisite orders" to begin work immediately. Soon thereafter the delegate requested an additional $200,000 to complete the route.[19]

At the height of the Indian war, army road builders had completed the Portage Road around the Cascades of the Columbia and a road from Cowlitz Landing to Steilacoom. In addition, Anderson had secured an appropriation of $35,000 for continuation of the road north from Steilacoom to Bellingham Bay where the army established a new post. But W. W. DeLacy surveyed this route in 1857 and reported that it would cost at least $77,000. This persuaded the army to expend the available moneys to complete the road only as far as Seattle and to construct a short section from Bellingham Bay to Whatcom. Stevens introduced bills to complete work on these and other projects already started. Included were requests for $45,000 for the Steilacoom to Bellingham Bay route, $40,000 to complete work between Vancouver and Cowlitz Landing (a route that had not been improved previously due to the availability of river transportation), $8,000 to improve the pack trail from Vancouver to the Cascades of the Columbia, and $20,000 for the road over Naches Pass (to include funds to reimburse settlers for work done in 1853). Stevens also proposed new routes which included a road from the mouth of the Columbia River to Olympia via Grays Harbor, a road from Olympia to Port Townsend, and a Seattle to Fort Colville route over Snoqualmie Pass. The total appropriation came to $160,000. Stevens argued justifiably that the Indian war had proved the need for improved transportation, but during his four years in Congress, aside from the Mullen Road, Stevens had little success in squeezing the funds requested from the federal treasury. A rough trail was opened from Seattle to Whatcom, and $10,000 was expended on a similar trail from Cowlitz Landing to Monticello, but no other improvements were made except through scattered local efforts by settlers.[20]

There were several reasons for the failure to secure additional funds. The Thirty-fifth and Thirty-sixth Congresses were notably more conservative than their predecessors in appropriating funds for internal improvements in the territories. In addition, Congress was expending large sums for military and Indian purposes in Washington Territory, and there were limits to its largess. Finally, it was clear that the main east-west and north-south routes had been completed in one form or another, and Congress was inclined either to let the territory wait for further funds or to force the citizens to improve the connecting routes by their own efforts. Stevens understood this reasoning and, once he had secured the Mullan Road appropriations, was inclined to believe other issues took precedence. In his view the Mullan Road was more important than all of the other projected roads combined; it was not the same as a railroad, but it was the next best thing.

The Mullan Road legislation was one facet of Stevens' effort to make immigration to Washington Territory more attractive. Between 1853 and 1858, population growth and economic development in the territory fell far short of even the most pessimistic predictions made on the eve of territorial status. Precise population figures are not available, but the votes cast for delegate increased by only a few hundred between 1854 and 1857, with part of that increase probably due to the greater interest in the latter race. James Swan estimated that the population had doubled from 4,000 in 1853 to 8,000 in 1857. This was overly optimistic, but even if true, immigration would have been minimal. The popularity of California, the pall cast by the Indian war, and the economic depression that hit the nation in 1857 all partially explain the slow growth.

Stevens was convinced that the difficulties of travel and misinformation about the territory were the major obstacles hindering rapid growth. The first problem could be eliminated by improved roads and eventually by railroads, and the second could be at least minimized by an intensive propaganda effort. As an example of current reports about the territory circulating in the East, Stevens might have pointed to an article in *Harper's Weekly* which noted:

The commonly received notion of Washington Territory makes of it a country wild and rugged, made up chiefly of thickly-wooded mountains and steep ravines, having an unkind climate vibrating between a drizzle and a raw fog, robbed somehow of its due share of fair vivifying sunshine, and inhabited by Indians the chief end and aim of whose existence is depriving white settlers of that valuable and ornamental appendage, the scalp.[21]

While he was delegate, Stevens took every opportunity to extol the territory's virtues; he wrote letters to newspapers, offered advice to emigrants, and spoke to organizations such as the American Geographic and Statistical Society. He tried to dispel the notion that the northern latitudes of the West were a barren wasteland, and stressed the good river transportation plus the advantages of the new Mullan Road. He predicted that once the Indian treaties were ratified, the frontier would move west at a rate of 200 or 300 miles a year which would mean that a railroad could be profitable almost from its initiation. Stevens continued to hear that the weather was objectionable, but to this he replied that the "idea of ice and snow is the veriest myth which ever hung around the brains of sensible men." When speaking to his colleagues in Congress, Stevens continued to push the advantages of Puget Sound as a gateway to Asia. He focused specifically on the Amur River, then the boundary between Russia and China. If this river were opened to free trade by Americans, he predicted that the United States could exchange tobacco, guns, cotton, and cutlery for wool, hides, and the Siberian camel, which would be "so well adapted for the transportation of army supplies in the interior of our continent." As Perry's successful mission to Japan in 1853–54 was still titillating the imagination, it appeared to many that the delegate from Washington had a valid argument. His greatest propaganda effort was his two-volume final report on the railroad survey published in 1859. It is likely that the thorough explanation of the route's advantages contained in that report helped persuade Congress to charter a northern transcontinental line in 1864, two years after approval of the central route.[22]

One bugbear that continued to plague the territory was the location of the international boundary. After the controversy over the Hudson's Bay Company claims and the San Juan boundary, Stevens had attempted to play down the border dispute, particularly after the start of the Indian war when the territory was forced to appeal to the Hudson's Bay Company for aid. On one occasion he did tell James Douglas that he had seen an 1849 map by Arrowsmith which showed the boundary running through Haro Strait, but he quickly added that whatever their differences on this point, he wished continued harmony and good feeling in their relationship. When he became delegate, Stevens immediately adopted a more strident attitude toward Great Britain and predicted that trade competition in the Orient would eventually result in conflict.

His good relationship with James Douglas ended with the start of the Fraser River gold rush in 1858. As that area had no government except that imposed by the company, Douglas assumed responsibility. Following traditional British policy, he reserved mineral rights for the Crown, required all miners to pay a monthly license fee, and limited the right of trade and navigation to British subjects and vessels. This policy contrasted with American custom which conveyed mining rights to the discoverer and allowed administration of mining districts by claim clubs or miners' organizations. Many Americans, including Stevens, protested Douglas' decrees. The delegate fired off a series of letters to Secretary of State Lewis Cass arguing that the British policy was intolerable on the grounds that the United States had allowed foreign nationals into her mining areas and it ill behooved the British to restrict Americans in British Columbia when the Company enjoyed special privileges in Washington Territory.[23]

Stevens did not point out that the Company's rights in the territory were tolerated only because of an international treaty, and he conveniently forgot to mention the aid extended by the Company during the Indian war. Stevens told Cass that even if Douglas had authority to govern the miners, which he doubted, it could not be allowed because the promulgations came in conflict with "Young America." He fumed that the policy was "so arrogant and proscriptive that people should not submit to it for a moment." Americans were not subject to the "domineering and intolerant rule of any trading company." Cass promised to inquire, but expressed confidence that Americans would be treated the same as British subjects. He cautioned that many of the points touched upon by the delegate related to the internal affairs of another nation which the government had no desire to become involved in. Stevens took the hint and made no further inflammatory statements. He was satisfied that he had done his duty for the American miners. The British Secretary of State for Foreign Affairs informed the administration that his country wished to be as liberal as possible toward American citizens, and this satisfied Cass. The return of most American miners to the United States in the fall ended the possibility of an international incident, and when British Columbia became a Crown colony (with Douglas as governor), it left no doubt of British sovereignty in that region.[24]

Douglas soon had ample opportunity to exercise his new authority when the Pig War brought the simmering dispute over the San Juan boundary to a boil in 1859. Those who believed Stevens was the guiding hand behind everything that happened in the territory gave him credit or blame for the actions of General William Harney which threatened to bring the two countries to war. For example, George McClellan claimed the two men wished to start a war with Great Britain to diffuse the sectional conflict between the states. Hazard Stevens asserted that his father manipulated both Harney and Governor Gholson and forced them to take a strong stand which, according to Hazard, saved the San Juan Islands for the United States. After the earlier dispute, both factions had continued to occupy the islands, but there were few new settlers until the spring of 1859 when Americans, some of whom were disappointed gold seekers, took up claims and tipped the population, balance in favor of their country. One of the settlers, Lyman Cutler, who lived near to the Hudson's Bay Company headquarters on San Juan Island, carried on a running dispute with Company men over proper ownership of the island. Cutler was particularly upset by the depredations of Company animals, and on June 15 he killed a pig rooting in his rudely fenced garden. The affair could easily have been forgotten, but when General Harney visited the island a few weeks later, he ordered troops in—a move that he justified as necessary protection from the threat of northern Indians. This action resulted in a confrontation that was not resolved for almost a year, and that several times threatened a shooting war.[25]

The most recent and thorough history of the Pig War places responsibility for the dangerous situation squarely on the shoulders of General William Harney. The general had a history of scrapes and disputes with both superiors and subordinates during his long career. He had been court-martialed before the Mexican War for occupying Mexican territory without authority and for refusing to obey an order from General Scott transferring him to another command. Stevens admired Harney for his brave, bold action at Cerro Gordo which carried the hill and the battle. This was the highlight of Harney's career and won not only Stevens' praise but that of General Scott. When Stevens was thinking of generals who might replace Wool, Harney came to mind. In 1858, when the Department of Oregon became a separate military district, Stevens urged that either J. F. K. Mansfield or Harney be appointed, and the latter was named in September. By the time Harney arrived in the Northwest the campaign of Wright and Garnett to avenge the defeat of Steptoe was well under way, and he played almost no part in it. During the ensuing winter he managed to antagonize most of his subordinates with arrogant actions. Keith Murray concludes that Harney was "emotionally unstable and lacked judgment," and that the decision to occupy San Juan Island was his alone, although "one cannot determine a century later what Harney's motives were for preparing to occupy disputed territory without orders."[26]

When Stevens arrived in Washington Territory in the spring of 1859 to campaign for reelection, he had been gone for a year and a half. He was busy with the campaign and did not see Harney frequently, although he visited socially with the general at Fort Vancouver in the spring and early summer. Neither Harney nor Stevens was aware of the pig incident when Harney started down the Sound on a routine inspection tour. Therefore the delegate could not have influenced the general's snap decision to order Captain George Pickett to occupy San Juan Island. After the fact, in August, Stevens visited Pickett's camp and talked with Harney. The delegate did not protest Harney's action. He agreed with the general's intention to strengthen the American claim and, even if Stevens disagreed with Harney's method, he would not allow the American position to appear disunited by engaging in bickering. It is likely, based on Stevens' earlier behavior relative to the islands, that he would not have acted as Harney did, but would have relied upon verbal protests until higher authorities decided upon a policy. Stevens indicated his less-than-enthusiastic approval of Harney's move by maintaining a discreet silence.

Stevens feared that General Scott, who had gone to the Northwest, would prove too conciliatory, and that he would remove Harney, but did nothing to forestall either. It is clear that Stevens did not want to give up the San Juans, but he resisted the temptation to fight Harney's battles. He had other problems and was content to let the two generals fight it out without his help. When the delegate returned to Washington D.C., he claimed, "The San Juan matter was all cut and dried before I got here." Scott prevailed, the crisis was defused, and Harney was transferred—despite his violent objections—to another department. Through the rest of his career, even during the most desperate years of the Civil War, he was assigned to unimportant positions with little responsibility.[27]

When his second term as delegate began, Stevens was still deeply involved with achieving Congressional approval of the treaties and with issues related to the Indian war. These sensitive issues were one good reason why he wished to avoid in-

volvement in the politically explosive situation involving Harney. From the time Stevens first arrived in Washington as
delegate in 1857, payment of the war debt by Congressional redemption of territorial scrip and policies pertinent to the Indians received his highest priority. Ratification of the treaties
was most important, but there were a number of related issues
such as division of the Oregon superintendency, appropriations
for the Indian department, punishment of those Indians whom
Stevens considered murderers, and opening of land east of the
Cascade Mountains to settlement. Although miffed by the actions of some treaty signatories, Stevens decided to push for ratification of all treaties. He argued that there were some in each
tribe who "do not deserve that they [the treaties] be confirmed,"
yet "that will be the easiest disposition of the matter." He realized that failure to ratify would leave the army in control of the
area east of the mountains, which meant that it would remain
closed to settlement for an indefinite period. He persistently opposed further "illegal" exclusion of new settlers and urged
Wright and Steptoe to allow old settlers to return. They acquiesced to the latter demand because the Indians wished to
trade with these men for cattle and other goods. Stevens also
recognized that new settlers, or miners, could create problems,
particularly if there were no treaties. He had predicted that if
large numbers of miners had gone to Colville in 1857, there
would have been trouble, and, while he was still in the territory,
he had urged many to wait for more "definite and peaceable"
conditions—admitting, however, that he had "no authority to
prevent their going."[28]

    In an attempt to bring about punishment of the Indians who
(he believed) had instigated war and committed murder, Stevens presented a brief to officials in the capital. He argued that
the tribes understood that when the war ended they "were to
submit to such terms as might be dictated by the government."
According to Stevens, Charles Mix, acting commissioner of Indian affairs, agreed that punishment was necessary to sustain
the government's prestige and to prevent further outbreaks. But
Secretary of the Interior Jacob Thompson insisted that the key
point was whether or not Wright had extended amnesty to the
Indians. Stevens claimed that he had not, but General Clarke,
after consulting with Wright, said that a general pacification
had been agreed to. Stevens asked that the army prove the existence of this policy, but Thompson refused to act unless the
army specifically denied pacification existed. Stevens finally had

to give up; he muttered that nothing could be done except to see that such a policy was never implemented again. When Leschi was executed later, Stevens regarded it as a symbolic punishment of all the Indians he considered murderers. He predicted Leschi's execution would serve as ample warning to any future troublemakers.[29]

Stevens and Joe Lane were more successful in securing approval of an emergency deficiency appropriation which paid for the extraordinary expenses of the Oregon and Washington superintendencies during the war. However, the economy-minded Thirty-fifth Congress cut Nesmith's requests for new funds by fifty percent, and most other superintendents fared as poorly. Stevens complained that it was a hard Congress to deal with; they "were determined to reduce expenses and in some things to an unreasonable extent." Of more importance to Stevens, however, was ratification of the Indian treaties. He spent countless hours talking to members of the Indian Affairs Committee of the Senate, and he received strong support from the superintendent of Indian affairs and Lane. Stevens argued that the treaties were essential to preserve permanent peace, and that it was the duty of the government to act "with some little show of justice to the aboriginal inhabitants of the country." He told Congress that the treaties were fair to both parties because he "did not endeavor to drive a bargain but proposed to do what was just as between the two races." Wool was equally determined to block the treaties, at least those concluded at Walla Walla, and many members of Congress agreed with the general that the treaties had caused the war. The Senate compromised by appointing a special commissioner, Christopher Mott, who was instructed to investigate the Indian department and make such recommendatons as he thought appropriate, with special attention given to the desirability of approving the various treaties. In a test vote, the Senate tentatively approved the treaties 22 to 15 and postponed the final vote until the session beginning December 1858.[30]

The outbreak of Indian hostilities that summer made Mott's report superfluous. The gold rush to the Fraser River aroused new interest in the Colville mines, and two miners were killed. Steptoe, unaware of the earlier warnings to Stevens not to come north of the Snake River, recommended sending an expedition north as a show of force. This led to his defeat, and General Clarke immediately ordered Wright and Garnett into the field to punish the offenders. Stevens exlaimed, "Steptoe's defeat has made a great sensation here, and the true mode of managing the Indians is generally acknowledged." With immense satisfaction he reported, "The sentiment of condemnation of the temporizing measures of the military is universal and overwhelming. The officers whose counsels here lead to it, have pretty much lost all reputation they ever had." At Stevens' urging the War Department transferred one regiment from Utah and ordered 400 recruits sent to the West from New York. The delegate assured Nesmith that the "War Department seems determined to prosecute the Indian war vigorously, and are satisfied that it is a matter that should no longer be trifled with." Stevens boasted that Steptoe's defeat indicated "something was rotten in Denmark," and "quietly observed 'The Indians who whopped Steptoe, the Volunteers whipped.' " Although his conclusion was not accurate, Stevens could construe the military events in the territory to his advantage. He did not mention Chief Spokane Garry's warning not to cross the Spokane River, nor did he hint that Steptoe's expedition had antagonized the Indians just as the volunteers had provoked them in 1855–56. There is little doubt that Stevens' presence in Washington D.C. placed him at a distinct advantage in interpreting events and influencing policy. He was the resident authority on the Northwest, and few in 1858 were inclined to question his judgment.[31]

In response to Stevens' urging, Congress created the Department of Oregon as a separate military division. It also accepted his argument that ratification of the treaties was necessary to prevent further outbreaks. In April 1859 Congress ratified all the Washington treaties with little opposition, although it was not until the next session that funds were appropriated to put them into effect. The tortuous history of the treaties, from Stevens' appointment as superintendent in 1853 until ratification six years later, well illustrated the weaknesses of the treaty system. From the beginning, difficulties in communication led to delays, and the start of hostilities resulted in the treaties becoming the scapegoat for the war, which in turn created further delays. The dispute between Stevens and the army created its own set of problems as did the myth that the Indians had a choice as to whether or not they would give up a large portion of their lands. The transition for the Indians might have been easier if the policy of Wool and Wright had prevailed east of the Cascades. This would not have been feasible indefinitely, but it would have provided time for the tribes to adjust to the inevitable. On the other hand, if Stevens had enforced the treaty provisions strictly, many difficulties might likewise have been avoided. But Stevens did not possess the proper temperament or personal qualities, including flexibility, tact, and humility, that were necessary to prevent bloodshed for both races under the ground rules established by the treaty system.[32]

The other major political issue was payment of the war debt. In January 1856 Stevens had ordered that scrip be issued to pay the expenses of raising and equipping volunteers. This action fit a pattern adopted previously on the frontier in time of emergency. Oregon, for example, issued scrip during the Cayuse War and did so again in 1855–56. The refusal of Stevens and Curry to allow most of the volunteers to be mustered into the service of the United States added a new element, and Wool's caustic attacks upon the volunteers cast further doubt over the chances of eventual redemption of the scrip. Washington Territory issued its first scrip on February 4, 1856, and the paper continued to appear until the end of 1857, although the great bulk of the notes were issued before the fall of 1856. In all there were 4,229 separate pieces of Washington scrip ranging in face value from $6 to $10,000 with a total value of $1,614,128.09. Scrip in the larger amounts was issued to firms like the Hudson's Bay Company, which sold the territory at least $58,650 in goods during 1856. Other holders of large amounts of the paper included the Puget Mill Company (the store owned by Indian agent Enoch Fowler in Port Townsend), L. Snow and Company, Henry Yesler, and William Saywood.[33]

In 1856, Lane and Anderson asked Congress to commit itself to pay the war debt, but appropriations were held up by Wool's letters, which accused the civilian authorities of making war "for the sake of plundering the national treasury." Joe Lane replied with emotion to Wool's charges, asserting that if the army's policy had been followed, "Every man, woman, and child, would have been cruelly slaughtered." He asked his colleagues if they believed that an American changed in character when he moved to the Pacific Coast, or if they thought, "their hearts have ceased to pulse with patriotic devotion to our country's flag and our country's honor." The Oregon delegate argued that the settlers had humanely extended civilization to the Indians but it had been cruelly rejected. He asked, "Who that acknowledges the right of the white race to occupy and improve the land of the natives (and I know of no one who will deny it)—who that acknowledges such right will deny to them the right of self-defense when assailed in their pioneer homes?" Lane warned, "American blood is being shed—ay, sir, and on our own soil." Anderson berated some Congressmen, particularly abolitionist Joshua Giddings, for giving the Indians characteristics taken from the novels of Cooper. Anderson eagerly informed the abolitionists that many Indians were slaveholders, and all were a "compound of cruelty, vindictiveness, treachery, and ingratitude." The rhetoric had good effect; no congressman wished to dispute the arguments, and in any event the facts of the distant conflict were not very clear to those in the nation's capital. Still, the House Committee on Military Affairs noted the large amount of the claim as well as the difference of opinion between the civilian and military authorities and recommended that Congress gather more information before taking action.[34]

J. Ross Browne was appointed as a special agent by the Interior Department to investigate the causes of the war, the handling of the Indians, and expenditures of the Indian department, while the secretary of war was instructed to appoint a commission which would examine the war debt of the two territories. In 1857 Browne submitted a long report that absolved Stevens and the treaties of any blame for the war and suggested that the territorial officials had no choice in the raising of volunteers. It was, said Browne, a case of fighting or suffering the destruction of the territories. The agent admitted that he did not understand the details of expenditures made in Washington, and complained, "The accounts become complicated, and it is utterly impracticable for any person with the partial data before him, presenting only one view of the question to disentangle them." Still, he believed that most of the war expenditures were justly made and that Stevens' accounts could be trusted because even the most belligerent opponent had never accused the governor of "application of public moneys to his own emolument or to pecuniary speculation of any kind." Stevens was not in the territory when Browne made his investigation, but Lane and the agent became close friends during Browne's stay in Oregon. Although Stevens was pleased by the report, the citizens of Port Townsend were not amused by Browne's description of that community which depicted both Indians and whites as drunken degenerates and concluded that it would be difficult to find a worse town anywhere in the world. James Swan, a booster of Port Townsend's commercial future, dismissed Browne as "a writer more witty than reliable."[35]

Stevens tried unsuccessfully to secure the appointment of William Miller to the three-man commission appointed by Secretary of War John B. Floyd, but he had no reason to complain of the men named: Lafayette Grover, Rufus Ingalls, and U.S. Army Captain A. J. Smith. Grover, a respected citizen and early settler of the Willamette Valley, was the brother of Cuvier Grover. He was sympathetic to the volunteers—as was U.S. Army Captain Rufus Ingalls, who was also Stevens' third cousin and good friend. The only questionable member from Stevens' point of view was Smith. The commission defined its task as a matter of ascertaining the number of volunteers who served, the length of service, and the expenses necessarily incurred. They accepted the vouchers of the territorial quartermasters at face value and made no attempt to investigate the necessity of expenditures or the validity of prices charged. In their final report the commission noted that certain irregularities appeared in the volunteers' accounts, but they believed that these were honest mistakes resulting from the necessarily "quite precipitous" efforts to get a force into the field. The report essentially supported the Oregon and Washington claims and was the basis for a recommended payment of approximately $4,500,000 to Oregon and $1,500,000 to Washington.[36]

When Congress reconvened at the end of 1857, Stevens and Lane used the reports of the commission and J. Ross Browne to justify the war claims. Their first opportunity to raise the issue came when the House considered a bill to pay James Douglas $7,000 for arms sold by the Hudson's Bay Company to Washington Territory. Douglas had reimbursed the Company out of his own pocket, and was pressuring the State Department for repayment. When the measure came to the floor on May 13, 1858, Lane introduced a rider providing for payment of all war claims. He was ruled out of order, but the delegate took the opportunity to argue that Douglas should not be singled out for repayment. When Lane finished, Stevens gained the floor, and, as it was late in the day, he kept his remarks brief. Stevens defended the volunteers, who he claimed had saved his life when he returned from the Blackfoot council. He also said that Douglas's claim was just and deserved to be paid but that the citizens of Oregon and Washington were equally deserving. According to Stevens, "every member" listened carefully to his remarks.[37]

The favorable reports of the various investigators and the vigorous arguments of the two delegates did not guarantee easy sailing for the debt measure. Quite the contrary. General Wool, from the headquarters of the Eastern Department of the Army

in Albany, New York, sent out a barrage of criticism. He fired a
heavy salvo early in 1858 when he submitted a long report by
Captain Thomas Jefferson Cram of the Topographical Engineers, a member of Wool's staff when he was in the West. Cram
entitled his report "Topographical Memoir of the Department
of the Pacific," but it was more a survey of Indian policy than
an attempt to add to geographic knowledge. The captain found
little to praise in either the physical resources or the citizens of
Washington territory, and concluded that the whole area north
of the Columbia River would have been best left as one vast Indian reservation, arguing, "It is certainly not to be denied, by
any sensible man who has examined it carefully, that the
United States realized from Great Britain but very little that is
at all valuable or useful to civilized man." Cram's report mixed
truth, half-truth, distortion, and pure fabrication in about equal
amounts. An example of the latter was his account of the miners who went to Colville in 1855.

The bare recital of some of the crimes committed by these Anglo-Saxon devils, in human shape, is sufficient to cause the blood of every virtuous man,
whether of red or white skin, to boil with deep indignation. They were not
satisfied with stealing the horses and cattle of the Indians, but they claimed
the privilege of taking and ravishing Indian women and maidens *ad libitum*.

Cram did make some telling points, however. He justifiably accused the Oregon volunteers of inciting the fight with Peopeomoxmox in December 1855, for example. It was easy, Cram
charged, "to draw or provoke the Indians into a fight, and after-
wards justify the act, particularly as in such cases there is only
one side whose story is seldom, if ever, told to the world." Cram
concluded that the best policy in the future would be to assign
control of Indian affairs over to the army. Wool endorsed the
report and added remarks that reiterated that the war had been
less to defend the whites from Indian attack than "to promote
ambitious and speculating schemes." The general asserted that
"powers greater than belong to the President were exerted to
carry on the war, by fitting out expeditions ... which were
wholly unnecessary and under no circumstances called for."[38]

James Swan predicted that Stevens would emerge victorious
in the end, and that despite his efforts the general would not be
successful "in pulling the *wool* over the eyes of the people." In
his arguments before various committees of Congress and on the
floor of the House, Stevens had the advantage of presenting the
facts as he interpreted them without the fear of contradiction
from anyone who had been in the Northwest during the war.

Some of the governor's actions were questioned, however, particularly Shaw's expedition east of the mountains and the failure to muster volunteers into the regular service. To these Stevens responded that the army's failure to provide him protection on his return from the Blackfoot council had convinced him that "a proper self-respect and regard for public safety made it incumbent on us to manage our own affairs." As for Shaw's expedition, Stevens claimed that when Wright failed to occupy the Walla Walla Valley the expedition became necessary because the Nez Perce needed protection and had asked for troops. Stevens also charged that Cram had accepted rumors as fact and hinted that the officer had received most of his information from half-breeds who were more sympathetic to the Indians than to the whites. He disputed Cram's account of Peopeomoxmox's death, arguing that the chief, the leader of the hostiles in that vicinity, was killed trying to escape. Stevens claimed, "The Indians, whether friendly or hostile, were sacred in the camps of the volunteers."[39]

Stevens, like Cram, mixed truth with falsehood. He showed that army officers had called upon the territory for volunteers in 1855, and he asked that those who thought the citizens profited from the war should consult the reports of Browne and others, which indicated widespread destruction and economic stagnation in the Northwest. Stevens' most telling points were made when he, for the sake of argument, accepted the charges leveled at him by the military. Suppose, Stevens said, that the treaties had caused the war, that some vagabonds had committed outrages on the Indians, and that scoundrels profited excessively from the conflict. What, he asked, as governor, should he have done? Once the war started, was it his duty to allow the Indians to lay waste the settlements and destroy innocent people? He was faced with a war when he returned from Fort Benton and, he insisted, it was his responsibility to protect the territory. Warming to the task, the delegate asked his colleagues,

What account would an executive have had to render, who, when he heard that the Indians were devastating the settlements, burning the houses, and massacring the women and children, had declined to protect those settlements on the ground that here and there a white man had outraged the Indians, and driven them to arms?

If the treaties had caused the war,

Was it the fault of those Territories? Was the appointment of commissioners, the calling together of councils, and the forming of treaties their act? Not at all. It was the act of your Congress. It was done under the orders of your President.

This was an argument difficult to refute. Representatives from frontier states sprang to the support of Stevens and Lane. The opposition nevertheless still queried if the war had been conducted with prudence and economy or if the two territories had squandered the public treasury unnecessarily. It was primarily for this reason that the House sent the war-debt issue to a subcommittee chaired by C. J. R. Faulkner of Virginia.[40]

Stevens was disappointed at the further delay but he believed that the main point had been carried. The action of the House implied approval, and the question was no longer if the debt would be paid, but how much. Faulkner's committee referred the whole matter to the third auditor of the Treasury, Robert J. Atkinson, for his scrutiny and ultimate recommendation. This was not good news for Stevens because Atkinson was well known to all territorial officials as a vigilant, indefatigable protector of the public purse. He was also reputed to be a friend of Wool and could be relied upon to spare no effort in turning up irregularities in the volunteers' accounts. The *Pioneer and Democrat* complained that Atkinson was opposed to the claims and would "expend what little brain he has in a nervous shaky effort to report adversely."[41]

Atkinson made use of the various reports, vouchers, and returns compiled by the Grover-Ingalls-Smith commission but complained that the information was fragmentary. It was clear that the auditor suspected that volunteer quartermasters and purchasing agents had expended funds unnecessarily and had paid prices higher than the going rate. To ascertain normal cash prices in the Northwest during the period of the war, Atkinson compared purchases made by army quartermasters with those of the volunteers. He found that Lieutenant Withers at Fort Vancouver paid an average of $124 for horses and $158 for mules. Most of the horses bought by the volunteers cost from $200 to $500; and, although prices for mules varied greatly, one volunteer quartermaster paid an average of $400 for sixteen animals. Similarly, prices paid by volunteers were more for forage, flour, beef, and wages for packers and laborers—sometimes double or triple the prices paid by the army.[42]

Atkinson criticized the volunteer service for allowing many men to hold two jobs and to claim pay for both. Doty, Shaw, Craig, Fitzhugh, Tilton, Lander, and Major Rains were among those so paid. Another was A. H. Robie, who, Atkinson complained, had so mixed his accounts as Indian agent and volunteer quartermaster that the business of the two departments could not be separated. The treasury investigators also discovered that many volunteers continued to live at home and engage in their normal occupations while drawing pay and rations from the volunteers. Men who were discharged for disobedience or who had not been sworn in properly were listed on the roles and continued to receive pay until their full units were disbanded. The auditor found that large quantities of pants, shirts, boots, saddles, and other equipment were often issued to companies shortly before their enlistments expired while other large quantities of goods were not properly accounted for. Complaint was also made of numerous extra charges by the quartermasters for meals or special services that they claimed were furnished. Even Atkinson did not know how to characterize the list of hospital stores found in the accounts of Warren Gove, quartermaster stationed at Steilacoom. The hospital supplies consisted of two bottles of oil, one bottle of mustard, seven bottles of pepper, 98½ gallons of whiskey, 76 gallons of brandy, 300 gallons of vinegar, 63½ pounds of tea, 64 barrels of salt, and 51 barrels of salmon. The auditor laconically observed that this return was a "curiosity."[43]

Stevens replied that the initial cost for raising an army was necessarily great, and in addition the cost per man was much greater when the soldiers served for only a few weeks rather than a period of several years. He argued that the government had saved money as it was cheaper to raise volunteers in an emergency than to keep large numbers of regulars posted on the frontier in times of peace. He defended the amounts paid to the volunteers as justified because they had to build roads and forts and care for their animals with no extra help or pay. Stevens' arguments had some validity. It is not surprising that the records were incomplete; the volunteers began without any organization and lacked the necessary vouchers and forms for proper bookkeeping. The volunteers had to pay higher prices than the Regular Army because there was less certainty that the seller would be paid. Scrip circulated at a discount, and sellers raised prices to protect themselves from further devaluation of the territorial paper. Prices were also driven up, for both regulars and volunteers, by increased demand. Stevens believed he was in no position to quibble over prices in the middle of a war and instructed Miller and his subordinates to pay whatever was necessary to acquire essential supplies. Miller admitted to Atkinson that he paid high prices at times, but claimed he did the best he could under the circumstances. As to the high wages paid some employees, Miller gave the example of an occasion when he allowed $30 a day for an expressman going over Naches Pass. This, Miller said, was an unusual circumstance, but the trip was extremely hazardous, and no one could say that the money had not been earned. One quartermaster, Charles Weed, admitted that he had stockpiled, but explained that he bought goods when they were available because he did not know how long the war would last, or when he would next be able to obtain supplies. Warren Gove claimed that he had kept all his accounts in plain form because he had never seen an army account book. He did not think it was fair for the auditor to expect them to follow the "pettyfogging forms" the army had been developing for seventy years.[44]

As the debate between territorial officials, the army, Congress, and the Third Auditor unfolded with first one side and then the other seeming to have the advantage, the territorial scrip fluctuated in value. The paper varied from as high as 50¢ for every dollar to as low as 15¢, the latter value occurring early in 1857 when many believed Wool would be able to block payment of the debt. After Stevens won nomination as a candidate for delegate the value began to move up, with one storekeeper advertising he would buy all the scrip brought to him. Stevens' victory in the election kept the scrip on an upward course and in 1858–59 it was generally worth 30¢ or 40¢ on the dollar. One argument used by opponents of debt repayment was that the scrip had fallen into the hands of speculators who had paid the original holders only a fraction of the value. Naturally much of the scrip changed hands in the natural course of business transactions, but although some eastern interests did buy scrip, most of it was still held in the Northwest in 1861. Washington D.C. interests had purchased $30,000 in scrip at a rate of 33¢ to 40¢, and Stevens' brother Oliver, then a Boston lawyer, had purchased smaller amounts at about the same price for clients.[45]

All the parties who held scrip provided goods or cash in return for assuming a risk. When the final payments were made, neither investors nor the original holders of the scrip profited unduly. The debt was discharged at about 50¢ on the dollar, which meant that Oliver Stevens' clients, for example, received a return of 25 to 50 percent on their investment spread out over a period of two to four years. It is impossible to compute the average return, but at a time when safe investments paid 10 or

12 percent a year, a return on scrip of 35 percent for three years would make it a normal return. There is little reason to believe that many people made a "killing" by speculating in territorial scrip. It likewise does not appear that the volunteers were guilty of large-scale fraud or graft. The huge expenditures were caused by demand, inexperience, and confusion. Most fraud that did occur was petty and usually resulted from a lack of understanding of the law and proper procedures. Volunteers, for example, assumed incorrectly that they were entitled to a new outfit before they returned home because they had worn out their clothes while serving the territory.

Atkinson's report raised more questions for Congress than it answered. He presented the facts and figures as he interpreted them, but he did not recommend payment or nonpayment of any item. In February 1859 the House passed the buck back to the Third Auditor by presenting him with guidelines and asking him to make specific recommendations. Atkinson was to determine who had been legally enrolled in the volunteer service, to disallow compensation higher than that allowed by the army for comparable ranks or duties, to cancel double pay, and to judge all claims in relation to the prices then current. Atkinson told Congress that he needed a special appropriation to allow investigators to go to the Northwest, but receiving none he had to rely on communications with citizens, volunteers, and army personnel in an attempt to meet the requirements of the Congressional request. The auditor complained that many of his letters went unanswered and that those who did reply usually had a stake in the claims. He also found it difficult to secure additional information on muster rolls because Oregon officials insisted that they had sent all available documentation. Atkinson's efforts were even further hampered by the untimely death of acting governor Charles Mason, who had been attempting to cooperate with the auditor.[46]

In his final report Atkinson recognized that it was doubtful if any of the volunteers not mustered into the service of the United States Army had a claim to any compensation. But the auditor was determined not to decide that politically touchy question; he recommended that all duly enrolled volunteers receive compensation and left it to Congress to include or exclude those not mustered into federal service. Atkinson allowed each man $2 a day, the amount provided for by the volunteer service, but reduced the additional daily allowance to men who furnished their own horses from $2 to 40¢. (He ignored a request of the Washington legislature asking for a land grant of 160 acres for each veteran.) Similar reductions were made for those who received extra clothing or supplies. The elimination of double pay reduced the debt by $79,000. The most difficult decisions came over the amounts paid by the volunteers for supplies. Atkinson admitted that he had insufficient information to determine if the supplies were needed in all instances, or to know where the goods went after they were purchased. In his report Atkinson assumed that the vouchers were for the most part valid, but, based on existing cash prices in the Northwest, he established a scale which reduced most of the amounts paid in scrip by the volunteer service. Whereas the volunteers paid an average of $275 for horses, he allowed $180–$240 for American breeds and $50–$90 for Indian horses. The auditor allowed $1.33 a bushel for oats, $8 a barrel for flour, 10½¢ a pound for beef, and 50¢ rather than $1 for meals, although all prices were adjusted to allow for differences between the Willamette Valley, Portland, and Puget Sound. The claims of both territories were reduced from a total of $6,011,457.36 to $2,714,808.55, a reduction of 55 percent.[47]

It is unlikely that territorial officials expected to receive any more than half of their claim. The *Pioneer and Democrat* had predicted a final payment of between one and two million dollars. Stevens and Lane knew that they had to push final approval of the claim through Congress in the teeth of the sectional conflict which made any territorial business difficult to transact. Hearings were held in 1860 by House committees, and the old questions of the validity of the war and the necessity of the volunteers arose once again and were again countered by Stevens and Lane. House and Sentate committees finally accepted the auditor's report in April 1860, to the immense relief of Delegate Stevens. Final passage occurred in 1861.[48]

In May 1859 Stevens returned to the territory to campaign for reelection, his support stronger than ever. William Miller had been a tower of strength for the delegate, as he kept him informed of events in the territory and made certain that Stevens' efforts in the capital were well publicized. There was little doubt that Stevens had done a superlative job for his constituents in his first two years. The primary issue used against him was the failure of Congress to approve the war debt, yet it was argued that it had been approved in principle and that the next session would determine the final amount.

Stevens was also fortunate that the political opposition remained disorganized. National political issues were still relatively unimportant in the territory, and the Republicans had strong organizations only in King and Pierce counties. Even the *Puget Sound Herald,* which replaced the *Washington Republican* as the Steilacoom newspaper in March 1858, was not blatantly anti-Stevens. For example, the editors praised the "worthy delegate" for his vigorous efforts to secure payment of the war claims. Still, some factionalism appeared in the Democratic county conventions that met in the spring of 1859. In part the split followed the breakdown of the national party into Douglas and Buchanan camps, but it was mostly a pro-Stevens, anti-Stevens division. In Clark County, Charles Carter complained, "A particular party or clique seem to own this place, and seem to want to exclude all others who see fit to differ with it. . . . It appears to be the determination of Governor Stevens and his satellites to either rule or ruin." These critics were a small minority, and they usually avoided direct criticism of the delegate in favor of an attempt to elect uncommitted or anti-Stevens delegates to the territorial convention. Some posed as pro-Stevens men in the hope that they could be elected as delegates and then vote against him. Few of the opponents' subterfuges worked; most of the delegates who arrived in Olympia for the convention on May 16 were committed to Stevens.[49]

When Stevens landed at Vancouver in early May, he was met at the wharf by several hundred supporters, a forty-two gun salute, and "deafening cheers." He remained in Vancouver for three days to give an address (which recounted his activities as delegate) and to attend a grand banquet and ball given in his honor at which music was played by the 4th Infantry band. Stevens could reflect that circumstances had changed during his twenty-month absence; the Indians had been chastised and the army was providing entertainment for his benefit. He hurried on to Olympia to consult with his friends before the convention opened. He need not have worried; his allies dominated the affair. Edmund Fitzhugh was again the chairman, and men like Wiley, Maxon, Van Bokkelin, Miller, Fowler, and Seth Catlin were among the delegates. They endorsed the platform of the 1856 national convention and the policies of President Buchanan, applauded Stevens' work as delegate, and, as usual, called for a transcontinental railroad and for the end of Hudson's Bay Company rights.[50] On the first ballot Stevens was nominated for a second term with all but four of the sixty votes.

The weakness of the opposition was revealed when the Republicans refused to name a candidate, choosing rather to run William Wallace as an Independent in the hope they could at least lay the groundwork for future campaigns. The candidates traveled together down the Sound and on May 20 began a speaking tour that moved steadily south, with usually one and sometimes two debates each day. Wiley declared that Wallace would have to "move his boots" if he hoped to keep up with the delegate. For the next seven weeks the candidates covered the populated areas of the territory from the Canadian boundary to Walla Walla. Stevens emphasized his record in Congress and attacked the report of the Third Auditor. Wallace countered that the auditor had some valid complaints, a position that did not win many votes. He also declared that, as the next Congress would be Republican, he would be more acceptable than a Democrat. Wallace knew he did not have many issues and relied on his humor and oratory to win votes; he was a vigorous stump speaker who entertained isolated frontier audiences with his tales. Stevens, in contrast, was generally serious when he discussed the issues affecting the territory. At Kitsap, Wallace spoke for an hour, and one listener reported that he vilified the whole Democratic party "starting with the President, working his way down and only skipping the Third Auditor." Wallace brought a laugh with his description of Stevens running through the capital trying to hold Buchanan's coattails with one hand and Douglas's with the other. But reports from along the campaign route indicated that although Wallace got the laughs, Stevens made the arguments and "floored" Wallace on every point. Stevens' friends skewered Wallace as a broken-down political hack who had run in the past as a Whig, Know-Nothing, Republican, and Independent. Stevens depicted his opponent as "a mere objector." He confided to Miller, "I have a most profound contempt for the man and perhaps do not take sufficient pains to conceal it."[51]

Stevens' opponents once again raised the drinking issue. It was claimed, "In consequence of his hospitable entertainment at Bellingham Bay, the Governor did not meet his engagements in Clallam County." Stevens told Miller that the tour down the Sound had left him so weak and exhausted that he was almost prostrated six times during a speech in Olympia. As the campaign moved south he regained his strength and finished the canvass strongly with no missed engagements and fewer opposition charges of excessive drinking. The Wallace supporters then turned to their second perennial issue, martial law. The *Puget Sound Herald* facetiously called for Stevens' reelection because: his actions during martial law had saved every man, woman, and child in Pierce County from death; he tyrannically deposed the chief justice; he promised passage of the war debt, which was now delayed only because of his fight with Wool; and, "Like his perfect counterpart Napoleon he knew no criteria but self-interest." These arguments were to no avail; Stevens was returned to Congress with 61 percent of the vote (1,684 to 1,091).[52]

As usual, Stevens did least well in Pierce and King counties, but he also lost Jefferson and Kitsap, the latter by a narrow margin. The delegate had a large majority in Clark, and won in Walla Walla County by the seemingly suspicious vote of 163 to one. Settlers east of the mountains, however, had every reason to vote for Stevens and against the opposition. Wallace's supporters had no comment on the Walla Walla results, but they did claim that transient miners and sailors illegally voted in Whatcom County. One resident of that county accused Edmund Fitzhugh of discouraging a challenge by one citizen by telling the protester he would get "his d----d head knocked off his shoulders." The objector, perhaps remembering that Fitzhugh had once killed a man, took the hint and left. Stevens' majority would have been even larger had the votes from pro-Stevens Spokane County not been lost through bungling. Officials had failed to locate polling places in time for the election.

Stevens remained in the territory until mid-September, primarily to supervise construction of farm buildings and the breaking of ground at his home on the edge of Olympia. He visited Captain Pickett's camp on San Juan Island and made a few public appearances, but primarily he rested and prepared for the opening of Congress in December. Perhaps he sensed that political events in the coming year would require all his energy.[53]

Second Term: National Politics

The Congress which convened in December 1859 anticipated more than anything else the fateful 1860 presidential campaign. In his first term Stevens had tried to avoid national issues, particularly those with sectional overtones. This task was made easier by his lack of a vote and the expectation by Congress that delegates would not become involved in concerns that did not directly affect their territories. Although Stevens privately debated Kansas, popular sovereignty, and slavery, in public he wisely focused on measures that affected the Northwest. Even in his 1859 campaign he spoke little on national issues except to condemn the evils of Black Republicanism. But like every politician of the 1850s, Stevens eventually had to assume a stance on slavery, sectionalism, and the impending division in the Democratic party. It was apparent when he took his seat for a second term that he supported the President and that he was allied with Joe Lane on national as well as Northwest issues. Stevens' stance was one more of principle than expediency. When he was with the Coast Survey in the early 1850s, firsthand observance of the increasing sectional antagonism had convinced him that the primary issue was salvation of the Union, which meant protection of states' rights no matter how distasteful those rights. He continued to believe that slavery was wrong, but at the same time he deprecated attacks by abolitionists which drove the South into a pugnacious, defensive stance. Still, if a choice had to be made, Stevens knew he would fight to save the Union. For this reason he sympathized with the efforts of Pierce and Buchanan to accommodate the South. Joe Lane had arrived at almost the same position, and their political cooperation, forged on a commonality of regional interests, broadened to embrace national concerns as well.

Joe Lane had split from Asheal Bush and the Salem Clique in 1858, but he was able to parlay his great personal popularity into a seat in the Senate upon the admission of Oregon as a state in February 1859. Along with the second senator, Delazon Smith, Lane began to build a machine which he hoped would maintain his power base in Oregon and project him into the national political picture. Congress had approved Oregon statehood by a narrow margin when fifteen Republicans abandoned their party's stand against the measure. On the evening of the crucial vote, Stevens introduced the new senator from the balcony of Lane's hotel room to a crowd of celebrants which included the serenading Marine band. As early as 1856 Stevens had suggested that Lane would make good pesidential timber, and a small boom was under way in 1859–60. In ordinary circumstances Lane would not have received serious consideration, but everyone knew that 1860 would not be an ordinary presidential campaign. Rough, unpolished, almost the eastern stereotype of a frontier politician, Lane heard critics say that he lacked the learning and imagination to become president. But Lane was also a proven vote-getter who had taken the right stands on the issues. Theoretically this son of the Old Northwest, resident

of the Pacific Northwest, and friend of the South could unite
the three sections into a winning combination. In this eventuality, Stevens could prove a valuable ally as he possessed many
qualities, as Lane freely admitted, that the prospective candidate lacked.[54]

While Congress debated for two months over the choice for
speaker, Stevens worked behind the scenes to assure passage of
the war-debt measure, the final piece of legislation he had vowed to obtain when he was elected in 1857. During his final
months as delegate, he continued to work for appropriations for
roads, public buildings, and a naval yard on Puget Sound. Separation of the Oregon and Washington Indian superintendencies
also remained a concern. But once payment of the war debt
seemed assured, Stevens felt he could turn more of his attention
to the rapidly deteriorating national scene.

Election of the speaker did not ease tensions, which by April
became so intense that many House members came to the
chambers armed. On April 5, after Owen Lovejoy, the brother
of murdered abolitionist Elijah Lovejoy, addressed the House,
Representatives Roger Pryor of Virginia and John Potter of
Wisconsin almost became involved in a fight on the floor. Later
Pryor challenged the Northerner to a duel, but rejected the
bowie knives named by Potter as weapons unworthy of a gentleman. Each man then accused the other of cowardice. Stevens laconically observed that there was "a pretty good state of feeling." The Democratic convention met in April, and Stevens was
selected to head the Oregon delegation. He predicted that the
convention would eventually turn to either John C. Breckinridge
or Lane.[55]

During the third week of April, Stevens arrived in Charleston
where he found rooms renting for an exhorbitant $5 a day and
the temperature hovering unseasonably near 100 degrees. He
hoped that the convention would deadlock, forcing North and
South to turn to the West for a compromise candidate—a man
of the people, who in the fashion of Andrew Jackson or William
Henry Harrison would sweep the country. It was a possibility.
Oregon and California were in a position to hold the balance of
power in Charleston because there were fifteen Southern and
sixteen Northern delegations. In the first key convention vote,
Stevens and Gwin of California voted with the South to elect
Caleb Cushing, an enemy of Douglas, as permanent chairman.
The convention agreed to adopt the platform before choosing a
candidate, and after almost two days and nights of bitter de-

bate, the platform committee submitted a document drafted by the coalition of South and West. Essentially it followed a position earlier spelled out by Jefferson Davis which called for protection of property by the federal government whenever and wherever necessary. When the platform reached the convention floor, the Douglas supporters succeeded in substituting a plank calling for reliance upon the federal courts to decide the issue of protection of property. That move wrecked the convention; nine Southern delegations walked out. The Oregon delegates were in a quandary, but after wiring Lane, who had remained in Washington D.C., they decided to stay in the convention, as did the border states, in an attempt to block the nomination of Douglas and put through a compromise candidate like Lane. When the convention resumed the day after the Southern walkout, it was first decided that the succesful candidate would need two-thirds of the original number of delegates certified, or 202 votes. Stevens placed Lane in nomination, but in the early balloting he received only six votes while Douglas had over 145. When voting began the next day Lane's support climbed to a high of 20¼ votes while Douglas had as many as 152 or a majority of the delegates still in attendance. Stevens, among others, urged the Douglas people to agree to a compromise candidate, virtually anyone but Douglas, whom they refused to have "thrust down our throats." But Douglas's managers would not give up, and, after fifty-seven ballots, they suddenly moved to adjourn to meet six weeks later in Baltimore.[56]

Before the Baltimore convention met on June 18, the Constitutional Union party named John Bell and the Republicans turned to the relatively unknown Abraham Lincoln. The Southern delegations expected to be reseated at Baltimore, and Stevens went to the convention hoping that the party could be saved and Lane nominated. Like other politicians, his closeness to events led Stevens to assume that the intraparty conflict would be resolved because the Democrats had always compromised differences in the past. Until the Baltimore convention Stevens did not fully realize the extent of the divisions forcing the party apart. Stevens was named to the important credentials committee, and he told Lane that the Southern delegations would be allowed to return. He was wrong. The Douglas faction was determined to control the Baltimore proceedings. After four days of bitter wrangling, in which Stevens had a major role, the credentials committee seated newly elected Douglas delegations from several of the Southern states. During the night, before the report went to the convention, Stevens wrote a minority report signed by nine other members of the committee which called for the seating of all the Charleston delegations. He argued that it was a question of either seating those selected through the regular party processes or giving the seats to those chosen by irregular methods. Stevens suggested that the Southern delegates had not resigned when they walked out but had merely withdrawn to consult with their constituents. Just before the two reports were presented, there was an ill omen: the stage covering the orchestra collapsed with a great crash, spilling people into the pit. When the vote was finally taken, the minority report was rejected 100½ for and 150 opposed, and the split in the party was confirmed.[57]

Douglas's opponents withdrew, and the Little Giant was nominated with near unanimity by the delegates who remained. Unlike the Charleston convention, the Oregon and California delegates joined the other bolters, who held their own convention in a nearby hall. The 105 delegates adopted a platform and nominated John C. Breckinridge of Kentucky for president and Joe Lane for vice-president, while Stevens was named chairman of the newly formed Democratic National Party Executive Committee. Stevens' staunch fight on behalf of the coalition had put him in the limelight. It is possible that Jesse Bright, an old friend of Stevens, and one of a triumvirate of Senators who had managed the anti-Douglas forces, played a key role in the appointment. The energetic westerner was a logical choice to run the campaign. He was well known in all sections of the country, yet he had not acquired numerous political enemies as had men like Bright, who had been on the national scene for many years. Stevens' prominent position in the new party, which claimed to be the true Democratic party, seemed to prove his boast that he had "made more reputation than anyone" at the convention.[58]

Stevens established party headquarters at 28 Four and a Half Street in the capital, where he began efforts to build a political organization, to raise funds, to write speeches and pamphlets, and to distribute information to the newspapers. As during the days of the Indian war, it seemed that he had thousands of details and dozens of people to attend to all at the same time. The major thrust of Stevens' speeches and statements was designed to discredit Douglas and insure that the Breckinridge faction emerged as dominant in the party after the election. He was highly critical of Douglas's course at the conventions, which he labeled a policy of rule or ruin. Stevens dismissed the Baltimore gathering as "a theatrical affair" marked by tricks and chicanery. Douglas's nomination had not been sanctioned by two-thirds of the delegates, and Stevens noted that the two-thirds rule had historically bound the party together by "bands of steel."[59]

Stevens had the major responsibility for organizing mass rallies and soliciting speakers because Breckinridge and Lane followed the traditional pattern of making few public appearances. Early in July, at a rally in Washington, Buchanan formally endorsed the Breckinridge-Lane ticket. Stevens urged Pierce to lend his support. He told the former president that few could speak to the heart of the American people as well as he, and asked, "Could we have the power of your speech on the stump." As the campaign moved into the fall, Stevens distributed a compilation of documents, which included the platform, sketches of the candidates, and speeches by prominent party members. At a large rally at Cooper Union, New York, typical posters appeared announcing, "The Rail-Splitter Shall Not Split the Union," "John Brown was a Squatter Sovereign," "Joe Lane Was Fighting the Battles of his Country in Mexico when Abe Lincoln was Voting Against Supplies for the Soldiers," and "Let Millions Join the Loud Refrain—Hurrah for Breckinridge and Lane."[60]

The Democratic National Party Executive Committee decided to concentrate their efforts on a few key states like New Jersey and Pennsylvania, as well as New England, to keep them out of the Lincoln column. It was their belief that by winning in all or even some of these states, the election might be thrown into the House of Representatives. In this effort Stevens had the advantage of President Buchanan's support, which gave him access to federal patronage, but he complained that although some "noisy partisans" were removed from office, the Buchanan administration would not do enough. Pierce indicated some of the problems of using patronage when Stevens asked him about certain New Hampshire postmasters accused of supporting Douglas. Pierce replied with alarm that the men in question were good Democrats, and he hinted that it might be a plot by the Douglas people to sow disaffection among their opponents.[61]

Despite frantic efforts Stevens faced insurmountable problems in the management of the campaign, not the least of which was money. In the North he could not compete with Douglas's fund-raising organization led by August Belmont. The Douglas people controlled most state parties outside the South as well as most Democratic newspapers. During the final days Stevens focused on New Jersey and Pennsylvania, but he was increasingly less optimistic. The pessimism was justified; Breckinridge failed to carry any state outside the deep South except Maryland, and Lincoln swept to victory in the electoral college. Stevens nevertheless declared that he had "done right in . . . the Presidential canvass and I know the future will show it."[62]

With his fling at national politics nearing an end, at least temporarily, Stevens told William Miller that he would accept a third term as delegate if the party wanted him. However, his new national prominence made this possibility unlikely. Democrats in Washington Territory were discouraged both by the Republican victory and by Stevens' support of Breckinridge. In addition, some supporters thought he had neglected territorial affairs while seeking political fame. Edmund Fitzhugh, who was in Washington D.C. in 1860, wrote that Stevens had not acted with his usual promptitude in having Selucious Garfielde, a defector to Republicanism, removed from the land office. Others grumbled about the delegate's support of Michael Simmons, who was also accused of jumping to the Republican party. It was true that minimal territorial legislation passed during the first session in 1860, but with adjournments for the conventions and campaign, little business was accomplished anywhere in the country. Stevens did manage favorable action on the war debt, and Garfielde was removed in the summer of 1860. The President had moved slowly on Garfielde because the confusion of political allegiances in 1860 made caution necessary, as the case of the New Hampshire postmasters indicated. Simmons was a perplexing problem; Stevens had secured his reappointment as Indian agent in 1857 despite opposition from many in the territory. The two men were not close personally, and Stevens knew that Simmons resented the close supervison of his activities during the war. But he also thought that Simmons had done well under the circumstances and deserved reappointment. However, in 1860 Simmons openly supported the Republican party, and some of Stevens' friends reminded him that he had been warned.[63]

Stevens probably hurt himself most by a sudden cessation of communications to his friends in the territory except for William Miller. He explained that he was simply too busy after April to write, but many supporters were miffed and concluded that the delegate was no longer interested in territorial affairs and would not be returning. Others, who disliked Stevens' support of Breckinridge, or who were old enemies, used his silence to write him off for 1861. Edmund Fitzhugh, who had ambitions to become delegate, continued to pose as a friend of Stevens but wrote a series of damning letters to the territory from Washington D.C. Pretending to write with a heavy heart, he said that Stevens had become a changed man who neglected the business of the territory, harbored delusions of political grandeur, refused to listen to advice, and drank heavily. Fitzhugh solicitiously promised Miller that he would stay in the capital to look after Stevens and do his best to prevent him from harming himself or the territory.[64]

There was a grain of truth in all of Fitzhugh's statements, although they were grossly exaggerated. It later became clear that Fitzhugh had betrayed Stevens, but in the interim his letters did great harm, particularly in influencing Miller, who was the key to Stevens' chances for reelection. Fitzhugh's charges came at an inopportune time, for Miller was already agitated by the delay in dividing the Oregon superintendency of Indian affairs. Stevens had promised that Congress would act on this matter soon after the session began in 1859, and it had been agreed that Miller would receive the post. The confused state of Congress delayed action, but Miller began to think, particularly after hearing from Fitzhugh, that Stevens had deserted him. He finally poured out his suspicions to the astonished delegate, who had no knowledge of his friend's disaffection. Stevens assured Miller that he was his truest friend and any allegation to the contrary was "pure slander." Once Stevens returned to the territory the two men became close friends again, but Miller's coolness toward Stevens in late 1860 and early 1861 hurt Stevens' reputation in the territory and his chances for reelection.[65]

The long-downtrodden political opposition in the territory sensed that their day was coming and leaped to the attack. A new Republican newspaper, the *Washington Standard,* appeared in Olympia after Lincoln's election and joined the *Puget Sound Herald* in opposition to Democrats in general and Stevens in particular. They knew that if the delegate could be brought down the party would be in complete disarray. John Murphy, editor of the *Standard,* labeled Stevens a rank disunionist and secessionist. A rumor circulated that Stevens owed the government at least $40,000 as the result of the disallowance of expenditures in the Indian department. Even Miller was at the point where he did not know what to believe, and as one of Stevens' bondsmen, he asked the Treasury Department for information on his accounts. When Stevens finally learned of the charge, he denounced it as "silly," and produced a letter from the Second Auditor which indicated that the national government owed Stevens $214.56.[66]

Stevens was shocked that rumors had been accepted as truth not only by his enemies but by his friends. He told Miller he was mortified that "no voice was raised in my defense. All know that I have never speculated, lived economically and gave all my attention to public business." Miller, at least, was well aware that Stevens was right and had good reason to be aggrieved. The delegate wearily reminded his friend that he had been a disbursing officer for public funds since he was twenty-three, and hoped never to be one again. At that moment he no doubt meant it. In the summer of 1860 he had been at the head of a national party, and in Washington Territory his power seemed unchallenged. He had succeeded in justifying his course of action as governor, and the future, although containing uncertainties, looked bright. Only a few months later the Democratic party was split, the future of the Union was in doubt, and Stevens was under attack in his own territory, where his party and even his closest political ally suspected him of negligence and crimes.[67]

As 1860 drew to a close, Stevens watched four Southern states leave their seats in Congress. He did not recognize the right of secession and hoped that some means might be found to prevent the breakup of the Union. He told Miller, "I have used every exertion in connection with other men to prevent the secessionist movement." Stevens supported every effort to keep the Union together, including endorsing the Crittenden Compromise. But his characteristic optimism that human effort could solve any problem began to erode as more states left the Union. At the end of January he declared, "Dissolution is not threatened. It is history." Accurately predicting that the border states would join the Confederacy if a physical collision occurred, he criticized the Republicans' indifference to the crisis. In early 1861, as Stevens brooded over the Union and his own future, he became despondent and for a time began to drink heavily and frequently. This period passed, and in the closing weeks of the Buchanan administration he roused himself to a final, furious effort on behalf of territorial measures.

Congress finally acted on the war debt and gave its approval to the recommendations of the Third Auditor, as Stevens had expected, but a near obstacle arose when Buchanan expressed reservations. The delegate, however, called on the president to convince him that he should sign the bill. Stevens also finally persuaded Congress to divide the Oregon and Washington Indian superintendencies, and, to demonstrate his loyalty to Miller, nominated him as the new Washington superintendent although he knew the Lincoln administration would promptly remove him. Congress appropriated funds for a new land office, and Stevens spent many hours consulting with departments on proposals for new government buildings in Olympia, even making a design for the capitol. Stevens was aided in these efforts by the advantageous position of the western congressmen, who held the balance of power between the Douglas Democrats and the Republicans, both of whom wished to control the lame-duck Congress. In addition there were rumors that the West Coast might secede to form a Pacific Confederacy. The rumors were never more than that, and Stevens would have adamantly opposed any such notion. The delegate was in a favorable position as all sides courted his favor during the session.[68]

Immediately after Lincoln's inauguration, Stevens left the capital to catch a steamer from New York, reaching the Columbia River at almost the same hour as the guns fired on Fort Sumter. He found that former friends like Benjamin Shaw were not convinced that his return was in the best interests of the party. Shaw believed that Stevens' stand in the Presidential race had weakened the party in the territory and had left the delegate vulnerable to those who wanted "to kill King Isaac to get his position." In his usual earthy manner Shaw complained that Stevens "has had his head under water, but his arse has been in full view." He suggested that the Democrats cut themselves off from the delegate while trying to keep the party alive for the next four years. Stevens noted many "lukewarm friends" who were exaggerating the extent of the opposition to help bring about his defeat. There were also friends who were genuinely surprised that he had returned. Miller had heard from a trusted source in the East as late as February that Stevens would not be a candidate despite the delegate's assertions to the contrary. Stevens found that little had been done in his behalf although the territorial convention was only a month away.[69]

Stevens threw himself into the campaign beginning with an impressive speech at Vancouver which listed his accomplishments during the years as delegate, explained his actions in the 1860 canvass, and averred his devotion to the Union. His friends were pleased and his enemies disheartened by the sudden appearance of the vigorous, fire-breathing delegate who showed little evidence of ill health, dissipation, or secessionist sympathies which rumors had recounted. It was the same Isaac Stevens they had come to admire or hate. He quickly convinced several prospective candidates like Lloyd Phillips (an old friend from Vancouver) and Judge William Strong to withdraw. He also wrote to allies to profess continued friendship and to ask their support. Stevens then made a quick trip to Walla Walla to mend fences in that old political stronghold, and returned to Vancouver assured that areas east of the Cascades still supported him.[70]

Stevens' appearance in the territory signalled the beginning of a vicious attack by the Republicans; they knew that he was the only man who could prevent them from assuming political control of the territory. Selucius Garfielde, who had bolted the Democratic party in 1859, began running for delegate on the Democratic ticket as early as the summer of 1860. He hoped that if he were successful the Republicans would support him or in the event he failed he could then run as a Republican. Some of the kinder appellations applied by Stevens' friends to Garfielde were "treacherous," "sweet scented pup," and "egregrious ass." These terms had some validity, but he was also an effective speaker with great personal charm and a political shrewdness that often brought him out on top as the political winds shifted. Garfielde and the Republicans aimed all their artillery at Stevens, continuing to accuse him of defaulting on his debt to the government, of harboring secessionist sympathies, and of being the moving force in an attempt to form a Pacific republic. The *Washington Standard* claimed that he had been greeted at Vancouver by a welcoming committee of one. The *Standard's* description of Stevens' return to Olympia was more graphic. Early one morning the editor supposedly looked out the window and observed a long-eared Cayuse, "and upon his back the infintesimal specimen of humanity known as I. I., slowly picking their way into town."[71]

Stevens answered the opposition with a long speech at Olympia on May 4 before a large crowd. He reviewed his accomplishments in Congress, but he placed particular emphasis on national events. He charged that Lincoln and his party had to bear the responsibility for secession, but he did not believe that Lincoln's election justified the South's actions. The delegate declared that during the period between the election and inauguration he had worked to save the Union.

I conceived my duty to be to stop disunion, and accordingly I exerted myself
to this end. I conferred with Southern men and urged them to oppose disunion at home, assuring them that Republican ascendancy would be short
lived, and would fall to pieces by its own weight in the attempt to carry on
the government.

War, Stevens argued, would make the situation worse, as a Confederate victory would destroy the Union, while a victory by the
North would lead to despotism over the South or perhaps over
the whole country. There was some irony in Stevens' sudden
fear of military despotism, but he proved an accurate prophet of
future events.[72]

The county conventions confirmed that Stevens controlled the
areas east of the Cascades, but there were splits in other counties and some elected both pro- and anti-Stevens slates of delegates. The usual anti-Stevens sentiments existed in Pierce and
King counties and Garfielde had strong support in Kitsap. In
Clark, the perennial candidate, Columbia Lancaster, was able to
rally Stevens opposition to his banner. But Stevens went to
Vancouver for the territorial convention convinced that he had
at least thirty-three firm votes, more than enough to win renomination.

As a veteran of Charleston and Baltimore, Stevens should
have known that nothing could be taken for granted in political
affairs. The convention opened on May 13 with J. J. Van Bokkelin in the chair, and the anti-Stevens delegates immediately
questioned the voting procedures by suggesting that proxy votes,
as allowed in the past, should not be permitted. It was agreed
to let the chairman decide, and Van Bokkelin ruled out the
proxies. This decision virtually ended Stevens' chances for nomination as a large number of delegates from east of the mountains had not made the long trip in person. Even many of Stevens' supporters on the Sound saw no reason to attend, as one
member of the delegation could just as easily cast several votes.
It was clear that Van Bokkelin, considered a strong Stevens
man, had bolted to the opposition. It is likely that Van Bokkelin was resentful because Stevens had not worked for Frost's
reappointment at the end of 1860, although Stevens had done
the best he could when he prevented Frost's removal. The delegate believed that Frost and Van Bokkelin were in his debt; obviously they thought otherwise.[73]

The convention dragged on for four long, rancorous days even
though half of Stevens' support had been eliminated by the proxy
decision. Van Bokkelin was elected as permanent chairman by a

vote of 18-16, and the anti-Stevens faction decided that regular election procedures had not been followed in Shoshone (the newly created county that included present central and southern Idaho and western Wyoming), or Walla Walla, Klickitat, and Snohomish—all Stevens strongholds. They gave the Shoshone votes to other delegates and overrode objections by the usual 18-16 vote. At this point a number of Stevens' delegates walked out of the convention, and Stevens withdrew as a candidate. A wild scramble for votes took place, and on the first sixteen ballots more than twenty individuals received votes. The balloting went into a second day with the contest evolving into a Lancaster and Garfielde battle. Stevens supporters who remained threw their votes to Lancaster who fell only two short of a majority. But he could get no closer; Garfielde won on the twenty-fifth ballot.[74]

Garfielde accepted the nomination, and the convention then called on Stevens to speak. In his farewell address to the territory it was clear that Stevens was already more concerned with battles in the East than with the political fight that had just ended. He took a swipe at the nominee when he promised to support Garfielde even though he had defected in 1859. Stevens added, "In the minds of some there are doubts as to the fairness of your nomination." The departing delegate thanked the citizens for supporting him for eight years and, he declared, "I have nothing to explain, to retract or to apologise for." He told the delegates it was not a time for "mournfully looking to the past," for the Union was in danger, and it became the duty of all patriots to respond. Stevens said he was convinced that even if the South's grievances were magnified 10,000 times, secession would be the worst possible remedy. "Let the doctrine be admitted that one state can break up the compact without the consent of the others and anarchy will reign, and all hope of regulated liberty will be at an end."[75]

Stevens' friends correctly assumed that Garfielde had won the nomination through irregular if not fraudulent methods. But if they had not been uncertain of Stevens' candidacy and his good faith, a less hasty campaign might have accumulated sufficient delegates that no amount of maneuvering would have changed the final result.

Stevens was not inclined to pine over the lost nomination. Even before the convention met, he had decided to offer his services to the Union Army. When the convention adjourned, he wrote to the Secretary of War and boarded the first available steamer for San Francisco. His departure left the territory with a sense of loss, and many, even those who had opposed a third term, believed that he had been used badly. Almost all recognized that he stood above anyone else in the territory in ability, intelligence, energy, and courage. Few could deny the territory's debt for his herculean effort on the survey or his work to publicize that route. His record as delegate was a model of dedication on behalf of the territory. Those who had disputed and disagreed with Stevens usually did so because he at times carried out policies by methods which stretched or exceeded the limits of his power. Stevens' overlapping titles and responsibilities contributed to his assumption of absolute power and stimulated his natural energies to the extent that his zeal became excessive. There is no doubt that philosophically Stevens believed in democracy, the separation of powers, and the sharing of responsibility. But he was a man of action, and in the heat of political, physical, or intellectual battles, he often reacted more to the contingencies of the moment than to sober thought or calm reflection. When contemporaries described Stevens, they usually spoke of energy, force, zeal, or action, and when he failed, it was because he let these characteristics dominate equally important human characteristics of patience, humility, and compromise.[76]

THE
GENERAL

As Isaac Stevens traveled from New York toward Washington
D.C. during July 1861, the first major engagement of the war
was unfolding near the capital at Bull Run. The mass confusion, bloodshed, and heroics brought home to the picnickers,
who came out from the city to watch, that modern warfare was
not a pleasant experience. The retreat of the Union Army to the
capital threw the city's population into hysteria, but the disorganized Confederate forces failed to follow up the victory.
When he reached the city, Stevens again offered his services to
Secretary of War Simon Cameron, clearly expecting an appointment as brigadier general because of "large military experience
since I left the army and my position before the public." Appointments to important military positions, particularly in the
early days of the war, were rife with political overtones. Unfortunately for Stevens, his career had been all too public. He protested in vain that despite his support of Southern political doc-
trines he had always been a Union man. Stevens pointed to his
efforts between the election and inauguration on behalf of the
Union, and declared, "This secession movement must be put
down with an iron hand." These facts, plus the North's desperate need for competent military leaders, dictated that he should
receive an appointment, but military considerations were secondary to a man like Cameron, a wily politician from Pennsylvania. To Cameron it appeared the height of political folly to
commission as a Union general the man who had headed the
Breckinridge campaign.[1]

Further opposition came from Winfield Scott, still the ranking
general in the army, who indicated that he opposed any appointment for Stevens because he drank excessively. The general

359

may have believed this, but relations between the two men had been anything but cordial since the publication of Stevens' book on the Mexican War. Scott had supported Wool during the Indian war, and when the commanding general went to Washington Territory during the San Juan crisis, he found Stevens in the opposing camp. Scott was not a man who forgot or forgave. Stevens soon recognized the situation and decided the only alternative was a direct appeal to the president. He was granted an interview in late July but was only one of hundreds asking Lincoln for political or military office. Many were unqualified or incompetent, and Lincoln was in turn amused or irritated by the great stampede. He may not have been aware of Stevens' military deeds, but he was fully cognizant of his recent political record. Lincoln believed that a primary purpose of military patronage was to insure the support of various ethnic, social, or political groups for the war effort. Breckinridge Democrats were not high on the list of priorities. He listened to Stevens' plea, but politely refused to intervene, at least for the moment.[2]

Stevens was despondent. He could understand political defeat, but found it hard to accept the administration's rejection of his military services when the nation was threatened. It hurt even more when he saw men who he knew lacked the necessary ability or training assuming important military posts. The fact that George McClellan, who had won minor military but major propaganda victories in western Virginia, was becoming the toast of the capital did not lift his spirit. Stevens fancied that a personal vendetta existed, and he toyed with the notion of returning to Meg and the children in Newport to remain there for the duration of the war. Stevens did not carry out this threat because the state governors began clamoring for his services.

The Regular Army had been reduced to little more than 13,000 officers and men by 1860; it was clear that the majority of fighting units would, as usual, be composed of volunteers raised by the states. The day after Fort Sumter, Lincoln had called on the governors for troops. They responded eagerly, but they found it easier to raise men than to find competent officers to lead them. Learning that Stevens had been refused a commission in the Regular Army, the governors of Massachusetts and Rhode Island each offered him a colonelcy in command of a volunteer regiment. Governor John Andrew of Massachusetts apologetically explained that the rank would be only temporary until he could find a brigade that would entitle Stevens to brigadier-general rank. But Stevens preferred, if possible, to work

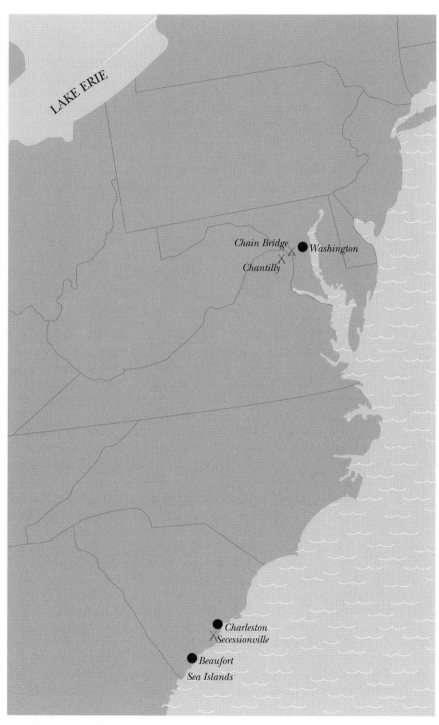

LAKE ERIE

Chain Bridge ✕ ● Washington

Chantilly

● Charleston
✕ Secessionville

● Beaufort
Sea Islands

Civil War Campaigns

with regulars. When he recovered from his pique, Stevens resumed talks with administration officials, who were more amenable once the implications of the defeat at Bull Run began to sink in. Cameron told Stevens that he could not offer an appointment as general, but that a colonelcy in the 79th Regiment of New York Volunteers was open. This was an outfit that had been badly cut up at Bull Run, and although they were volunteers, Stevens, given the choice, preferred to accept his command from the federal government rather than a state; he was determined to prove to the administration that he could do the job. He saw the position as the first step toward eventual command of a corps or an army.[3]

At virtually the same time Cameron made Stevens a colonel, the president offered McClellan command of the Army of the Potomac in place of Irvin McDowell, who had become the scapegoat for the defeat at Bull Run. The dashing McClellan instilled new confidence in the capital. The new general cleared the boisterous, drunken soldiers from the streets and set to work to mold a mass of humanity into a disciplined fighting army. McClellan was hailed as the "Young Napoleon"—an appellation which particularly rankled Stevens, who predicted, "McClellan is one of the bubbles in this contest and will soon burst." Stevens consoled himself with the thought that he could return to a political career in the Northwest when the war was over. William Miller had assured him that the party would wait out the war, that Washington would then be made a state, and that Stevens would serve "for many a long year in the U.S. Senate." Stevens dreamed of a similar future, but he was forced to deal with the realities of the present.[4]

The 79th New York, called the Highlanders because of the predominance of Scotsmen in its ranks, was stationed near the Potomac River as part of the ring of troops protecting the capital. When Stevens took command on August 11, after a week's visit to Newport, he found them dispirited, undisciplined, and surly. Their commander (James Cameron, the War Secretary's brother) had been killed and the Regiment had suffered 197 other casualties. They were particularly opposed to Stevens because he had been selected by the Secretary of War instead of being elected democratically. (Stevens was one of the first officers appointed by the administration as one means of bringing the volunteers under the control of the federal government.) To make matters worse, just before Stevens' appointment Cameron had been obliged to revoke a furlough he had ordered for the entire regiment.[5]

The rumor that there would be no leave was circulating as Stevens arrived in camp, and the coincidence led to the false belief that he was responsible. His reception was openly hostile. Two days later Stevens asked for resignations from a number of officers, including his second in command, Lieutenant Colonel Samuel Elliott, who had hoped to win election as colonel and who abetted the rising discontent. When Stevens ordered the command to strike their tents to move to a new camp, the mutiny which had been building since Bull Run broke out. All except two companies that contained new recruits refused to obey. Stevens boldly circulated through the camp threatening and cajoling the men, but after several hours he had made little headway. The situation degenerated further when many of the men proceeded to get drunk. Stevens reluctantly called for help, whereupon other forces surrounded the camp, arrested the ringleaders, took the colors from the regiment, and marched the reluctant troops to the new camp, which was located, some wags said appropriately, near the Maryland Insane Asylum.[6]

With the mutiny crushed, Stevens immediately imposed a regimen of strict discipline and constant activity. He held daily inspections, ordered long drills, had the men survey the countryside for information for a topographic map, and took them on ten-mile marches. But he also held out the carrot when he worked to get leaves for as many men as possible. Stevens promoted the more able young sergeants, and appointed his son, a student at Harvard, to serve as his adjutant. In September the regiment took up defensive positions on the Virginia side of the Chain Bridge, northwest of the capital. Stevens tried to keep liquor away from the troops, and when it was revealed that a sutler had ignored orders, Stevens had his whiskey dumped, tied the man to a tree, and distributed his foodstuffs to the troops. After several hours the sutler was released and sent packing. Stevens was in his proper element as colonel of the Highlanders. His qualities of force, courage, and even arbitrariness, which had led to difficulties in Washington Territory, were needed in the Army of the Potomac. His ability recognized, he was soon given the command of the First Brigade in General William F. Smith's division. The army slowly began to resemble a disciplined force, and Stevens' command soon became a model for others to imitate.[7]

Stevens' friends bombarded Lincoln and his cabinet with requests for his promotion. They noted his success with the Highlanders, stressed his military experience, and hinted that he might resign if not promoted. Someone in the administration brought these facts to McClellan's attention, but he blocked any action. Still, on September 28, 1861, Stevens was commissioned a brigadier general from Washington Territory. Stevens insisted upon this identification with Washington, which seemed to substantiate his promise to William Miller: "If life is spared me, I shall be in the Territory again."[8]

The First Brigade, which included the Highlanders, the 6th Maine, and the 2nd and 3rd Vermont, was ordered to reconnoiter as far as Lewinsville, six miles to the west. Confederate forces commanded by J. E. B. Stuart bombarded the force with artillery fire, but Stevens had orders not to precipitate an engagement. After completing the scout he returned to the Chain Bridge. Stevens complained that McClellan suppressed his role in leading the reconnaissance, but was mollified by the return of the Highlanders' colors and news of his promotion. McClellen, however, complimented Stevens' troops in a report to General Scott, claiming that his men "came back in perfect order and excellent spirits. They behaved most admirably under fire. We shall have no more Bull Run affairs." Early in October Smith's division was part of a force that occupied a defensive position along the line reconnoitered by Stevens. The brigade took up a position near Falls Church where they felled trees, cleared brush, and constructed fortifications along the perimeter. Stevens was critical of this strictly defensive posture, but he kept his comments private. On October 16 he unexpectedly received orders to leave his command and report to General Thomas W. Sherman at Annapolis. In a farewell address to his troops, Stevens praised the Highlanders for their loyalty in the weeks since the abortive mutiny, and they indicated their devotion by shouting from the ranks, "Tak' us wi' ye."[9]

The Sea Islands Campaign

Stevens was greeted at Annapolis by General Sherman who had requested him as one of his three brigade commanders. Sherman had been in his last year at West Point during Stevens' first and had served in the artillery in Florida and with Taylor in Mexico. Stevens was pleased because he knew that Sherman was a thorough professional with ability and judgment. It was also a pleasure to be out from under McClellan's command. His joy increased upon learning that he would participate in a combined army-navy expeditionary force that would launch a daring attack against the Sea Islands off the coast of South Carolina. If successful it would boost sagging morale. The islands would also serve as a base for blockade operations and perhaps as a jumping off point for attacks on nearby Savannah or Charleston.[10]

Sherman granted Stevens' request to add the Highlanders to his Second Brigade of the Expeditionary Corps, along with the 50th and 100th Pennsylvania (which also had many Scots), and the 8th Michigan. At Fortress Monroe they rendezvoused with a mixed fleet of sail and steam vessels under Commodore Samuel F. DuPont, and after a week spent in overloading the fleet with horses, cannon, men, and supplies, they started south with each steam vessel towing a sailing ship. Three days out at sea a violent storm scattered the fleet and came close to destroying the entire force. Stevens was on the *Vanderbilt,* a side-wheeler donated to the navy by Cornelius Vanderbilt. The storm, plus the added strain of towing a large four-masted ship, almost caused the side-wheeler to founder, and they were forced to cut the sailing vessel loose. The next day the *Vanderbilt* found herself in calm seas with no one in sight, and Stevens opened sealed orders which directed the corps to seize Port Royal. They were the first to arrive. For a time they feared the rest of the fleet had been lost, but the remaining vessels began straggling in, except for two that had been driven ashore and two others that sank.[11]

The storm left the expeditionary force in disarray: the 12,000 men and hundreds of horses had little water; the landing gear was lost when the *Winfield Scott* jetisoned her cargo to keep afloat; and the Confederates had time to prepare while the Union forces regrouped. The Confederates, however, were outnumbered three to one, and their commander, General Thomas Drayton (whose brother commanded one of the Union gunboats), did not have ready access to reinforcements.

On November 7, the navy began bombarding the two fortifications guarding Port Royal. DuPont led his gunboats into the harbor single file, and for several hours they circled slowly while pouring a steady fire into the Confederate positions. The army waited nervously in the transports anchored just outside the harbor, but no attack was necessary because the forts had been abandoned at some point during the shelling. When the troops landed, they encountered only Confederate casualties. The goods strewn along the road toward the mainland indicated a hasty retreat. As they moved onto the neighboring islands, they found that these had been abandoned with equal haste by owners and overseers, who seized a few belongings and fled to the fortifications at Savannah.[12]

No one had anticipated that the Sea Islands would fall with such ease, and Sherman had no orders except to capture and secure the islands. The thought immediately occurred to Sherman and his brigade commanders that they might have an opportunity to launch a quick strike at either Charleston or Savannah. Stevens, who was acquainted with Savannah and its fortifications as a result of his inspection tour in 1848, urged an immediate movement upon the city. He argued that the sparsity of troops at Port Royal indicated that they would not encounter serious resistance. If he were wrong they could retreat to Port Royal and the protection of the navy gunboats. After a long discussion he was overruled by Sherman, who was supported by the other brigade commanders, Egbert L. Viele and Horatio Wright. They believed that Stevens' assessment was probably correct, but they had doubts as to how long they could hold the city and as to the permanent value of such a dash. In addition, Sherman was by nature cautious and not inclined to undertake an ambitious venture without specific orders from Washington. Both sides had valid arguments: the capture of Savannah would have given a great lift to Northern morale, but if they lost the city after a short time the effort would be wasted. There is little doubt that if Stevens had been in command he would have attempted a preview of William T. Sherman's march through Georgia. But Thomas Sherman wrote to McClellan, who had since replaced Scott as general-in-chief, indicating that as he understood it the "object of the expedition" called for him to open the harbors, which was "all that I can do at present with the resources available."[13]

With his decision made, Sherman set up headquarters on the most southerly island, Hilton Head, where the troops set to work bringing supplies ashore and building fortificatons. After a month, Stevens was ordered to take his 2nd Brigade to Port Royal Island, where he established headquarters at Beaufort.

Beaufort was often described as the Southern Saratoga, and if any area in the South came close to matching Northern notions of great plantations, large white-columned mansions, and fields filled with slaves, it was the Sea Islands, which Beaufort served as the social capital. The planters came in summer to escape the heat and disease of the cities. While they enjoyed the sea breezes, overseers supervised the care of the valuable long-staple cotton that could be grown successfully in few places outside of the Sea Islands. On November 7 many of these planters watched the naval action at Port Royal from their rooftops, and, when defeat was certain, they fled, leaving rich furnishings and great houses to the enemy. They also left 10,000 or 11,000 slaves, who assumed the sole purpose of the invasion was to grant them freedom.

For Northern soldiers and abandoned slaves, as well as white Southerners who crossed stealthily from the mainland, the temptations of the riches offered by the deserted plantation homes proved too much to resist, and the weeks following the invasion saw a saturnalia of looting, plundering, and general destruction. Stevens was sent to Port Royal Island to end the chaos, to secure the island from Confederate attack, and to do something about the slaves, now officially classed as contraband. The first priority was to restore order. Three days after the landing Sherman had decreed that looters would be court-martialed and subjected to severe penalties. The proclamation had little effect as Stevens found that looting had "reached alarming magnitude." A detail he sent to stop the marauders joined in the festivities and, when arrested by a third party, were found in possession of horses, chickens, hogs, and one dried sheepskin. Stevens termed it a "most disgraceful scene of plunder," and charged the senior officer with disobedience and conduct unbecoming an officer. By the end of the year the men were under control, partly because they had worked the looting out of their systems, and partly because the officers had time to impart some discipline to the troops, a majority of whom started the expedition as raw recruits. One of these men later said that Stevens' "strict discipline" was resented, but that when the brigade came under fire they were grateful.[14]

When Stevens occupied Port Royal Island on December 7, it was discovered that Confederate forces were erecting a battery at the ferry on the Coosaw River, which separated the island from the mainland. In addition they had driven piles into the river above and below the ferry to prevent attack by Union gunboats. Stevens had orders not to cross the river, but he was able to reduce the battery with fire from the island. However, the Confederates immediately began new fortificatons a mile and a half upstream from the ferry. Stevens convinced Sherman to permit him to lead a combined army-navy attack against the

new work and to clear the Confederates away from the mainland areas abutting Port Royal Island. He gathered up a large
number of flatboats used to transport cotton, requisitioned three
gunboats from Commodore DuPont, and set to work removing
the obstructions from the river. In the early morning hours of
January 1 Stevens moved his brigade across the river on the un-
wieldly flatboats five miles downstream from the Confederate
position.

The crossing went slowly. They were hampered by darkness,
the current, and the ponderous craft, but they met no opposition, and at dawn they began marching through the forest. Stevens kept the gunboats advised of the forward position of the
troops, which allowed the vessels to sweep the woods with
grapeshot just ahead of the advance. The whole operation proceeded smoothly, and the Confederates abandoned the fort after
offering only scattered resistance. Stevens had strict orders not to
follow so he leveled the fortification, took possession of a twelve-
pound cannon, and, on January 2, returned his force to the island. In high spirits, Stevens wrote Sherman, "I hope the general commanding may be gratified with our celebration of New
Years Day." Although there had been some delay and confusion
in the night crossing of the river, the operation was a success,
the troops believed they had won a great victory, and Stevens
again displayed imagination by innovative use of the navy sig-
nal corps in coordinating the land-sea advance.[15]

The victory of Port Royal Ferry gave Stevens and his troops
their first taste of battle, but it proved to be the last hostile action in that sector for the next several months. Stevens turned to
drilling his troops and had to resort to the old devices of marches, reconnaissances, and topographical surveys to keep the men
occupied. The elegant town of Beaufort, with its beautiful gardens, mild climate, and splendid quarters, provided some compensation for the lack of activity. Stevens set up his headquarters in an "extremely elegant" house once occupied by the
Presbyterian minister. The town contained a library housed in a
neoclassical building designed by Thomas Wren, and Stevens
turned part of his leisure time to reorganizing the collection. He
ordered the books recatalogued, with private collections maintained separately with the owner's name inscribed on the flyleaf.
He also began conducting courses for his young officers in
which he lectured on tactics and strategy. One aide boasted that
it was "the best managed brigade" in the command, but Stevens was left with much free time, and in "sheer despair" he

read all the novels in the library with the "same vigor and energy" as if he were conducting a campaign. He complained to Meg, "I am very weary at my position here. I have literally nothing to do, except to perfect the discipline of my Brigade." The post was so dull that Meg came to Beaufort for a visit in March and remained for a month. She, at least, enjoyed the peacefulness of the island, which was blossoming out with magnolias, yellow jasmine, roses, and acacia. The call of the mockingbird mixed with the notes of the Highlanders' bagpipes as they serenaded her in the lush garden next to headquarters.[16]

It was not all sweetness and light at Beaufort. Stevens suffered from intermittent attacks of yellow fever. More annoying was the case of William Lilley, whom Stevens had appointed brigade quartermaster on the basis of an acquaintance Stevens made with Lilley during the 1860 presidential campaign. For the most part Stevens had selected a loyal, capable staff, but in Lilley he discovered, as Lincoln had also learned, that political friends did not make thè best military appointees. In December Sherman had expressed some doubts about Lilley's ability, but Stevens defended him—only to discover a month later that the quartermaster was not keeping proper records and had neglected to order needed supplies and ammunition. Lilley reacted to Stevens' censure by spreading vicious gossip through the camp. He was dismissed from the service. Lilley immediately traveled to Washington D.C. where he gained the ear of Stevens' political enemies, who eagerly listened to the quartermaster's tales, which included a charge that Stevens was completely inebriated during the Port Royal Ferry engagement. Stevens' appointment as brigadier general still needed the approval of the Senate, and it was held back as a result of the slanders. Sherman warned, "I think you had better look to this thing, for enemies I find work in the dark and when unexpected." W. J. A. Fuller, a prominent lawyer and Democrat in New York, whose son was in the Expeditionary Force, intervened on Stevens' behalf, but it was only when Sherman returned to Washington in April that the Senate was convinced of Lilley's fabrications and went ahead with Stevens' confirmation of rank.[17]

Distressing as these personal problems were, the major issue Stevens faced was that of the slaves. It was an issue complicated by civilian-military conflicts, the logistics of caring for more than 10,000 people, and the absence of a federal decision on the legal status of the slaves. Sherman's declaration that the abandoned slaves were contraband along with other property averted a hard political decision at least temporarily. When Stevens took possession of Port Royal Island he had orders to use the so-called contrabands to pick cotton, construct roads, or do any work he thought necessary. By December much of the stored corn and meat on the island had been eaten or carted off, and many of the Negroes were short on supplies for the winter. In addition, the invasion had occurred soon before the yearly clothing issue was due and the old clothing was in tatters. DuPont and Sherman made a joint appeal to Northern charitable organizations for supplies.

It soon became apparent that the government was more concerned with cotton than with the Negroes. The first evidence of activity was the appearance of cotton agents sent by Secretary of the Treasury Salmon P. Chase, who appointed a veteran cotton broker, William Reynolds, to supervise the activity. Reynolds arrived in the islands in December, and the military feared that the Treasury agents would take command. Commodore DuPont remarked, only half facetiously, that there seemed to be an agent with the rank of captain for every bale of cotton on the islands.[18]

As most of the cotton (and Negroes) were on Port Royal Island, Stevens was directly affected. He protested vehemently to Sherman about the activities of the cotton agents who worked under the supervision of the quartermaster, Lieutenant Rufus Saxton, in the days before Reynolds arrived. Saxton had been one of Stevens' associates on the railroad survey, but the general bitterly complained that the quartermaster had delegated authority to the agents, which derogated Stevens' power and opposed military propriety and usage.

I am perfectly aware that the Commanding General does not intend to and will not permit any interference with my proper authority, and I take it for granted that he has that entire confidence in my absolute integrity and business capacity which has been conceded to me through an arduous and various public service, in peace and war, in the regions of civilization, and in the vast wilderness, during nearly an entire quarter century, and I trust that he will admonish the Chief Quartermaster to be careful not to give orders, that by inexperienced men in civil life, shall be construed as giving them command and control over general officers. I trust we are not reviving the early experiences of the French Revolution when unscrupulous and selfish citizens were given the control of armies and commanders, and when their sirocco and poisonous breath blasted the fairest reputations.

Stevens' letter was primarily a reaction to the activities of William Nobles, a hot-tempered, strident cotton agent who squabbled with numerous individuals on the islands. Nobles had demanded troops and transportation to aid him in collecting cotton on Ladies Island, which was separated from Port Royal Island by the Beaufort River. Stevens coldly informed him that the troops were engaged in collecting supplies but that he was free to collect all the cotton he wished through his own efforts. He ordered Nobles not to establish his headquarters in Beaufort and cautioned him to keep out of the army's way. Saxton immediately told Stevens that Nobles had misunderstood instructions; the agent had been given no authority to order troops. Sherman praised Stevens for his efforts to that point and assured him that his authority would not be undermined, but he indicated that the agent might be allowed any wagons not in use to help expedite removal of the cotton. Somewhat mollified, Stevens assured Saxton that he had thought he had reason to complain of his orders, but "very probably I was mistaken." He promised to do "all I can to facilitate operations."[19]

The temporary truce was broken by the arrival of Reynolds, who urged his agents to put all the Negroes to work picking and transporting cotton. The agents did not need much prodding; they received a percentage of the profit from each bale. But the stepped-up effort led to new friction and recriminations. Nobles told Sherman that the Pennsylvania Roundheads of Stevens' command had seized his transportation, harassed the Negroes, stolen property, and defaced a tomb by forcing off the doors. Stevens denied all the charges. He said he would stand by the facts as reported by his officers. Reynolds then seized the Beaufort library for shipment to New York, an act that Stevens protested on the grounds that the books were safe and were of great service to his troops. Thereafter he cooperated with the cotton agents only to the extent that his orders absolutely required.[20]

In addition to the army and the Treasury agents, a third group began to appear on the streets of Beaufort before the end of 1861. These were representatives of antislavery, missionary, and philanthropic groups sent from the North to improve the physical and moral condition of recent slaves, and to aid in moving them toward complete emancipation. Having read official and private letters and the reports of at least one newspaperman, they were well aware of the situation on the islands and the plight of the Negroes. Radical members of the Lincoln administration wished to aid these missionaries, although Republican moderates would have preferred to ignore both them and the contraband problem.

At almost the same time Treasury Secretary Chase sent Reynolds south, he asked Edward Pierce, a young Boston lawyer and antislavery spokesman, to report on conditions and make recommendations relative to the former slaves on the Sea Islands. Pierce was hesitant but finally agreed, and he arrived at Beaufort in mid-January. Pierce developed an immediate antipathy toward Reynolds and his agents, who he believed were using the Negroes for their own enrichment. He objected to the agents' practice of paying the Negroes primarily in food and supplies because the system lent itself to fraud and perpetuated a system close to slavery. In addition, the Boston lawyer wanted the Negroes to plant corn and other crops for their self-support but the cotton agents naturally wished all energies devoted to a new cotton crop. In February Pierce was joined by the Reverend Mansfield French, who was sponsored by the American Missionary Association and who, like Pierce, was to recommend measures that would improve the condition of the Negroes. The two men returned north together after agreeing that they would rally support in New York and Boston. Pierce stopped in Washington to visit President Lincoln. The president complained impatiently that he could not be bothered with such matters, but he did direct Chase to give the philanthropist any instructions he thought judicious. In March a shipload of recruits, which included clerks, doctors, teachers, divinity students, railway agents, and professed socialists departed for the Sea Islands. Sherman received the band and quickly sent them to Stevens, who mused that here was a further source of grief in a war that for him had contained more politics than military action. He would no doubt have heartily agreed with Commodore DuPont, who wrote, "We have had all kinds of agents out here [:] cotton collectors, statistic collectors, humanitarians [,] philanthropists, etc., the best among them the people of God, starting schools." DuPont complained that they all differed with each other on nearly everything, "agreeing only on one, abuse of the Generals."[21]

While Salmon Chase dispatched agents and missionaries, Sherman was left in the dark as to the proper policy of the army toward the Negroes. In December he reported to the commanding general that most Negroes would willingly remain on the plantations, but he predicted that they would do little work without direction. He urged, "It is really a question for the government to decide what is to be done with the contrabands." In January the general was still waiting for a reply—and he continued to ask what should be done. Finally in February, without guidance, he formulated a policy in General Order No. 9. Because, he said, the Negroes had been abandoned by their masters, faced anarchy and possible starvation, and were existing in a state of "abject ignorance and mental stolidity," he ordered all the plantations grouped in districts under the authority of an agent who would organize the "willing blacks" into work parties while seeing that they received proper food, clothing, and remuneration. Further, Sherman ordered,

Until the blacks become capable of themselves of thinking and acting judiciously, the services of competent instructors will be received—one or more for each district—whose duties will consist in teaching them, both young and old, the rudiments of civilization and Christianity—their amenability to the laws of both God and man—their relations to each other as social beings and all that is necessary to render them competent to sustain themselves in social and business pursuits.[22]

Stevens, and most of the officers and men in the command, believed Sherman's order was a mistake. When the islands were first occupied, Stevens had suggested that they follow local custom as closely as possible in their handling of the Negroes. In this way they could gain the support of the loyal citizens, who would help bring South Carolina and the other states back into the Union. But Stevens was thinking of the climate of opinion in the South when he had been in Charleston in 1860, and, like Lincoln, he overestimated the strength of the Unionists once the fighting had begun. Stevens declared, "If this war is to be simply a war of emancipation, and not a war to enforce the constitution and the laws, my services are not needed. I shall in that case return to the Northwest and help build up that portion of our country." One historian has suggested that the army of Jefferson Davis contained about as many abolitionists as that of Abraham Lincoln. Sherman's command was no exception. Most of the troops agreed that they did not wish to fight in an abolitionist crusade.[23]

Stevens told Sherman that his order was a mistake because it would drive the border states still in the Union into the Confederacy; he believed the order amounted to emancipation and hoped the administration would revoke the action. Sherman denied that emancipation was his intent; he insisted that he had acted strictly as a soldier with a practical problem. He had responsibility for 10,000 people for whom a policy was essential before the spring planting season. They had to be put to work under supervision, Sherman reasoned, and the Treasury agents and missionaries provided ready-made supervisors. Stevens was still unhappy, as he thought they should insist that all Negroes, not just "willing blacks," be made to work. He also believed that to teach them to think and act judiciously was a task that the army was not prepared to handle.[24]

Stevens was correct when he argued that the army was not equipped to educate the Negroes, but the missionaries who came from the North were eager to accept the challenge. They descended, Hazard said, "like the locusts of Egypt . . . male and female, all zealously bent on educating and elevating the 'freed-men.' " The officers on Stevens' staff were inclined to poke fun at the young humanitarians, who called themselves Gideon's Band, and amusement increased when the mission group spent most of a month in Beaufort squabbling in unchristian fashion. Stevens had doubts that the Gideons would accomplish any-thing practical, but as time passed he became more sympathetic to their efforts. It was clear to him that, unlike the Treasury agents, Gideon's Band were sincere, if at times fumbling, in their desire to help the Negroes.

The general and Edward Pierce were drawn together by com-mon antipathy toward the cotton agents, Nobles in particular. Nobles's anger grew as both Stevens and Pierce complained of his actions, and in May, when the cotton agent encountered Pierce in Hilton Head, he beat him severely before soldiers could rescue the missionary leader. Nobles was ordered north on the next steamer, and both Stevens and Pierce believed they had been vindicated.

Despite the Nobles-Pierce incident, army, cotton agents, and missionaries began to function less at cross purposes by spring. Each had certain areas of authority and expertise, and it was a matter of cooperating within the confines of a few small islands or creating complete chaos. The agents supervised the cotton crop, the missionaries began the process of education, and the army preserved order. Stevens did his best to prevent harass-ment of the Negroes and to stop the stealing of their food. He issued army rations to Negroes considered "cases of destitution," while he backed up attempts to put the plantations on a system-atic basis by arresting "refractory persons" and by threatening to use the ball and chain on hard cases. With relative harmony prevailing, Stevens was shocked when the *New York Tribune* charged that his command had treated the Negroes cruelly and had frustrated the efforts of Gideon's Band. The culprit proved to be a correspondent who had visited Beaufort, and who had

believed the army was not moving fast enough to suit his abolitionist principles. The missionaries, as well as the army, denied
the *Tribune's* allegations. By summer both the missionaries and
Stevens had modified their positions. Gideon's Band members
realized that it would take more than a proclamation to bring
the slaves into American society, and Stevens had become convinced that slavery would soon end throughout the country. He
believed it was his duty to do what he could "firmly and kindly" to "protect the colored people."[25]

While Stevens dealt with slaves, missionaries, and Treasury
agents, he wished that he might be somewhere else, anywhere
fighting was taking place. He followed developments closely,
and devised strategy that he sent to Bache, Meigs, and other
friends. He quickly placed his finger on a primary weakness of
the Northern effort when he declared that McClellan and other
generals were moving too cautiously with "too much tenderness
for the battlefield." Harking back to Napoleon, and his own experience, Stevens argued that an army's spirit was the single
most important factor, and the increased morale of a victory
more than made up for the casualties suffered. He told Bache,
"They must summon the men of brains, experience, and will
and energy to the posts of responsibility or we shall be misera-
bly whipped." His old friend Lee was an excellent tactician,
Stevens admitted, but he suggested that Lee could be defeated
by pushing him with little respite, which would not allow time
to plan a defense.

Stevens wrote a "Brief Memoir in Relation to the War"
which he sent to Senator Henry Rice of Minnesota with instructions to circulate to others with influence. He correctly criticised
the administration for its plan of simultaneous attacks on many
fronts. Stevens urged moving with overwhelming force at one
decisive point, which might be in western Kentucky and Tennessee with the immediate objective Memphis and the ultimate
objective the opening of the Mississippi Valley. At the same
time the navy should give up its small expeditions on the coast
and concentrate on New Orleans. While the Union concentrated
on the Mississippi, the blockade should be tightened and the
army in Virginia placed in a strictly defensive position. Stevens
dismissed the importance of Richmond as an objective. He argued, "At Richmond should be struck the last and not the first
great blow of the war." As Stevens wrote, General Grant was
preparing to strike at Forts Henry and Donelson in the first step
of the long struggle that ended at Vicksburg. However, the ad-

ministration did not make the commitment to the Mississippi
Valley that either Grant or Stevens would have wished. In fact,
there is no indication that Stevens' memoir had any more influence than Stevens had had in August 1861 when he made
similar suggestions to the Secretary of War. The Union eventually followed Stevens' plan virtually to the letter, but only after
many more months of the piecemeal effort focused on Richmond.[26] Although it was frustrating to watch the course of military events in other theaters, it was even worse to be isolated
from activities taking place within Sherman's command. Sherman decided that they had little to fear from the Confederates
as long as they kept at least a brigade on Port Royal Island.
Thus, Stevens had to remain stationary while Viele's brigade laid
seige to Fort Pulaski, and Wright seized Jacksonville and Fer-
nandina, Florida.

The absence of a Union Army general staff, and the coordinated planning such a staff could have provided, proved to be a
serious detriment to the Expeditionary Corps. Sherman and Stevens developed plans to take either Charleston or Savannah, but
they required the cooperation of the navy and the approval of
higher authorities. Most of the responsibility for such decisions
fell on McClellan, whose preoccupations with his own army precluded an examination of the possibilities for large-scale operations in South Carolina and Georgia. The siege of Fort Pulaski
dragged on for several weeks, and during this time the Confederates were able to send reinforcements to that sector. Although Stevens was impatient for action, he became aware of
the problems Sherman faced in an attempt to mount a campaign. When some Northern politicians placed the blame for
the inactivity on Sherman and suggested that Stevens replace him,
Stevens quickly defended his superior and disavowed any connection with the critics. Despite differences of opinion on some
matters such as the Negro question, the mutual respect of the
two men deepened during their association on the Sea Islands.
Stevens regretted his superior's caution but respected his fairness, honesty, and professonalism. Sherman admired Stevens for
the same reasons, and when forced to disagree, Sherman did so
with tact and with assurance that he held "an exalted opinion"
of Stevens' talents and personal character.[27]

Stevens was upset when Sherman was replaced by General
David Hunter in March 1862. From the start of the expedition,
radical politicians, including those in Lincoln's cabinet, believed
that the Sea Islands offered an excellent opportunity to force the

government to come to terms with the slavery issue. Stevens had believed that Sherman moved too far in his Order No. 9; the radicals did not think he went far enough. The radicals implied that Sherman was not a competent military man, a charge the *New York Times* echoed when it praised Hunter's appointment because he was a true soldier while at the same time indicating that Sherman was too political. This assessment completely reversed the facts, and the *Times* completed the distortion by indicating that Stevens was at odds with his commander and waited "chafing under the inaction imposed upon him by the incompetency of General Sherman." At the same time, the Department of the South was created. Hunter was assigned overall command of the department as well as that of the northern division, while the southern division, which included the Sea Islands, came under the command of General Henry W. Benham.[28]

David Hunter graduated from West Point in 1822 and served continuously in the army except for one six-year period. Wounded at Bull Run, he was named to relieve Fremont in the western department in October 1861. Hunter was a competent, energetic general who sympathized with the political views of the radicals. The portly Benham was at West Point with Stevens for two years and had ranked first in the class of 1837. He was well known to Stevens as their paths had crossed many times, but few of their encounters had been friendly. Benham had served under Wool in Mexico, and in 1853 he took Stevens' place in the Coast Survey, where, Benham alleged, he had straightened out the mess Stevens left behind. Early in the Civil War, Benham served in West Virginia, where he was censured by General Rosecrans for attacking too rapidly at Carnifex Ferry in September. Two months later he was criticized for allowing defeated Confederate forces to slip away. Benham was a competent engineer but not a good general; there were few men Stevens would have been less eager to see as his immediate superior.[29]

Hunter and Benham arrived in the new department at the beginning of April and immediately ordered Wright's brigade to return from Florida. They also asked the officers' wives to leave immediately for the North. Before Meg departed she saw Benham in Hilton Head strutting about "in high feather acting like a spread eagle" boasting that he would soon take Charleston. He did not inspire Meg's confidence, and she darkly observed, "I regret his being placed in command at Hilton Head." On his second day in command, Hunter declared that slaves who had fallen into government hands as a result of the Port Royal attack were free; soon thereafter he likewise included all Negroes in the department.[30]

In March, before he was replaced, Sherman had received orders, which probably emanated from Secretary of War Edwin Stanton, to recruit the Negroes as soldiers. Sherman argued that the Negroes were uneasy because of rumors that they would be sold in Cuba and that any sudden movement of the type proposed would create great alarm. He suggested enrolling a small number for a limited period with the promise that they would be returned to the islands. Although many radicals and abolitionists had advocated using former slaves as troops, those who were close to the situation, such as the members of Gideon's Band, knew that Sherman was right. One of the band, Susan Walker, had tried to inspire the Negroes to fight, but she found that they had no desire to oppose their former masters. Walker concluded that the Negroes could be forced to fight, but that none would voluntarily leave the islands.[31]

In May, Hunter ordered Stevens to collect all the able-bodied male Negroes within his command and send them to Hilton Head for muster into the army. Stevens, as might be expected, was extremely critical of Hunter's order. He knew that the Negroes did not want to serve, and he believed that they would make poor soldiers for anything but menial tasks because they still feared their former masters. In any event, Stevens preferred that the war be won solely with white troops. But despite his personal feelings, he obeyed and had his men move rapidly so the news would not spread and result in panic. He told his officers to reassure the recruits that they would be well treated, but at each plantation there were loud lamentations and cries of grief as the men were marched off. Within a few hours, 600 Negroes were on their way to Hilton Head. Edward Pierce immediately added his protest to Stevens'. He called the order arbitrary and told Hunter the men were needed to work on the plantations. Hunter bowed to the pressure, although he kept the men Stevens had already sent. In the future, Hunter said, he would accept volunteers, to whom he promised to issue free papers at the time of enlistment. The 600 men were organized into the first Negro unit in the army, with volunteers from Stevens' brigade serving as officers. The government ignored Hunter's action, and officially the unit did not exist, but abolitionists and radicals acclaimed the general's policies. Stevens morosely com-

plained, "Very strange things are being done in this department," and urged men like James Nesmith, then a senator from
Oregon, to work to have Hunter's measures overturned. He
threatened to resign and pleaded with Nesmith, "Will you get
me transferred where I can do service?" Lincoln overruled the
radicals on May 20 when he revoked the order freeing the
slaves, while at the same time he called on the border states to
consider implementing voluntary emancipation.[32]

Secessionville

As Lincoln acted, it also appeared that military activity
would resume in the department. Benham commenced feverish
preparations for a strike against Charleston. He saw an opportunity to send Stevens and Wright to join General Robert Williams, already on James Island (near Charleston) with his brigade. He planned to send Stevens by sea while Wright traveled
overland from Edisto Island, where his troops were camped. Stevens was disappointed with the plan partly because Benham
had reduced an all-out attack by Stevens to destroy the Sav-
annah-Charleston railroad to nothing more than a diversionary
raid. Stevens had contemplated wrecking that rail line since first
coming to Beaufort. In addition, Stevens was dubious about the
prospects of the Charleston campaign because of transportation
problems. He warned that Wright could not make his way over
the swamps, rivers, and small islands in time to make an attack
before the Confederates reinforced their defenses. They would
both need to go by sea, which was impossible, or postpone the
attack. But Benham insisted on implementing his plan.[33]

On June 2 Stevens' brigade sailed from Hilton Head and that
evening moved up the Stono River, which had been secured by
Union gunboats. The next morning they landed on James Island and fought a brief skirmish with Confederate troops who
had come from Charleston to test Union strength before withdrawing. Stevens grumbled, as they waited for Wright to arrive,
that they would either sit there for six months or make an attack for which they were ill-prepared. Stevens had yearned for
action, but he was not so eager that he wished any part of foolish, ill conceived plans. He confided to Meg that Benham was a
vacillating imbecile, a nuisance, and an ass utterly unfit for
command. Since the war began, he told Meg, the army had
placed him in positions where he could accomplish little but
which subjected him to "extreme mortification and annoyance."
He mused, "It may yet even teach me patience." Wright did

not arrive until June 8. He told a harrowing tale of a week of constant toil, loading and unloading rafts, crossing rivers, and sloughing through swamps. Benham reorganized his force into two divisions and one brigade with Stevens in command of the second division.[34]

Meanwhile, the Confederates, anticipating that a large force was gathering for an attack, had worked feverishly to perfect their fortificatons built at a narrow neck of the island. They constructed a parapet sixteen feet high, protected on both flanks by water and in the front by a deep ditch. Eight heavy guns were brought in, and the work was christened Fort Lamar after the commander, T. G. Lamar of the South Carolina Artillery. When Hunter arrived, he observed the strength of the Confederate defenses, ordered Benham not to attempt a battle, and returned to his headquarters. Following Hunter's orders, Stevens established a battery to bombard Fort Lamar, which the Union forces called Secessionville, and the invasion force dug entrenchments to fortify their position. For a week Stevens' men labored around the clock while he complained bitterly that Hunter had 400 Negro troops basking in the sun at Hilton Head.[35]

The Union guns destroyed one of the Confederate batteries but did little damage to the fortification itself. Benham, however, had convinced himself that his force of 12,000 men could take Charleston and raise the American flag over the city where the war had begun. Ignoring Hunter's orders of June 10 to make "no attempt to advance on Charleston," Benham went ahead with plans for a major attack. At Stevens' suggestion the Confederate positions were probed to see if there was any flanking route around Fort Lamar. These efforts proved fruitless, and Stevens concluded that there would be no attack. Benham was not ready to give up. On June 15 he decided that the increasing numbers of Confederates made an immediate attack imperative. He called Stevens, Wright, and Williams to his tent and ordered a frontal attack the next morning. The three commanders all voiced their objections: they argued that the shelling had had little effect; that volunteers had seldom, if ever, successfully stormed works of that kind; and that it was only a "bare possibility" that they could succeed. Stevens added that he would obey all orders of a superior officer to the best of his ability, but that personally he objected to the attack. He wrote to Meg that he feared the worst, but, "We shall try to prevent a disaster from occurring."[36]

Benham selected Stevens' division for the dubious honor of leading the assault with Wright and Williams joining from the flanks once Stevens hit the center. At 1:00 on the morning of the sixteenth, Stevens moved his men forward through the woods, capturing enemy pickets as they went. The attack had to be made across a cotton field about 200 yards wide with water and marsh on either side. In addition to the ditch in front of the fort, there was a ditch and hedge about 500 yards from the work. The Confederates had six guns in the fort and numerous sharpshooters were posted in pits and in the brush. Stevens and Wright had argued that if Benham insisted upon an attack, they should first use all their firepower for a heavy bombardment, but the general insisted upon a surprise attack at dawn. The movement of 4,000 men through a woods infested with pickets could not go long undetected, and the Confederates were well aware of the impending attack long before it was launched.[37]

The 8th Michigan and Stevens' pride, the 79th New York Highlanders, led the charge, running over the broken rows of cotton in the face of murderous fire. At the hedge the attack slowed because the only feasible crossing was through a narrow opening. It was amazing that elements of both regiments reached the foot of the parapet before falling back. While the charge was in progress, Stevens tried frantically to bring up troops to follow in the footsteps of the leading regiments. In the confusion of the half-light of dawn, burdened with the fatigue of their earlier efforts and loss of sleep, the men moved slowly, not reaching the hedge until the first charge was starting to fall back from the fort. All the troops on the field gathered behind the protection of the hedge until Benham ordered Stevens to break off the attack. They retreated in good order and reached camp by 10:00 the same morning. The narrow limits of the battlefield had prevented most of Wright's or Williams' force from participating in the action, which had lasted only a half hour. The Union troops, mostly Stevens' division, had 685 men killed or wounded. More than 25 percent of the 8th Michigan and 79th New York were casualties, as were thirteen of the twenty-two officers of the 8th Michigan. A correspondent of the *New York Times* called the charge "as mad as that of the Light Brigade," and so it was. The Highlanders, among others, had shown incredible bravery and discipline, in which Stevens took pride, but there was little to be grateful for when so many lives had been unnecessarily wasted. Stevens had been calling for offensive action in the department for many months, but he did not want an impossible attack and was bitter at the folly of the Secessionville action.[38]

Benham, having been ordered not to fight a battle, told Hunter that they had conducted a reconnaissance in force and that "the main object of the reconnaissance was accomplished in ascertaining the nature of the fort, and the position in front on our right as also the character of the ground in advance of our left." Benham praised the courage of the men and lauded "the careful arrangement and skilful disposition of the forces of General Stevens guided as they were by his own cool courage." In an address to his division, Stevens said they had covered themselves with glory, but that he shared their grief that many of their best men lay beneath the ground. He assured them, "You did not seize the fort because it was simply impossible." In private his outrage grew as he contemplated the results. He condemned the "blustering, blundering, foolish, unprincipled Benham," and averred, "Six to seven hundred killed and wounded men cry out against him." Hunter was equally shocked by the disaster and immediately removed Benham from command, sending him north under arrest.[39]

Benham mounted a furious attack in Republican newspapers, which attempted to shift the blame to Stevens. Insisting that the ill-fated frontal assalt was nothing more than a reconnaissance in force, Benham produced correspondence indicating that Stevens had previously recommended "a reconnaissance" as proof that he was responsible for the debacle. Benham also stated that if Stevens had not delayed the attack and had kept to the time-table, they would have surprised the enemy and carried the fort. Stevens knew that the stories were printed for political reasons, but he could not restrain himself from replying, and he received permission to publish his version in the press. Professor Bache kept him posted on Benham's tactics, but urged his friend to ignore the attacks; the public was becoming disgusted with the increasing reports of petty bickering by Union generals. Thereafter Stevens kept quiet, and in August Benham was removed from the rolls of the army.[40]

At the end of June Hunter withdrew the Union forces from James Island, sending Wright back to Edisto Island and returning Stevens to Beaufort, where he would be second in command to Rufus Saxton. Hunter had faith in Stevens as a military commander and did not blame him for Secessionville, but Stevens was openly critical of radical policies, and Hunter wanted someone less controversial in command in an area where the main problems continued to be political, not military. As Stevens returned to the Sea Islands, he dejectedly wondered why he was returning to Beaufort when his country desperately needed him in Virginia. He promised Meg that he would soon resign and attempt to get a command in the West, "unless it be avowedly made a war of negro emancipation," in which case he would no longer participate. Stevens was buoyed by the support of his troops, whose devotion to their general had increased after the battle at Secessionville. Junior officers and men in the ranks praised their leader for courage in the face of fire and for his efforts in their behalf. The Highlanders in particular were dogged in devotion to the "prodigious little man," and insisted they would fight for no one else. They firmly believed that if the little general "with his big shaggy head" were in command of an army, he would soon set the enemy to dancing. After the battle the Highlanders presented Stevens with a solid gold scabbard, silver spurs, and a letter of appreciation framed in a silver case. He was deeply moved, and he told Meg that only his "splendid troops" did not ignore him.[41]

In desperation Stevens wrote directly to the President to advise that all military operations in the Southern Department be ceased and the troops sent to either the army of McClellan or that of General John Pope. The forces in the department did not, he believed, have sufficient strength or a proper base to effectively strike Charleston or Savannah. He pleaded with Lincoln, "Give us the opportunity to share the dangers of our comrades in arms. Let us feel that we are doing good service for our country—that we are really helping in the grand contest of the war." Lincoln, Stanton, and Hunter independently came to the same decision as Stevens at almost the same time. Their primary reason for calling the forces north was the course of events in Virginia during June and July. McClellan had finally begun his long-awaited move against Richmond by taking his forces to the peninsula by sea. In June it appeared that he would be successful, and Lincoln created a new Army of Virginia under John Pope to move on Richmond from the north and catch the Confederates in a pincers. But this plan was frustrated when McClellan was defeated in the Battle of Seven Days and began withdrawing from the peninsula. More troops would now be needed to regenerate the offensive.[42]

Chantilly

In mid-July Stevens' and Wright's divisions were ordered to Virginia. As he happily steamed north on the *Vanderbilt,* Stevens concluded that the only proper course was to join the armies of Pope and McClellan on the Potomac and begin anew from that point. On July 16 Stevens' division set up camp at Newport News, where it was assigned as the First Division of the 9th Army Corps under the command of General Ambrose Burnside, with Jesse L. Reno and John G. Parke joining Stevens as the division commanders. The situation for Stevens seemed to be brightening; Burnside had won a reputation as one of the best corps commanders in the army, and Pope, whose army they would join, was known as a fighter. In addition, Henry Halleck had been named general-in-chief in an attempt by Lincoln to coordinate all army operations. At Newport News Stevens talked with General George Cullum, who had become Halleck's chief-of-staff, and discovered that both his old friends agreed with the view that the Union forces should regroup on the Potomac. It appeared that events were starting to move, and Stevens had reason to believe there would be positive results.[43]

The troops remained in camp organizing and preparing equipment until the early part of August. Stevens took the opportunity to attempt to secure Hazard an appointment as colonel of a Massachusetts volunteer regiment. Oliver, Charles Stevens, and others pressured Governor John Andrew to grant the request, but he argued that the only opening was with an Irish regiment, and he had to name an Irishman or at least a Catholic as commander. Hazard continued as his father's adjutant.

The corps left Newport News by steamer for Fredricksburg, where they remained until August 14. While they waited for orders to move north to join the rest of Pope's army, they heard reports of fighting as Stonewall Jackson began to attack Pope's scattered forces before they could link up. An engagement took place near Cedar Mountain on August 9 which led Pope to order Reno's and Stevens' divisions to that area. Pope ascertained that Lee was pumping troop reinforcements to Jackson as McClellan backed off the peninsula. To meet that threat he intended to mass all the divisions of his army on the Rappahannock River. As Stevens moved toward Cedar Mountain he wrote Meg that they would soon have an overwhelming force; the troops were in fine spirits, he was in good heath, many old friends were around him, and "events look promising."[44]

On August 24 Stevens' men were fired upon by Confederate cavalry at Sulphur Springs, in the first hostile action they had seen since coming north. At this point the two armies faced each other with Pope reinforced to 75,000 men and Lee commanding 55,000. Lee probed the Union lines, then decided to split his forces in a daring move typical of his sagacity. A force under Jackson moved to the north clear around the Union army and placed itself between Pope and Washington D.C. It was the type of action that Stevens knew Lee would take if given the chance. On August 25, while Stevens moved east to Warrenton Junction, Jackson silently left the line of the Rappahannock, slipped around the Union flank and struck Pope's supply depot at Manassas Junction the next day. Pope was confused, as Lee had hoped. He refused to believe that a large Confederate force was behind him. If Pope had moved the troops at Warrenton Junction to Manassas Junction, Jackson would have been cut off. But the Union commander delayed. Finally he marched toward Centreville, where contact was made on August 28 when Jackson blocked the route of part of the Union force.[45]

The next day the Confederates took up a defensive position with their left on Bull Run and the majority of the troops behind a cut made for a yet-uncompleted railroad. Pope had 62,000 men available, but he attacked in uncoordinated, though fierce, thrusts that Jackson's well-protected troops were able to repulse one at a time. By eleven in the morning Jackson had been reinforced by 30,000 men brought up by Longstreet. Throughout the day Pope continued the piecemeal attacks. One of these was led by Stevens' old lieutenant, General Cuvier Grover, whose brigade on the Union center was ordered to make a bayonet charge across the railroad cut. Grover attacked in late afternoon, supported by units from the divisions of Kearney, Reno, and Stevens. Stevens' men charged through a small woods and over the cut, where they engaged in heavy fighting against vastly superior numbers for about fifteen minutes until forced to withdraw with heavy casualties. Stevens' horse was shot from under him, but after the retreat he was seen calmly walking out of the woods followed by a tall orderly carrying his saddle. It was a terrible, bloody day for the Union army, but in the center of the action Stevens could only see a small fraction of the total picture; he charged when ordered, and retreated when it was impossible to sustain an advance. Pope, who should have seen the large picture, did not know that Longstreet had come up and was convinced that continued pressure would

crack Jackson's line. At the end of the day he wired Lincoln
and Halleck that he had won a great victory and would continue the attack the next morning if Jackson did not retreat during
the night. The following day Lincoln learned that Pope was
mistaken—it was Secessionville again but on a much larger
scale.[46]

Early on the morning of August 30, Stevens met with the other generals at Pope's headquarters. Pope told them, as he had
told Lincoln the previous evening, that they had won a victory.
Stevens was astonished, for it appeared to him that Jackson had
held his position and that the Union army had taken heavy
casualties. He spoke out, and many agreed with him, but others
believed a continued attack would succeed. Pope ordered Stevens to take out a reconnaissance to test Jackson's line. Moving
forward with 100 men of the Highlanders he found the enemy,
as expected, strongly entrenched. Pope refused to accept this
evidence that Jackson's force was in a position where it could
resist any Union attack. Supported by his corps commanders,
Heintzelman and McDowell, Pope ordered the battle renewed.
A strong force was mobilized to hit Jackson's center, while Stevens and Kearny were ordered to hold the right flank near Bull
Run. In the meantime General Lee arrived on the scene, waited
for Pope to attack, and then counterattacked with Longstreet
against the Union left. That flank began to recoil, and General
John Reynolds personally galloped to report the alarming news
to Pope. Pope again refused to believe his staff, but he was finally convinced by the enraged Reynolds to send cavalry to investigate further. The news proved correct, and Pope's army
made an orderly retreat across Bull Run only after desperate
fighting at Henry House Hill. Stevens and his men had done
their job by holding the right flank and protecting the retreat,
although they knew at the beginning of the day that they "were
going into the jaws of death itself."[47]

After Stevens' men crossed Bull Run, they found the main
road toward Centreville jammed with men and wagons. He
pulled his exhausted troops off the road, where they slept during
the night as the rest of the army moved toward Washington.
The next morning they followed, marching through a drizzle.
Stevens received orders to act as a rear guard and was reinforced with two batteries and a cavalry brigade. While Pope
continued the retreat toward Washington, Stevens took up a defensive position to await a Confederate probe. But when the attack failed to materialize, Stevens guessed that Lee might again

be trying to move around Pope to strike him "under the ribs."
He was right. Jackson had marched toward Fairfax Courthouse
in an attempt once again to place himself between Pope and
Washington.[48]

The next day, September 1, Pope became aware of Jackson's
route and ordered Stevens, reinforced by elements of Reno's
now scattered division, to head overland to intercept the Confederates on the Little River Pike. As the force approached the
turnpike near Chantilly they encountered Jackson's troops in
cornfields and woods next to the road. Stevens moved the men
through a marsh and came out on the same railroad cut that
had caused so much grief at Bull Run. As the advance skir-
mishers passed beyond the cut, a regiment of Confederates rose
in the grass before them, and the Union force retreated. Stevens
ordered a charge. The division forced the Confederates out of the
grass and back through a cornfield toward the woods, but the
enemy main force poured a withering fire into the Union ranks.
Hazard was hit in the arm and hip. His father ordered him
helped off the field, and then leaped forward to lead the charge.
Stevens seized the flag of the Highlanders from a fallen color
bearer and dashed forward across the field shouting, "Highlanders, my Highlanders, follow your general!" The division responded, recklessly forcing the Confederates to retreat into the
woods.

At the height of the charge a sudden thunderstorm broke over
the battlefield; and as the lightning flashed and the thunder
joined the roar of the guns, a bullet struck Isaac Stevens in the
temple. He fell dead clutching the colors in his hands.[49]

EPILOGUE

General Stevens' courageous, gallant action seemed to fulfill his prophecy that he would play a major role in the war or die in the process. His picking up the flag and leading the charge may have been an impulsive gesture resulting from the heat of battle and the wounds to his son. But perhaps, too, it was part of his urge to capture glory even if it meant death. He died as he had lived, scorning opposition and tempting fate.

Stevens' body was taken from the field by his grieving men and sent to Washington D.C., where John Hayes, an old boarding-house friend from the Coast Survey days, took charge. At Meg's request the funeral and interment took place in Newport. The funeral attracted politicians from throughout the Northeast, including the governors of Massachusetts and Rhode Island, military men who could be spared from active duty, Professor Bache and numerous members of the Coast Survey, family, friends, and acquaintances. Meg's brother-in-law, the Reverend Charles Brooks, who had married Meg and Isaac in that same city twenty-one years before, presided at the funeral. Subsequently the city of Newport appropriated funds for a granite obelisk to be placed at the grave bearing the inscription

In memory of Major-General Isaac Ingalls Stevens, born in Andover, Mass., March 25, 1818, who gave to the service of his country a quick and comprehensive mind, a warm and generous heart, a firm will and a strong arm, and who fell while rallying his command with the flag of the Republic in his dying grasp, at the battle of Chantilly, Va., September 1, 1862.

Others in the Northeast and the Pacific Northwest joined in the eulogies. Typical was a long poem published in the *Boston Commonwealth* which began:

He fell—that glowing eye
In sudden night was quenched;
But still the flag he lifted high
And onward bore to victory,
In his dead hand was clenched.

Of all the eulogies, none would have pleased Stevens more than a passing reference made by Abraham Lincoln in an answer to rebukes for naming prominent Democrats like Stevens as generals.

In sealing their faith with their blood, Baker, and Lynn, and Bohlen, and Richardson, Republicans, did all that men could do; but did they any more than Kearny, and Stevens, and Reno, and Mansfield, none of whom were Republicans, and some, at least, of whom, have been bitterly and repeatedly denounced to me as secessionist sympathizers?

Isaac Stevens would have wished no more fitting epitaph then the recognition that he had done his duty.[1]

Stevens was posthumously promoted to major general, to rank from July 4, 1862. There is little doubt that greater military responsibilities awaited if he had survived Chantilly. John Hayes reported that a cabinet member told him that at the moment of Stevens' death, Lincoln was considering elevating him to command of the Army of Virginia. Generals E. O. C. Ord and George Ruggles both later remembered that they had heard the same rumors. It is possible that the rumors had some validity, although elevation to a corps command was more probable. Stevens had in good measure the qualities that Lincoln was looking for in a commanding general: he was not overly cautious like McClellan or excessively rash with the lives of his men like Pope. Stevens' understanding of proper tactics; his organizational ability, energy, courage, and zeal; and the love borne toward him by his troops were all sound reasons for high-level command. But more important than these was his uncanny ability to see clearly the war in its broadest scope. As early as 1861 he predicted the strategy that ultimately produced victory for the North. He also knew what kind of men such a strategy demanded and predicted the ultimate downfall of commanders (such as McClellen) who lacked the aggressive spirit to make that strategy work.[2]

Hazard Stevens continued the Civil War career that his father was denied. After two months spent recovering from the wounds received at Chantilly, he returned to the Ninth Corps as inspector general in the Third Division commanded by General

George W. Getty. He served with Getty at Fredericksburg and at the siege of Fort Huger. In mid-1863 Hazard went with Getty to the Sixth Corps of the Army of the Potomac. He served in the battles of Grant's final campaign against Lee, beginning with the Wilderness (where he took a minie ball below the knee) and continuing to Appomattox. Getty wrote:

I was an eye-witness to Stevens's courage and daring in every battle in which the Divisions I had the honor to command were engaged from Fredericksburg to the closing scene at Appomattox. . . . At the battle of the Wilderness I remember he was wounded, but never left the field, and remained with the Division and behaved in his usual gallant manner in all the battles of the Army of the Potomac.

On April 2, 1865, Stevens was brevetted brigadier general at age twenty-three, which made him, Hazard later claimed, the youngest general in the war.[3]

The young general declined an offer to remain in the peacetime army with the rank of major. A key factor in this decision was his financial responsibility for his mother and three younger sisters (ages eighteen, fifteen, and fourteen at the end of the war). Isaac Stevens had left them only a small inheritance, which consisted primarily of the house and farm outside Olympia. Meg, Hazard, and the girls returned to the Northwest, where Hazard became the agent for the Oregon Steam Navigation Company at Wallula. Meg and the girls took up residence in Portland. In 1868 old friends of his father secured Hazard the position of collector of internal revenue at Olympia, and the family returned to their old home. While collector, Stevens read law with Elwood Evans, the lawyer who had once opposed his father on martial law and Indian policy. In 1870 Stevens became an attorney for the Northern Pacific Railroad, with the major responsibility of prosecuting theft of timber from land granted to the company. While in Olympia he was appointed by President Grant to investigate the claims of British subjects on the San Juan Islands (which had been assigned to the United States in 1872), and he organized a successful effort to build a railroad to connect Olympia with the Northern Pacific, which had bypassed the community fifteen miles to the east. Stevens proved to be a "chip off the old block" in all of these endeavors.[4]

The feat for which Hazard Stevens was best remembered during this time in Olympia was his successful ascent of Mt. Rainier in August 1870. Stevens organized a small party to undertake what was then considered an impossible feat. After seventeen days he and P. B. Van Trump made it to the summit to become the first known conquerors of the mountain that dominated the landscape of the territory on which his father had had such an important influence.[5] (Stevens Canyon and Van Trump Park are named after these two men.)

The illness of one of Hazard's sisters in 1874 led Meg and the girls to move back to Boston, and Hazard followed the next year. Hazard continued his career as a lawyer and dabbled in politics, serving in the Massachusetts General Court (legislature), but never achieving election to Congress—a position he eagerly sought. Susan and Kate married, but Hazard, his mother, and Maude continued to live together in a house they had built in Dorcester. Meg never remarried. Her only forays into public life were periodic pleas to Congress to recognize the validity of claims her husband made for reimbursement of expenditures while in public service. She died in 1914 at the age of ninety-five. Hazard outlived his mother by four years before he suffered a fatal stroke during a visit to Washington State to dedicate an Indian war monument near Goldendale. Eventually Kate returned to Olympia, where she lived in the family home and became something of a local celebrity and a pleasant, if slightly eccentric, reminder of a distant past until her death in 1941.[6]

NOTES

See List of Abbreviations, pp. 445-48.

Where a note cites more than one item of correspondence in a collection, each item is separated from the others with a semicolon. Such sets are normally followed by the designation for the collection, which is separated from the set—and from other citations—also with a semicolon. Example: Bache to Pierce, May 1, 1856; Pierce to Bache, May 3, 1856; Pierce Papers; etcetera.

Chapter 1
Of New England Puritans and Pioneers

1. The Stevens family first became taxpaying landowners in the 1530s, perhaps beneficiaries of the Crown's distribution of monastery lands.

2. Curtis Nettles, *The Roots of American Civilization*, 2nd ed. (New York: Appleton, Century, Crofts, 1958), pp. 68-69; Edmund S. Morgan, *The Puritan Dilemma* (Boston: Little, Brown & Co., 1958), Chap. 2; Wallace Notestein, *The English People on the Eve of Colonization* (New York: Harper & Row, 1954), Chap. 7.

3. Marcus Hansen, *The Atlantic Migration* (Cambride, Mass.: Harvard University Press, 1940), p. 31; Morgan, *The Puritan Dilemma*, pp. 28-33.

4. The passengers on the *Confidence* included Sarah Osgood and her family, ancestors of Isaac Osgood, who was associated with Isaac Stevens in building coastal forts and with the Pacific railroad survey. Horace Stevens, "The Ancestors of Major General Isaac Ingalls Stevens", SHSW, pp. 1-2; Charlotte H. Abbott, "Early Records of the Stevens Family of Andover," North Andover Historical Society, North Andover, Mass.

5. Claude Fuess, *Andover: Symbol of New England* (Andover, Mass.: Andover Historical Society, 1959), pp. 9, 17, 31.

6. Horace Stevens, "Ancestors," SHSW, p. 4; Sarah L. Bailey, *Historical Sketches of Andover* (Boston: Houghton, Mifflin and Co., 1880), pp. 23-25, 155.

7. Joseph married Mary Ingalls, with whose family Stevenses frequently intermarried.

8. The oldest son of John Stevens had died in a campaign against Louisburg (1689), during the first English-French conflict in the New World.

9. Andover and North Andover developed as separate communities. The ancestors of Isaac I. Stevens were associated primarily with the area that came to be known as North Andover.

10. Horace Stevens, "Ancestors," SHSW, pp. 3, 6.

11. T. R. Hazard, *Recollections of Olden Times* (n.p., 1879), p. 227.

12. Horace Stevens, "Ancestors," SHSW, p. 6; H. S., *Life,* 1:4–5.

13. When Isaac I. Stevens died the farm went to his brother Oliver. Upon Oliver's death in 1908 it consisted of 200 acres, a house, and ten large farm buildings. The farm is still owned by members of the Stevens family, who have maintained the home much as it was in the nineteenth century. Horace Stevens, "Ancestors," SHSW, p. 6; H. S., *Life,* 1:6; Edmund Leland, "Marble Ridge Farm," ms., SHSW, pp. 2–4.

14. For example, the Cummings family included one of the fourteen proprietors of Dunstable.

15. Leland, "Marble Ridge Farm," p. 3; H. S., *Life,* 1:11–12; George Mooar to Hazard Stevens, November 9, 1899, HSUO.

16. H. S., *Life,* 1:7. At the time Hazard wrote, only Oliver, the youngest of Hannah's children, survived, and he had been two years old when she died.

17. Sarah Cummings to Hannah Stevens (sister of IIS), June 20, 1834, Stevens Family Papers, WSL.

18. Aaron Cummings to Isaac Stevens, November 12, 1835, Stevens Family Papers, WSL; H. S., *Life,* 1:8–9.

19. The children of Hannah and Isaac were Hannah, 1815–1840; Susan, 1817–1841; Isaac, 1818–1862; Elizabeth, 1819–1846; Sarah Ann, 1822–1844; Mary Jane, 1823–1847; and Oliver, 1825–1908.

20. H. S., *Life,* 1:14.

21. Hazard Stevens, manuscript copy of "Life of IIS," HSUO, pp. 12–13. Incidents and judgments unfavorable to the family were deleted from the original manuscript by Hazard.

22. Ibid., p. 15; H. S., *Life,* 1:17. Nathaniel Stevens returned from the ill-fated Maine venture soon after his brother's injury and established a mill on Lake Cochichewick in 1813. He took advantage of the War of 1812 to gain a market and subsequently was among the first to accept technological advances. By the end of the 1820s Nathaniel was one of the richest men in the area. Contemporaries described him as remarkably energetic, with a tenacity that yielded to no obstacle. Similar terms would later be used to describe his nephew Isaac. The mills in North Andover remained in operation and were controlled by the Stevens family until the 1960s. Fuess, *Andover,* pp. 255–57; Bailey, *Historical Sketches,* pp. 589–90.

23. Leland, "Marble Ridge Farm," SHSW, pp. 4–5.

24. Isaac Stevens, Sr., to IIS, November 9, 1835, May 1, 1836, February 27, 1838; Aaron Cummings to Isaac Stevens, Sr., November 12, 1835; IISUW; Edward Pessen, *Jacksonian America: Society, Personality, and Politics* (Homewood, Ill.: Dorsey Press, 1969), Chap. 2.

25. IIS to Susan Stevens, February 28, 1836; IIS to Hannah Stevens, September 30, 1838; IISUW.

26. IIS to Isaac Stevens, Sr., December 17, 1837, August 21, November 17, 1838, April 13, 1842; IIS to William Stevens, October 21, 1839; IISUW.

27. S. R. Hall to Lewis Cass, October 22, 23, 1834; John Richardson to Cass, November 15, 1834; A. R. Baker to Cass, November 19, 1834; NA, RG 94; Records of the Adjutant General's Office, United States Military Academy Cadet Application Papers (M688), R 94; Claude Fuess, *An Old New England School: A History of Phillips Academy Andover* (Boston: Houghton, Mifflin and Co., 1917), pp. 209, 211, 215.

28. Sarah Cummings to IIS, March 11, 1830, Stevens Family Papers, SHSW; IIS to William Stevens, June 12, 1833, IISUW; IIS to Cass, March 11, 1835, U.S. Military Academy Cadet Application Papers.

Chapter 2
First in the Class

1. IIS to Susan Stevens, June 21, 1835, Stevens Family Papers, WSL; IIS to William Stevens, June 13, 1835, IISUW.

2. Stephen Ambrose, *Duty, Honor, Country: A History of West Point* (Baltimore: Johns Hopkins Press, 1966), p. 90.

3. Ibid., pp. 72–73, 89–91.

4. Ibid., pp. 119, 129–30. The system of Congressional appointments was less democratic than previous methods of selection, for it placed a premium upon direct access to senators or representatives. If Gayton Osgood had not been a friend of the Stevens family or if Isaac had not had powerful political friends like William and Nathaniel Stevens or Nathan Hazen, it is doubtful that even the best recommendations from his mentors would have proved sufficient to gain an appointment.

5. U.S., Congress, House Report 303, 24th Cong., 2d sess. [306], pp. 17–29; Ambrose, *Duty, Honor, Country*, pp. 108–11, 119–24.

6. IIS to Susan, June 21, 1835, Stevens Papers, WSL.

7. Joseph B. James, "Life at West Point One Hundred Years Ago," *Mississippi Valley Historical Review* 31 (June 1944): 23; IIS to Susan, June 21, 1835; IIS to Isaac Stevens, Sr., July 2, 1837; Stevens Family Papers, WSL; IIS to his sisters, September 8, 1835; IIS to Isaac, Sr., September 2, 1836; Henry Stevens to IIS, January 22, 1838; IISUW; Hazard Stevens, manuscript copy of "Life of IIS," HSUO, p. 56.

8. IIS to Isaac, Sr., May 22, 1836, July 2, 1837, Stevens Papers, WSL; IIS to Aaron Cummings, August 30, 1835; IIS to William Stevens, August 16, 1836; IIS to Isaac, Sr., November 17, 1838; Henry Stevens to IIS, January 22, 1838; IISUW.

9. H. S., *Life*, 1:43; George W. Cullum, *Biographical Register of the Officers and Graduates of the U.S. Military Academy at West Point*, 2 vols. (New York: D. Van Nostrand Co., 1868), 1:616–19. Carpenter served in the Seminole War and at

396 ISAAC I. STEVENS

a series of frontier posts from Wisconsin to Texas. He was killed at the battle of Stone River in December, 1862, four months after Stevens' death. Bacon also served in the Seminole War and on the frontier. He died in Mexico City as a result of wounds sustained in the battle for the capital in the Mexican War. Stevens was wounded in the same battle.

10. H. S., *Life,* 1:26.

11. IIS to William Stevens, December 5, 1835; IIS to Isaac, Sr., December 20, 1835; IIS to Susan, February 23, 1836; IISUW; Ambrose, *Duty, Honor, Country,* pp. 91–93.

12. H. S., *Life,* 1:26; U.S., Congress, House Doc. 2, 26th Cong., 1st sess. [363], *Report on the United States Military Academy,* p. 323; IIS to William Stevens, December 5, 1835; February 1, 1836; IIS to his sisters, September 8, 1835; IISUW; Ambrose, *Duty, Honor, Country,* p. 132; Stephen Ambrose, *Halleck: Lincoln's Chief of Staff* (Baton Rouge: Louisiana State University Press, 1962), pp. 4–5.

13. IIS to Isaac, Sr., January 20, 1838, Stevens Family Papers, WSL; Ambrose, *Duty, Honor, Country,* pp. 80–81; *Report on the United States Military Academy,* pp. 223–24.

14. IIS to Isaac, Sr., December 5, 20, 1835; IIS to his sisters, September 8, 1835; IIS to William Stevens, July 6, 1836; IISUW.

15. At the end of the January examinations in his second year, Stevens slipped to second in French, but was first again in June. Combined with his usual first in mathematics, the fourth in drawing, and decreased demerits (which moved him to seventeenth on the conduct role), Stevens had no trouble ranking first overall. He easily maintained this position during his final two years. IIS to William Stevens, July 6, 1836; IIS to Isaac, Sr., March 11, June 18, 1836; IIS to Susan, March 5, 1836; IIS to Elizabeth Stevens, March 5, 1836; IISUW; H. S., *Life,* 1:27.

16. IIS, "West Point Notes" (box 7), IISUW; Ambrose, *Duty, Honor, Country,* pp. 96–97; H. S., *Life,* 1:41; R. Ernest Dupuy and Trevor N. Dupuy, *Military Heritage of America,* (New York: McGraw-Hill & Co., 1956), pp. 191–93.

17. James, "Life at West Point," pp. 24–25; IIS to Susan, September 5, 1837; IIS to Isaac, Sr., January 20, 1838; Stevens Family Papers, WSL; Hazard Stevens, manuscript copy of "Life of IIS," HSUO, p. 51.

18. IIS to Isaac, Sr., November 17, 1838; IISUW; IIS to Isaac, Sr., May 26, 1836; Stevens Family Papers, WSL.

19. IIS to Nathan Hazen, November 5, 1837, IISUW; IIS to Hannah Stevens, January 27, 1838, Stevens Family Papers, WSL.

20. IIS to Oliver Stevens, October 28, 1838; IIS to Hannah, January 27, 1839; IIS to William Stevens, January 13, 1839; Prospectus for the *Talisman* (box 7), essays written by IIS for the *Talisman* (box 7); IISUW.

21. Susan to IIS, February 18, 1836 (this letter is misdated as 1835); Elizabeth to IIS, July 10, 1836; Isaac, Sr., to IIS, October 29, November 9, 1835, February 7, 1836; IISUW.

22. Hannah to IIS, December 7, 1835, December 15, 1837, October 29, 1838; IIS to Hannah, September 30, 1838; IIS to Isaac, Sr., December 17, 1837; IISUW; IIS to Hannah, January 27, 1838, Stevens Family Papers, WSL; H. S., *Life,* 1:59.

23. He later complained that the *Democratic Review* had become "a mere party concern" and replaced it with the *North American Review*.

24. Elizabeth to IIS, July 10, 1836; IIS to Hannah, January 27, 1837, September 30, 1838; IIS to Isaac, Sr., November 17, 1838; IIS to Susan, September 18, 1838; IISUW; IIS to Susan, September 5, 1837 Stevens Family Papers, WSL.

25. Isaac, Sr., to IIS, February 27, September 8, 1838; IIS to Oliver, October 28, 1838, December 15, 1840; IIS to Isaac, Sr., November 17, 1838, January 17, 1841 (this letter is misdated as 1840); IISUW.

26. IIS to Isaac, Sr., November 17, 1838, IIS Memo to H. L. Smith on Carlyle (box 7); IISUW.

Chapter 3
The Young Lieutenant

1. At one time Stevens assumed he would end up fighting the Seminoles. The war still dragged on in 1839 but his ranking assured he would not go to Florida. He wondered why 6,000 fighting men could not subdue 1,000 poorly equipped Indians, and came to the conclusion that the generals were a poor lot except for the retired Andrew Jackson. He dismissed Winfield Scott as a leader who made a great noise but effected nothing. Stevens judged that the Seminole war "cannot add to the military glory of any concerned with it," and was glad to be far removed from the action. Col. Joseph Totten to Major Richfield Delafield, April 11, July 3, 1839, Totten Letters; IIS to Totten, July 17, 1839; IIS to Isaac, Sr., May 22, 1836, July 2, 1837; Stevens Family Papers, WSL; IIS to William Stevens, January 13, 1839; Henry L. Smith to IIS, July 20, September 12, 1839; IISUW.

2. I. L. Folsom to IIS, April, 1842; IISUW.

3. Nine of thirty-one resigned, two were deceased, and one had been dropped from the service.

4. IIS to William Stevens, August 5, 1840; IIS to Isaac, Sr., October 14, 1840; IISUW; Robert Weigley, *The United States Army* (New York: Macmillan Co., 1967), p. 169.

5. Nathan Hazen to IIS, October 4, 1840; IIS to William Stevens, August 5, 1840; Henry L. Smith to IIS, October (or November), 1840; IISUW.

6. Zealous B. Tower to IIS, September 27, 1839, IISUW; H. S., *Life,* 1:62.

7. The house was located in the middle of Newport near the waterfront. Large, comfortable, and built in typical Newport style (with the entrance almost in the street), the house had a small pediment over the door, and a sparse, neoclassical style. The home is presently preserved as a historic site.

8. Benjamin Hazard's ancestors on both sides of the family became freemen of Boston prior to 1636. The maternal ancestors of Margaret's mother came to Massachusetts from Wales in 1634 and settled in Newport in 1639. Lyman-Hazard genealogy, HSUO; Meg to Mary Hazard, 1840; Meg to Mary, April 30, 1839, February 15, 1841; HSUO. Meg identified her rejected suitor only as

Henry. Meg had a habit of partially dating or not dating many of her letters, but the approximate dates of most can be determined by internal evidence.

9. Meg to Mary, 1839 (or 1840), December 2, 1840, HSUO; H. S., *Life*, 1:65; Elizabeth to IIS, August 25, 1839; Hannah to IIS, October 20, 1839; B. F. Tilden to IIS, October 22, 1839; Henry L. Smith to IIS, December 5, 1839, April 27, July 15, 1840; IISUW.

10. Henry Halleck to IIS, November 11, 1840; IIS to Isaac, Sr., September 24, 1841, marriage certificate (box 7); IISUW.

11. Weigley, *United States Army*, pp. 163–65; U.S., Congress, House Doc. 2, 36th Cong., 2d sess., [363], *Report on the United States Military Academy*, p. 225.

12. Totten was pleased with Stevens' work, and he was promoted to first lieutenant in July, 1840. It is likely that the rapid promotion was awarded primarily for his West Point record and as an inducement to remain in the service. Of the other men in the class of 1839 who went into the Engineer Corps, one, Robert Q. Butler, died in 1843, and the other three were not promoted until 1845. George W. Cullum, *Biographical Register of the Officers and Graduates of the U.S. Military Academy at West Point*, 2 vols. (New York: D. Van Nostrand Co., 1868), 1:94–96, 573–75; Totten to James Mason, September 16, 1839, August 23, 1841, Totten Letters; Totten to Mason, December 24, 1840, LOE.

13. Totten to Mason, August 4, 1841, Totten Letters; IIS to Isaac, Sr., September 24, 1841, IISUW.

14. Totten wearily responded to an allegation of favoritism toward certain cadets by stating that the same charge had been made and disproved so often that it hardly seemed necessary to deny it once again.

15. Henry Stevens to IIS, May 3, 1840; IIS to Isaac, Sr., November 16, 1840; IISUW; Totten to Senator Franklin Pierce, February 17, 1841; Totten to Secretary of War, Joel Poinsett, December 8, 1840; Totten to Secretary of War, John C. Spencer, November 18, 1841; Totten, Memorandum, March 16, 1842; Totten to Sylvanus Thayer, April 7, June 24, 1842, Totten Letters; U.S., Congress, House, Doc. 206, 26th Cong., 1st sess., [368], *Report from the Secretary of War on a System of National Defense*, pp. 1–5, 37, 41, 78–79, 87.

16. Totten to Poinsett, February 20, 1839, July 28, 1840, Totten Letters; *Report from the Secretary of War on a System of National Defense*, passim.

17. The fort was not located in New Bedford proper but across the bay in the community of Fairhaven. IIS to Totten, September 20, 21, 30, November 5, December 1, 1841, January 4, 1842, EDLR; Lt. George Welcker (Assistant to the Chief Engineer), to IIS, September 24, October 18, November 8, 1841; Totten to IIS, September 25, November 3, 1841; LOE; U.S., Congress, House Report 327, 29th Cong., 1st sess. [489], *Report on Fortifications at New Bedford.*

18. IIS to Totten, March 30, May 3, 1842, EDLR; Totten to IIS, April 4, 1842, LOE.

19. IIS to Totten, April 12, July 1, August 1, October 1, 7, 1842, EDLR; Totten to IIS, April 4, 1842, LOE.

20. IIS to Sarah Ann Stevens, January 14, 1842; Meg to Mary, October 13, 19, 27, 1841, January 27, 1842; Stevens Family Papers, WSL; Meg to Mary, September 29, November 11, 1841, September 10, 1841; IIS to Isaac, Sr., September 21, 1842; HSUO.

21. IIS to Isaac, Sr., June 8, 1842, IISUW. He also hired an Irish girl as a servant, but muttered that she was "strong as a horse, but not so ready or capable." IIS to Isaac, Sr., August 18, September 21, 1842; HSUO.

22. Meg to Mary, September 10, 1842; IIS to Isaac, Sr., January 22, 1843, HSUO; IIS to Isaac, Sr., February 8, April 13, November 6, 1842, Stevens Family Papers, WSL. Stevens' youngest sister, Mary, wrote that a fugitive, who was the blackest person she had ever seen, spent a night at their farm. Because she had a dark complexion, Mary lightheartedly suggested that, as they hit it off, it might have proved a good match for each. Mary to IIS, June 19, 1842; IISUW.

23. IIS to Isaac, Sr., February 15, 1841; IIS to Meg's sister Emily, n.d.; Stevens Family Papers, WSL; Oliver to IIS, June 25, 1840; B. F. Tilden to IIS, August 1, 1840; IISUW.

24. Totten asked for $150,000 for the fort at the narrows of the Penobscot near Bucksport and planned that it would have a garrison of 500 men and 148 guns. For Portsmouth he requested $300,000 for works to hold 750 men and 150 guns and for Portland, $48,000. Many of the engineer officers lobbied vigorously for approval of the projects. James Mason wrote an article on the defense of the Northeast frontier which was printed in a number of newspapers. Totten to Joel Poinsett, February 20, 1839; Totten to John C. Spencer, August 20, 1842; Totten Letters; IIS to Isaac, Sr., August 21, 1838, IISUW; *Report from the Secretary of War on a System of National Defense,* pp. 44–45; U.S., Congress, House Doc. 227, 26th Cong., 1st sess., [368], *Resolution of Citizens of Prospect, Maine, in Favor of Fortifying Penobscot Bay*; Henry Halleck, Military Notebook, June, 1843, Henry Halleck Papers, L.C.

25. IIS to Isaac, Sr., January 22, 1843, HSUO; IIS to Isaac, Sr., March 10, 1843, Stevens Family Papers, WSL; IIS to Totten, December 1, 1842, January 4, March 3, 1843, EDLR; Totten to IIS, March 23, April 8, 1843, LOE; Henry L. Smith to IIS, December 6, 1841, IISUW.

26. Totten to IIS, July 5, 27, August 1, 1843, LOE; IIS to Totten, July 29, 1843, EDLR.

27. When Stevens later tried to buy land next to Fort McClary, the owner on one side asked $600 an acre and the owner on the other side asked $125. The $70 offer therefore seemed a bargain. Totten to IIS, September 14, 1843, March 16, April 27, January 4, July 12, 1844, LOE; IIS to Totten, March 5, 1846, EDLR; Totten to Capt. John Sanders, June 14, 1841, Totten Letters.

28. Stevens lent his brother several hundred dollars, a loan he could ill afford, to finance his education. Oliver was a bright student but conscientiously followed a resolution to "take things fair and easy and not fret our gizzard to pieces." Oliver to IIS, September 11, 1843, August 4, 1846, IISUW.

29. Henry L. Smith was one officer who often complained that Totten did not understand his problems, and who wished that the Chief Engineer would leave most decisions to men in the field. IIS to Oliver, May 13, 1844; IIS to Isaac, Sr., June 24, 1844; HSUO; IIS to Oliver, April 17, 1844; IIS to Isaac, Sr., April 26, 1844; Stevens Family Papers, WSL; IIS to Totten, May 1, 13, 17, June 25, July 10, August 7, October 21, 1844, EDLR; Totten to IIS, April 27, June 7, July 13, 1844; Totten to Henry W. Benham, July 11, 1843; LOE; Henry L. Smith to IIS, December 6, 1841, IISUW.

30. A similar newspaper voucher submitted by Robert E. Lee was disallowed on the same day.

31. Totten to IIS, March 7, July 2, 12, September 9, 1845, May 21, 30, June 24, November 19, 1846, LOE; IIS to Totten, August 11, 1845, May 27, June 10, 1846, EDLR.

32. H. S., *Life,* 1:88; IIS to Oliver, May 13, 1844, HSUO.

33. IIS to Totten, July 24, 1844, June 5, July 4, 6, 1846, EDLR; George Welcker to IIS, August 3, 1844, LOE; *Portsmouth Journal,* July 6, 1844.

34. Totten to IIS, December 14, 1846, LOE.

35. IIS to Totten, October 21, December 7, 1844, EDLR; George Welcker to IIS, July 19, 1844, LOE; IIS to Isaac, Sr., November 6, 1843, IISUW; IIS to Oliver, February 3, 1843; IIS to Isaac, Sr., July 24, 1843; Stevens Family Papers, WSL.

36. Meg to Mary, February 28, 1845, HSUO; IIS to Isaac, Sr., July 24, 1843, Stevens Family Papers, WSL; N. B. Weston to IIS, February 3, 1846; George Shepard to IIS, February 11, 1846; A. P. Peabody to IIS, February 15, 1846; J. E. H. Smith to IIS, March 11, 1846; IIS to Oliver, October 22, 1846; IISUW.

37. Oliver to IIS, March 16, 1844; Isaac, Sr., to IIS, November 5, 1846; Isaac, Sr., to Meg, July 12, 1847; Meg to IIS, August 4, 1844; IISUW; H. S., *Life,* 1:87; Hazard Stevens, ms. copy of "Life of IIS," HSUO, p. 79.

38. Virginia's death was partially assuaged by the birth of Susan in November, 1846. IIS and Meg to Harriet Hazard, December 8, 1845; IIS to Elisa Lyman, December 14, 1845; Stevens Family Papers, WSL.

Chapter 4
In the Halls of the Montezumas

1. George B. McClellan to his sister, May 3, 1846, George B. McClellan Papers, LC.

2. IIS to Totten, June 24, 1845, October 19, 1846, EDLR; George Welcker to IIS, October 23, 1846, IISUW.

3. He encountered opposition when the Adjutant General refused to pay for the ads and circulars which Stevens claimed raised more recruits than if two recruiting sergeants had been sent into the field. Totten intervened to force payment and ordered Stevens to continue his efforts. IIS to Totten, November 5, 17, 1846, EDLR; Totten to IIS, December 16, 1846, LOE.

4. *Portsmouth Journal,* September 12, 1846; IIS to G. R. Jones, March 28, 1847; General William Worth to Capt. H. L. Scott, AAA, September 16, 1847; Ezra Clark to Hon. R. P. Dunlap, February 2, 1847; George Evans to William L. Marcy, February 15, 1847; AGO, Mexican War, LR; IIS to Unknown, January 20, 1842, Letterbook, 1849–51, IISUW.

5. Oliver to IIS, February 15, 1845, IISUW; Frederick Merk, *The Oregon Question* (Cambridge, Mass.: n.p., 1967), pp. 212–18.

6. Stevens hired a nineteen-year-old Irish lad who had just enlisted in the Massachusetts volunteers as a servant. He also had time to visit the theater to view mass precision dancing by a Chinese troup which was the current sensation in Boston. IIS to Totten, December 21, 22, 1846; Totten to George W. Cullum, December 22, 1846; LOE; IIS to Totten, December 26, 1846, EDLR; IIS to Meg, January 1, 12, 13, 1847, December 29, 1846; IIS to Oliver, December 20, 1846; IISUW.

7. IIS to Totten, January 11, 12, 1847; IIS to Capt. Benjamin Alvord, January 12, 1847; EDLR; George Welcker to IIS, January 14, 1847, LOE; IIS to Meg, January 27, 1847; Engineer Order No. 1, December 22, 1846; IISUW.

8. IIS to Meg, February 21, 1847, IISUW; IIS to Meg, March 10, 1847, Stevens Papers, SHSW; Quartermaster's Report from Brazos, November 1, 1846, AGO, Mexican War, LR.

9. Totten to General Winfield Scott, March 13, 18, 19, 1847; Totten to Officers of Engineers, March 19, 1847, Totten Letters; Gustavus Smith to Winfield Scott, AGO, Mexican War, Misc.; General Orders No. 33, February 25, 1847, NA, RG 94, Mexican War, General and Special Orders, February 18–December 18, 1847; IIS to Meg, March 10, 27, 1847; Abstract of Operations at Vera Cruz as Regards the Working Parties of Lt. Stevens, Engineer, March 1847; IISUW; Justin H. Smith, *The War With Mexico,* 2 vols. (New York: Macmillan Co., 1919), 2:27–36.

10. H. S., *Life,* 1:232; IIS to Meg, March 27, April 3, 1847, IISUW; IIS, *Campaigns of the Rio Grande and Mexico* (New York: D. Appleton Co., 1851), pp. 107–108.

11. Stevens also acquired a new servant, an old career soldier, who he later dismissed as a drunkard. IIS to Meg, April 10, 1847; IIS, Mexican War Journal, March 28, 1847, IISUW; George Meade, *The Life and Letters of George Gordon Meade,* G. G. Meade, ed., 2 vols. (New York: Charles Scribner's Sons, 1913), 1:192–93.

12. Totten to Scott, March 28, 1847, Totten Letters. The engineer officers were Stevens, James Mason, John Smith, Robert E. Lee, P.G.T. Beauregard, Gustavus Smith, Zealous Tower, George McClellan, and J. G. Foster.

13. IIS to Meg, April 12, 1847, IISUW.

14. IIS, Mexican War Journal, April 14–18, 1847, IISUW; IIS to Meg, April 18, 1847, Stevens Family Papers, WSL; Theodore Eckerson to Hazard Stevens, April 4, 1877, HSUO; Douglas S. Freeman, *Robert E. Lee,* 4 vols. (New York: Charles Scribner's Sons, 1934–35), 1:238–41; T. Harry Williams, ed., *With Beauregard in Mexico* (Baton Rouge: Lousiana State University Press, 1956), pp. 32–34.

15. Freeman, *Lee,* 1:242–46; IIS, Mexican War Journal, April 16–18, 1847; IISUW; IIS, *Campaigns of the Rio Grande and Mexico,* pp. 54–56; IIS to Meg, April 18, 1847; IIS to Isaac, Sr., April 9, 1847; Stevens Family Papers, WSL; U.S., Congress, Ex. Doc. 1, 30th Cong., 1st sess. [277], *Mexican War Reports.*

16. IIS, Mexican War Journal, April 19, 1847; IIS to Meg, April 22, 1847; IISUW.

17. Dupuy and Dupuy, *Military Heritage of America,* pp. 160–61; IIS to Meg, April 18, 1847, IISUW.

18. Stevens remained unimpressed by the Mexican people, although he found the upper class elegant and dignified. He observed that one wealthy merchant of Puebla had offered his services as a spy for $5,000, and concluded that many Mexicans would be willing to serve as agents for the right price. Catholic services fascinated him, but he felt obliged to dismiss the ceremony and pageantry as a "pagan corruption" of American Catholicism. IIS to Meg, February 21, April 22, May 1, June 3, 1847, IISUW; IIS to Isaac, Sr., May 6, 26, 1847, Stevens Family Papers, WSL; IIS, *Campaigns of the Rio Grande and Mexico*, pp. 11–12; IIS, Mexican War Journal, April 21–30, 1847, IISUW; Capt. J. L. Irwin to Capt. H. L. Scott, AAA, July 23, 1847, AGO, Mexican War, Misc. Colonel Totten and most other Regular Army men agreed that reliance upon volunteers was a mistake. Totten to Joel Poinsett, November 27, 1846, Totten Letters.

19. IIS, Mexican War Journal, May 5, 15, 23–26, 1847, IIS to Meg, April 22, May 1, 1847, IISUW.

20. IIS, Mexican War Journal, June 3–July 25, 1847, IISUW.

21. IIS to Meg, August 22, 1847, IISUW; Williams, *With Beauregard in Mexico*, pp. 41–42.

22. In his report Major Smith said, "He [Stevens] persevered until night but with no result except to conclude that there was no practical route in that direction." Major J. L. Smith to Capt. H. L. Scott, AAA, August 27, 1847, AGO, Mexican War, LR.

23. IIS, Mexican War Journal, August 19, 1847; IIS to Meg, August 22, 1847; IISUW; Williams, *With Beauregard in Mexico*, pp. 47–49; Smith, *War With Mexico*, 2:99–106.

24. The two days of fighting resulted in Mexican losses of 700 killed and 800 captured. IIS to Meg, August 22, 1847; IIS, Mexican War Journal, August 19, 1847; IISUW.

25. On August 19–20, in the fighting at Contreras and Churubusco, Scott lost 133 killed, 865 wounded, and 40 missing—a total of about one-seventh of his force. IIS, Mexican War Journal, August 19, 1847; IIS to Meg, August 22, 1847; IISUW; Smith, *War With Mexico*, 2:113–18; W. H. French to Hazard Stevens, June 5, 1877; Truman Seymour to Hazard Stevens, March 28, 1877; HSUO.

26. IIS, Mexican War Journal, August 19, 1847; IIS to Meg, August 22, 1847; IISUW.

27. IIS, Mexican War Journal, August 21–September 7, 1847; IIS to Meg, August 22, 1847; IISUW.

28. Major Smith suffered from a hernia, but Stevens did not accept that as a valid reason for inactivity. IIS, Mexican War Journal, September 6–11, 1847, IISUW; Major J. L. Smith to Capt. H. L. Scott, AAA, September 26, 1847, AGO, Mexican War, LR.

29. IIS, Mexican War Journal, September 8–13, 1847, IISUW. General Worth reported that Stevens displayed the "gallantry and skill which so eminently distinguished this [Engineer] Corps." Gen. William Worth to Cap. H. L. Scott, AAA, September 16, 1847, AGO, Mexican War, LR; Smith, *War With Mexico*, 2:161–62.

30. IIS, Mexican War Journal, September 13-30, October 1, 12-24, November 2-3, 14, 20, December 4, 9, 1847, IISUW.

31. IIS, Mexican War Journal, September 11-12, 1847, IISUW; Gen. Winfield Scott to William L. Marcy, September 18, 1847, AGO, Mexican War, LR.

32. In a period of less than a week, six of the nine engineer officers were wounded: Lee, Beauregard, Tower, Mason, Foster, and Stevens—the latter three suffering serious injuries. IIS, Mexican War Journal, September 11-12, 1847, IISUW; AGO, Mexican War, Misc.

Chapter 5
To the Coast Survey

1. Brevets amounted to honorary advances in rank and were a common form of military reward in the nineteenth century. A controversy arose after the Mexican War as to whether the promotions should carry advances in pay as well as rank. Many mistakes were made in granting brevets: Stevens was not directly involved in the battle at Chapultepec; McClellan was brevetted for an action he never saw; Gustavus Smith received only one brevet and Zealous Tower none. The oversights, obvious as they were, proved difficult to rectify. Totten to George W. Cullum, April 19, 1847, Totten Letters; IIS to Meg, January 23, 1848; J. G. Foster to IIS, February 6, 1848; IISUW; Certificates of Promotion, Stevens Family Papers, WSL.

2. Stevens sang the praises of General Scott to the administration, which was an honest but politically injudicious action.

3. Oliver later inquired whether their father had remarked on the "performance" after one occasion when they made particularly heavy inroads on the cider. Oliver to IIS, January 27, March 25, 1848, IISUW.

4. J. G. Foster to IIS, February 6, 1848; Meg to IIS, February 21, 1847; Meg to Isaac, Sr., July 5, December 4, 1847; Isaac, Sr., to IIS, December 8, 1847; IIS to Meg, July 8, 1847; IISUW; H. S., *Life*, 1:227-28.

5. IIS to Oliver, March 15, 1848; IIS to Meg, July 8, 1847; IIS to Isaac, Sr., February 28, 1848; IISUW; H. S., *Life*, 1:229.

6. Totten to IIS, January 22, March 6, 20, 1848, LOE; IIS to Totten, March 3, 15, 30, 1848, EDLR; IIS to Oliver, March 15, 27, April 1, 1848, IISUW.

7. IIS to Totten, April 24, May 9, July 15, 1848, EDLR; Totten to IIS, July 10, 1848, Totten Letters; Totten to IIS, July 13, 1848; Capt. Fred A. Smith, Assistant of the Chief Engineer, to IIS, April 3, May 1, 11, 1848; LOE.

8. IIS to Totten, May 9, October 18, 1848, EDLR; Fred Smith to IIS, June 15, 1848; Totten to IIS, July 13, 1848; LOE; IIS to Totten, July 15, 1848; George Cullum to IIS, May 12, 1848; Oliver to IIS, May 15, 1848; IISUW.

9. IIS to Mary Hazard, September 18, 1848, HSUO; IIS to Oliver, December 8, 1848, IISUW.

10. IIS to Totten, July 29, 1848, May 1, 1849, EDLR; IIS to Mary Hazard, September 18, 1848, February 3, 24, November 21, 1849, January 2, 1850, HSUO; IIS to Oliver, December 8, 1848, IISUW.

11. The concerned officers included Col. Sylvanus Thayer, Col. Joseph F. K. Mansfield, Col. Robert E. Lee, Major William Fraser, Major John G. Barnard, Lt. Col. James Mason, Major P. G. T. Beauregard, Capt. J. M. Scarritt, Major Zealous Tower, Capt. Gustavus Smith, Capt. George McClellan, Capt. John G. Foster, Capt. Henry Halleck, and Major Isaac I. Stevens. Memorial of Brevet Officers of Engineers to Totten, July 26, 1849, EDLR; James Stuart to George McClellan, September 26, 1848, George McClellan Papers, LC.

12. IIS to Fred A. Smith, April 11, May 12, 1849; IIS to James Mason, April 11, 1849; IIS to J. G. Barnard, May 19, 1849; IIS, Circular to the Brevetted Officers of Engineers, May 29, 1849; IIS to Totten, July 26, May 10, 1849; Letterbook, 1849–51; IISUW; Totten to Secretary of War, G. W. Crawford, December 15, 1849, EDLR.

13. IIS to Fred A. Smith, May 12, 1849; IIS to J. G. Barnard, May 19, 1849; Letterbook, 1849–51, IISUW.

14. Alexander Dalles Bache to IIS, August 7, 1849; Bache to A. A. Humphreys, September 3, 1849; Bache to George W. Cullum, August 6, 1849; Totten to Bache, July 16, August 2, 1849; Cullum to Bache, July 7, 1849; Bache Corres.; Totten to Cullum, July 27, 1849, Totten Letters.

15. IIS to Fred A. Smith, August 15, 19, 1849, IISUW; Fred A. Smith to IIS, September 14, 1849, LOE.

16. A. Hunter Dupree, *Science in the Federal Government* (Cambridge, Mass.: Harvard University Press, 1957), pp. 29–30, 52–55, 104; CS, Annual Report; *DAB*, 1:461–62.

17. Dupree, *Science in the Federal Government,* pp. 100–104; CS, Annual Report, 1850; IIS to Bache, September 19, 1850, Bache Corres.

18. IIS to Oliver, October——, 1849, October 29, 1849, IISUW; IIS to Bache, November 7, 1850, Bache Corres.

19. IIS, Annual Report of the Assistant in Charge of the Office, November 11, 1850, November 15, 1851, CS, Annual Report, 1850, 1851; IIS to Bache, December 13, 1849, September 11, 1851; Samuel Manning to IIS, September 4, 1851; IIS to Manning, September 5, 1851; Wilson Fairfax to Bache, April 17, 1850; Bache to Henry Benner, April 17, December 12, 1850; CS, Corres. with Assts.; Bache to IIS, November——, 1850, Bache Corres.; Wilson Fairfax to IIS, November 8, 1850; CS, Letters and Papers Rec.

20. It is not surprising that William McNeil Whistler, who became an engraver with the Survey soon after Stevens left, would attempt to amuse himself by adding seagulls and other embellishments to his coast profiles; he was dismissed after a few weeks. William McClery to IIS, 1850; Wilson Fairfax to IIS, April 1850; Bache to IIS, November 22, 1850, August 13, 1851, CS, Letters and Papers Rec.; IIS, Annual Report of the Assistant in Charge of the Office, November 11, 1850, November 15, 1851, CS, Annual Report, 1850, 1851; IIS to Bache, July 20, 24, December 30, 1850, CS, Corres. with Assts.

21. This was the beginning of a long association with Saxton, who served with the railroad survey and with Stevens on the Sea Islands during the Civil War. IIS to Bache, September 19, October 15, 1851, June 1, 1852, CS, Corres. with Assts.; Bache to IIS, January 12, 1850, CS, Letters and Papers Rec.; IIS, Annual Report of the Assistant in Charge of the Office, November 15, 1851, February 15, 1853, CS, Annual Report, 1851, 1853.

22. IIS to Bache, September 3, 16, 17, 18, 19, 1850, Bache Corres.; IIS to Bache, August 31, 1850; IIS to William Gwin, September 9, 1850; IIS to M. Dickinson, September 17, 1850; Richard Cutts to Bache, August 24, 31, 1850, CS, Corres. with Assts.; Bache to IIS, January 16, 1850, CS, Letters and Papers Rec.; Jefferson Davis to IIS, January 17, 1850, NA, RG 23, Coast Survey, Letters Received by the Assistant in Charge of the United States Coast Survey Office, Miscellaneous.

23. Bache to IIS, July 14, August 5, 1852; IIS to Bache, November 23, 1850; Bache Cores.; IIS to Meg, September 29, 1850, IISUW.

24. The new baby was born on April 28, 1850, and named Gertrude Maude (the family called her Maude). IIS to Bache, April 3, 1850; IIS to Meg, August 29, September 5, 6, 16, 1850; Meg to IIS, March 27, 1850, September 8, 1850; John L. Hayes to IIS, April 3, 1850; IISUW; IIS to Bache, April 20, 1850; Bache Corres.; IIS to Bache, April 29, 1850, CS, Corres. with Assts.

25. Bache to IIS, April 3, 1850, CS, Letters and Papers Rec.; Totten to IIS, February 27, 1851, LOE; IIS to Totten, September 30, 1850, May 14, October 11, 1851, EDLR; Totten to Bache, May 28, 1850, Totten Letters; IIS to Bache, April 20, 1850, Bache Corres.

26. IIS to Bache, May 14, 15, 28, July 12, 1850, August 1852, Bache Corres.; IIS to Bache, May 16, 25, 1850, April 17, 1851, CS, Corres. with Assts.; IIS to Meg, September 5, 16, 1850, February 24, 1851; Theodore Woodman to IIS, March 15, 27, 1852; IIS to Woodman, March 19, 1852, IISUW; H. S., *Life*, 1:257, 264-65.

27. IIS to Meg, July 27, 1851, IISUW; Meg to Mary, December 5, 1849, HSUO.

28. IIS, Memorandum on Promotion Lieutenants in Staff Corps to Captain after Fourteen Years Service (box 6); IIS, Memorandum Comparing Years of Service in Rank for American and English Officers (box 6); IIS, Circular letters to Officers of Engineers, July 12, September 13, 1852; IIS to H. L. Kendrick, July 28, 1851; W. R. Palmer to IIS, July 1, 10, 1852; William Rosecrans to IIS, July 2, 1852; G. A. Gilmore to IIS, July 21, 1852; IISUW; H. S., *Life*, 1:258-59.

29. IIS, Notes on Fortifications (box 6); IIS, Article on National Defense (box 7); Review by Commander S. F. DuPont on the National Defense (box 6); Jeremy F. Gilmer to IIS, March 9, 1852; Joseph F. K. Mansfield to IIS, April 9, 1852; J. M. Scarritt to IIS, April 18, 1852; Zealous Tower to IIS, June 1, 1852; George Cullum to IIS, September 3, 1852; P. G. T. Beauregard to IIS, September 23, 1852; G. A. Gilmore to IIS, September 27, 1852; IISUW; Totten to IIS, February 18, 1852, Totten Letters.

30. Ord and Stevens discussed possible railroad routes to the Far West. Stevens advocated a humane but vigorous policy toward the Indians; he urged that they be supplied by the government until they could be educated into new ways of providing for their sustenance. IIS, Article on Artillery (box 7); IIS, Article in Regard to the Staff Bill to Secure the Services of Competent Officers in the Staff Departments of the Army (box 6); IIS, Notes on Military Service in Texas (box 7); IIS to H. L. Kendrick, July 28, 1851; IIS to William Hardee, September 8, 1851; L. Sitgreaves to IIS, July 16, 1852; E. O. C. Ord to IIS, July 23, 1852; IISUW; IIS to Isaac, Sr., February 13, 1851, Stevens Family Papers, WSL; IIS to Totten, March 1, 1851; IIS to Henry Hunt, May,

1851; IIS to Gustavus Smith, May, 1851; IIS to William Hardee, July 28, 1851; Letterbook, 1849–51, IISUW.

31. A number of officers wrote about their experiences in Mexico. Many, such as P. G. T. Beauregard, primarily to emphasize their own efforts in the war. This was not Stevens' objective; he scrupulously avoided mention of his accomplishments and took equal pains not to overplay the role of the Engineer Corps. T. Harry Williams, ed., *With Beauregard in Mexico* (Baton Rouge: Louisiana State University Press, 1956), p. 4; IIS to Isaac, Sr., October 24, 1847, HSUO; Joseph F. K. Mansfield to IIS, May 3, 1850; Frederick Bowen to IIS, August 24, 1850; IIS to Bache, May——, 1850; IIS to D. Appleton and Co., May——, 1851; IIS to Gustavus Smith, May, 1851; Letterbook, 1849–51, IISUW; IIS to Bache, June 14, 1851, Bache Corres.; IIS, *Campaigns of the Rio Grande and Mexico,* pp. 12–13.

32. IIS to Henry Hunt, May, 1851, Letterbook, 1849–51, IISUW.

Chapter 6
In the Footsteps of Lewis and Clark

1. Roy Nichols, *Franklin Pierce; Young Hickory of the Granite Hills,* 2d ed. (Philadelphia: University of Pennsylvania Press, 1958), pp. 205, 209; IIS et al., *Vindication of the Military Character and Services of General Franklin Pierce* (n.p., 1852); IIS to Isaac, Sr., October 24, 1847, HSUO. The *Boston Post* letters appeared in the newspaper on June 10, 11, 15, 18, and July 1, 1852. Nathaniel Hawthorne was another Massachusetts man who used his pen in Pierce's behalf; he wrote the official campaign biography and was rewarded with the counselor post at Liverpool.

2. Oliver to IIS, June 18, July 14, 1852; Charles G. Green to IIS, 1852; Henry L. Hunt to IIS, August 21, 1852; Isaac, Sr., to IIS, July 2, 1852; John L. Hayes to IIS, April 10, 1850; J. G. Foster to IIS, August 24, 1852; Z. B. Tower to IIS, August 25, 1852; Daniel Sanders to IIS, October 21, 1852; J. Addison Thomas to IIS, September 11, 1852; IISUW; IIS to Franklin Pierce, September 25, 1852, Pierce Papers; H. S., *Life;* 1:256.

3. Oliver to IIS, October 30, 1852; George Cullum to IIS, November, 1862; William Rosecrans to IIS, November 5, 1852; Clipping from *Newport Daily News,* October 18, 1852 (box 3); IISUW.

4. George Cullum to IIS, November, 1852; D. Leadbetter to IIS, December 16, 1852; J. G. Foster to IIS, September 1, 1852; IISUW.

5. IIS to Oliver, December 8, 1849, IISUW; IIS to Mrs. Benjamin Hazard, February or March, 1850, HSUO.

6. Stephen A. Douglas to Pierce, March 7, 1853; Hannibal Hamlin to Pierce, March 7, 1853; E. K. Smart to Pierce, March 7, 1853; T. J. D. Fuller, Moses McDonald, and John Applegate to Pierce, March 5, 1853; Robert J. Walker to Pierce, March 5, 1853; Jeremiah Clemens to Pierce, March 5, 1853; James Shields to Pierce, March 8, 1853; Solon Borland to Pierce, March 7, 1853; NA, RG 69, "Department of State, Appointment Files, Pierce and Buchanan Administrations."

7. IIS to Jefferson Davis, March 21, 1853; IIS to William L. Marcy, March 22, 1853; IIS to Robert McClelland, March 22, 1853, LRPRRS; William H. Goetzmann, *Army Exploration in the American West, 1803–1863* (New Haven: Yale University Press, 1959), pp. 276–77.

8. IIS to Jefferson Davis, March 25, 1853, LRPRRS. Appointment to the survey came unofficially on or about March 25, Stevens' birthday, and officially the appointment dated from April 8.

9. IIS to Davis, March 25, 31, 1853, LRPRRS; Totten to IIS, March 30, 31, 1853; Totten to Davis, April 3, 1853, Totten Letters; IIS to Totten, March 21, September 19, 1853, EDLR.

10. *DAB,* 10:569; E. Douglas Branch, "Frederick West Lander, Road-Builder," *Mississippi Valley Historical Review* 26 (September 1929): 172–73; IIS to Davis, March 25, 31, April 1, 1853, General Orders (written by IIS, but signed by Jefferson Davis), April 8, 1853, LRPRRS.

11. Special Orders No. 7, Headquarters of the Army, April 14, 1853; IIS to John Evans, April 11, 1853; IIS to J. G. Cooper, April 12, 1853; IIS to George Suckley, April 12, 1853; IIS to Suckley and Cooper, April 15, 1853; IIS to Isaac Osgood, April 25, 1853; LRPRRS; Robert Taft, *Artists and Illustrators of the Old West, 1850–1900* (New York: Charles Scribner's Sons, 1953), pp. 8–14; David I. Bushnell, "John Mix Stanley, Artist-Explorer," *Annual Report, 1924* (Washington, D.C.: The Smithsonian Institution, 1925), pp. 508–10. In 1853, 152 of Stanley's paintings were in the Smithsonian, and by 1865 (when a fire destroyed the collection) it had grown to more than 200. *Annual Report, 1853* (Washington, D.C.: The Smithsonian Institution, 1854), pp. 241–42; Richard Evans, "Dr. John Evans, U.S. Geologist, 1851–61," *Washington Historical Quarterly* 26 (April 1935): 84–85.

12. Simpson did send four guides to Fort Gerry. IIS to A. J. Donelson, April 7, 1853; IIS to Rufus Saxton, April 29, 1853; IIS to Beekman DuBarry, April 26, 1853; LRPRRS.

13. IIS to Rufus Saxton, April 26, 1853; IIS to Quartermaster General Thomas Jessup, April 12 1853; Jessup to Major David H. Vinton, April 12, 1853; LRPRRS.

14. IIS to Davis, April 1, 1853; Rufus Saxton to T. S. Everett, April 14, 1853; LRPRRS. This letter is signed by Saxton, Everett's immediate superior, but the original is written in Stevens' hand.

15. IIS to Abiel Tinkham, May 8, 1853; IIS to Saxton, May 13, 1853; LRPRRS. Stevens called the Souris River by its English translation, the Mouse River.

16. *New York Tribune,* June 3, 1853; RES, 12:36.

17. IIS to Davis, June 3, 1853, RES, 1:33, 12:36, 38; H. S., *Life,* 1:305; Suckley Journal, May 25, June 3, 4, 1853; George Suckley to Mary Suckley, June 6, 1853; George Suckley Letters, Bieneke Library.

18. RES, 12:37–39; Lander to IIS, May 22, 1853; IIS to Lander, May 31, 1853; IIS to Tinkham, May 31, 1853; RES, 1:14–18; IIS to Meg, June 10, 1853, IISUW.

19. RES, 12:40–42, 47, 55; IIS to Davis, June 10, 1853; RES, 1:18; IIS to Meg, June 10, 1853, IISUW. One report said the twenty-five men were either dismissed or decided to leave the survey party. *New York Tribune,* August 5,

1853; Suckley Journal, June 5, 29, 1853, George Suckley Papers, The Smithsonian Institution Library, Washington, D.C..

20. RES, 12:42–43, 51–52; George Suckley to John Suckley, June 20, 1853, Suckley Letters; Suckley Journal, June 12, 21, July 11, 1853.

21. RES, 12:50–53, 58–59; Order No. 8, June 19, 1853, Miscellaneous papers, Suckley Papers.

22. RES, 12:52–55, 58, 62–64; IIS to Davis, July 4, 1853, RES, 1:19–20; unidentified newspaper clipping, September 6, 1853, IISUW.

23. RES, 12:73–76.

24. *New York Tribune,* September 13, 1853; RES, 12:83–85; IIS to Davis, July 4, August 8, 1853; Cuvier Grover to IIS, August 7, 1853 [Report on the "Dead Colt Hillock" Line]; A. J. Donelson to IIS, March 8, 1854 [Navigability of the Missouri]; RES, 1:19–21, 222–23, 231–47.

25. RES, 12:86; Suckley Journal, August 7, 1853.

26. Stevens was impressed by the strength of the Blackfoot Indians and sensed that they would be worthy adversaries if not placated. He made an exception of the Gros Ventres, who he believed were "a simple-minded race, easily influenced, and very kindly disposed towards the whites." RES, 12:85, 88–89, 93. A detailed account of the incident on the Little Muddy River was not found.

27. Suckley to IIS, August 26, 1853, Suckley Letters; RES, 12:89–92; Order No. 11, August 19, 1853; Donelson to Davis, November 27, 1854, RES, 1:41–42, 635.

28. George Stevens to his sister, Sue, September 10, 1853, IISUW; RES, 12:100.

29. IIS to Davis, September 8, December 1, 1853, RES, 1:23–24, 72; U.S., Congress, Senate Doc. 29, 33rd Cong., 1st sess. [695], *Report of the Secretary of War on the Pacific Railroad Surveys,* p. 3.

30. John Mullan graduated from West Point in 1852. *DAB,* 12:319; RES, 12:105–106.

31. John Mullan to IIS, January 20, 1854 [Report of an Exploration from Fort Benton to the Flathead Camp. . . .], RES, 1:301–319; 12:123–25.

32. RES, 12:107, 111–15; Order No. 18, September 15, 1853, RES, 1:33.

33. Among other things, Stevens ordered Doty to investigate the feasibility of turning the Blackfeet to agriculture. Alice E. Smith, *James Duane Doty* (Madison: University of Wisconsin Press, 1954), pp. 329, 348–49; Doty to IIS, December 15, 1854 [Report of a Survey from Fort Benton. . . along the Eastern Base of the Rocky Mountains. . . .]; Doty to IIS, December 28, 29, 1853; Doty, [Meterological Observations Made at Fort Benton]; RES, 1:441–46, 543–53, 572–84; IIS to Doty, five letters, all dated October 3, 1853, IISUW; RES, 12:113.

34. RES, 12:119–22.

35. Ibid.; Marshall Sprague, *The Great Gates: The Story of the Rocky Mountain Passes* (Boston: Little, Brown and Co., 1964), p. 154.

36. RES, 12:122–23, 127–28, 164–65; Mullan to IIS, November 19, 1853 [Report of the Exploration from Cantonment Stevens to Fort Hall and Back. . . .],

Mullan to IIS, January 21, 1854 [Report of a Reconnaissance from the Bitter Root Valley to Fort Hall. . . .], RES, 1:319-49.

37. George Suckley to Rutsen Suckley, December 9, 1853, Suckley Letters; Suckley Journal, October 7, November 10, 1853; RES, 12:151.

38. Benjamin Alvord to McClellan, June 21, 1853, McClellan Papers, LC.

39. RES, 12:137; IIS to McClellan, December 8, 1852; IIS to P. G. T. Beauregard, March 18, 1853; Beauregard to McClellan, March 3, 1853; McClellan to his brother, Arthur, April 14, 1853; McClellan to his mother, July 12, 1853; McClellan Journal, June 27, July 18, 1853.

40. McClellan Journal, August 9, 1853; McClellan to his brother, John, September 18, 1853; McClellan Papers.

41. McClellan privately expressed doubt that the whites could keep their promises, and he was particularly apprehensive that whites who violated Indian rights would not receive punishment. McClellan Journal, August 9, 11-16, 18, 23, 1853.

42. Stevens never criticized McClellan for not examining the western side of Snoqualmie or any other pass. McClellan Journal, August 20-26, 31, September 7-15, 1853; McClellan to his mother, September 11, 1853; McClellan Papers.

43. McClellan Journal, September 21, October 10, 1853; McClellan to his brother, John, September 18, 1853; McClellan to his mother, November 24, 1853; McClellan Papers.

44. F. W. Howay et al., "Angus McDonald: A Few Items of the West," *Washington Historical Quarterly* 8 (July 1917): 197; RES, 12:147-149.

45. McClellan Journal, October 22-29, 1853, McClellan Papers; RES, 12:147-49.

46. McClellan Journal, November 7-8, 1853; IIS to McClellan, November 5, 8, 1853; Frederick Lander to McClellan, November 8, 1853; McClellan to Lander, November 8, 1853; McClellan Papers; RES, 12:154-55.

47. McClellan Journal, November 9, 15, 1853.

48. Philip H. Overmeyer, "George B. McClellan and the Pacific Northwest," *Pacific Northwest Quarterly* 32 (January 1941): 36, 43, 49, 57, 59-60. Overmeyer is critical of McClellan's leadership during the entire survey. It is possible that Overmeyer was looking forward to McClellan's Civil War failures in his interpretation of the McClellan of 1853. McClellan to his mother, November 24, 1853; McClellan to his brother John, November 28, 1853; McClellan Papers; McClellan to J. G. Cooper, December 19, 1853, J. G. Cooper Papers, Sutro Library, San Francisco; RES, 12:163. In 1855 McClellan went to Europe as a military observer and discovered he disliked Europe as much as West Point, Mexico, Texas, and the Pacific Northwest.

49. RES, 12:163-67; Abiel W. Tinkham to IIS, June 19, 1854 [Railroad Report of the Practicability of the Snoqualmie Pass and the Obstructions to be Apprehended from Snow]; Tinkham to IIS, July 19, 1854 [Report as to the Railroad Practicability of the Line of the Marias Pass, of the Northern Little Blackfoot Trail, and of the Southern Nez Perces Trail]; RES, 1:184-86, 276-81.

50. RES, 12:173-76.

51. Goetzmann, *Army Exploration in the American West,* p. 278; idem, *Exploration and Empire* (New York: Alfred A. Knopf, 1966), pp. 281, 285–86; IIS to Henry Halleck, January 2, 1854, IISUW.

52. RES, 1:87–88, 96–101, 111–12, 117–19, 143–45.

53. Ibid., 1:128–40.

54. Stevens estimated that it was 14,400 miles from Liverpool to Shanghai via the Cape of Good Hope and 10,800 miles via North America. Ibid., 1:114–15; Henry Nash Smith, *Virgin Land* (Cambridge, Mass.: Harvard University Press, 1950), Chaps. 1, 2.

55. RES, 1:10–12; E. G. Beckwith, "Report of Exploration for the Pacific Railroad by Capt. J. W. Gunnison," Ibid., 2:81.

56. Ibid., 1:10-12. Davis assigned Andrew A. Humphreys, Stevens' predecessor on the Coast Survey, and Gouvernor K. Warren to make a supplementary report on the various railroad surveys. They are more favorable to the northern route than Davis, noting the generally favorable grades and the good connections with river transportation on the Missouri and Columbia rivers. Warren and Humphreys did take issue with Stevens on the total amount of arable soil along the route and the snow depth in the Cascades. Working from figures that gave the annual precipitation at Fort Steilacoom, they estimated snowfall on Snoqualmie Pass at twenty feet. A. A. Humphreys and G. K. Warren, "An Examination . . . of the Reports of Explorations for Railroad Routes. . .," RES, 1:39-51.

57. Goetzmann, *Army Exploration in the American West,* p. 306.

58. Ibid., p. 334; RES, 12:196; Taft, *Artists and Illustrators of the Old West,* pp. 15–21.

59. Taft, *Artists and Illustrators of the Old West,* pp. 275–76.

60. S. F. Baird, "Memoranda in Reference to the Natural History Operations," RES, 1:9-11; Suckley Journal, May 25, 27, 1853.

61. George Gibbs to McClellan, May 1, 1854; John Evans to A. A. Humphreys, January 13, February 9, 14, 1855; Northern Survey Corres. Evans did not believe the intermountain region could sustain a dense population, but he did think it could support grazing and a limited farm population. This view was not as far from Stevens' position as Evans seemed to believe.

62. Volumes 8, 9, and 10 of RES contain the Smithsonian Institution's report on birds, fish, and reptiles for all of the survey parties. See also Ibid., Vol. 12, Book 2.

63. Ibid., Vol. 12, Book 2; Chaps. 1, 2, and 3.

64. Ibid.

65. George Gibbs did most of the work on Indian tribes although John Mullan and James Doty contributed shorter sketches of the Flathead and Blackfoot Indians. Gibbs was an apt student of Indian culture. After the survey he continued to compile dictionaries of Indian languages. The survey report included a census of the tribes between the Sound and the Nez Perce country and Gibbs's account of customs, previous contacts with whites, and suggested future policy. George Gibbs to McClellan, March 4, 1854, [Report on the Indian Tribes of the Territory of Washington]; Mullan to IIS, November 18, 1853, [Report on the Indian Tribes in the Eastern Portion of Washington Ter-

ritory]; Doty to IIS, December ——1853, [Report on the Indian Tribes of the Blackfoot Nation]; RES, 1:402–446.

66. The impact of Lewis and Clark's journey on the American image of the Northwest is described in John Logan Allen, *Passage Through the Garden* (Urbana: University of Illinois Press, 1975); RES, 12:242.

67. RES, 12:171, 239–42; IIS to Humphreys, December 6, 1856, Northern Survey Corres.

68. RES, 12:197–98; D. W. Meinig, "Isaac Stevens: Practical Geographer of the Early Northwest," *The Geographical Review* 45 (October 1955): 542–52.

<hr />

Chapter 7
The Governor

1. U.S., Congress, House, *Congressional Globe,* February 8, 1853; *Columbian,* October 23, 1852. See also the issues of September 18, 25, October 2, 16, November 6, December 11, 1852.

2. William Strong, "History of Oregon," p. 4, Bancroft Library; Delancey Floyd-Jones to his sister Sarah, March 31, 1853, Floyd-Jones Papers, Bancroft Library.

3. Strong, "History of Oregon," p. 38.

4. U.S., Congress, House, *Congressional Globe,* February 8, 1853.

5. James E. Hendrickson, *Joe Lane of Oregon* (New Haven: Yale University Press, 1967), p. 59.

6. Jefferson Davis to Franklin Pierce, December 9, 1852; Lane to Pierce, March 11, 1853; Stephen Adams to Pierce, March 11, 1853; J. Patton Anderson to William L. Marcy, March 15, 1853; Anderson to Davis, March 27, April 6, 1853; Appointments.

7. Democratic State Central Committee [Indiana] to Pierce, January 12, 1853; Lane to Pierce, March 6, 1853; Jesse Bright to Marcy, March 15, 1853; Edward Lander to Marcy, March 28, 1853; Caleb Cushing to E. Louis Lowe, August 18, 1854; John K. Miller to Marcy, April 30, 1853; Miller to Pierce, March ——, 1853; John Rives to Pierce, May 27, 1853; E. D. Potter to Marcy, May 31, 1853; Obediah B. McFadden to Cushing, August 15, 1853, May 16, 1854; Appointments; Hubert Howe Bancroft, *History of Washington, Idaho, and Montana* (San Francisco: The History Co., 1890), p. 80; *Pioneer and Democrat,* June 11, 1853; Hendrickson, *Joe Lane,* pp. 63, 74, 81–82, 84–85.

8. Governor Phillip Allen to Pierce, May 31, 1853; IIS to James Mason, May 20, 1853; Charles Mason to John Lee, June 13, 1853; Rhode Island Congressional Delegation to Pierce, June 4, 1853; NA, RG 69, "Department of State, Appointment Files, Pierce and Buchanan Administrations."

9. *Pioneer and Democrat,* April 30, May 7, December 3, 1853.

10. Ibid., April 30, May 28, 1853.

11. The Organic Act for Washington differed from its immediate predecessors primarily by deleting the governor's absolute veto over acts of the territorial legislature, and by allowing missionaries 640 acres at each of their mission

sites. The latter provision was also part of the Oregon Organic Act. Francis N. Thorpe, ed., *The Federal and State Constitutions, Colonial Charters, and other Organic Laws . . .,* 7 vols. (Washington, D.C.: Government Printing Office, 1909), 7:3963–68; *Pioneer and Democrat,* April 30, May 28, 1853.

12. IIS to Citizens of Washington Territory, 1853, McClellan Papers, LC; IIS to McClellan, April 26, 1853, LRPRRS; IIS to J. Patton Anderson, April 18, 1853; IISUW.

13. IIS to McClellan, April 26, 1853; IIS to Davis, May 8, 1853; LRPRRS; Davis to IIS, April 14, 1853; Davis to McClellan, May 9, 1853; NA, RG 107, "Records of the Office of the Secretary of War (M 6), 'Letters Sent Relating to Military Affairs, 1800–89.' "

14. *Pioneer and Democrat,* July 16, 23, 1853.

15. Edward Allen later complained that the going rate for labor was $3.00 a day and that McClellan agreed to this figure. McClellan Journal, September 12, 1853; Articles of Agreement Between A. W. Moore and George McClellan, September 13, 1853; Edward Allen to McClellan, December 22, 1853; McClellan to Davis, December 22, 1853; McClellan Papers; Blanche Mahlberg, "Edward J. Allen, Pioneer and Roadbuilder," *Pacific Northwest Quarterly* 44 (October 1953): 157–60.

16. *Pioneer and Democrat,* August 13, September 24, October 8, 1853; Davis to McClellan, May 26, 1854; Davis to Lt. Richard Arnold, May 19, 26, 1854; Sec. of War, LS; Theodore Winthrop, *The Canoe and the Saddle* (Tacoma: Tichnor and Fields, 1913), pp. 82–83.

17. Message of IIS to Second Annual Session of the Washington Territorial Legislature, December 5, 1854; Charles M. Gates, ed., *Messages of the Governors of the Territory of Washington to the Legislative Assembly, 1854–1889,* University of Washington Publications in the Social Sciences, vol. 12 (Seattle: University of Washington Press, 1940), pp. 10–14; IIS to G. N. McConaha, March 9, 1854, Miller Papers. In 1858 Congress rejected a request for $10,000 to complete the Fort Steilacoom to Walla Walla road. Interior Dept., Terr. Papers.

18. U.S., Congress, Senate Doc. 357, 61st Cong., 2d sess., "Treaty Establishing Boundary West of the Rocky Mountains," *Treaties, Conventions, International Acts, Protocols, and Agreements . . . ,* 2 vols., 1:656–58; James O. McCabe, *The San Juan Water Boundary Question,* Canadian Studies in History and Government, no. 5 (Toronto: University of Toronto Press, 1964), pp. 3–7; Marcy to IIS, June 3, 1853, Miller Papers.

19. William F. Tolmie to IIS, December 27, 1853; IIS to Tolmie, January 9, 1854; IISUW; Peter Skene Ogden and Dugald MacTavish to IIS, January 16, 1854; G. Sammosy to IIS, March 22, 1854, Miller Papers.

20. "Treaty Establishing Boundary West of the Rocky Mountains," *Treaties, Conventions. . . ,* 1:657–58.

21. IIS to Marcy, June 21, 1854, U.S., Congress, Senate Ex. Doc. 37, 33rd Cong., 2d sess. [752].

22. Ibid.

23. Ibid.; *Pioneer and Democrat,* December 24, 1853.

24. The License of Exclusive Trade actually expired in 1859. At that time the United States government, claiming that Company rights had lapsed, took control of Fort Vancouver while encouraging settlers to encroach on other

Company lands. These actions led to a reopening of negotiations and resulted in the 1869 agreement that provided for a payment of $450,000 to the Hudson's Bay Company and $200,000 to the Puget Sound Agricultural Company. *Pioneer and Democrat,* January 28, July 8, 1854, January 20, 1855; IIS to Lane, July 15, 18, 1854, Elkanah Walker Papers, Huntington Library, San Marino, Calif.

25. Ebey's predecessor, Simpson P. Moses, established a precedent for active customs collectors when he organized a relief party to rescue the passengers and crew of the *Georgiana* (wrecked off the Queen Charlotte Islands) who had been taken prisoner by the Indians. The federal government censured Moses and refused to pay the expenses of the rescue party, although Congress later relented and picked up the tab. In 1853 Ebey wrote the Secretary of the Treasury indicating that he considered the San Juan Islands part of the United States and would act accordingly until otherwise advised. George Gibbs stated that Ebey acted on his own authority when he placed an official on the islands. One of Ebey's associates in the events of the spring of 1854 was Abe Benton Moses, the brother of Simpson Moses. George Gibbs to McClellan, May 1, 1854, McClellan Papers; Bancroft, *History of Washington,* pp. 56–58; I. N. Ebey to Secretary of the Treasury, James Guthrie, September 29, 1853, Records Relating to the NW Boundary; Evans Journal, May 12, 1853, Elwood Evans Papers, Bieneke Library.

26. McCabe, "San Juan Water Boundary Question," pp. 11–14; IIS to James Douglas, May 12, 1855; Douglas to W. J. Smith, September 28, 1855; Marcy to IIS, July 14, 1855, U.S., Congress, House Ex. Doc. 65, 36th Cong., 1st sess. [1051], *Affairs in the Department of Oregon* [Correspondence relating to the San Juan Islands]; Douglas to IIS, April 26, 1855, Records Relating to the NW Boundary.

27. *Pioneer and Democrat,* December 3, 10, 1853.

28. Clark was allotted five representatives for a voting population of 466, or one representative for every 93 voters; Thurston received one representative for every 95 voters, and Pierce (the other large county), one representative for every 92 voters. The smaller counties, having populations ranging from 61 to 111, each received one seat. B. F. Yantis organized the Union Party, a split off from the Democratic party. It did not survive the election, and both Yantis and Simmons were brought into the Democratic party with appointments as Indian agents. Bancroft, *History of Washington,* pp. 62, 71–73; *Pioneer and Democrat,* January 14, 21, 1854; Wilfred J. Airey, "A History of the Constitution and Government of Washington Territory" (Ph.D. diss., University of Washington, 1945), p. 34.

29. Message of IIS to the First Annual Session of the Legislative Assembly of Washington Territory, February 28, 1854, Gates, *Messages of the Governors,* pp. 3–9.

30. Ibid. Stevens was presumably thinking of a 640-acre claim, which had become standard in the Northwest, but he did not give a specific figure. The Homestead Act of 1862 was less liberal, alloting only 160 acres after five years residence. The Oregon Donation Act of 1850 allowed married women to hold land; Stevens' proposal thus went a step further by giving the right to single women also.

31. Ibid.

32. *Pioneer and Democrat,* February 18, 1854; IIS to Doty, March 27, 1854; IIS to Daniel Hazard, May 26, 1853; IISUW.

33. Hazel Mills, "Governor Isaac I. Stevens and the Washington Territorial Library," *Pacific Northwest Quarterly,* 53 (January 1962): 1–12.

34. Ibid. The library was located in rooms rented from Father Pascal Richard. The first librarian was B. F. Kendall, one of Stevens' aides on the survey. In 1854 each territorial library received an additional $500 from the federal government. Message of IIS to the First Legislative Assembly..., Gates, *Messages of the Governors,* p. 8; NA, RG 56, "Accounts of Legislative Expenses, 1854, Washington Territory, "Treasury Department, Miscellaneous Treasury Accounts;'" IIS to Robert McClelland, August 15, 1854, Interior Department, Terr. Papers.

35. Charles M. Gates, *The First Century at the University of Washington, 1861–1961* (Seattle: University of Washington Press, 1961), pp. 3–7; Merle Curti and Vernon Carstensen, *The University of Wisconsin,* 2 vols. (Madison: University of Wisconsin Press, 1949), 1:64.

36. When in San Francisco he visited with Henry Halleck, who had left the army to practice law in California. H. S., *Life,* 1:425–27; Isaac, Sr., to IIS, December 18, 1853, IISUW.

37. Hazard Stevens incorrectly stated that Davis made a request for a deficit appropriation only after Stevens had arrived in Washington D.C. and forced the Secretary of War to act. The dispute over the disallowance of certain claims made by Stevens as a consequence of the railroad survey continued even after his death. The Treasury Department disallowed per diem of one dollar for Army officers, certain mess bills, payment for bedding and other personal equipment abandoned by Tinkham's men in the Bitterroot Mountains, pay of $200 a month to Isaac Osgood, and the other items listed in the text. IIS to Bache, February 11, 1854; R. J. Atkinson to Honorable James Hale, March 22, 1864; IISUW; Davis to IIS, April 12, August 22, September 13, 1854, Sec. of War, LS; A. A. Humphreys to Secretary of War, Joseph Holt, January 31, 1861; IIS to Davis, November 15, 1854; Correspondence of Northern Survey.

38. The report of the various surveys which had been scheduled for early 1854 did not appear until 1855. Stevens, despite the scope of the northern survey, had completed the task while most of the other parties were still in the field. G. H. Warren to Major William Emory, July 16, 1854; IIS to Humphreys, September 26, 1854; Donelson to Davis, November 14, 1854; Correspondence of Northern Survey.

39. This was true not only in official reports but also in private letters. For example, he wrote to Professor Bache, "The geography of the Cascades has been admirably described by Capt. McClellan...." IIS to Bache, February 11, 1854, IISUW.

40. IIS to McClellan, May 10, June 2, September 27, 1854; Robert L. Harris to McClellan, December 6, 1854; Eugene Webster to McClellan, December 16, 1854; McClellan Papers; IIS to Humphreys, September 26, 1854, Correspondence of Northern Survey.

41. A. W. Tinkham to Humphreys, September 18, 1855; Donelson to Humphreys, November 27, 1854; Donelson to Davis, June 8, 1855; George Gibbs to John Lambert, April 20, 1855, Correspondence of Northern Survey.

42. H. S., *Life*, 1:431; Columbia Lancaster to McClellan, May 8, 1854; Davis to IIS, August 18, 1854; Sec. of War, LS; IIS to James Campbell, December 17, 1853; IIS to Thornton Jenkins, February 9, 1854; IISUW.

43. IIS to Commissioner of the General Land Office, John Wilson, December 28, 1853, John Wilson to Robert McClellan, Feb. 23, 1854; Interior Department, Terr. Papers; Philip Thomas to Pierce, May 8, 1854; John E. Howard to Pierce, May 11, 1854; NA, RG 48, "Records of the Office of the Secretary of the Interior, Appointment Papers, Washington Territory;" James Tilton to Secretary of the Interior, September 20, 1855, U.S., Congress, House Ex. Doc. 1, 34th Cong., 1 sess., [840], *Annual Report of the Secretary of the Interior*.

44. W. Turrentine Jackson, *Wagon Roads West* (Berkeley: University of California Press, 1952), p. 96.

Chapter 8
The Great White Father

1. H. S., *Life*, 1:433-36; Margaret Stevens, "Notes of a Journey of Governor Stevens and Family ... 1854," Stevens Family Papers, WSL.

2. Ibid.

3. Ibid.

4. Ibid.

5. Ibid.; Meg to her sister, Nancy, February 17, 1855; Meg to her mother, February 18, 1855; IISUW; H. S., *Life*, 1:442-45.

6. Ibid.; Meg to Mary, February 1, 1856, Stevens Family Papers, WSL.

7. A measure giving women the right to vote narrowly failed, and a proposal to exclude slaves and free Negroes from the territory did not receive support. Airey, "History of the Constitution and Government of Washington Territory" (Ph.D. diss., University of Washington, 1954), pp. 38, 42; *Journal of the House of Representatives of the Territory of Washington*, 1st sess. (Olympia, 1855), pp. 61-62, 148-170; *Journal of the Council of the Territory of Washington*, 1st sess. (Olympia, 1855), pp. 34, 38, 126-130; *Statutes of the Territory of Washington*, 1854, 1st sess. (Olympia, 1855), p. 53; George Gibbs to McClellan, May 1, 1854, McClellan Papers, LC.

8. Airey, "History of the Constitution and Government of Washington Territory," pp. 41-42; *Statutes of the Territory of Washington, 1854*, p. 64 and passim; Gibbs to McClellan, May 1, 1854, McClellan Papers; Edmund Meany, *History of the State of Washington* (New York: Macmillan Co., 1946), pp. 163-64.

9. Statement of John Clendenin and J. Patton Anderson, April 15, 1854; Mason to Secretary of the Treasury, James Guthrie, April 1, 1854; IIS to Guthrie, June 10, 1854; NA, RG 56, Treasury Department, "Letters from Executives of Territories;" Mason to Elisha Whittesley, January 9, August 10, December 22, 1854, January 5, 1855, NA, RG 217, First Comptrollers Office, "Letters Received, Territorial;" Account of Legislative Expenses, 1854, Statement of Mileage and Salary for Legislators, February 27, 1854, Abstract of Disbursements on Account of the Expenses of the Legislative Assembly of the Territory of Washington for the Year Ending June 30, 1854, NA, RG 217, Miscellaneous

Treasury Accounts (Charles Mason); Mason to Whittesley, Mar. 20, 1854, NA, RG 217, First Comptrollers Office, "Miscellaneous Letters Received;" Whittesley to Mason, August 11, 1855, NA, RG 217, First Comptrollers Office, "Letters Sent, Territorial."

10. Journal of the Council of the Territory of Washington, 2d sess. (Olympia, 1855), pp. 149–55.

11. William Hagan, *American Indians* (Chicago: University of Chicago Press, 1961), p. 55.

12. U.S., Congress; Senate Misc. Doc. 59, 36 Cong., 1 sess. [1038], p. 20; House Misc. Doc. 47, 35 Cong., 2d sess., *Protection Afforded by Volunteers to Overland Immigrants.*

13. Father Pascal Ricard to Reverend J. B. A. Brouillet, October 12, 1855, J. B. A. Brouillet Papers, YVRL; Hazard Stevens, "The Pioneer and Patriotism," *Washington Historical Quarterly* 8 (July 1917): 174–76; Major Gabriel Rains to Major Edward D. Townsend, January 29, 1854, DOP, LR.

14. George Simpson, *Narrative of a Journey Round the World,* 2 vols. (London: Lea and Blanchard, 1847), 1:179. An officer at Fort Steilacoom reported that the Indians near the fort were perfectly harmless and kept the post supplied with fish and game. Delancy Floyd-Jones to his sister, Sarah, March 3, 1853, Floyd-Jones Papers, Bancroft Library; Meg to her mother, February 18, 1855; Meg to her sister, Nancy, February 17, 1855; IISUW.

15. U.S., Congress, Senate Ex. Doc. 34, 33d Cong., 1st sess. [698], IIS to Commissioner of Indian Affairs, George Manypenny, December 26, 1853.

16. Arthur A. Denny, *Pioneer Days on Puget Sound* (Seattle: The A. Harrison Co., 1908), pp. 74–76; George Gibbs Journal, March 9–22, 1854, Records Relating to NW Boundary; IIS to Comm. of Indian Affairs, December 21, 1854, WSIA.

17. Commissioner Manypenny explained that Governor Stevens underestimated the cost of goods and transportation. IIS to Manypenny, December 26, 1853; Manypenny to Secretary of the Interior, Robert McClelland, February 6, 1854; U.S., Congress, Senate Ex. Doc 34, 33d Cong., 1st sess. [698].

18. Colonel B. F. Shaw, "Medicine Creek Treaty," *Proceedings of the Oregon Historical Society, 1903* (Salem, 1906), pp. 27-29.

19. H. S., *Life,* 1:454. It is not always completely accurate to refer to "tribes" or "chiefs" in western Washington because of the loose organizational patterns, but for convenience these terms are used.

20. Records of the Commission to Hold Treaties with the Indian Tribes in Washington Territory and the Blackfoot Country, December 7, 25, 1854, RPC; James Swan, *The Northwest Coast* (Fairfield, Wash.: Ye Galleon Press, 1966), pp. 338, 341.

21. During the Indian war some whites charged that Leschi's name was forged, and that he had refused to sign the treaty. There is no evidence to support this view; the record indicates that no chief at the council objected to the treaty. In any event, Stevens would not have resorted to forgery. No chief who signed one of Stevens' treaties ever said that he had not signed or that he had been forced to sign. Treaty with the Nisqually, Puyallup ... , Dec. 26, 1854, RPC.

22. IIS to Comm. of Indian Affairs, December 30, 1854, RPC; B. F. Shaw to the editor (*Portland Oregonian?*), January 14, 1904, Benjamin F. Shaw Papers, Oregon Historical Society, Portland.

23. George Gibbs proceeded to lay out the reservations at Nisqually Flats and Commencement Bay. At the latter location the timber was so thick that he could only run the lines a short way back from the beach, but he rationalized that it made no difference as the Indians would only use the shore area. During the survey some Indians told him they wanted an additional reservation established, but Gibbs said he "shut them up by telling them it was too late to talk about that." Acting Commissioner of Indian Affairs, Charles E. Mix to IIS, August 30, 1854, WSIA, R7, LR; RPC, December 26, 27, 1854; Gibbs to IIS, January 5, 1855.

24. George Gibbs Journal, Jan. 12, 1855; RPC, January 5–22, 1855.

25. Ibid., January 22, 23, 1855.

26. Ibid., January 25, 1855.

27. Ibid., January 25, 1855; Gibbs Journal, January 25, 1855.

28. RPC, January 26, 1855; *Pioneer and Democrat,* February 3, 1855.

29. RPC, January 30, 31, 1855.

30. *Pioneer and Democrat,* February 3, 17, 1855.

31. IIS to William Tappen, March 23, 1854, WSIA, R 1, LS; Tappen to IIS, December 15, 1854, January 18, February 6, 14, 1855; Tappen to Mason, June 19, 1854, WSIA, R 17, "Letters from Employees Assigned to Columbia River or Southern District...."

32. Swan, *Northwest Coast,* pp. 330–38; Gibbs Journal, February 22–26, 1855.

33. Swan, *Northwest Coast,* pp. 344–49; Gibbs Journal, February 27–March 3, 1855.

Chapter 9
Amid Fluttering Plumes

1. McClellan Journal, August 17–23, 1853.

2. At about the same time Lieutenant Saxton, traveling to his rendezvous with the eastern survey party in the Bitterroot Valley, met with the Cayuse Indians, who, like the Yakimas, left the meeting with a fear of future white settlements. Ibid.; McClellan to IIS, August 22, 1853, WSIA, R 23, Misc. LR.

3. IIS to A. J. Bolon, March 23, 1854, WSIA, R 1, LS.

4. IIS to Skloom, March 22, 1854; IIS to A. J. Bolon, March 23, 1854; IIS to Comm. of Indian Affairs, January 11, 1855; Father A. M. Blanchet to IIS, December 21, 1854; WSIA, R 1, LS.

5. Doty Journal, RPC, March 31–April 4, 1855; IIS to Comm. of Indian Affairs, May 3, 1855, Washington Territory, Governor's Correspondence, 1853–55, Letterpress Book, WSL.

6. Doty Journal, March 31–April 4, 1855.

7. Ibid., April 17, 18, 1855; Doty to IIS, March 4, 26, April 3, 21, 1855, WSIA, R 23, Misc. LR.

8. IIS to Doty, May 20, 1855, WSIA, R 1, LS; Robert H. Ruby and John A. Brown, *The Cayuse Indians* (Norman: University of Oklahoma Press, 1972), Chap. 11 and pp. 189–93.

9. IIS to Doty, May 20, 1855; IIS to Comm. of Indian Affairs, May 1, 1855; WSIA, B 1, LS. Doty and the local settlers waiting at the treaty ground for the governor concluded "that neither the Cayuse or the Walla Walla will enter into a treaty and in case they are urged to do so, will create a disturbance and break up the council." Doty Journal, May 18, 1855.

10. Doty Journal, May 21, 22, 1855.

11. Kip Journal, May 24, 1855; Doty Journal, May 24, 1855; Richard Lansdale Diary, May 24, 1855, Bieneke Library. Kip estimated a total of 2,500 Nez Perce, but Lansdale said there were 500 warriors, and Doty listed 600 warriors with another 300 Indians in camp. Lansdale and Doty are probably closest to the actual figure.

12. Kip Journal, May 26, 1855; Lansdale Diary, May 26, 1855; Doty Journal, May 25, 26, 1855.

13. Craig had lived with the Nez Perce Indians for a number of years, and they had faith in him. This could not be said of the other translators, but the proceedings were apparently recorded as faithfully as human frailty allowed. Lansdale Diary, May 28, 29, 1855; RPC, May 28, 29, 1855.

14. RPC, May 30, 1855.

15. Ibid., May 31, 1855; Lansdale Diary, May 28–June 2, 1855.

16. RPC, June 1, 2, 1855.

17. Ibid., June 4, 1855; Lansdale Diary, June 4, 1855.

18. RPC, June 5, 1855; Lansdale Diary, June 5, 6, 1855; Kip Journal, June 5, 1855.

19. RPC, June 7, 8, 1855; Kip Journal, June 7, 1855; Doty Journal, June 4–8, 1855; Lansdale Diary, June 6, 7, 1855.

20. Lansdale Diary, June 9, 1855.

21. On the evening of June 8 Skloom said he still opposed the treaty, but the next day he accepted his brother's decision. Doty Journal, June 8, 9, 1855; RPC, June 9, 1855.

22. RPC, June 9, 1855; Doty Journal, June 9, 1855; Lansdale Diary, June 9, 1855.

23. Apparently Hazard Stevens was responsible for the story that the Cayuse Indians were the authors of a plot to murder the whites at the council. He suggested that Lawyer foiled their designs by moving his tent near that of the governor's and placing him under his protection. None of the men who kept journals mentioned the incident, nor does the governor. The whites did know the Cayuse Indians were hostile and expected that there might be treachery. It is possible that Hazard remembered this and that faulty recall led him to manufacture a specific incident. William C. McKay, like Hazard Stevens writing many years later, indicated that when Kamiakin signed the treaty, he bit his lips so hard that the blood ran. The recollections of Hazard Stevens, McKay, and others, written after the passage of time, are suspect when not

confirmed by eyewitness accounts of the council; time always colors memory, particularly when events become as controversial as the Walla Walla Council. H. S., *Life*, 2:47–48; William C. McKay Papers, Umatilla County Library, Pendleton, Ore.; William Brown, *The Indian Side of the Story* (Spokane: C. W. Hill Printing Co., 1961), pp. 98–100; Francis Haines, *The Nez Perces* (Norman: University of Oklahoma Press, 1955), p. 122; RPC, June 11, 1855; Doty Journal, June 11, 1855.

24. Charles J. Kappler, ed. and comp., *Indian Affairs, Laws, and Treaties*, 4 vols. (Washington, D.C.: Government Printing Office, 1904), 2:694–705.

25. Stevens was again concerned that officials in Washington D.C. would think he had been too generous. He explained to the Commissioner that large reservations were necessary because the tribes had many horses and cattle. IIS to Comm. of Indian Affairs, June 12, 1855, WSIA, R 1, LS; Doty Journal, June 11, 1855.

26. This wording appeared in the Nez Perce and Yakima treaties. The treaty for the Cayuse, Walla Walla, and Umatilla Indians was more specific as it included the phrase "any lands not actually enclosed by said Indians." Kappler, *Indian Laws and Treaties*, 2:694, 699, 703; IIS to A. J. Bolon, March 23, 1854, WSIA, R 1, LS; *Pioneer and Democrat*, April 21, 1855.

27. *Pioneer and Democrat*, June 29, August 3, 1855.

28. Doty Journal, June 12–17, 1855; Lansdale Diary, June 13–15, 1855; RES, 12:207–209.

29. Doty Journal, June 26, July 7, 1855; RES 1:148.

30. RPC, July 9, 1855.

31. Ibid., July 10, 11, 1855.

32. Ibid., July 11, 1855; Robert I. Burns, *The Jesuits and the Indian Wars of the Northwest* (New Haven: Yale University Press, 1966), pp. 91–92; IIS to Rev. Adrian Hoecken, July 11, 1855, WSIA, R 1, LS.

33. RPC, July 13, 1855.

34. Article XI of the treaty read:
It is moreover provided that the Bitter Root Valley, about the Loo-lo fork, shall be carefully surveyed and examined, and if it shall prove, in the judgment of the President to be better adapted to the wants of the Flathead tribe than the general reservation provided for in this treaty, then such portions of it as may be necessary shall be set apart as a separate reservation for the said tribe. No portion of the Bitter Root valley, above the Loo-lo fork, shall be opened to settlement until such examination is had and the decision of the President made known. Kappler, *Indian Laws and Treaties*, 2:722–25; RPC, July 16, 1855.

35. IIS to Comm. of Indian Affairs, July 17, 1855, WSIA, R 1, LS.

36. H. S., *Life*, 2:95–98.

37. Lansdale Diary, August 18, 20, 1855; Lansdale Diary, August 21, 1855, Bieneke Library; *DAB*, 4:592–93.

38. RPC, August 15, 1855; William Tappen to IIS, September 6, 1855; IIS to Comm. of Indian Affairs, September 18, 1855; IIS and Cumming to Comm. of Indian Affairs, October 22, 1855; RPC.

39. Cumming to Comm. of Indian Affairs, September 19, 1855; IIS to Comm. of Indian Affairs, September 20, 27, 1855; Cumming to Doty, September 25, 1855; IIS to Doty, September 27, 1855; Cumming to IIS, September 27, 1855; Official Journal, October 16, 1855; RPC.

40. Official Journal, October 17, 1855; Cumming to Doty, October 21, 1855; IIS to Doty, October 22, 1855; RPC; Kappler, *Indian Laws and Treaties,* 2:736–39.

41. John C. Ewers, *The Blackfeet* (Norman: University of Oklahoma Press, 1955), pp. 226–36.

Chapter 10
Broken Faith or Broken Promises?

1. Hubert Howe Bancroft, *History of Washington, Idaho, and Montana* (San Francisco: The History Co., 1890), p. 109, footnote; Michael Simmons to IIS, March 26, 1855, WSIA, Letters from Agents Assigned to the Puget Sound District, R 9.

2. Typical of the miners was Edward Eldridge, who came over Naches Pass with two friends at about the time of the Matisse incident. When this party reached the Yakima Valley, they became confused by the many trails, headed northeast, and wandered into an Indian camp, where they were closely questioned. Eldridge and his friends claimed that they were Hudson's Bay Company employees, a story the Indians doubted. Nevertheless the gold seekers were released and put on the right trail to Colville. Eldridge found little gold at the diggings and started back to the Sound in mid-September with a party of sixteen others, none of whom, Eldridge claimed, were armed. They struck out for Fort Walla Walla, which was deserted; but, turning toward The Dalles, Eldridge's party caught up with the post's fleeing inhabitants. When Eldridge arrived in Olympia he discovered that he had been reported dead. Throughout this venture Eldridge accepted the danger of Indian hostility as being no more a hazard of wilderness travel than the possibility of drowning in a river or freezing in a winter storm. He never considered the danger great enough to postpone his travels. Edward Eldridge, "Sketch of Washington Territory," Bancroft Library; Charles Mason to George Gibbs, September 14, 1855, Mason Letters, Bieneke Library; A. H. Robie to IIS, January 2, 1857, WSIA, Letters from Employees Assigned to the Columbia River, or Southern District, R 17; Gibbs to IIS, August 7, 1855, WSIA, Misc. LR, R 23; Bancroft, *History of Washington,* p. 109, footnote; A. J. Splawn, *Ka-Mi-Akin, Last Hero of the Yakimas* (Portland: Kilham Stationery and Printing Co., 1917), pp. 39–41. On September 14 the *Pioneer and Democrat* reported that affairs in the territory were at a standstill, that it was a period of stagnation, and that "dreams of quick riches must give way." *Pioneer and Democrat,* August 10, 21, September 14, 28, 1855.

3. Splawn, *Last Hero of the Yakimas,* pp. 41–43; Lucullus V. McWhorter, *Tragedy of the Whak-Shum* (Yakima: n.p., 1937), pp. 11–15. Splawn and McWhorter based their accounts on conversations with the Yakima Indians many years after the event. They agree that Bolon's mission did not antagonize the Yak-

imas, and they argue, despite the charges of the Catholic missionaries, that Bolon was on good terms with most of the Yakima chiefs.

4. The Yakimas believed that the killing of Bolon disgraced the tribe, and they expressed reluctance even many years later to talk about it. Splawn, *Last Hero of the Yakimas,* pp. 42–43; *Pioneer and Democrat,* October 12, 1855.

5. *DAB,* 20:513–14; Harwood P. Hinton, "The Public Career of John Ellis Wool" (Ph.D. diss., University of Wisconsin, 1960), see in particular chap. 3.

6. Wool to Jefferson Davis, January 7, 1854; Wool to Col. S. Cooper, AAG, January 19, 1854; Wool to Lt. Col. Lorenzo Thomas, AAG, February 28, 1854; Major Gabriel Rains to Major E. D. Townsend, AAG, January 29, 1854; U.S., Congress, House Ex. Doc. 88, 35th Cong., 1st sess. [956]; Correspondence Between the Late Secretary of War and General Wool; E. D. Townsend to Lt. Col. Benjamin Bonneville, September 13, October 2, 1854; Capt. A. J. Smith to E. D. Townsend, September 1, 1854; Benjamin Bonneville to F. S. Brent, September 21, 1854; Gabriel Rains to Benjamin Bonneville, December 8, 1854; Wool to Joe Lane, March 29, 1854; Records of Tours of Service in the Department of the Pacific, Wool Papers.

7. Wool to Lane, March 29, 1854; Wool to Davis, January 29, 1855; Bonneville to Townsend, January 7, 1855; Rains to Townsend, January 2, 1855; Wool Papers; Doty to IIS, March 4, 1855, WSIA, Misc. LR, R 23.

8. Moshell claimed that one reason for killing Bolon was to avenge Haller's attacks in Snake Country. McWhorter, *Tragedy of the Whak-Shum,* p. 15; Granville O. Haller, *The Dismissal of Granville O. Haller . . .* (Paterson, N.J.: Daily Guardian Office, 1863), pp. 36–39; Haller Journal, October 6, 7, 1855, UWL; William Brown, *The Indian Side of the Story* (Spokane: C. W. Hill Printing Co., 1961), p. 140; Fort Dalles, Order No. 78, September 30, 1855, Granville Haller, Copy of Remarks on Muster Roll for September and October 1855, DOP, LR; Splawn, *Last Hero of the Yakimas,* pp. 46–48.

9. Haller claimed that Rains initially planned to send only one company of fifty-one men to the Yakima country. Haller, *Dismissal,* p. 37; Wool to Commanding General, April 2, 1856, Indian Disturbances; H. Dean Guie, *Bugles in the Valley* (Yakima: n.p., 1956), p. 28; A. H. Sale, "Indian War Recollections," *Oregon Native Son* 1 (January, 1900): 493; A. B. Roberts, "The Yakima War of 1855," *Clark County History* 8 (1967): 237.

10. Splawn, *Last Hero of the Yakimas,* pp. 48–49; Commander of Post, Fort Vancouver to AAG, November 16, 1855, DOP, LR.

11. Wool to Thomas, October 19, 1855, Wool Papers; Wool to Commanding General, April 2, 1856, Indian Disturbances; *Puget Sound Courier,* September 7, 28, October 19, November 23, 1855; *Pioneer and Democrat,* October 19, 26, 1855.

12. Mason to Rains, September 22, 26, October 14, 1855; Rains to Mason, September 26, 29, Oct. 9, 1855; James Douglas to James Tilton, November 6, 19, 1855; Indian War Docs.

13. Mason to George Curry, October 20, 1855; Curry to Mason, October 22, 1855; Mason Letters; Rains to Townsend, October 22, 1855 DOP, LR; Wool to Thomas, May 15, 1856, U.S., Congress, House Ex. Doc. 118, 34th Cong., 1st sess. [859], "Correspondence on Indian Hostilities in Oregon and Washington."

14. Haller, *Dismissal,* p. 41; Rains to Townsend, October 22, 1855, DOP, LR; William F. Tolmie to Mason, October 23, 1855, Mason Letters; *Pioneer and Democrat,* November 9, 1855.

15. Martin F. Schmitt, ed., *General George Crook, His Autobiography* (Norman: University of Oklahoma Press, 1960), pp. 26–27. George Hunter recalled that during the march to The Dalles, he and several friends turned their coats inside out to look like red Indian blankets and appeared on a distant hill in full view of the column. A company of volunteers set out in hot pursuit and, after a long chase, the pranksters wheeled and revealed their identity. A court martial was called but the only sentence was a lecture on the danger of wearing out horses needlessly. George Hunter, *Reminiscences of an Old Timer* (San Francisco: Crocker, 1887), pp. 109–15; Cyrus Walker, "Reminiscences of the Yakima War," *Oregon Native Son* 1 (January 1900): 448; Kelly Mercer, "Diary of Company A, November 22, 1855, Bieneke Library.

16. Rains experimented with land mines during the Seminole War and developed them further during the Civil War. They were deemed too barbaric for use against troops, so Rains was transferred to river defenses where he managed on one occasion to cause $4,000,000 in damage to federal ammunition barges and warehouses at City Point, Virginia. Rains's subordinate officers in the Yakima campaign included Lt. Philip H. Sheridan; Capt. Edward O. C. Ord, who was a classmate of Stevens at West Point, and who became a prominent Civil War general; and Capt. David A. Russell, who served as a Union general until killed in battle in 1864. Guie, *Bugles in the Valley,* p. 38.

17. Commander of Post, Fort Vancouver to AAG, November 16, 1855; Capt. E. O. C. Ord, Charges and Specifications Preferred Against Major G. J. Rains, Fourth Infantry, December 9, 1855, DOP, LR; Guie, *Bugles in the Valley,* p. 33.

18. Haller, *Dismissal,* pp. 41–42; Ord, Charges against Rains, December 9, 1855, DOP, LR; Haller Journal, "Scout Into the Yakima Country Under Major Rains, Fourth Infantry," November 8, 9, 1855; P. H. Sheridan, *Personal Memoirs,* 2 vols. (New York: Webster, 1888), 1:54, 58–59.

19. Splawn, *Last Hero of the Yakimas,* pp. 50–51; Brown, *Indian Side of the Story,* pp. 140–41; Robert Ballou, *Early Klickitat Valley Days* (Goldendale, Wash.: Goldendale Sentinel, 1938), p. 334; Thomas Prosch, "The Indian War in Washington Territory," (Northwest Collection, University of Washington Library, Seattle Wash.), p. 8; Ezra Meeker, *Seventy Years of Progress in Washington* (Seattle: n.p., 1921), p. 358; Ord, Charges against Rains, December 9, 1855, DOP, LR. Rains claimed that two Indians were killed by the howitzers. Rains to Mason, November 12, 1855, Indian War Docs. Haller noted that Rains had ordered that only vegetables could be taken, but the mission was "being cleaned out." One Catholic soldier saved some relics, which he turned over to Haller for safe keeping. Haller Journal, November 10, 11, 13, 1855; Sheridan, *Personal Memoirs,* I:61–62, 64, 66; Burns, *The Jesuits and the Indian Wars of the Northwest* (New Haven: Yale University Press, 1966), pp. 129–30; Pascal Ricard to Mr. Secretary & Governor, December 1, 1855, Mason Letters; Ricard to J. B. Brouillet, November 9, 1855; Louis S. D'Herbomez to Ricard, December 12, 1855, Father J. B. Brouillet Papers (typescript copies translated from French), YVRL.

20. Hinton, "Wool," pp. 325–35; Townsend to Wool, November 28, 1855, DOP, LR; Wool to Commanding General, April 2, 1856, Indian Disturbances.

21. Hinton, "Wool," p. 340; Mason to George Gibbs, Jan. 9, 1856, Mason Letters.

22. Mercer, "Diary of Company A," December 4–7, 1855; T. C. Elliott, "The Murder of Peu-Peu-Mox-Mox," *Oregon Historical Quarterly* 34 (June 1934): 123–30; Joseph F. Santee, "The Slaying of Peo-Peo-Mox-Mox," *Pacific Northwest Quarterly* 25 (April 1934): 128–32; Hunter, *Reminiscences of an Old Timer,* p. 142; *Pioneer and Democrat,* January 18, 1856; Angus McDonald to IIS, January 27, April 6, 1856, WSIA, Misc. LR, R 23; Thomas Cornelius to his wife, Florentine, November 1855, November 19, 1855, Thomas Cornelius Papers, Huntington Library, San Marino, Calif.

23. Mercer, "Diary of Company A," November 29, December 8–21, 1855, January 1, 13, 28, February 7, March 5, 1856; Cornelius to his wife, December 27, 1855, January 12, February 6, April 14, 1856, Cornelius Papers; J. Orin Oliphant, ed., "Journals of the Indian War of 1855–56," *Washington Historical Quarterly* 15 (January 1924): 11–31.

24. Doty Journal, RPC, October 28–December 1, 1855.

25. Ibid., October 28–December 1, December 3, 1855.

26. Ibid., December 4, 1855.

27. Ibid.

28. IIS to Commanding Officer of the Troops in the Field or at The Dalles, November 26, 1855, DOP, LR.

29. Stevens argued that Elijah's killers escaped because California society was in an unsettled state in the early 1850s. Doty Journal, December 4, 1855.

30. Ibid., December 5, 1855.

31. Ibid., December 6–17, 1855.

32. IIS to James W. Wiley, December 13, 1855, published in *Pioneer and Democrat,* January 11, 1856; Message of IIS to Third Annual Session of the Legislative Assembly of the Territory of Washington, January 21, 1856, Charles M. Gates, ed., *Messages of the Governors of the Territory of Washington to the Legislative Assembly 1854–1889,* University of Washington Publications in the Social Sciences (Seattle: University of Washington Press, 1940), 12:25.

33. Mercer, "Diary of Company A," December 20, 1855; Doty Journal, December 20, 1855.

34. Mason to Rains, September 22, 1855, Indian War Docs.; John Cain to B. F. Shaw, October 25, 1855, Bieneke Library; Townsend to Wool, November 28, 1855, DOP, LR.

35. Shaw later reported that "it was impossible" to protect the friendly Walla Walla and Cayuse Indians. Shaw to Wool, January 12, 1856, DOP, LR; Doty Journal, December 21, 1855–January 1, 1856; IIS to Major M. A. Chinn, December 25, 1855, WTVP, Gov. Corres., LS.

36. The messengers killed were both prominent citizens—Abe Benton Moses and Joseph Miles (a lawyer in Olympia). Mason to Isaac Sterret, October 18, 1855; Mason to Lt. John Withers, November 3, 1855; Mason to Chief of Ordnance, Benicia, November 23, 1855; WTVP, Gov. Corres., LS; James Tilton to James Douglas, November 1, 1855; Tilton to Gibbs, November 11, 1855; James Tilton Papers, Bieneke Library.

37. Maurice Maloney to Rains, October 29, 1855; Maloney to Mason, November 6, 1855; John Nugen to Mason, October 30, 1855; Indian War Docs.; Bancroft, *History of Washington*, pp. 118–19.

38. Maloney to Mason, November 6, 1855; Nugen to Tilton, November 4, 1855; E. D. Keyes to Mason, December 7, 1855; Indian War Docs.; E. D. Keyes, *Fifty Years' Observation of Men and Events* (New York: Charles Scribner's Sons, 1884), pp. 251–53; Bancroft, *History of Washington*, pp. 122–23.

39. Margaret White Chambers, "Reminiscences," Northwest Collection, UWL, Seattle, pp. 41, 47; Arthur Denny, *Pioneer Days on Puget Sound* (Seattle: The A. Harrison Co., 1908), pp. 83–84; Tilton to Gibbs, two letters of November 25, 1855, Tilton Papers.

40. *Pioneer and Democrat*, January 4, 18, 25, 1856; *Puget Sound Courier*, January 25, 1856.

41. IIS, Third Annual Message, January 21, 1856, Gates, *Messages of the Governors*, p. 25; IIS to Shaw, February 20, March 12, 1856, WTVP, Gov. Corres., LS.

42. IIS to Keyes, January 20, 1856, WTVP, Gov. Corres., LS; IIS, Third Annual Message, January 21, 1856, Gates, *Messages of the Governors*, p. 27.

43. One settler, whose family had known Leschi for many years, claimed that he harbored resentment toward whites after a white soldier stationed at Fort Steilacoom married his sister and then left her behind when he was transferred. When the girl returned home in disgrace, her father took to the woods for three days, remaining on all fours and howling like a wolf to indicate that he had been debased lower than a dog. Early in January 1856 the army tried to seize Leschi near the mouth of the Puyallup River, but the chief refused to come aboard the *Beaver*, a craft the military had borrowed from the Hudson's Bay Company. Sarah McAllister Hartman, manuscript, Bieneke Library; Maloney to Keyes, January 8, 1856; James Alden to Secretary of the Navy, J. C. Dobbin, January 7, 1856; DOP, LR; Keyes to Mason, January 6, 1856, Indian War Docs.

44. Gardner Allen, ed., *The Papers of Francis Gregory Dalles* (New York: Naval History Society, 1917), pp. 203–205; Charles M. Gates, ed., "Seattle's First Taste of Battle, 1856," *Pacific Northwest Quarterly* 47 (January 1956): 1–8; William Woods complained that when twelve marines made a charge to drive the Indians back, none of the local citizens would join them. William Woods to Gibbs, February. 4, 1856, George Gibbs Letters, Bieneke Library.

45. IIS, Third Annual Message, January 21, 1856, Gates, *Messages of the Governors*, p. 27–28.

46. IIS to Doty, March 8, 1856, WTVP, Gov. Corres., LS.

47. IIS to Shaw, February 20, 1856, IIS to P. Wells, February 29, 1856; WTVP, Gov. Corres., LS.

48. IIS to Isaac Ebey, March 7, 1856, WTVP, Gov. Corres., LS; William Packwood to Tilton, February 26, March 5, 1856; J. J. Van Bokkelen to Tilton, February 20, 1856; WTVP, Adj. Gen., Corres., LR).

49. Andrew J. Chambers, "Recollections," Northwest Collection, UWL, pp. 33–34; "Autobiography of John Rogers James," *Told By The Pioneers*, 3 vols. (n.p.: Washington Pioneer Project, 1937–38), 2:91–92; IIS to Calvin Swindal, March 29, 1856; IIS to Gilmore Hays, March 29, 1856; WTVP, Gov. Corres.,

LS; Joseph White to Tilton, May 2, 1856; Swindal to Tilton, May 2, 1856; U. B. Hicks to Tilton, May 3, 1856; WTVP, Adj. Gen., Corres., LR. The White-Swindal feud continued to simmer. After a month passed, White charged that Swindal had fired at a bird while on a scout in violation of standing orders. He demanded that Swindal pay the usual penalty of extra guard duty, but the captain refused and, in turn, accused White of disobeying orders. The bitterness remained until the volunteers were discharged.

50. IIS to Gilmore Hays, February 25, 1856, WTVP, Gov. Corres., LS.

51. Record of Scrip Issued, Governor's Letterbook, Washington State Archives, Olympia; IIS to George Curry, February 17, 1856; IIS to Shaw, February 17, 1856; WTVP, Gov. Corres., LS; R. S. Robinson to W. W. Miller, February 14, 1856; Franklin Matthias to Miller, February 29, 1856; M. B. Millard to Miller, August 4, 1856; WTVP, Quartermaster and Commissary Correspondence.

52. IIS to Hays, February 20, 1856; IIS to Miller, February 20, 1856; WTVP, Gov. Corres., LS; Keyes to Mason, January 4, 1856; Capt. William C. Pease to Tilton, April 2, 1856; Mason to Col. J. W. Ripley, December 12, 1855; Indian War Docs.

53. William Wells to IIS, March 5, 1856, WTVP, Gov. Corres., LR; IIS to Shaw, March 16, 1856, WTVP, Gov. Corres., LS; Bancroft, *History of Washington,* pp. 163–64.

54. Wool told Stevens that he was not aware that the governor was in danger on his return from the Blackfoot country, and he denied recalling troops sent to Stevens' aid. Wool condemned the activities of the Oregon volunteers in the Walla Walla Valley, particularly the killing of Peopeomoxmox. The general warned that brutal actions "may have caused feelings difficult to overcome." IIS to Wool, December 23, 1855, January 29, 1856; Wool to IIS, February 12, 1856; Miller Papers; Lt. Col. Theodore Nauman to D. R. Jones, April 25, 1856, DOP, LR; *Pioneer and Democrat,* February 22, 1856.

55. Stevens told Wool to waste no tears on Peopeomoxmox, who he claimed had plotted to kill his party on the return from the Blackfoot council. There is no evidence to support this charge. Wool refused to answer this letter and had it returned to the governor, which effectively ended further communication. IIS to Wool, March 15, 20, May 12, 1856, Miller Papers; IIS to Mason, February 23, 1856, WTVP, Gov. Corres., LS; IIS, Third Annual Message, January 21, 1856, Gates, *Messages of the Governors,* p. 26; *Pioneer and Democrat,* February 15, 1856.

56. Keyes, who became second in command on the Sound after Casey arrived, was an 1832 graduate of West Point who had taught at the Military Academy as well as serving as an aide to General Scott. Like Casey he became a Union general and fought in a number of battles starting with First Bull Run and including McClellan's peninsular campaign.

57. IIS to Casey, February 2, 17, 18, 21, 1856; Tilton to Casey, February 19, March 2, 1856; Casey to Tilton, February 19, 1856; Casey to IIS, March 7, 1856; Miller Papers; Keyes, *Fifty Years' Observation,* pp. 257–61.

58. Casey to IIS, March 12, 15, 1856; Casey to Tilton, March 12, 1856; Tilton to Casey, March 10, 1856; IIS to Casey, two letters of March 16, 1856; Miller Papers.

59. Mason to John Cain, October 12, 1855; IIS to Mason, June 14, 1855; WSIA, LS, R 1.

60. Commissioner of Indian Affairs to IIS, March 4, April 19, 1856, WSIA, Letters from the Comm., R 7; Sidney S. Ford, Sr., to IIS, March 20, October 10, 1856, WSIA, Letters from Employees Assigned to the Western, or Coast, District, R 16.

61. Travers Daniel to IIS, April 12, May 24, 1856; Ford, Sr., to IIS, August 20, 1856; WSIA, Letters from Employees Assigned to the Western, or Coast District, R 16; IIS to Ford, Sr., July 15, 1856; IIS to A. J. Cain, August 31, 1856, WSIA, LS, R 2.

62. Edmund Fitzhugh to IIS, February 3, 22, March 28, May 11, 1856; Enoch Fowler to IIS, March 7, July 22, 1856; WSIA, Letters, R 10.

63. Nathaniel Hill to IIS, March 31, April 7, May 1, June 16, September 30, 1856, WSIA, Letters, R 10; Nathaniel Hill, "Washington Territory Sketches," manuscript, Bancroft Library.

64. D. S. Maynard to IIS, February 9, 19, March 11, September 14, 1856; H. Haley to IIS, April 22, May 2, 15, July, 1856; George Paige to Maynard, January 20, 1857; Paige to IIS, May 13, 1857; WSIA, Letters, R 10.

65. H. Haley to IIS, April 22, May 2, 15, July, 1856, WSIA, Letters, R 10; IIS to Haley, April 14, 1856; IIS to Commissioner of Indian Affairs, November 1, 1856; WSIA, LS, R 2.

66. Paige to IIS, September 26, October 31, November 6, 1856; James Goudy to Paige, November 21, 1856; WSIA, Letters, R 10; Casey to IIS, July 21, October 20, 1856, Miller Papers.

67. IIS to Local Indian Agents, April 13, 1856; IIS, Address to the Indians Brought in by Mr. Yesler from Seattle, May 11, 1856; IIS to Richard Lansdale, June 1, 1856; WSIA, LS, R 2; Commissioner of Indian Affairs to IIS, December 4, 1855, April 19, 1856; WSIA, Letters from the Comm., R 7.

68. Nathaniel Hill to Michael Simmons, September 30, 1856, WSIA, Letters, PSD, R 10; IIS to Commissioner of Indian Affairs, May 5, 1856; IIS to Maynard, February 12, 1856; IIS to Edmund Fitzhugh, March 3, 1856, WSIA, LS, R 2.

69. Sidney Ford, Jr., to IIS, May 3, 1856, WSIA, Letters, R 10; IIS to Commissioner of Indian Affairs, May 5, 31, 1856, WSIA, LS, R 2.

Chapter 11
Martial Law

1. Message on Martial Law; Hugh Goldsborough to George Gibbs, January 4, 1856, George Gibbs Letters, Bieneke Library.

2. Martial Law, Vindication. In his "Vindication," Stevens argued: "It is simply a question as to whether the executive had the power, in carrying on the war, to take a summary course with a dangerous band of emissaries, who have been the confederates of the Indians throughout, and by their exertions and sympathy can render, to a great extent, the military operations abortive."

3. Robert S. Rankin, *When Civil Law Fails: Martial Law and Its Legal Basis in the United States* (Durham, N.C.: Duke University Press, 1939), pp. 35, 38–41.

4. The unfortunate Doty remained on the Sound, and Stevens eventually relented to the extent that he gave him a job as clerk in the Indian department. Doty continued to drink heavily and committed suicide in June 1857. IIS to William F. Tolmie, March, 1856, Miller Papers; Tilton to Tolmie, March 2, 1856, James Tilton Papers.

5. Message on Martial Law, Testimony of George Gallagher.

6. *Ibid.*; H. J. G. Maxon to Tilton, March 30, 31, April 11, 1856, WTVP, Adj. Gen., Corres., LR; IIS to Casey, March 31, 1856; Casey to IIS, March 31, 1856; Miller Papers.

7. Wallace had run for territorial delegate in 1854; when the Indian war started, he raised a company of volunteers and participated in the campaign in 1855 and early 1856. Tilton to Wallace, October 31, 1855, William Wallace Papers, UWL; Martial Law, Vindication, April 3, 1856.

8. Tilton to Casey, April 2, 1856; Casey to IIS, April 3, 1856; IIS to Casey, April 7, 1856, Miller Papers; IIS to Warren Gove, April 8, 1856, WTVP, Gov. Corres., LS.

9. IIS to Shaw, April 29, May 4, 1856; IIS to Edward Lander, May 5, 1856; WTVP, Gov. Corres., LS.

10. F. N. Chenoweth to Lander, April 30, 1856; IIS to Lander, May 4, 1856; Lander to IIS, May 4, 1856; Shaw to IIS, May 5, 1856; Miller Papers.

11. Martial Law, Vindication, Shaw to IIS, May 10, 1856.

12. IIS to Lander, May 5, 1856; Lander to IIS, May 5, 1856; IIS to Shaw, May 6, 1856; Miller Papers; Martial Law, Vindication, "Vindication" and "Proceedings of a Meeting of the Bar, Third Judicial District, Washington Territory . . . May 7, 1856."

13. Ibid.

14. Ibid.; IIS to Shaw, May 15, 1856, WTVP, Gov. Corres., LS.

15. B. F. Kendall to Gibbs, May 10, 1856; Gibbs to Elwood Evans, May 12, 1856; Miller Papers.

16. Capital letters are those of Gibbs and Goldsborough; in the final draft sent to Marcy the word "diminutive" is eliminated. Gibbs and Goldsborough to Marcy, May 11, 1856, Miller Papers.

17. IIS to Bluford Miller, May 15, 1856, WTVP, Gov. Corres., LS; Martial Law, Vindication; Lander to Marcy, May 22, 1856; Gibbs and Goldsborough to Marcy, May 19, 1856.

18. Ibid., Gibbs and Goldsborough to Marcy, May 19, 1856.

19. "Proceedings of the Commission Convened on the 20th of May, 1856 . . . ," WTVP, Gov. Corres.

20. Message on Martial Law, F. N. Chenoweth to Wallace, Gibbs, and Clark, May 15, 1856; IIS to Shaw, May 21, 22, 1856; Elwood Evans to William Bigler, May 19, 1856; Miller Papers; Martial Law, Vindication, Gibbs and Goldsborough to Marcy, May 19, 1856.

21. IIS to Shaw, two letters of May 18, 1856, May 21, 1856, WTVP, Gov. Corres., LS.

22. Message on Martial Law, F. N. Chenoweth to Marcy, June 8, 1856, and F. N. Chenoweth, "Opinion, May 24, 1856."

23. IIS to Pierce, May 23, 1856; IIS to F. N. Chenoweth, May 28, 1856; IIS to Victor Monroe, May 28, 1856; Chenoweth to IIS, May 29, 1856; Evans to Gibbs, May 26, 1856; Miller Papers; IIS to Shaw, May 24, 1856, WTVP, Gov. Corres., LS. Elwood Evans charged that this letter to Shaw was written by Stevens after May 24, probably on May 25, and was pre-dated to give the impression that the governor was ending martial law for his own reasons and not because of Chenoweth's decisions. IIS to Victor Monroe, May 25, 1856, ibid.; Message on Martial Law, Chenoweth to March, June 8, 1856.

24. A footnote to this episode involved the clash between Stevens and Company A, 2nd Regiment of the volunteers. Company A contained King County recruits and the ranking officer was Arthur Denny, a political opponent of the governor. Although most of the territorial volunteers supported the governor throughout the martial-law crisis, the members of Company A signed resolutions of opposition and later refused to obey orders to march to a new camp. Stevens sent Edmund Fitzhugh to persuade the company members to remove their names from the resolution and to threaten them with dishonorable discharge if they did not. All but a few refused and were dishonorably discharged with six months pay withheld. The territorial legislature investigated and voted, strictly on party lines, to require the governor to pay the forty-four men their full compensation. The same legislature condemned the governor for calling martial law. The governor ignored that body's actions, and a subsequent legislature overturned the condemnation. As territorial delegate, Stevens' requests for payment of the war debt included full payment for the members of Company A, probably to avoid giving an explanation of the reasons for the dishonorable discharges. Fourth Legislative Session of the Territory of Washington, Dec. 1, 1856, Council Journal (Olympia, 1857), pp. 51–57, 98, 111, 179; Fourth Legislative Session of the Territory of Washington, December 1, 1856, House Journal (Olympia, 1857), pp. 88–90, Appendix C, "Testimony on Final Muster Role of Company A, 2nd Regiment, W. T. Volunteers, pp. LXVII–LXXXIII; Message on Martial Law; IIS to Shaw, May 30, 1856, WTVP, Gov. Corres. LS; *Pioneer and Democrat,* July 11, 1856.

25. U.S., Congress, Senate, *Congressional Globe,* July 2, 1856.

26. *Ibid.*; Senate, July 2, 1856, January 31, 1857; House, January 31, 1857. Virtually all the verbal opposition to martial law came from members of the Democratic party.

27. *New York Times,* August 7, October 3, 1856; Gibbs and Goldsborough to Marcy, May 11, 1856; Marcy to IIS, September 12, 1856; Miller Papers. In August, Pierce and Joe Lane agreed that Lane would become governor if Stevens' removal became necessary, as appeared likely at that point. When news arrived that martial law had ended, Lane's nomination was dropped. Nichols, *Franklin Pierce: Young Hickory of the Granite Hills,* 2d ed. (Philadelphia: University of Pennsylvania Press, 1958), p. 573.

Chapter 12
Return to Walla Walla

1. At least two letters written in 1856 reflect the possible influence of too much whiskey—or, perhaps, fatigue. They are rambling and repetitive, very

unlike the usual crisp and logical, although at times lengthy, communications sent by Stevens. IIS to Pierce, August ——, 1856, Miller Papers; IIS to Shaw, February 18, 1856, WTVP, Gov. Corres., LS.

2. Meg to Mary, February 1, 1856, Stevens Family Papers, WSL; Meg to Mary, February 14, 1856; IIS to Meg, August 19, 25, 1856; HSUO.

3. IIS to Adj. Gen. Barnum, Oregon Volunteers, February 17, 1856; IIS to Curry, February 17, May 22, 1856; IIS to Columbia Lancaster, February 17, 1856; IIS to M. R. Hathaway, February 17, 1856; IIS to Shaw, February 17, 18, 20, 1856; IIS to C. P. Higgins, February 17, 1856; IIS to W. H. Pearson, February 17, 1856; WTVP, Gov. Corres., LS.

4. Wright spent the remainder of his career in the Northwest. From 1861 to 1864 he commanded the Department of the Pacific, moving on to take command of the District of California in 1865. On July 30, 1865, sailing north to take command of the Department of the Columbia, he drowned in a shipwreck off the Oregon coast. Keyes, *Fifty Years' Observation of Men and Events* (New York: Charles Scribner's Sons, 1884) p. 285; IIS to Curry, May 22, 1856, WTVP, Gov. Corres., LS; Wool to Casey, February 12, 1856, DOP, LS; Harwood P. Hinton, "The Public Career of John Ellis Wool" (Ph.D. diss., University of Wisconsin, 1960) pp. 347-49; Rodney Glissan, *Journal of Army Life* (San Francisco: A. L. Bancroft, 1874), p. 320.

5. L. W. Coe to Putnam Bradford, April 6, 1856, Coe Manuscript, Bieneke Library; William Lucas to William Wallace, April 6, 1856, William Wallace Papers, UWL; Lt. Col. Theodore Nauman to D. R. Jones, April 25, 1856; Wright to D. R. Jones, April 4, 5, March 7, 25, 1856; DOP, LR; Philip H. Sheridan, *Personal Memoirs,* 2 vols. (New York: Webster, 1888), 1:73-75.

6. Lt. P. H. Sheridan to Lt. Col. Thompson Morris, April 1, 1856; Lt. Henry Hodges to D. R. Jones, April 4, 1856; DOP, LR.

7. *Pioneer and Democrat,* April 4, 18, 1856; U.S., Congress, Senate Ex. Doc. 66, 34th Cong., 1st sess., *Report of the Secretary of War on Indian Disturbances in the Territories of Washington and Oregon*; Wool to Lorenzo Thomas, May 15, 1856; Wright to D. R. Jones, April 18, 1856; Wright to Curry, April 27, 1856; DOP, LR. It was John Pope, not Wool, who first bragged that his headquarters was in the saddle.

8. IIS to Wright, April 2, 24, 1856; Wright to IIS, April 10, 27, 1856; Miller Papers.

9. IIS to Wright, May 8, June 18, 1865; Wright to IIS, April 27, 1856; Wright to Shaw, May 27, 1856; Miller Papers.

10. Wright to D. R. Jones, May 1, 3, 6, 8, 9, 11, 15, 18, 30, June 11, July —— , 1856, DOP, LR; Wright to IIS, June 20, 1856, Miller Papers.

11. IIS to Sidney Ford, Sr., May 18, 1856; IIS to Shaw, June 5, 1856; WTVP, Gov. Corres., LS; Wright to D. R. Jones, July 7, 9, 1856, DOP, LR.

12. Wright, unlike Stevens, was extremely patient in his dealing with the Yakimas. His troops spent much of June and July in camp simply waiting. Granville Haller observed that Wright would not let the troops do anything to alarm the Indians, and he complained that the colonel appeared more concerned with the neatness of the soldiers' hair and beards than with the Indians across the river. Haller wrote of "time hanging heavy in camp," and he idled away the hours reading *Modern Flirtations* and *Caroline Tracy the Spring Street Milliner's Apprentice.* Granville O. Haller, "Journal of a Third Expedition

Into the Yakima Country Made in the Summer of 1856 Commencing in May," June 1–4, 9, 10, 30, 1856, Haller Journal; Wright to D. R. Jones, July 7, 9, 1856, DOP, LR.

13. Wright to W. W. Mackall, two letters of July 18, July 25, 27, August 3, 6, 1856, DOP, LR.

14. Wright to J. F. Noble, July 15, 1856; Wright to Thompson Morris, July 26, 1856; Wright to IIS, August 1, 1856; IIS to Wright, July 3, August 3, 1856; Miller Papers; A. L. Coffey and William Sharp to J. Patton Anderson, June 7, 1856, Bieneke Library.

15. Walter W. DeLacy, "Itinerary of March," June 12, 16, 21, 26, 30, July 4, 1856, Miller Papers; IIS to Shaw, July 10, 1856, WTVP, Gov. Corres., LS.

16. DeLacy, "Itinerary of March," July 8–11, 1856, Miller Papers; Maxon's Company to Shaw, July 12, 1856, WTVP, Southern Battalion Communications.

17. DeLacy, "Itinerary of March," July 13–22, 26, 1856; D. F. Byles, "Indian Wars of 1855–56," pp. 1–4, Northwest Collection, UWL; Wright to Mackall, October 31, 1856 (includes statement made by Howlish-Wampum), DOP, LR.

18. IIS to Shaw, August 2, 1856, WTVP, Gov. Corres., LS.

19. Lansdale Diary, Nov. 7, 1855, Mar. 31, 1856; Lansdale to IIS, October 2, 3, November 7, December 1, 1855; January 1, April 1, June 30, 1856; John Owen to Doty, April 25, 1857; WSIA, Letters from Employees Assigned to the Eastern District, or Flathead Agency, and the Blackfoot Agency, R 22; Council Held at the Mission of St. Ignatius, March 24, 1856, WSIA, Records in Relation to Treaties, R 26; Seymour Dunbar, ed., *The Journals and Letters of Major John Owen*, 2 vols. (New York: E. Eberstadt, 1927), 1:123, 138.

20. Father Anthony Ravalli to William Craig, January 24, March 22, 1856; Angus McDonald to IIS, May 13, 1856; WSIA, Letters from Employees Assigned to the Nez Perce and Umatilla Agencies, R 21; McDonald to IIS, January 27, April 6, May 15, 1856, WSIA, Misc. LR, R 23.

21. Craig to IIS, March 22, 1856; IIS to Craig, April 9, 1856; WSIA, Letters from Employees Assigned to the Nez Perce and Umatilla Agencies, R 21; IIS to Commissioner of Indian Affairs, May 25, 1856, WSIA, LS, R2.

22. Craig to IIS, June 30, 1856, WSIA, Letters from Employees Assigned to the Nez Perce and Umatilla Agencies, R 21; Spokane Garry and other chiefs to IIS, June 4, 1856, WSIA, Misc. LR, R 23.

23. IIS to A. J. Cain, July 30, 1856, WSIA, LS, R 2.

24. IIS to Lansdale, June 1, 1856; IIS to Michael Simmons, June 4, 1856; IIS to Commissioner of Indian Affairs, August 18, 1856; IIS to J. F. Noble, August 3, 1856; IIS to A. J. Cain, August 3, 16, 1856; WSIA, LS, R 2; Pinkney Lugenbeel to Wright, July 27, August 3, 1856, DOP, LR.

25. Wright to Mackall, August 17, 1856, DOP, LR; IIS to Craig, August 23, 1856; IIS to Commissioner of Indian Affairs, August 31, 1856, WSIA, LS, R 2; IIS to E. J. Steptoe, August 25, 1856, Miller Papers; Spokane Garry to IIS, September 12, 1856, WSIA, Misc. LR, R 23; DeLacy, "Itinerary of March," August 25, 1856, Miller Papers; John Allen to friend Murray, August 24, 1856, Misc. letter, Northwest Collection, UWL.

26. Steptoe to father, Dr. William Steptoe, October 9, 1855, August 22, 1856, Edward J. Steptoe Papers, UWL; IIS to A. H. Robie, August 31, 1856,

NOTES PAGES 296–310

WTVP, Gov. Corres., LS; IIS to Steptoe, August 31, September 1, 4, 1856; Steptoe to IIS, September 1, 4, 1856; Miller Papers.

27. Steptoe to IIS, September 1, 4, 10, 1856; IIS to Steptoe, September 10, 1856; Miller Papers.

28. H. S., *Life,* 2:213–15.

29. Ibid., 2:216–19.

30. William Brown, *The Indian Side of the Story* (Spokane: C. W. Hill Printing Co., 1961), pp. 169–76; M. P. Burns to IIS, September 18, 1856, WTVP, Gov. Corres., LR.

31. IIS to Jefferson Davis, October 22, 1856, Miller Papers; Wright to Mackall, November 15, 1856, DOP, LR; Steptoe to sister, Nannie, October 27, 1856, Steptoe Papers.

32. IIS to Jefferson Davis, October 22, 1856; Steptoe to IIS, September 19, 1856; Miller Papers; Wright to Mackall, November 15, 1856, DOP, LR.

33. The fighting in 1858 began when Steptoe was sent north of the Snake River with troops and was attacked, just as Garry had predicted in 1855. Steptoe's defeat near Rosalia led to retaliation later in the year by forces under Colonel Wright who defeated and punished the offending Indians at the battles of Spokane Plain and Four Lakes. Steptoe was criticized for not taking adequate precautions during his march into Spokane country. One possible explanation is that he did not expect serious difficulties because his relationship with the Indians had been good during the two years after the second Walla Walla council. It is also possible, but less likely, that failing health impaired his judgment. A brain tumor had begun to afflict Steptoe in 1857 when he wrote his sister: "This past winter has been especially grievous to me—sick, isolated, brooding painfully over the past and almost hopelessly on the future, I have grown ten years older in one, apparently." Steptoe to sister, Nannie, October 27, 1856, April 5, 1858, Steptoe Papers; Steptoe to Mackall, September ———, 1856 (this note is undated; it was written on a small scrap of paper while Steptoe was escorting Stevens back to The Dalles); Wright to Mackall, October 16, 30, 31, November 15, December 7, 1856; Steptoe to Wright, November 20, 1856; Robert Newell to Wool, October 11, 1856; DOP, LR.

34. IIS to Steptoe, November 22, 1856; IIS to Davis, October 22, November 21, 1856; Miller Papers.

35. IIS to Commissioner of Indian Affairs, November 1, 1856, WSIA, LS, R 2; IIS to Wright, October 4, 1856; Wright to IIS; October 4, 1856; Miller Papers.

36. IIS to Casey, October 20, 1856; Casey to IIS, October 20, 21, 1856; Miller Papers.

37. *Pioneer and Democrat,* November 28, 1856; "Narrative of James Longmire," *Told By The Pioneers,* 3 vols. (n.p.: Washington Pioneer Project, 1938), 1:142–43; James Goudy, "An Account of the Capture and Killing of Quiemuth," Bieneke Library; IIS to A. J. Cain, October 13, 1856; IIS to Sidney Ford, Jr., October 20, 1856, WSIA, LS, R 2.

38. *Pioneer and Democrat,* November 28, 1856; IIS to Commissioner of Indian Affairs, April 3, 1857, WSIA, LS, R 2; IIS to Wesley Gosnell, November 14, 1856, WSIA, LS, R 2; John B. Allen, "Leschi vs. Washington Territory,"

Washington Territory Reports 1 (Seattle 1906): 14–29; Wright to William Wallace and Frank Clark, July 17, 1857, Miller Papers; Hubert Howe Bancroft, *History of Washington, Idaho and Montana,* (San Francisco: The History Co., 1890), p. 172.

39. Stevens wanted all the treaties ratified (except the Yakima treaty, and the Cayuse, Walla Walla, and Umatilla treaty), because, he argued, "It would be idle and trifling to think of treating with tribes who have violated treaties." IIS to Sidney Ford, Sr., November 22, 1856; IIS to Commissioner of Indian Affairs, November 1, 1856; WSIA, LS, R 2; IIS to A. H. Robie, December 4, 1856; IIS to A. J. Cain, December 26, 1856; IIS to Commissioner of Indian Affairs, December 12, 1856, February 2, 1857; WSIA, LS, R 3.

40. IIS to Commissioner of Indian Affairs, June 2, 1857; IIS to James W. Nesmith, May 1, 1857; WSIA, LS, R 3.

41. *Pioneer and Democrat,* January 29, February 5, 1858; Bancroft, *History of Washington,* pp. 172–73.

42. *Truth Teller* (Steilacoom, Washington Territory), January 3, February 25, 1858. The listed editor was "Ann Onymous."

Chapter 13
The Delegate

1. IIS to William Miller, August 31, 1856, Miller Papers; A. J. Cain to IIS, May 14, September 11, 1856, WSIA, Letters from Employees Assigned to the Columbia River, or Southern, District, R 17.

2. *Pioneer and Democrat,* June 20, 1856. (This issue is dated May 9 on the front cover and June 20 inside. There were no issues between these two dates.) Also see Ibid., July 11, August 1, 1856.

3. Ibid., June 27, 1856, April 10, June 12, 1857; *Washington Republican,* June 12, 19, 1857.

4. *Pioneer and Democrat,* May 15, 1857. The incumbent delegate, J. Patton Anderson, had hopes of renomination, but family illness prevented his return to the territory. It is doubtful that Anderson could have defeated Stevens in any event. Anderson never did return to Olympia, but remained in the South and joined the Confederate Army at the beginning of the war. He served well as a division commander under General Hardee. Stevens' term as governor expired in March 1857, but, as was customary, he remained in office until a successor was named. Franklin Mathias to Miller, April 14, 1857; J. Patton Anderson to Miller, February 18, March 17, 1857; A. J. Cain to Miller, March 18, August 9, 1857; Miller Papers.

5. *Washington Republican,* May 19, 1857; *Pioneer and Democrat,* May 15, 1857.

6. *Washington Republican,* May 29, June 19, 1857; *Pioneer and Democrat,* June 19, 26, 1857.

7. *Pioneer and Democrat,* June 26, July 3, 10, 1857; *Washington Republican,* June 19, July 3, 1857; August Kautz Journal, June 22, July 1, 1857, UWL.

8. Abernethy to Wallace, December 19, 1857, Wallace Papers; Abernethy to Elwood Evans, August 11, 1857, Elwood Evans Papers, Bieneke Library; *Pio-*

neer and Democrat, July 24, September 11, 1857.

9. *Pioneer and Democrat,* February 7, 1857.

10. *Pioneer and Democrat,* September 4, 11, 18, October 30, 1857; Meg to Mary, April –, 1858, Stevens Family Papers, WSL.

11. Ibid., Meg to Mary, Spring 1858; Meg to Mary, March 20 –, 1857, January 20, 24, 31, 1860; Meg to her Mother, March 25, 1857, February 26, 1860, HSUO.

12. James Swan to *Pioneer and Democrat,* December 22, 1856, James Swan Letters, Northwest Collection, UWL; J. Patton Anderson to Miller, March 31, May 3, July 3, 18, December 17, 1856, Miller Papers.

13. IIS to James W. Nesmith, November 19, December 2, 17, 1857, IISUW.

14. F. N. Chenoweth to J. S. Black, December 26, 1857; Chenoweth, Selucious Garfielde, and George Corliss to Black, April 19, 1858; IIS to Black, 1858, March 8, June 23, 1858, Appointments.

15. IIS to Black, March 8, June 23, 1858; Obediah McFadden to Black, November 7, 1857; William Gwin to Black, March 15, 1858; Edward Lander to J. Patton Anderson, December 14, 1856; H. J. G. Maxon and other citizens to Black, April 19, 1858; Petition of Seventy-five Citizens of Pierce County to Frank [sic] Pierce, 1858; Lander to Lane, June 19, 1858; Lane to Buchanan, June 22, 1858; Appointments; IIS to Miller, March 19, June 3, 17, 19, 1858, Miller Papers. Obediah McFadden remained on the bench and became chief justice. Lane tried without success to secure an appointment for Lander as minister to Paraguay or Venezuela.

16. IIS to Miller, April 4, 1858; Morris Frost to Miller, August 24, 1857; Miller Papers; IIS to Black, August 19, 1858, Appointments; James W. Buchanan to Peter Daniel, March 6, 1859; Travers Daniel to President Buchanan, April 25, 1859; IIS to President Buchanan, March 30, 1857; Morris Frost to Howell Cobb, March 9, 1859; NA, RG 56, "Department of the Treasury, Collector of Customs Applications."

17. One friend of the President pleaded with him not to appoint McMullin governor of Kansas as that territory had suffered enough. DOS, Appt. File, Thomas Shankland to President Buchanan, March 21, 1857. McMullin told the district convention in Virginia that he was not a candidate for renomination to Congress, but suggested that if they found him the best man for the job he would not refuse. He was not renominated, but the convention suggested that he be named to another office. DOS, Appt. File, "Address of Fayette McMullin to the Members of the Democratic Convention of the 13th Congressional District of Virginia," March 14, 1857; Officers of the Democratic Convention, Marion, Virginia, to President Buchanan, March 19, 1857; A. J. Cain to Miller, August 9, September 6, 1857; A. J. Cain, Sr., to Miller, September 7, 1857; Miller Papers; McMullin to R. M. Walker, April 3, 29, 1858, Charles Mason Letters. William Strong once translated a speech to say "what I thought the governor ought to have said." Strong, "History of Oregon," pp. 78–79, Bancroft Library.

18. It was charged that McMullin came to Washington Territory to shed one wife and acquire another, which he did. But his primary reason for becoming governor was political not marital. McMullin served in the Confederate Congress and died in Virginia in 1880 as the result of a train accident. McMullin

to Lewis Cass, April 16, 1858; Mason to Cass, June 21, 1858; Charles Mason Letters; A. J. Cain to Miller, June 3, 19, 1858; IIS to Miller, June 28, December 17, 1858; Miller Papers; IIS to Buchanan, September 30, 1858; IIS to Cass, November 9, 1858, January 18, 1859; Miller to Buchanan, December 12, 1857; Petitions on Mason's behalf from Citizens of Washington Territory, July, 1858; DOS, Appt. File.

19. In January 1857 the Washington Legislature, at Stevens' request, passed an act incorporating the Northern Pacific Railroad Company. Prominent in that action, in addition to Stevens, were William Strong, Arthur Denny, W. S. Ladd, and prominent Minnesota and Wisconsin citizens. James Doty, Sr., persuaded the Wisconsin Legislature to also incorporate the company. IIS to Miller, April 18, May 3, 1858, Miller Papers; IIS to *New York Journal of Commerce,* March 31, 1858, printed in *Pioneer and Democrat,* June 4, 1858.

20. *Pioneer and Democrat,* March 19, 26, January 29, 1858; IIS, Memorandum on Construction of Military Roads, February 9, 1858; IIS to Jefferson Davis, Chairman, Military Committee, and Stephen A. Douglas, Chairman, Committee on Territories, May 25, 1858, IISUW; W. Turrentine Jackson, *Wagon Roads West* (Berkeley: University of California Press, 1952), pp. 96–106; May Pickett, "Forty Years on Bellingham Bay" (Master's thesis, University of Washington, 1924), p. 15; U.S., Congress, House, *Congressional Globe,* March 4, 1858, May 12, 1860.

21. McMullin estimated the population to be about 7,000 at the end of 1857. *Harper's Weekly,* August 22, 1857; IIS, "A Circular Letter to Emigrants," February 1, 1858, IISUW.

22. IIS to Miller, June 28, 1858, Miller Papers; IIS to Lewis Cass, June 3, 1858, printed in *Pioneer and Democrat,* August 20, 1858; IIS, "A Circular Letter to Emigrants," "Speech on the Pacific Railroad, 1858," "Address on the Northwest to the American Geographic and Statistical Society, 1858," IISUW.

23. IIS to Miller, June 28, 1858, Miller Papers; IIS to Nesmith, August 3, 1858; IISUW; IIS to Cass, May 18, 1858, printed in the *Pioneer and Democrat,* August 20, 1858; IIS to Cass, June 29, 1858, printed in the *Pioneer and Democrat,* September 3, 1858; IIS to Cass, July 21, 1858, printed in the *Pioneer and Democrat,* September 24, 1858.

24. Ibid.; Cass to IIS, July 28, 1858, printed in the *Pioneer and Democrat,* September 24, 1858.

25. Keith Murray, *The Pig War,* Pacific Northwest Historical Pamphlet No. 6 (Tacoma: Washington State Historical Society, 1968), pp. 21, 32–36; *Oregon Statesman,* October 22, 1940; H. S., *Life,* 2:293.

26. The *Pioneer and Democrat* was also of the opinion that responsibility for the San Juan affair rested with "Harney and on him alone." *Pioneer and Democrat,* August 18, 1859; Murray, *The Pig War,* pp. 15–21, 35; IIS to Miller, July 18, 1858, Miller Papers.

27. Stevens gave a major address to the Steilacoom Library Association in September, 1859, and it is significant that he did not mention the San Juan controversy. *Pioneer and Democrat,* September 16, 1859. After his return to Washington D.C., Stevens did not correspond with Harney, although the general sent him copies of two letters to the Adjutant General that protested Scott's intention to remove him and to eliminate the Department of Oregon. William S. Harney to AAG, two letters of November 17, 1859, NA, RG 393,

"U.S. Army Continental Commands, 1821–1920, Department of Oregon;" IIS to Miller, December 4, 1859, January 16, 1860, Miller Papers; H. S., *Life,* 2:292.

28. IIS to Steptoe, February 10, 1857; IIS to A. H. Robie, February 9, 1857; WSIA, LS, R 3; Wright to Mackall, December 8, 1856; Steptoe to Wright, December 5, 1856; DOP, LR. Wool's successor, Newman S. Clarke, continued the ban on settlement until October 31, 1858. IIS to Nesmith, January 18, 1858, IISUW.

29. IIS to Nesmith, December 19, 29, 1857, January 18, 1858; IIS to Charles Mix, December 28, 1857; IISUW.

30. U.S., Congress, House, *Congressional Globe,* December 23, 1858; IIS to Nesmith, December 17, 1857, January 18, June 3, 19, 25, 1858, IISUW.

31. IIS to Nesmith, July 18, August 3, 20, 1858; IIS to B. F. Yantis, June 28, 1858; IISUW.

32. IIS to Nesmith, April 22, 1859, IISUW.

33. Record of Scrip Issued, Governor's Letterbook, Washington State Archives, Olympia, Wash.

34. U.S., Congress, House Report 195, 34th Cong., 1st sess. [868], *Expenses of the Oregon and Washington Indian War*; Joseph Lane, Speech on Suppression of Indian Hostilities, April 2, 1856, May 7, 1856, IISUW; U.S., Congress, House, *Congressional Globe,* August 6, 1856.

35. U.S., Congress, House Ex. Doc. 39, 35th Cong., 1st sess. [955], *Report of J. Ross Browne*; James Swan, "Washington Sketches," p. 8, Bancroft Library.

36. When the commission spent several weeks in Olympia, Rufus Ingalls stayed at the Stevens' home. Meg to Mary, March 15, 25, 1857, HSUO; U.S., Congress, House Ex. Doc. 45, 35th Cong., 1st sess. [955], *Report of Commission to Ascertain Expenses of the Indian War.*

37. IIS to Meg, May 17, 1858, Miller Papers; U.S., Congress, House, *Congressional Globe,* May 13, 1858.

38. U.S., Congress, House Ex. Doc. 114, 35th Cong., 1st sess. [1014], T. J. Cram, *Topographical Memoir of the Department of the Pacific,* pp. 66–69, 80–88, 98, 122, 124–25.

39. James Swan to *Pioneer and Democrat,* December 22, 1856, Swan Letters, UWL; U.S., Congress, House, *Congressional Globe,* May 31, 1858; "Remarks of Isaac I. Stevens on the War Expenses of Washington and Oregon Made Before the Committee of Military Affairs of the House," Mar. 15, 1860, printed in the *Pioneer and Democrat,* May 18, 1860.

40. Ibid.

41. IIS to Miller, June 19, 1858, Miller Papers; *Pioneer and Democrat,* April 22, 1859.

42. U.S., Congress, House Ex. Doc. 51, 35th Cong., 2d sess. [1006], *Claimes Growing Out of Indian Hostilities in Oregon and Washington, Report of the Third Auditor.*

43. Ibid.

44. After the war the volunteers auctioned their horses, wagons, weapons, and other supplies at various places, but mostly at Vancouver. Stevens said that the equipment sold for more than the volunteers had originally paid. This was

true in some instances, but the auditor complained that many items were sold for a fraction of their cost. This was partly explained by the sharp decrease in demand for some equipment after the war. U.S., Congres, House, *Congressional Globe*, May 31, 1858; Miller to *Pioneer and Democrat*, printed in the issue of June 10, 1859; *Pioneer and Democrat*, June 17, 24, 1859.

45. *Pioneer and Democrat*, May 15, 1857, Nov. 19, 1858; Oliver Stevens to Miller, August 3, 1858, Miller Papers; Thomas Prosch, "The Indian War in Washington Territory," Northwest Collection, UWL, p. 15; U.S., Congress, House Misc. Doc. 88, 40th Cong., 2d sess., *Communications on Oregon Indian War Claims*.

46. U.S., Congress, House Ex. Doc. 11, 36th Cong., 1st sess. [1046], *Report of the Third Auditor of the Treasury*.

47. Ibid.

48. *Pioneer and Democrat*, March 11, 1859; U.S., Congress, Senate Report 161, 36th Cong., 1st sess. [1039], *Report on Payment of Expenses*. Stevens and Lane succeeded in attaching an amendment allowing claiments to bring new evidence which would allow payment of higher amounts than those allowed by the auditor. Most of the scrip was redeemed between 1861 and 1864, although the Treasury Department was still making payments and hearing evidence in the 1870s. The records of the individual claims are in the National Archives.

49. IIS to Nesmith, April 22, 1859, IISUW; *Puget Sound Herald*, December 24, 1858, February 11, 1859; *Pioneer and Democrat*, February 11, 18, March 4, 1859; A. J. Cain, Sr., to Miller, April 24, 1859; S. B. Curtis to Miller, April 25, 1859; Miller Papers.

50. *Pioneer and Democrat*, February 18, March 18, May 13, 20, 1859; *Puget Sound Herald*, May 27, 1859.

51. Even more contemptible to Stevens was the defection of a Democratic appointee to the land office, Selucius Garfielde, who came out for Wallace. Garfielde was wily, unscrupulous, and an effective political speaker. Stevens warned that someone would have to follow him on the stump to counter his arguments. Joe Lane wrote an open letter which praised Stevens for his "energy, talent, and learning," attributes that had made him a commanding influence with Congress, the President, and government department personnel. Lane called Stevens "the best working man that I ever knew." The *Puget Sound Herald*, which was supporting Wallace, sourly complained of the Lane-Stevens alliance, editorializing that they "tickle each other with twaddle and baby talk." *Pioneer and Democrat*, May 20, June 3, 10, 17, 24, 1859; *Puget Sound Herald*, May 13, 20, 1859; Rufus Ingalls to Miller, June 20, 1859; Seth Catlin to Miller, June 14, 1859; IIS to Miller, June 5, 15, 20, 1859; Lane to Miller, February 15, 1859; Miller Papers.

52. *Puget Sound Herald*, June 10, 17, 1859; IIS to Miller, June 15, 1859; Miller Papers.

53. *Puget Sound Herald*, July 15, 1859; *Pioneer and Democrat*, August 12, 1859, Miller Papers.

54. Among others, Lane split with Nesmith. This placed Stevens in an awkward position as he had worked closely with Nesmith; he had even defended him in Congress from political attacks. Stevens chose Lane over Nesmith and, by the start of the 36th Congress, the relationship between Stevens and Nesmith was cool. James E. Hendrickson, *Joe Lane of Oregon* (New Haven: Yale University Press, 1967) pp. 202–203, 219–23.

55. Washington and the other territories were not allowed representation in the convention. Stevens cast a proxy vote for one of the Oregon delegates who could not make the long journey east. IIS to Miller, April 19, 1860, Miller Papers; Roy Nichols, *The Disruption of American Democracy* (New York: Macmillan Co., 1948), pp. 286–87.

56. Hendrickson, *Joe Lane of Oregon,* pp. 224–27; Nichols. *Disruption of American Democracy,* pp. 296–307; William B. Hesseltine, ed., *Three Against Lincoln: Murat Halstead Reports the Caucuses of 1860* (Baton Rouge: Louisiana State University Press, 1960), pp. 45–46, 61, 68–87, 98–100; Robert W. Johannsen, *Stephen A. Douglas* (New York: Oxford University Press, 1973), pp. 749–59.

57. *Minority Report of Mr. Stevens, Delegate From Oregon* (Washington, D.C.: n.p., 1860), pp. 3–4; Nichols, *Disruption of American Democracy,* pp. 313–14; Hesseltine, *Three Against Lincoln,* pp. xvi–xvii, 214–20, 223–25. Before the convention gathered in Baltimore, Douglas said publicly that the bolters should not be seated. Johannsen, *Stephen A. Douglas,* pp. 762–63, 768–69.

58. IIS to Miller, August 8, 1860, Miller Papers; Nichols, *Disruption of American Democracy,* pp. 317–18; Hendrickson, *Joe Lane of Oregon,* pp. 230–31; Hesseltine, *Three Against Lincoln,* p. 236.

59. IIS, " 'Address to the Democracy,' Speech on the Occasion of a Serenade for Gov. Dickinson," August 1, 1860, printed in *Pioneer and Democrat,* October 5, 1860. Douglas was equally determined that his faction would control the party after the election and was fighting Breckinridge more than Lincoln. Johannsen, *Stephen A. Douglas,* p. 778.

60. IIS to Pierce, July 20, 26, 1860; Pierce to IIS, July 30, 1860; Pierce Papers; "Speech of President Buchanan, July 9, 1860," *Breckinridge and Lane Campaign Documents* (Washington City: n.p., 1860); Lucille Stillwell, *John Cabell Breckinridge* (Caldwell, Idaho: Caxton Press, 1936), p. 87. "Gathering at the Cooper Institute," *Breckinridge and Lane Campaign Documents.*

61. IIS to Pierce, July 20, 26, 1860; Pierce to IIS, July 30, 1860; Pierce Papers; IIS to Miller, August 8, 10, September 12, 1860, Miller Papers.

62. Nichols, *Disruption of American Democracy,* pp. 336–37; IIS to Miller, September 12, 1860, Miller Papers.

63. Fitzhugh to Miller, April 3, 1860; IIS to Miller, July 10, August 8, September 12, 1860; William Morrow to Miller, June 13, July 11, November 21, 1860; O. B. McFadden to IIS, April 11, 1860; Democratic Party of Washington Territory to IIS, March 15, 1860; Miller Papers.

64. A. J. Cain, Sr., to Miller, September 16, 1860; O. B. McFadden to Miller, August 15, 1860; William Morrow to Miller, March 7, 1860; Fitzhugh to Miller, April 3, July 22, 1860; Ibid.

65. IIS to Miller, November 13, 1860; Miller to IIS, October 6, 1860; Ibid.

66. IIS to Miller, January 4, February 11, 1861, Ibid.; *Puget Sound Herald,* April 18, 1861; *Washington Standard,* Olympia, April 13, 1861; *Pioneer and Democrat,* February 1, 1861.

67. IIS to Miller, January 4, February 11, 1861, Miller Papers.

68. Nichols, *Disruption of American Democracy,* pp. 389–90; IIS to Miller, January 4, 22, February 11, March 8, 1861, Miller Papers; *Pioneer and Democrat,* April 5, 1861; IIS to *Pioneer and Democrat,* printed in issues of January 3, 10, 21, 1861, December 10, 17, 1860.

69. Shaw to Miller, November 30, 1860; Edward Furste to Miller, February 25, 1861; IIS to Miller, March 8, April 14, two letters of April 15, 1861, Miller Papers.

70. *Washington Standard,* April 20, 1861; Tilton to IIS, February 8, 1861; IIS to Miller, April 14, 15, 1861; John Mullan to Miller, April 19, 1861; Edward Geary to Miller, April 30, 1861, Miller Papers.

71. *Washington Standard,* April 13, 20, 27, May 7, 11, 1861; J. S. Jaquith to Miller, May 24, December 6, 1860; Fitzhugh to Miller, July 19, 1859, Miller Papers.

72. *Pioneer and Democrat,* May 10, 1861; *Washington Standard,* May 11, 1861.

73. *Pioneer and Democrat,* May 24, 1861; IIS to Miller, May 10, 1861; George Paige to Miller, April 27, 1861; Paige to IIS, April 20, 1861; S. B. Curtis to IIS, April 23, 1861; Miller Papers; *Washington Standard,* May 11, 1861; IIS to Howell Cobb, April 16, June 9, 1860, Collector of Customs Applications.

74. *Pioneer and Democrat,* May 24, 31, 1861.

75. *Ibid.*; Miller to Jas. Biles, May 9, 1861, Miller Papers.

76. Garfielde's nomination divided the Democratic party, and he did not receive the support of Republicans as he had hoped. Garfielde had been too clever; the Republicans ignored him and Democrats denounced his nomination as a fraud. The *Pioneer and Democrat,* along with many other Democrats, supported the candidacy of Edward Lander on the Union ticket. This made it easy for the Republicans to elect William Wallace, who suddenly suffered from an embarrassment of riches as Lincoln offered him the governorship; he declined the offer after he was elected delegate. Stevens did not comment on the campaign after his convention speech, but he probably would have picked Lander as the lesser of three evils. He respected Lander despite the martial-law dispute but could not abide either Wallace or Garfielde. IIS to Nesmith, May 22, 1861, IISUW; IIS to Secretary of War, May 22, 1861, NA, RG 94, "Department of War, Office of the Adjutant General, Letters Received, 1800–1890;" Shaw to Miller, May 29, 1861, Miller Papers; *Pioneer and Democrat,* May 24, 31, 1861; *Puget Sound Herald,* July 11, 1861; *Port Townsend Register,* July 10, 1861.

Chapter 14
The General

1. IIS to Secretary of War, June 16, 1861, AGO, LR; IIS to Totten, June 19, 1861, IISUW.

2. Oliver Stevens to IIS, August 15, 1861, IISUW; T. Harry Williams, *Lincoln and His Generals* (New York: Alfred A. Knopf, 1952), pp. 10–11.

3. IIS to Simon Cameron, July 30, 1861, AGO, LR; John Andrew to IIS, August 10, 1861; IIS to Bache, August 12, 1861; T. G. Hazard to IIS, August 15, 1861; IISUW.

4. IIS to Miller, October 23, 1861, Miller Papers; IIS to Totten, June 19, 1861; Miller to IIS, October 11, 1861, IISUW.

5. H. S., *Life,* 2:321–22.

6. Thirty-five men were arrested, of which fourteen were soon returned to the regiment while the rest were imprisoned in the Dry Tortugas until February, 1862. William T. Lusk, *War Letters of William Thompson Lusk* (New York: n.p., 1911); Lusk to his mother, August 17, 1861, Ibid.; H. S., *Life,* 2:323–26.

7. IIS to Miller, October 19, 1861, Miller Papers; IIS to Gen. Rufus King, September 18, 1861; IIS to Secretary of War, September 18, 1861; Report of Capt. John Talloner, September 19, 1861; Statement of Charles Nagle, September 10, 1861; Simon Cameron to IIS, September 28, 1861; AGO, LR.

8. Those who urged Stevens' promotion included seventy-nine members of the Rhode Island legislatue, the two powerful Republican senators from Massachusetts, Henry Wilson and Charles Sumner, and Congressman Israel Washburn. Old friends like Professor Bache, Montgomery Meigs, and A. A. Humphreys also applied pressure on the administration in Stevens' behalf. Hazard said his father sent him to see the president in September. After spending hours in the president's anterooms with numerous other supplicants, Hazard spoke to one of the Negro doorkeepers, who, when he learned that the Stevens in question was the same man who had often visited President Buchanan, arranged an interview with Lincoln. Hazard said that Lincoln immediately issued an order for his father's promotion. This was not true, but the rest of the story may be valid. Stevens, among other reasons, wished to have his commission list him as a resident of Washington Territory because he was sensitive to criticism he received during the 1860 campaign when he was called a citizen of Oregon. This had resulted from his membership in the Oregon delegation to the Democratic convention and the subsequent assumption by many eastern newspapers that he was a resident of that state. H. S., *Life,* 2:333–35; Memorial from Legislature of Rhode Island to the President, August 9, 1861; Israel Washburn to the President, September 3, 1861; Harrison Richie to IIS, September 4, 1861; M. C. Meigs to the President, September 7, 1861; AGO, LR; IIS to Miller, April 8, 1862, Miller Papers; Frederick A. Aiken to IIS, September 28, 1861; Aiken to William Seward, September 25, 1861; Oliver to IIS, September 30, 1861; IISUW; Lincoln to McClellan, September, 1861, as cited in Roy Basler, ed., *The Collected Works of Abraham Lincoln,* 9 vols. (New Brunswick, N.J.: Rutgers University Press, 1953), 4:504.

9. IIS to Miller, October 23, 1861, Miller Papers; Brig. Gen. Stevens to 3rd Brigade, Smith's Division, October 16, 1861, IISUW; H. S., *Life,* 2:329–32; McClellan to Scott, September 11, 1861; IIS to Brig. Gen. William Smith, September 13, 1861; Rebellion Records, 1:5·167–72.

10. *DAB,* 17:92.

11. Special Order No. 18, October 17, 1861, General Order No. 19, October 23, 1861, Expeditionary Orders; IIS to Meg, October 24, 1861, IISUW; Lusk to his mother, October 21, 25, 1861, Lusk, *War Letters;* Thomas Sherman to E. D. Townsend, AAG, August 20, 1861; Sherman to Rufus Saxton, September 13, 1861; Sherman to M. C. Meigs, October 27, 1861; Expeditionary Orders, LS.

12. Sherman to AAG, November 8, 1861, Ibid.; Hazard Stevens to Meg, November 4, 1861, Stevens Family Papers, WSL; H. S., *Life,* 2:347–48.

13. Sherman to AAG, November 17, 27, 1861, Expeditionary Orders, LS; IIS to Miller, December 5, 1861, Miller Papers; H. S., *Life,* 2:349–50.

14. Louis H. Pelouze to IIS, November 25, December 5, 1861, Expeditionary Orders, LS; Lusk to his mother, November 9, 1861, Lusk, *War Letters*; IIS to Sherman, November 23, December 8, 1861, Expeditionary Orders, LR; General Order No. 24, November 11, 1861, General Order No. 40, December 18, 1861, Expeditionary Orders.

15. Stevens' force suffered casualties of one killed, one missing, and nine wounded. He assessed Confederate losses as "heavy". Sherman to IIS, December 10, 1861, Expeditionary Orders; IIS to Sherman, two letters of December 8, 1861, two letters of December 9, 1861, December 10, 1861; IIS to Lt. Col. Bernholts, December 8, 1861; IIS to Pelouze, December 12, 15, 18, 31, 1861, January 3, 1862; IIS to S. F. DuPont, January 3, 1862; IIS to Albert Myer, January 3, 1862; Expeditionary Orders, 2nd Brig. Corres.; Pelouze to IIS, December 27, 1861; Sherman to L. Thomas, AAG, December 10, 1861; Expeditionary Orders, LS; IIS to Pelouze, January 3, 1862; Sherman to L. Thomas, AAG, January 4, 1862; *Rebellion Records*, 1:4:46–53. Sherman wrote the commanding general that Stevens' attack was a complete success, and said that Stevens was so well known for his "zeal and energy" that it was necessary only to note the "clever and happy results."

16. IIS to David Hutchinson, December 20, 1861; IIS to Pelouze, February 8, 1862; Expeditionary Orders, 2nd Brig. Corres.; "Roll of Non-Commissioned Officers and Privates Employed on Extra Duty as Mechanics at Beaufort Library, S. C., during the Months of January and February, 1862" (box 6), and IIS to Meg, February 16, 1862, IISUW; Lusk to his mother, December 10, 1861, February 16, 1862, Lusk, *War Letters.*

17. Some senators who disliked Stevens because of his association with the Breckinridge campaign were eager to embrace any charge against him. IIS to Pelouze, December 17, 1861, January 21, 25, 1862; IIS to Lilley, March 24, 1862; Expeditionary Orders, 2nd Brig. Corres.; Sherman to IIS, February 12, 16, April 13, 1862; IIS to Bache, February 14, 1862; Bache to IIS, February 24, April 12, 1862; IIS to Nesmith, February 17, 1862; IIS to W. J. A. Fuller, March 15, 1862; IIS to Meigs, March 26, 1862; Fuller to IIS, February 27, March 24, 1862; IISUW.

18. Willie Lee Rose, *Rehearsal for Reconstruction* (New York: Bobbs-Merrill Co., 1964), pp. 18–20, 25; Pelouze to IIS, December 7, 1861, Expeditionary Orders, LS.

19. IIS to Nobles, December 10, 1861; IIS to Sherman, three letters of December 10, 1861; IIS to Pelouze, December 12, 1861; IIS to Lt. Cross, Commanding on Ladies Island, December 12, 1861; IIS to Saxton, December 13, 1861; Expeditionary Orders, 2nd Brig. Corres.; Pelouze to IIS, December 11, 1861; Sherman to IIS, December 11, 15, 1861; Ibid., LS.

20. IIS to Pelouze, January 11, February 8, 1862, Expeditionary Orders, 2nd Brig. Corres.; Pelouze to IIS, December 26, 1861; Ibid., LS.

21. DuPont to Henry Winter Davis, February 25, 1862, quoted in Rose, *Rehearsal for Reconstruction*, pp. 21–25, 26, 34, 45.

22. Sherman to L. Thomas, AAG, December 15, 1861, January 15, 1862, AGO, LR; General Orders No. 9, February 6, 1862, Expeditionary Orders.

23. IIS to Sherman, December 17, 1861; Hazard Stevens to Dr. Peck, March 14, 1862; Expeditionary Orders, 2nd Brig. Corres; IIS to Bache, February 16, 1862, IISUW.

24. IIS to Bache, February 16, 1862; IIS to Sherman, February 17, 1862; Sherman to IIS, February 20, 1862; IISUW.

25. Rose, *Rehearsal for Reconstruction,* pp. 65–71, 142; IIS to Col. Farnsworth, February 12, 17, 1862, Expeditionary Orders, 2nd Brig. Corres.; W. T. Lusk to Dr. Trimble, March 11, 1862; Hazard Stevens to Capt. Ely, March 14, 1862; Hazard Stevens to Major F. L. Hagadorn, April 17, 1862; Hazard Stevens to Dr. Peck, April 11, 1862; IIS to Pelouze, March 26, 1862; IIS to Capt. Dimmock, March 27, April 7, 1862; IIS to Lt. Col. Bernholts, March 31, 1862; Expeditionary Orders, 2nd Brig. Corres.; *New York Tribune,* February 14, 1862; W. J. A. Fuller to IIS, March 12, 1862; IIS to Fuller, March 24, 1862; IISUW.

26. IIS to Bache, February 18, 1862; IIS to Fuller, March 15, 1862; Bache to IIS, February 24, 1862; IISUW; Sherman to McClellan, December 19, 26, 1861, AGO, LR.

27. Sherman to IIS, February 20, 28, 1862; IIS to Fuller, March 15, 1862; IISUW; Sherman to McClellan, December 26, 1861, AGO, LR; McClellan to Sherman, February 14, 1862, *Rebellion Records,* 1:4:225.

28. Fuller to IIS, March 24, 1862, IISUW; *New York Times,* March 21, 1862; Rose, *Rehearsal for Reconstruction,* pp. 144–45.

29. *DAB,* 2:178–79, 9:400, 17:92. Sherman served with Halleck in the West in 1862 and then went to the Gulf Coast where he lost a leg at Port Hudson in 1863. Benham was also critical of Stevens' efforts (in the early 1850s) to raise the status of the Engineer Corps; he claimed that he had a better plan. Benham to William Rosecrans, August 11, 1852, April 11, 1853, Henry W. Benham Papers, Rutherford B. Hayes Library, Fremont, Ohio; Sherman to IIS, April 13, 1862, IISUW.

30. Meg to Bache, April 8, 1862, IISUW; Benham to Wright, April 2, 1862, Expeditionary Orders, Dept. South, LS.

31. Sherman to AAG, March 8, 1862, Expeditionary Orders, LS; Benham to IIS, May 11, 1862, IISUW; Rose, *Rehearsal for Reconstruction,* pp. 145–46.

32. IIS to Meg, May 12, 13, 1862; IIS to Benham, May 13, 1862; IIS to Nesmith, May 13, 1862; IISUW; Lusk to his mother, April 3, 1862, Lusk, *War Letters;* IIS to Benham, May 12, 1862, Expeditionary Orders, 2nd Brig. Corres.; Rose, *Rehearsal for Reconstruction,* pp. 146–48; Hunter to IIS, May 8, 1862, Hazard Stevens, Circular From Headquarters, 2nd Brig., Northern District, Dept. of the South, May 11, 1862; Edward Pierce to S. P. Chase, May 12, 1862; G. M. Wells to Pierce, May, 1862; L. D. Phillips to Pierce, May 13, 1862; *Rebellion Records,* 3: 2:30, 52–54, 58–60.

33. On April 11 Fort Pulaski fell to Viele and the new generals received credit although they had had no part in the seige. In May Viele's brigade was sent to Virginia to participate in an attack on Norfolk. IIS to Benham, May 23, 31, 1862; Benham to IIS, May 18, 28, 30, 1862; IISUW.

34. IIS to Meg, June 11, 1862, IISUW; H. S., *Life,* 2:390–92.

35. IIS to Capt. Ely, June 8, 1862; IIS to Capt. Sealy, June 10, 1862; IIS to Benham, June 11, 1862; IIS to Capt. B. F. Porter, June 11, 1862; Expeditionary Orders, 2nd Brig. Corres.

36. IIS to Meg, June 15, 1862; IIS to Hunter, July 3, 1862; IISUW; *New York Times,* June 28, 1862.

37. Benham to Hunter, June 16, 1862, Expeditionary Orders, Dept. South, LS; Hazard Stevens to Capt. Sears, June 15, 1862, Ibid., 2nd Brig. Corres.; IIS to Hunter, July 8, 1862; IIS to Wright, June 19, 1862; *Rebellion Records,* 1:14:48–50, 58–64.

38. Benham to Hunter, June 16, 1862, Expeditionary Orders, Dept. South, LS; General Order No. 26, 9th Army Corps, 2nd Division, June 18, 1862, II-SUW; *New York Tribune,* July 17, 1862; *New York Times,* June 28, July 17, 1862; *New York World,* June 28, 1862; H. S., *Life,* 2:412. Hazard was in the midst of the fighting during the attack. The Confederate losses were 204. Hunter to Edwin Stanton, June 23, 1862; IIS to Wright, June 19, 1862; *Rebellion Records,* 1:14:41–85.

39. Benham to Hunter, June 16, 1862, Expeditionary Orders, Dept. South, LS; General Order No. 26, 9th Army Corps, 2nd Division, June 18, 1862; IIS to Meg, June 21, 26, 30, July 9, 19, 1862; IIS to W. J. A. Fuller, July 10, 1862; IISUW.

40. Benham, after constant pleading, was restored to rank in February 1863. Although he never again commanded men in battle, he did good service building pontoon bridges, and was in charge of the Engineering Brigade of the Army of the Potomac. *DAB,* 2:179; IIS to editor, *New York Times,* July 18, 1862; Bache to IIS, July 3, 16, 17, 24, 1862; Wright to IIS, August 9, 1862; II-SUW. Wright, like Bache, advised Stevens to avoid a newspaper battle as he predicted that Benham was finished in any event. IIS to Capt. G. W. Smith, June 22, 1862, Expeditionary Orders, 2nd Division Corres.; Lusk to John Adams, June 17, 1862, Lusk, *War Letters.*

41. Lusk to his mother, February 16, June 10, 1862, Lusk, *War Letters;* IIS to Bache, June 22, 1862; IIS to Meg, June 26, 28, 30, July 9, 1862; IISUW.

42. IIS to Lincoln, July 8, 1862, IISUW.

43. IIS to Meg, July 14, 1862, IISUW; H. S., *Life,* 2:423–24.

44. IIS to Major Lewis Richmond, July 22, 29, 1862; IIS to Col. Carter, August 10, 1862; IIS to Hazard, August 5, 10, 1862; John Pope to Jesse Reno, August 14, 1862; Oliver to IIS, July 29, 1862; Charles Stevens to IIS, July 31, 1862; IISUW; John Andrew to IIS, July 29, 1862, HSUO; Itinerary of the First Division, 9th Army Corps, Brig. Gen. Isaac I. Stevens Commanding, Aug. 4–31, 1862, *Rebellion Records,* 1:12, part 2: 544–45.

45. Pope to Reno, August 20, 21, 1862; IIS to L. Thomas, AAG, August 26, 1862, 9th Army Corps, 2nd Division Corres.; IISUW; Itinerary of First Division, 9th Army Corps, Aug. 4–31, 1862, *Rebellion Records,* 1:12, part 2: 544–45.

46. T. Harry Williams, *Lincoln and His Generals,* pp. 157–58; H. S., *Life,* 2:454–59; Itinerary of First Division, 9th Army Corps, August 4–31, 1862, *Rebellion Records,* 1:12, part 2: 544–45; Maj. Gen. Samuel P. Heintzelman to Col. George Ruggles, October 21, 1862; Brig. Gen. Philip Kearny to George Ruggles, August 31, 1862, *Rebellion Records,* 1:14, part 2: 413, 416.

47. Union casualties at Second Bull Run were 16,000, 21 percent of the force; Confederate casualties were 9,200, 19 percent. Stevens' division had losses of 95 killed, 585 wounded, and 67 missing. H. S., *Life,* 2:426–67; George Ruggles to Hazard Stevens, April 4, 1900, HSUO.

48. Robert Amour, manuscript, HSUO; H. S., *Life,* 2:477–81.

49. Lusk to his mother, September 4, 1862, Lusk, *War Letters*; Robert Amour, manuscript, HSUO; H. S., *Life*, 2:481–86; Itinerary of the First Division, 9th Army Corps, September 1–October 31, 1862, *Rebellion Records*, 1:14, part 1: 431–32.

Epilogue

1. Mrs. E. F. Lusk to William Lusk, September 9, 1862, Lusk, *War Letters*; Lincoln to Schurz, November 24, 1862, Basler, ed., *Collected Works of Abraham Lincoln*, 5:510; H.S., *Life*, 2:498–501.

2. H.S., *Life*, 2:498; E. O. C. Ord to Hazard Stevens, August 4, 1877; George Ruggles to Hazard Stevens, April 18, 1877; HSUO.

3. *A Brief Sketch of the Life of General Hazard Stevens* (Boston: Geo. H. Ellis Co., 1908), pp. 9–13.

4. Ibid., pp. 13–15; Hazard Stevens to Moses Stevens, March 17, 1897, II-SUW.

5. *Sketch of Life of Hazard Stevens*, p. 16. Stevens published an account of the ascent in the November 1876 issue of *Atlantic Monthly*.

6. Ibid., pp. 16–19; Hazard Stevens to Edwin Stanton, September 25, 1865, IISUW; F. A. Vanderlip to Hazard Stevens, January 24, 1900, HSUO. Only one of the Stevens' children (Susan, who married Richard Eskridge, an army career officer) had children. Five of Susan's children lived to maturity, and all but one were born at army posts in the West.

LIST OF ABBREVIATIONS

AGO, LR — NA, RG 94, Department of War, Office of the Adjudant General, Letters Received 1800–1890.

AGO, Mexican War, Misc. — NA, RG 94, Office of the Adjutant General, Mexican War, Army of Occupation, Miscellaneous Papers.

Appointments — NA, RG 60, General Records of the Department of Justice (N198), Records relating to the U.S. Attorneys and Marshals, Washington, 1853–1902

Correspondence of Northern Survey — NA, RG 48, Records of the Office of the Secretary of the Interior (M126), Correspondence of the Office of Explorations and Surveys Concerning Isaac Stevens' Survey of a Northern Route for the Pacific Railway, 1853–61

CS, Annual Report — NA, RG 23, Coast Survey, Superintendent's Report and Accompanying Papers, Annual Report, 1850

DAB — *Dictionary of American Biography,* 22 vols. (New York: Charles Scribners Sons, 1928–58)

DOP, LR — NA, RG 393, United States Army Continental Commands, 1821–1920, Department of the Pacific, Letters Received

DOS, Appt. File — NA, RG 69, Department of State Appointment Files, Pierce and Buchanan Administrations

Doty Journal — James Doty, Journal of Operations . . . , NA, RG 75, Documents Relating to Negotiations of Ratified Treaties with Various Indian Tribes, 1801–09 (T494) R5

EDLR — NA, RG 77, War Department, Engineer Department, Letters Received, 1840–52

445

Expeditionary Orders	NA, RG 393, Records of United States Continental Army Command, 1821–1920, Expeditionary Corps, General and Special Orders
Haller Journal	Granville O. Haller, Journals, University of Washington Library, Seattle, Wash.
H.S., *Life*	Hazard Stevens, *The Life of Isaac Ingalls Stevens,* 2 vols. (Boston: Houghton, Mifflin & Co., 1900)
HSUO	Hazard Stevens Papers, University of Oregon Library, Eugene, Ore.
IIS	Isaac Ingalls Stevens
IISUW	Isaac Ingalls Stevens Papers, University of Washington Library, Seattle, Wash.
Indian Disturbances	U.S., Congress, Senate Ex. Doc. 66, Report of the Secretary of War on Indian Disturbances in the Territories of Washington And Oregon, 34th Cong., 1st Sess. [822]
Indian War Docs.	*Indian War Messages and Documents.* Documents, Vol. 1, Historical Miscellany, Northwest Collection, University of Washington Library, Seattle, Wash.
Interior Dept., Terr. Papers	NA, RG 48, Records of the Office of the Secretary of the Interior, Territorial Papers (M189), Washington, 1854–1902
Itinerary of March	Itinerary of March of Right Wing of 2nd Regiment Washington Territory Volunteers Under Col. Shaw, June 12–August 29, 1856 . . . , William Winlock Miller Papers, Bieneke Library, Yale University, New Haven, Conn.
Kipp Journal	F. G. Young, ed., "The Indian Council at Walla Walla, May and June, 1855, by Col. Lawrence Kipp, U.S.A. A Journal, *Sources of the History of Oregon,* Vol. 1, pt. 2 (Eugene: University of Oregon, 1897)
Landsdale Diary	Richard Landsdale, Personal Diary, and Official Diary. Bieneke Library, Yale University, New Haven, Conn.
LC	Library of Congress
LOE	NA, RG 77, War Department, Engineering Department, Letters to Office of Engineers, 1840–52.
LR	Letters Received
LS	Letters Sent
LRPRRS	Letters Relating to the Pacific Railroad Survey; found in IISUW

Martial Law, Vindication	U.S., Congress, Senate Ex. Doc. 98, 34th Cong., 1st Sess. [823], Message of the President . . . Proclamation of Martial Law . . . , Vindication of Governor Stevens . . . , May 10, 1856
Mason Letters	Charles Mason Letters, Bieneke Library, Yale University, New Haven, Conn.
Rebellion Records	*The War of Rebellion: A Compilation of the Official Records of the Union and Confederate Armies,* 4 series, 130 vols. (Washington, D.C.: Government Printing Office, 1880–1902)
McClellan Journal	George B. McClellan Papers, Library of Congress
Meg	Margaret Lyman Hazard Stevens, Isaac I. Stevens' wife
Message on Martial Law	U.S., Congress, Senate Ex. Doc. 41, 34th Cong. 3d Sess., [881], Message of the President of the United States . . . Respecting the Proclamation of Martial Law in Washington Territory, United States vs. Charles Wren, Lynn A. Smith, and John McLoed, June 2–5, 1856
Miller Papers	William Winlock Miller Papers, Bieneke Library, Yale University, New Haven, Conn.
NA	National Archives

Newspapers
   The Columbian
   Pioneer and Democrat
   Puget Sound Herald
   Puget Sound Courier
   Washington Standard
	Olympia, Oregon Territory
	Steilacoom, Washington Territory
	Steilacoom, Washington Territory
	Steilacoom, Washington Territory
	Olympia, Washington Territory

Pierce Papers	Franklin C. Pierce Papers, Library of Congress
Records Relating to N.W. Boundary	NA, RG 76, Records of Boundary Claims, Commissions, and Arbitrations (T606), 1853–1901
RES	U.S., Congress, Senate Ex. Doc. 46 [992], and House Ex. Doc. 91 [791], *Reports of Explorations and Surveys to Ascertain the Most Practicable and Economical Route for a Railroad from the Mississippi River to the Pacific Ocean.*
RG	Record Group
RPC	NA, RG 75, Documents Relating to the Negotiation of Ratified and Unratified Treaties with Various Indian Tribes, 1801–69 (T494), R5.
SHSW	State Historical Society of Washington, Tacoma Wash.

Stevens Family Papers, WSL	Stevens Family Papers, 1822–1913 (microfilm), Washington State Library, Olympia, Wash.
Swan Letters	The James Swan Letters, Northwest Collection, University of Washington Library, Seattle, Wash.
Tilton Papers	James Tilton Papers, Bieneke Library, Yale University, New Haven, Conn.
Totten Letters	NA, RG 77, War Department, Engineer Department, Official Letters of Colonel Joseph G. Totten, Chief Engineer, 1839.
UWL	University of Washington Library, Seattle, Wash.
Wool Papers	John E. Wool Papers, New York State Library, Albany, N.Y.; State Historical Society of Washington, Tacoma, Wash. (microfilm)
WSIA	NA, RG 75, Records of the Bureau of Indian Affairs (N5), Records of the Washington Superintendency of Indian Affairs, 1853–74
WSIA, Letters, PSD	NA, RG 75, Letters from Employees Assigned to Local Agencies of the Puget Sound District
WSL	Washington State Library, Olympia, Wash.
WTVP, Gov. Corres., LS	Washington, Territory, Washington Territory Volunteer Papers, 1855–57, Governor I. I. Stevens, Correspondence, Outgoing, Washington State Library, Olympia, Wash.
YVRL	Yakima Valley Regional Library, Yakima, Wash.

NOTE ON SOURCES

This essay on sources is not meant to be exhaustive, but to serve two purposes: to identify more fully the major collections used and to point to sources that supplement or offer greater detail on topics touched upon in the text. The footnotes should be consulted for additional references not listed here.

General

The personal papers of Isaac I. Stevens and his family are located in several collections as the manuscripts were dispersed following Stevens' death. The largest collection is the eight boxes in the manuscript collection of the University of Washington Library. The bulk of this material covers Stevens' life from his entrance into West Point through 1853. A few of the letters in the University of Washington collection have been published in: John S. Richards, ed., "Letters of Governor Isaac I. Stevens, 1853–54," *Pacific Northwest Quarterly* 30 (July 1939): 301–37, and J. Ronald Todd, ed., "Letters of Governor Isaac I. Stevens, 1857–58," *Pacific Northwest Quarterly* 31 (October 1940): 403–59. The Hazard Stevens Papers at the University of Oregon library contain the manuscript of Hazard's biography of his father, letters written and received by Hazard while conducting research, a large number of letters written by his mother, and some Isaac I. Stevens letters as well as material relating to other members of the Stevens' family. A small but valuable collection of Stevens' family papers has been microfilmed by the Washington State Library, Olympia. This collection was recently acquired from Mrs. Helen Eskridge by the Eastern Washington Historical

449

Society. The Washington State Historical Society has a few Isaac I. Stevens papers. The large William W. Miller collection at Yale University contains much Stevens material. Most of Stevens' letters in this collection are to Miller or to other political associates in the Pacific Northwest or to army officers.

There are two previously published biographies of Isaac I. Stevens. Hazard Stevens, *Life of Isaac Ingalls Stevens*, 2 vols. (Boston: Houghton, Mifflin & Co., 1900) is a classic example of a biography designed to justify the actions of the protagonist. Hazard freely deleted injurious material, twisted facts, or, most usually, gave only one side of the story. Some chapters, such as the one on the Mexican War, constitute a reproduction of his father's journals and selected letters, or parts of letters which are edited without indicating deletions. In this volume I have accepted Hazard's version only when it can be confirmed by other evidence. Hazard is most useful in his chapters on the Civil War, which are fuller than the account in this book. Hazard had the advantage of witnessing many of the Civil War events he described. Joseph T. Hazard, *Companion of Adventure* (Portland, Ore.: Binfords and Mort, 1952) is a brief biography apparently based entirely on Hazard Stevens. It is a condensation of the earlier work and is aimed at a high school-level audience. It is of little value. The best brief sketch of Stevens is Scott H. Paradise, "Isaac Ingalls Stevens," *The Phillips Bulletin* (October 1932), pp. 7–16. Rose M. Boening, "Bibliography of Isaac I. Stevens," *Washington Historical Quarterly* 9 (July 1918): 174–96, is incomplete and out of date. An interesting study by a communications student is Caleb W. Prall, "A Study of the Method of Persuasion in Selected Speeches Delivered by Isaac Ingalls Stevens" (Master's thesis, University of Washington, 1943).

Chapter 1

The well-preserved colonial Massachusetts town records, as well as the strong historical sense of the Stevens family, makes the early history of the family relatively easy to trace. Two accounts by members of the family are particularly useful: Horace Stevens, "The Ancestors of Major General Isaac I. Stevens" and Edmund Leland, "Marble Ridge Farm," both typescripts in the Washington State Historical Society. Also useful are Charlotte Abbot, "Early Records of the Stevens Family of Andover,"

North Andover Historical Society, and *Vital Records of Andover, Massachusetts to the End of the Year 1849,* 2 vols. (Topsfield, Mass.: Massachusetts Historical Society, 1912). Two excellent histories of Andover which contain information on the Stevenses are Sarah L. Bailey, *Historical Sketches of Andover* (Boston: Houghton, Mifflin & Co., 1880) and Claude Fuess, *Andover: Symbol of New England* (Andover: Andover Historical Society, 1959). Fuess is also the author of *An Old New England School: A History of Phillips Academy Andover* (Boston: Houghton, Mifflin & Co., 1917). Letters of recommendation to West Point are in the National Archives, Record Group 94, "Records of the Adjutant General's Office, United States Military Academy Cadet Application Papers" (M688).

Chapter 2

The Stevens collections at the Washington State Library and the University of Washington contain numerous letters sent and received by Isaac I. Stevens from his father, brother, sisters, uncles, and cousins during his years as a cadet. These letters were the major source for this chapter. The best account of West Point during this period is Stephen Ambrose, *Duty, Honor, Country: A History of West Point* (Baltimore: Johns Hopkins University Press, 1966). See also Sidney Forman, *West Point: A History of the United States Military Academy* (New York: Columbia University Press, 1950). Extremely useful is George W. Cullum, *Biographical Register of the Officers and Graduates of the U.S. Military Academy at West Point,* 2 vols. (New York: D. Van Nostrand and Co., 1868). Typical of the numerous government investigations of the Military Academy are the reports contained in U.S., Congress, House Report 303, 24th Cong., 2d sess. [306] and U.S., Congress, House Document 2, 26th Cong., 1st sess. [363]. The Stevens papers at the University of Washington include some of Stevens' class notes and the essays he wrote for the *Talisman.*

Chapter 3

There is no account of the Corps of Engineers during the pre-Civil War era, but Robert Weigley's excellent history *The United*

States Army (New York: Macmillan Co., 1967) is of some use. The basic source for the Corps is found in the National Archives, Record Group 77, "War Department, Engineer Department." They contain letters sent and received by the office of the chief engineer. The same record group contains the Official Letters of Colonel Joseph G. Totten, Chief Engineer, 1839–53. The title is a misnomer as many of the letters are private or semi-private and are kept separate from Totten's official letters, although division is not precise. Also helpful are government reports such as U.S., Congress, House Doc. 206, 26th Cong., 1st sess. [368], *Report From the Secretry of War on a System of National Defense.*

As with the Stevenses, there is extensive information on the Lyman-Hazard families. The Hazard Stevens Papers at the University of Oregon contain a Lyman-Hazard geneology. Also useful are "The Old Hazard House," *Newport Historical Society Bulletin,* 33 (July 1920); Caroline E. Robinson, *The Hazard Family of Rhode Island* (Boston: the author, 1895); and Lyman Coleman, *Geneology of the Lyman Family in Great Britain and America* (Albany: J. Munsell, 1872).

Chapter 4

The Corps of Engineer records continue to be an important source on the Mexican War. Records in the National Archives relative to the Mexican War are scattered and unorganized, but useful materials in Record Group 94 are: "Office of the Adjutant General, Mexican War, Army of Occupation, Letters Received, Nov. 1846–47"; "Office of the Adjutant General, Mexican War, Army of Occupation, Misc. Papers"; and "Mexican War, General and Special Orders, February 18–December 18, 1847." In addition to his letters home, Stevens kept an abstract of operations at Vera Cruz and a journal which covered most of his year in Mexico. These are in the Stevens Papers at the University of Washington. Isaac I. Stevens, *Campaigns of the Rio Grande and Mexico* (New York: D. Appleton Co., 1851) is a general history of the war and does not focus on Stevens' experiences. The best accounts of other engineers who served in Mexico with Stevens are Douglas S. Freeman, *Robert E. Lee,* 4 vols. (New York: Charles Scribner's Sons, 1934–35) and T. Harry Williams, ed., *With Beauregard in Mexico* (Baton Rouge: Louisiana State University Press, 1956). See also Williams' *P. G. Beauregard: Napoleon in Gray* (Baton Rouge: Louisiana State University Press, 1957). Biographies of George McClellan contain little on his Mexican War career, but the George C. McClellan Papers, Library of Congress, contain a number of letters written from Mexico. Still the most thorough account of the war is Justin H. Smith, *The War with Mexico*, 2 vols. (New York: Macmillan Co., 1919).

Chapter 5

As with the Engineers, there is no history of the Coast Survey although A. Hunter Dupree, *Science in the Federal Government* (Cambridge, Mass.: Harvard University Press, 1957) has a good brief account. The appropriate records in the National Archives are in Record Group 23, "Coast Survey: Correspondence of Alexander Dalles Bache, 1843–65"; "Superintendent's Report and Accompanying Papers"; "Letters Received from the Superintendent and Papers Received by Assistant in Charge of the United States Coast Survey Office"; "Correspondence with Assistants in Office"; and "Letters Received by the Assistant in Charge of United States Coast Survey Office." The Stevens Papers at the University of Washington contain articles and memorandums relating to Stevens' efforts on behalf of the engineer officers and attempts to reorganize the army.

Chapter 6

For the Presidential campaign of 1852 see the Franklin Pierce Papers, Library of Congress; I. I. Stevens, et. al., *Vindication of the Military Character and Services of General Franklin Pierce* (n.p., 1852); and Roy Nichols, *Franklin Pierce: Young Hickory of the Granite Hills,* 2d ed. (Philadelphia: University of Pennsylvania Press, 1958). Letters supporting Stevens' appointment as governor are in the National Archives, Record Group 69, "Department of State, Appointment Files, Pierce and Buchanan Administrations."

The best general history of the railroad surveys of the 1850s is William H. Goetzmann, *Army Exploration in the American West, 1803-1863* (New Haven: Yale University Press, 1959). I disagree with certain of Goetzmann's interpretations as they relate to the northern route. More general but also useful is Goetzmann's *Exploration and Empire* (New York: Alfred A. Knopf, 1966). A standard work is Robert R. Russel, *Improvement of Communication with the Pacific Coast as an Issue in American Politics* (Cedar Rapids, Iowa: Torch Press, 1948). George L. Allright, *Official Exploration for Pacific Railroads, 1853-1855* (Berkeley: University of California Press, 1921) has been superceded by Goetzmann as has Martha Dobbins, "Governor Stevens' Pacific Railroad Survey" (Master's thesis, University of California, 1916). The official reports of the railroad surveys were published by both houses of Congress in twelve volumes (with the last volume in two books) between 1855 and 1860. Volume 1 contains a general report by Jefferson Davis on the various routes, but most of the volume is Stevens' "Report of Explorations for a Route for the Pacific Railroad near the Forty-Seventh and Forty-Ninth Parallels of North Latitude from St. Paul to Puget Sound," *Reports of Explorations and Surveys to Ascertain the most Practicable and Economical Route for a Railroad from the Mississippi River to the Pacific Ocean,* (U.S., Congress, House Ex. Doc. 91, 33rd Cong., 2d sess.,[791]). Stevens' final report was published by Congress in 1859 as volume 12, (U.S., Congress, Senate, Ex. Doc. 46, 35th Cong., 2d sess.,[922]), and was reprinted in 1860 in two books (U.S., Congress, House, Ex. Doc. 56, 36th Cong., 1st sess., [1054 & 1055]). Other volumes of the reports which contain references to the northern route are volumes 7, 8, and 9 on zoology and botany of the surveys, U.S., Congress, Senate, Ex. Doc. 78, 33rd Cong., 2d sess., [765, 766, 767]), and G. K. Warren's review of Western exploration, 1800-1857, published as volume 9 in 1859, U.S., Congress, House Ex. Doc. 91, 33rd Cong., 2d sess., [791].

During preparations for the survey, Stevens kept copies of his correspondence relating to the survey in a separate ledger which is in the Stevens Papers at the University of Washington (Letters Relating to the Pacific Railroad Survey). Letters relating to the post-survey collection and publication of results are in the National Archives, Record Group 48, "Records of the Office of the Secretary of the Interior (M 126), Correspondence of the Office of Explorations and Surveys Concerning Isaac Stevens' Survey of a Northern Route for the Pacific Railway, 1853-61." Valuable sources of information are the George Suckley Letters,

Bieneke Library, Yale University, New Haven, Conn., and the George Suckley Papers at the Smithsonian Institution Library, Washington D.C. There is some scattered material on the survey in the Smithsonian Institution Manuscript Collections. Indispensable are George McClellan's letters and journal, both in the McClellan Papers, Library of Congress. Philip Overmeyer, "George B. McClellan and the Pacific Northwest," *Pacific Northwest Quarterly* 32 (January 1941) is overly critical of McClellan.

Information on various members of the survey party can be found in: Stephen D. Beckham, "George Gibbs, 1815-1873 Historian and Ethnologist" (Ph.D. diss., UCLA, 1969); E. Douglas Branch, "Frederick West Lander, Road-Builder," *Mississippi Valley Historical Review* 16 (September 1929): 172-87; Robert Taft, *Artists and Illustrators of the Old West, 1850-1900* (New York: Charles Scribner's Sons, 1953); David I. Bushnell, "John Mix Stanley, Artist-Explorer," *Annual Report, 1924* (Washington, D.C.: The Smithsonian Institution, 1925); Richard Evans, "Dr. John Evans, U.S. Geologist, 1851-61," *Washington Historical Quarterly* 26 (April 1935): 83-89; Addison Howard, "Captain John Mullan," *Washington Historical Quarterly* 25 (July 1934): 185-202; and Alice E. Smith, *James Duane Doty* (Madison, Wis.: University of Wisconsin Press, 1954). Letters from the survey party appeared in the *New York Tribune* and letters from Stevens to Stephen A. Douglas are printed in Robert W. Johannsen, "Reporting a Pacific Railroad Survey: Isaac Stevens' Letters to Stephen A. Douglas," *Pacific Northwest Quarterly* 47 (October 1956): 97-106. A superb article is D. W. Meinig, "Isaac Stevens: Practical Geographer of the Early Northwest," *The Geographical Review* 45 (October 1955): 542-58. See also Meinig's *The Great Columbia Plain* (Seattle: University of Washington Press, 1968). Some of Stanley's and Sohon's sketches are reproduced in William H. Goetzmann, "The Grand Reconnaissance," *American Heritage* 23 (October 1972): 44-59, as well as in the 1859 reports. An analysis of American perceptions of the Pacific Northwest is John Logan Allen's, *Passage Through the Garden* (Urbana: University of Illinois Press, 1975).

Chapter 7

Although it contains errors of fact and interpretation, still the most useful volume for the history of Washington during the territorial period is Hubert Howe Bancroft, *History of Washington, Idaho and Montana* (San Francisco: The History Company, 1890). Edmond Meany, *History of the State of Washington* (New York: Macmillan Co., 1946) is less satisfactory than Bancroft, but helpful on some points. See also Clinton A. Snowden, *History of Washington,* 4 vols. (New York: The Century History Co., 1909) and George Fuller, *A History of the Pacific Northwest* (New York: Alfred A. Knopf, 1931, 1947). The early county histories are useful sources of information, but the reader needs to be aware that the usual purpose was to glorify the early settlers. Most helpful were: W. D. Lyman, *History of Walla Walla County* (n.p.: W. H. Lever, 1901); William F. Prosser, *A History of the Puget Sound Country* 2 vols. (New York: Lewis Publishing Co., 1903); and W. P. Bonney, *History of Pierce County,* 3 vols (Chicago: Pioneer Historical Publishing Co., 1927). An anti-Stevens work is Ezra Meeker, *Pioneer Reminiscences of Puget Sound* (Seattle: Lowman and Hanford Stationery and Printing Co., 1905).

The best source for the formation of Washington Territory is the *Columbian* (later the *Pioneer and Democrat*), published in Olympia. The Oregon newspapers are also useful as is the U.S., Congress, *Congressional Globe.* A thorough, sound account of Joe Lane's political career is contained in James E. Hendrickson, *Joe Lane of Oregon* (New Haven: Yale University Press, 1967). William Strong's manuscript entitled "History of Oregon" (Bancroft Library, Berkeley, Calif.) contains reminiscences of the early territorial period. The Organic Act can be found in Francis N. Thorpe, *The Federal and State Constitutions, Colonial Charters, and Other Organic Laws . . . ,* 7 vols. (Washington, D.C.: Government Printing Office, 1909). The story of filling the territorial offices is contained in the Appointment Files of the Department of State (cited in the previous chapter); the National Archives, Record Group 60, "General Records of the Department of Justice (M 198), Records Relating to the Appointment of Federal Judges and U.S. Attorneys and Marshalls, Washington, 1853-1902"; and Record Group 48, "Records of the Office of the Secretary of the Interior, Appointment Papers, Washington Territory." The most convenient source for the annual messages of Stevens and Mason to the territorial legislature is Charles M. Gates, ed., *Messages of the Governors of the Territory of Washington to the Legislative Assembly, 1854-1889* University of Washington Publications in the Social Sciences, vol. 12 (Seattle: University of Washington Press, 1940).

In addition to the Stevens papers and the William Winlock Miller Collection, other collections of personal papers useful for this period are the George B. McClellan Papers, Library of Congress; Elkanah Walker Papers, Huntington Library, San Marino, Calif.; Joseph Lane Papers, Indiana University Library, Bloomington, Ind. (microfilm copies, University of Oregon Library); Charles Mason Letters, Bieneke Library, Yale University, New Haven, Conn.; and the Elwood Evans Papers at the Bieneke Library.

In addition to previously listed sources, road building in Washington is discussed in W. Turrentine Jackson's admirable monograph *Wagon Roads West* (Berkeley: University of California Press, 1952). Blanche Mahlberg provides information on Edward Allen in "Edward J. Allen, Pioneer and Roadbuilder," *Pacific Northwest Quarterly* 44 (October 1953): 157–60. See also National Archives, Record Group 48, "Records of the Office of the Secretary of the Interior, Territorial Papers (M 189), Washington, 1854–1902." A thorough discussion of early land surveys is in Frederick Yonce, "Public Land Disposal in Washington" (Ph.D. diss., University of Washington, 1969). A detailed discussion of Stevens' efforts to collect a library is Hazel Mills, "Governor Isaac I. Stevens and the Washington Territorial Library," *Pacific Northwest Quarterly* 53 (January 1962): 1–16. Charles M. Gates has a brief discussion of early attempts to found a university in *The First Century at the University of Washington, 1861–1961* (Seattle: University of Washington Press, 1961).

The boundary dispute is discussed in James O. McCabe, *The San Juan Water Boundary Question*, Canadian Studies in History and Government, No. 5 (Toronto: University of Toronto Press, 1964); Keith Murray, "The Pig War," *Pacific Northwest Historical Pamphlet No. 6*, (Tacoma: Washington State Historical Society, 1968); and Barry M. Gough, "British Policy in the San Juan Boundary Dispute, 1854–72," *Pacific Northwest Quarterly* 62 (April 1971): 59–68. The treaty establishing the boundary is found in U.S., Congress, Senate Doc. 357 (2 vols.), 61st Cong., 2d sess., *Treaties, Conventions, International Acts, Protocols, and Agreements*. Correspondence relating to the boundary dispute is contained in Record Group 76, "Records of Boundary and Claims Commissions and Arbitrations (T 606), Records Relating to the Northwest Boundary, 1853–1901"; U.S., Congress, Senate Ex. Doc. 37, 33rd Cong., 2d sess., [752]; and House Exec. Doc. 65, 36th Cong., 1st sess., [1051], *Affairs in the Department of Oregon.*

Chapters 8 and 9

The history of territorial government during the first year is found in *Journal of the House of Representatives of the Territory of Washington,* First Session (Olympia, 1855); *Journal of the Council of the Territory of Washington,* First Session (Olympia, 1855); and *Statutes of the Territory of Washington,* 1854 (Olympia, 1855). A competent treatment of constitutional issues is Wilfred J. Airey, "A History of the Constitution and Government of Washington Territory" (Ph.D. diss., University of Washington, 1945). Mercedes S. Gleason, "The Territorial Governors of the State of Washington: 1853–1889" (Master's thesis, University of Washington, 1935) is of little use for either fact or interpretation. There is scattered information on the territorial government in the various department records in Washington D.C., particularly in the National Archives, Record Group 48, "Records of the Office of the Secretary of the Interior, Territorial Papers (M 189), Washington, 1854–1902"; Record Group 56, "Treasury Department, Letters From Executives of Territories"; Record Group 217, "First Comptrollers Office, Letters Received, Territorial, and Miscellaneous Letters Received"; and Record Group 217, "Miscellaneous Treasury Accounts." Two perceptive discussions of inherent problems within the territorial system are John Smurr, "Territorial Constitutions: A Legal History of the Frontier Governments Erected by Congress in the American West, 1787–1900" (Ph.D. diss., Indiana University, 1960) and Kenneth N. Owens, "Pattern and Structure in Western Territorial Politics," *Western Historical Quarterly* 1 (October 1970): 373–92.

Although there is considerable literature on nineteenth-century Indian wars, work on Federal Indian policy is less abundant. An indispensable book is Francis Paul Prucha, *American Indian Policy in the Formative Years* (Cambridge, Mass.: Harvard University Press, 1962). Also see Ronald Satz, *American Indian Policy in the Jacksonian Era* (Lincoln, Neb.: University of Nebraska Press, 1975). A short survey of policy is found in William Hagan, *American Indians* (Chicago: University of Chicago Press, 1961). A good work on the Pacific Northwest is Alban W. Hoopes, *Indian Affairs and their Administration, with Special Reference to the Far West, 1849–1860* (Philadelphia: n.p., 1932). See also Charles F. Coan, "The Federal Indian Policy in the Pacific Northwest, 1849–1870" (Ph.D. diss., University of California,

1920); Coan, "The First Stage of the Federal Indian Policy in the Pacific Northwest, 1849–1852," *Oregon Historical Quarterly* 22 (March 1921): 46–89; William M. Neil, "The Territorial Governor as Indian Superintendent in the Trans-Mississippi West," *Mississippi Valley Historical Review* 43 (September 1956): 213–37; Francis Haines, "Problems of Indian Policy," *Pacific Northwest Quarterly* 41 (July, 1950):203–12; and Douglas Martin, "Indian-White Relations on the Pacific Slope, 1850–1890" (Ph.D. diss., University of Washington, 1969). Charles E. Garretson, "A History of the Washington Superintendency of Indian Affairs, 1853–65" (Master's thesis, University of Washington, 1962) is superficial.

For the state of Indian-white relations in Washington and Oregon in the years prior to 1855 see: J. B. A. Brouillet Papers, Typescript, Yakima Valley Regional Library, Yakima; Hazard Stevens, "The Pioneer and Patriotism," *Washington Historical Quarterly* 8 (July 1917): 172–79; Floyd-Jones Papers, Bancroft Library, Berkeley; U.S., Congress, Senate Misc. Doc. 59, 36th Cong., 1st sess. [1038]; Senate Ex. Doc. 34, 33rd Cong., 1st sess., [698]; and National Archives, Record Group 393, "United States Army Continental Commands, 1821–1920, Department of the Pacific, letters Received and Letters Sent." The correspondence between the officers stationed in the Department of the Pacific is a valuable source for army opinion and policy throughout the period of the Indian wars.

A basic source for the treaty negotiations is "Records of the Washington Superintendency of Indian Affairs, 1853–74," in the National Archives, Record Group 75. It is available on microfilm (M 5, 26 rolls) and comprises a rich mine of information for Stevens' policy and the administration of Indian affairs to 1874. An equally valuable group of records is in Record Group 75, "Documents Relating to the Negotiation of Ratified and Unratified Treaties with Various Indian Tribes, 1801–69" (T 494). James Doty's journal is contained within these papers. Other personal accounts of the various treaty negotiations are George Gibbs' journal, which can be found in the Records Relating to the Northwest Boundary Survey (cited above); James Swan, *The Northwest Coast* (Fairfield, Wash.: Ye Galleon Press, 1966); Colonel B. F. Shaw, "Medicine Creek Treaty," *Proceedings* (Salem, Oregon Historical Society, 1906); Benjamin F. Shaw Papers, Oregon Historical Society, Portland; George B. McClellan Papers, Library of Congress; F. G. Young, ed., "The Indian Council at Walla Walla, May and June, 1855, by Col. Lawrence

Kip, U.S.A., A Journal," *Sources of the History of Oregon,* vol. 1, Pt. 2 (Eugene: University of Oregon, 1897); Richard Lansdale, Personal Diary, Bieneke Library, Yale University, New Haven. Lansdale is more laconic and less well-known than Kip, but may be the more accurate observer. A second Lansdale diary at Yale is labeled "Official Diary," and it contains some pertinent information. The Joel Palmer Papers, Oregon Historical Society, Portland, and the L. V. McWhorter Papers, Washington State University Library, Pullman, Wash., contain little relating to the treaty negotiations. For papers of two Indian agents see Robert Fay Papers, Washington State Library, Olympia and Nathaniel Hill, manuscript, Bancroft Library, Berkeley. The Indian treaties are contained in Charles J. Kappler, comp. and ed., *Indian Affairs, Laws and Treaties,* 4 vols. (Washington D.C.: Government Printing Office, 1904).

Secondary works dealing with the treaties, tribes, or personalities involved in the negotiation vary greatly in quality and objectivity. A brilliant work and the best source for the Flathead Council is Robert I. Burns, *The Jesuits and the Indian Wars of the Northwest* (New Haven: Yale University Press, 1966). Equally important for the Nez Perce perspective on the events of the period is Alvin M. Josephy, *The Nez Perce Indians and the Opening of the Northwest* (New Haven: Yale University Press, 1965). Three books by Robert H. Ruby and John A. Brown are valuable although overly sympathetic to the Indians: *Half-Sun On The Columbia* (Norman: University of Oklahoma Press, 1965); *The Spokane Indians* (Norman: University of Oklahoma Press, 1970), and *The Cayuse Indians* (Norman: University of Oklahoma Press, 1972). John C. Ewers has written a solid history, *The Blackfeet* (Norman: University of Oklahoma Press, 1958). Less satisfactory is Francis Haines, *The Nez Perces* (Norman: University of Oklahoma Press, 1955). There is no history of the Yakima tribe, but every historian of the tribe must consider A. J. Splawn, *Ka-Mi-Akin, The Last Hero of the Yakimas* (Portland: Kilham Stationery and Printing Co., 1917). Two works written from the Indian point of view are John Beeson, *A Plea for the Indians* (New York: Beeson, 1858) and William Brown, *The Indian Side of the Story* (Spokane: C. W. Hill Printing Co., 1961).

Chapter 10

An excellent biography of Wool is Harwood P. Hinton, "The Public Career of John Ellis Wool" (Ph.D. diss., University of

Wisconsin, 1960). There are voluminous Wool papers for his years on the Pacific Coast. Most of the correspondence between Stevens and Wool is in the Miller Collection at Yale. This collection also contains correspondence between Stevens and Wright, Casey, Steptoe, and other military officers. The previously cited records of the Department of the Pacific naturally contain Wool's orders and correspondence to his subordinates. Also useful are the John E. Wool Papers, New York State Library, Albany (microfilm, Washington State Historical Society, Tacoma), and U.S., Congress, House Ex. Doc. 88, 35th Cong., 1st sess., [956], "Correspondence between the Late Secretary of War and General Wool." For the army perspective on the Indian war see Granville O. Haller, *The Dismissal of Granville O. Haller* ... (Paterson, N.J.: Daily Guardian Office, 1863) and Haller Journals, University of Washington Library, Seattle; H. Dean Guie, *Bugles in the Valley* (Yakima: n.p., 1956); P. H. Sheridan, *Personal Memoirs* 2 vols. (New York: Webster, 1888); E. D. Keyes, *Fifty Years' Observation of Men and Events* (New York: Charles Scribner's Sons, 1884); and the Edward J. Steptoe Papers, University of Washington Library, Seattle. Wright's letters from the Yakima Valley are published in William N. Bischoff, "The Yakima Campaign of 1856," *Mid-America* 31, new series 20 (July 1949): 163–205. See also Bischoff, "The Yakima Indian War, 1855–1856" (Ph.D. diss., Loyola University of Chicago, 1950).

Diaries, personal accounts, and reminiscences by volunteers or settlers include: J. W. Reese, "The Exciting Story of Fort Henrietta," typescript, Umatilla County Library, Pendleton, Ore.; Edward Eldridge, "Sketch of Washington Territory," Bancroft Library, Berkeley; A. H. Sale, "Indian War Recollections," *Oregon Native Son* 1 (January 1900): 210–14; A. B. Roberts, "The Yakima War of 1855," *Clark County History* 8 (1967); George Hunter, *Reminiscences of an Old Timer* (San Francisco: Crocker, 1887); Cyrus Walker, "Reminiscences of the Yakima War," *Oregon Native Son* 1 (January 1900):447–48; Kelly Mercer, Diary of Company A, Bieneke Library, Yale University, New Haven; Thomas Cornelius Papers, Huntington Library, San Marino, Calif.; Arthur Denny, *Pioneer Days on Puget Sound* (Seattle: The A. Harrison Co., 1908); Robert Ballou, *Early Klickitat Valley Days* (Goldendale: Goldendale Sentinel, 1938); George Blankenship, *Lights and Shades of Pioneer Life on Puget Sound* (Olympia: n.p., 1923); U. B. Hicks, *Yakima and Clickitat Indian Wars* (Portland: Himes, 1886); Margaret White Chambers, "Reminiscences," and

Andrew Chambers, "Recollections," Northwest Collection, University of Washington Library, Seattle; Sarah McAllister Hartman, Typescript, Bieneke Library, Yale University, New Haven; "Autobiography of John Rogers James," *Told By The Pioneers,* 3 vols. (n.p.: Washington Pioneer Project, 1937-38); D. F. Byles, "Indian Wars of 1855-6," typescript, Northwest Collection, University of Washington Library, Seattle; and Denys Nelson, "Yakima Days," *Washington Historical Quarterly* 19 (April, July 1928): 45-51, 117-33. See also Clarence B. Bagley, ed., "Attitude of the Hudson's Bay Company During the Indian War of 1855-56," *Washington Historical Quarterly* 8 (October 1917): 291-307.

Papers of territorial officials not previously cited are the papers of James Tilton and George Gibbs, Bieneke Library, Yale University, New Haven, and the George Law Curry Letters, Oregon Historical Society, Portland. The major source for the activities of the Washington volunteers are the Washington Territory Volunteer Papers, 1855-57 in the Washington State Library, Olympia. The papers are divided into various categories: Governor I. I. Stevens, Correspondence, Incoming and Outgoing; Quartermaster and Commissary Correspondence; Quartermaster Vouchers, Abstracts, and Receipts; Washington Territory, Secretary, Correspondence; Southern Battalion, Correspondence; and Adjutant General, Correspondence. A Governor's Letterbook and the records of territorial scrip are housed in the Washington State Archives, Olympia. Many of the letters relating to the Indian war cited above can also be found in Indian War Messages and Documents, 1856 vol. 1, Historical Miscellany, Northwest Collection, University of Washington Library, Seattle. An identical volume is the misnamed *Message of the Governor of Washington Territory* (Olympia, 1857).

For accounts of specific events during the Indian war see the following. For the death of Bolon: A. J. Splawn, *Ka-Mi-Akin, The Last Hero of the Yakimas* and Lucullus V. McWhorter, *Tragedy of the Whak-Shum* (Yakima: n.p., 1937). McWhorter's interviews and notes are in the L. V. McWhorter Papers, Washington State University Library, Pullman. For the death of Peopeomoxmox: T. C. Elliott, "The Murder of Peu-Peu-Mox-Mox," *Oregon Historical Quarterly* 35 (June 1934): 123-30; Joseph F. Santee, "The Slaying of Peo-Peo-Mox-Mox," *Washington Historical Quarterly* 25 (April 1934): 128-32. For the attack on Seattle there are numerous accounts—among them: Gardner Allen, ed., *The Papers of Francis Gregory Dalles* (New York: Naval History Society, 1917) and Charles M. Gates, ed., "Seattle's First Taste of Battle, 1856," *Pacific Northwest Quarterly* 47 (January 1956): 1–8. A general history is Francis Fuller Victor, *The Early Indian Wars of Oregon* (Salem, Oregon: F. C. Baker, 1894). See also Roy Lokken, "Frontier Defense in Washington Territory, 1853–1861" (Master's thesis, University of Washington, 1951).

Information and correspondence on the Indian wars (much of it duplicated in sources already cited) is contained in U.S., Congress: House Ex. Doc. 1, 34th Cong., 1st sess., [840]; Senate Ex. Doc. 66, 34th Cong., 1st sess., [822]; House Ex. Doc. 93, 34th Cong., 1st sess., [858]; House Ex. Doc. 118, 34th Cong., 1st sess., [859]; House Misc. Doc. 116, 35th Cong., 1st sess., [963]; Senate Misc. Doc. 59, 36th Cong., 1st sess., [1038]; House Ex. Doc. 112, 35th Cong., 1st sess., [958]; and House Ex. Doc. 29, 36th Cong., 2d sess., [1097].

Chapter 11

A good history of martial law is Robert S. Rankin, *When Civil Law Fails: Martial Law and Its Legal Basis in the United States* (Durham, N.C.: Duke University Press, 1939). An excellent article is Roy Lokken, "The Martial Law Controversy in Washington Territory, 1856," *Pacific Northwest Quarterly* 43 (April 1952): 91–119. An earlier and less useful account is Samuel Cohn, "Martial Law in Washington Territory," *Pacific Northwest Quarterly* 27 (July 1936): 195–218. The Washington Territory Volunteer Papers and the William Miller Papers, both previously cited, are important sources for martial-law material. Other important documents are contained in U.S., Congress: Senate Ex. Doc. 98, 34th Cong., 1st sess., [823], *Message of the President of the United States communicating ... copies of papers relating to the Proclamation of Martial Law in Washington Territory;* and Senate Ex. Doc. 41, 34th Cong., 3rd sess., [881], *Message of the President of the United States ... Respecting the Proclamation of Martial Law in Washington Territory.* Also of use are the William Wallace Papers, University of Washington Library, Seattle. For a brief account of Wallace's career see Annie L. Bird, "William Henson Wallace, Pioneer Politician," *Pacific Northwest Quarterly* 49 (April 1958): 61–76. Another of the Steilacoom lawyers is treated by Willis A. Katz, "Benjamin F. Kendall, Territorial

Politician," *Pacific Northwest Quarterly* 49 (January 1958): 29–39. For George Gibbs see Vernon Carstensen, ed., *Pacific Northwest Letters of George Gibbs* (Portland: Oregon Historical Society, 1954). The Company A controversy is contained in the House and Senate Journals for the Fourth Legislative Session (Olympia, 1856). All of the correspondence is in Appendix C, Fourth Legislative Session of the Territory of Washington, December 1, 1856, House Journal (Olympia, 1857).

Chapter 12

Most of the sources used in this chapter are cited previously in Chapters 8, 9, or 10. An eyewitness account of the Cascade massacre is in the Coe manuscript, Bieneke Library, Yale University, New Haven. For Shaw's expedition, Walter W. DeLacy, "Itinerary of March of Right Wing of Second Regiment of Washington Territory Volunteers Under Lt. Col. Shaw, June 12–August 29, 1856 . . . ," contained in the Miller Papers, Yale, is indispensable. The Edward J. Steptoe Papers, University of Washington Library, Seattle, contain letters from Steptoe to his family written from Washington Territory. For the killing of Quiemuth there are two contemporary accounts: "Narrative of James Longmire," *Told By The Pioneers,* 3 vols. (n.p.: Washington Pioneer Project, 1937–38); and James Goudy, "An Account of the Capture and Killing of Quiemuth," Bieneke Library, Yale University, New Haven. For the trial of Leschi see John B. Allen, reporter, *Washington Territory Reports* 1 (Seattle, 1906). The two issues of the *Truth Teller,* published by Elwood Evans in Steilacoom, are also useful for the Leschi affair. The Elwood Evans Papers, Bieneke Library, Yale University, New Haven, contain newspaper clippings and articles written by Evans on the Leschi trial and other events in the territory during this period. For the San Juan crisis see U.S., Congress, House Ex. Doc. 65, 36th Cong., 1st sess., [1051].

Chapter 13

The James Swan Letters, Northwest Collection, University of Washington Library, Seattle, contain comments on Stevens' work as delegate; also see the James W. Nesmith Papers, Oregon Historical Society, Portland. In addition to the appointment files of the Department of State and the papers pertaining to appointments of Federal Judges and Marshals cited previously, see National Archives, Record Group 56, "Department of the Treasury, Collector of Customs Applications." The Stevens Papers, University of Washington, contain articles, memorandums, and speeches by Stevens on military roads, the Pacific railroad, and the prospects of the Pacific Northwest. Contemporary views of the Far West are discussed in Howard Kushner, "Visions of the Northwest Coast: Gwin and Seward in the 1850s," *Western Historical Quarterly* 4 (July 1973): 295–306. The Record of Scrip Issued is in Governor's Letterbook, Washington State Archives, Olympia. Government documents on the payment of scrip include U.S., Congress: House Report 195, 34th Cong., 1st sess., [868], *Expenses of the Oregon and Washington Indian War*; House Ex. Doc. 39, 35th Cong., 1st sess., [955], *Report of J. Ross Browne*; House Ex. Doc. 45, 35th Cong., 1st sess., [955], *Report of Commission to Ascertain Expenses of the Indian War*; House Ex. Doc. 114, 35th Cong., 1st sess., [1014], *T. J. Cram, Topographical Memoir of the Department of the Pacific*; House Ex. Doc. 51, 35th Cong., 2d sess., [1006], *Claims Growing Out of Indian Hostilities in Oregon and Washington, Report of the Third Auditor*; House Ex. Doc. 11, 36th Cong., 1st sess., [1046], *Report of the Third Auditor of the Treasury*; and Senate Report 161, 36th Cong., 1st sess., [1039], *Report on Payment of Expenses*. See also National Archives, Record Group 217, "Third Auditor, Letters Sent, Oregon and Washington Indian War Claims"; and "Third Auditor, Register of Claims, Oregon and Washington Indian Wars." An account of J. Ross Browne in the Northwest is contained in Richard Dillon, *J. Ross Browne, Confidential Agent in Old California* (Norman: University of Oklahoma Press, 1965); see also Lina Browne, ed., *J. Ross Browne: His Letters, Journals and Writings* (Albuquerque: University of New Mexico Press, 1969).

For the Presidential campaign of 1860, in addition to Hendrickson's *Joe Lane of Oregon,* see Roy Nichols, *The Disruption of American Democracy* (New York: Macmillan Co., 1948) which is a standard, comprehensive account. For Douglas's position, Robert W. Johannsen's, *Stephen A. Douglas* (New York: Oxford University Press, 1973) is thorough and perceptive. An excellent account of the various conventions is William B. Hesseltine, ed., *Three Against Lincoln: Murat Halstead Reports the Caucuses of 1860* (Baton Rouge: Louisiana State University Press, 1960). Stevens' report on the seating of the Charleston bolters at Baltimore was published as *Minority Report of Mr. Stevens, Delegate From Oregon* (Washington D.C.: National Democratic Executive Committee, 1860). A good picture of the Breckinridge campaign emerges from *Breckinridge and Lane Campaign Documents* (Washington City: n.p., 1860). The definitive biography of Breckinridge is William C. Davis, *Breckinridge Statesman, Soldier, Symbol* (Baton Rouge: Louisiana State University Press, 1973). A trenchant article on territorial politics in this period is Robert W. Johannsen, "National Issues and Local Politics in Washington Territory, 1857–1861," *Pacific Northwest Quarterly* 42 (January 1951): 3–31. The same author's *Frontier Politics on the Eve of the Civil War* (Seattle: University of Washington Press, 1955) deals mostly with Oregon. See also Robert Johannsen, "A Breckinridge Democrat in the Secession Crisis, Letters of Isaac I. Stevens, 1860–61," *Oregon Historical Quarterly* 55 (December 1954): 283–310.

Chapter 14

An excellent account of Lincoln's relationship with the military is T. Harry Williams, *Lincoln and His Generals* (New York: Alfred A. Knopf, 1952). A valuable account of the social and political problems of the Sea Islands after their capture by the Union Army is contained in Willie Lee Rose, *Rehearsal for Reconstruction* (New York: Bobbs-Merrill Co., 1964). One of Stevens' aides later published full and informative Civil War letters which contain much information on Stevens—William T. Lusk, *War Letters of William Thompson Lusk* (New York: n.p., 1911). Much of the military correspondence and reports are contained in *The War of the Rebellion: A Compilation of the Official Records of the Union and Confederate Armies* 4 series, 130 vols. (Washington D.C.: Government Printing Office, 1880–1902). Despite their bulk, the published records contain only a relatively small portion of the records of the war. For the complete story consult the National Archives, Record Group 393, "Records of United States Army Commands, 1821–1920: Expeditionary Corps, Letters Sent and Letters Received"; "Expeditionary Corps, General and Special Orders"; "Expeditionary Corps, 2nd Brigade Correspondence"; "Ninth Army Corps, Second Brigade Correspondence"; "Department of the South, Letters Sent and Letters Received"; and "Ninth Army Corps, Second Division Correspondence." The New York newspapers, particularly the *New York Times,* carried stories from the Sea Islands and published the controversy between Benham and Stevens. The Henry W. Benham Papers, Rutherford B. Hayes Memorial Library, Fremont, Ohio, contain little on this period of Benham's career. Useful information is found in National Archives Record Group 107, "Records of the Office of the Secretary of War, Letters Received, 1801–70 (M 221), and Letters Sent Relating to Military Affairs, 1800–89" (M 6). See also Record Group 94, "Records of the Adjutant General's Office, Letters Sent, 1800–90" (M 565).

INDEX

469